WHARRAM

A Study of Settlement on the Yorkshire Wolds, XII

THE POST-MEDIEVAL FARM AND VICARAGE SITES

by

C. Harding, E. Marlow-Mann and S. Wrathmell

with contributions by R. McNeill Alexander, Craig Barclay, James Barrett,
Wendy Carruthers, E. Ann Clark, Peter Davey, Peter Didsbury, Chris Dyer, Geoff D. Gaunt,
Alison R. Goodall, Ian H. Goodall, Allan Hall, H. Leaf, David Neave, Ray Perry,
Richard T. Porter, Jenny Price, Jane Richardson, Ian Riddler, Bryan Sitch,
A.M. Slowikowski, John Southey, John Tibbles, Marijke van der Veen, John G. Watt,
Siobhan Watts, Susan R. Watts, Hugh Willmott, Susie White and John Wood

Illustrations by

Mark Chisnall, Katherine Hunter, Jerneja Kobe, Emmeline Marlow-Mann, Cecily Marshall
and Chris Philo

York University
Archaeological Publications 14

© Wharram Research Project and Department of Archaeology, University of York, 2010
ISBN 978 0 946722 21 1

Edited by: E. Ann Clark and S. Wrathmell
Published by: University of York
Typeset by: Archaeological Services WYAS
Printed by: Short Run Press Limited, Exeter

This publication has been made possible by a grant from English Heritage

Wharram: A Study of Settlement on the Yorkshire Wolds
General Editor: S. Wrathmell

Vol. I⁺   *Domestic Settlement 1: Areas 10 and 6* (1979)
                 Society for Medieval Archaeology Monograph 8. £7.00

Vol. II   *Wharram Percy: The Memorial Stones of the Churchyard* (1983)
                 York University Archaeological Publications 1. £4.00

Vol. III*⁺   *Wharram Percy: The Church of St Martin* (1987)
                 Society for Medieval Archaeology Monograph 11. £17.50

Vol. IV   *Two Roman Villas at Wharram le Street* (1986)
                 York University Archaeological Publications 2. £5.00

Vol. V   *An Archaeological Survey of the Parish of Wharram Percy, East Yorkshire.
                 1. The Evolution of the Roman Landscape* (1987)
                 British Archaeological Reports, British Series 172. £12.00

Vol. VI*   *Domestic Settlement 2: Medieval Peasant Farmsteads* (1989)
                 York University Archaeological Publications 8. £10.95

Vol. VII   *Two Anglo-Saxon Buildings and Associated Finds* (1992)
                 York University Archaeological Publications 9. £7.50

Vol. VIII*   *The South Manor Area* (2000)
                 York University Archaeological Publications 10. £18.00

Vol. IX*   *The North Manor Area and North-west Enclosure* (2004)
                 York University Archaeological Publications 11. £22.00

Vol. X*   *Water Resources and their Management* (2005)
                 York University Archaeological Publications 12. £19.50.

Vol. XI*   *The Churchyard* (2007)
                 York University Archaeological Publications 13. £25.00

Vol. XII*   *The Post-medieval Farm and Vicarage Sites* (2010)
                 York University Archaeological Publications 14. £27.50

Vol. XIII   *A History of Wharram Percy and its Neighbours* (2011)
                 York University Archaeological Publications

* These volumes are available from Oxbow Books, 10 Hythe Bridge Street, Oxford, OX1 2EW
⁺ These volumes are available from Customer Sales and Services, Maney Publishing, Suite 1C,
  Joseph's Well, Hanover Walk, Leeds LS3 1AB

Cover: remains of the early 19th-century farmhouse looking south

Contents

List of Plates

List of Figures

List of Tables

ix

Summary

The present volume is the penultimate report on excavations at the English deserted medieval village site of Wharram Percy, in North Yorkshire. It charts the history of settlement at Wharram from the early 16th to the early 19th centuries, the period which began with the destruction of the medieval farming community and its open-fields, and ended with the abandonment of the one remaining farmstead occupying the former village site, and of the adjacent vicarage. The volume details the significant but unevenly surviving documentary sources relating to the final depopulation of the village, and to the vicarage and farmstead which continued for three centuries to occupy the valley terrace immediately to the north of the churchyard. It also details the very fragmentary structural sequences excavated in each of these homesteads and attempts, not entirely successfully, to relate the documents to the building remains. More successfully, the late 18th and early 19th-century houses are related to contemporary local buildings traditions.

The artefacts associated with the two homesteads are catalogued, illustrated and discussed in detail, as they constitute one of the most significant and extensive assemblages of material culture from a small rural community of this period. The ceramics, clay tobacco pipes and vessel glass are among the categories of artefact recorded in unparalleled numbers from this type of settlement. The chapters relating to environmental evidence include not only a full faunal analysis but also a detailed report on the *in situ* charred remains of the crops that were being stored in the vicarage barn when it was destroyed by fire in 1553.

Zusammenfassung

Der vorliegende Band ist der vorletzte Bericht über die Ausgrabungen der mittelalterlichen Wüstung Wharram Percy, North Yorkshire, England. Er behandelt die Siedlungsgeschichte in Wharram vom frühen 16. bis in das frühe 19. Jahrhundert. Dieser Abschnitt umspannt die Zeit von der Auflösung der mittelalterlichen ländlichen Gemeinde und der dazugehörigen Ackerfluren (*open fields*) bis zu dem Wüstfallen des schließlich einzig verbleibenden Gehöfts auf dem ehemaligen Dorfgelände und des angrenzenden Pfarrhauses. Der Band stellt die bedeutenden, jedoch lückenhaften schriftlichen Quellen mit Angaben zur endgültigen Aufgabe des Dorfes dar sowie jene Informationen zum Pfarrhaus und zum Gehöft, die – auf der Talterrasse unmittelbar nördlich des Friedhofes gelegen – die ältere Ansiedlung drei Jahrhunderte überdauerten. Darüber hinaus werden die äußerst fragmentarischen Befundabfolgen, die in den beiden untersuchten Gehöften archäologisch belegt sind, dargestellt. Es wird – wenngleich nicht ganz erfolgreich – versucht, die schriftlichen Quellen mit den Befunden in Verbindung zu bringen. Ungleich direkter ist hingegen die Verknüpfung der Gebäude des späten 18. und des frühen 19. Jahrhunderts mit den regionalen Bautraditionen.

Die Artefakte, die den beiden Gehöften zugeordnet werden können, wurden katalogisiert, sind illustriert und werden im Detail diskutiert. Sie stellen eins der bedeutendsten und umfangreichsten Inventare materieller Kultur einer kleinen, ländlichen Gemeinde dieser Periode dar. Keramik, Tonpfeifen und Glasgefäße gehören zu den Artefaktkategorien, die hier in für ländliche Siedlungen einzigartig großer Zahl ausgegraben worden sind. Die Kapitel zur Archäobotanik und –zoologie beinhalten nicht nur eine vollständige Analyse der Fauna, sondern auch einen ausführlichen Bericht über die im Zuge des Brandes der Pfarrscheune im Jahre 1553 *in situ* verkohlten Getreidereste.

Résumé

Ce volume est l'avant-dernier rapport concernant les fouilles sur le site du village médiéval anglais abandonné de Wharram Percy, au North Yorkshire. Il trace l'historique du peuplement de Wharram, du début du 16ème siècle au début du 19ème siècle, la période qui commença par la destruction de la communauté agricole médiévale et de son système de champs ouverts, et qui se termina par l'abandon de la dernière ferme qui restait encore sur le site de l'ancien village, et du presbytère avoisinant. Ce volume donne des détails sur les sources documentaires restant encore, lesquelles sont considérables mais incomplètes, concernant le dépeuplement final du village, ainsi qu'au sujet de la ferme et du presbytère, lesquelles continuèrent trois siècles durant à occuper la terrasse sur la vallée immédiatement au Nord du cimetière. Il donne également des détails sur les séquences structurales très fragmentaires fouillées dans chacune de ces demeures, et il s'efforce, sans y réussir entièrement, d'établir des liens entre les sources documentaires et les vestiges des bâtiments. Il réussit bien mieux à établir des liens entre les maisons de la fin du 18ème siècle et du début du 19ème siècle d'une part, et les traditions de construction locale contemporaine d'autre part.

Les objets fabriqués associés aux deux demeures sont catalogués, illustrés et discutés de manière détaillée car ils représentent l'un des ensembles de culture matérielle les plus significatifs et les plus importants en provenance d'une petite communauté rurale de cette période. La céramique, les pipes à tabac en argile et les vaisseaux en verre se trouvent parmi les catégories d'objets fabriqués enregistrés en quantités sans parallèle et découverts dans ce type de peuplement. Les chapitres qui traitent des indices environnementaux comprennent non seulement une analyse complète de la faune mais aussi un compte-rendu détaillé des restes carbonisés in situ des récoltes qui étaient entreposées dans la grange du presbytère lorsqu'elle fut détruite lors d'un incendie en 1553.

Preface and Acknowledgements

The excavations that are the subject of this volume explored the sites of the post-medieval farmstead and the late and post-medieval vicarage. They lie in a part of the village area described for convenience, both during the excavations and in the post-excavation phase, as the North Glebe Terrace. The terrace is that part of the valley in which the cottages and medieval church now stand – a partly artificial terrace that has probably been augmented on numerous occasions, both by landslips and by human effort, during the lifetime of the settlement. 'Glebe' refers to the core ecclesiastical holding on the terrace, and 'north' relates to that part of the terrace lying north of the churchyard. As will become evident in the excavation and discussion chapters of this report, there is considerable overlap between the northern part of the churchyard, excavated as Site 26 and reported in the churchyard volume (*Wharram XI*), and the southern parts of the vicarage Sites 54 and 77 described in this volume. Though the present volume has been constructed as a 'stand-alone' report, access to the previous volume would probably be of benefit in a number of respects.

Since the publication of the first volume in 1979, each of the definitive Wharram excavation reports has been devoted to a particular group of sites, rather than to a particular theme or chronological period. Yet in practice it has frequently proved possible to combine considerations of geography, theme and chronology: thus *Wharram VII* and *VIII* were concerned with Wharram's Anglo-Saxon occupation, *Wharram IX* with its Late Iron Age and Roman settlement, *Wharram X* with the management and use of its water resources, and *Wharram XI* with the graveyard and its contents. Similarly *Wharram XII*, though constructed to report a group of adjacent excavation sites on the North Glebe Terrace is also, effectively, a report on the whole of the post-medieval settlement, which was in the form of a small hamlet occupying this part of the old village site from the 16th to the early 19th centuries. For this reason the reports on post-medieval artefacts, notably the clay tobacco pipes, coins and pottery vessels, deal with these elements of Wharram's material culture from all the excavation sites across the whole village area. In practice, the numbers of such items recovered from excavation sites in other parts of the village area, though significant are not substantial, and on present evidence (though this may change with future investigations) there is little evidence of homesteads outside the North Glebe Terrace at least from the 17th century onwards.

Preparations for the excavation of the post-medieval sites began in 1977, when R.T. Porter located, as accurately as possible on the modern map, the buildings, trackways and fences shown on 19th-century maps, in particular on the earliest known estate plan, made in

1836. That plan showed a large building, subsequently demolished, just south of the surviving cottages. In the late 1970s this was assumed to have been the vicarage, and the outbuildings marked on its north side (including a range that became the cottages), were thought to have belonged to the vicars: hence the references to vicarage outbuildings in the earliest interim reports on the Site 51 excavations. It was not until 1980 that the unexpected discovery of foundations belonging to an 18th-century building further south, on Site 54, led to a reassessment of the documentary evidence, and to a recognition that the Site 54 building was actually the vicarage. The building immediately south of the cottages on the 1836 plan was therefore a post-medieval farmhouse, with its outbuildings to the north in Site 51. Thereafter, Sites 51 and 74 became the main excavation areas designed to recover the plan of the post-medieval 'farmstead' (the term used here to denote both the farmhouse and its outbuildings), and Sites 54 and 77 became the principal investigations of the 'vicarage' (again, denoting both the vicar's dwelling and associated outbuildings).

The excavations discussed here were sponsored by the Department of the Environment, later English Heritage, and carried out under the auspices of the Medieval Village (now Medieval Settlement) Research Group. The direction and administration of the project were in the hands of the late John Hurst and the late Maurice Beresford, the latter assisted by Francesca Croft. As always the late Mrs Joan Summerson and the Milner and Veysey families provided valuable organisational assistance throughout.

The supervision of work on Site 51, which ran from 1978-88, was carried out in various seasons by R. Daggett, G. Hutton, A. Josephs, B. van Maanem, P. Ottaway, M. Smith and S. Wrathmell. Site 74 (1985-9) was supervised by A. Gilmour with the assistance of A. van Bentham, P. Richardson and S. Ware. The structural investigation of the cottages was carried out immediately after the end of the 1990 excavations by A. Gilmour, A. Josephs and S. Wrathmell. On the vicarage, Site 54 (1979-86) was supervised by C. Harding (with G. Foard in 1979-80), assisted in various seasons by J. Humphrey, G. Hutton, S. King, M. Smith and J. Watt. Site 77 (1984-90) was supervised in the first year by M. Atkin, subsequently by J. Wood, with the assistance of L. Abrams, J. Dunk, D. Gilding, G. Hutton, P. Kennedy, P. Richmond and A. Towle.

Charlotte Harding wishes to thank many friends and colleagues who assisted, both on and off-site, with the excavation and interpretation of this site. Particular thanks are due to Sheila King and Jonathan Watt, Ann Clark and Stuart Wrathmell, the late John Hurst and the late Maurice Beresford, for support and encouragement. In addition she would also like to thank Ann Foard, Glen Foard, Julie Humphrey, Graham Hutton and Mike Smith for help on site, Sebastian Rahtz and Dan Smith for photographs, and Guy Beresford and Barbara Hutton for comments on structural details of the vicarage. For help with the preparation of the publication thanks are due to Emmeline Marlow-Mann; the late Ian Goodall kindly made some very useful observations on the vicarage building plans.

Ann Clark wishes to thank all those who took part in the processing of finds, especially those who struggled with the vast quantities of iron! As always, the staff at English Heritage's Centre for Archaeology have been helpful and patient in the location and movement of large numbers of boxes. She would also like to thank the staff at Archaeological Services, WYAS, especially Zoe Horn, Alison Morgan and Jane Richardson who have frequently facilitated the finds work in numerous ways, as well as Alison Goodall who kindly facilitated the completion of the ironwork report after the death of Ian Goodall. She is also grateful to David Crossley for his support and comments, and, in particular, to Peter Brears whose initial enthusiasm helped us to realise the potential of this assemblage, and whose wide-ranging conversations have been so helpful during the preparation of this report.

Stuart Wrathmell wishes to thank those who helped with the preparation of the site reports, and with the analysis of the documentary sources. Much of the initial work in preparing the Site 77 excavation records for post-excavation analysis was carried out by David Gilding and Barbara Johnson. Christopher Whittick's help with documentary sources, particularly those relating to ecclesiastical cause papers, was invaluable. David and Susan Neave also provided guidance and assistance with documentary sources more generally, as did staff of the Borthwick Institute for Archives at the University of York, the Museum of English Rural Life at the University of Reading, The National Archives and the North Yorkshire County Record Office. Finally, he would like to thank David Crossley for providing support and guidance in relation to many aspects of the structure and content of this volume.

R.T. Porter would like to thank Mr Howard Peach for information on Richard Allen's diary transcripts. Thanks are due to Koen de Groote, John Cotter, Anne Jenner and other members of the Medieval Pottery Research Group for help with the identification of the continental and other fine wares. Polydora Baker, Senior Zooarchaeologist with English Heritage, identified a number of the bird bones when the reference material available to the author proved insufficient. Her willingness to give advice on some of the identifications is gratefully acknowledged.

Wendy Carruthers is grateful to Donna Isaacs for efficiently sorting most of the rich flots, and would especially like to thank Marijke van der Veen for undertaking the Canoco analysis and making valuable suggestions regarding the interpretation. She is grateful to the following people for their help: a number of people looked at *Anguina tritici* samples or drawings and gave information and their opinions on the identification, including Allan Hall (University of York), John Southey (BPGS), Ray Perry (Rothamsted Research), Margaret Redfern (BPGS), Rosemary Bayles (NIAB), Brian Kerry (Rothamsted Research) and John Letts (Heritage Harvest). Kath Hunter managed to make the galls look beautiful in her drawings. She is also grateful to Chris Dyer for providing references and information about cereal storage and quantification, and for commenting on this report.

Wharram XII has been sub-edited and desk-top published by Chris Philo. The drawings are credited individually within the captions. Susanne Atkin created the index, and the foreign language summaries have been prepared by Emma Bentz and Charlette Sheil-Small. Peggy Pullan assisted in the finds administration for the post-excavation analysis. The editor's are grateful to English Heritage's project manager Dave MacLeod, for his guidance and support.

It has, regrettably, been necessary in several recent volumes to record the deaths of scholars who have been closely involved in the Wharram Project at various stages over the past sixty years. In this volume it is our sad duty to record the death of Keith Allison, editor of the first six East Riding volumes of the Victoria History of the County of York. Keith was one of the pioneers of research on deserted villages – he was one of the main contributors to the studies of deserted villages in Oxfordshire and Northamptonshire published by the Medieval Village Research Group in 1965 and 1966 – and he was also one of the first diggers to join Maurice Beresford in 1950. His continuing support for and advice on the Wharram project was acknowledged by Maurice and John in the first volume of this series. The present volume has benefited considerably from the research included in his book on *The East Riding of Yorkshire Landscape*, originally published in 1976.

Fig. 1. Map of north-east England showing the position of Wharram Percy and other locations mentioned in the text. (C. Philo)

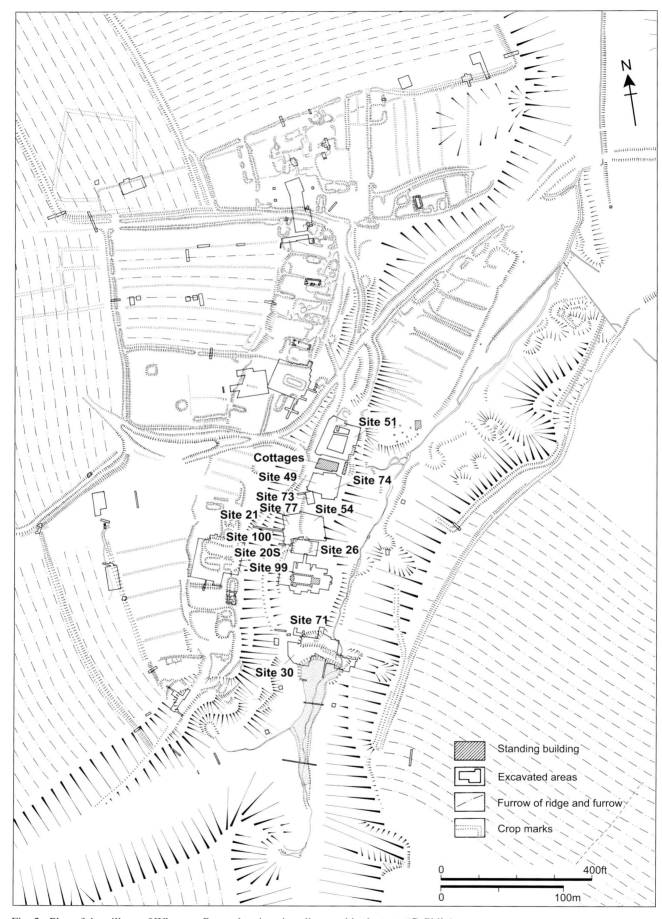

Site 51

Cottages
Site 49
Site 73
Site 77
Site 21
Site 100
Site 20S
Site 99

Site 74
Site 54

Site 26

Site 71

Site 30

Standing building

Excavated areas

Furrow of ridge and furrow

Crop marks

0   400ft

0   100m

Fig. 2. Plan of the village of Wharram Percy showing sites discussed in the text. (C. Philo)

Part One
Documentary Evidence

In many of the documents cited in this part, the opening of the year is reckoned to be 25 March. These dates have been revised, so that all years start at the beginning of January. In the quotations, except those extracted from other publications, spellings and numerals have been modernised for greater clarity but grammar, abbreviations and the use of capital letters are as in the originals. Words which are now obsolete have been defined according to Wright 1880.

1 Farming, Farmers and Farmsteads from the 16th to 19th centuries
by S. Wrathmell

The end of the medieval village and its open-field agriculture

There is only one direct record of acts of depopulation at Wharram Percy. It is an abstract of evidence given to a national commission of enquiry set up in 1517 to investigate the enclosure of land, and the conversion of arable farms to pasture, that had occurred since the first anti-depopulation legislation of the late 1480s (Leadam 1892, 172-6). It states that at Wharram Percy in the said East Riding four messuages (houses) and four ploughs had been thrown down after the aforesaid Feast of St Michael, and that the Baron of Hylton, John Holtby and John Hansby were tenants of a free tenement there:

'*Et quod apud Wharrom percy in dicto Estriding post predictum Festum sancti michaelis iiij^{or} messuagia & iiij^{or} aratra prosternuntur. Eo [sic] quod Baro de Hylton Johannes Holtby & Johannes Hansby sunt tenentes liberi tenementi inde*'
(Leadam 1893, 247)

The Hiltons of Hylton Castle, County Durham, had been lords of the manor since the beginning of the 15th century (*Wharram I*, 20), and the two other people named were probably feoffees of the Hiltons, following Leadam's suggestion.

The date of this group of evictions is not recorded; nor, indeed, can we be certain that all four occurred at the same time. They can, however, be assigned to the period after Michaelmas 1488, the time of the first general anti-enclosure legislation, and on the basis of the form of the entry, Maurice Beresford argued that they are likely to have taken place between 1488 and 1506 (*Wharram I*, 7).

We know from earlier records that these four messuages were not the only inhabited houses in 15th-century Wharram: inquisitions *post mortem* of 1436 and 1458 both record the existence of sixteen messuages belonging to manorial tenants (*Wharram I*, 13). What we do not know, despite searches among the relevant historical sources, is whether the sixteen houses documented in 1458 continued to be occupied for the next thirty years, or whether there had already been a decline in this number before the recorded evictions.

Nor do we have information on the impact of depopulation on Wharram's remaining householders. Those who were left may have continued to farm their open-field bovate or 'oxgang' holdings as their predecessors had done for centuries, interspersed with untenanted and uncultivated lands. On the other hand, there may have been an engrossment of holdings, the surviving families taking over lands formerly cultivated by their departing neighbours.

In the face of all this uncertainty there is now one newly identified piece of evidence that can be deployed to document the process of depopulation. It is provided by a witness in a suit or 'cause' of dilapidations, brought before the court of the archbishops of York in 1555 (Borthwick CP G.917 and G.3537). The cause itself will be considered more fully in Chapter 2, but part of it concerned the vicarage barn, which had been destroyed by fire two years earlier during the incumbency of Marmaduke Atkinson, vicar from 1540 to 1554 (Lawrance 1985, 71). The barn had not been rebuilt, and the newly instituted vicar, William Firby, claimed that it should have been. Atkinson, who had resigned to take up Bainton rectory, responded that insufficient corn could be grown on the vicar's two oxgangs of arable land to justify its rebuilding.

A series of witnesses provided depositions in support of Atkinson. One of them was Robert Pickering of Raisthorpe, a 'husbandman' or farmer aged about 70, who deposed that 28 years before (i.e. in 1527) the town (or township) had been laid to grass:

'that there belongeth to the vicarage of Wharram Percy two oxgangs of Land whereof when there was the most corn that he knew growing upon them there was not above three loads of Corn of both oxgangs since the town was Laid to grass which is 28 years since...'
(Borthwick CP G.917)

Whatever the changes that had taken place in the 15th century, in terms of reduced areas of cultivation or engrossing, Pickering's statement indicates a general conversion of arable to pasture in 1527, an event that signifies the formal end of open-field farming at Wharram Percy, and with it the demise of its medieval farming community.

The pastoral conversion of 1527 must have been carried out by, or with the agreement of the lord of the manor, Sir William Hilton; but Pickering's deposition indicates that the vicarage lands continued to be cultivated. Since the early 14th century, the advowson of

1

the church, the rectory and the vicarage with its glebe lands had belonged to the Augustinian priory of Haltemprice at Cottingham, near Hull, passing to the crown when the priory was suppressed in 1536 (see Chapter 2). They therefore lay outside Hilton's control. Thomas Marwen of Acklam, aged 30, another of Atkinson's witnesses, confirmed the continued cultivation of the glebe into the 1540s:

'that he was Tenant to the said Sir Marmaduke Atkinson of the vicarage of Wharram Percy by the space of five years wherefore he knoweth there was… two oxgangs of Arable Lands and certain Grass to the quantity of two acres as is articulate whereof was growing one year accounted with another six Loads of Corn and two loads of hay or thereabouts the which did Extend to the sum of ten shillings for so he this deponent hath paid to the vicar for it'
(Borthwick CP G.917)

It seems that the two oxgangs belonging to the vicarage were not the only lands that continued for a time in cultivation. Also outside manorial control was another two bovate holding belonging to a chantry in St Martin's church, which passed to the crown after the suppression of chantries. According to William Holme of Raisthorpe, aged 60:

'there belongeth but two oxgangs of Arable Land and Scarce two Acres of meadow to the said vicarage of Wharram Percy over and besides his pension in money which he Receiveth at the King's and queen's majesties hands And that there hath not grown upon the said two oxgangs of Land for this twelve years last past above two or three Loads of Corn in one year so far as he could Extend it And that by his Estimation there did not grow upon the said meadow above two Loads of hay For he saith that he helped to occupy and mow the Arable Land and meadow belonging to a Chantry which one Sir William Burneby this Examinate's uncle had at Wharram Percy and hath every as much arable Land and meadow belonging to it as the vicarage hath twelve years or thereabouts before he died And by all that time he had not in the best year of his arable Land above three loads of Corn and of his meadow above two Loads of hay And it was better then than it is now'
(Borthwick CP G.917)

It is hard to imagine the appearance of the former townfields at this time, with extensive stretches of grassed-over ridges interspersed with a few scattered strips still under cultivation (and presumably, therefore, fenced off).

The yields claimed in depositions on behalf of Atkinson can be contrasted with the estimates made by Firby's witnesses, who focused mainly on what the two oxgangs *should* bear. In supplementary evidence William Stanesby, vicar of Wharram le Street, claimed:

'that if the vicar at Wharram Percy for the time being might be permitted to plough his arable ground through the Fields as other townships thereabouts doth his two oxgangs of Land were able to bear by his estimation one year with an other sixteen Loads of Corn'
(Borthwick CP G.3537)

Broadly speaking, the depositions as a whole suggest that the yields were less than a quarter of what they should have been, presumably because of increased contamination by weeds and grasses, and it seems that by 1555 cultivation of the vicarage strips had ceased. Robert Holme of Raisthorpe, husbandman, aged about 30 deposed:

'that he hath helped to lead the Corn and hay belonging the vicarage of Wharram Percy once or twice about fifteen or sixteen years since [in about 1540] And he saith that there was not above two loads of hay and three Loads of Corn at such time as he led the same For he saith that there is but two oxgangs of Land and certain pieces of meadow Lying abroad one from another And as for the oxgangs of land it is not tilled [as other Lands be therabouts *deleted*] but lies Sward'
(Borthwick CP G.917)

What of the former lands of the manorial tenants, laid down to grass in 1527? An earlier cause in the archbishop's court provides some information about what happened to them. It was a tithe cause (Borthwick CP G.314), brought in 1543-4 by the then vicar Marmaduke Atkinson against John Thorpe of Appleton near Malton. Atkinson had recently taken to farm from the crown the rectory of Wharram, which included all the tithes of the parish, and he claimed that Thorpe had underpaid tithes of lamb and hay. 'Mr Thorpe', as he was called by Atkinson's witnesses in their depositions, was evidently a grazier of substance: by his own (conservative) estimate, in that year he had pastured within the bounds of the parish no fewer than 24 score ewes, 17 score wethers (castrated rams) and 14 score hogs (weaned young sheep, before first shearing).

None of the documents relating to this cause specifies the township(s) affected, because the tithe covered the parish as a whole; but there is circumstantial evidence that the pastures in question were in Wharram Percy township, put to grass sixteen years earlier. That evidence is contained in the deposition of one of Atkinson's witnesses, Thomas Carter of Towthorpe, aged 36. He stated that he had known John Thorpe for four years and deposed as follows:

'he saith that he this deponent was an inhabitor of the said town of Wharram Percy unto martinmas Last and dwelt there the space of three years And Further said that he had this present year ten sheep of his own which went in a pasture where the said Mr Thorpe's sheep went And he this deponent saith that he could neither go to nor fro to Fodder his said sheep but he must needs see them... And also he saith that George Alan and george gurwell then his [Thorpe's] shepherds did give in so many... [sheep?] for the kings tax'
(Borthwick CP G.314)

Atkinson's witnesses all gave evidence as to how they knew the numbers of sheep pastured by Thorpe. The others stated that they had viewed the grounds where the sheep were kept. Carter's response to the same question referred to his residence in Wharram Percy town(ship), a response that would be meaningless unless the sheep had been in the same township. Furthermore, Carter's period of residence there seems to have coincided with the length of his acquaintance with Thorpe.

Carter was not the only inhabitant of Wharram Percy in the 1540s. One of his fellow witnesses was described as 'Johannes Willson de Wharompercie', the place-name clearly referring to the township rather than the parish on this occasion, as all the other deponents are identified by township. Similarly in a further tithe cause of 1548 (Borthwick CP G.379), brought by Robert Geyre, farmer of the tithes of Thixendale, three of the deponents seem to have been residents of Wharram Percy township: Michael Taylor, John Botterell and John Holme (Purvis 1949, 35-6).

It is clear, therefore, that a few farmers, or rather, perhaps, smallholders and farm labourers, continued to inhabit Wharram Percy township in the decades after its pastoral conversion. Yet there is no reason to doubt that the entire township, save for the vicarage and chantry oxgangs and possibly a few garden plots, was at this time given over to animal husbandry, and was mainly in the hands of a non-resident grazier. Before the end of the 16th century, however, a new farm had been established at Wharram, and cultivation of a minor but significant part of the township area had resumed.

Farming, farmers and farmsteads, *c.* 1570 to 1770

In 1573 Matthew Hutton, dean and future archbishop of York, purchased the manor of Wharram Percy from the Hiltons (Feet of Fines: Collins 1888, 34). It was said to include a 'messuage with lands', implying a single farm holding and farmstead, setting the pattern of land use for the next two centuries. The non-resident grazier of the 1540s had been replaced by a resident farmer who rented the whole of the township, including the former chantry lands that were now part of the manor, and probably also the glebe lands by arrangement with the vicar (see Chapter 2).

A decade after Hutton's purchase, the 1584 Muster Roll provides another glimpse of Wharram Percy's inhabitants. It records four (unnamed) 'ablemen' in the township (Brooks 1951, 77). Beresford suggested that these four might have been at Wharram Grange (*Wharram I*, 14, n.30), a farm over a kilometre north of Wharram Percy village site, in Wharram le Street township (*Wharram X*, 21). This cannot be correct, however, as in 1584 the Grange was combined with Wharram le Street in a separate entry (Brooks 1951, 75).

Though the status of these able men is unknown, one was presumably a tenant farmer occupying Matthew Hutton's messuage and lands; and though they are unnamed, they may have included members of the

Weddell and, or Milner families who, severally or jointly, are likely candidates for the position of principal farming family at Wharram Percy in the closing decades of the 16th century. William Milner appeared in the lay taxation record of 1598 as the sole payer in the township (TNA PRO E179/204/353) and, as we shall see in Chapter 2, Michael Milner of Mowthorpe and Leonard Weddell (the latter recorded at Wharram Percy in 1586) were joint tenants of the vicarage in 1604.

In September, 1605 Hutton leased to Margery Weddell, widow, then of Clifton, York, and Robert Weddell her son, the manor, grounds, meadows and pastures of Wharram Percy, along with the chief house of the manor which they were required to repair, maintain and uphold (NYCRO ZAZ 10). Margery is likely to have been the widow of Leonard, taking on a new tenancy after his death.

The lease imposed conditions requiring the maintenance of quickset hedges, and restricting the amount of land that could be brought into tillage. They:

'also shall well and sufficiently ditch and set with quickwood or cause to be well and sufficiently ditched and set with quickwood all the outer hedges in and about the said grounds and closes of the said Manor and pastures of Wharram Percy aforesaid in all places there where quickwood hath been set and now decayed… [and the tenants shall not] plough rip up or keep hereafter in tillage any grounds above specified at any time during the said term other then those grounds which now at this present or within these twenty years last past have usually been ploughed and occupied in tillage yearly' (NYCRO ZAZ 10)

The lease was to run for twelve years, and it may have been at its expiry that the tenancy of Wharram Percy farm passed to John Richardson. In 1604 Richardson had married Ellen Weddell of Wharram Percy, plausibly the daughter of Leonard and Margery and sister of Robert (Paver's Marriage Licences: Clay 1889, 460), and in 1626 Petronel Richardson of Wharram Percy, probably their daughter, was licensed to marry William Gray, the vicar of North Grimston (Paver's Marriage Licences: Clay 1903, 162).

Richardson was clearly a man of substance: in 1626 and 1629 he was the sole taxpayer at Wharram Percy (TNA PRO E179/204/434, E179/205/459) and, as John Richardson of Wharram Percy, he had to compound for failing to take a knighthood at the coronation of Charles I (Baildon 1920, 106). He occupied the manor and lands of Wharram Percy until 1636, when they were leased by Mathew Hutton, grandson of the archbishop, to Sir John Buck of Filey. In 1638 Richardson was said to be late of South Wharram alias Wharram Percy, now of North Grimston (Hull University Archives, DDSY 66/26).

The lease of 1636, a stage in the process of the sale of the estate to Sir John Buck, contained similar conditions to those of 1605, but added a few more details which clarify the kind of farming that was taking place in this period. Sir John covenanted that he would not bring into tillage any land that had not been ploughed within the previous twenty years:

'and the same also to be such parcels of the same, as shall not in any one year exceed one hundred acres of the inclosed grounds and four hundred acres of the pastures at large which are not inclosed'
(Reading UL, Ms EN 1/2/296)

These details indicate that Wharram was run on the basis of an 'infield-outfield' system of farming, signified by the enclosed and unenclosed grounds.

Alan Harris has noted that restrictions on the extent of cultivation were frequently included in 17th and 18th-century leases of Wolds grazing lands (Harris 1961, 87). The reason for them is that long established grass would, when ploughed and sown for the first time, produce high yields: Harris quotes William Marshall's comment in relation to the late 18th-century improvement of the Wolds, that 'old turf, when newly broken up throws out immense crops of oats' (Harris 1961, 86). Yields could not, though, be maintained without the sustained application of manure: the grasslands could be ruined, and short-term gain for the tenant could result in longer-term damage for the landowner.

Wharram Percy was just one of many Wolds townships where an infield-outfield system of cultivation was practised during the 17th and 18th centuries. The infield was land that was regularly cultivated, and consequently had to be heavily manured, though on the Wolds, unlike other infield-outfield regions in Britain, there seems to have been a fallow between successive crops (Harris 1961, 24). The outfield was cultivated less frequently, in a manner again described by Harris:

'The Yorkshire outfield was divided into furlongs, one or more of which was ploughed and sown in succession, as a local correspondent of the Royal Society explained in the sixteen-sixties: "They have in many townes 7 fields and ye swarth of one is every yeare broken for oates and lett ly fallow till itts turne att 7 yeares end, and these seven are outeffeilds"'
(Harris 1961, 24-5)

In the late 18th century, Isaac Leatham of Barton, near Malton, weighed up the merits and demerits of outfield cultivation:

'The greater part of the Wold townships which remain open have a large quantity of out field in ley land, that is land from which they take a crop of corn every third, fourth, fifth or sixth year, according to the custom of the township; after which they leave it without giving it any manure or fallow, in the same situation as when they reaped the crop, on this grass ley, and on the fallows, the sheep are depastured, and are folded on the latter at night, a practice destructive both to the land and sheep. The fold conducted in this manner is beneficial to the arable land, but the farmer does not consider how much he robs his pasture land, while he saves his money for the moment, by manuring land without being obliged to purchase manure'
(Leatham 1794, 42)

If the cultivated part of Wharram's infield was fallowed between crops, as elsewhere on the Wolds, then the land under regular cultivation may well have amounted in total to about 200 acres, given the infield limit in 1636. Its primary function was probably to supply the needs of the farm, rather than to generate crops for sale. In terms of the market, Wharram Percy was still very much a sheep farm.

This is certainly the impression given in the earliest known detailed record of the farm and house, the probate inventory of William Botterell of Wharram Percy, dated 30 March 1699 (Borthwick, Probate Records, Buckrose Deanery: see Beresford and Hurst 1990, 111):

	£ s d
'In the Parlour	
Inprimis His purse and Apparel	30-00-00
one Bed Bedstead and Bedding	02-10-00
one Chest with Linen	05-10-00
A Table Carpet, 3 Chairs with other Utensils	01-00-00
In the fore Room	
Eleven pewter Dishes 6 plates and 2 pewter Tankards a Chamberpot salt together with other small pieces of pewter	01-10-00
A Cupboard Table Wheel 5 Chairs & other Implements therein	01-10-00
In the Kitchen	
A Brass pots [sic] Kettels pans & other small pieces of the same metal	03-10-00
two Tables with other Implements	00-10-00
In the milk house	
one Kimlin [salting tub] Churn Bowls with other wood Vessel	01-15-00
In the fore Chamber	
Two Beds Bedsteads with Bedding and other small Utensils therein	09-01-00
In the Parlour Chamber	
Wool and other Implements	51-00-00
In the Kitchen Chamber	
A servants Bed and Bedding with other Implements therein	01-03-04
Ten Cows	30-00-00
Eight Oxen	28-00-00
Eight young Beasts	11-00-00
Corn in the Barn and Chamber	18-00-00
Oats sown and ploughing the ground	12-00-00
Eight horses old and young	20-10-00
A Wain Ploughs Harrows and other necessaries belonging husbandry	04-10-00
Swine	07-06-00
Ewes	150-00-00
Wethers	80-00-00
Hogs	27-00-00
sacks winnowing cloth Bushels stuttells [?] Leaps Riddles sieves with other Implements	00-10-00
	497-15-04

Of the animals listed in the inventory, sheep of all kinds made up nearly 73% of the estimated value of livestock, with draught animals – horses and oxen – and followers accounting for 17%. The herd of ten dairy cows represented little more than 8% of the total. Oats had been sown, probably earlier that month, and the crop was valued at £12. There was a further £18 worth of unspecified corn in the barn and chamber to furnish the farm's needs until harvest time. This can be compared with the £51 valuation of 'Wool and other Implements' in the Parlour Chamber. The bulk of the wool clipped in the previous summer had presumably been already sold. Half a century earlier, Henry Best of Elmswell, near Driffield, had written that:

'Wee usually sell our wooll att hoame… Those that buy it carry it into the West towards Leeds, Hallifax and Wakefield; they bringe (with them) packe-horses and carry it away in greate packes. These wool-men come and goe continually from Clippinge-time till Michaellmasse' (Woodward 1984, 28-9).

Perhaps William Botterell had made enough money by the previous October to be able to keep a quantity of fleeces over winter, to be sold at higher prices before the start of the next clipping season (in the following June: see Woodward 1984, 22).

Harris's analysis of inventories for the period 1688-1738 provides a context for the brief references to crops in the Botterell document. On the lower slopes of the Wolds, wheat with some rye, and barley occupied a large share of the sown lands, the rest being taken up with oats, beans and peas. The inventories for farms on the high Wolds are not as helpful, but Harris has supplemented them with other sources. They indicate that wheat was less important here, and that barley was the main crop: 'the high Wolds remained a barley rather than a wheat area throughout the eighteenth century' (Harris 1961, 25-6).

As for the house, it is probably the same as the one recorded in the 1674 Hearth Tax, assessed at three hearths (Beresford and Hurst 1990, 102). The taxpayer was then listed as 'Mr [Thomas] Bacon', but he was clearly not the occupant. He lived at Wharram Grange, a six-hearth house on which he also paid tax. Bacon was a relation of the landowners, the Bucks, by marriage, and had been trustee of the dower settlement for Sir John Buck's widow in 1649 (Reading University EN1/2/302). The three-hearth Wharram Percy farmhouse may already have been occupied by the Botterell family.

The ground-floor rooms named in the inventory were the parlour, fore room, kitchen (all heated) and milk house, the first three having chambers above. The fore room was evidently the household's main living and dining room, the parlour Botterell's private room and bedroom. The wool stored in the chamber above the parlour would have provided excellent loft insulation against the cold during the previous winter months (the inventory being made in March), as well as being by far the most valuable 'household item' and therefore

requiring a secure location. This is in line with the advice given by Henry Best, that:

'Your roome wheare your wooll lyeth shoulde allwayes bee bordened under foote, because that earthen, bricke, and stone floores are allwayes moist and dampish and suffer not wooll to dry. Your wooll should allwayes bee kept under locke and key, not onely to preserve it cleanely from dirte and dust, but allsoe from the fingers of theevish and ill-disposed servants.'
(Woodward 1984, 26)

The other two chambers may represent the sleeping quarters of other members of the family (in the fore chamber) and of servants (in the kitchen chamber); but if so, the generous provision of upstairs accommodation is unusual for the Wolds in this period, according to one study (Harrison and Hutton 1984, 238). The rooms might just have been used for the storage of bedding and other items. Botterell had married Mary Read in 1690, and from his will and the parish registers appears to have had, in October 1698, three surviving daughters, two of them born in 1694 and 1697 (Borthwick PR WP1).

The Botterell's house has been identified with the earliest structural remains excavated on Site 74 (Period 2, pp 33-6). An attempt is made in Chapter 28 to reconcile the documentary and archaeological evidence for both this and the later farmhouse and outbuildings.

The inventory does not, of course, indicate the geographical extent of Botterell's farm, but it may well have encompassed the entire township, with some 200 acres of infield and extensive undivided sheepwalks beyond. This would certainly be in keeping with the early 17th-century references to the manor and its chief house. To the north of Wharram Percy, the farmers of Wharram le Street continued to live on the medieval village site and to farm open-field arable holdings (Beresford and Hurst 1990, 107), whilst the tenants of Wharram Grange, part of the Buck estate since the late 16th century (Reading University EN 1/2/285, 288), farmed the lands that had once belonged to the medieval grange of Meaux Abbey, in the western part of Wharram le Street township. The immediate post-Dissolution buildings of Wharram Grange farm were almost certainly located in the former grange precincts on the boundary of Wharram Percy and Wharram le Street townships (*Wharram X*, 2-5), but by the time of the Hearth Tax, Thomas Bacon's home was probably already in the location of the present Wharram Grange, on the Wold top 1.8km to the north-west of Wharram Percy church (see Fig. 5).

Wharram Percy, Wharram Grange and Wharram le Street were all in the hands of the Buck family in the mid-18th century, when they appeared in a rental entitled 'Lady Bucks Estate' (NYCRO ZQG XIII/11/1/12: see Plate 1). The document is undated but includes among the tenants William Read, who died in April 1752 (Borthwick PR WP1). Though Wharram Percy had probably been a single holding in earlier times, at the date of the rental it was held as two separate tenancies, one on the east side of the Beck (the precursor of Bella Farm), the other on its west side (later Wharram Percy Farm).

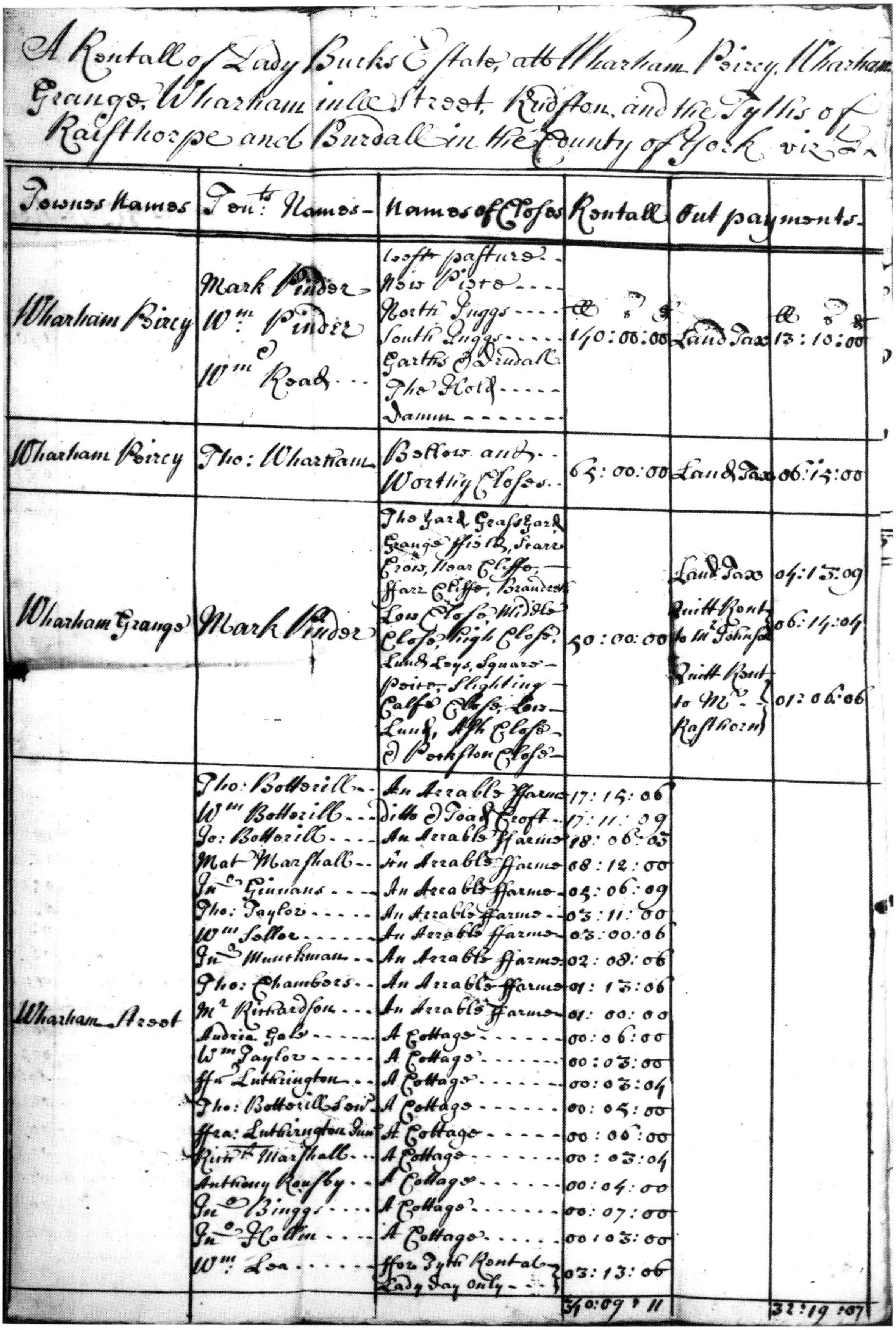

A Rentall of Lady Bucks Estate, att Wharham Pircy, Wharham Grange, Wharham inle Street, Kudston, and the Tyths of Raisthorpe and Burdall in the County of York viz.

Townes Names	Ten.ts Names	Names of Closes	Rentall	Out payments	
Wharham Pircy	Mark Pinder / W.m Pinder / W.m Road	Crofft pasture / New Pire / North Juggs / South Juggs / Garths & Drudall / The Hold / Damm	£ s d / 1/0:00:00	Land Tax	£ s d / 13:10:00
Wharham Pircy	Tho: Wharham	Bellow and Worthy Closes	65:00:00	Land Tax	06:15:00
Wharham Grange	Mark Pinder	The Yard Grassgard, Grange fflith, Starr Cross, Near Cliffe, Farr Cliffe, Brandeth Low Close Middle Close, High Close, Land Leys, Square Poior, Slighting Calfe Close, Low Lund, High Close & Porkston Close	50:00:00	Land Tax / Quitt Rent to M.r Johnson / Quitt Rent to M.r Rasthorn	04:15:09 / 06:14:04 / 01:06:06
Wharham Street	Tho: Bottrill	An Arrable ffarme	17:15:06		
	W.m Bottrill	ditto & Road Croft	17:11:09		
	Jo: Bottrill	An Arrable ffarme	18:06:03		
	Mat Marshall	An Arrable ffarme	08:12:00		
	Jn.o Ginnans	An Arrable ffarme	04:06:09		
	Tho: Taylor	An Arrable ffarme	03:11:00		
	W.m Soller	An Arrable ffarme	03:00:06		
	Jn.o Munkman	An Arrable ffarme	02:08:06		
	Tho: Chambers	An Arrable ffarme	01:15:06		
	M.r Rickardson	An Arrable ffarme	01:00:00		
	Audria Gale	A Cottage	00:06:00		
	W.m Taylor	A Cottage	00:03:00		
	ffra. Luthrington	A Cottage	00:03:04		
	Tho: Bottrills son	A Cottage	00:04:00		
	ffra: Luthrington Jun	A Cottage	00:00:00		
	Ruth Marshall	A Cottage	00:03:04		
	Anthony Rousby	A Cottage	00:04:00		
	Jn.o Biggs	A Cottage	00:07:00		
	Jn.o Hollin	A Cottage	00:03:00		
	W.m Loe	ffor Tyth Rentall Lady day only	03:13:06		
			340:09:11		33:19:07

Plate 1. Rental of Lady Buck's Estate (NYCRO ZQG XIII 11/1/12), published by kind permission of North Yorkshire County Record Office.

The rental does not record the sizes of the Wharram Percy holdings, but there is for each of them a column recording the 'Names of Closes'. West of the Beck, Mark and William Pinder and the aforementioned William Read paid £140 for their holding, including the closes named West Pasture, New Piece, North and South Ings, Garths and Druedale, The Hold and Dam. On the east side of the Beck were 'Bellow and Worthy Closes', which at the time of the rental were leased for £65 by Thomas Wharham of Wharram le Street (Beresford and Hurst 1990, 112-13).

Most of the names of the closes listed in the mid-18th-century rental also appear on the earliest-known estate map for Wharram Percy, William Dykes' plan of 1836, and by combining the two sources of information it is possible to make a rough estimation of the location and size of the infield and outfield, the enclosed and unenclosed lands of 1636 (see Figs 3 and 4).

'Worthy', meaning 'enclosure', is the name attached to two fields south-east of the church in 1836. They lay on the plateau above the steep-sided valley, and had clearly been formed from one original enclosure. The location of Bellow Close is unknown, but it may be represented by Kiln Close and Home Close, where the new farmstead called Bella was erected in the 1770s (see below).

The closes recorded on the west side of the Beck were more numerous. 'Dam' is clearly the field containing the pond, and 'The Hold' is presumably the area later occupied by Nut Wood ('Holt' on the 1836 map: see Fig.7 below). The 'Garths' may also have been in the valley, though they might equally have been on the plateau in the area of the former tofts and crofts. 'North Ings' is so named in 1836; 'South Ings' was presumably Ings Meadow in 1836, lying south of North Ings. 'Drudale', the other name that appears both in the rental and on the map, is the one given to a series of fields running westwards from the churchyard and dam field.

On the 1836 map the southern and western edges of the Druedale fields are marked by a continuous, convex boundary of the kind that is most readily associated with a primary 'intake' from a larger area unenclosed land. The North and South Ings meadows have a continuous eastern boundary, following the top of the steep-sided valley called, in 1836, Ings Brow. If the rental's 'West Pasture' can be identified with the 1836 Hog Walk (there is nothing either to substantiate or refute this), and if the rental's 'New Piece' became Birdsall Close (despite two fields east of Worthy having this name in 1836), then the 17th and early 18th-century enclosed ground of Wharram Percy, its cultivated infield and enclosed pastures, can be seen to form two coherent blocks of land, close to the former village site on either side of the Beck.

These 'closes' would, essentially, have supplied the farm's corn, hay and cattle-pasture requirements. Draught animals and dairy cattle would have grazed the Cow Pastures that encompassed much of the lower, eastern half of the medieval village site, by the side of the Beck, as well as the Ings Brow fields which occupied the valley further north. Druedale itself, occupying the southern part of Druedale fields, would have been another strip of enclosed permanent pasture with access to water.

According to the figures given on the 1836 map, the 'Worthy' block east of the Beck amounted to just over 40 acres. The main block of putative enclosed grounds west of the Beck would have covered rather more than 250 acres. Together, these represented a little over 20% of the whole township. Apart from 'Bellow' close and the pastures by the Beck, the rest of its territory would have been unenclosed grazing lands for sheep, with very restricted access to water.

The mid-18th-century rental, recording as it does two different holdings on each side of the Beck, might be taken to indicate that the Bellow-Worthy closes were never in fact part of the Wharram Percy infield; that they had a separate origin. It seems however, an odd choice of location for enclosed fields if they were created by a tenant of Wharram le Street, given that there is no indication they were furnished with their own farmhouse or outbuildings before the 1770s (see below). It seems much more likely that the Wharram Percy infield had originally been created on both sides of the Beck, but that access to the eastern part had become difficult because of land slips where the springs on the west side of the valley issue close to the cross-valley trackway. Landslips in this area occurred in earlier times (*Wharram XIII*, forthcoming) and still occur.

At Wharram Percy, therefore, the abolition of the medieval open-field system in 1527 did not lead to an 'enclosed' landscape in the sense of being completely divided up into a series of smaller hedged or fenced fields. The bulk of its territory remained undivided, individual furlongs of its old ploughing ridges perhaps being fenced temporarily and ploughed from time to time to supplement the crops from the in-grounds.

Wharram was not unique on the Wolds in having such characteristics: it was one of a number of properties that Harris has described as 'being at once physically open yet technically inclosed' (Harris 1961, 29). He identified several townships, among them Cowlam, Croom and Arras, where early depopulation and conversion of arable to pasture had not been accompanied by full enclosure; where the landscape remained open well into 18th century, although the common fields had disappeared long before. 'Where subdivision fences did occur they were usually of a temporary nature, and were raised as required to fence off plots of ground for occasional cultivation' (Harris 1961, 29-30).

Susan Neave's discussion of another example, Eastburn in Kirkburn parish, suggests an experience very similar to that of Wharram Percy, though here depopulation came about a century and a half later. Between 1664 and 1666 the whole of Eastburn was acquired by John Heron of Beverley, who emptied the settlement. Its fate was recorded in the witness statements associated with a tithe cause which came before the archbishop's court in 1682. Deponents claimed that Heron had pulled down most of the houses and converted the township to pasture. Again, however, it was not

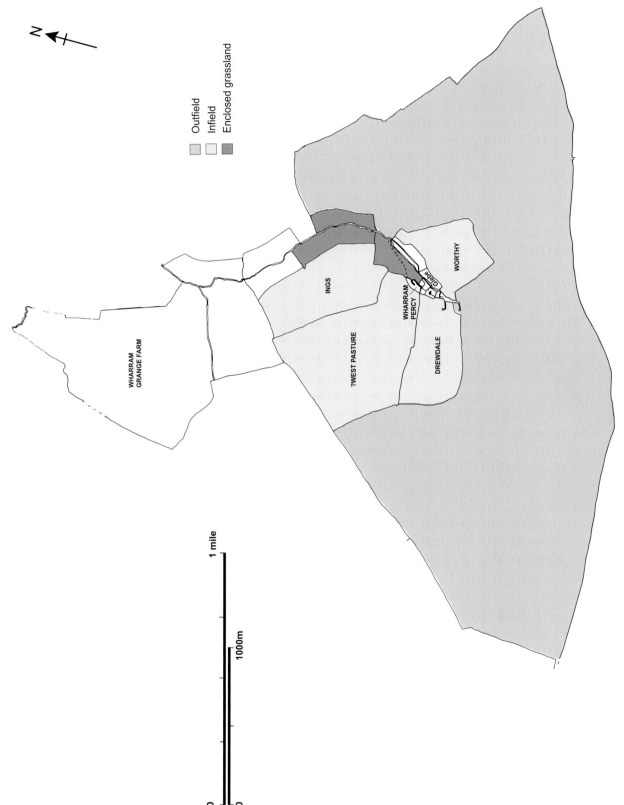

Fig. 3. The infields and outfields of Wharram Percy. (E. Marlow-Mann, after Wm Dykes 1836)

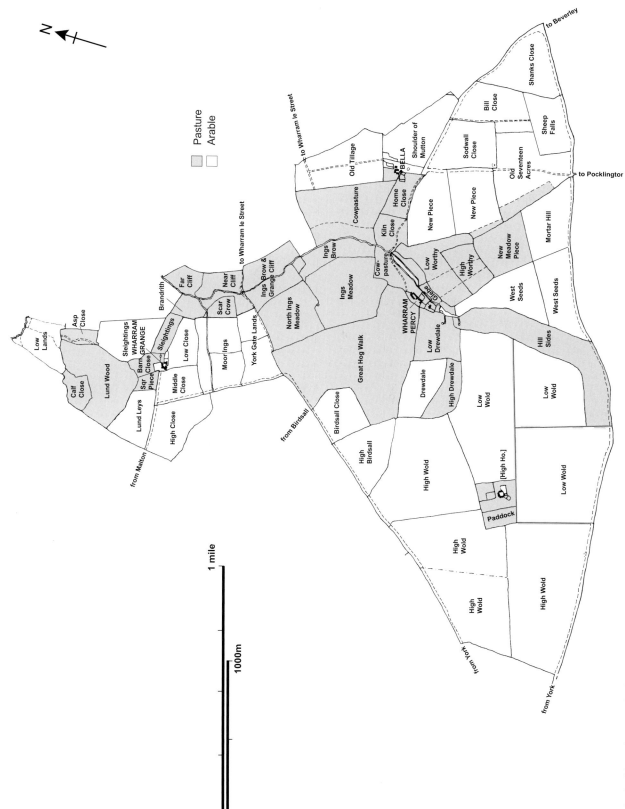

Fig. 4. Arable and pasture lands. (E. Marlow-Mann, after Wm Dykes 1836)

Pasture
Arable

9

physically enclosed: following depopulation the township was used as a sheep walk (Neave 1993, 133).

Such farms were thought by Leatham to have originated as ancient demesne lands (land formerly occupied by a lord of a manor for his own immediate use), rather than as depopulated former open-field townships. Some may, of course, have originated in this way, though others did not:

'Besides the open or uninclosed townships, and those recently inclosed, there are several others which are a sort of ancient demesne or inclosure. These commonly have a large quantity of land belonging to them without subdivision fences, which land generally consists of extensive pastures, sheep walks, or rabbit warrens, and some closes near the homestead'
(Leatham 1794, 42)

In the 18th century there were also, as Leatham implies, numerous unenclosed Wolds townships still occupied by village communities whose tenants continued to farm open-field holdings – though probably in many cases the open fields had been reduced to much smaller areas of infield (see Hayfield 1991, 33). The different tenurial characteristics of these townships and the depopulated sheep-walks can be seen in the Wharram parishes, in the mid-18th-century Buck rental (see Plate 1). The Wharram Percy and Wharram Grange farms, with a handful of tenants and lands recorded in the form of named closes, contrast markedly with the entries for Wharram le Street, in which ten tenants had 'An Arable Farm' each, and a further nine had 'A Cottage'. Wharram le Street was still at this time an unenclosed, open-field township (see Beresford and Hurst 1990, 115).

Improvement farms and farmsteads, *c.* 1770 to 1850

Enclosure and subdivision were, however, soon to overtake both the open-field townships and the open sheep-walk farms, bringing a degree of homogeneity to the Wolds landscape that had been absent since the end of the Middle Ages. Harris has calculated that the period 1730-1810 saw 206,000 acres of the Wolds being divided up, with only 20,000 acres remaining unenclosed after the latter date (Harris 1961, 62). Posts and rails were used to fence the new fields, along with quickset hedges, as the readily available chalk was inappropriate for the construction of stone walls (Harris 1961, 63).

Wharram Percy's main period of improvement came in the 1770s, and it was instigated by Sir Charles Buck. Numerous accounts and receipts survive among the Cholmeley of Brandsby MSS to document the process (NYCRO ZQG XIII/11/2). The improvements encompassed the laying out and fencing of new fields for Bella and Wharram Percy farms, created out of previously undivided pastures.

In March 1776 Sir Charles paid 16s 6d 'for his proportion of the Tax for the Inclosure of Wharram', and

this record is followed by numerous vouchers for ditching, for fencing with posts and rails, and for hedging with quicksets, as well as for the purchase of gates. Hedges were still being planted in 1779. The payment in 1776 for 'digging and completing a Pond forty five feet Diameter upon Bellow pasture' was presumably for the construction of a dewpond associated with the newly laid out fields (see Hayfield and Brough 1986-7).

The estate plan of 1836 shows clearly the abutment of these new field boundaries on to the ring-fence of the former 'ingrounds' (Fig. 4). It also shows that, in 1836, the lands newly enclosed in 1776 were largely under crop, whilst large parts of what had probably been infield had been put down to grass. Presumably the old infield, under regular cropping for up to two centuries, had become exhausted, whereas the 'old turf' was still very productive.

The creation of new fields on the Wolds was sometimes accompanied by the erection of farmsteads in new locations, to serve farms carved out of outlying parts of newly enclosed townships, or to serve existing farms from more convenient sites. Elsewhere, old farmsteads containing mud, chalk and thatched buildings were demolished and replaced by brick and pantile houses and outbuildings (Harris 1961, 70-72).

Sir Charles' improvement of his Wharram estate involved the erection of a new farmstead at Bella, and the rebuilding of Wharram Grange (Fig. 5). At Wharram Percy the works were much more limited, being confined mainly to the creation of a new water supply and the erection and repair of outbuildings. In 1774 its tenant farmer was John Monkman (rent £145), and the Monkman family remained tenants of Wharram Percy until 1807 (Beresford and Hurst 1990, 112; Birdsall Estate Office, Wharram Deed Box, 1807 lease).

Wharram Percy's new water supply was installed by the end of December 1766, when John Sollit presented a bill for sinking a well at Wharram Percy at a cost of £10 11s 9d. It required 'sinking and soughing' for a depth of 18 yards. There is no indication of why a new supply was needed; it is a matter that will be discussed in Chapter 28 (p. 351). More easily understood is the requirement for a new supply to the new farmstead at Bella, installed the previous March. For that, Sollit submitted a bill for 'sinking a well… upon Bellow' at a cost of £31 13s 2d. It was 40 yards deep; of this, 20 yards involved 'Blasting' and cost £15. More modest sums were paid for 'claying' and walling the well.

As for Sir Charles's improvements to the buildings, work had begun in March 1774 at Wharram Grange, starting with 'Pulling down the Thatch and Roof of the Old House'. It continued with the purchase of building materials, and payments for construction work on the house, the stables, the beast house and the granary. In February 1776 work began on Bella farmhouse, with the purchase and transportation of brick, tile and stone, the last quarried from Grimston Hill. Later purchases of materials included Hildenley stone for hearths, plinths,

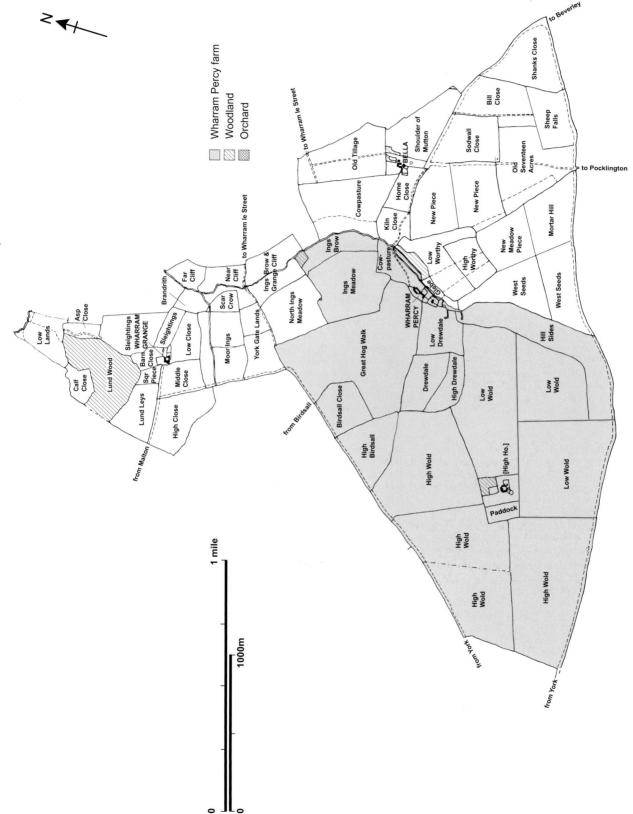

Fig. 5. The three farms of Wharram Percy, Bella and Wharram Grange in the 18th and 19th centuries. (E. Marlow-Mann after W. Dykes 1836)

N

Wharram Percy farm
Woodland
Orchard

1 mile

1000m

0

to Beverley

to Pocklington

Shanks Close

Bill Close

Sheep Falls

Sodwall Close

Old Seventeen Acres

Shoulder of Mutton

BELLA

Old Tillage

Cowpasture

Home Close

Kiln Close

New Piece

New Piece

Mortar Hill

to Wharram le Street

Low Worthy

High Worthy

New Meadow Piece

West Seeds

West Seeds

Ings Brow

Ings Meadow

Cowpasture

Glebe

WHARRAM PERCY

Low Drewdale

Hill Sides

to Wharram le Street

Far Cliff

Near Cliff

Ings Brow & Grange Cliff

North Ings Meadow

Brandrith

Scar Crow

York Gate Lands

Great Hog Walk

Drewdale

High Drewdale

Low Wold

Low Wold

Asp Close

Low Lands

Sleightings

WHARRAM GRANGE

Sleightings

Low Close

Moor Ings

Calf Close

Lund Wood

Sqr Barn Piece Close

Middle Close

Lund Leys

High Close

from Malton

from Birdsall

Birdsall Close

High Birdsall

High Wold

Paddock

[High Ho.]

Low Wold

High Wold

High Wold

High Wold

from York

from York

11

jambs and mantles. The final bills for Bella seem to have been for carpentry, paid in 1778, including work on the stables, beast houses and other outbuildings. In 1780 Sir Charles turned his attention once more to the Grange, and built a new barn there.

It is the absence of an initial payment for demolition work on an old house at Bella, similar to that recorded for Wharram Grange, which supports the suggestion that the farmstead for this holding was erected on a new site. A summary of monies owed to James Slee for day works in December 1776 includes a payment for 'Labourers Levelling the Buildings & Clearing away the Rubbish' for 67 days; but it does not indicate the location of the buildings in question.

The problem of determining the location of the various works arises because the lists of work at Bella are intermixed with items that record contemporary but more limited work at Wharram Percy, and many of the entries in the accounts do not distinguish between Bella and Wharram Percy. There are, however, enough references to show that rebuilding at the former village site was confined to the outbuildings and did not include the house. For example, the carpentry bill paid in October 1778 was itemised thus:

'Bill for Carpenter's Work at the House at Bella   81:15:8
Bill for Dᵒ at Wharram Percy, the Barn
Stables Beast Houses etc at Bella   44 :1:4'

Similarly, William Rowland, who acted as quantity surveyor for the operations, submitted a bill to Sir Charles for his work in 1777-8 'to taking dimensions & measuring all the Mason's work for Dᵒ [the house at Bella] likewise Monkmans Barn & Stable [at Wharram Percy]'. There is nothing in the surviving vouchers that could refer to a new house at Wharram Percy itself. This is, of course, contrary to the previously published assumption that a new farmhouse was built on the village site as part of these improvements (see e.g. Beresford and Hurst 1990, 112, 117). The possible identification of 'Monkman's barn' in the archaeological remains on Site 51 (Chapter 5), and the re-dating of improvement farmhouse excavated on Site 74 (Chapter 4), are considered further in Chapter 28.

The following summary of works at Wharram Percy includes only those entries specifically identified as relating to that place; others, unidentified, *may* have been but are excluded here. The initial activity seems to be recorded in a 1776-7 summary account of payments owed to James Slee for day works at Wharram Percy and Bella. Between 29 April and 12 May 1776, labourers spent 18 days 'digging Earth at Wharram Percy' at a cost of £1 16s 0d. A receipt signed by Richard Waite in the following August records the payment of a further £18 16s 7d for 'Digging away and levelling some hundred and four Yards (Cubic) of Earth from John Monkman's barn'.

James Slee erected over 71 roods of stone walling for John Monkman's new barn and, in August of the same year, his masons spent five days repairing Monkman's dairy. They spent another three 'Laying Sleepers John Monkmans Barn floor', with labourers 'digging & Serving them'. In November, tiling was repaired on an unspecified building at Wharram Percy, and masons spent 6 days 'Repairing Jnᵒ Monkmans Shade', again with labourers serving them. This last building was perhaps his waggon shed. Among the items of 'masons work' for which Slee was paid were eight stone arches at Wharram Percy costing £1 in total, and building the granary steps at a cost of £1 1s 0d. In January and March 1777, 2200 bricks were taken to Wharram Percy.

A carpenter's bill for 'Monkman Barn at Wharram Percy', undated but in the 1776-7 bundle, provides the cost of purchasing and installing a wide range of items, including (in order of appearance) rafters, joists to the stable, barn floor boards, chamber boards, two granary doors and frames, three stable doors, four barn doors and frames, eight 'picking holes' (i.e. pitching holes), one two-light window frame, one frame and door 'under styes', 18 lintels for doors and windows and '90 foot of plain Plinth in the Granary'. Several entries provide detailed calculations of the linear and/or area dimensions of the timberwork as well as the cost, though the numbers are not always easy to interpret. The relevant ones are (including errors of arithmetic):

	£ s d
95ft 4in by 15ft 2in Rafter is = to 29 sq yds = 82ft 9in at 6s per sq yd	8-18-10
Joists to the Stable 30 foot 6in by 20 is = to 6 sq yds = 10ft at 5s per sq yd	1-10-6
Barn Floorboards & Joists 14-9 by 17ft 10in is = to 2 sq yds = 63ft at 5s	0-13-0
Planks to Dᵒ laying 29 yards 2ft at 6d per yard	0-14 -6
Chamber boards 29ft by 18ft is = to 58 yards at 7d is = to	1-13-10

The range of buildings called Monkman's barn seems to have incorporated a stable and granary as well as the barn itself. The granary may have been at first-floor level, reached by the (?external) steps constructed by Slee. It may have been set over the stable, on the stable joists. It is interesting that both the mason's and the carpenter's accounts indicate that the barn was at least partly floored with timber boards set on joists or sleepers (perhaps the threshing floor).

The entry concerning the laying of planks for the barn floor can be interpreted as indicating that the floor area covered by planking was a little over 29 square yards. If the first two sets of figures in the preceding entry ('barn floorboards and joists') indicate the dimensions of this part of the barn, they could be interpreted as meaning that it was 14ft 9in by 17ft 10in, equivalent to just over 263 square feet, or just over 29 square yards. The coincidence of the two area dimensions lends confidence to the interpretation of the first two sets of figures in the 'joists to the stable' entry in a similar fashion: that the stable measured 30ft 6in by 20ft. The final 'chamber boards' entry clearly indicates a room measuring 29ft by 18ft.

Assuming these three spaces were contained in a single range, and the range was one room deep, there should be a common distance recorded in all of them, being the width of the building (or of this part of the building). There is no single figure, but three are close: 17ft 10in for the barn joists, 20ft for the stable joists and 18ft for the chamber. Why the discrepancies? The joists for the barn floor need not have been tied into the wall foundations, whereas the stable joists (assuming they supported a first-floor room) will have been set into the walls on each side, requiring a greater length. The planking for the chamber floor will, however, have been flush against the inner faces of the chamber walls. Therefore the slight variations in measurement add weight to this interpretation.

If these assumptions and calculations are correct, then the building had an internal width of 18ft, with two rooms at ground level: a 30ft 6in long stable and 14ft 9in long 'barn' with a boarded floor. It has to be said, however, that a total of four barn doors seems excessive for a room of this size (not to mention eight pitching holes); this again suggests that the joists and planking for the barn floor were confined to a strip between two opposed doors used for threshing.

The chamber could have been the room above the stable: it may in fact have been the granary, as its internal dimensions would give a perimeter measurement of 94ft, only slightly greater than the figure of 90ft for the 'plinth' in the granary. Adding the length of the plank-floored barn and stable together gives a recorded length of just over 45ft, or 15 yards. With an external width of about 7 yards, the recorded area of the building would have been about 105 square yards. If this area had been cleared of earth a yard deep, its cubic volume would have been similar to that recorded in Richard Waite's bill, but this seems a very substantial accumulation of soil. A depth of half a yard would an area of about 30 yards by 7 yards. This might explain the 95ft 4in figure at the beginning of the entry for rafters, giving us the length of the building; on the other hand, the second measurement, 15ft 2in, seems most likely to be the length of the rafters on each side of the building, the length required to run them from the tops of the external faces of the walls to the ridge. It may be, therefore, that the 95ft 4in figure needs dividing by two to give the length of roofing works, bringing the distance closer to the 45ft figure.

The 71 roods of stone walling built by Slee should give a better indication of the range's overall dimensions; but this is another figure that is difficult to interpret. A bill for further walling in 1779 (see below) included an entry for 20 rood 58ft at 6s 6d, the total cost being £6 16s 0d. This indicates that a rood was equivalent to 63ft, and therefore that 71 roods measured 4,473ft. But this is presumably not a simple linear measure, but one that takes account of the height of walling as well as its length.

In 1779 there was further work at Wharram Percy, and rather confusingly this also related to a barn – whether the one recorded in 1776-7 or another is impossible to say. An account 'viewed' by Rowland and submitted by him to Sir Charles includes payment to James Slee for 'putting down the old Barn and Repairing the walls that was Thought proper to Stand'. A further account from Slee in the same year, which is titled Wharram Percy but does not specify particular buildings, lists the following works:

To Walling 20 Rood 58 foot at 6s 6d per rood is = to	6-16-0
To Tiling & pointing = 14 sq yd 5 foot at 4s per sq yd is = to	2-16-0
To Paving 24yds 8ft at 3d per yard is = to	0- 6- 2½
To 8 Corbels at 2s 6d Each	1- 0- 0
To Ridging 20 yards at 1s 2d per yard is = to	1-16-2
To Coping & ridging laying on 51 yards at 3d per yard is = to	0-12-9

In October of that year William Thirk acknowledged receipt of money for various carpentry works including 'to the Barn at Wharram percy to 3 door frames', and the same month a bill was paid for taking 1500 tiles to Wharram.

Some thirty years later, the number, function and condition of the buildings associated with the three farms were recorded in an estate valuation. The manuscript book is dated 1806, and survives among the records held in Lord Middleton's estate office at Birdsall. Wharram Grange Farm was then let to Thomas Rivis at an annual rent of £208, and its buildings and fields were described as follows:

'The Buildings consist of a New Dwelling House, built with Stone and covered with Tile, containing two Parlours, four Lodging Rooms, Kitchen, Backkitchen and Dairy. One two-Stall Stable, one Stable for eight Cart Horses, two Houses for six Cows each, Foal Shed, Waggon Shed and Granary over, and a Barn, all in Good Repair, Stone and Tile… The Buildings on this Farm are all new and in good Repair. The Grounds are tolerably well subdivided with Quickset Fences which are in pretty good Order. The Tillage Land is in general good Turnip and Barley Soil, but is not adapted to the growth of Wheat, the Tenant can never be certain of a fair Crop of that Article.'

The farmhouse at Bella, basically the one still standing there, received a much less satisfactory report. The farm was let to John Botterell at an annual rent of £299:

'The Buildings consist of a Mansion House, the Walls are ill built, with Brick on the outside, and Chalk Stone within, through which the Rain penetrates very much, and is covered with Blue Westmorland Slate, containing two Parlours, Butlers Pantry, Kitchen, small Dairy, Laundry, Brew & Bake House, and good Cellars; Two Staircases, four Bed Rooms and four Garrets - Coal House, two Stables, four Stalls each, and Granaries over – Two Cow Sheds, Foal House, Pigsty and a good Barn, Brick and Tile – One two Stall Stable, Waggon Shed, Cart Shed and Carpenters Shop, Chalk Stone and Tile… The Buildings on this Farm are very good, except the Dwelling House, which has been so shamefully built, that it will require some ingenuity to prevent the Rain penetrating through the Walls. The Grounds have been pretty well subdivided, and the Quickwood has been taken Care of, which, in general, makes good Fences. The Tillage Land is of a dead cold Nature, except the old Tillage No. 6 – it however grows Grass Seeds tolerably well, and (like Wharram Percy Farm) it is better calculated for Oats than any other Sort of Grain, nor is it safe for a Turnip Crop.'

The tenant of Wharram Percy Farm was recorded initially as Francis Monkman, though this was subsequently amended to Francis Gofton, who paid an annual rent of £433:

'The Buildings consist of a Dwelling House, in bad Repair, containing two Parlours, Kitchen, Dairy, and four Lodging Rooms, Stone and Tile. A New Barn, two Thru-Stall Stables and Granary, Brick and Tile; small Waggon Shed, Cow House, Duck House, Pigsties and Coal Shed, Stone and Tile. Detach'd – A Waggon Shed, Stone and Thatch… Most of the Buildings on this Farm are in a decayed State, and very insufficient for a Farm of such Magnitude, it is necessary a New Dwelling House, and other Conveniencies, should be built. The Fences on the High Grounds, are principally sod Walls, and, of course, are good for nothing. A great Part of the High Wold, now in Grass, has formerly been plough'd, and no doubt, according to Custom, it has been laid down extremely poor, all of which, and the Tillage in this Farm, except No. 30, 39 & 40 is of a cold dead Nature, Oats only should be sown, tho' it is by no means certain of bringing a fair Crop either of that Grain, or Turnips.'

The valuation confirms the position inferred from the 18th-century building accounts: that Grange Farm had been rebuilt in its entirety in the 1770s; that the Bella Farm buildings had been erected at the same time (albeit inadequately, as far as the house was concerned), but that only the barn (with stable and granary) had been newly built at Wharram Percy. The two parlours of the Wharram Percy house were presumably the parlour and fore room of the 1699 inventory; the increased number of upper 'lodging rooms' may be associated with improvements which included covering the roof in tiles. Only one of the outbuildings was still covered in thatch.

The surveyor's recommendation that Wharram Percy needed a new dwelling house seems to have been acted upon at some point during the next 25 years, for an inventory of Wharram Percy farmhouse dated November,

1830, clearly describes an entirely different building (NYCRO ZPB III 6/4/3), the foundations of which were excavated on Site 74 (Period 4, pp 37-41). The inventory was of goods and chattels belonging to John Cattle, the tenant, which had been distrained on behalf of the owners because Cattle was £400 in arrears with his rent:

'In the Dwellinghouse
Front Room
    Secretary & Book Case containing a number of Books
    3 Tables - 7 Chairs – Stool – Celleret – Barometer
    Fire Iron & Fender - Carpet

In the Kitchen
    Mangle – Clock - 4 Tables 6 Chairs -

Front Chamber (No. 1)
    3 Beds, Bedsteads &c - 3 Chairs – Looking Glass - Desk

Front Chamber (No. 2)
    Bed, Bedstead & Hangings - 4 Chairs

Servant Girls Room
    2 Bedsteads, Bed etc.

Back Room
    One Bed, Bedstead etc. – Desk - 7 Chairs - Table, Stove

Men Servants Garret
    8 Bedsteads Beds etc

In the Barn
    A quantity of Barley threshed & unthreshed

In the Stable
    One Ride Horse – one Poney – 3 Saddles - 3 Bridles

Upon the Farm
    Thirteen Draught Horses & Gearing - 4 Waggons
    one Cart – 12 Harrows - 4 Ploughs – 1 large
    Hay Stack - part of another Hay Stack – 5 -
    Wheat Stacks - six Oat Stacks - 500 Sheep –
    13 Milch Cows - 12 Calves – Machine Fan
    12 Pigs'

When exactly did this much larger farmhouse replace the old building? An entry for 1807 in Lord Middleton's Note Book (Birdsall Estate Office: Wharram Archive notes) refers to the building of a new house, barn and stables at Wharram, so it may be that the surveyor's

Table 1. Census information. (House names deduced by R.T. Porter)

Date	1801	1811	1821	1831	1841
No. of houses:	3	4	3	2	3
(inhabited by one family each)	WP Farm Bella Vicarage	WP Farm Bella High Ho. Vicarage	WP Farm Bella High Ho.	WP Farm Bella	WP Farm Bella High Ho.
No. of males:	21	26	31	22	28
Uninhabited:	0	0	1 Vicarage	1 High Ho.	0

recommendation had an immediate response. On the other hand, we cannot rule out the possibility that this entry refers, at least as far as the barn and stables are concerned, to the erection of the present Wharram Percy farmstead, called High House in the 1820s to 1840s, standing in an isolated position on the Wold top about 1.4km to the south-west (see Fig. 5).

High House included a dwelling by the time of the 1811 census. R.T. Porter has provided the accompanying table (Table 1), drawn from census returns and recording the number of houses in the parish between 1801 and 1841 (see *Wharram III*, 16-20). He has deduced the names of the various inhabited and uninhabited dwellings; he suggests that in 1831 the vicarage was deemed to be a ruin rather than an uninhabited dwelling, and that the lack of occupants at High House in the same year may be related to John Cattle's bankruptcy.

What was the purpose of the High House farmstead? Some of the new Wolds farmsteads erected on new sites seem to have been intended as subsidiary groups of buildings for existing farms, rather than as the main farmsteads for newly created holdings. Colin Hayfield has studied several examples in the Wharram area: they were ranges of barns and other storage buildings, sometimes accompanied by a cottage or larger dwelling house, set round foldyards, where cattle were stored over winter. The dung generated by the cattle could be spread on surrounding fields, which were otherwise difficult to manure from the distant main farmstead (Hayfield 1991, 33-45). Keith Allison says of them:

'Such farmsteads usually comprised a small foldyard, a barn and a cottage, and frequently they took the name High Barn or Wold Barn… The 1,000-acre Burdale farm had two of these smaller units, situated on the higher land north and south of the valley in which the main farmstead lay.'
(Allison 1976, 164).

There can be little doubt that High House was conceived as one of these subsidiary farmsteads. Along with the farmhouse north of the church, it remained part of a single tenancy for over three decades. A letter of June 1831 indicates that John Cattle had occupied the two sets of farmsteads and outbuildings (Birdsall Estate Office, Wharram Deed Box: Wharram Archive notes). In 1841 the Goftons, the new tenants who had replaced Cattle, numbered four people and were recorded at the village farmstead along with two female servants and seven resident labourers. At High House there was one female servant and eight agricultural labourers.

Within a decade, however, the farmstead on the village site had been demolished, and R.T. Porter has provided a further note on the dating of this event. The farmhouse north of the church was still marked on Wise's Railway Plan dated 29 November, 1845 (see *Wharram X*, 261, where it is wrongly ascribed to the engineers, Birkinshaw and Dickens). The west range of the courtyard outbuildings had, however, already been demolished, and it is likely that the house went soon afterwards. It is

recorded as an earthwork on the Ordnance Survey 6 Inch map for which the final field examination took place in 1850 (see Margary 1991, ix).

The 1851 census records the Goftons at Wharram Percy New House, along with thirteen resident labourers. Low Houses, the present cottages, contained a labourer with his family and a shepherd's wife and her family. The cottages continued to be occupied until 1976, when the last one was vacated.

The new farmhouses were more spacious, providing accommodation for farm labourers as well as the farmer's family. At Cottam, for example, to the south-east of Wharram, there had been significant depopulation in the first half of the 18th century, with all but four of the nine houses and cottages being demolished after 1719, and only one family resident there by 1743 (Neave 1993, 134). Yet Harris records that in 1841, the two inhabited farmsteads there had no less than 41 occupants (Harris 1961, 99).

The increasing population on the Wolds in the early 19th century, after a long period of decline, reflects an enormous increase in the amount of cultivated land that accompanied the enclosure of the old sheep pastures and rabbit warrens, especially during the first four decades of the century. The fertility of the arable lands was now maintained by new crop rotations, incorporating new crops such as turnips and seeds, and by the use of new fertilisers. New feeding-stuffs were introduced, and cattle were brought in and stored in fold yards over winter, their primary purpose being to convert straw into manure as a way of maintaining the fertility of the arable lands (Harris 1961, 61-2, 102-5). The layout and function of the farm buildings that supported the new agricultural practices on the Wolds have been discussed elsewhere (see Hayfield 1991; Hayfield 1998, 113-21; Beresford and Hurst 1990, 120-21).

2   The Rectory, Chantry House and Vicarage from the 14th to 19th centuries
by S. Wrathmell

The rectory, vicarage and chantry house *c.* 1300-1550

The church of Wharram Percy is believed to have been established at the beginning of the 11th century, but there are few documentary references to its patrons and incumbents before the late 13th century (*Wharram III*, 21-23 and 27-30; *Wharram XI*, 327; *Wharram XIII*, forthcoming). At the beginning of the 14th century, the rector of Wharram Percy church was Master William Skeldergate. He had been appointed by Robert Percy, lord of the manor, who held the advowson, the right to appoint its incumbent. Skeldergate had, in turn, appointed a vicar, Henry Barkeby, to carry out parochial duties on his behalf. By March 1301, however, Barkeby was dead and Skeldergate obtained the archbishop's permission to consolidate the vicarage with the rectory, as he 'resides and intends to reside' (*Reg Corbridge I*, 165).

Skeldergate died in January 1308, and Robert Percy presented his own younger son, Henry Percy, clerk, as rector (*Reg Greenfield III*, 128). Unlike Skeldergate, Henry was largely an absentee rector, obtaining a series of licences for absence to study (Lawrance 1985, 69). The provisions he made for the 'cure of souls' in his absence are unknown, but in 1312 his incumbency was challenged by Gerald Salvayn, lord of Thixendale and Raisthorpe, who procured the presentation of his own son George Salvayn, clerk, to the living (*Reg Greenfield III*, 199). The case dragged on for a number of years, but Henry eventually prevailed.

It was probably after legal proceedings had ended that Robert Percy also granted to Henry his interest in the advowson of Wharram Percy. The process of transfer was completed when Robert quitclaimed his rights to Henry in September 1320 (Bodleian Library, Dodsworth 76, f.162r). Within two years, however, Henry had sold his interest in the advowson to Geoffrey Scrope (Feet of Fines: Roper and Kitching 2006); the king licensed the transaction in June, 1322 after an Inquisition *ad quod damnum* (*Cal PR 1321-4*, 136). Thereafter, Scrope presented three further rectors, the first of them in July 1323. The archbishop's register does not indicate whether Henry Percy had died or resigned (Lawrance 1985, 69).

Scrope's interest was short-lived. His friend Thomas Wake of Liddell had recently founded the Augustinian priory of Haltemprice at Cottingham, near Hull, and in February, 1327 Scrope was given licence to grant to the priory the advowson of Wharram Percy (*Cal PR 1327-30*, 14). The right of presentation remained with the priory until its suppression in 1536, when Haltemprice's rights and properties passed to the king.

The terms of Scrope's grant were set out in letters of authorisation issued by the archbishop and dated 17 November 1327. Archbishop Melton granted Haltemprice authority to appropriate the church of Wharram Percy to their own uses, and to take possession, without any further request to the archbishop, on the resignation or death of the current rector Sir John de Aldeburgh, whom the archbishop had admitted and instituted on Haltemprice's presentation.

There was to be a perpetual vicar with cure of souls, to be presented by Haltemprice to the archbishops (or the dean and chapter *sede vacante*) and to be admitted and instituted by the archbishop or dean and chapter, for whose support the archbishop reserved an adequate portion of the fruits of the church, set at 40 marks (£26 13s 4d), to be paid to the vicar on the feast of St Martin (30 November) and Whitsun; he also reserved an annual pension of two marks (£1 6s 8d) to be paid from the church by Haltemprice to the archbishop (or the dean and chapter *sede vacante*), in compensation for his loss of the income of the church, which hitherto had been accustomed to be governed by a secular rector during vacancies and paid to the archbishops, since from the date of the appropriation the vacancies would be shorter.

The grant was to enable Haltemprice to support four chaplains, two at Haltemprice of which one was to be of the Holy Spirit with prayer and memorial of souls, and the other for the souls of William and Constance the parents of Sir Geoffrey Scrope and of the same Sir Geoffrey and his wife Yvette after their deaths celebrating each day, and two at the church of Wharram Percy, one of the Blessed Virgin with prayer and memorial of souls, and the other celebrating daily for the souls of William and Constance, their sons Thomas and William, and for the souls of Sir Geoffrey Scrope and his wife Yvette, Sir Henry Scrope and Master Stephen Scrope, which Geoffrey gave the advowson of Wharram Percy to Haltemprice (Borthwick Register 9, f.308).

Haltemprice was, however, inadequately endowed (*Wharram III*, 22), and its financial difficulties led, in 1440, to a new ordination which substantially reduced the vicar's portion. The letters of Archbishop John Kempe, dated 27 April 1440, set out the following terms. The present vicar of Wharram Percy and his successors should have the cure of souls of the parishioners and administer the sacraments, and to that end should be bound personally 'to inhabit a dwelling-house (*mansum*) in the vill of Wharram Percy by the church, disposed and ordained for this purpose of old'; the present vicar and his successors to receive £11 6s 4d for his upkeep and that of a decent and sufficient chaplain to celebrate in the vills of Thixendale and Raisthorpe, to be paid by Haltemprice every year; the present vicar of Wharram Percy and his successors to have a garden by the dwelling-house, 'as it is now enclosed', and two bovates of arable land in the fields and territory of the vill of Wharram Percy belonging to the prior and convent (Borthwick Register 19, f.195).

The 1440 ordination, therefore, specified which house the vicars should occupy: one next to the church, probably erected soon after the appropriation in 1327. It also seems to infer that there may have been some difficulty in persuading previous vicars to live there. This accords with the scattered references to vicars' dwellings in the first half of the 14th century, which indicate that some of them occupied houses belonging to the manor, located perhaps at the opposite end of the village.

The first of these references is in the inquisition *post mortem* after the death of Robert Percy, held in June 1323. It begins with the capital messuage, or manor house, worth 3s 4d a year; then it deals with 'another house that the vicar of Wharram was accustomed to inhabit', worth 12d a year; then it goes on to value the demesne oxgangs before detailing the rents and other dues from the tenantry (TNA PRO C134/75/15 m.3). This seems to indicate that the vicar's house lay within the demesne holding. Similarly, when Eufemia, widow of a later lord of Wharram Percy, was assigned a third part of the manor as dower in 1368, she was given 'a messuage which Master Peter Lyelff, formerly vicar of the church of Wharram, lately held, and a cottage called "le Prestehous", with a close and land annexed, in recompense of her dower of the chief messuage of the manor' (*Cal IPM XII*, 183).

The vicar's house itemised in 1323 was worth just under a third the value of the capital messuage, indicating that it would have represented an appropriate level of compensation for the loss of a third of the manor house. Therefore it is probable that the two references, in 1323 and 1368, are to the same property. Peter Lyolf had been vicar from 1338 until his death in 1349 (Lawrance 1985, 69), so it may be that the appropriation of the church by Haltemprice had initially made little impact upon the residential arrangements of the vicars. It is interesting in this context to note the action begun in 1370 by the prior of Haltemprice against Adam Gemelyng, vicar of Wharram Percy, for waste in the lands, houses, woods and gardens at Wharram Percy demised to Adam for a term of years (Baildon 1895, 82).

Whatever the date of its erection or length of use, there is no reason to doubt that the 1440 vicarage was the same modest property as that entered by Marmaduke Atkinson a century later, containing a house and also a barn to accommodate the produce of the two oxgangs of arable that had been assigned to the vicar. The revenues and lands enumerated in 1555 reflect closely those of 1440:

'[The vicarage] had no tithes oblations lands grounds commodities nor profits pertaining or belonging to the same saving one yearly annual pension or sum of £11 6s 8d which hath and ought to be paid yearly… by the proprietors… also two oxgangs of arable lands and certain grass meadow or *ynge* ground to the quantity of two acres of land…'
(Borthwick CP G.3537)

A large part of the barn, along with charred remains of the crops it had contained, was excavated in Site 77 (see Chapter 9).

Of the other ecclesiastical dwellings in the village, the rectory seems to appear only once in the documentary sources. It occurs in the 1368 assignment of dower, one of the assigned properties being 'a waste toft formerly in the tenure of Broune Robyn next the rectory, with the lands belonging thereto; similar waste tofts formerly in the tenures of William Whyt and Emma Henrykesson…' (*Cal IPM XII*, 183).

This indicates that the rectory was adjacent to one or more of the farmsteads formerly in the occupation of manorial tenants, but it does not, of course, give any indication of the part of the village in which it was located. We can assume that the residence of, successively, Master William Skeldergate and Henry Percy (albeit only very occasionally for the latter), will have been substantial and appropriate to men who also held a park and a pond (presumably used as a fishery) from the lord of the manor (Bodleian Library, Dodsworth 76, f.162r; *Wharram X*, 8).

The use of the rectory after the 1327 appropriation is unknown, though it may well have been leased out. The rectory barn, however, assuming it was located next to the house, would presumably have still been used for the collection and storage of all the parish tithes before their sale or transfer to Haltemprice.

The final ecclesiastical component of the village was a chantry house. Though two chantries had been set up in the church at the time of appropriation, they are not mentioned in 1440 and had probably, therefore, failed by then. Another one was, however, set up in the 15th or early 16th century (presumably after 1440), as it is recorded at the time of its suppression. According to the particulars for the sale of its lands, drawn up in June 1552, it was called the chantry of Towthorpe in the parish church of Wharram Percy. At the time its lands were said to be two oxgangs containing 16 acres in the tenure of the vicar, Marmaduke Atkinson, and let year on year for 13s 4d (TNA PRO E315/68, f.439v). This land holding was the subject of William Holme's deposition in the dilapidations cause of 1555-6 (see Chapter 1).

The name of the chantry indicates some connection with the township of Towthorpe, which formed the eastern end of Wharram parish, or with a family named after that place. It has been a source of some confusion (e.g. *Wharram III*, 7), as there was also a chapel at Towthorpe itself, dedicated to St Katherine. The survey of colleges, chantries, chapels etc. undertaken by the archbishop in 1546 records that the incumbent of the chapel at Towthorpe, Robert Boynton, had a stipend of £4 13s 4d paid by the farmer of Towthorpe tithes (TNA PRO E301/66, no.152). The chapel was said specifically to have no lands or tenements, and so is clearly distinguished from Towthorpe chantry. In the previous year Boynton, St Katherine's last incumbent, had brought a cause of defamation against John Reves of Towthorpe. Reves had been heard to say, in the churchyard of Wharram Percy, that in the 'town' where he came from Boynton had got a man's daughter with child; Reves was also alleged to have called Boynton a 'whore master' (Borthwick CP G.338).

The house of the chantry chaplain can be roughly located, though again in post-suppression documents. Another of the depositions in the 1555-6 dilapidations cause was Thomas Marshall's testimony about the location of the vicarage barn: '[there] was a laith standing at the North end of the Vicarage to the chantry house ward' (Borthwick CP G.3537). This indicates that the chantry house was north of the vicarage house, and separated from it by the vicar's barn. We know that from 1440 the vicarage was next to the church, and it was common for the houses of chantry chaplains also to be located close to the church (Cook 1947, 50-51).

The vicarage in the mid-16th century

The most detailed documentation for the vicarage dates to the mid-16th century and has already been quoted extensively in Chapter 1. It is the partial record of proceedings in a cause of dilapidations brought in the court of the archbishop of York. The plaintiff was William Firby, vicar of Wharram Percy, who had been admitted to the living in December 1554 (Borthwick, Admissions

Index). The accused, or 'respondent', was Marmaduke Atkinson, who had preceded Firby as vicar of Wharram, but had resigned to become rector of Bainton. The forms of ecclesiastical court proceedings at York have been summarised by Purvis (1953, 66-7), and provide the context for understanding the surviving documents.

The first surviving document is a statement by the prosecution setting out Firby's case in a series of numbered 'articles'. The defence then made 'personal responses' on Atkinson's behalf, denying or qualifying the facts that had been alleged in the articles. The prosecution then produced witness statements to support Firby's allegations, in the form of depositions that addressed each of the articles in numerical order. The deponents also had to provide the court with information as to how long they had known each party, how old they were and where they lived. Most witnesses had little or nothing to depose in relation to at least a few of the articles; but through their detailed testimony on others, they have provided a considerable amount of information on the vicarage, its lands, and indirectly on the agrarian landscape of Wharram Percy in the first half of the 16th century (see Chapter 1).

The second stage of the proceedings mirrored the first, beginning with a series of articles on behalf of the defence. Responses by the prosecution followed, and then witness statements supporting the articles set out by the defence. A third stage followed, because the prosecution wished to add further articles to its original series of charges.

Atkinson made a second set of personal responses to the further articles, and there was a second series of witness statements on behalf of the prosecution. Finally, the process was mirrored yet again, with Atkinson setting out articles and providing depositions from witnesses, and Firby setting out his personal responses.

The documents surviving from this cause are in two bundles at the Borthwick Institute for Archives, University of York. Most of the items are in CP G.3537: these include the two sets of articles submitted by each party, the two sets of personal responses provided by each party and three of the four sets of depositions. The final items in the bundle are an 'additional position' or statement in relation to one of Atkinson's articles, and a sheet of paper which summarises the dimensions of the vicarage buildings, both extant and demolished. The second bundle, CP G.917, contains the fourth set of depositions. The documents that do not seem to have survived are the initial ones setting up the cause, and the final one giving the court's sentence.

Not all the documents are dated, but all except one can be grouped together and placed in chronological order (Table 2). This is because the responses, depositions and additional positions can be matched up with the numbers and content of the four sets of articles, and some of the sets of articles refer directly to depositions in support of the previous set of articles. Therefore we are able to follow the flow of claim and counter-claim, back and forth between the parties, through the four groups of documents.

Table 2. Chronological list of groups of surviving documents recording the 1555-6 Dilapidations Cause, with Borthwick references.

Groups	Content	Medium	Date	Reference
Group 1	Articles by WF against MA	Large sheet of parchment with small piece sewn on	undated	CP G.3537
	Personal responses of MA	Sheets of paper	?23 May 1555	CP G.3537
	Seven depositions for WF starting with Thomas Jeb	Sheets of paper	11 June 1555	CP G.3537
Group 2	Articles by MA referring to above depositions	Large sheet of parchment	undated	CP G.3537
	Personal responses of WF	Sheets of paper	15 July 1555	CP G.3537
	Nine depositions for MA starting with William Holme	Sheets of paper	29 October 1555	CP G.917
	Additional position by WF referring to above depositions	Small sheet of parchment	undated	CP G.3537
Group 3	Articles by WF against MA	Small sheet of parchment	undated	CP G.3537
	Personal responses of MA	Sheets of paper	30 July 1555	CP G.3537
	Three depositions for WF starting with vicar of Acklam	Sheets of paper	30 July 1555	CP G.3537
Group 4	Articles by MA referring to above depositions	Large sheet of parchment	undated	CP G.3537
	Personal responses of WF	Sheets of paper	17 April 1556	CP G.3537
	Six depositions for MA starting with Michael Tailor	Sheets of paper	17 July 1556	CP G.3537
?	Summary of sizes of various buildings	Sheet of paper	undated	CP G.3537

MA = Marmaduke Atkinson
WF = William Firby

Group 1 documents

The original allegations were made by Firby early in 1555, following his institution the previous December (Lawrance 1985, 71). The general thrust of his complaint was summarised in the fourth article: that the chancel of the parish church and the vicarage houses and buildings were ruined and dilapidated and had been since the time of Atkinson's incumbency. Article five mentions in particular a barn or laith of six posts or crucks that had stood in the vicarage in Atkinson's time, but was there no longer:

'*Item ponit et Articulatur quod tempore incumbentie dicti vicarii in dicta vicaria fuit quoddam horreum anglice* a barn or Laith of six posts or crucks…'

It would, according to article six, cost £6 13s 4d to rebuild. The phrase 'posts or crucks' recurs in the depositions, the ambiguity perhaps reflecting the different building traditions of the Wolds and of the York area where the cause was heard. The former was within the region of cruck building, the latter in the post-and-truss zone (*Wharram VI*, 3-5).

As far as the chancel was concerned, Atkinson's response was to confirm its ruinous condition, both during his incumbency and at the time of his resignation. Its maintenance and repair were not, however, his responsibility, but the rector's. The rectory had been in the possession of Haltemprice Priory at its dissolution, and so now belonged to the crown. Therefore the chancel's repair was a matter for the king and queen (Philip and Mary).

With regard to the barn, his response was that when he entered the vicarage (in 1540: Lawrance 1985, 71) the buildings had all been under one roof, with a house at one end and a barn at the other, but that they had been burned down in 1553:

'that at this respondent entering to the said vicarage there was a house and a laith of six posts or more builded all under one roof and this respondent used the one end for his dwelling and the other end for his corn and hay the which houses by chance of fire was burned in the night season about two years since'

Later supplementary evidence by Atkinson refines the date of the fire to Lent, 1553, that is, to the month of February or March in that year.

The first four depositions on behalf of Firby were made by a yeoman, a husbandman, a wright and a labourer from Askham Bryan and Copmanthorpe to the south-west of York, some 20 miles away. All had known Firby for many years, but they were not acquainted with Atkinson, nor with conditions at Wharram Percy during Atkinson's incumbency. Thomas Carter of Copmanthorpe, for example, said he had nothing to depose in relation to the former barn, except that 'neighbours' said there had been one there. Firby had clearly brought them in as men he could trust to give him valuations relating to the costs of dilapidations and estimates of yields from the glebe lands.

He also, however, had statements from three husbandmen of Thixendale, men whom he had known for only a short time but who had known Atkinson for many years. The first, Thomas Marshall, was able to give more details about the vicarage buildings before the fire, and widened the argument from the simple presence or absence of a barn. He deposed that the buildings which stood there when Atkinson entered the vicarage comprised a barn, stable and house, and were far more extensive than those which Atkinson had erected after the fire, and which existed at the time Firby entered the vicarage:

'the which laith he saith was builded at the stable end and he saith the mansion house stable and laith were all builded under one roof'

'he thinks a laith of six posts or crucks will cost at least building and setting up seven pounds and he saith that there Lacks of the building which was builded at the time of the said Sir Marmaduke Atkynson's entry to the said vicarage and the most part of his incumbency thereunto the same was burned with fire which is about two years since at the east end 28 foot and at the end to the church ward 40 foot…'

Though this deposition refers to the 'east end' of the vicarage, all but one of the other statements indicate that before the fire the vicarage buildings had run north to south. Hugh Collome of Thixendale, for example stated that the laith had stood at the north end of the vicarage, in the direction of the chantry house; he also implies it was a three bay building, though this is difficult to reconcile with only six posts or crucks:

'that the time of the said Sir Marmaduke Atkynson's incumbency in the said vicarage unto the houses were burned which was in lent last two years since that was a laith standing at the North end of the Vicarage to the chantry house ward of three rooms which he saith was at the end of the mansion house of the said vicarage and under one roof and he saith that there lacks of the building which was there before the burning of the said vicarage at the North end the whole room where the laith stood which is 28 foot…'

Group 2 documents

In the articles for the defence, Atkinson confirmed the layout of the vicarage buildings at the time of his induction:

'*Item quod tempore admissionis et inductionis dicti domini marmaduci ad dictam vicariam* all and singular houses and buildings belonging to the said vicarage were builded under one Roof viz one little house with a chamber over it a little house used for a kitchen and one little house used for a laith and at that time there was no more houses nor buildings belonging the said vicarage'

He also said that he had erected new buildings after his admission and before the fire, at considerable cost to himself; that the fire was not caused by his negligence, that the buildings he erected after the fire were sufficient without a barn, and that they were in good repair at the time of his resignation.

Husbandmen of Raisthorpe and Towthorpe gave statements in support. Their testimony in relation to the necessity or otherwise of a vicarage barn, linked to estimates of the yields of corn and hay from the glebe land, has already been discussed in Chapter 1. They also confirmed that Atkinson had spent significant sums on new buildings both before and after the fire. William Holme of Raisthorpe deposed:

'that he hath Seen at Divers times before the said vicarage was burnt by Chance of fire many workmen at the said vicarage And he did see many things new made about the house which he believeth cost the said Sir Marmaduke above £20'

'that he hath viewed the house at Wharram Percy And that there is sufficient Room to Lie all the corn and hay belonging the said vicarage in And as much building and better building now than there was when the said Sir Marmaduke came unto it'

William Bennet of Raisthorpe said:

'that the vicarage and houses about the same was new builded by the said Sir Marmaduke since they were burnt which cost him as he believeth by his estimation £20 or more'

Robert Pickering of Raisthorpe could supply even more detail, having himself participated in the work:

'that by his Estimation the building of the houses Stuff and workmanship for the vicarage of Wharram Percy cost the said Sir Marmaduke £10 and above for he see three Carpenters there half a year and he this Examinate wrought there thatching six weeks and after him was there two thatchers and six wallers by the space of six weeks of his certain Knowledge'

Group 3 documents

Firby resumed his attack with additional articles, and with clerical support in the shape of depositions by the vicars of Acklam, Fridaythorpe and Wharram le Street. The allegations still included the issue of the barn, and the need for a place to store corn, but the focus shifted to a comparison of the dimensions of the present vicarage with those of the pre-fire buildings, elaborating upon the earlier depositions that the new building was shorter than the old at both ends. Atkinson's response introduced new arguments: that there had been void ground between the old buildings, and so the total roofed area had been no greater than now; and that since the fire he had erected not only a new vicarage but also another building containing a kitchen, stable and hen house.

'he saith that whatsoever it lacks in the ends he believeth that there was as much ground that stood void betwixt the houses of the old building as that Lack extendeth unto. And considering another house which is new builded of three Rooms that is to say for a kitchen stable and a hen house being Distant about 40 foot from the new mansion house articulate there is as much building there and rather more than was when he came first unto the said vicarage'

The three vicars conducted the first recorded earthwork survey at Wharram Percy on 26 July 1555. Robert Ellerton, vicar of Acklam, deposed:

'that being at Wharram Percy upon friday last accompanied with the aforesaid Sir William Stanesby and Sir William Marshall as is above specified they measured the Situation of the old building to be 42 yards and a half of Length and the new building to be 22 yards and half'

'that the said new building Lacketh also in Length of the old building as appeareth by the ground whereupon the old building was situate and builded twelve yards at the one end and eight at the other…'

Group 4 documents

The final group of documents includes Atkinson's reply to the additional articles submitted by Firby, and they give the most detailed account of the vicarage buildings. They start with Atkinson explicitly retracting his earlier statements that when he entered the vicarage all the buildings were under one roof. His final articles elaborate his response to Firby's additional articles, in which he had mentioned for the first time an area of void ground 'betwixt the houses':

'*Item ponit et articulatur… quod tempore inductionis Dicti marmaduci ad dictam vicariam ac diu antea* There was two Sundry houses then belonging unto the said vicarage which was then builded in and under two Sundry Roofs the one of the said houses then being distant from the other house about forty foot'

'that both the said houses at the time of the said Induction of the said Sir Marmaduke was then in Length about 24 yards and in breadth as yet doth and shall appear by the groundwork walls and foundations of the said houses yet remaining'

'*quod dictus marmaducus post Inductionem suam…* did build at his costs and charges in and upon the void ground aforesaid then being as is aforesaid betwixt the said two houses two fair parlours two Chimneys and four high chambers and also he builded at his costs and charges two outshots viz one at the end of the said houses then being about four yards long and another outshot at the other end of the said houses then being about four yards long, the said outshots being of breadth as the other houses <were> whereunto they were builded and annexed…'

It was as a result of his own building works that the vicarage came to be a single range all under one roof, and 'was 42 yards long And of breadth as yet shall and doth appear by the groundwork walls and foundations of the said houses…'

Once more the farmers of Raisthorpe and Towthorpe (but not Thixendale) made statements in support of Atkinson. On 17 July 1556, Michael Tailor of Towthorpe recorded the results of a second formal survey of the pre-fire vicarage earthworks, stating:

'that he this deponent three weeks since or thereabouts at the Desire of Sir Marmaduke Atkinson Accompanied with William Holme William Hogeson Robert Ryves John Bottrell [blank] vicar of Acclam and Sir William Stayneby [William Firby deleted] did go and measure the old buildings belonging the vicarage of Wharram Percy with the new building there And he saith that the hall house of the new building doth contain in Length 25 yards and a half and in breadth six yards And that there is a new house that stands where no house stood before which doth contain in length 12 yards and a half and five yards in breadth Also there was another building which was for ducks Swine and pullen [poultry] pulled down by the vicar that now is which doth contain by the measure of the Eystre which is the baulk of the Length of the house seven yards in Length and two yards and a half in breadth And he this deponent saith that there is void ground at the south end of the hall newly builded which was parcel of the old building thirteen yards and a half of Length and of breadth seven yards And at the north end nine yards and a half of Length and seven yards of breadth in place whereof the new house aforesaid was builded And he saith that there was of void ground of the old building as doth appear by the foundations of the walls to this deponent's judgement To the quantity of fifteen yards in length and twelve yards in breadth at the entering of the said Sir Marmaduke to the said vicarage'

With regard to the buildings erected by Atkinson before the fire, he stated:

'that the said Sir Marmaduke did cause two parlours two chimneys [three chambers deleted] to be builded in the waste ground as is articulate and also he builded two outshots whereof he hath deposed in his depositions in this court before Christmas last'

Robert Ryvar, labourer provided supporting evidence on the pre-fire buildings erected by Atkinson, and indicated they were built in about 1546:

'that about six years after the said Sir Marmaduke was instituted vicar of Wharram Percy he this examinate saith that the said Sir Marmaduke did cause to be builded two fair parlours two chimneys and two chambers and one outshot which this deponent did thatch himself at the west side of the said house and these he saith was builded of the waste ground of the said vicarage'

He was also involved in the second survey:

'that he this deponent about Pentecost last past at the desire of the parson of Baynton [Atkinson] and Sir William Firbie vicar of Wharram Percy accompanied with Michael Tailor George Andro William Holme vicar of Acclam and vicar of Wharram in the street and William Hodgeson did measure the said grounds and by their measure he saith there is 25 yards of the hall house new builded and six yards of breadth wheron the old building at the time of building [sic] of the house was before and

a kitchen builded where there was no building at the time of the burning of the said vicarage of twelve yards long and five yards of breadth and the said parson Baynton soon after he came to the vicarage did build a swine house or hen house of eight yards long and two yards broad and further he saith that there is thirteen yards at the west [recte: south – as in other depositions] end of the house now builded void ground whereupon building was set before it was burned and the north end of the said house he saith that there is nine yards whereupon there was building before it was burnt and now none and further he saith that the new building now belonging to the vicarage with the ground which was waste whereupon the parson of Bainton did build two parlours two chimneys and two chambers which did contain fifteen yards of length to this examinate's judgement and about five yards breadth is as much building and more as was of the ground belonging to the said vicarage when the said parson entered to the same according to their measuring aforesaid'

William Hodgson, husbandman, was able to support Atkinson's modified testimony as to the buildings that were there in 1540:

'that there was two houses at the entry of the said Sir Marmaduke to the said vicarage and a vacant place distant betwixt them how far certainly the said vacant place was he cannot depose but he saith he knoweth that there was two such houses for he was a scholar at the said time and at commons in the vicarage with one Thomas Carter and learned with Sir Thomas Hurre'

He also provided more details on the buildings erected by Atkinson before and after the fire:

'that the said Sir Marmaduke about six years as he remembereth after he came to the said vicarage and took induction there did build a parlour a buttery a double chimney four chambers viz three little chambers and another chamber wheron joists were laid and the same uncovered and with those houses he filled the vacant room which was betwixt the said houses and also he builded one outshot at the end of the house towards the church and an other outshot off the backside of the house which he did make a bolting house and a larder house of'

'that the hall house now builded by the said Sir Marmaduke was as broad within half a yard as the other was which was burned of this deponent's own sight for he did see and view the site of the old house when this hall house new builded was set up and a part of the new house was set where one of the walls of the other old house which was burned stood…'

William Holme of Raisthorpe, husbandman, 60, confirmed that in 1540 there were two buildings with a gap between them, and gave details about two outshots also erected by Atkinson:

'that at the entry of the said Sir Marmaduke to the said vicarage there was two buildings and a vacant place betwixt them about fifteen yards of which vacant place the said Sir Marmaduke before the houses was burned did build two parlours two chimneys two chambers of this deponent's knowledge and sight and also did build at the end of the house towards the church an outshot for hens and such like and also he builded another Outshot off the backside of the said house for a larder house…'

John Botterell, husbandman, was another participant in the 1556 survey:

'that betwixt Easter and pentecost last past he this deponent at the request and consent of Sir Marmaduke Atkynson priest and Sir William Firbie vicar of Wharram Percy was at the measuring of the houses now builded and belonging to the said vicarage of Wharram Percy accompanied with the vicar of Wharram of the street vicar of Acclam William Hodgeson Michael Tailor George Andrewe and William Holme and also he saith that the said Sir Marmaduke Atkynson and Sir William Firbie was present and see the measuring of the said houses. And he saith the hall house now builded and other houses being under one roof is 25 yards of length and six yards of breadth. Another house being a Kitchen and other buildings under one roof twelve yards length and five yards breadth. Another Little house of seven yards length and two yards breadth which was measured by the aistre [a house or its parts] or roof of the house which house was standing when the parson of Baynton went from the vicarage and since fallen down. Also there is thirteen yards at the South end of the hall house wherupon there hath been building and now void ground And at the North end of the said house there is nine yards of waste ground wherupon there hath been building…'

Analysis of evidence for the vicarage buildings, 1540-54

It is possible to distil from all these articles, responses and depositions a coherent and detailed building history for the vicarage between 1540 and 1554, and a broad indication of the size of its component structures despite variations in the measurements provided by each party. R.T. Porter, the Wharram project surveyor, has analysed the internal consistency of the surveys, and has used the figures from the vicars' survey to generate the diagrams in Figure 6, showing the pre-fire and post-fire building plans. Given that the excavation of Site 77 revealed what was unquestionably part of vicar Atkinson's burnt-out barn, it was anticipated that the reconciliation of the documentary evidence and the structural remains would be straightforward. This was not in fact the case, as will be seen in Chapter 28.

When Atkinson entered the vicarage there were two separate buildings: one a dwelling with a kitchen and a chamber over, and the other a barn. The barn was about 8 yards (7.32m) long and 7 yards (6.4m) wide, and the house (and kitchen) would have been about 17 yards (15.54m) long. The gap between them was 15 yards (13.72m) long, and its breadth was said to be 12 yards (10.97m), though the documents give no indication of what delimited the measurement of breadth. Their orientation may have been broadly north to south (though perhaps more north-east to south-west, to account for the discrepant orientations), with the barn at the north end.

In about 1546 (according to Robert Ryvar), Atkinson built a block between them containing two heated parlours, with chimneys, on the ground floor, and chambers above. He also erected two outshots: one at the south end of the house for hens and/or pigs, and one along the west side as a larder. The parlour block linked the formerly separate barn and dwelling, creating a continuous roof about 42^1/$_2$ yards (38.86m) long. We are not told whether the roof ran in a straight line, or whether it covered buildings set on differing alignments. In either case, when a fire broke out one night in February or March, 1553, the whole range was consumed except for the hen house.

Atkinson constructed its replacement during the next twelve months, before resigning to take up Bainton rectory. The new hall was about 22^1/$_2$ yards (20.57m) long by 6 yards (5.49m) wide, and was set partly on the site of the old building. The area of the former barn was, however, outside the new vicarage, as was a stretch of the old vicarage to the south of the new one. It may be that part of the central area of the earlier vicarage was also left outside the footprint of the new one. Nowhere is the orientation of the new hall specified. Atkinson also built an entirely new range, containing stables and a kitchen (or perhaps brew house – one of the deponents calls it an ale house), about 13 yards (11.89m) distant from the hall in a place where there had been no buildings before (at least as far as the deponents were aware). It measured 12 yards by 5 yards (10.97m by 4.57m).

The chantry house and vicarage from the late 16th century to mid-19th century

After the dissolution of Haltemprice priory, the advowson, rectory and revenues of Wharram Percy church remained in the crown's possession for nearly half a century. The tithes of the various constituent townships were initially farmed out on short-term leases, those of Wharram Percy township on at least two occasions to the vicars. At the time of the dissolution they were farmed by John Smith, the last vicar presented by Haltemprice (TNA PRO C66/1025, m.45), and a few years later by vicar Atkinson, who initiated a tithe cause against John Thorpe in 1543 (see Chapter 1). In 1545 the tithes were leased for 21 years by Thomas Kydall of York (*LP Henry VIII, 20, pt 1, 682*).

The chantry lands, too, seem initially to have been farmed out on short term leases. On 30 June 1552 particulars were drawn up for the sale of the chantry's two oxgangs which were then said to be held year on year by vicar Atkinson. The purchaser was to have the issues of the lands from the previous Easter (TNA PRO E315/68, f.439v). It has not been established whether the lands were immediately sold, but if there was a delay, it could be that Atkinson, not the purchasers, received the issues of the lands that year; and *if* the oxgangs were still being cultivated, their produce might then have formed part of the vicarage barn contents the following spring (see Chapter 24).

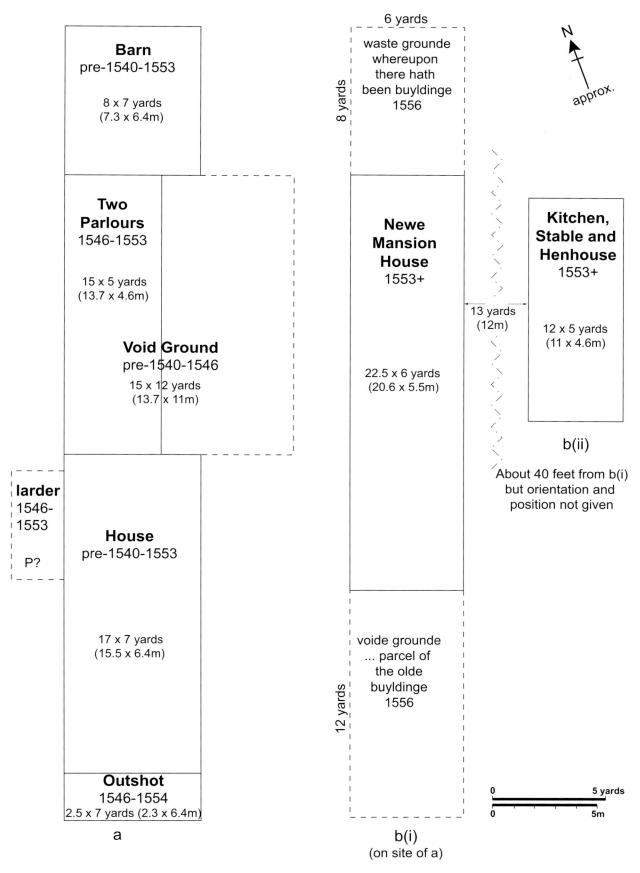

Fig. 6. The vicarage buildings as described in the documentary evidence: a. pre-1553, b. post-1553. Approximate dimensions in yards. P?=position and size not stated. (E. Marlow-Mann after R.T. Porter)

In 1566, on the expiry of the Kydall lease, Richard Marks was granted the tithes of Wharram Percy and Burdale, after offering to build within two years a barn to house these tithes either in Wharram Percy or Burdale (TNA PRO C66/1025, m.45). In 1570 Marks initiated a tithe cause against William Drew. He claimed Drew had, in and since 1567, pastured 'in certain closes or grounds within the said parish of Wharram Percy lately common' numerous geld beasts, draught beasts (oxen and horses), sheep and lambs, cows and calves, and he had not paid his tithes (Borthwick CP G.1793). He had also, it was alleged, cleared and converted for his own use up to 60 waggon-loads of timber from the place called 'le Sydebanke'.

The Sidebank, also named the Wood, was one of two small parcels of land which in 1563 had been identified as 'lands concealed from Her [Majesty] since the dissolution of the monasteries'. It was described as 'two acres and called Wharram Wood'; the other was 'an acre called Wharram Dam'. Both were 'now or recently' in the tenure of the rector of Bainton (i.e. Marmaduke Atkinson: TNA PRO C66/999, m.18). The two parcels together were said to amount to four acres, in particulars for grants of crown lands audited in 1567 (TNA PRO E318/36/1972). Their location and earlier history will be discussed further in *Wharram XIII*.

These 'concealed lands' were soon afterwards acquired from the crown by Matthew Hutton, dean and later archbishop of York. Having purchased the manor from Sir William Hilton and others in 1573 (see Chapter 1), he bought the advowson and tithes of Wharram Percy in January 1582 (*Wharram III*, 24), and also acquired the chantry lands. Later that year, Hutton entailed his property, including Wharram Percy, on his son Timothy, and on Timothy's lawful heirs. The grant of the manor and tithes included all the houses, lands and tenement called chantry lands, a parcel of meadow called the Dam and a parcel of land called the Sidebank (NYCRO ZAZ 10).

The chantry house survived into the 17th century, achieving notice in the 1605 lease of the manor and lordship of Wharram Percy to Margery and Robert Weddell (see Chapter 1):

'And also all the houses and land there sometime belonging to the late Chantry called Tolethrop chantry founded in the parish church of Wharram Percy aforesaid and also two parcels of ground called the side bank and dam within the said lordship…[the tenants to] repair maintain and uphold the chief house of the said Manor and the chantry house aforesaid, and all other edifices houses and buildings to the said Manor or to the said Chantry house [belonging]'
(NYCRO ZAZ 10)

Thirty years later, the lease of the estate to Sir John Buck, the first stage in the Bucks' purchase of Wharram Percy, used much the same wording (Reading UL, Ms EN 1/2/296), but no subsequent reference to the chantry house has been identified.

As for the vicarage, William Firby, plaintiff in the dilapidations cause, remained vicar of Wharram Percy until his death. He was succeeded in January 1576 by Thomas Pearson, who was already vicar of Wharram le Street, and who continued to serve both parishes until his death in 1618 (Lawrance 1985, 66, 71). Though Firby had been resident in the parish (and presumably continued to inhabit the vicarage), Pearson was not, and visitations record his neglect of the property. In 1586 it was reported that 'the vicarage houses [buildings] are in great decay' (Borthwick V.1586 CB f.125v), though the extent of the 'decay' is uncertain: the house itself was evidently still standing, and was still used by Pearson when he came to the church. For in the same year James Grainger brought a cause of defamation against Pearson. Pearson's response was that:

'[he] being in the vicarage of Wharam Percy in the month of october late and there keeping posession peaceably in his said vicarage alone The said James Grainger came to the window of the said vicarage accompanied with six or seven other persons and called on this respondent and said priest open the Door…'
(Borthwick CP G.2248)

In a visitation of 1600, Pearson was found to have given no sermons at Wharram Percy in the previous year (Borthwick V.1600 CB1 f.110r), and four years later was said to have let the vicarage to two farmers. He had:

'let forth his vicarage So that he… [missing] dwell of it and having Let the vicarage house to Leonard Wooddell and Michaell Millner of Mowthrope the said houses are in ruin and decay'
(Borthwick V.1604 CB f.114v)

Pearson was ordered to repair it before the Feast of St Martin. Leonard Weddell had been associated with Wharram Percy from at least 1586, when he had been charged by the vicar with irreverent behaviour, and with allowing a great dog to cause a disturbance in the churchyard (Borthwick V.1586 CB f.126r). He was presumably the husband of Margery Weddell who, as a widow, leased the manor, tithes and former chantry property in 1605, along with her son (Chapter 1).

Beresford identified resident and non-resident vicars on the basis of parish register entries: whether they were married or buried at Wharram Percy, and whether their children were baptised there. He argued that between Pearson's death, in 1618, and 1747 there is sufficient evidence to suggest that successive vicars were resident. Thereafter, the evidence indicates at least some periods of non-residence until the demolition of the vicarage, in or shortly after 1834 (*Wharram III*, 30-31).

Though we can expect the vicarage to have become dilapidated at the beginning of the 17th century, when vicar Pearson let it out, the succession of resident incumbents from 1618 to 1747 presumably kept it in repair, and at least some of their successors may also have done. The only information on the house in the 17th century is that provided by the Hearth Tax returns during the incumbency of vicar Luck (called 'Luckock' in the 1674 returns, when he paid tax on two hearths: Beresford and Hurst 1990, 102).

Though the glebe terriers survive from the 17th century, the first, brief mention of the vicar's house occurs in a terrier of 1716 (Borthwick, Ter. K Wharram Percy 1716). It lists 'A House with a Stable, an Orchard, Garden & Backyard containing by Estimation an Acre of Ground'. In 1743 it is described as 'A Vicarage House a Stable and some other Conveniences, the Yard in which the House stands…'. Much more detail is provided in the 1764 terrier, though we have no way of knowing whether the detailed record was made because the house was newly rebuilt:

'*Imprimis* A Vicarage House consisting of three Rooms below Stairs with a Pantry annexed all in one Straight Building nineteen yards long and four and $^1/_2$ Wide, two Rooms flagged and one floored with Deal; Above Stairs 4 Chambers only of the Same Dimensions viz- Nineteen Yards long and 4 Yards and half Wide, with a false Roof, without any Garrets, The Timber of the House consists of Ash Wood and Deal Poles A Stable Eleven Yards long and five Wide' (Borthwick, Ter. K. Wharram Percy 1764)

This was undoubtedly the building excavated as Structure K in Site 54 (see pp 107-110).

The same description as that in 1764 appears also in the 1770 terrier, but from 1777 onwards it became:

'*Imprimis* A Vicarage House Nineteen Yards long and four yards wide, Two Rooms flagged and One floored with Deal – A Stable Eleven yards long and five Wide, The whole Building covered with Thatch as also the House…'. (Borthwick, Ter. K. Wharram Percy 1777)

R.T. Porter has provided the following notes on the final years of the vicarage house, during the incumbency of Richard Allen. Allen had been curate of Wharram Percy from 1784 to 1788, when he was admitted vicar. He had no other living at that time, nor until the following year, when he also became curate of Kirby Grindalythe. He may have lived in the Wharram Percy vicarage house from 1784 to 1788, and possibly until 1798 when he also became curate at both Little and Great Driffield. According to a transcript of his diaries (East Riding Archives and Local Studies Service YE/B/ALL), which covers the years 1828, 1830 and 1832, Allen was resident at Little Driffield during this period. He had probably lived there since acquiring the curacy. In the years 1828-9 he had a curate at Wharram Percy, Matthew Welburn, but we are not told Welburn's place of residence, nor that of any earlier curates.

The diary transcripts contain a few references to the vicarage house at Wharram Percy. The first, in July 1828, simply records: 'Received a letter from Mr Cattle informing me that part of the house was fallen'. Cattle was the tenant of Wharram Percy farm, and he rented the glebe lands from Allen. We cannot prove that the house in question was the vicarage rather than Cattle's farmhouse; but it is hard to imagine why Cattle would write to Allen in the latter case, and even less why Allen should then enter it into his diary.

In July 1832 the transcript records: 'Visited Wharram Percy, where we met with a kind reception. The vicarage house much out of repair. Considered it best to defer this business till next spring'. A month later, however, he recorded: 'My nephew and Mr Croxton sounded Mr Duncan, steward for Lord Middleton, respecting Wharram Percy.'

Lord Middleton may already have been planning to unite the two Wharram vicarages, though he did not become patron of Wharram Percy until the following year when he purchased the Wharram estate from the descendants of the Bucks (*Wharram III*, 25). Allen died in January, 1833 (*Gentleman's Mag.* 103, 1 March 1833, 282), and the vacancy provided the opportunity for Middleton to petition for unification. The surviving record, seeking the annexation of Wharram Percy to Wharram le Street, confuses the names of the two places:

'That the Vicarage House of Wareham alias Wharram Percy is a mere cottage and has been for many years inhabited by a Cottager but the Vicarage House at Wareham alias Wharram Percy [*sic*], although it is not at present fit <dilapidated> for the residence of the Vicar is capable of being made so and is conveniently situated for both the Parishes' (Borthwick PR/WS 7/2).

Given the outcome, it was clearly the 'mere cottage' that was Wharram Percy; indeed, the phrase is repeated in its final appearance, in a terrier of 1853. This notes the union with Wharram le Street 'in or about the year 1833' and goes on to record that:

'The old Vicarage House was a mere Cottage with a Stable adjoining both covered with Thatch. The House & Stable which were much dilapidated were both taken away on the Union with Wharram in the Street being effected. There is an Orchard planted with Fruit Trees adjoining the Site of the Vicarage House which together with what was the back yard of the House, contained by estimation one acre…' (Borthwick, Ter. K. Wharram Percy 1853)

3 Cartographic Evidence for the Post-medieval Farmstead, Cottages and Vicarage
by R.T. Porter

This concluding chapter of Part One provides an analysis of the cartographic and written sources relating to the size, shape, boundaries and features of the farmstead and the adjacent land in the 18th and 19th centuries. It is based on a much longer, detailed archive report prepared by the author, and has been edited for this volume by E. Marlow-Mann and S. Wrathmell. The excavation of the farmhouse (Site 74) and outbuildings (Site 51) are detailed in Chapters 4 and 5. The land to the south and east of the farmstead formed part of the glebe land, belonging to the vicar; for a detailed description of this see *Wharram XI*, 4-7.

Pre-1829 maps

The earliest cartographic representation of the buildings and roads at Wharram Percy is Jefferys' map, published 1775 (surveyed *c*.1767-69 by J Hodskinson; Fig. 7). This shows a short stretch of fenced road running north from the church, passing to the west of two buildings, presumably the vicarage and the farmstead. The representation of the church is identical to those at Kirby Grindalythe, Fridaythorpe and Birdsall. The road joins the Birdsall – Sledmere road and follows the old hollow-way eastwards towards the (post-survey) Bella Farm. On the more accurate and detailed Greenwood map (1818; surveyed 1815-17; Fig. 7) the Birdsall – Sledmere road is again shown, with a branch (only a footpath in 1850) towards Wharram le Street. The north – south road previously shown by Jefferys can be taken as passing between the two pairs of buildings and, having crossed the dam, is then depicted heading south up Deep Dale

towards Raisthorpe. The church symbol is placed well west of this road, for clarity. The four buildings are a schematic representation of the courtyard farm, farmhouse and vicarage. The pecked line east of these buildings along the beck clearly represents the farm boundary between Wharram Percy Farm and Bella Farm.

Bryant's map of 1829

The first map to name the Vicarage at Wharram Percy is Bryant (1829; surveyed 1827-1828; Fig. 7). The road ('Good Cross or Driving Road' – Bryant 1829) from the church and farmstead towards Bella is, however, mis-orientated almost east-west rather than north-south; the following notes use corrected directions rather than those from the map.

Four buildings are shown, in addition to the church. One is west of the road, almost opposite the church, but still on the terrace. This may possibly be the vicar's

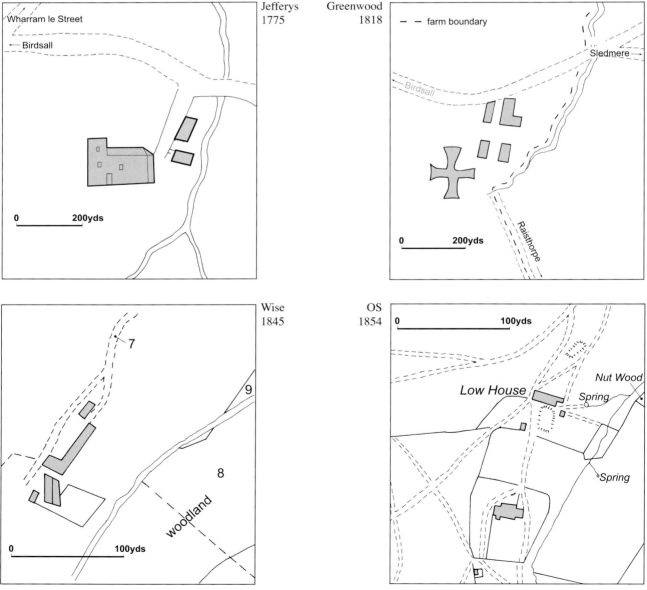

Fig. 7. Redrawings of historical maps. (E. Marlow-Mann after R.T. Porter)

stable, whose exact location is uncertain. Alternatively, it could be the building shown by Dykes (1836) south-west of the farmhouse and dubbed tentatively the 'farmer's stable', which was certainly west of the road.

The other three buildings are all north of the church and east of the road, as on Jefferys 1775. The first of these is clearly labelled 'Vicarage'; this actual naming of a building as 'Vicarage' must not be confused with the description of the benefice, which appears against the names of most churches on the Ordnance Survey maps.

The second building, aligned north-south and fronting onto the road, represents the farmhouse; it is labelled 'House'. Immediately to the north is the third building, at right angles to the road: this is in the position of the South Range of the courtyard farm, but is perhaps meant to represent the whole of the courtyard.

Westward and southward from the church, tracks ('Lanes and Bridle Ways' – Bryant) run up to 'Wharram High Ho.' (name and track shown for the first time) and

up 'Wharram Dale' (Deep Dale) towards Raisthorpe. As on Jefferys 1775 and Greenwood 1818, a track heads north-westwards from the farmstead area over the Wold top to Picksharp Farm and Birdsall.

William Dykes' plan of 1836

The earliest plan covering Wharram Percy Farm, Bella and Wharram Grange so far known is by William Dykes, surveyed 1836. There are two versions: Dykes 1836a is his 'fair plot' on paper, at a scale of 1:2376, while 1836b is a reduced version on parchment, at 1:7128, similar in content to 1836a but omitting chain-lines and gates. An extract showing the settlement area, based on 1836a, appears in Figure 7. A redrawing of the full area covered by Dykes's plans appears as Figure 5.

Dykes 1836a shows the farmhouse (not labelled on original) on an almost exact north-south alignment, at an angle of approximately 90° to the South Range of the

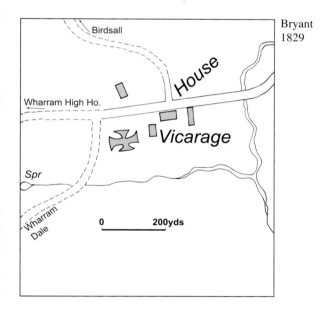

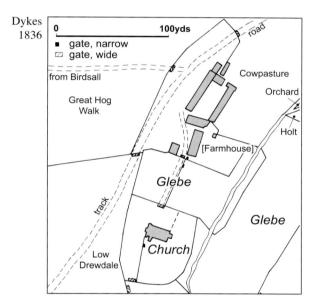

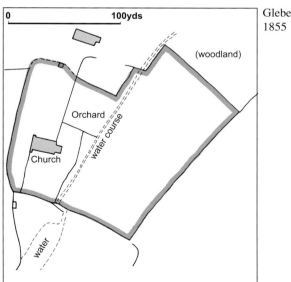

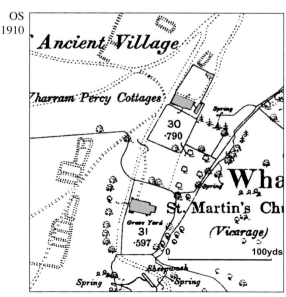

outbuildings, which were laid out around a rectangular courtyard immediately to the north. The West and East Ranges are on a more north-east to south-west alignment, with the North Range at right angles to them. The North Range is divided into two parts with a gap in between; the eastern end of the North Range projects beyond the East Range, so this gap is not central to the courtyard. Two extensions to the north are shown, on the same alignment as the West Range. To the west of the southern end of the farmhouse is a roughly square building, discussed above as the possible 'farmer's stable'.

A small square outhouse, of uncertain function, is shown east of the farmhouse. One suggestion is that this may have been the farmer's privy, approached via the gap between the north wall of the farmhouse and the south wall of the South Range. It may be significant that, because of the orientation of the Farmhouse (Fig. 8), this gap could be maintained at 2m only by setting back the east end of the south wall of the South Range, a feature which survives in the modern Cottages (see Fig. 26). This suggests that access between the Farmhouse and the South Range was required for a small cart – perhaps the building was a pit privy needing periodic emptying. An alternative suggestion is that the small outhouse contained the 1776 well – see the discussion in Chapter 28.

The farmstead is enclosed by fences on all but the north-east side, separating it from the Great Hog Walk and, assuming a gate across the gap in the North Range, from the Cowpasture. The only 'road' labelled as such runs north-east along the modern track towards Bella and thence 'to Beverley'. In the other direction, one track comes across the Great Hog Walk 'from Birdsall' and another heads south-westwards up the terrace-way to High House.

A third track sweeps south along the west frontage of the farmhouse (Dykes 1836b) and across the glebe, virtually over the site of the Vicarage (not marked), but does not enter the Churchyard or proceed across the dam. Its absence from Dykes 1836a implies that the stretch through the churchyard was not clearly defined on the ground. However, the western area of the churchyard, possibly used for grazing, was fenced off from the burial area. In the north-east of the map extract, small portions of the farmer's Orchard on the valley floor and of Nut Wood, here designated 'Holt', appear for the first time.

Wise's railway plan of 1845

Wise's deposited plan for the Malton and Driffield Junction Railway (1845; Fig. 7) is just one of the suite of documents relating to the Act (9&10 Vict. lxxvii; House of Lords Record Office) authorising the construction of this railway. A railway survey included all features within the limits of deviation (here 100 yards either side of the proposed centre line) and the complete boundaries of properties of which any part commenced within the limits (Adams 1913, 201, citing Castle 1847); 'properties' in this case would include 'enclosures'.

The excerpt shown on Figure 7 is over 100 yards beyond these limits, but portions of the two wooded areas to the north-east fall within them: west of the beck is parcel 9 'orchard and watercourse', occupied by William Smith Gofton (the farmer); east of the Beck is parcel 8 'plantation and watercourse' (the 'Nut Wood' of OS 1854). The depiction of the farmstead can only be regarded as a bonus, and the further south the map extends, the less reliable the information will be.

The most important evidence the map provides is for the loss of the West Range farm buildings, their function presumably transferred to High House. No credence, however, can be given to the depiction of the farmhouse as a very oblique parallelogram, though the inclusion of the centre-line is of interest. The omission of the 1836 fences north and west of the farmstead may be accepted as a genuine landscape change, since it seems unlikely that Wise would have neglected to show them while at the same time including the short fences south and east of the farmstead.

More problematic is the woodland shown immediately east of the farmhouse, representing a southern extension of Nut Wood along the eastern valley side, which is not seen in either 1836 or 1850. This may simply have been hillside scrub if no longer grazed following the vicar's departure perhaps 50 years earlier.

The alignment of the extreme south of the 'Public Highway from Wharram le Street to Wharram Percy' (parcel 7), which is beginning to pass west of the 'farmer's stable', can be ignored. Of more interest, however, is a track, depicted for the first time, using the north entrance to the courtyard; this track is also visible as a hollow-way on the ground.

Ordnance Survey map of 1854

The Ordnance Survey six-inch map was published in 1854, but was stated to have been surveyed in 1850-51. In practice, this would be the date at which the manuscript plans were certified as fit for publication, but the date of final field examination could be a year earlier (Margary 1991, ix; Oliver 1996). The actual survey date of the Figure 7 extract (which omits the contours, and the earthworks on the plateau) is here usually cited as 1850: by then the farmstead had been relocated to the wold-top site at High House (Bryant 1829). On the Terrace, only the South Range survived, now named Low House.

The site of the Farmhouse is shown as an upstanding earthwork, with hachures defining the outer edges of the walls and the east wall defined additionally by hachures on its inner edge. For the formation of such an earthwork at least a couple of years should be allowed between demolition (i.e. about 1847-8) and survey; if the demolition of the West Range seen on Wise 1845 was part of a continuing process, that suggests that the Farmhouse was destroyed in 1846-7. Taken together, OS and Wise thus give a date for demolition of the Farmhouse of c. 1847. The South Range appears unchanged except for a small extension on its east side. The possible 'farmer's stable', and the privy or well, south-west and east of the farmhouse site, are still present; the latter probably served Low House after the demolition of the Farmhouse.

The only other visible remains of the farmstead is an earthwork representing its most northerly building, a thin detached structure, shown on Dykes 1836 and Wise 1845. The West and East Ranges have left no trace, and the twin north to south tracks run partly over their sites.

The farmstead/glebe fences of 1836 are still intact in 1850, but the only other surviving fence associated with the farmstead is a short one running up the hillside from the west end of Low House; this was shown pecked, possibly under construction, in 1845.

The route to the dam, and thence to Raisthorpe and Thixendale, is now shown completely; its course across the glebe passes east of the Vicarage site to enter the Churchyard at a point distinctly further east than was shown in 1836. On entering the Churchyard it bifurcates either side of the northern internal churchyard fence, one track passing through the possible grazed western area, the other proceeding to the rather steeply sloping south-east corner.

Bushes are shown in the portion of the glebe east of the track, labelled 'Orchard' in 1855 and known from the Terriers to have been orchard since the 18th century. The OS map, however, does not use here the distinctive orchard symbol, perhaps implying some neglect of the glebe orchard at this period.

A steep path leads from the east end of Low House down to the spring: when this was investigated in 1989 no dating evidence was found, as the low rectangular stone enclosure (0.69 x 0.81m) around it was not dismantled. This apparent use of the spring in 1850 may support the identification of the small outhouse as a privy rather than a wellhouse. A further path runs eastwards down the hillside from this outhouse almost to the Beck.

Although 'Low Houses' was inhabited by two families in the 1851 Census, no fences appear to demarcate any gardens in 1850. The short fence west of Low House, described above, would protect the area south of Low House against livestock, but only if there were a further fence, not on OS 1854, running east of the house; there was a fence in this position in 1836 and 1845. The presence of the farmhouse earthwork helps to confirm the impression that there were but limited gardening activities associated with Low House up to 1850, and certainly none on the north side, where no fences at all can be seen or inferred. Across the valley, 'Nut Wood' is now so named for the first time.

Glebe plan of 1855

The 'Plan of the Church Yard & Glebe Land adjoining situate at WHARRAM PERCY referred to in the preceding Terrier' (1855; Fig. 7) relates to the Terrier of 1 August 1853. The Orchard, named on a map for the first time, is now again fenced off from the glebe to the west, but it is smaller than in 1836 as its western boundary follows the line of the 1850 track. This fence line created

a low earthwork beneath it at the east edge of the terrace, the orchard being entirely on the slope down to the Beck and on the valley floor itself. It is fenced off from the steep valley side east of the churchyard, as on Dykes 1836, but not on OS 1854.

The western section of the farmstead/glebe fence is now shown pecked, and passes on the north side of the supposed 'farmer's stable'. The fence south of this has disappeared to form one large paddock extending from this 'stable' to the south-west corner of the churchyard; the whole of this was 'now let by the Vicar to Mr. W.S. Gofton at the annual rent of two pounds' (1853 Terrier). This building, while obviously no longer the farmer's personal stable next to his residence, has thus become appurtenant to the farmer's grazing rights over the glebe. North of the glebe, a fence runs across the site of the farmhouse and curves eastwards down the valley side, but with a long break in its run on the steepest slope.

Maps of 1855-1888

A major property re-demarcation exercise took place on the terrace between 1855 and 1888, representing perhaps the final consequences of the 1840s removal of the farmstead to the Wold Top, though also influenced by the change in estate ownership, and removal of the Vicarage in 1834; the fields themselves were redesigned in the 1840s, as evidenced in part by Wise 1845. The western portion of the Churchyard was taken into Low Drewdale field, and the remainder refenced; the east boundary already has a distinct reverse-S bend in 1855, as depicted on OS 1890, marking a departure from the original hedgerow. Gardens were provided to the north and south of the tenanted Cottages, extending some 9m south into the former glebe. The precise date of these gardens is not known; the best estimate for the laying out of the gardens is c. 1856-72, logic suggesting the desirability of the Cottages having gardens as early as possible within this range.

Maps of 1890 and 1910

Low House, formerly the South Range, was renamed on the OS 1890 map (surveyed 1888) as 'Wharram Percy Cottages' and internal divisions mark out three separate dwellings. The OS maps of 1890 and 1910 (surveyed 1909; Fig. 7) represent the internal party walls in a generalised way, but erroneously add a superfluous line at the W end, apparently creating a fourth tiny cottage with no front door.

Although it is not readily apparent here, the west wall of the Cottages, and the north-south internal walls, are at an angle of 81° to the east-west walls. The orientation of the west wall in fact follows that of the West and East Ranges of the courtyard farm, and is in turn followed by the West and East fences of the post-1855 Cottage gardens. This angle, which makes maximum use of the limited flat land on the terrace, also approximates to that of the late 17th-century farmhouse (see Chapter 28).

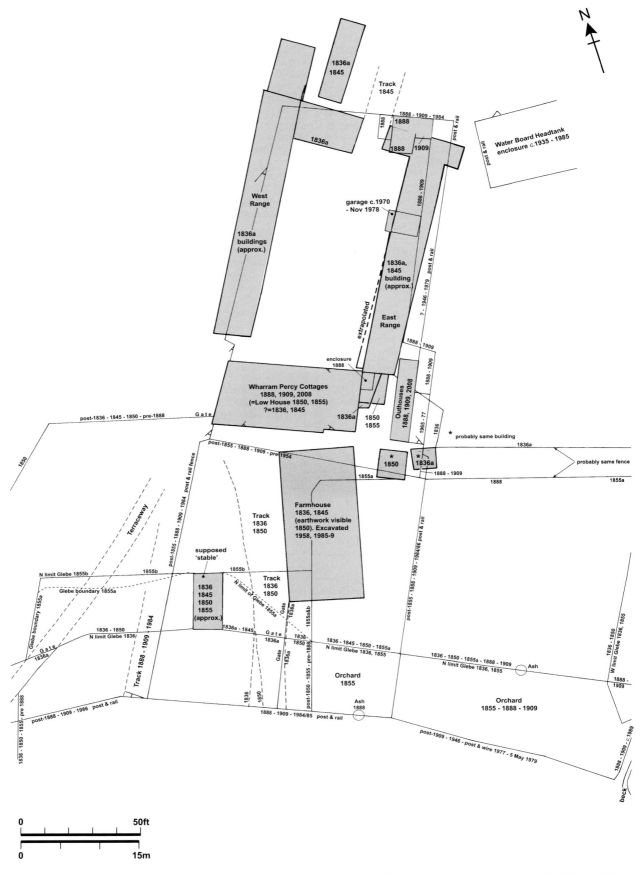

Fig. 8. Location of farm buildings, mainly from cartographic evidence; for continuation southwards, see Fig. 9. (E. Marlow-Mann, after R.T. Porter)

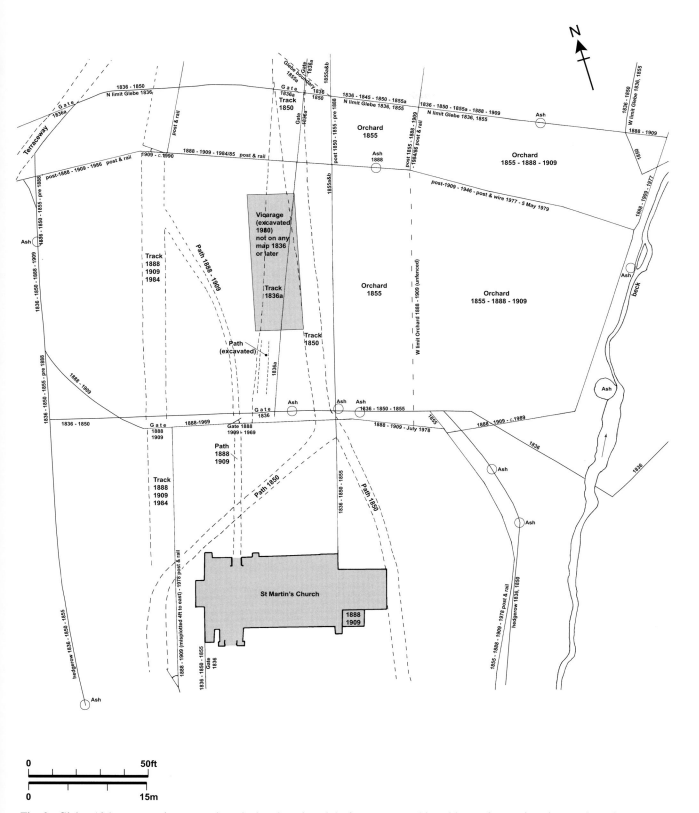

Fig. 9. Glebe, 18th-century vicarage and north churchyard, mainly from cartographic evidence; for continuation northwards, see Fig. 8. (E. Marlow-Mann, after R.T. Porter)

The Cottages on the OS county plans (OS 1890 and 1910) are shown *c.* 3-4m too far north; this seems to have been a cartographic error in 1888 in the course of replotting from the field books of the 1850 survey. East of the Cottages is a long narrow building, about 10.9m by 2.36m, divided into six rooms – storage and toilet facilities replacing the presumed earlier single privy. The land surrounding the Cottages was divided into a north and south garden area. In view of the close correlation between the 1888-1909 fences and the post-and-rail fences surveyed at 1:120 in the 1960s, it is presumed that at least the perimeter fences of the gardens were post-and-rail from the beginning, but the earliest positive information is in a photograph of the Church, provisionally dated to *c.* 1890.

The south garden contains the sites of the early 19th-century farmhouse and its possible privy and stable, which both survived perhaps a decade longer than the farmhouse itself. None of these three buildings seems to have had any topographic expression from 1888 onwards. No paths or outbuildings are shown in the south garden in 1888 or 1909, and no buildings are visible in the south-west two-thirds of the garden on a Lister picture postcard of *c.* 1907 (Gofton 1948).

The southernmost 9m of the south garden occupies part of the mid-19th-century glebe. The remains of the old Vicar's Orchard formerly extended into what by 1888 was the south-east part of the garden. In 1888 the Orchard was shown braced to the Cottage gardens, to make a single parcel (parcel 30) of 0.790 acre, suggesting that it was assumed to have been appropriated to the cottages. By 1909, however, the Orchard had once again been united (parcel 30a) with what remained of the glebe.

The north garden included the Cottages and the area to the south, up to the boundary with the south garden. In the north-east corner a group of small buildings and associated enclosures (perhaps a pigsty) were present in 1888 and, with some rearrangement, in 1909. The west fence was laid out down the middle of the former west range of the Courtyard Farm, while the north and east fences also partly overlie the north and east ranges, thus echoing the earlier pattern.

OS 1890 shows a single row of coniferous trees (identified as larch from 1954 photographs) extending eastwards down the valley side immediately east of the cottages. It is conceivable that these had been planted as a rudimentary shelter belt to the farmhouse that was destroyed *c.*1847. The spring was still shown to the east, but with no approach track.

The full record of cartographic representation of buildings, fences and trackways is shown on Figure 8 (farmhouse, outbuildings and cottages) and Figure 9 (vicarage, glebe and northern part of churchyard).

Part Two
Excavation of the Farmstead Sites
by E. Marlow-Mann and S. Wrathmell

4 Site 74

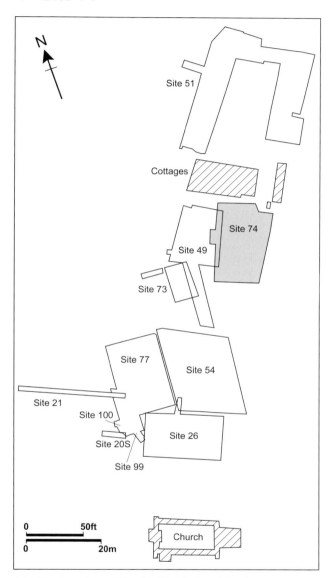

Fig. 10. Location of Site 74. (E. Marlow-Mann)

Site 74 was excavated over a period of five seasons, from 1985 to 1989, with the aim of displaying to visitors the foundations of the late 18th and 19th-century farmstead. As a result the excavation depth was limited but it was possible to reveal a succession of structures perhaps dating from the 16th century, with unexcavated medieval structures probably lying beneath. Unfortunately no section drawings from the excavations have survived within the archive.

Site 74 was previously reported in *Interim Reports 1985, 15; 1986, 12-14; 1987, 12-14; 1988, 7-8; 1989, 6.*

Until 1980, this structure was erroneously referred to as the 'post-medieval vicarage' in the project literature.

Period 1 (?17th century) (Fig. 11)
The structural remains uncovered beneath the Period 2 farmhouse building were allocated to Period 1. Very few features survived and the best preserved was a fragment of wall (366) approximately 0.6m thick in the north-east corner of the excavation. Although less than 2m of the chalk block wall survived it was possible to see that it ran in a north-east to south-west direction. To the west of this wall were the remains of a yard surface (367), comprising a loose greyish-brown silt with chalk inclusions, overlain by a chalk pebble surface (370) probably used as a cobbled track. To the west of the east wall of the Period 4 farmhouse was a small patch of demolition debris (373) associated with the Period 2 farmhouse and a deposit of loose black-grey sand rich in charcoal and coal (360). The latter has been interpreted as an area of burning beneath the Period 2 tiled floor but it was not clear to what it related. To the south a layer of compacted blackish-grey sandy silt with chalk inclusions (341), extent unknown, served as a sub-floor base on top of which the Period 2 floor was constructed. The further investigation of these features lay outside the aims of excavation.

The Period 1 remains were initially thought to date to the 16th century or earlier; but the amount of 15th-century pottery was small, and there was an almost complete absence of 16th-century material. In Didsbury's view (Chapter 13) any 16th-century or early 17th-century farmhouse was located elsewhere, a view shared by Davey and White (Chapter 18). Furthermore, the finds indicated that there had clearly been much disturbance of these layers in relatively recent times, although no recent cut features were distinguished during the excavation.

Period 2 (2nd half of 17th century) (Figs 12 and 13)
The remains of Period 2 were more substantial than Period 1: a building, probably only one room deep and four rooms long, ran at least 15.5m north-east to south-west with a width of 5.5m. The eastern wall (351) was the best preserved and was of chalk block construction approximately 0.5m thick. The alignment of the wall changed about 6m from the southern end. The southern return wall (292) was of a similar construction to the east wall. The entire building was extensively robbed of building materials, presumably for the Period 4 farmhouse. Nothing had survived of the west wall but the line of a robber trench. The northern wall was not apparent and probably lay beyond the limits of excavation.

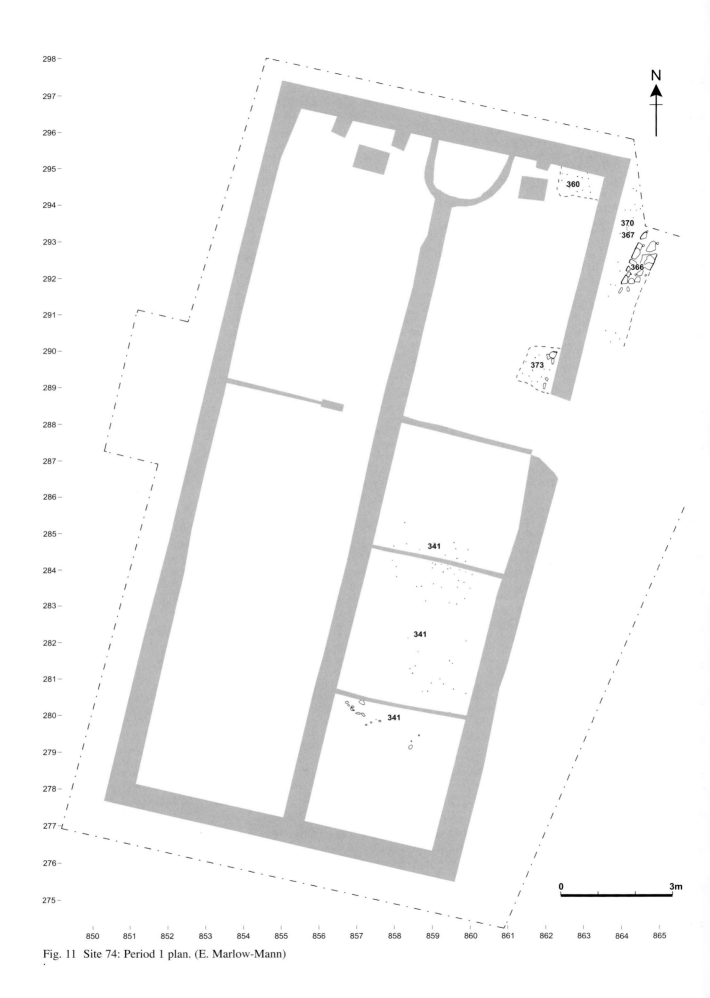

Fig. 11 Site 74: Period 1 plan. (E. Marlow-Mann)

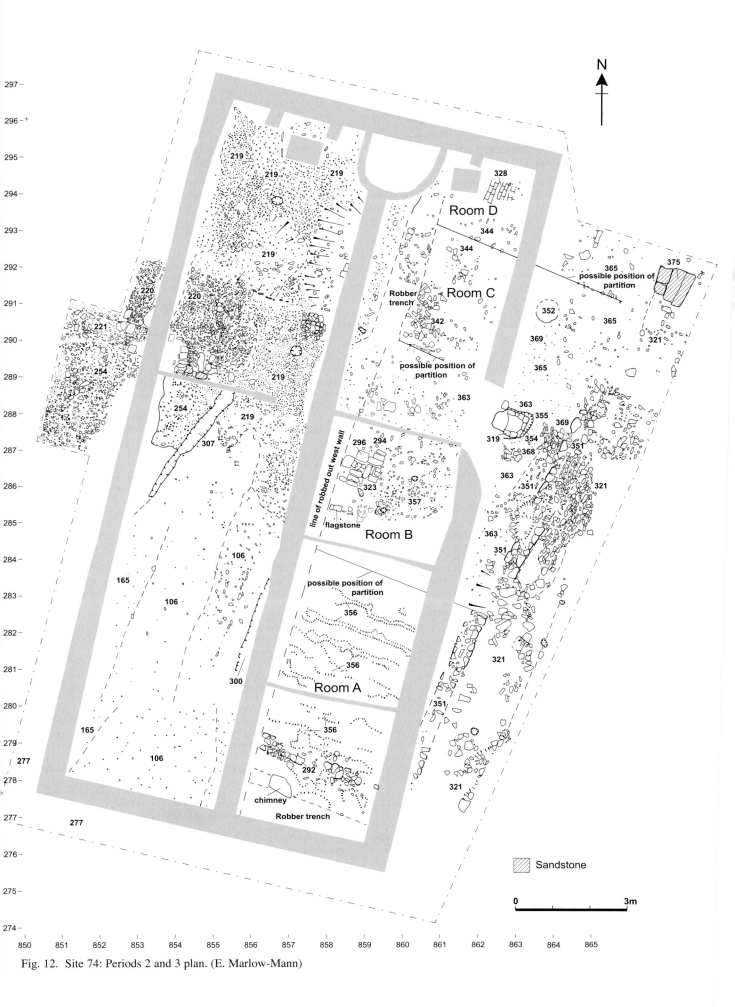

Fig. 12. Site 74: Periods 2 and 3 plan. (E. Marlow-Mann)

Room A, the southernmost room, was approximately 5.5m x 5m. Slots (356) cut into the sub-floor Period 1 layer (341) ran the width of the room suggesting joists for supporting a timber floor, although no further evidence survived. The fireplace associated with this room was situated in the southern wall (292): a large chalk block (no context number) on the outside of this wall indicated the remains of the chimney-stack base, the remainder having been robbed out.

The next room to the north, Room B, was presumably partitioned off from Room A but no partitioning was evident in the archaeological record. A line has been marked on Figure 12 to indicate its probable position based on the northern extent of the floor joist slots in Room A. Room B's dimensions are therefore approximately 6m x 5m. A flat flagstone floor (296) was laid upon a bedding layer of loose soft yellow-brown sand (323) which, in turn, overlay a compacted reddish-brown chalky pea-grit layer (357), probably also used as a floor make-up layer. Two post-holes (no context numbers) cut through this deposit but their function is not known. Layer 294, a crumbly grey silt with coal inclusions, appeared in plan to butt against the flagstones although their relationship was unclear at the time of excavation. It was interpreted as being a possible floor layer but it is also possible that it served as a make-up layer for the flagstones. The northern part of Room B consisted of a layer of hard yellow sand with chalk and pea-grit (363), probably a floor make-up layer, and this deposit continued into Room C. A pathway (220) to the west, discussed below, indicated that an entrance probably existed in the western wall at the northern end of Room B, but no archaeological evidence remained. An ash pit (319), comprising a square structure using chalk blocks and bricks within the construction cut (355) and with a fill of hard compacted chalk rubble (354), was situated at the north end of the room, towards the eastern wall. Layer 369 comprised a hardened chalk mettling surface and this layer was overlain by a deposit of chalk blocks (368), apparently a fragment of walling, possibly the side of the hearth.

The partitioning between Rooms B and C was once again unclear. A line of edging stones north-west of the ash pit may mark the position of a doorway threshold, but whether this was the line of the room division depends on which way the hearth faced. Room C, to the north, approximately 3.5m x 5m, primarily consisted of a continuation of layers 363 and 369, and an area of hard orange sand with chalk and flint inclusions (342). Many broken flagstones were scattered around this room making it likely that it was also flagged. The function of a circular mortar feature with its fill of compact yellowish-brown silty sand and worn chalk pebbles (352) is unknown. Throughout Rooms C and D were general dumps of mixed rubble (344 and 365), possibly demolition debris.

Room D, the northernmost room of the building, measured approximately 5.5m in width; the north wall was not reached in excavation. The room was floored with either brick or tile: the floor had not survived but impressions left in the underlying grey-brown silty mortar layer (328) were still visible. An area of large sandstone blocks (375) probably marks an external threshold to an eastern doorway. The eastern wall did not survive in Room D but its line may have continued, meeting the inner edge of threshold 375. No partition is evident between Rooms C and D but a line has been included on Figure 12 to indicate its possible position.

To the east of the building the ground was made up of a greyish-black sandy silt deposit with chalk cobbles (321) which could indicate a pathway to the eastern doorway. Numerous small post-holes (no context numbers) cut through this deposit but no pattern could be discerned. Some later post-holes had been inserted through the eastern wall, damaging its line.

To the west of the building were deposits suggesting yard surfaces and a garden. The surfaces were made up mostly of a brownish-yellow mortar packed surface (219); depressions in this surface perhaps indicating that it had supported stone paving. Two post-holes (no context numbers) were cut through surface 219 but their purpose was not clear. A distinct cobbled surface (220) comprising light grey sand with embedded flint, sandstone and chalk formed a pathway from the west which presumably led to the main entrance to the house. A possible wall (221), made of compacted rubble set into mortar, may have been a boundary between the path and the yard area to the south. A slight edge represented the northern boundary of the pathway. The main stones of the wall had not survived. To the south of this cobbled path surface 219 continued and would probably have joined up with the chalk-metalled surface (254) to the west; a later gully (307) destroyed any evidence of an intersection. Deposit 300, further south, probably represented the fill of the robber trench marking the line of the west wall.

The date of construction of the Period 2 farmhouse seems to lie in the second half of the 17th century: a clay pipe stem from below the construction layer in Room D (344) is likely to date to the first half of the 17th century; and the floor bedding in Room B (323) contained a clay pipe bowl unlikely to have been deposited before 1660. The pottery takes the construction of the building even later, with Staffordshire vessels of c.1690-1714 from the floor make-up.

Period 3 (2nd half of 17th century to end of 18th century) (Fig. 12)

The deposits of this period represent the period of occupation of the Period 2 farmhouse and external areas.

A greyish-brown silt deposit with a heavy concentration of coal (230, not illustrated) covered much of surface 219. The area south was built up using a crumbly brownish-grey silt with clay, tile and chalk pebbles (299, not illustrated); this levelled the ground in preparation for a chalk gravel layer (106). To the west a deposit of chalk gravel and brick fragments (165) may have been a surface layer or simply an area of dumped material. An area of blackish-grey soil (277) which ran

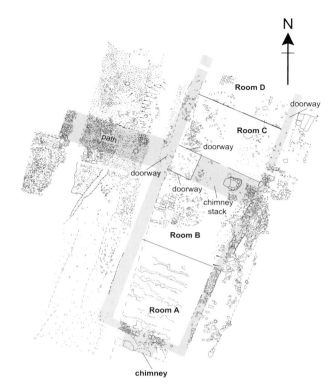

Fig. 13. Site 74: simplified interpretative plan of Period 2 farmhouse. (E. Marlow-Mann)

around the southern end of the site seems likely to have been part of a garden.

Discussion

It is almost certain that this farmhouse is the one referred to in the will of William Botterell made in 1699 (see p. 4), although the pottery from its construction phase suggests it may have then been a relatively new building. The dwelling is described as having four ground-floor rooms: a parlour, a 'fore room', a kitchen and a milk house; it also records three rooms above the first three ground-floor rooms listed. If this identification is correct, the parlour would be Room A, the 'fore room' Room B, the kitchen Room C and the milk house Room D. The inference that Room D or the milk house was single storey supports the fact that it may have been separate from the rest of the house and had its own entranceway, represented by the threshold of large sandstone blocks (375). This would also help explain the use of a brick or tile floor in this room. No evidence of a staircase was found: it would probably have been of timber construction. The description of a building in the valuation of 1806 (see p. 13) also seems to agree with the remains of this building. The ground floor is described as having two parlours, a kitchen and a dairy which would correspond with Rooms A, B, C and D respectively. The second storey comprised four lodging rooms; if the milk house was single storey, these lodging rooms must have been above Rooms A, B and C, with the fourth room indicating a subdivision. The cobbled pathway (220) to the west of the building presumably led to the front door and a small entranceway. The 'fore room' (Room B) and

the kitchen (Room C) would each have had a fireplace; little archaeological evidence remained to indicate exactly where these were positioned, but they would probably have shared a chimney stack. The chimney for the parlour (Room A) was in the south wall. The change in alignment of the east wall suggests that, as with the late medieval buildings on the plateau (*Wharram VI*), the farmhouse was cruck-built, with the walls constructed in sections rather than continuously. In Chapter 28 David Neave provides a further discussion of the plan form and construction of the building, and relates it to other vernacular houses in the region.

This house was originally thought to have been swept away during the Improvements of the 1770s, but as indicated in Chapters 1 and 28, the association of early 19th-century pottery with the occupation of this building demonstrated that previous assumptions were wrong. The ceramic record (including the clay pipes) consistently demonstrates that the end of Period 3 came only in the early 19th century.

Period 4 (post-1806, pre-1830) (Fig. 14; Plates 2-5)
The Period 4 farmhouse was constructed on a north-east to south-west alignment, on a slightly different line from its predecessor, with dimensions of 20m x 9.5m. The east and north external walls (130) were about 0.6m thick and were constructed with a chalk and sandstone rubble fill, faced with sandstone blocks, some of which were reused from an earlier building. Wall 130 survived to a

Plate 2. Site 74: general view of Period 4 farmhouse looking south.

Fig. 14. Site 74: Periods 4 and 5 plan. (E. Marlow-Mann).

Plate 3. Site 74: general view of Period 4 farmhouse looking south.

Plate 4. Site 74: Period 4 farmhouse; double oven (228) and ash pits, looking north.

maximum height of three courses. The foundation cuts (283 and 329) were uncovered, filled with orangey sand with grit and rubble (284, 330 and 347; 335 not illustrated). The south and west walls (100) comprised chalk and sandstone blocks, brick-faced externally in English garden-wall bond, surviving to a maximum height of six courses; they were constructed within a foundation trench (231/247) with an undescribed fill (248). The headers and stretchers depicted on Figure 14 indicate the varying heights of the surviving wall levels. The building was two rooms deep and divided down its long axis by a stone wall (154). This internal dividing wall was constructed using chalk and sandstone blocks, to a maximum surviving height of three courses, within the foundation trench (290; 233 and 297b not illustrated), backfilled with a clayey silt and gravel deposit (289; 234 not illustrated); it was presumably a load-bearing wall supporting the first-floor joists. Part of this wall was later robbed out but the fill of the ensuing trench, dark crumbly sand with chalk, brick and gravel inclusions (198) marked the wall's original line. The building seems to have been divided into seven ground-floor rooms, including the entrance hall.

Within Room 1, dimensions 4m x 7.5m, a semicircular oven (228) built of sandstone and chalk blocks, was set in its north-east corner and extended into Room 3 (Plate 4). Against the north wall was a fireplace (204A and 205A), 2m wide and 0.5m deep and furnished with a stone-lined ash pit (196), 0.75m x 1m. The depth of the ash pit was not recorded. It contained early 19th-century pottery and pipe stems as well as ash (181) from coal and wood. Part of the ash pit was robbed out but its extent could be traced from the robber trench (197). The floor was made up with a layer of compacted mortar and pea-grit (199) and surfaced with white mortar and pantile inclusions (232), only a small area of which survived along the central wall.

Room 2 was separated from Room 1 by a single-skinned brick wall (104) surviving only one course high and possibly represented the footing for a timber partition. The doorway was to the east, next to the central wall 154, the eastern end of the brick wall appearing to be a larger stone, possibly indicating a threshold. Room 2, measuring approximately 1.5m x 4m, was the entrance hall to the farmhouse, with a doorway in the western wall south of the brick partition wall. The floor seemed to be surfaced with compacted white chalk with trampled rubble material (102); this surface continued partway into Room 6 and it is probable that this layer was actually part of the construction debris or a make-up layer and not a true floor surface.

Room 6, measuring approximately 9m x 4m, was divided from Room 2 by a single-skinned brick partition (105A), only a portion of which has survived. There was an extension southwards from this partition, the function of which was unclear; it was possibly the remnant of a stairwell. No floor surfaces were associated with this room and it seems probable that it had a timber floor,

Plate 5. Site 74: Period 4 farmhouse; brick partitioning between rooms, looking north.

although no joists or slots to support one are evident. A deposit of dark greyish-brown compacted clayey silt with chalk scatters (340) was visible towards the central wall underlying a pea grit layer (339, not illustrated); these deposits made up a bedding layer for the farmhouse foundation. A single post-hole (no context number, Fig. 14) to the south end of the internal dividing wall 154 probably indicates post-demolition activity.

The rear half of the house was noticeably narrower than the front range, being on average only about 3.5m wide. Room 3, the north-eastern room measuring 3.75m x 7.5m, contained the eastern half of a semicircular oven (229) exposed in Room 1. In the centre of the north wall was the stub wall of another fireplace (no context number) corresponding in position to that in Room 1. It was marked by an associated ash pit (223), 0.85m x 0.65m, this time brick-lined with a slate base. The ash pit was filled first with a browny-yellow compact sand with brick and mortar inclusions (225, not illustrated) sealed by a greyish-white ashy sand with a mortar-rich fill (224, not illustrated), presumably representing demolition rubble. Several sandy silt deposits containing pea-grit, mortar and rubble (241, 242 and 246) covered the northern part of the room. These may have been demolition material or possibly a base layer for the brownish-yellow pea-grit and silt make-up which covered the rest of the room. A small post-hole (no context number) in the north-east corner of the room, along with two (no context numbers) set in the east and central wall, probably represent post-demolition activity. A portion of the east external wall is missing at the south end of this room and this is likely to have been the location of a doorway given that one was not evident in the surviving stretch. There was nothing to indicate a hallway or lobby area. A blackish-grey silty clay deposit (238) ran along the east side of the central wall and presumably served as a floor make-up layer (or was possibly demolition material). Running along the outside of the east wall by Room 3 was a layer of crumbly grey sandy silt with 40% chalk inclusions (310) possibly a path leading to the door.

Room 4, measuring 3.5m x 3.25m, was partitioned off from Room 3 by a single skinned brick wall (142), surviving two courses in height. The doorway from Room 3 into Room 4 seemed to be in the north-west corner of the room where a few flagstones on the threshold survived. A compacted mortar-rich surface (244) served as make-up for the floor.

A further single-skinned brick partition wall (also numbered 142) survived to a maximum of six courses, within foundation cut 336. The wall separated Rooms 4 and 5 and a gap in the western portion suggested a doorway. Room 5, dimensions 4m x 3.5m, had a raised area in the north-west corner of the room, a layer of mortar, pea-grit and rubble (267), probably demolition debris used as make-up material. From this doorway the floor level dropped approximately 0.2m to a loose whitish-grey plaster-rich layer (314) which was probably a floor base. Salt residues were apparent on the walls and it may be that Room 5 was a curing room for meat.

Room 7, measuring 3.5m x 3.5m, was divided from Room 5 by a further single skinned internal brick partition wall (141), six courses high. The layer of demolition debris (267) used in Room 5 was used as a possible make-up layer for the greyish-white sandy floor surface 268. A gap in the partition indicated that access to Room 5 was through the brick wall. Two post-holes (no context numbers) along the inside of the external wall again represent post-demolition activity.

The revised dating for the construction of this farmhouse is supported by pottery from Room 1, which provides a *terminus post quem* of c. 1800-1810.

Period 5 (early 19th century to 1850)
Period 5 represents activity associated with the occupation of the Period 4 farmhouse, though not much of that had survived the building's demolition, and there was considerable post-demolition contamination, as evident in the pottery record.

Discussion
Two sources assisted with the understanding of the room functions of the Period 4 to 5 farmhouse: a bankruptcy inventory of John Cattle dated 1830 (see p.14) and comparison with the present Wharram Percy farm on the Wold top. Though important, it should be noted that the bankruptcy inventory only lists personal belongings within a room; where no belongings are present, the room is not listed. Given the circumstances in which the inventory was drawn up, the contents listed under the various rooms may not be a clear guide to the former functions of those rooms.

The western brick-faced half of the building would have been for the farmer's use, the brick facing marking the most fashionable side. The doorway in Room 2 would have provided direct access onto the courtyard and village track. Room 1, the front room containing the smaller part of the oven (228), would have therefore been the farmer's kitchen. According to the inventory the kitchen contained a mangle, a clock, four tables and six chairs. Room 6 would have been the farmer's parlour. As with the Period 2 farmhouse and the vicarage, this was the best room of the house and is likely to have had a timber floor although no evidence survived in the archaeological record. This room was listed as containing a secretary, bookcase and books, three tables, seven chairs, a stool, a cellaret, a barometer, fire irons and fender, together with a carpet (possibly referring to a table carpet). The eastern, rear, half of the house was devoted to utility rooms and the servants' and farmhands' accommodation. The rooms were narrower but the Room 3 oven was larger, which suggests that the servants and labourers numbered more than the farmer's family. Room 4 was possibly the pantry, presumably serving both labourers and the farmer; it is possible that there was a doorway in the spine wall to allow the farmer access to this room. Room 5's plaster-rich floor layer was probably a preparation layer for a flagged floor. The room itself was likely to have been a dairy although there was little archaeological evidence to support this. The first floor would have been similarly divided with separate staircases and divided sleeping quarters. The inventory lists two front chambers, a servant girls' room, a back room and the men servants' garret, all of which contained beds. Most of the ground-floor rooms had no good floor surfaces surviving, suggesting that they were tiled or flagged and that such reusable materials were removed when the building was demolished. Very little of the Period 5 occupation layers survived due to the building's demolition in the mid-19th century and subsequent activity.

The plan form of this building, and its relationship to other farmhouses of this period on the northern Wolds, are discussed by Neave in Chapter 28.

Period 6 (1851 to 20th century)
The Period 4 farmhouse was recorded on the Dykes plan dated July 21 1836, however, the OS 1854 map, surveyed in 1850-51, shows the earthwork remains of the building, indicating that the farmhouse had by this time been demolished. All activity associated with the demolition of the building and subsequent use of the area as a garden for the Wharram cottages have been assigned to this period. Period 6 therefore comprises many deposits of rubble debris, numerous post-holes, pits and cesspits. The area was so disturbed that further interpretation is of little use.

The south range of outbuildings was converted into cottages around the same time that the Period 4 farmhouse was demolished. The second storey of the cottages has a facing of reused broken bricks probably derived from the demolition of the farmhouse. The window and doorway lintels and sills also did not quite fit the cottage openings, and were clearly reused from the farmhouse window and doorway openings.

5   Site 51

Site 51 was excavated over a period of eleven seasons, beginning in 1978 and concluding in 1988 with the site being laid out for display to the public. Map evidence of 1836 (see Chapter 3) indicates four ranges of farm buildings to the north of the post-medieval farmhouse, surrounding an open courtyard. Only the South Range has survived, converted into the present cottages; the gardens to the north of the cottages covered the remains of the other ranges which had been demolished before the end of the 19th century. The erosion caused by gardening, often involving the use of a plough, destroyed most of the stratigraphic information on the East and North Ranges. The courtyard area was so disturbed that the present-day surface was below that of the early 19th-century courtyard. Only the West Range was partially spared, lying beyond the garden boundaries, therefore providing the most useful information on these buildings (Plate 9).

Site 51 was previously reported in *Interim Reports 1978, 12-13; 1979, 9; 1980, 14; 1981, 8-9; 1982, 18-20;*

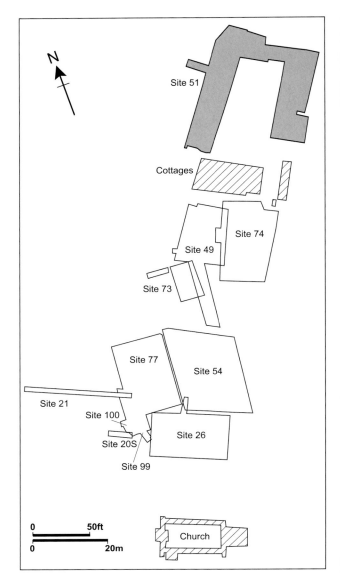

Fig. 15. Location of Site 51. (E. Marlow-Mann)

1983, 15-17; 1984, 15-16; 1985, 14-15; 1986, 12; 1987, 10-12; 1988, 7.

West Range

Period 1 (medieval) (Fig. 16; Plate 6)
The first period represents features that pre-date the Range's construction. Although the aim of the excavations was to display the post-medieval farm buildings, some limited investigation was undertaken to determine whether the site supported earlier archaeology. Damaged portions of the flooring of Room 4 and of the southern extension of the West Range were removed, revealing a series of medieval deposits and structural remains.

A chalk rubble wall footing (1043) was revealed running in a general north to south direction suggesting the main east wall of a building with the returning wall visible at the southern limit of excavation. A group of chalk blocks (1067) may have functioned as a pad-stone for a vertical timber. Wall 1043 was cut at some point

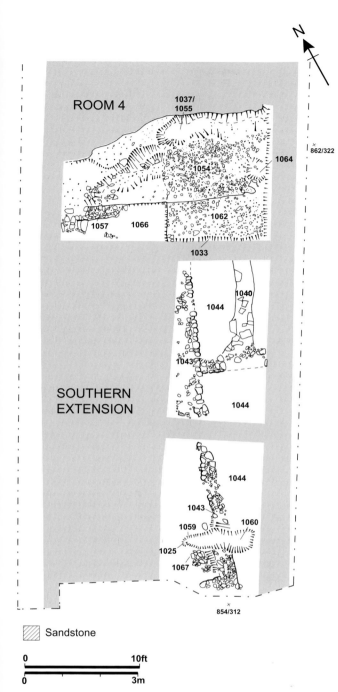

ROOM 4

1037/
1055

1064

862/322

1054

1057   1066

1062

1033

SOUTHERN
EXTENSION

1040

1044

1043

1044

1044

1043

1059   1060

1025

1067

854/312

Sandstone

0   10ft

0   3m

Fig. 16. Site 51: West Range, Period 1 plan. Shaded areas mark later floors and walls left *in situ*. (E. Marlow-Mann)

before Period 2.1 by a linear feature (1059) filled with brown clay and small chalk inclusions (1060). This, in turn, was cut by a small post-pit (1025). The rubble remains of a further wall (1040) ran parallel to 1043 and joined or butted against a wall running east-west (no context number) – the poor preservation of 1040 made the nature of the intersection impossible to determine. The east-west wall was of similar construction to wall 1043 which it abutted and probably signified an extension to the building. The entire building was surrounded by a burnt surface layer (1044) sloping west-east, dropping approximately 0.3m over a distance of 2.7m.

Beneath the West Range Room 4 a cellar or undercroft had been carefully cut about 0.2m deep into the natural chalk (1066) providing a level floor. A fragment of wall (1057) was revealed, built in the same style as 1043, possibly the northern return wall of the building. This seemed to line the edge of the undercroft but the wall was not removed and their relationship was not established. A possible surface (1054) made up of very sticky brown clay with chalk inclusions was apparent although it was unclear to which part of the building it related. It seemed to be outside the boundary of the building as far as the limited excavation evidence showed and may have been related to the area of terracing on the north side of the cellar. Interpretation of the relationship of these features to 1040 and 1044 was hindered by a later possible robber trench (no context number) and its unexcavated fill (1062) which had destroyed any information at this level. Surface 1054 was cut by a gully (1037/1055) and an unexcavated sub-rectangular feature (1064). This in turn was cut by the foundation trench (1033) for the later West Range south wall.

Discussion

The Period 1 features described above could possibly indicate a cruck-built peasant dwelling, dimensions unknown. Feature 1067 could have supported a cruck blade; unfortunately the western side of the building which may have revealed an opposing timber base did not lie within the excavated area. The layer of burnt material (1044) suggests that a fire caused the building's destruction. There was some associated pottery of the 12th to 14th centuries. It is unlikely that the undercroft was related to the peasant dwelling: on its floor was a coin of Henry I (see *Wharram XI*, 303, no. 9).

Period 2.1 (late 18th century to early 19th century)
(Fig. 17; Plate 7)
The initial construction of the West Range has been assigned to Period 2.1 incorporating the internal features and surfaces of its four rooms together with the construction of a metalled track along the west side of the building.

This construction phase produced a building 21m x 6.6m externally which had been terraced into the natural chalk slope. The exterior walls were approximately 0.6m thick and were constructed of chalk blocks (518, Fig. 18, S.CC, S.AA and S.BB; Fig. 20, S.DD) with an outer protective skin of brick (519) on the north and west walls only. The eastern external wall along Rooms 2 and 3 was not apparent and it is possible that this section may have been open to the courtyard. Alternatively, erosion may simply have removed this stretch of walling in its entirety. The building was divided into four rooms utilising timber partitioning; a southern extension was added in Period 2.3.

Room 1 at the north of the building, measuring approximately 3.4m x 5.4m, was terraced into the bedrock, consolidating areas of rubble bedrock with soft chalk surfacing. Six large post-pits (711, 696, 721, 709, 562 and 713) contained vertical timbers. Two pits (709

Plate 6. Site 51: Period 1 structure, with Period 2.3 cobbled stable adjacent, looking west.

Plate 7. Site 51: Period 2.1; view from north end of west wall, with the North Range remains to the top of the picture, looking east.

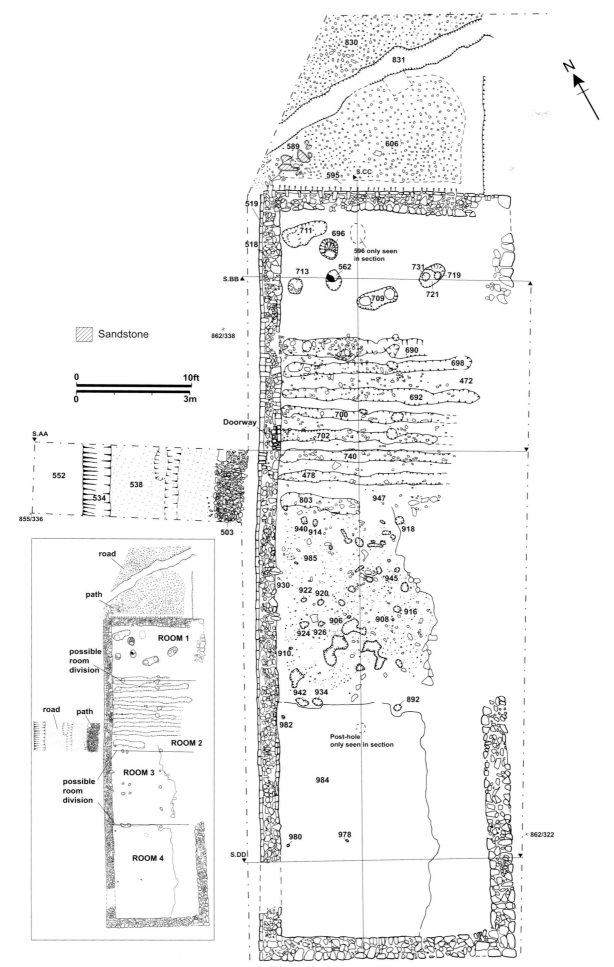

Fig. 17. Site 51: West Range, Period 2.1 plan, with smaller simplified plan of main features. (E. Marlow-Mann)

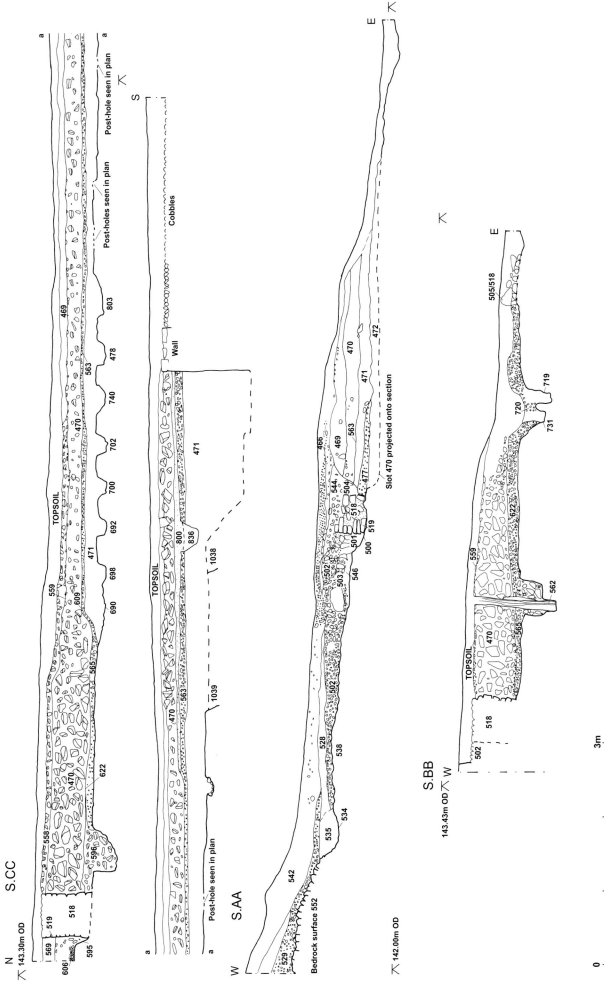

Fig. 18. Site 51 sections. (E. Marlow-Mann)

and 711) contained two post-pipes: one vertical and the other set at 45 degrees as a bracing post. These features were covered by a chalk surface (565, shown only in section, Fig. 18, S.CC and S.BB; Fig. 19) which, in turn, was repaired with a pinkish-white deposit of mortar and chalk (622). This surface was clearly laid around post 562 (Fig. 18, S.BB) and over its stone packing. Although there is no section evidence for post-holes 711, 696, 721, 709 and 713, it is possible that these were constructed in the same way. Posts 719 and 731 may have also followed this sequence but erosion had destroyed the relevant information. Although the east wall had been partly robbed in the 20th century, the pattern of wear on the floor indicated a doorway at the south end of this wall. There was no surviving division between Rooms 1 and 2, although it seems likely that some form of partitioning must have existed given the apparently differing functions of the two rooms.

Room 2, to the south, approximate dimensions 5m x 5.4m, had slots (690, 698, 692, 700, 702, 740, 478 and 803) running east-west, cut through a hard chalk surface (472) and centred about 0.6m apart. This suggests a raised timber floor. 'Post-holes' and packing stones set within these trenches may indicate supports for the floor joists. A brick threshold marked the remains of a doorway in the west wall and a patch of mortar flooring (477, shown in section only, Fig. 18, S.AA) just inside the entrance had superseded at least part of the timber floor.

Room 3, with dimensions approximately 5m x 5.4m, was floored with a worn, uneven compacted chalk surface containing large inclusions (985). Into this surface five stake-holes (918, 945, 916, 892 and one unnumbered) were cut running lengthways along the middle of the room; post-holes 942 and 934 suggested timber partitioning between Rooms 3 and 4. The interior of the chalk-block external walls of Rooms 3 and 4 had been faced with mortar. Four pairs of post-holes (934 and 942, 924 and 926, 920 and 922, 940 and 914) were set in the floor on the west side of the room. The other pairs had evidently been positioned next to the partition walls, the inner pairs arranged symmetrically towards the centre of the room. Numerous other stake-holes and stone fragments littered the floor indicating a room in constant use with many repairs and improvements.

The southern room of Period 2.1, Room 4, measured approximately 6.1m x 5.4m. Stake-holes (980, 978 and 982) indicated possible internal divisions. These were cut into a level compacted clay surface with chalk pebble inclusions (984). New post-holes (812, 826, 828, 836, 840, 842 and 844, not shown in plan or section) were later cut, presumably either to repair existing partitioning or to create new internal divisions.

About 0.3m west of the West Range wall the bedrock was cut away in the form of a shallow step; this proved to be the foundation trench cut (500, shown in section only, Fig. 18, S.AA) for the west wall, filled with a light yellowish-brown clayey loam with chalk chips and gravel (501). It was unclear to what extent this step was a pre-Range feature but there must have been some drop or

slope since the bedrock surface beneath the West Range follows a similar level to the base of the foundation trench. On the west, the trench had been cut through a deposit of dark grey sticky clay (545, not illustrated) containing a single brick of an entirely different type from those used in the West Range walls. These deposits seemed to be make-up layers for a path which consisted of a limestone cobbled surface (503) about 0.8m wide following the wall and extending over the foundation trench fill. A road made up of a compacted pebble surface (538) ran along the west side of this path, with a shallow but well-defined ditch (534) on the west cut into the natural bedrock (552) to catch water running off the hillslope. A second shallow depression (no context number) on the east was interpreted as wear-marking. This road and path should probably be assigned to this phase of the range although the road could predate its construction.

To the north of the West Range was a series of surfaces constructed of layers of pebble and flint. The relationship of these surfaces to the foundation trench (595) of the north wall of the West Range was uncertain but it seemed likely that they were either earlier than or contemporary with the West Range construction and therefore probably relate to the path and road to the west of the building. The lowest surface excavated was a chalk and pea grit surface (663, not illustrated) and this probably equates to 538 to the west. A flint surface (830, Fig. 20, S.WP51/85/10a and S.WP51/85/10b) raised the trackway approximately 0.15m and this was level with a flint and sandstone surface (606, Fig. 18, S.CC) to the south. These were separated by a drainage ditch (831, Fig. 20, S.WP51/85/10b) which ran approximately east-west. An area of sandstone flagging (589) associated with surface 606 at the north-west corner of the West Range may indicate a continuation of path 503. A row of post-holes (no context numbers, not shown in plan or section) beneath the later wall (526, Fig. 19) possibly indicated the line of an earlier boundary.

Discussion
The central positions of posts 562 and 731 (or 719) are likely to have been supports for a loft. The function of the other post-holes is not clear, although the braced posts in pits 709 and 711 presumably formed similar functions. It is likely that Room 2 was a grain store with a raised, boarded floor. The sets of four post-holes in Room 3 perhaps indicated feeding troughs or racking of some kind. There was nothing to indicate the function of Room 4. An attempt is made in Chapter 28 to relate this building to the documentary evidence provided by the building accounts of the mid-1770s. The site finds did not provide significant evidence for the date of its construction.

Period 2.2 (late 18th century to early 19th century)
(Fig. 19)
In Period 2.2 the main building was extended, with the addition of two rooms to the south end of the range,

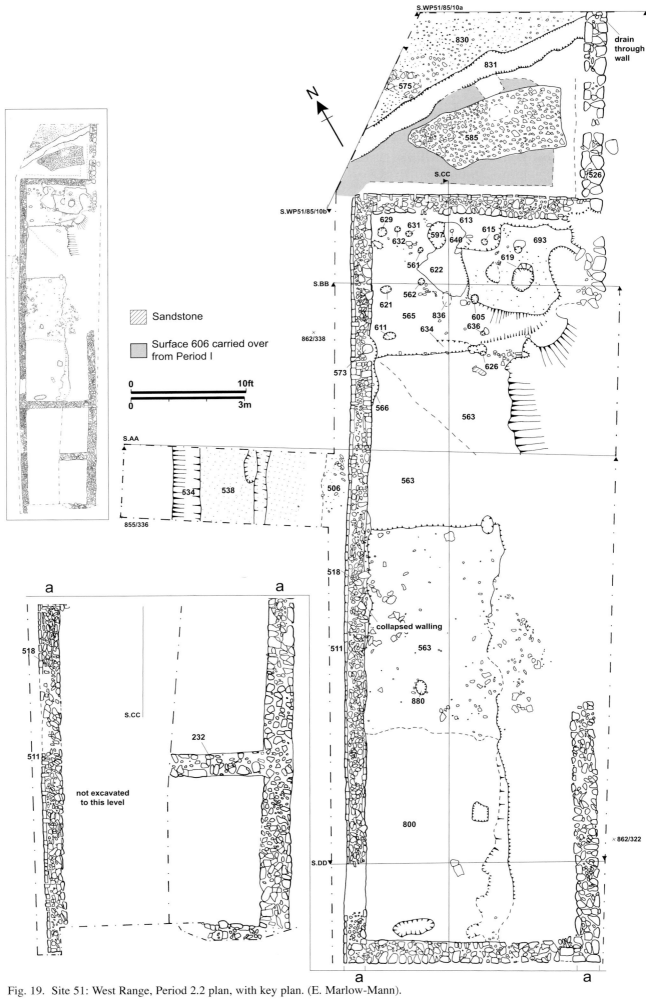

Fig. 19. Site 51: West Range, Period 2.2 plan, with key plan. (E. Marlow-Mann).

increasing its length to approximately 30m and bringing it to within 2m of the South Range. The internal partitioning was altered and the floor levels were raised.

Room 1 remained approximately the same size and was separated from Room 2 by post-holes (573 and 626) and a chalk, limestone and brick partition slot (634). The floor level had been raised approximately 0.8m above surfaces 565 and 622 and was then surfaced in the north-east corner with a solid chalk pebble floor (693). Many post-holes (619, 615, 613, 640, 597, 631, 632, 629, 621, 611, 636, 605, and two post-holes with no context number) cut through these surfaces but no pattern was discernible and their function remained unclear. The floors were laid around post 562 from Period 2.1 (Fig 18, S.BB) indicating that the post was still in use, perhaps supporting a loft. Post 561 may have been the post-pipe from the Period 2.1 post-hole 696, again with the raised floors being laid around it. Post-holes 621, 629 and 631 may also have represented the continuation of timbers from Period 2.1 (post-holes 713 and 711 respectively). The floor surface appeared to be very disturbed, perhaps indicative of heavy use and repairs. Two sets of four post-holes along the west wall were noted during excavation but it was not possible to identify these from the records.

Room 2 became slightly smaller, approximately 4.8m x 5.4m, and its partitioning with Room 3 was only noticeable through a change in the floor level, with the floor in Room 2 being approximately 0.18m lower, although this was not clear in section. A post-hole (no context number) on the line of this floor-level change may indicate part of a timber partition, the opposing post-setting perhaps having been lost under collapsed walling. The floor surface was levelled with a clay loam deposit (471, shown in section only, Fig. 18, S.CC and S.AA) and the room was surfaced with a chalk and mortar floor (563, Fig. 18, S.CC and S.AA) approximately 0.05-0.1m deep. The floor level had been substantially eroded about 0.5m over a distance of 3.8m to the east along the middle of the room and this line was continued through Rooms 3 and 4.

Rooms 3 and 4 appeared to have been amalgamated in this period, although a division may have existed without leaving any trace in the flooring. They were surfaced with a continuation of 563 from Room 2. Three post-hole features (880, and two post-holes with no context numbers) cut this surface but seem unrelated and their function is not clear.

Two rooms were added to the south end of the building. The exterior walls were constructed in the same manner as the main building with the west wall being brick-faced; the two rooms were separated for at least half their width by a stone wall (232) about 0.6m thick running east-west. The western half of the extension was not excavated below the later Period 2.3 cobbled surface so it was not clear whether this east-west wall ran the

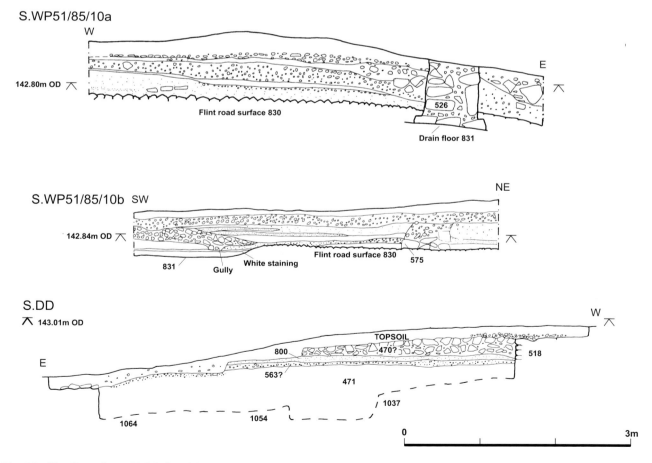

Fig. 20. Site 51 sections. (E. Marlow-Mann)

Plate 8. Site 51: Period 2.3, cobbled stable with Period 1 features underneath, looking south.

whole width of the building. The eastern half was excavated down to a sloping surface (no context number), interpreted as an eroded layer of sub-floor filling. No doorways were revealed within the limits of excavation.

To the west of the building the foundation trench fill (501) of the west wall was overlain with a mortar layer incorporating light grey clayey loam and 20% chalk inclusions (506). The road (538) and ditch (534) probably continued to function as before. North of the range a wall (526, Fig. 20, S.WP51/85/10a; Fig. 22 S.WP51/84/7) was built running north from its north-east corner; it was a similar thickness to the West Range walls but the chalk blocks used were larger and it did not have the brick facing. To the west of this wall was a flint cobble path (585) overlying surface 606. A small gap in wall 526 may indicate access for the path although it was unclear whether this was deliberate or due to the wall's poor state of preservation. A conduit (no context number, Fig. 20, S.WP51/85/10a) was built as the wall was constructed allowing drainage ditch 831 to continue to function. As the road surfaces continued to build up it seemed clear that the road was diverted northwards at the time wall 526 was constructed. Structure 575 was constructed on the Period 2.1 flint surface, 830, which was still in use. The structure might be a patch of rubble or perhaps a post-setting, although when seen in section (Fig. 20, S.WP51/85/10b) it appears more likely to have been another wall, perhaps related to 526.

Discussion
Once again the finds failed to provide dating for these modifications to the West Range; nor was there any relevant documentary evidence. Wall 526 northwards of the West Range may have been the west wall of the North Range; unfortunately not enough survived to establish this definitively.

Period 2.3 and 2.4 (19th century) (Fig. 21; Plates 6 and 8)
Period 2.3 and 2.4 cover the final building modifications followed by demolition and later sequences. The exterior of the building remained unchanged save for the addition of a doorway in the west wall; the main internal modifications involved reflooring.

Room 1's dimensions remained the same with a partition indicated by a post-hole (560) and its possible counterpart to the east (no context number). A cart rut (544) made after the building was demolished destroyed any evidence of a post-hole along the west wall which may have formed a line with these. A north-south division was also indicated by post-pipes 561 and 562, continuing in use from Period 2.1 and which may also have lined up with 560. The western half of the room was built up about 0.5m with a sandy chalk make-up layer (470, Site 51, Fig. 18, S.CC, S.AA and S.BB) and surfaced with chalk cobbles (559). The north-eastern half retained the chalk flooring (693) from Period 2.2; this was set about 0.3m below 559. A deposit of brown

50

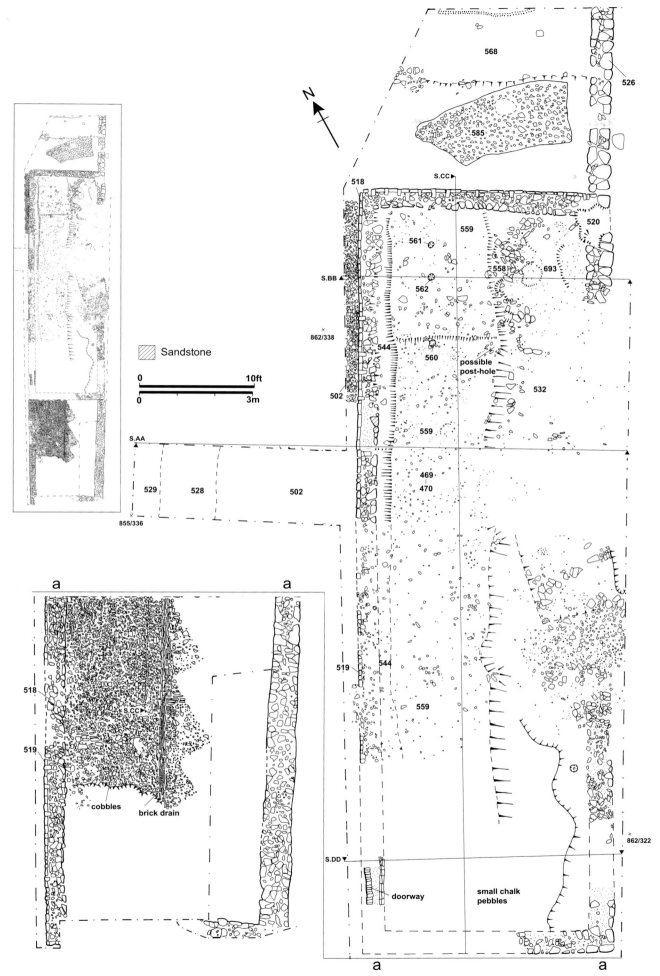

Fig. 21. Site 51: West Range, Period 2.3 and 2.4 plan, including key plan. (E. Marlow-Mann)

51

loam with chalk and brick (558) was associated with the demolition of the West Range. A modern pit (520) had been cut through the north-east corner of Room 1.

Rooms 2 to 4 appeared to have been amalgamated with all internal partitioning removed. The floors had been raised approximately 0.25m by sand and chalk gravel deposits (800 and 470, Fig. 18, S.CC, S.AA and S.BB; Fig. 20, S.DD) and were surfaced with the chalk cobble floor (559) used in Room 1; the floor level was approximately 0.2m below that of Room 1. The eastern side of the building was eroded, with large patches of chalk rubble presumably from the destruction of the eastern wall (Plate 9). A doorway (no context number) was placed in the west wall in the southern corner of what had previously been Room 4, visible as a brick threshold. A band of headers on edge formed the external threshold and its surface was level with the surrounding brick skin level. On the inner wall edge, set lower down, was another line of bricks which may have supported the inner face. The threshold stone would therefore be about 0.15m deep although the actual stone was missing; in its place were smaller stones, mortar and fragments of brick which may have been introduced when the threshold was removed. The doorway was blocked at some point later in this phase and prior to the building's demolition.

The two southern rooms of the extended building were floored with a cobbled surface (no context number); this overlay the partition wall (232) indicating that the separate rooms had been combined. A brick drain (no context number) ran north-south through the centre of the room.

The exterior track was raised again with a closely packed flint surface (502, Fig. 18, S.BB and S.AA), probably contemporary with the internal floor resurfacing 559. North of the West Range and to the west of wall 526 an area of small chalk surfacing (568, Fig. 22, S.WP51/84/7) was built up from the earlier surface (830) and this, in conjunction with 585, is likely to have been a continuation of 502 from the west of the West Range. A very small gully (no context number) ran through 568 at the north end of the site and may have been a small drainage channel or a cart rut. The western side of surface 502 was later overlain by brown loam hillwash deposits (528, 529 and 542 (in section only), Fig. 18, S.AA). Modern road surfacing of flint, brick and chalk hardcore (466) covered the track to the east, partly overlaying the West Range features.

Discussion
The absence in this phase of archaeological evidence for internal partitions or other features makes it difficult to assign a function to the main part of the building. It does seem likely that the southern extension served as a stable.

Plate 9. Site 51: general view of the site showing the extensive plough damage and garden erosion.

52

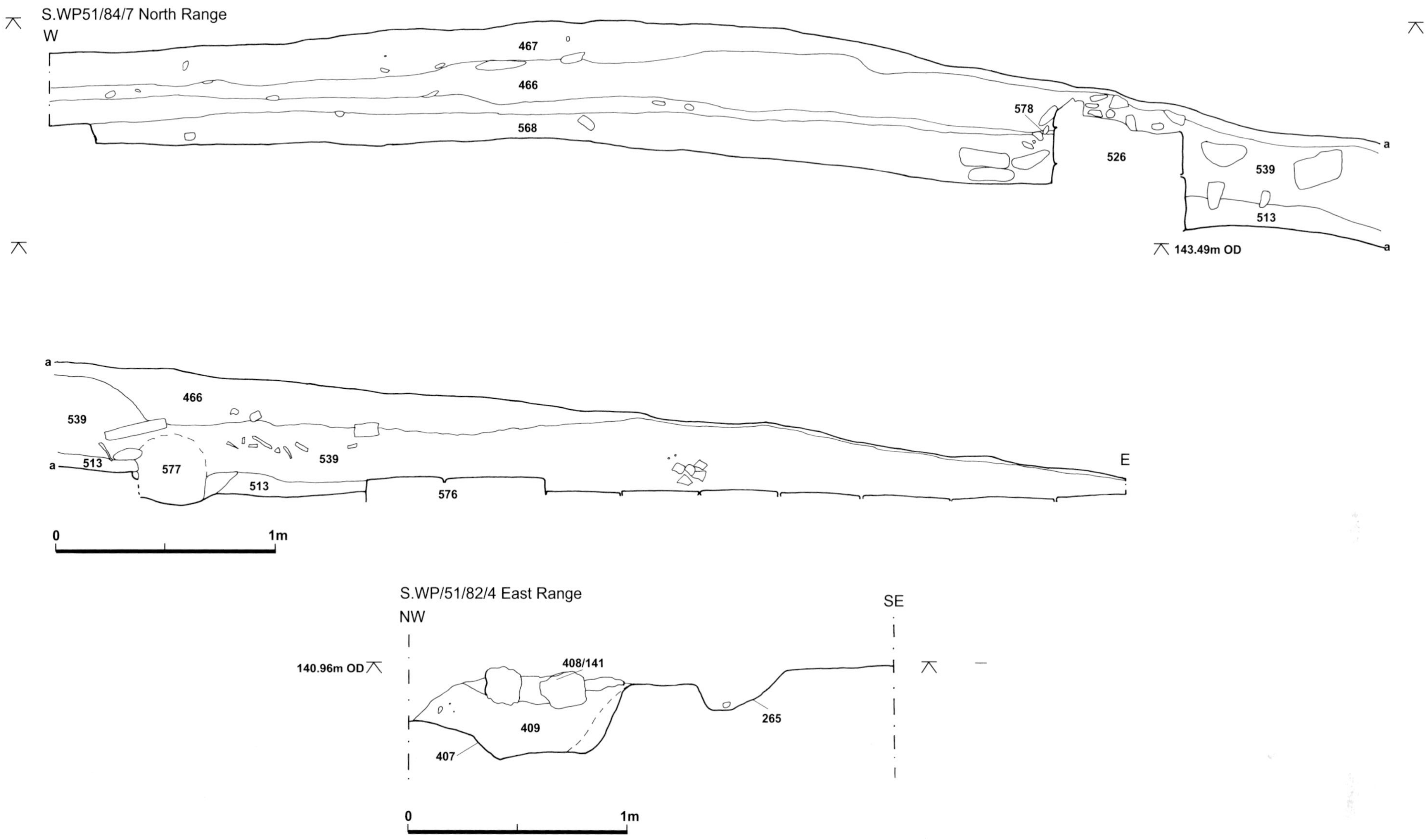

S.WP51/84/7 North Range

W

467
466
568

539
513
526
578

143.49m OD

S.WP/51/82/4 East Range

NW

140.96m OD

SE

265

408/141
409
407

E

466
539
513
576
577
513
539

1m
0

Fig. 22. Site 51 sections. (E. Marlow-Mann)

53

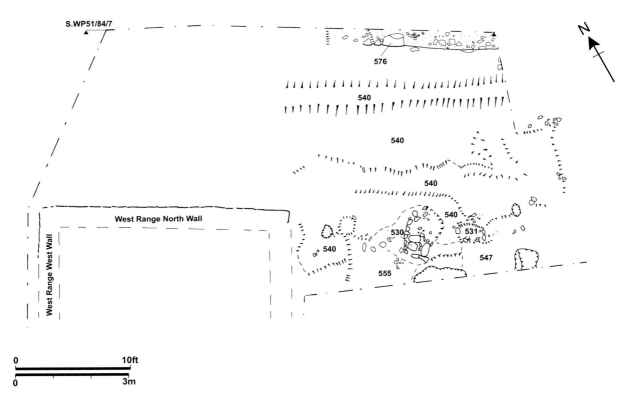

Fig. 23. Site 51 North Range Period 1 and Period 2 plan. (E. Marlow-Mann)

North Range

Period 1 (medieval) (Fig. 23)

Very little remained of the North Range due to extensive gardening and disturbance, and the little that was revealed was very ephemeral. A few features seemed to pre-date the range of post-medieval buildings and these were within a terrace (555) cut into the slope of the bedrock. The surface of 555 was aceramic, although it was sealed by layers containing medieval pot. Beneath this surface a black humic loam layer (547) was revealed, extending to a depth of 0.5m in places. This loam proved to be an undisturbed medieval occupation layer, containing 13th and 14th-century pottery and it seems clear that there were more medieval layers beneath the limits of excavation. Several post-holes (no context numbers) were revealed in this context but no pattern could be discerned and their function was unknown; it is possible that they held timbers for structural supports.

The structures uncovered consisted of part of a wall foundation (530) incorporating dressed sandstone blocks, presumably from the church or a manor house, and a hearth (531).

Period 2.1 (medieval to early 20th century) (Fig. 23)

Further terracing with a surface of a yellowish-brown deposit with chalk pebble inclusions (540) to the north contained the structural remains of a wall of mortared chalk blocks with a dressed outer face (576, Fig. 22, S.WP51/84/7).

Discussion

It is possible that the Period 1 features belonged to a peasant house in the row of crofts running along the valley terrace, the south end having been lost with the construction of the post-medieval farm buildings and later activity.

Cartographic evidence (Dykes 1836 and Wise 1845; see Chapter 2) indicates two outbuildings to the north and north-east of the West Range – there is some discrepancy between Dykes 1836a and 1836b and the extents of the eastern outbuilding are unclear. It is possible that wall 576 represents the south wall of the eastern outbuilding, while wall 526 of the West Range may represent the east wall of the western outbuilding. Archaeological evidence indicates that wall 576 was later than wall 526, suggesting that the eastern outbuilding was built after the western extension.

East Range (Fig. 24)

NB East Range periods do not relate to other periods in Site 51.

Period 1

This phase consists of contexts related to the construction or make-up of Period 2 features.

Labels within the figure:
376/337
334
393
319
312
303
336
323
280
306
367
S.51/82/4
399
183
267
360
379
372
267
164
357
885/320
152
347
265
141
267
875/320
150
152
152
153
141
153
152

0   3m

Fig. 24. Site 51 East Range plan. (E. Marlow-Mann)

Period 2 (12th century to 20th century)

Extensive use of the area as a garden and as a site for refuse pits destroyed almost all the archaeological evidence relating to the East Range: a single wall and some later post-holes are all that remained.

Part of a two to three-course high, chalk block wall (141, Fig. 22, S.WP51/82/4) approximately 0.5m wide which ran north-east to south-west was revealed. The absence of other associated walls led the excavators to suggest that the remainder of the building was to the west, and of timber construction. The only evidence in support of this interpretation consisted of two large sandstone blocks (no context number, not shown on plan), one possibly *in situ*, which could have supported a series of bays or arches. A packed angular chalk surface (372) covered the putative interior of the building. R.T. Porter's reconciliation of the various 19th-century plans of these buildings (Fig. 8) suggests, however, that wall 141 may have been in fact the west wall of the range rather than its east wall, as it appears to have occupied a line that would bring its southern end close to the north-east corner of the cottages (see Fig. 141). An area of hard-packed reddish-brown clay with chalk inclusions (323) extended westwards from the northern end of wall 141 through which was cut a series of post-holes (367, 336, 334, 393, 319, 312, 303, 280 and 306). An evenly spaced line of post-holes (150, 347, 357, 360 and 183) running north-east to south-west, on a slightly different alignment to the wall and cutting it, suggested the possibility of a later timber structure, perhaps associated with the post-holes at the north end.

On the east side of the wall a closely packed chalk rubble surface (153) was overlain by a hard-packed weathered flint surface (152) and it seems likely that, if the second of the alternative interpretations is the correct one, this was internal flooring of the Range. Slightly overlying this flint sufacing was a narrow layer of plaster and mortar (267), interpreted as demolition phase debris.

Period 3 (20th century?)

This period consists of deposits related to the disuse of Period 2 structures.

Discussion

The archaeological evidence of the East Range could indicate, as suggested during the excavations, an open-fronted building used possibly as a cart or wagon shed, such as those surviving at Towthorpe and the Wharram Percy farms. On the other hand, if the wall that survived to be excavated was in fact the west wall of the range, its function cannot be determined from its archaeological remains. The function of the group of post-holes at the northern end of the building was also uncertain. They may have been related to the building shown, on late 19th-century plans, at the north end of the East Range, adjoining the entrance to the courtyard and forming the eastern part of the North Range. Alternatively they could have been more recent, perhaps a garden shed.

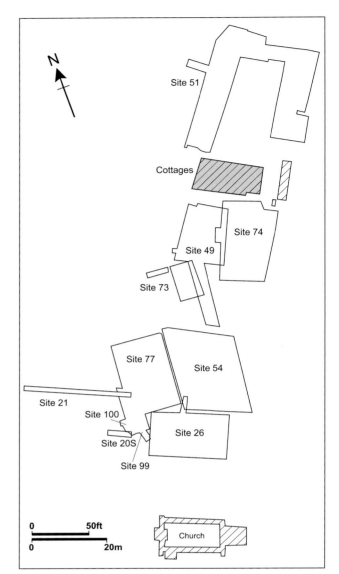

Fig. 25. Location of the cottages. (E. Marlow-Mann)

6 Cottages (Fig. 25)

The standing structure of the cottages was finally investigated at the end of the Wharram Percy excavations in August 1990. The aim was to see if any more could be learnt about the original use of the South Range of outbuildings belonging to the 18th-century farmstead. The reconstruction of these outbuildings as cottages had left few earlier features visible externally. Therefore attention was focused on the inner faces of the walls, with horizontal strips of plaster removed at a height of 1.3m above the internal floor levels to locate blocked openings. The plaster on the north wall was cut away between 0.4m and 0.6m above the internal floor level.

Period 1 (late 18th century to early 19th century)

The original building (Fig. 26) was 18m by 8.5m, narrowing to 8m at the eastern end. It was a one-storey, two to three-roomed building constructed with chalk blocks. The marked disparities in north to south and east to west

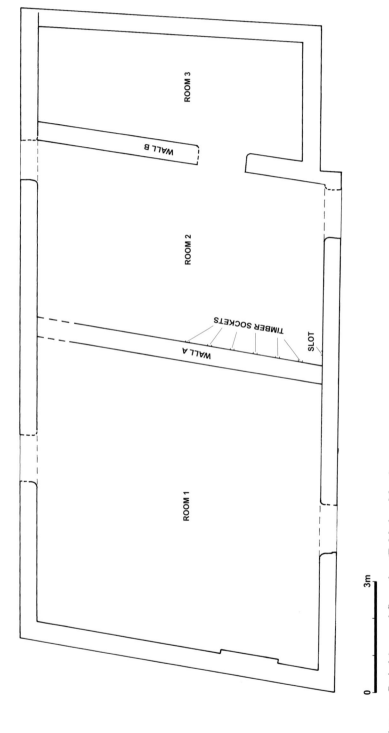

Fig. 26. Cottages: Period 1 ground-floor plan. (E. Marlow-Mann)

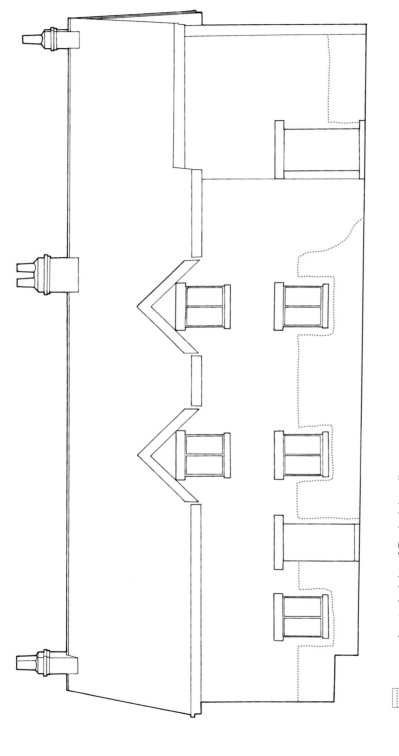

approximate height of Period 1 walls

0   3m

Fig. 27. Cottages: Period 2, south elevation. (E. Marlow-Mann)

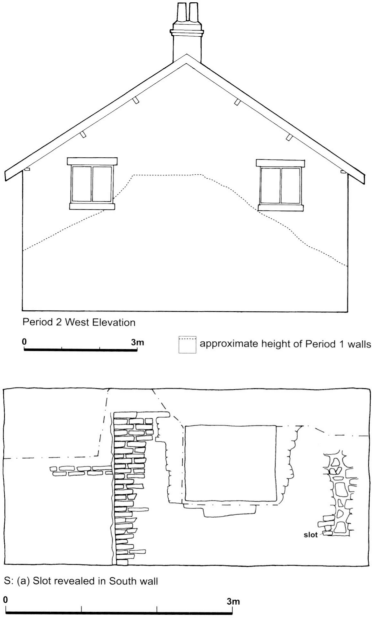

Period 2 West Elevation

0 _____ 3m

approximate height of Period 1 walls

S: (a) Slot revealed in South wall

0 _____ 3m

Fig. 28. Cottages: Period 2, west elevation and section. (E. Marlow-Mann)

alignments suggest it was already a modification of an earlier building, though no evidence could be seen that would have indicated the form of this earlier structure. The external walls were 0.45m-0.55m thick and were faced externally with brick. The Period 1 facing survived to a height of approximately 1.73m, just below the first window lintel on the south side (Fig. 27). It used English Garden Wall bond and probably represented the full height of the Period 1 building's walls. The original western gable wall was visible within the external wall (Fig. 28). The east wall seemed to be original Period 1, built to sill level, then rebuilt above; the north wall was completely refaced in Period 2, which concealed the Period 1 openings.

Rooms 1 and 2 were originally combined as one large room with four entranceways. At some stage in Period 1, Wall A (Fig. 26) was added. This butted against the south

wall, indicating that it was built after initial construction. At the north end, where it would have met the north wall, the brickwork was not tied into the chalk blocks on the east side. Room 1 measured 7.65m by 7.6m and must have been separate from the rest of the building as there was no evidence of a doorway within Wall A. The room contained two opposing entranceways, blocked over in Period 2: one in the south wall and one in the north wall. The southern doorway, with a width of 1.3m, was in the centre of the wall, 3.2m from the west wall, with rounded interior corners. The brick was tied into the chalk walling. The northern doorway was off centre, being 3.8m from the western wall. The eastern side of this entranceway was not revealed but its position could be plotted, on the assumption that its width was the same as that of its counterpart. No further openings were exposed.

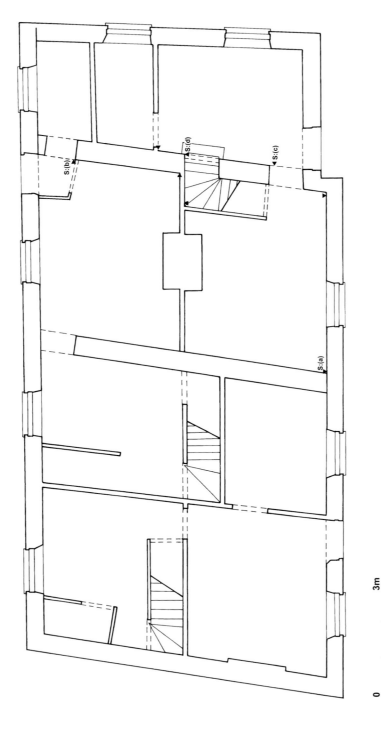

S₍(b)

S₍(d)

S₍(c)

S₍(a)

0   3m

Fig. 29. Cottages: Period 2 ground-floor plan. (E. Marlow-Mann)

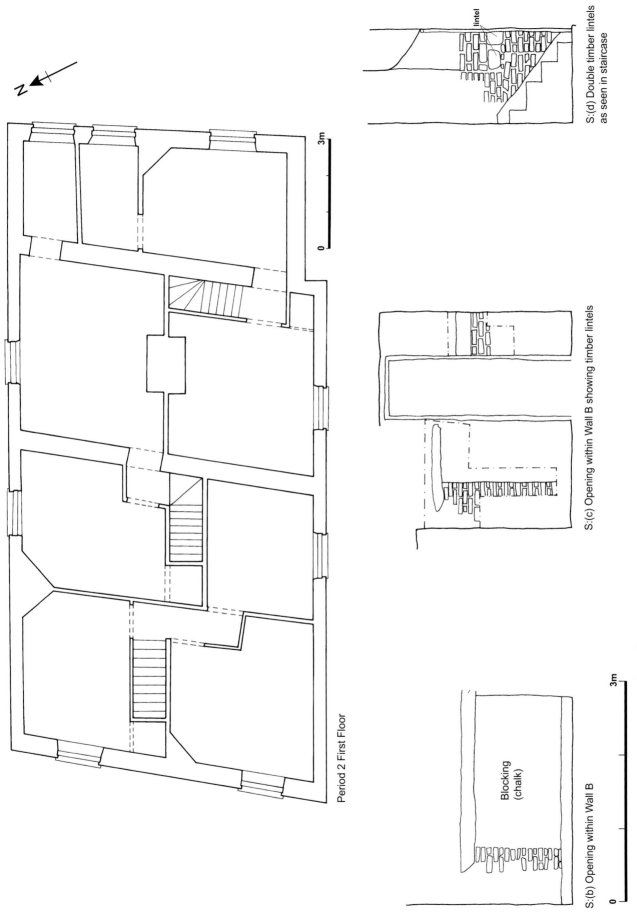

N

Period 2 First Floor

0   3m

S:(d) Double timber lintels as seen in staircase

lintel

S:(c) Opening within Wall B showing timber lintels

Blocking (chalk)

S:(b) Opening within Wall B

0   3m

Fig. 30. Cottages: Period 2 first-floor plan and ground-floor sections. (E. Marlow-Mann)

Room 2 (Fig. 26), 4.75-4.95m by 7.7m, also contained two doorways, blocked in Period 2. The western edge of the doorway in the southern wall was situated 1.4m from the eastern wall; the eastern edge was not revealed. The northern doorway, approximately 1.1m wide, was exposed 1.05m from the eastern wall in the same position as the present entranceway. Both doorways had rounded brick internal corners and the reveals were tied into the chalk block walling. Wall B was bonded into the chalk block south wall. The northern end was interrupted by a Period 2 doorway but enough remained to show that it abutted the north wall. This suggested that this section of the northern wall was added when the Period 2 doorway was inserted, the original wall perhaps having been damaged during the work. Wall A contained sockets for timbers approximately 100mm by 100mm scantling, at 600mm intervals. The timbers would have been 1.35m above floor level and may have extended the full length of the wall, although they were only visible in the southern half of the room. A slot (Fig. 28 S:(a)) was revealed in the south wall. This may have housed a supporting beam for the outer ends of the timbers discussed above, the whole perhaps part of a feeding trough.

Room 3 (Fig. 26) was an irregular shape, measuring 2.55-3.30m by 7.05m. Externally, the north wall of the cottages appeared continuous from one end to the other, encompassing the north end of Room 3. The interior of the eastern wall butted against the north wall, indicating that the eastern wall was rebuilt at some stage in Period 1. The outer brick facing below 1m, however, was continuous around the corner to the north wall, suggesting that this area of refacing was all done at the same time, after the wall was rebuilt. The relationship of the southern wall with the eastern wall was not investigated so it was unclear how much of the walls had been reworked and whether both had been rebuilt. The southern jamb of a doorway (Fig. 26) was revealed in wall B with a rounded doorjamb; the position of the northern jamb has been estimated.

Period 2 (mid to late 19th century)
A second, gabled, storey was added to the outbuildings in Period 2 when they were converted into the present three cottages. Internal brick walls and doorways were added and three staircases inserted. The cottages had two doorways in the south wall and one door in the north wall, suggesting three separate dwellings. The heightened cottage walling was faced in brick using English bond above the Period 1 structure (Fig. 27). The 'headers' consisted of broken brick ends, evidently reusing materials from an earlier structure. The north wall (Plate 8) was constructed of sandstone blocks up to sill level and then faced in English bond, probably indicating a refacing in Period 2, although it was not clear why sandstone blocks were used for the lower courses instead of brick; it is possible that the sandstone courses belonged to Period 1. It seemed likely that all the building materials used to convert the range to cottages, including the sandstone lintel and sills of door and window openings, were recycled from the demolition of the farmhouse.

Discussion
The alignment of the east and west walls of Rooms 1 and 2 corresponded with the alignment of the East and West Ranges of Site 51; however, it was unclear why the north and south walls of the cottages were not at right angles to the east and west walls. The North Range was also on a different alignment and the irregular layout of the farmstead was perhaps influenced by topography and pre-existing structures. The unusual shape of Room 3 was dictated by the limited space left next to the East Range.

Period 1 of the cottages, as the South Range of the farmstead, must have been contemporary with the main use of the West Range, Periods 1-2; the West Range pre-Period 1 was on a very different alignment from the cottages. As the Period 2 cottages evidently used material from the demolished farmhouse, their change in function coincided with the abandonment of the farmstead and was, therefore, contemporary with Site 51 Period 2.4.

7 Sites 11 and 49

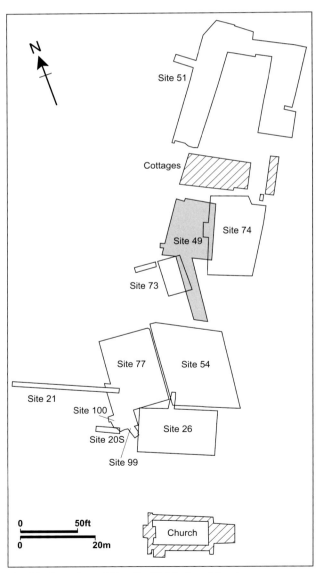

Fig. 31. Location of Site 49. (E. Marlow-Mann)

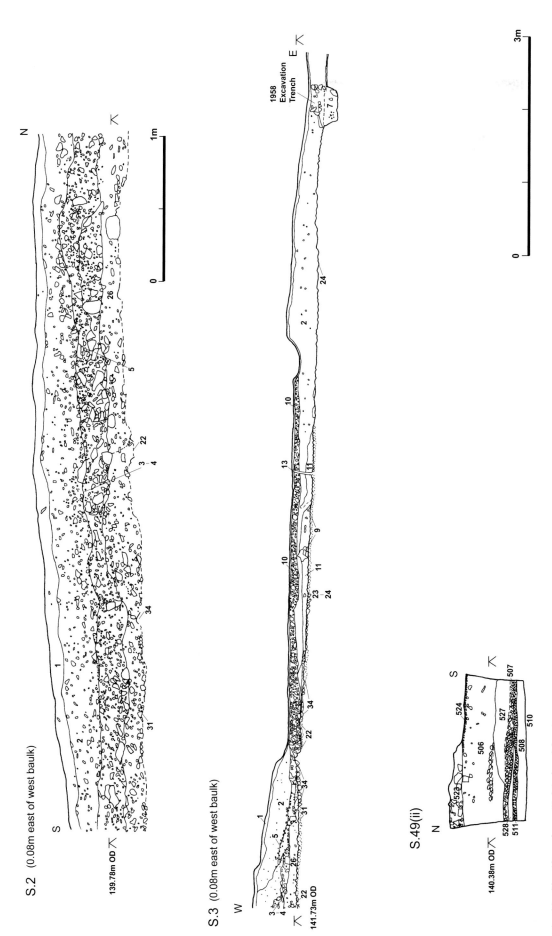

S.2 (0.08m east of west baulk)

S.3 (0.08m east of west baulk)

S.49(ii)

Fig. 32. Site 49 sections. (E. Marlow-Mann)

63

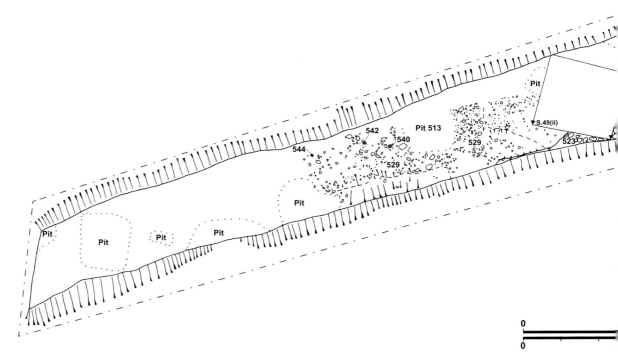

Fig. 33. Site 49: Period 2 plan. (E. Marlow-Mann)

Site 11 relates to the initial phase of trenching in the area of the farmhouse. It was begun when one of the 1958 excavation rubbish pits encountered an ashlar wall. The building's foundations were uncovered but all further work was carried out as Site 74 for the farmhouse and Site 49 for the courtyard.

Site 11 was previously reported in *Interim Report 1958, 1.*

Site 49 was situated south of the cottages and west of the farmhouse. Excavation began in 1978-79 and continued in 1983-84 with the intention of uncovering the farmyard and trackway shown on 19th-century maps. A trench (7, initially Site 11, shown only in section, Fig. 32, S.3) was dug in 1958 along the walls of the farmhouse in order to reveal the building's exact location and size. As a consequence of this some important stratigraphic information has been lost. This trench was later incorporated into the Site 49 excavations. The extension running southwards from the main excavation represents an attempt to trace the line of the road from the corner of the cottages to the line of the southern garden fence through an area heavily disturbed by modern rubbish and

cesspits (513 (=Pit 1, Site 73); 502 (not illustrated), and unnumbered pits, Fig. 33). Several of the pits were excavated and the contents recorded prior to being cut back into a box section about 1m deep in order to provide information on the terrace make-up.

Site 49 was previously reported in *Interim Reports 1978, 12; 1979, 9; 1983, 17-18; 1984, 16.*

Period 1 (Iron Age/Romano-British to 15th century)
The natural chalk bedrock (510, Fig. 32, S.49(ii)) was overlain by a buried soil layer (508) *c.* 0.14m deep containing bone and handmade pottery, possibly Iron Age in date. Covering this was a layer of pea-grit (511) *c.* 0.04m thick overlain by chalky hillwash deposits (528).

A surface made up of heavily compacted chalk pebbles (22, Fig. 32, S.2 and S.3) was revealed and may represent the earliest surviving trackway. It was well worn and showed signs of having been repaired frequently with chalk fragments (31, Fig. 32, S.2 and S.3; 35, not illustrated) suggesting a long exposure. The surface was not removed.

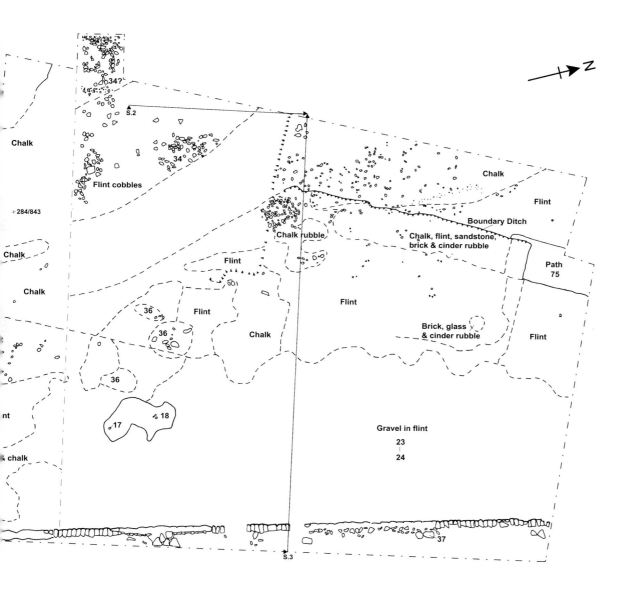

Z

Chalk

34?

S.2

34

Flint cobbles

+284/843

Chalk

Chalk

Chalk

36

Flint

36

36

18

17

nt

& chalk

Chalk rubble

Flint

Chalk

Chalk

Flint

Chalk

Flint

Boundary Ditch

Chalk, flint, sandstone,
brick & cinder rubble

Path
75

Brick, glass
& cinder rubble

Flint

Gravel in flint
23
24

37

S.3

Period 2 (17th century to late 19th century) (Fig. 33)
Several layers of probable destruction debris (33 (not
illustrated); and 36), used to level the area immediately to
the west of the farmhouse, were overlain by a series of
stone deposits consisting mainly of gravel and flint (23
and 24, Fig. 32, S.3). The exact purpose of these deposits
is unknown but they were possibly used to create a yard
for parking and turning carriages. A plaster and brick pad
(18) was uncovered on top of the yard surface, the
function of which remains unclear. Some brick fragments
(17) bonded to this surface perhaps represented the base
for a structure or feature.

Approximately 4m to the west of the western
farmhouse wall and roughly overlying the earlier surface
22, the deposits were much more irregular, including
coarse components of chalk, flint and cement cobbles
(34, Fig. 32, S.2 and S.3). This surface contained ridges
and depressions consistent with a well-used trackway.
Some deposits (3, 4 and 5, Fig. 32, S.3; 20, not illustrated)
were identified as areas of road repair, indicating a
continuous period of use and maintenance. Although the

trackways were exposed running north-south with an
approximate total width of 4.5m, their precise eastern
limits were confused by the presence of the yard. The
western side lay under the present track to St Martin's
Church and was not excavated.

The tracks were overlain by humic deposits (26, Fig.
32, S.2 and S.3; 32, not illustrated) possibly representing
an old turf line. A possible boundary ditch or robbed-out
wall foundation trench (no context number) was also
uncovered; this cut through a packed crushed white chalk
deposit (75) representing a well-used pathway.

In the southern trench extension loam deposits (506
and 527, Fig. 32, S.49(ii)) made up the ground level
beneath the road. The road surface, approximately 2.5m
wide, consisted of a hard packed cobbled surface (524
(=11, Site 73, Period 2)), with possible wheel depressions,
overlain by a coarser hard packed chalk rubble layer (523
(=2, Site 73, Period 2)). A series of post-medieval
depressions (529; 533, not illustrated) ran along the line of
the road, culminating in a hollow (no context number)
c.1m deep and *c*. 0.75m wide, filled with building rubble.

Period 3 (late 19th century to 20th century)
A line of Period 3 stake-holes (540, 542 and 544) followed a similar alignment to the Period 2 depressions (529 and 533). Up to 1m of topsoil (1) and overburden (2) built up across the site, consisting of garden soil and accumulated spoil from pit digging. The remainder of contexts from Period 3 consist of activities associated with excavation and with the use of the area as a garden and yard for the cottages. As such the contexts were too recent and disturbed to warrant further discussion.

8 Site 73

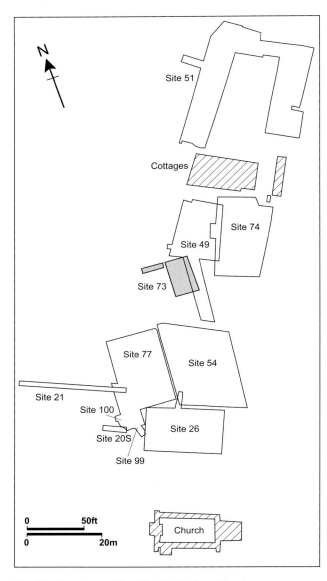

Fig. 34. Location of Site 73. (E. Marlow-Mann)

Dug over two seasons in 1983 and 1984 as an extension to Site 49, Site 73 covered an area approximately 10m x 5.5m between the present and former roads. A small structure was identified on maps of 1836-1855 as a stable (see Chapter 3) and the aim of excavation was to locate and interpret this building prior to public display. The site had been extensively disturbed by 19th and 20th-century gardening and by modern rubbish and cesspits (6, 10, 12, 13 (=513, Site 49) and 17, Fig. 35). Several of these were emptied (6, 10, 13 and 17) and the sections drawn which, combined with the pit excavations in Site 49, provided a comprehensive picture of the terrace build-up. An extension trench, 5.75m x 1m, was opened to the west to investigate whether any pre-19th-century archaeology survived beneath the 19th/20th- century road (Fig. 35).

Site 73 was previously reported in *Interim Reports 1983, 18-19; 1984, 16.*

Period 1 (?pre-medieval)
The natural periglacial chalk and clay (32 and 42, not illustrated; 112, Fig. 36, S.a) was overlain by a clean hillwash layer (103 and 104, Fig 36, S.a) which appeared to have been levelled in the medieval period to make a platform for building. The buried soil layer (508, Fig. 32, S.49(ii)) revealed in Site 49 did not extend into Site 73. A possible post-hole (no context number, Fig. 36, S.b) was revealed in section, filled with chalk rubble from the overlying layer. It is possible that this layer equates with context 35 from Period 2, although this was unlabelled on the section drawing.

Period 2 (16th century to 19th century?) (Fig. 35; Plate 10)
Where undisturbed by pits the surface of the site consisted of a number of chalk rubble and cobble surfaces (63, 51, 121, 90, 35, 131, 80, 98 and 115) containing little dating evidence. A clay soil deposit with bones and charcoal (55) in the north-east corner may have been a yard surface but it was unclear to what this would have related. In the south-west corner of the site was a group of features including remnants of walls (9 and 92), heavy cobbles (8), post-pits (no context numbers) and a beam slot (no context number). The cobble surface (8) was built up by a layer of dark soil with chalk inclusions (88) which overlay a deposit of hard-packed yellow chalky clay with large chalk inclusions (35) covering the southern half of the site. The fragment of mortared ashlar wall (9), running north-east to south-west with a thickness of approximately 0.5m, was plastered both sides suggesting an internal dividing wall and this was supported by the cobbles (8) on each side of it, presumably indicating the main floor surface inside the building. A layer of black ash (no context number, Fig. 36, S.b) suggested that the building was destroyed by fire. A further patch of walling (92) at the south-east end of Pit 17 appeared to be running south-east to north-west and it is possible that this was an external wall, although the rubbish pits had destroyed any further evidence of this structure. These features continued into the unexcavated areas to the south and west. Although not datable, it was noted at the time of excavation that these features bore a resemblance to external surfaces and structures north of the 18th-century vicarage site (Site 54 Periods 6-7). They did not appear to correspond with the stable structure indicated on the maps (Chapter 2).

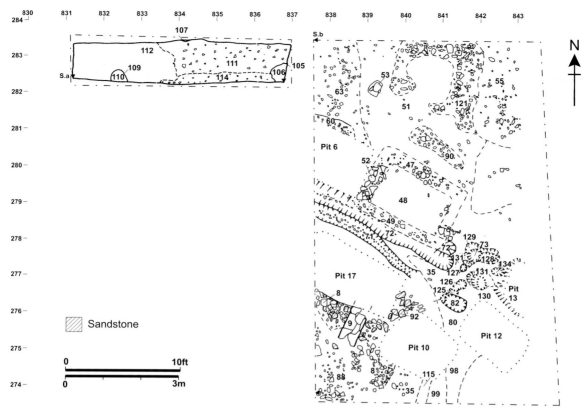

Fig. 35. Site 73: Period 2 plan. (E. Marlow-Mann)

Plate 10. Site 73; general view of the site, looking west.

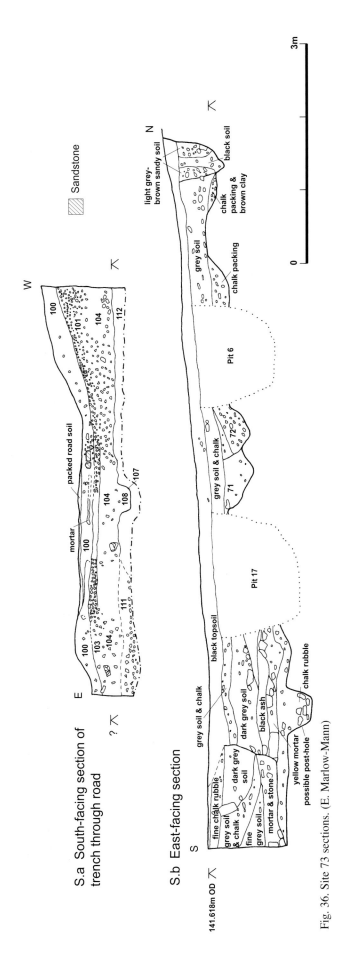

S.a South-facing section of trench through road

S.b East-facing section

Fig. 36. Site 73 sections. (E. Marlow-Mann)

To the north of this structure lay a series of east-west gullies (71 and 72, Fig. 36, S.b) possibly marking a late division between the vicarage and farmstead areas. The ditches culminated to the east in a collection of intercutting post-pits (82, 125-130, 73 and 134) of varying dates which appeared to mark the boundary's junction with the road and perhaps mark gate posts.

In the centre of the excavated area a structure measuring 1.9m by 2.6m was revealed. It had wall foundations approximately 0.4m thick. The north-east to south-west walls (52) were composed of chalk rubble blocks about 0.20m across and the northern wall (47) was probably of similar rubble construction (although the context records omit any description). The southern wall (49) may have been built into gully or trench 72. A hard packed chalk surface (48) seemed to cover the inside of the building and may have been a contemporary floor surface.

A group of three rounded stones (53), about 0.4m in diameter, was perhaps the base of a pillar. Its position was very close to the supposed south-west corner of the stable (Chapter 2) and it is possible that this feature base was all that remained of the structure.

Several hillwash deposits (101, 103 and 104, Fig. 36, S.a) were revealed in the extension trench to the west, with a maximum depth of 0.70m down to the periglacial chalky clay (111 and 112). These contained medieval pottery presumably washed or tipped down from the tofts above. Three pit features (105, 107 and 109) were revealed cutting through into the natural chalk but their purpose remained unclear.

It was noticeable that very little 18th-century cultural material was recovered from Site 73. Surface debris may have been cleared and redeposited elsewhere in the early 19th century but there is no evidence to support this. With the close proximity of Low House Farm and the vicarage it does, however, seem anomalous that little 18th-century pottery was deposited.

Period 3 (19th century to early 20th century)

A hard packed chalk surface with brick fragments (102, not illustrated) was overlain by topsoil and overburden (100) and this may represent part of a former road surface, although it was not clear how recent this layer was. The remainder of the Period 3 contexts consisted mainly of modern pits (6, 10, 12, 13 and 17), post-holes and disturbed deposits and will not be discussed further.

Part Three
Excavation of the Vicarage Sites

9 Site 77

by E. Marlow-Mann and S. Wrathmell
based on an archive report by J. Wood

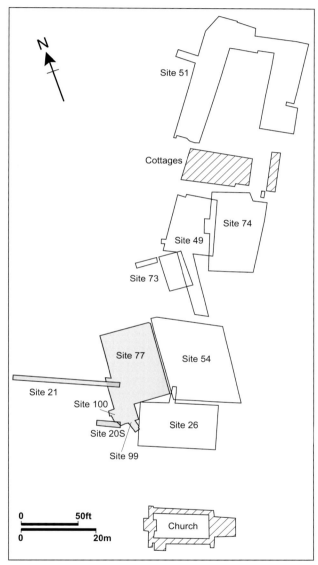

Fig. 37. Location of Site 77. (E. Marlow-Mann)

Excavations on Site 77 were undertaken to investigate the substantial building remains uncovered within three earlier trenches in the western valley side in 1971 (Sites 20N, 20S and 21, see *Wharram XI*). Once the 19th-century track to the church was moved in 1984 it became possible to begin a large open-area excavation to reveal the full structural remains of what was interpreted as a sequence of vicarage buildings. Work was undertaken

over a period of seven years, from 1984 to 1990: excavation in 1984 was overseen by Malcolm Atkin with subsequent work supervised by John Wood. The specific objective of the excavations was to uncover the remains of vicarage buildings which preceded those already identified in Site 54 (Chapter 10); there was no attempt to excavate levels earlier than those that had accumulated in the later Middle Ages. Four extensions to Site 77 - Sites 20S, 21, 99 and 100 - have already been discussed in *Wharram XI* and that volume should be consulted for more detailed information. The results of those excavations are, however, summarised here and incorporated into relevant phases of Site 77. The rubble dumps which covered much of this site generally do not add greatly to our understanding of the structural sequence and it has, therefore, been decided to base this report around the fragments of walling and associated surfaces that remained once the debris had been cleared. The relationship of the structural remains described below to the vicarage buildings in Site 54, to the east, and the buildings in Site 26, to the south, will be considered in Chapters 10 and 28.

The site was opened in 1984 using an open area planning system laid out on the Ordnance Survey metric grid. The excavation was divided into three plan areas, and each new plan recorded a number of changes at a time. It became apparent quickly that this system would not work in the conditions of Site 77. Site 54 was already being excavated using single context recording, but because of concerns about possible difficulties over context relationships if the system was not implemented satisfactorily, an attempt was made at developing a compromise system, continuing Wharram's long history of experimentation in various aspects of excavation. Site 77 was then further divided into 5m grid squares. Each grid was then excavated in a manner similar to single context recording and attempts were made to transcribe the large area plans onto smaller sheets stored by grid square. It is clear from the records that this system led to deficiencies in the site archive, with lengths of walls or deposits stopping at the grid edge, not having been recorded in the adjoining grid square. It has also become apparent that some plans have been mislaid. After a couple of seasons of increasing stratigraphic complexity, resulting from episodes of levelling, terracing, demolition and hillwash, this system was seen to be unsatisfactory and a single context recording system was belatedly introduced.

Further problems were caused by the presence of a conduit trench which had been cut through the vicarage area, probably in the early to mid-18th century, to carry water from one of the southern springs to the farmhouse

Plate 11. Site 77: view of Period 1 barn looking west.

on Site 74. It ran south-west to north-east across the site and appeared to have destroyed many important relationships between walling fragments; it also made linking features on the east with features on the west side difficult and, in some cases, impossible. The recording of Sites 77 and 54 proceeded independently and the baulk between the two was unfortunately broadly along the line of a number of terracing cuts into the hillside, made for the construction of the later vicarage. It was therefore doubly unfortunate that such a key area should have had to be excavated at the end of the site's programme as a separate exercise and that, since the site excavation edges ran along, rather than crossed, the terracing cuts in the hillside, the scope for complexity and confusion was considerable. The excavators' barrow run was also situated on this baulk; although eventually removed and recorded, this did not help in linking the area to the Site 54 excavations.

Site 77 was previously reported in *Interim Reports 1984, 19-20; 1985, 17-20; 1986, 15; 1987, 14-16; 1988, 8-9; 1989, 6-9; 1990, 8-10.*

Period 1 (pre-1553) (Fig. 38)
At the northern end of the site was a building represented by two parallel lengths of walling which ran broadly north to south. The eastern wall (261 and 681) was 0.6m wide and it survived for a length of 7.85m constructed with chalk blocks and an occasional block of sandstone.

It was built on a rubble dump of orange clayey silt with chalk inclusions (704, not illustrated), which may have represented bonding material from an earlier structure. The western wall (56, 260, 641 and 586) was of similar construction; it survived for a length of 9.75m, to a maximum height of eight courses, with a width of 0.75-0.8m (Plates 11 and 12). The middle section of 56 was wider and looser and may represent the blocking of an original entrance (Fig. 45, wall 56); alternatively, it may have been related to Period 4 construction and the wall's reinforcement as a boundary. An area of orange pea-grit wall bonding material (713) at the south end of this wall suggested that it had formerly continued a further 0.7m southwards. Abutting 713 was an east to west linear deposit of light orange to burnt grey-black compacted pea-grit and cobbles (642=649) which was interpreted as a possible end wall or division. A later robber trench fill (339, Fig. 44) roughly corresponded with this and may have been a further indication of this wall line. It was not possible to determine the full extent of this building as the northern end lay under some 3m of overburden and was not excavated. It is clear from the Period 2 evidence that the building was a barn.

Within the barn floor area there was an uneven hard-packed chalky clay surface (716=719=660), likely to have been a floor surface; this was cut by a number of stake-holes and a linear feature of unknown purpose (717). Two trial trenches through this surface revealed

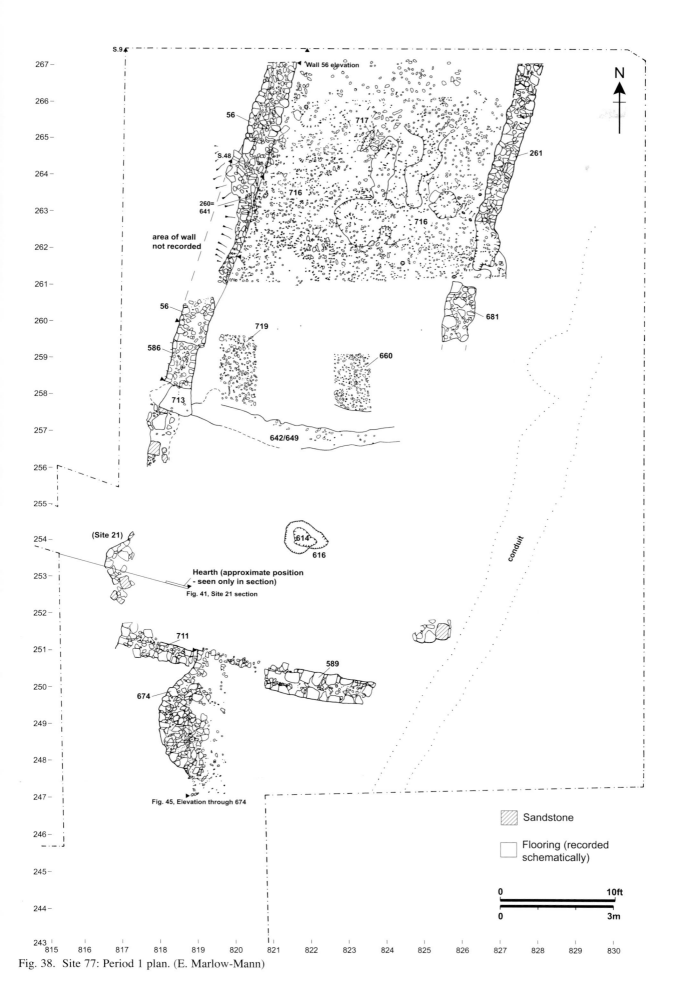

Fig. 38. Site 77: Period 1 plan. (E. Marlow-Mann)

Plate 12. Site 77: view of Period 1 barn, with burnt deposits, looking east.

two underlying surface-like layers of clay with pebble and cobble inclusions (680 and 702, not illustrated), themselves overlying a loose rubble dump of sandy soil with frequent rubble and pebble inclusions (710, not illustrated).

The barn area of the site was originally intended for public display (an intention that proved impractical) and it was therefore not excavated further. There were, however, possible buildings of an earlier date on a completely different alignment beneath it: besides the evidence from the trial trenches, a radar survey undertaken in 1989 (*Interim Report* 1989, 9) revealed a possible wall running 'diagonally' underneath the barn about 1m deep. A test pit through the barn floor that was intended to locate it failed to reveal any structural evidence. As GPR (ground-penetrating radar) was still experimental at this time, any data it revealed deserves to be treated with caution, and it should be noted that this exercise was undertaken primarily to test the GPR equipment rather than to investigate the archaeology.

South of the barn, the earliest structural feature was a large semicircular area of stonework (674, Fig. 45) built of chalk and sandstone, roughly coursed with a rubble core. It had a diameter of 3m and turned northwards at the north end. The stonework survived to a height of five courses. Nothing remained to indicate its continuation to the south or east. It may have been the base for a chimney or oven, or for a staircase. To the west of wall 674 was a

series of loose rubble deposits (631 and 698, not illustrated) which may have been used as levelling material.

A wall (711) ran westwards from the northern end of feature 674 and seems to have been a later addition, unless the northern end of feature 674 was cut through it. It was constructed of approximately 70% cobbles and was probably faced with chalk blocks although this is not clear from context records. It had a width of 0.5m and ran for a length of 2.1m; it then turned 90° to run northwards, on the same alignment as the barn walls although only a fragment, 0.55m in length, survived. It is possible that this fragment corresponded to a section of walling which incorporated a curved stone feature (no context number, Site 21, Fig. 41) discovered in a trial trench and also to a wall fragment (no context number) which abutted the south end of mortar deposit 713. This resulting wall alignment would appear, therefore, broadly to continue southwards the line of the west barn wall.

A further wall, 182, ran south south-eastwards from the west end of wall 711, as far as the southern end of the site where it was cut by the conduit trench. Wall 182 has here been assigned to Period 3.1 but, as outlined in Chapter 28, it might in fact belong to this phase instead: the evidence can be argued either way.

A layer of chalk cobbles and pebble rubble (608, not illustrated) represented construction debris associated with a further wall fragment (589) which was located east

72

Plate 13. Site 77: view showing curved feature in Site 21, wall 182, and layer of burning in the Period 2 barn visible in the baulk at the top, looking north.

of wall 711 on the same east to west alignment. It was built of chalk and sandstone blocks with a chalk rubble infill and an orange pea-grit matrix. It was 0.75m wide and survived for a length of 2.9m; it was truncated at both ends, although a line of rubble which spread westwards on the same alignment may represent its continuation. It is likely that wall 589 was a continuation of wall 711 although no direct relationship could be established.

To the north of wall 711 the remains of a hearth (no context number, Site 21, Fig. 41) was visible in section. It underlay the later Period 3.1 wall, 461, and was probably associated with the unnumbered curved stone feature from Site 21, Plate 13. A hard-packed dark ashen grey burnt area with chalk pebble inclusions (614) was contained within a hearth pit (616) cut into a compacted chalk floor (596). Its size and shape indicated that it was associated with the Period 3.1 hearth 595, but that it had been wrongly plotted in the field recording. East of this, just west of the conduit trench, an east-west wall (no context number) was partly recorded to a height of at least two courses. It appeared to be of chalk block construction with occasional sandstone; it was topped with a large chamfered sandstone block, but it was unclear whether this was *in situ*. Photographs of this area clearly showed that the wall underlay Period 3.1 features and it is likely, therefore, that it belongs in Period 1.

Period 2 (1553) (Fig. 39)
Period 2 was represented by a major burning event, specifically recorded in the barn area at the north end of the site. Much of its interior was covered in charcoal and the remains of burnt crops (559=643), which are discussed in detail in Chapter 24. This deposit was so rich that it was targeted for a specific sampling strategy. Further burnt deposits (647; 629 and 659, not illustrated) were also revealed but these were not extensively sampled.

These burnt deposits were overlain by patches of destruction rubble, indicating a period of deliberate backfilling. It was possible to identify individual dumps, possibly large barrowloads or cartloads, heaped against each other. These dumps were initially excavated separately but due to time constraints the remainder was removed in a single context. A significant number of these deposits contained large fragments of charcoal and burnt nails (622, illustrated; 320, 321, 449, 508, 545, 553, 561, 617, 653, 667, not illustrated. See Chapters 22 and 24). These presumably represented the collapse of the burnt building. Charcoal was present to a much lesser degree in many of the remaining deposits of this period (644, 665, 686, 696, illustrated; 204, 318, 606, 610, 612, 700, 706 and 715 not illustrated) and may have represented further destruction debris or levelling deposits. The buildings

Fig. 39. Site 77: Period 2 plan. (E. Marlow-Mann)

were evidently demolished almost to ground level, probably soon after the fire as the floor did not seem to have lain open for any great length of time; the ground was built up and levelled with the many rubble deposits available from the building remains.

Period 3.1 (1553 to 17th century) (Fig. 40; Plate 14)
A group of structures was built south of the Period 1 barn, overlying the earlier rubble deposits. A semicircular chalk wall with occasional sandstone blocks (220), 0.3m wide and facing east survived to a height of five courses. It formed a feature 2m in diameter which contained a rubble fill of orange-brown gritty sand with 70% stone inclusions and charcoal flecking (565). It may have been an oven foundation. Wall 220 appeared to turn north at the north-east corner of this feature; only a small fragment survived but it is probable that it joined with a robbed northern wall. Its line was probably represented by a raised linear deposit of browny orange silt and pebbles (435) which may indicate bedding material.

A narrow semi-circular wall of chalk blocks with sandstone fragments (348), also facing east and surviving to five courses, joined this circular feature to the south. A

mixed deposit of grey, black and brown soil with charcoal and pebble inclusions (593, not illustrated) represented its construction debris, while a bedding surface was indicated by a layer of orange-brown clayey silt with fine chalk inclusions and charcoal flecking (594, not illustrated). It surrounded a circular oven-type structure (595) constructed of chalk and flint blocks, sandstone and tile bonded with orange pea-grit, over which lay an ashy charcoal-rich layer (546, not illustrated).

Joining Structure 348 to the south was a narrow wall (146) which ran southwards (Plate 15). It was constructed of a rubble core and compacted grey-brown silty loam faced with chalk blocks. Only one block deep, about 0.2m wide, but surviving to a maximum height of four courses, it probably represented an internal wall. After 1.5m, wall 146 turned eastwards and continued for a surviving length of 3m; the cornerstone was sandstone. In line with this wall, 1.10m further east, was a pit or post-hole (712), 0.35m in diameter, which may indicate a wall or roof support; however, this may also have related to earlier structures in Period 1.

Apparently associated with these walls was a pale-coloured floor surface of fine pebbles and patches of

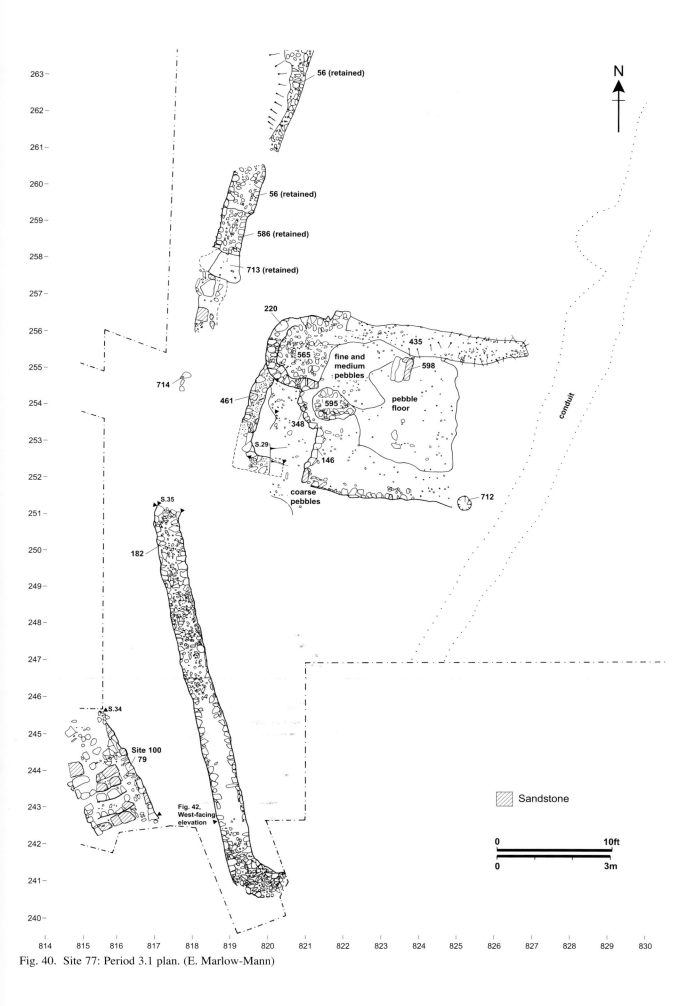

Fig. 40. Site 77: Period 3.1 plan. (E. Marlow-Mann)

Plate 14. Site 77: Period 3.1 features, with the Period 1 barn visible to the north, looking north.

Plate 15. Site 77: Period 3.1 wall 146, looking east.

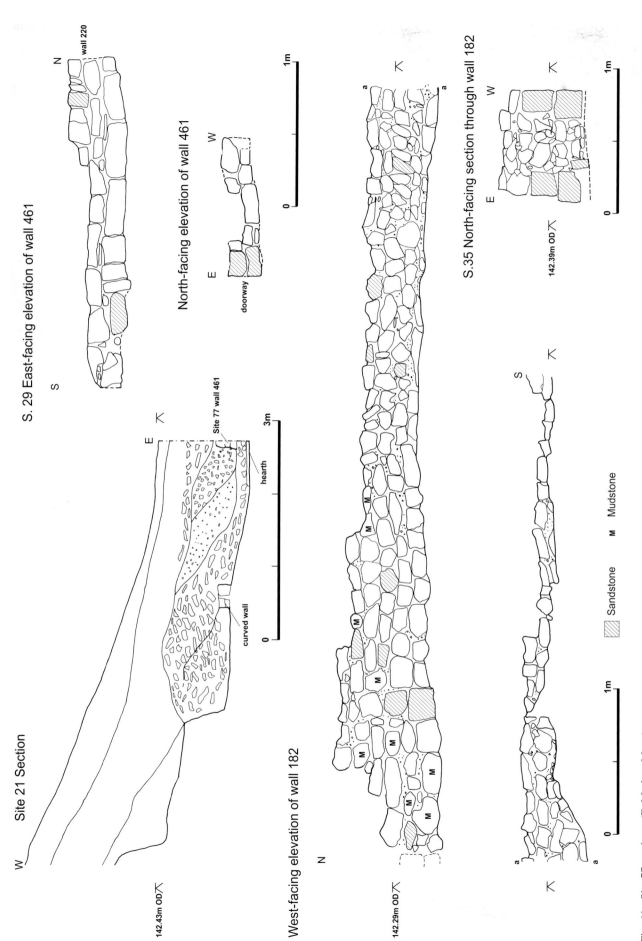

S. 29 East-facing elevation of wall 461

wall 220

N

S

North-facing elevation of wall 461

E

W

doorway

Site 21 Section

W

E

142.43m OD

3m

0

Site 77 wall 461

hearth

curved wall

West-facing elevation of wall 182

N

142.29m OD

0

1m

M

S. 35 North-facing section through wall 182

W

E

142.39m OD

0

1m

S

a

a

Sandstone

M Mudstone

Fig. 41. Site 77 sections. (E. Marlow-Mann)

Plate 16. Site 77: Period 3.1 features showing steps 79 and wall 182, looking west.

charcoal (no context number). On top of this surface a group of large dressed stones (598), burnt and possibly reused parts of a window, were set within a sandy deposit with fine pebble inclusions (624, not illustrated). This floor was surrounded on the west and south by a surface of fine and medium pebbles (no context number). No further structural remains survived eastwards of these features up to the edge of the conduit trench.

Wall 461 (Fig. 41, S.29) abutted the semicircular Structure 220 on its south-west side. This was a poorly constructed wall of roughly-worked chalk blocks with a pebble and sand make-up which survived to a maximum height of three courses. It turned eastwards on the same line as 146, although the corner was eroded prior to recording due to weathering between excavation seasons. Approximately 0.74m east of the supposed corner was the west side of an opening, 0.61m wide, and it is likely that this wall joined wall 146, making a small separate room measuring approximately 1.6m by 2m. The floor surface of this room consisted of a layer of coarse pebbles (no context number) which suggested a more hard-wearing use, possibly for an externally accessed store room. This surface continued outside the doorway into this room and extended in a south-west direction, although it was not recorded beyond this grid reference; this suggested a passageway. No evidence remained of any structures further south.

South-west of wall 461 a 10.5m stretch of north-north-west to south-south-east chalk-faced wall with a chalk rubble core (182, Fig. 41, S.35 and elevation) survived to a maximum height of five courses; it was 0.7m wide. There was no evidence of a construction cut and the wall was apparently built on the flat terrace cut from the hillside; sandstone roofing slabs were occasionally used as levelling for the base. Its northern end turned on to the alignment of the earlier west wall of the pre-fire vicarage, and northwards it seems to have incorporated the west wall of the vicarage and the west wall of the barn, creating an enclosure wall or revetment to hold back the hillside. This would also explain why the west wall of the Period 1 barn survived while the east wall was much more extensively robbed. A small fragment of walling (714) may indicate the remains of this wall in the area west of the structures of this phase, but the rest had evidently been robbed out: the sections (Fig. 41) of Site 21 showed no trace of wall 182 and it is clear that the wall had been removed at this point. Beyond the south end of Site 77, in its extension Site 99, wall 182 turned eastwards for approximately 1m to the edge of excavation, where it was cut by the conduit. It is clear that the wall continued eastwards across Site 26 as contexts 74 and 20 (*Wharram XI*, 45-9, fig. 39) for a further 20m.

West of this wall and in Site 100 was a flight of 'steps' (175-7=79, Site 100, Fig. 42; Plate 16) constructed

S.34 East-facing elevation of Site 100 Steps 79

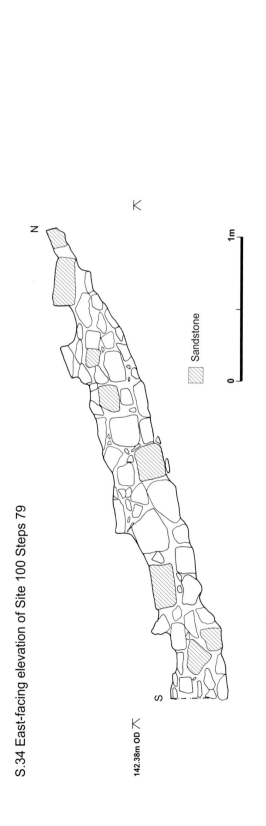

142.38m OD

Sandstone

0   1m

S.12 West-facing section along eastern baulk

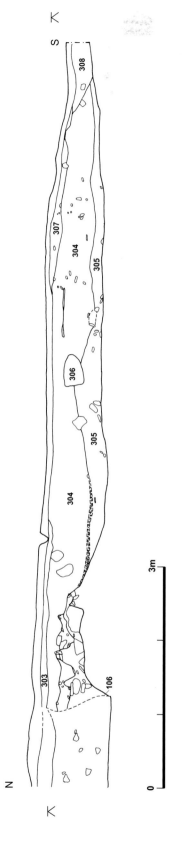

0   3m

Fig. 42. Site 77 sections. (E. Marlow-Mann)

mostly of chalk and sandstone blocks with the larger fragments forming the treads. They were only recorded for 3.25m running north-west to south-east, with a width of 1.65m, but they clearly gave access to a terraced trackway. (See *Wharram XI*, 59-60 for more detailed information on these remains). This area provided little dating or stratigraphic information. It would seem logical that the trackway ran along the outside of the enclosure wall, climbing the hillside, and has been assigned to this phase accordingly.

Period 3.2 (not illustrated)

A series of rubble dumps and wall collapse indicated the disuse of the Period 3.1 buildings. Deposits 347, 557 and 565 were located within the circular wall 220. They comprised high proportions of stone and cobble inclusions, with 347 made up of large sandstone blocks in pea-grit; these deposits may indicate the pushing in of the upper wall courses. The collapse of walls 348 and 146 was represented by rubble deposits 375/377 which included large quantities of cobble and pebble inclusions. Deposit 494 (not illustrated), west of wall 220, indicated the backfill of a robbing trench (no context number) which had removed part of the west wall of the Period 1 building. The remaining dumps suggested general demolition layers and probable deposits used for levelling the terrace.

Period 4 (17th century) (Fig. 43, Plate 17)

The main structural features of Period 4 lay east of wall 182, which probably continued in use, and to the east of the Period 3.1 structures and the conduit (106, Fig 77.5) Finds included the earliest distinctively post-medieval pottery. The surviving evidence suggested movement of the vicarage to the east in this period, but it may just reflect the impact of later terracing.

At the north-east corner of the site lay a mixture of rough walling deposits. Overlying an elongated rubble spread of coarse cobbles and pebbles (575, not illustrated), which may have been a foundation deposit or make-up layer, was feature 446. This consisted of irregular roughly hewn large chalk blocks with three squared blocks of sandstone and a large block of rough-hewn quartz; it may have represented the lower courses of wall 358 (see below). The feature ran northwards for a surviving length of 4.6m and entered the barrow run and eastern edge of excavation. Its associations in Site 54 are discussed in Chapter 10, Period 5. Among the large rubble was a gravelly layer with frequent chalk cobbles and rubble (499, not illustrated). The rubble included two keystones and it is possible that this deposit represented a collapsed archway. It is also possible that the keystones came from the church as reused building material; it should be noted that sandstone blocks from the church were also recovered from Site 54. Extending from the

Plate 17. Site 77: Period 4 features, looking north.

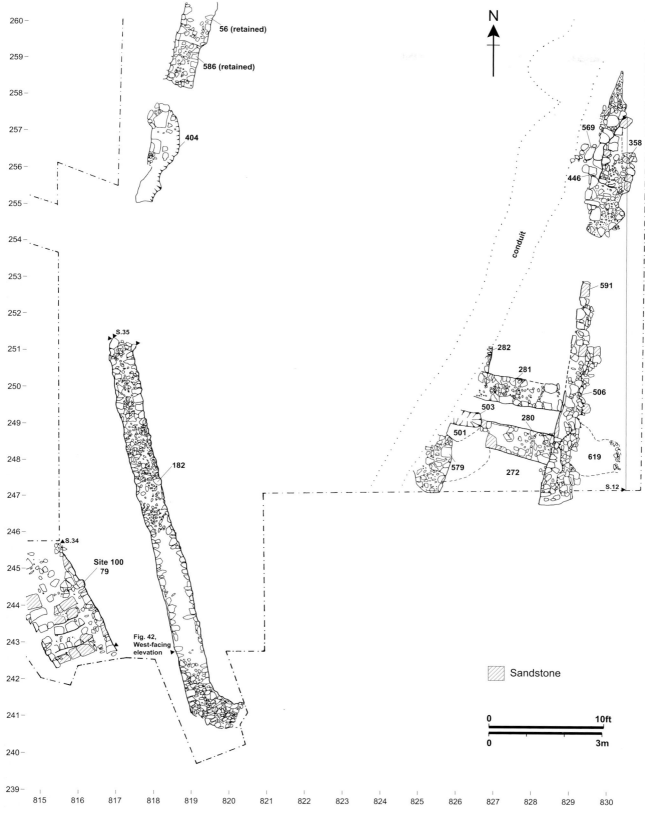

Fig. 43. Site 77: Period 4 plan. (E. Marlow-Mann)

81

west face of 446 was a fragment of chalk and sandstone block walling with chalk rubble (569); it was visible for only 0.5m to the east of the conduit trench and was not revealed further west.

Overlying deposit 446 to the north was a short length of chalk block walling incorporating some pieces of dressed sandstone (358). It ran north-east to south-west but its full extents were not clear from the records. An underlying cut (471, not illustrated) may represent its construction trench.

Located south of these features, after a gap of 1.3m and overlying a small spread of a rubble and cobble deposit (688, not illustrated) was a line of large chalk rubble infill of mid-orange-brown with frequent chalk pebbles (591 and 506). It ran roughly north to south and seems to have been the remains of a robbed-out wall. The rubble had a width of 0.45-0.85m, possibly representing a wall of width 0.75-0.8m, and it survived for a length of 6.2m.

Abutting the western edge of this wall-line at right-angles was a similar stretch of walling (281), surviving to a height of two courses and for a distance of 2.5m. It was 0.7m wide and was cut by the conduit to the west. Its construction consisted of an exterior face of roughly squared chalk and sandstone blocks with an internal rubble core. A small fragment of apparently added chalk walling (282) ran northwards from wall 281. It was recorded for a length of 0.7m where it was cut by the conduit; only the east face survived. It seems possible that walls 281 and 569 were contemporary, forming a structure 7.3m long and approximately 2.6m wide, taking wall 282 as its returning wall and assuming wall 282 was a similar thickness to 281.

To the south of wall 281, and roughly parallel to it, was a similar stretch of walling (280). Its construction was slightly different to 281, 280 comprising chalk blocks with occasional sandstone, with a thickness of 0.8m. It survived to a height of at least one course, and for a length of 2.1m where it was truncated to the west by a possible robber trench (503). This was, in turn, cut by the Period 5.2 conduit and no remains extended on the west side. Approximately at right angles to this wall line lay a probable southwards return wall for this structure. The wall (579) was built with large chalk blocks on the eastern face with a smaller chalk infill. The western side was damaged by the conduit but large chalk blocks were still apparent. A secondary robber trench (501) marked the north end of this wall where it would have met wall 280. Overlying several rubble deposits (458, 475 and 477, not illustrated) was a layer of packed silty clay with moderate inclusions of small sub-angular chalk and chalk pebbles (272). This probably represented the floor of this structure, which appeared to be about 2.5m wide. Although both 280 and 281 appeared to have been added to wall 591 it was not clear whether one predated the other or whether they were added at the same time.

To the east of wall 591, deposit 619 comprised a dump of chalk rubble that ran approximately east to west; this may indicate robbing of the wall.

Period 5.1 (17th century to late 18th century) (Fig. 44)

The buildings of Period 4 were destroyed, resulting once again in numerous demolition and rubble deposits. The ground level was built up in this way to a widespread surface layer, consisting of a yellow-brown fine silty loam with 50% chalk pebbles (144=168=185, Fig. 45, S.9). At the north end of the site, overlying this surface, a number of hillwash deposits (50, 200, 203 and 236, shown in section only, Fig. 45, S.9) accumulated over the Period 1 barn wall (56), to a depth of 0.8m, indicating the continued need for hillside revetments, seen now further east on Site 54. A new wall (117=77) was constructed to the south, overlying surface 144; it comprised irregular large angular chalk blocks and occasional sandstone blocks with a chalk core (153). It ran in a south-east to north-west direction and, due to much erosion where it lay beneath the 19th-century and later roadway, it survived only as two separate fragments spanning a distance of 8.5m. The western fragment (77) had a width of 0.45m but appeared to be missing its southern facing stones; the eastern fragment (117) had a width of 0.7m. This wall also included two reused pad-stones (48 and 149). A dark yellow-brown silty deposit with few chalk pebbles (162) was overlain by a similar deposit comprising 90% chalk pebbles and occasional sandstone (163). In plan this deposit resembled a return of wall 117, although no mention of this was made in the excavation records; the similarity was increased by the use of occasional sandstone which was also used in the construction of wall 117. To the south of wall 117 a surface deposit extended to the limits of excavation; this comprised a yellow-brown silty loam with 80% chalk rubble (165=181). The presence of wheel-ruts from the pre-1984 trackway were noted but not drawn. North of the wall 77 fragment was a deposit of cobbles, pebbles and silt (364) which was interpreted as a probable yard surface.

A small fragment of chalk block wall (389) which ran in a north to south direction was recorded on the western edge of the conduit. Very little survived but it may have been a turning point in a wall; this fragment was not recorded beyond the single grid square. A fragment of walling (231, Fig. 46) on a similar alignment was seen in section and on photographs to have survived to a height of five courses. It is possible that this represented a continuation of wall 389. Wall 231 also extended into Site 26 (walls 73 and 811, *Wharram XI*, fig. 44, Period 6.6) where they formed the east wall of a building with an entrance at its south-east corner.

A small deposit of cobble and pebbles, comprising chalk and sandstone in a silty matrix (401), outside the south-east corner of the excavation possibly represented the debris of a fragment of wall which ran approximately east to west; however, no edges to this feature were apparent and it may instead indicate demolition debris, possibly from Period 4 wall 591. Further north, a roughly-built right-angular deposit of large chalk cobbles and one large faced-sandstone block (478) was a more convincing fragment from a walled structure. It is

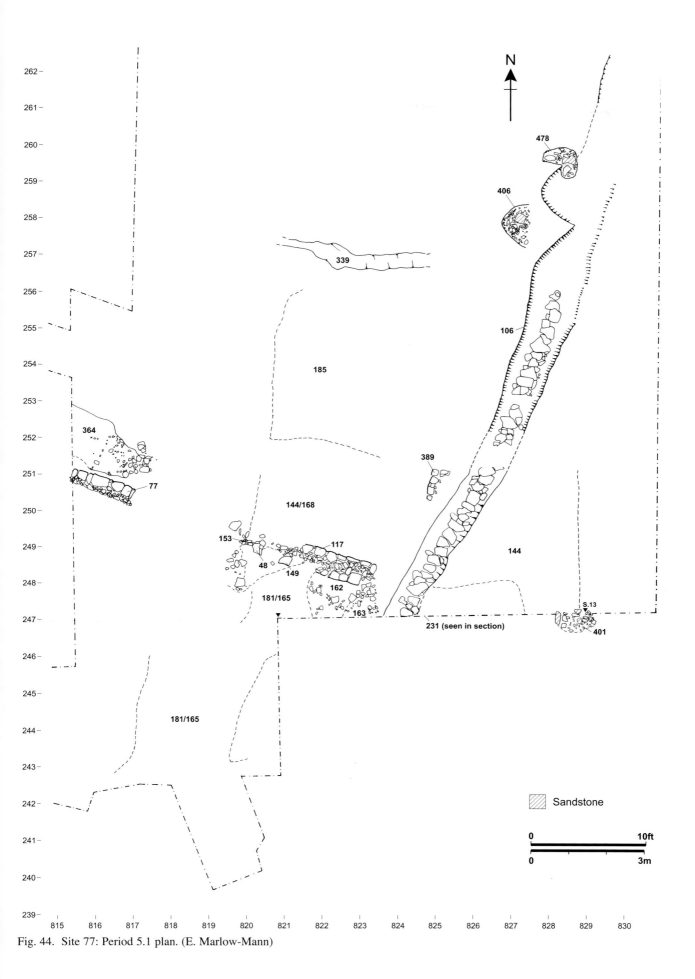

Fig. 44. Site 77: Period 5.1 plan. (E. Marlow-Mann)

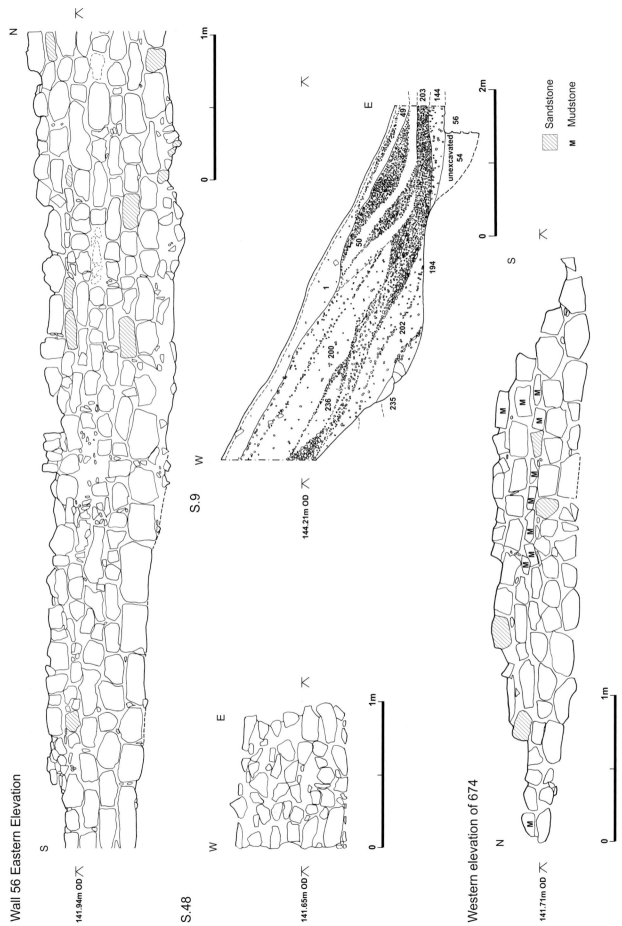

Wall 56 Eastern Elevation

S 141.94m OD

N

S.48

141.65m OD

W

E

1m

S.9

W

144.21m OD

E

1

50

203

49

144

56

unexcavated

54

200

236

202

194

235

2m

Western elevation of 674

141.71m OD

N

1m

Sandstone

M Mudstone

Fig. 45. Site 77 sections. (E. Marlow-Mann)

84

S.13 North-facing section along eastern end of southern baulk

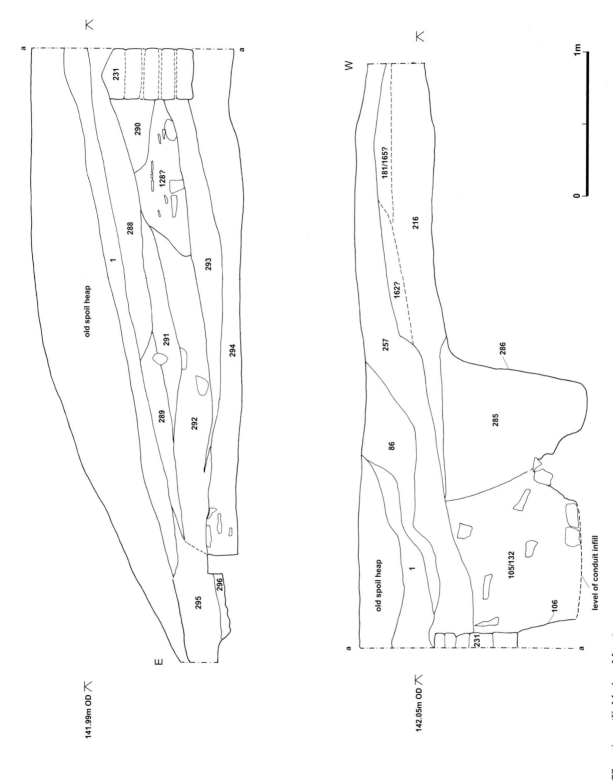

85

Fig. 46. Site 77 sections. (E. Marlow–Mann)

possible that a circular rubble dump of mostly chalk and some sandstone (406), located south-west of 478, was related to this structure. Although the phasing of 406 could not be tied down completely (it came after Period 2 and before Period 6), it seems likely to be related to structure 478 to which it lay in such close proximity. Any buildings of this phase have evidently been extensively robbed, possibly in conjunction with the construction of later buildings on Site 54.

Period 5.2 (Fig. 44)
Many of the structures and layers described above were cut by a trench dug for a water conduit (106, Fig. 46, S.13) which has, on the basis of pottery in its backfill layers, a *terminus post quem* of the early to mid-18th century (Chapter 13). The conduit comprised a vertical-sided trench, shelving at the base through natural chalk. The internal water channel (457, Fig. 44) was lined and capped with sandstone blocks (Fig. 65, S.64, Site 26). It was noted that the excavated material was backfilled immediately after the channel was built. As in Site 26, the water channel itself was made up of large and medium slabs of chalk and sandstone forming a stone-lined channel against the trench edge, and it was capped with large slabs of chalk and sandstone.

Period 6 (19th century to 20th century) (not illustrated)
Period 6 comprised a mixture of modern deposits, including topsoil and excavation debris, combined with natural hillwash and levelling material for the 19th-century roadway (see Chapter 3, Figs 8 and 9).

10 Site 54
by C. Harding

Introduction

The excavation aimed to continue the examination of the occupation sequence on the terrace around the church (Fig. 2). Structural remains had been identified to the west, beneath the trackway to the church, and it was planned to move this trackway further east so that excavation and possible display of the later vicarage buildings could commence. Before a new trackway could be constructed archaeological examination of this area was necessary.

The sequence and extent of excavated areas
(Fig. 47)

In 1979 an area 18m by 28m was opened: the southern boundary lay to the north of Site 26 and the northern boundary just outside the fence of the cottage garden.

The cobbled road (Period 7.8) was cleared and left *in situ* for use as the new trackway from the cottages to the churchyard. Conditions of excavation on the eastern side of the road were such that this area was not investigated further; excavation was thus limited to the area west of the road.

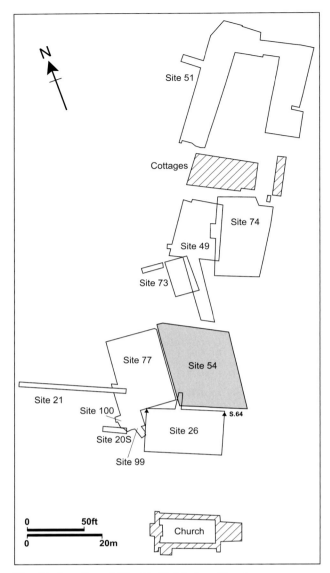

Fig. 47. Location of Site 54. (E. Marlow-Mann)

In 1984 the excavation area was further reduced. The isolated deposits in the triangular area north of the conduit (Period 7.6) were left as they would more readily be interpreted with deposits beyond the fence-line. Excavation then continued only in two areas because of time constraints: along the western and southern areas of the site (to facilitate links with the adjoining areas, Sites 77 and 26) leaving the north and east areas unexcavated between Periods 1 and 4.3. The surviving walls of Structure J (Period 6) were not removed as the feature was to be conserved for display.

The site was opened up by machine-stripping the topsoil, which clearly caused some damage and finds contamination at the north end of the site, there being no notion that an abandoned post-medieval building lay beneath; all further excavation was by hand.

Excavations revealed a continuous cycle of terracing which disturbed and truncated many features and deposits, resulting in the loss of a great deal of stratigraphic information. Further information and

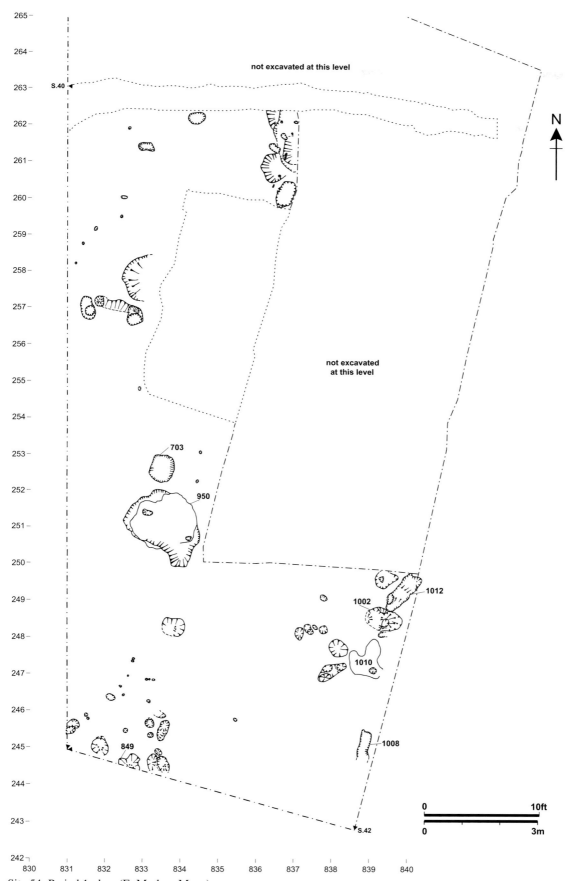

N

not excavated at this level

not excavated
at this level

S.40

703

950

1012

1002

1010

1008

849

S.42

0   10ft

0   3m

Fig. 48. Site 54: Period 1 plan. (E. Marlow-Mann)

stratigraphic relationships were lost during the winters between the excavation seasons: frosts and rain were particularly damaging to the deeper sections and the large post-medieval/modern features which intruded into the site.

Seasonal excavation continued until the end of July 1986; the site was laid out for presentation to the public in July 1989. Site 54 was previously reported in *Interim Reports 1979, 9-10; 1980, 14-15; 1981, 9; 1982, 20-22; 1983, 19-21; 1984, 17-19; 1985, 15-16; 1986, 14-15.*

Period 1 (Fig. 48)
The earliest activity here featured mainly clusters of post and stake-holes; several of these were clearly truncated, and some (1002 and 1012) originally contained two posts, although only one post-pipe was clearly discernible. Cut 703 probably represents a truncated or robbed post-pit or post-pad; if truncated its similarity to 602 (Period 4.1; Fig. 51) should be noted. Cut 950, although shallow, may have resulted from quarrying for chalk.

No coherent patterns indicative of structures could be identified: the intensity of later intrusive activity and of terracing across the site means that the survival of features at this level is unlikely to be representative of what was once there.

Period 2.1: Structure A (Fig. 49)
Sealing most of the Period 1 features were deposits (870, etc.) up to 0.2m thick. Those to the west on the more level terrace (636 and 934; Fig. 51 and Fig. 50) were more compacted and may have functioned as surfaces; to the east, silty deposit with angular chalk 965 (Fig. 50) and the eastern part of 725 did not appear worn and may represent rain-washed silts from up the slope.

Cutting through these surfaces and into Period 1 features were a number of assorted pits and post-holes. Cultural material was almost entirely absent; the sherds from the fill (947) of post-hole 948 dated possibly from the 12th or 13th centuries, while those from post-hole 798 may be intrusive. Given the considerable quantity of Romano-British material from the lowest levels of Site 26 to the south the contrast is notable and these features may thus relate to the similarly 'artefact-free' Period 2 post-Roman levels on Site 26.

A group of distinctive substantial features (780, 785, 816, 817, 825, 874, 876, 889, 918, and 1120), had several characteristics of note: depth mostly in excess of 0.5m, post-pipes, some of which were set at an angle with chalk packing and some of which had evidently decayed *in situ*. The slag, animal bone and knife blade (not extant) from 916 (not illustrated) suggest the proximity of domestic/agricultural activity; slag was also recorded in the fill of post-hole 777.

Together these formed roughly a 1.5m square timber structure, Structure A, with post-hole 788 and cuts 775, 777, 784 and 822 as possible repairs or additional bracing. The depth and spacing of all these cuts suggests a structure of some substance and height. A row of post-holes (798, 817 and 852; 908, Fig. 50, S.42) may belong with Period 1) and post-holes (927, 977, 970 and 958) to the east may also have been linked.

To the north-west of Structure A, a distinctive linear feature (954), function unknown, containing four separate post-holes, was cut into natural chalk and sealed by Period 2.2 rather than Period 2.1 surfaces. The general alignment of the cut follows that of the edge of the terrace and also the line of Structure A, which had been dismantled. For a very similar and possibly contemporary feature see Period 2.3 (Structure C).

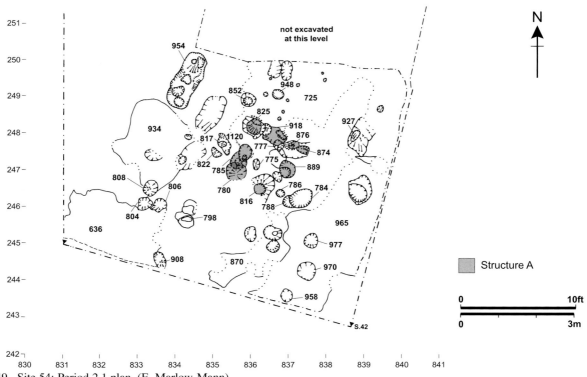

Fig. 49. Site 54: Period 2.1 plan. (E. Marlow-Mann)

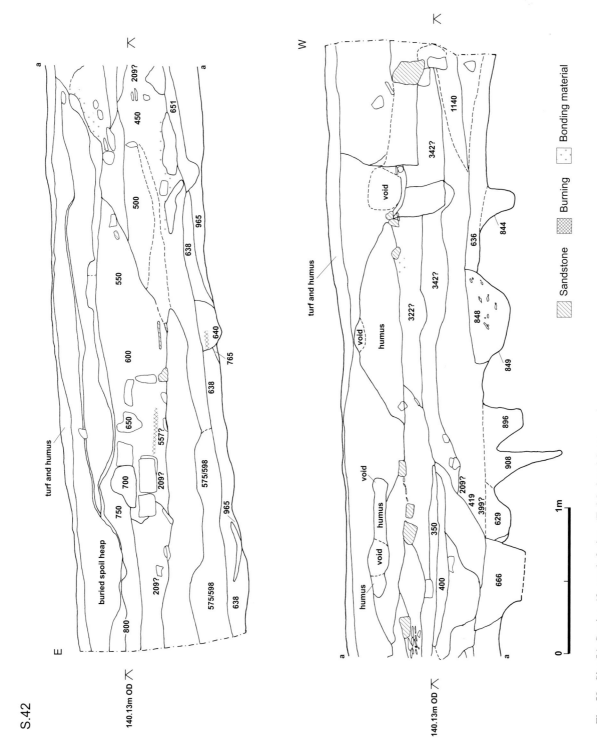

Fig. 50. Site 54: Section 42, north facing. (E. Marlow-Mann)

89

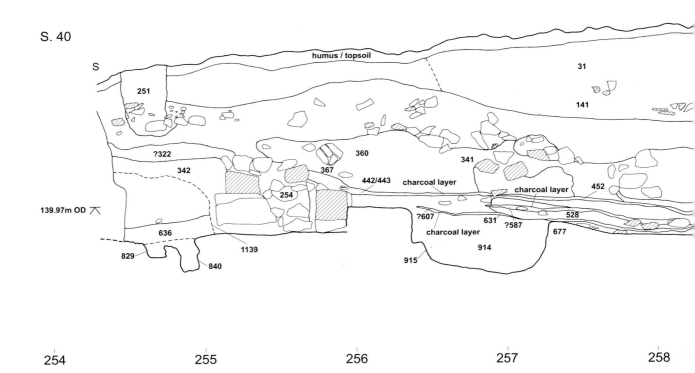

245 246 247 248 2

S. 40

S

251

humus / topsoil

31

141

?322

342

360

367

254

442/443

charcoal layer

341

charcoal layer

452

139.97m OD

636

1139

?607

charcoal layer

631 ?587

528

677

829

840

915

914

254 255 256 257 258

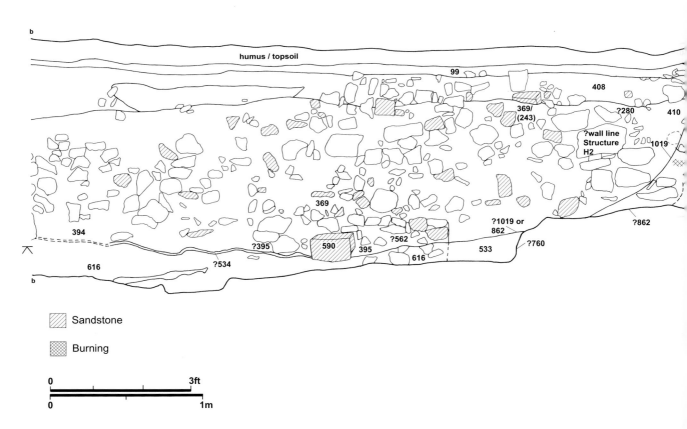

b

humus / topsoil

99

408

369/
(243)

?280

410

?wall line
Structure
H2

1019

394

369

?1019 or
862

?862

?395

590

395

?562

?760

?534

616

533

?760

616

Sandstone

Burning

0   3ft

0   1m

Fig. 51. Site 54: Section 40. (E. Marlow-Mann)

90

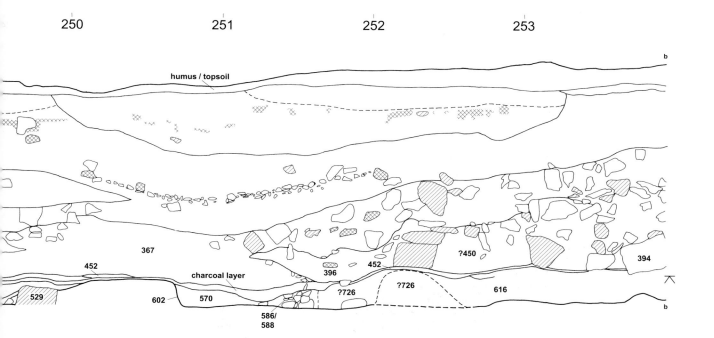

250 251 252 253

b

humus / topsoil

367

452

529

charcoal layer

602 570

586/
588

396 452 ?726 ?726

?450 616

394

b

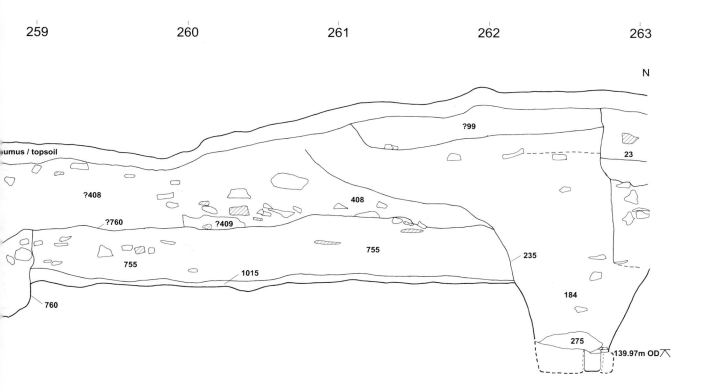

259 260 261 262 263

N

?99

23

humus / topsoil

?408

?760

?409

408

755

235

755

1015

760

184

275

139.97m OD

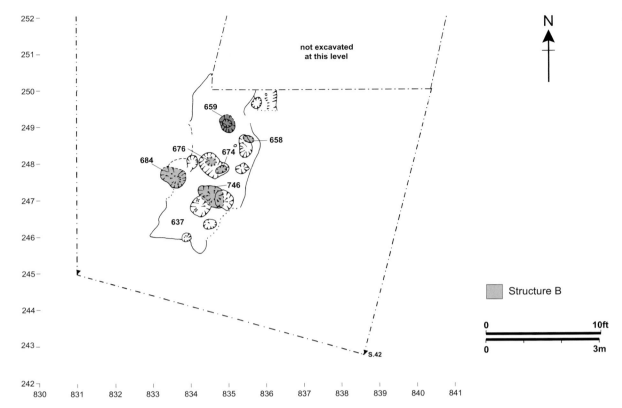

Fig. 52. Site 54: Period 2.2 plan. (E. Marlow-Mann)

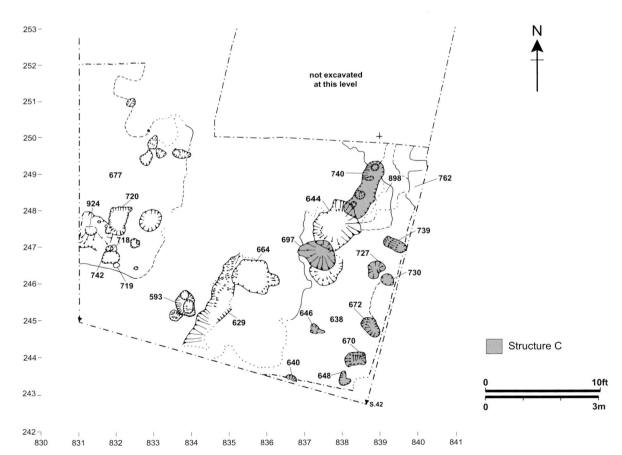

Fig. 53. Site 54: Period 2.3-2.4 plan. (E. Marlow-Mann)

Period 2.2: Structure B (Fig. 52)

Sealing several of the features west of Structure A was a deposit of silty clay (637), forming a level, but not compacted, surface. Some of the features cutting 637 shared distinctive characteristics of shape and arrangement. It is also of note that 659, 684 and 746 all appeared to have been deliberately dismantled and sealed off with sandstone blocks. These post-holes, along with 658, 674 and 676 represent a rectangular structure, Structure B, perhaps an extension or rebuilding of Structure A; overall dimensions would have been 1.2 x 1.8m.

The features to the west and south of this group (see also below, Period 2.4) may have been contemporary but, with the exception of 924 and 742/718-9 (Period 2.4), included no particularly similar features. Some may have been contemporary with Period 2.1 or with truncated gully 629 (Fig. 50; Period 2.3).

Period 2.3: Structure C (Fig. 53)

To the east of Structure A, a compact clay deposit (638; Fig. 50) represented a fairly evenly worn external surface with high proportions of animal bone concentrated in dump 762, indicating activity on the surface of 638.

Features cutting into this surface included linear cut 740 and its associated posts; 740 was distinctive and directly comparable in size and arrangement to 954 (Period 2.1). It is also of possible significance that post-hole 697 and scoops 640 and 646 were all in the same line; scoops 640, 646 (and 648) possibly mark depressions left by earth-fast posts, indicating a less substantial structure. From its size and plan, an industrial rather than structural or rubbish function might be suggested for squared cut 664, but there was no indication from its clean fill. To the east was a row of diverse post-holes (739, 727, 730, 672 and 670), with scoop 648 on a roughly parallel alignment to feature 740.

These post-holes appeared to have formed some sort of linear feature, Structure C. Although 638 sealed the north-east corner of Structure A (Period 2.1) it is possible that it continued in use, modified by Structure C, with post-hole 697 for example replacing 889.

Period 2.4 (Fig. 53)

Several of the disparate features cut into compact clay 677 (Fig. 51) appeared truncated (e.g. 924 and 915 (Fig. 51)) and it is possible that the surface of the deposit had been levelled at some stage. In plan, the features of this period do not appear connected and they had no apparent relationship to Structures A or B. Some may actually be contemporary with later groups, e.g. Periods 3 or 4.

Discussion

The rationale of the phasing is purely sequential in terms of deposits sealing or cut by various features. While subsequent deposits define some elements of the phasing sequence, other elements, only sealed by later deposits may have been contemporary. Structures A and B may well be contemporary and part of a single structure/function with Structure C a possible addition to A and in contemporary use with A and B.

The size and square shape of Structure A may ultimately prove to be diagnostic; the depth of its principal structural elements, 0.5-0.8m+, suggesting that either substantial height or weight were associated with its function.

The surfaces of Period 2.1 produced few finds as evidence of occupation/activity in the vicinity, in contrast to the features cut through 638 (Period 2.3) which contained a notably higher proportion of animal bone. The relative absence of ceramics makes any dating difficult to establish. The density of later intrusions, terracing and erosion makes it possible that the few medieval sherds are just as likely to be intrusive as the few Romano-British sherds are likely to be residual. The fill (643) of pit 644 in Period 2.3 however, contained a significant amount of medieval pottery, mainly of the 12th and 13th centuries.

Period 3.1: Structure D (medieval) (Fig. 54)

A series of levelling deposits accumulated over the Period 2 structures; as in other parts of the excavation area, the naturally sloping chalk had necessitated constant levelling-up (e.g. 650, Fig. 50; 649 and 597). An extensive area of part-compacted clayey loam (598, Fig. 50) with occasional large chalk and sandstone, increased in depth from 50mm to 300mm and sloped gently down to the east. The variable depth was possibly the result of accumulation against a barrier or obstruction beyond the eastern limit of excavation (*Wharram XI*, Site 26). Within 598 to the north was a lens of intense burning (574), up to 80mm deep, and clearly *in situ*; this suggests that 598 accumulated over a considerable period of time.

Protruding from the eastern edge of the excavation was a length of large chalk-faced walling (599). Two courses survived, the lower 1.2m wide, forming an offset both sides of the upper course (0.9m wide). This stub of wall, Structure D, extended 0.8m from the east section and was set directly on surface 598 with no construction trench. There was no evidence of the structure's original extent or function and, other than 598, no internal or external surfaces in association were identified. It was possibly truncated by terracing (see below), which may also account for the surviving irregular extent of 598.

Period 3.2 (medieval) (not illustrated)

Sealing wall footing 599 (Period 3.1) were deposits marking its disuse and the further clearance and levelling of the area. The rubble in deposits 575 (Fig. 50) and 560 was predominantly chalk possibly the destruction material of Structure D. Any western continuation of these features or deposits had been truncated or removed as part of the continual cycle of terracing and levelling.

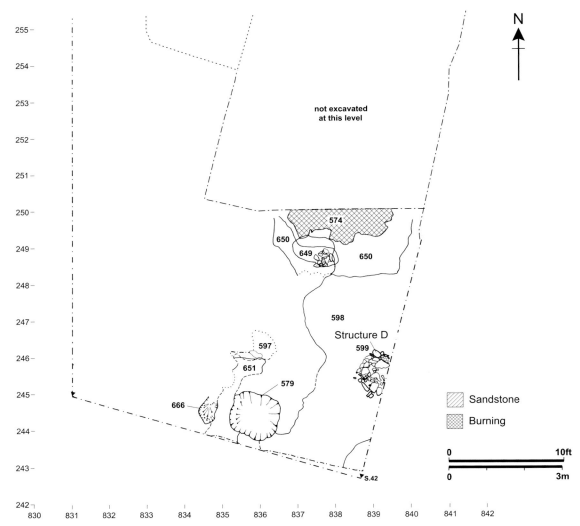

Fig. 54. Site 54: Period 3.1 plan (E. Marlow-Mann)

Period 3.3: Structure E (late medieval to 16th century) (Fig. 55)

Compacted deposits of silty clay with small chalk (480 and 557/558; Fig. 50) accumulated, forming an extensive area of level, but not heavily used, surfacing. The position of burnt timbers (420) at the edge of 557/480 is possibly significant. Cut into the western side of these deposits was a complex of shallow scoops, intercutting features (515; 542, 523 and 526, not illustrated), and dismantled posts (543 and 544, not illustrated) sealed by thick dumps of clay (548, not illustrated). The blocking of rectangular flat-bottomed post-holes 551 and 554 (not illustrated) by carefully laid large chalk blocks (545) in two courses was clearly deliberate consolidation. None of the fills contained any finds diagnostic of the function of these features.

These scoops were sealed by a further deposit to the west (416, not illustrated), up to 80mm deep and containing frequent animal bone. Cutting through it was cut 545/465 with cuts 469 to the north and 473 to the south, reusing stone feature 545 (see above) as a central dividing ridge. Set over the eastern half of 545, where it was only one course high, was a deposit of grey ash and charcoal (472) filling a squared depression with chalk blocks on the western and southern edges; in the centre

were lines of white ash in an F shape. Accumulated around 472, filling cut 465 and sealing 473 and 469 was mixed friable silt, with patches of charcoal (466, not illustrated), up to 60mm deep. This may also have been burnt *in situ*, probably as a result of the burning or firing of 472. Close by was burnt timber, 490. To the west and south were post-holes (460 and 457), scoop (440), and a shallow scoop (477) with seven stake-holes (483) cut through the base. The fill of 483 (478) contained a sherd of residual pottery of York Type A ware.

A dump of chalk rubble (479) provided a level construction base for wall footing 401 (Structure E). Large chalk and reused dressed sandstone, 0.6m wide by up to 0.2m high but not very well laid, survived for one course; the north side with sandstone was better-faced and set in/on a bed of clay. Any westward continuation of 401 (like Period 3.1 Structure D, wall 599) appears to have been truncated, although disturbed rubble extending a further 0.7m to the west may represent its original extent or the destruction of its upper courses. Its alignment was similar to 599 (Structure D) and it too may have been a footing for a timber superstructure or a boundary wall rather than part of a building: functional divisions within an external yard area.

94

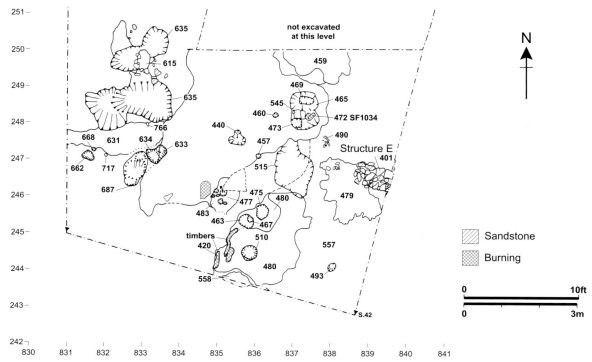

Fig. 55. Site 54: Period 3.3 plan. (E. Marlow-Mann)

The disposition of post-holes (493, 510, 463 and 475) similar in profile and size, was not obviously related to contemporary features. The clay fill of post-pipe 467 could have accumulated post-decay but the fills of 463 and 475 suggest that their posts were removed, 475 being consolidated with a large chalk block.

Small areas of probably truncated external surfacing (631, Fig. 51; 885, not illustrated) to the west were cut by shallow scoops, post-holes and stake-holes (615, 633-5, 662, 668, 687, 717 and 766), not apparently in any coherent pattern.

Discussion

This sequence of dumps, surfaces and structures represents typical external agricultural/domestic yard activity. The truncation of deposits and structures at the top (west) of the terrace slope helped maintain a level 'terrace' surface and reduced any 'build-up' against the hillside. The extent of the terracing is marked by the westward extents of the surfaces and wall footings of Periods 3.1-3. It should also be noted that similar sequences were identified on Site 26 to the south (Periods 4 and 5).

Wall footings 599 (Period 3.1) and 401 (Period 3.3) (Structures D and E) were approximately parallel, with the later footing displaced to the north. The progressive displacement of such structures northwards was also a feature of the sequences on Site 26 (*Wharram XI*). The external surfaces on the western side may have related to the contemporary vicarage which lay to the west (Site 77). For other interpretative possibilities see the overall discussion (pp 117-118; also Chapter 28). The date range of finds from these features is broadly medieval; Structure D contained a large amount of pottery ranging from the 12th to the 15th/16th centuries.

The carefully constructed two-phase feature 545/465 (Fig. 55) is difficult to identify as the first phase had no evidence of any associated burning. The burning associated with 472 was very intense, but possibly represents a single activity, not accumulated over a long period of time and there was no evidence of burning on the chalk blocks of 545 (Period 3.3). While no precise function for this feature can be identified, some sort of semi-industrial hearth, perhaps for repairs to agricultural tools or the production of nails, is presumed.

Period 3.4 (medieval to late 16th century) (not illustrated) In the north-west of the site, isolated by later terracing activity but broadly contemporary with these external features, was a small area of chalk cobbled surface (1015 Fig. 51) sealed by a dump of redeposited demolition debris that contained pottery of the 13th to 15th or 16th centuries (755, Fig. 51). This probably relates directly to structures on Site 77 to the west.

Period 4.1: Structure F (medieval to late 16th century) (Fig. 56)
A series of fragmentary surfaces (781, 661, 758, 603 and 642, illustrated; 580, 607, and 610, not illustrated), possible rubble foundations and pad-stones indicate the site of Structure F. It was defined by post-holes 584 and 585, rubble wall footings (529/626, Fig. 51) and possibly 530, in conjunction with cut 602 (shown only in section, Fig. 51) and surface 528 (Fig. 51). Cobbled surface 528 lay between 530 and 529, which were 1.70m apart. The surviving eastward extents of 530, 528, 529 and 608, as well as the extents of floors 603, 758 (Fig. 56), 607 and 610 (not illustrated), are all much the same, possibly truncated by later terracing. Wall footing 626 was

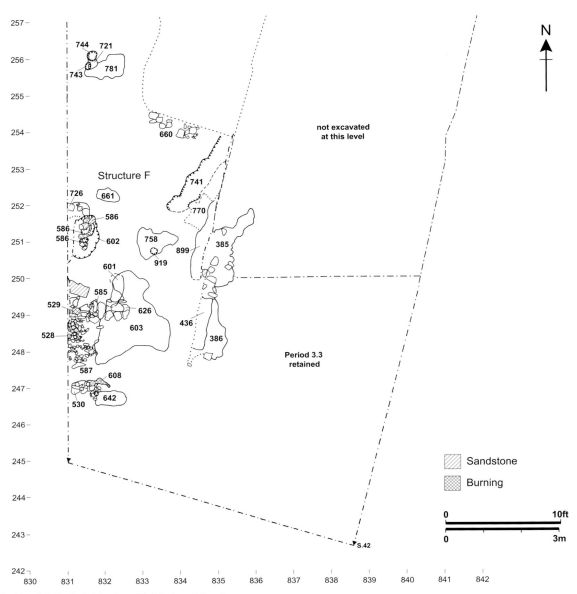

Fig. 56. Site 54: Period 4.1 plan. (E. Marlow-Mann)

identified as an extension of 529 and this appears truncated on the same line as 642. Post-holes 743 and 744 (replaced by pad-stone 721) possibly represented the northern extent of this structure.

A line of rubble (possibly a footing), 660, on an approximately north-west/south-east alignment, together with cut 741 approximately at right angles may represent part of the same or another structure. They were not precisely aligned to the other possible structural elements, but the rubble may have been displaced. Deposits 781, 770 and 899 were possibly parts of surfaces; any surfaces in use with these possible structural elements having been mostly removed by subsequent terracing and construction.

The regular edges and level surface of 436 suggest that it might have abutted a removed wall footing from Structure F, or even served as bedding for a wall footing itself. It provided a make-up for external surfaces 385 and 386, possibly constructed from worn cobbles, blocks of

worked sandstone, chalk limestone and flint. It is not clear whether these deposits, similar to 401 (and 479) (Period 3.3), originally extended further east or whether they merely formed a 'path' across the Period 3 surfaces. Equally, they may relate to unexcavated structures to the north or to later sequences of cobbled surfaces to the east (Period 5). At the level of 385 and 386 the decision was made to cease excavation in this area (see above): 385 is thus described as far as seen within this area while 386 was located to its full extent. The surfacing contained a sherd of 15th to 16th-century pottery.

Period 4.2 (medieval to late 16th century) (Fig. 57)

A terracing cut, 760 (Fig. 51), was identified extending from the western limit of excavation over a length of at least 4m (cut away to the north). Its depth and steepness varied and effectively terraced this area almost down to the natural chalk; the resulting surface provided a level platform for Structure G (see below). Structures F and G

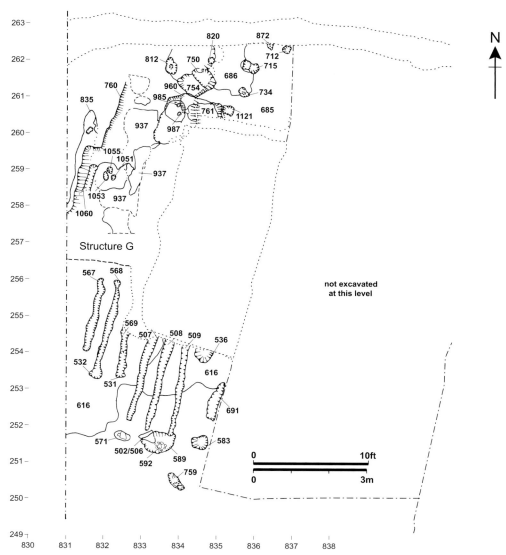

Fig. 57. Site 54: Period 4.2-4.3 plan. (E. Marlow-Mann)

were at the same absolute level making it impossible to prove with which structure the terracing cut was associated. Therefore, it is also possible that 760 was cut to provide a level platform for Structure F (Period 4.1); this would suggest that Structure F may have originally extended further north, but was partly levelled for the construction of Structure G. It is also possible that Structures F and G were ultimately part of the same building, on a similar alignment and footprint as the later Structure H (Period 5.2).

Other earlier terracing activity can be suggested from the persistent partial survival of deposits in some areas (see above, Periods 3 and 4.1) and accounts for the fact that in this area deposits of 15th to 16th-century date lie directly above natural chalk.

Period 4.3: Structure G (medieval to late 16th century) (Fig. 57; Plate 18)

Spreads of yellowish-brown clay (616, Fig. 51; 600, shown only in section, Fig. 50; 533 and 572, not illustrated) formed a fairly level surface over the northern

end of Structure F. Cutting this was a series of approximately parallel slots (507-509 and 567-569). Slots 567, 568 and possibly 569 were either positioned further to the north, or were much shorter than the others. Slots 568 and 569 seem originally to have ended in line with 567, but were later lengthened (531 and 532). The homogeneous burnt fills of these slots included moderate to frequent charcoal and there were also burnt patches on the surface of 616.

Together the slots formed supports for a suspended timber floor marking Structure G. It is probable that features to the east of 509 (536, 691, 583, and 759) were also directly associated. Slot 567 was only 0.5m from the western edge of the site and it is possible that similar features may have lain further west. At the south end of 507 was a rectangular deposit of sandstone blocks (571), possibly representing a post-pad. Similarly a deposit of sandstone rubble (592) against the southern edge of cut 589 was adjacent to the south end of 509. Opposite the south end of 508 were burnt clay (502) and a burnt post (506). Post-hole 583 may mark a further post in this

Plate 18. Site 54: slots in Structure G, looking west.

series. There were no artefacts or other evidence to suggest a function for this structure, but the slots may be compared with those from the Site 51 West Range (Fig. 17, Chapter 5).

Directly north of the slots was a series of fragmentary surfaces (835 and 937; 963 and 988 not illustrated) and post-holes (1051, 1053, 1055; 751 and 881 not illustrated) as well as a hearth pit (960) and parts of two slots (1060; 1043, not illustrated). The size and alignment of these slots were similar to those to the south, but their fills were not burnt. Hearth 960 appeared to have been subject to intense burning but not long-term use. The large rubble in the fill (761) was concentrated along the edge suggesting that it may have originally formed a surround to the hearth. Stake-holes 985, 987 and slot 1043 may have been associated structural elements. Although these features formed no overall coherent plan, they were broadly contemporary with Structures F and G and may relate directly to Structure G. Cobbled surfaces 685-6 (illustrated) and 1048 (not illustrated) were cut by a series of post-holes (812, 820, 872, 712, 715, 734 and 1121; 750/754, Fig. 50).

Finds from Period 4 include, for the first time in the sequence, post-medieval pottery. The late medieval Hambleton and Humber Wares in the Period 4.2 terrace cut (760) were accompanied by a sherd of Ryedale Ware dating to between the late 16th and early 18th centuries.

Period 5.1 (17th century) (Fig. 58)
A terracing cut (862, Fig. 51) extended from the western limit of excavation and mirrored cut 760 (Period 4.2). It is presumed to have served a similar function, levelling an external area where deposits had accumulated against the exterior of structures, in preparation for the construction of a new building.

Period 5.2: Structure H1 (17th century) (Fig. 58)
In the south-east corner of the site was a series of external surfaces, some of which may already have been in use

with Structures F and G. The clayey silts (399 and 209, shown only in section, Fig. 50, Fig. 51,) were compacted and trampled, and cut by a few post-holes (402, 405 and 407, not illustrated). They formed a fairly level surface with a combined depth up to 250mm; their composition of rain-washed silts suggested that they probably accumulated over a period of time. The extensive area of these surfaces marks a clear restructuring of the area after the Period 3 structures. Dump 271 appears to have been laid to level out hollows in the surface of Period 5.1 before resurfacing with 209.

In contrast, to the north was a level area of cobbled surfaces (138, 215-223, 225 and 267). To the north of these were compacted surfaces of clay with chalk chips and areas of burning (208, 259, 299, 361, 1130 and 1137). It was apparent that most of the features and deposits that cut through these surfaces (324, 327, 329 and 330) had been truncated, possibly by terracing for subsequent structures, and some of the compaction in this area may have resulted from the floors of a later building (Structure K, Period 7.1-2) built directly above. Note that the cobbled areas lay directly east of Structure G (Period 4.3) and the silty rubbles east of Structure F (Period 4.1). Most of these deposits remain *in situ* as excavation north of Grid line 250 ceased at this level.

To the south was a further construction or terracing cut (1139, shown only in section, Fig. 51). Sealing (and levelling) the remnants of Structures F and G were patchy compacted deposits of demolition debris (452 and 570, shown only in section, Fig. 51; 492 and 503, not illustrated), marking the disuse of these structures. Context 452 produced fifteen sherds, the largest and latest component being 17th-century Ryedale Ware.

Built into cut 1139 was wall footing 254 (Fig. 51). It was 0.8m wide, extending three courses (0.6m) high with the foundation course offset 40mm to the south on its outer face. The facing was composed of large chalk and sandstone blocks with a core of chalk and sandstone in a matrix of loose sandy clay. On part of the lower north (inner) face were traces of grey-white plaster *in situ*; further fragments of the same material were found in its demolition level, Period 6.3. The extent of 419 (Fig. 50), which was of 'bonding' type material, around the external south-east angle of 254, was probably the remains of construction material, or was applied to protect the lower chalk courses which would have been subject to frost damage if left exposed.

To the north of this wall was a sequence of heavily used clay floor surfaces (413, 443, 489, 488, 517 and 521; 562, Fig. 51), of which 517 contained two sherds of Ryedale Ware. Several of these surfaces had evidence of burning, and they contained a hearth (448). It is known from excavations on Site 77 to the west that Structure H's west wall (Site 77, 358) stood to a height of *c*.1.4m and was of the same construction as 254, possibly of one continuous build.

Cut 485 and post-hole 564, along with surviving wall stub 358 (Site 77), represent the northernmost surviving features associated with this structure, Structure H1.

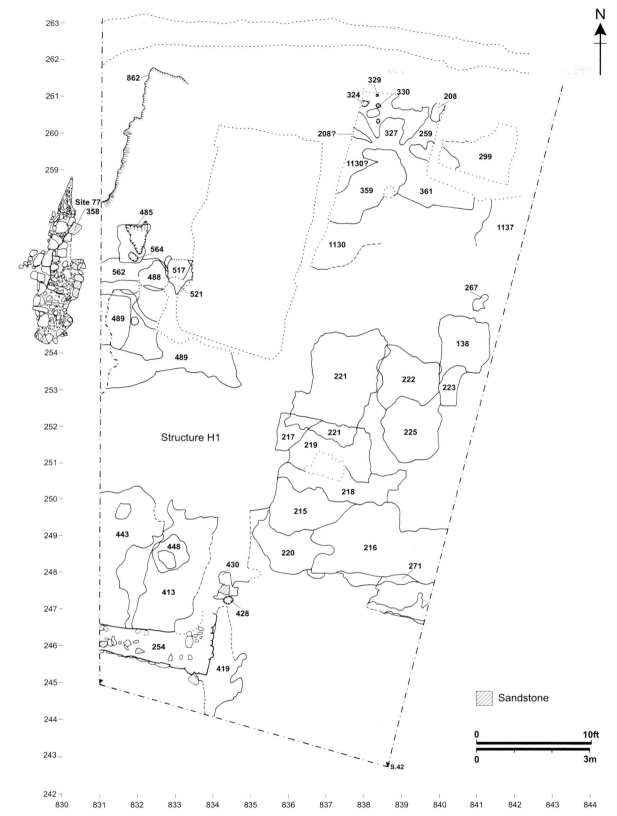

Fig. 58 Site 54: Period 5.1-5.2 plan (E. Marlow-Mann)

Although there was no surviving evidence for a north wall to this structure, terrace cut 862 (Period 5.1) suggests a possible maximum northern extent. It follows the alignment of wall 358 (Site 77) before turning east, just south of the conduit trench. The overall internal dimensions of this structure, Structure H1, could therefore have been c.5.0m by not more than 14m, with floor levels to the north at a higher level following the higher level of natural chalk.

To the east this structure would have had access on to the surfaces described above. Post-hole and mortar pad 428/430 may have served as door-post and threshold or, alternatively, may simply represent a main structural post position. No evidence of an east wall survived in this phase, but it is possible that wall 371 (see below Period 5.3, Fig. 59) was a rebuild of an earlier wall. This structure shares a similar alignment with Structures F and G.

Period 5.3: Structure H2 (17th century) (Fig. 59; Plate 19)

A sequence of clay surfaces (393, 411, 414, 415, 442, 451 and 453, not illustrated) mark resurfacing/repair mostly within the area of Structure H1 as a preparation for alteration or rebuilding of this structure. With the exception of 451 the surfaces all respected the line of wall 371 (see below) which may indicate that 411, 414 and 415 were actually contemporary with 371 or that they respected the line of a robbed Period 5.2 east wall or building line.

Laid on the surfaces of Period 5.2 and 451 was wall footing 371, of large and medium chalk and sandstone

Plate 19. Site 54: general view of Structure H looking north.

Plate 20. Site 54: possible refacing of wall 254/78, Structure H2, looking west.

Fig. 59. Site 54: Period 5.3-5.4 plan. (E. Marlow-Mann)

101

with some limestone, flint, tile and blocks of worked sandstone in the east face. It survived to a width of 0.7m and a height of one to two courses. The outer face was fairly regular but had collapsed inwards and the west face was less clear making it difficult to determine the precise line. The surviving sandstone blocks in the east face suggest that, along with 254/78 to the south, the whole length of the wall might have been faced (Plate 20).

The construction of 371 marks a second phase of Structure H1 and is designated H2. A repair to the outer face of wall 254 (Period 5.2) at the outer south-east corner comprised a single course of large (including some dressed) sandstone blocks (78). The gap between the reinforced corner of 254/78 and the surviving south end of 371 was 1.15m, fairly wide for an entrance but with the facing stones presumably having been robbed. Post-hole and mortar pad 428/430 (Period 5.2) continued in use as before. There was a deliberate blocking of the gap between walls 254/78 and the south end of 371 by a dump of rubble (334, unillustrated) and clay bonding material (253 and 256, not illustrated). The west wall (Site 77 wall 358) was retained and continued in use.

If the building originally extended as far north as terrace cut 862 (see above, Period 5.2), it then appeared to have been shortened, with the north wall of Structure H2 represented by the position of post-hole/post-pad 991/938 (Period 5.4, see below), replacing 485/564 (Period 5.2). No structural evidence of this wall survived on Site 54, due to the robbing suggested by robber cut 1019 (not illustrated) in Period 6.3 (see below). In Section 40 (Fig. 51) large chalk blocks in Grid 257 may represent the stub of the north wall at this same point, the surviving north end of wall 358. While the width would have remained the same, Structure H2, therefore, would have had an internal length of about 11m.

Discussion
Deposits 394-7, which included a near complete 16th or 17th-century costrel, together with 590, probably represented collapsed/robbed footings of stub or partition walls at right angles to the main axis of the structure. The large sandstone block in 396 (Fig. 51) may also have supported an internal division. There was no evidence as to whether these possible partitions were constructed at the same time as 371.

Period 5.4 (17th century) (Fig. 59)
To the north of this building, and probably contemporary with it, were dumps (e.g. 810; 882 and 922 not illustrated) of demolition debris used as levelling or make-up. Several pits (861, not illustrated; 991) were dug into these deposits: a possible pad-stone (938) had been carefully levelled and constructed in cut 991 but interpretation is difficult as it is a feature isolated by later intrusions (Periods 6.1 and 7.6). Its location directly against the edge of terrace cut 862 (Period 5.1) suggests that it may have been part of or directly contemporary with Structure H and it lies against the suggested line of the north wall of Structure H2.

Clay surfaces were laid over the dumps and debris but did not seal pad-stone 938. Although sloping, 836-8 extended as surfacing, probably external. The tendency of all the deposits was to be linear in plan, north to south, along the line of the natural terrace.

Period 6.1 Structure M (17th century) (Fig. 60)
In the north-west corner of the site the deposits were very similar to those in Period 5.4. Mostly these sloped down to the east and south, aligned north-south along the terrace, with characteristics suggesting levelling and dumping. The uneven mixed character of 433, 444, 756, 757 and 815 (not illustrated) suggests a make-up layer in preparation for possible surfaces 409 (Fig. 51 S.40) and 431. Layer 815 included Ryedale Ware, and surface 431 contained both Ryedale Ware and maiolica of the first quarter of the 17th century. Both 323 and 389 contained redeposited demolition material which suggests the demolition of some adjacent structure (probably on Site 77 to the west, but equally possibly to the north).

To the north of the later conduit cut (Period 7.6) the alignment of deposits similarly tended to be north-south. The western deposits contrasted markedly with those to the east down the slope. On compacted clay surfaces 374-5 there was no sign of wear on the rubble inclusions, suggesting possible 'internal' surfaces; cut into these was a rubble-filled feature (377/388) with a possible post setting at the west end. To the south were sandstone blocks (378) forming a possible pad-stone sealing a post-hole beneath. Down the slope to the east were compacted chalk and stone surfaces (381, 313, 317 and 339) notably worn in places; their function was clearly external (possible yard) surfacing. The bricks and sandstone in the fill of 363 (310) and the mortar deposit 383 were probably dumped material rather than *in situ* structural remains; 363 equated with 323 on the south side of the conduit cut. The ephemeral nature of this group of features and surfaces suggests some sort of dismantled yard structure, Structure M, rather than a building. Excavation did not continue below this level north of the conduit cut so it is also possible that not all these contexts were actually contemporary.

The sequences of dumping between surfaces suggest that either heavy use or persistent erosion was making resurfacing and levelling necessary. Few of the identified surfaces were heavily compacted and several deposits (e.g. 23) had a silty matrix, possibly the result of hillwash. Most were much deeper to the north and west and sloped fairly steeply to the south and east indicating that terracing and levelling were necessary, but perhaps not particularly successful. The linear arrangement of the deposits presumably reflected the prevailing alignment of contemporary structures as well as that of the natural hillside slope. The relative frequency of inclusions of domestic debris suggests that they served as external areas close to buildings. The finds, particularly to the south of the conduit, had a wide date range, the mixture probably resulting from redeposited material from Site 77 adjoining to the west.

Fig. 60. Site 54: Period 6.1-6.2 plan. (E. Marlow-Mann)

Period 6.2: Structure J (17th century) (Figs 60, 61 and 62; Plate 21)

Cutting through the north end of Structure H (Period 5) and through Period 6.1 dumps was a substantial sunken rectangular stone-lined room, set in construction cut 518. The walls were neatly constructed with a facing of roughly-dressed large limestone with occasional large and medium sandstone, chalk and burnt sandstone and a mixed rubble core. As the structure remains *in situ* the nature of the construction is only known at the upper level and, in section at the east end of the north wall, showing a rubble core and firm sandy clay matrix behind the facing. The dimensions of Structure J were 2.2m by 5m; the surviving heights of the walls ranged from 0.7m (south wall) to 1.95m (north wall) high, and their thickness ranged between 0.4m and 0.65m.

The north wall, 340 (Fig. 61) incorporated a neatly dressed recess, 0.33-0.27m (one block) deep and 0.7m wide, set into the interior wall face slightly to the west of centre; the base of the recess was 1.12m above the base of the wall and it extended up to the surviving top of the wall. There was evidence of slumping of the face of the west wall (624) (and the edge of cut 518) towards the centre. The north end of the wall was continuously bonded with 340 and the southern end with 623. The south wall (623) was keyed at the west and eastern ends into 624 and 622 (see below). The blocks of the lowest course of the east wall (622), predominantly sandstone, protruded slightly from the face (as with 340 and 623).

On the floor of the room, in the angle formed by walls 622 and 340, a series of large sandstone and limestone blocks (627), in a single course, extended 1.1m by 1.0m.

103

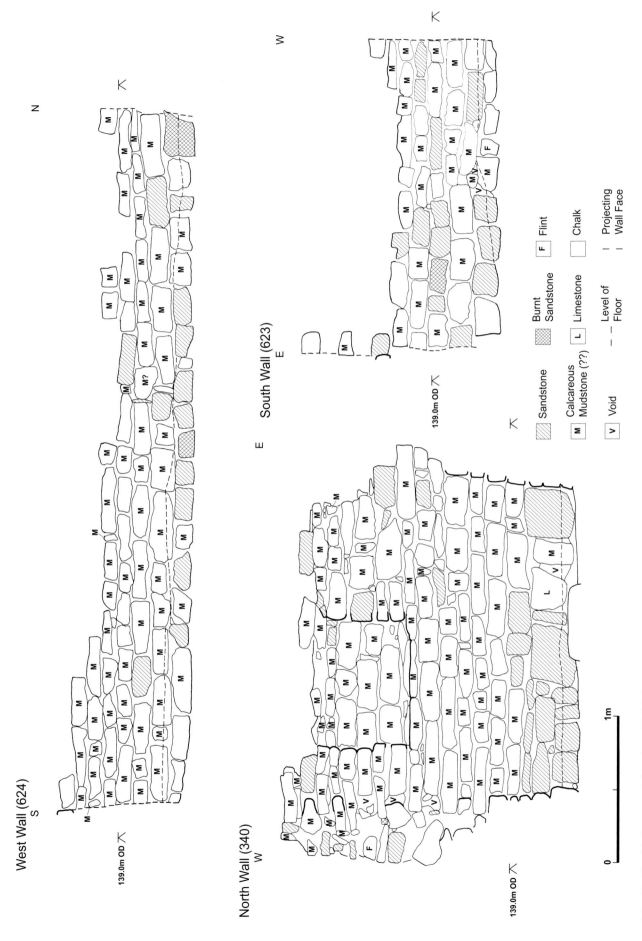

West Wall (624)

North Wall (340)

South Wall (623)

Sandstone

Burnt Sandstone

Flint

Calcareous Mudstone (??)

Limestone

Chalk

M Mudstone

Level of Floor

Projecting Wall Face

V Void

139.0m OD

139.0m OD

139.0m OD

0   1m

Fig. 61. Site 54: Structure J elevations. (E. Marlow-Mann)

104

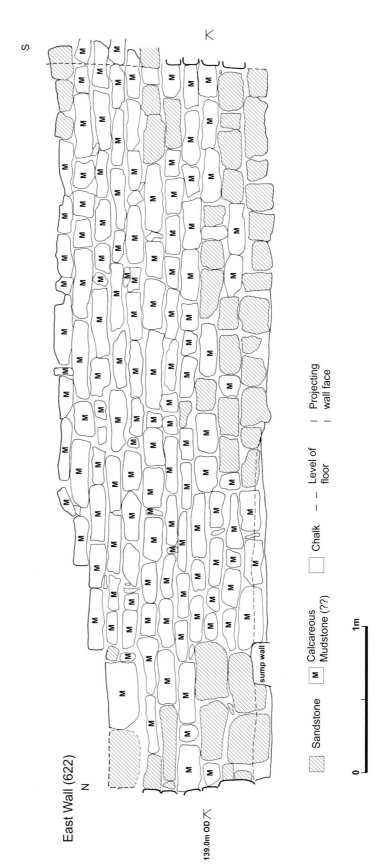

Fig. 62. Site 54: Structure J elevations. (E. Marlow-Mann)

East Wall (622)

N

S

139.0m OD

sump wall

Sandstone

M Calcareous Mudstone (??)

Chalk

—— Level of floor

I Projecting I wall face

0   1m

Plate 21. Site 54. Structure J, looking north.

Scarring on wall faces 340 and 622 suggest that originally the blocks, or possibly a timber superstructure, continued up the wall faces. The blocks were not bonded but set into floor bedding 625.

Discussion

These walls formed a substantial cellared structure, Structure J, and the quality of the masonry is distinctively superior to any other structure on Site 54 or Site 77. At the base of the walls sandstone predominated, and at the east end of 340 and the north end of 622 the very large sandstone blocks had distinct gaps between them. It was noted that after heavy rain all the water in the base of the cellar drained out through these gaps, suggesting that 627 could also have served as a sump or drain. The gaps may have been connected with a timber frame for steps, or shelving, running down from the north end of the east wall. The absence of some blocks at the northern upper face of 622 (which supported the later west wall of the vicarage (Period 7.1-2)) strengthens this possibility. Such a timber frame might have been positioned on the blocks of 627. Given the extensive survival of 340 it could be suggested that the recess in the north wall opened into a ventilation or light shaft and was not (primarily) intended as a shelf for storage. The uneven surface of floor bedding 625 probably resulted from the robbing of a floor of flagstones that survived only as fragments (1141) jutting out from the corner of walls 622 and 623.

The use of the structure is identified as that of a cool store, possibly a cellar or more likely a dairy cool-room. The quality and type of masonry are not paralleled by any other structure on this site, however there was fragmentary masonry of a similar type (and possibly date) on Site 26 at the north-west corner (Site 26, context 73, Period 6 Phase 6; Fig. 65, S64). This was also identified crossing into Site 77 as context 231 (Figs 44 and 46, S.13). A minimum overall height for this structure must be 1.8-9m.

Period 6.3 (17th century) (not illustrated)

Sealing the construction level of Structure J on the north side was a 'clean' uncompacted deposit of soft, pale mortar and small angular chalk (320), possibly bedding for a robbed paved surface of some sort, probably contemporary with Structure J and/or structures to the north (see Period 6.1); it contained mostly medieval ceramics. Compacted surfaces (410 and 424) over the site of Structure H2 contained late 16th to early 18th-century ceramics.

A major intrusive cut (1019, Fig. 51) was made through surfaces and deposits to the north (Period 6.1) down to the floor levels of Structure H2, facilitating the removal of its north and east wall which were pushed (or fell) inwards from the south end, and removing much of Structure J. Demolition material (e.g. contexts 353, 390, 391, 421, 455, 456, 461, 462, 471, 481, 516, 520, 566, 591, and 612-614,) mixed with domestic and other rubbish (e.g. contexts 516 and 614) was used to backfill Structure J up to the level of contemporary external deposits (see Period 5). Comparatively little larger rubble from the wall facings was noted; presumably this was carefully removed for reuse as was the flagstone flooring. Most of the deposits extended fairly evenly across the interior of the cellar suggesting that they did not gradually accumulate.

Large mixed, stony deposits (341, 367 and 369, Fig. 51, S.40; 241, 243, 245, 249, 260, 264, 266 and 412) suggested demolition debris from Structure H2 and the remains of structures on Site 77. The west wall of Structure H2 (Site 77 wall 358, Fig. 43) survived this robbing and was probably deliberately left *in situ* as a revetment against the encroaching hillside. Structure J was dismantled and backfilled before the final demolition of at least the north end of Structure H2, the debris from which spilled over the top of the fill of Structure J. Cut into the building debris which was left fairly level were three rubbish pits (321, 438, and 447) two of which contained animal skeletons, a near complete piglet (446) and a near complete calf (328).

Discussion

There was little evidence to suggest the length of time during which Structure J was in use. The few finds from the floor-bedding 625 (pottery and clay pipe stem) probably derived from the backfilling of Structure J rather than its construction. Didsbury's attribution of an early to mid-18th-century *terminus post quem* for Structure J's backfilling is supported by the glassware and clay pipe dating. From the evidence on Site 54 a probable reason for the dismantling of Structures H2 and J is that of the inherent instability of the hillside. The upper half of 622 leaned out towards the east in spite of the solid retaining deposits. This was opposite the slumping inwards of the west wall (624). This may have been the result of poor construction and a possible contributory factor to its disuse.

As already emphasised, repeated terracing and levelling has removed not only evidence of the nature of intervening periods of activity, but crucially, their relationships. The relationship of Structures H and J is defined by the demolition of J and the possibility that some of the material in the backfill of the cool-room came from H. Material interpreted as debris from H (Fig. 51) also spilled over the top suggesting that part of H on Site 54, probably the north wall, was at least standing. It is of course possible that the debris was from other structures to the west, Structure H (excluding its west wall which survived on Site 77) having been systematically robbed some time earlier.

Before the construction of the next building in this area (Period 7.1 below) major terracing and levelling took place.

Period 7.1: Structure K (18th century) (Fig. 63; Plate 22)

Wall footings and deposits formed the west, north and eastern sides of a building aligned north-south along the terrace, Structure K. The description of this structure is from south to north with details of subsequent alterations to some rooms at the end. It is clear that levelling and clearance of this area must have taken place prior to construction as the floors, east and south walls sit directly over external Period 3 surfaces. Robbing, collapse and spillage of the core material of the walls/footings meant that in places the wall-line was difficult to define; in other places, at the south-west corner for example, at the south end of 252 even plaster was still *in situ*. Initial machine clearance of the site also accounts for some of the intermixture of finds from the demolition material with the original levels beneath.

The walls were mostly constructed of a bonding material of firm silty clay with frequent small chalk and flint chips (e.g. 273). Variable proportions of reused sandstone blocks, bricks and other large/medium chalk and limestone rubble were included, sometimes surviving as wall-facing. At the south end, the west wall (252, 118 and 255) was clearly built into accumulated Period 5 and 6 deposits, reusing the surviving outer face of wall 78 (Period 5, Fig. 59) for support. Early 19th-century pottery from the wall indicated that one stretch at least had been rebuilt at that time. Further north the wall (101) rested in part on the surviving top of 622 (the east wall of Structure J, Period 6.2, Fig. 60).

The north wall (136) was set in a shallow trench (331, not illustrated); similarly, the north end of the east wall (234), which contained late 18th-century ceramics, was set in a shallow trench which appeared to be continuous with internal wall 258 (see below). The rest of the almost entirely robbed east wall, (205, 69, 224 and 210) was set on Periods 3-5 exterior surfaces. Approximately in the middle of this wall line, a break was marked by a worn threshold (73/71/121) comprising sandstone and limestone blocks, set on edge forming a kerb. The threshold make-up deposit (211, not illustrated) contained early 19th-century pottery.

At the south end this wall line was only really clearly defined by patches of sinkage, an eaves-drip line and the extent of internal floors. It is known that the south wall lay in the south baulk: as excavation on Site 26 had already taken place a very short distance to the south, it was clear that the size of the structure could be reliably estimated. The overall dimensions of Structure K were, internally, 17.7m (north-south) by 4.4m.

Rubble and clay deposit 112 and post-holes 156 and 181 formed the base of a partition towards the southern end of Structure K with a probable entrance offset from the east wall line forming a room to the south, designated Room 1. Although the southern outer wall of Structure K

Plate 22. Site 54. Structure K, Room 4A, looking north.

Plate 23. Site 54: Structure K, ash pit 1131, looking north.

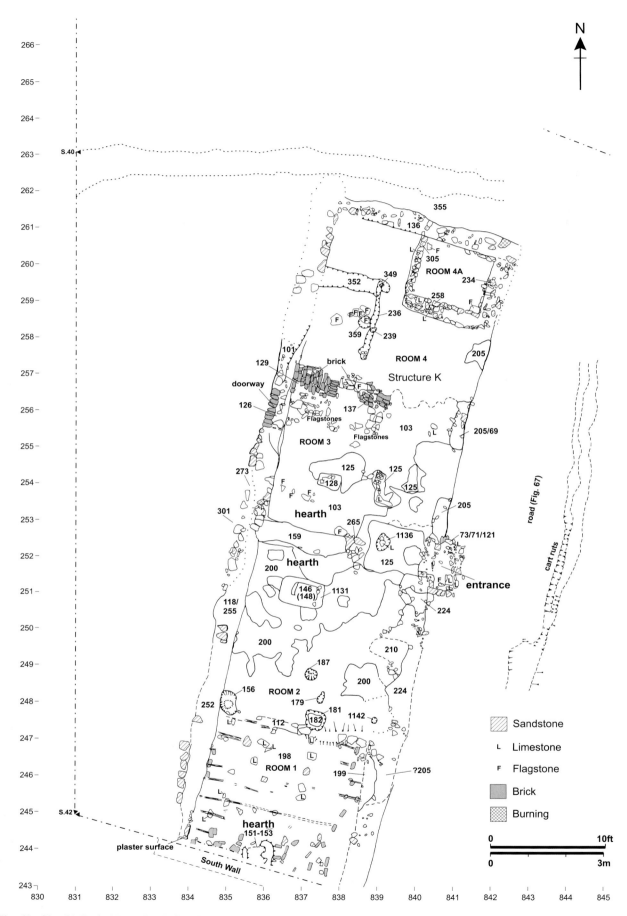

N

266 –

265 –

264 –

263 – S.40

262 –

261 –

260 –

259 –

258 –

257 –

256 –

255 –

254 –

253 –

252 –

251 –

250 –

249 –

248 –

247 –

246 –

245 – S.42

244 –

243 –

355

136

305
ROOM 4A
234
349
352
258
236
359
239
ROOM 4
205

101

129

brick

doorway

Structure K

126

137

Flagstones

Flagstones

103

ROOM 3

205/69

L

273

125
125
128
125

301

103

hearth

205

265

159

73/71/121
entrance

hearth
1136
L
125
200

118/
255

146
(148)
1131

224

200

210

200

187

224

156

ROOM 2

179

252

181

112

182

1142

198
L

199

ROOM 1

?205

L

L

hearth
151-153

plaster surface

South Wall

Sandstone

L Limestone

F Flagstone

Brick

Burning

0   10ft

0   3m

road (Fig. 67)

cart ruts

830 831 832 833 834 835 836 837 838 839 840 841 842 843 844 845

Fig. 63. Site 54: Period 7.1. (E. Marlow-Mann)

108

was in the baulk, the stone and clay hearth setting (151-3) was clearly built into this wall line. Post-hole 179 may have had a structural function in relation to this room division, or to the roof above. The joist supports (bricks, sandstone and limestone) and joists (198) would have supported a timber plank floor.

Deposits of clay with chalk chips (200; 145, not illustrated), which lay north of Room 1, represent the floor of Room 2, which had a hearth and ash-pit (1131; Plate 23). The clay floor deposit was probably bedding for a robbed flagstone floor. The lower fill (146) of the stone-lined (sandstone and limestone) ash-pit clearly represented accumulation during use, and the upper fill (148), deliberate backfill at the point of disuse. Presumably some sort of smoke-hood would have projected from the room division to the north (see below), although no post-holes or pad supports were identified. The ash-pit was not dismantled and remains *in situ*. The purpose of post-hole 187 in the middle of the room is not known.

The north wall footing of Room 2 (159 and 265) comprised very compacted rammed chalk. The area north of this was defined as Room 3. The extent of surface 100 (not illustrated) and its constituent similarity to 200 suggests a general floor-bedding/make-up. Some surviving fragments of flagstone flooring (103), mostly along the edges of the room, were also set on a lime mortar bedding, but it was impossible to identify whether any were original. It is possible that all the limestone elements were actually repairs and, in the case of those sealing the base of another ash-pit (128), certainly a secondary phase. Ash-pit 128 indicates that Structure K originally had back-to-back hearths in Rooms 2 and 3, set against the partition wall that divided the two rooms.

The extent of 125 marked a well-defined space between the east end of wall-line 159 and the threshold 121/71, possibly a later addition/repair in an access area or levelling for the slope noted down to the east. This area was defined as the lobby entrance although not separately numbered as a room.

Two further brick hearth settings (129 and 137) at the north end of Room 3, against wall line 134/130 (Fig. 64, Period 7.2) were composed of broken and fractured bricks and had clearly been considerably repaired. The bricks were burnt almost completely black in places and adjacent flooring had been cracked by the heat.

A line of bricks (126) set in the outer face of the west wall (101), the threshold of a doorway into Room 3, provided access to a yard area at the rear (west) of the building. The removal of the south wall of Structure J together with the south end of its west wall (see Period 6.3) had left the northern part of the west wall standing, forming, with the surviving north wall (340), a shelter, perhaps a porch, around this rear entrance to Structure K; this also acted as a barrier against hill-slip and rain-washed deposits accumulating in the space at the rear of the vicarage.

The threshold bricks (126) were set in a hard grey-white mortar in a row 0.9m long, with a further course of five bricks below at the south end (Plate 24). Some of the bricks were clearly reused, with the flagstones adjoining the bricks on the eastern (inner) side possibly associated with, or part of, floor 103 (see above). What was not clear was the nature of the division between this area and that to the north, Room 4, (but see Period 7.2 below). A linear rammed chalk feature (134; Fig. 64) in Period 7.2 probably formed a foundation/partition to the rear of

Plate 24. Site 54: Structure K, threshold 126, looking east.

hearth 137/129. It is possible that repairs to the hearths had obscured the line of an earlier/original partition.

At the northern end of the building was Room 4. Separate areas in the corner at the west end were formed by two shallow slots 236 (north-south) and 352 (east- west), and post-holes 239, 349 and 359, probably for timber partitions. A possible rubbish-pit (207, not illustrated) was located in the north-west corner. Fragments of flagstone and limestone indicated the former floor surface 171 (Fig. 64; Plate 25); this overlay a very mixed deposit (237, not illustrated), itself overlying a compacted coal dust deposit (335, not illustrated), which may have been a rough bedding surface. In the north-east corner was a more substantial stone-walled room (Room 4A); an east-west wall (258), mostly of sandstone, was set into a construction trench with a narrower north-south return (305), both of which survived two courses high, below the general floor level. The remains of flagstone flooring (306, not illustrated) at a lower level suggested that there had been a step down into this room, presumably a cool room or pantry. The apparently contemporary construction of 258 with external wall 234 suggests that this room was part of the original plan of the building, although wall 305 clearly butted the north wall (136).

Period 7.2: Alterations and repairs to Structure K (18th century) (Fig. 64)

Against the south wall in Room 1 a well-made hearth setting (109), comprising a fireplace of brick and burnt sandstone blocks with a mortared hearth area in front, replaced the earlier hearth (151-3, see above). This hearth sealed some of the edges of the floor joist supports. The largest sandstone block, measuring 0.72m by 0.12m by 40mm, may have been a reused lintel.

To the north in Room 2 there was evidence of a new hearth and possible reflooring. The original extent and composition of flagstone flooring 114 cannot be established. Some of it may well have been original (set on floor bedding 200 and in use with the hearth associated with ash pit 1131) while other patches sealed the edge of post-hole 156 (see above). It was not possible to distinguish the original from any subsequent repair but some of the flooring was of limestone slabs and probably represented a later repair. The infilling of ash-pit 1131 marked its disuse and a new hearth area (116-117) formed a level surface 30-50mm thick. This operated as an open hearth without a pit for the collection of ash. Parts of a free-standing grate or fire basket were found in the deposits sealing 117.

Wall 159 (Fig. 63), dividing Rooms 2 and 3, had been rebuilt at some stage, possibly at the same time as the fireplace in Room 2. Compacted deposits of bonding material and chalk rubble (119 and 120; 161 not illustrated) were rammed on top of 159, also sealing some of the flagstone flooring in Room 3 but not bonded into the external wall (118/101).

At the north end of the building in Room 4 the pantry or cool-room was remodelled. A smooth white plaster face (302; 336 not illustrated) 6mm thick was applied to the north and east walls (136 and 234) and was also noted on the northernmost blocks of the west wall (305, see above, Period 7.1); it also sealed the flagstone floor (306, not illustrated) but may have been part of the original scheme. The west wall was also heightened or rebuilt with a similar wall footing (135). This footing turned eastwards at its south end, sealing the original south wall footing (258), but not as far east as the main exterior wall line (234). Feature 213, which filled the resulting gap between, was very similar to the composition of the main wall (234) and it is possible that this was the entrance into the cool-room. No other possible point of access to this room was identified.

Brick surface 130, on the north side of slot 132, comprised red handmade bricks, set in three rows with a large sandstone block across the east end; it was probably robbed to the north and originally consisted of five rows. The bricks showed no evidence of burning and it is possible that they represented an unused hearth, an infill (with 132) of a cupboard/recess beside the west wall in Room 4, or just a patch of flooring.

Period 7.3: further robbing of Structure J and disuse/alterations to Structure M (18th century) (not illustrated)

A substantial cut, 370, into the surviving western wall stub (624) of Structure J (see Fig. 60, Period 6.2) would have robbed the remaining usable building stone and opened up the area at the rear of the vicarage.

To the north deposits 314 and 382 indicate resurfacing of Period 6.1 deposits. The composition of 312, a deposit of clay bonding-type material, was used here as a surface or make-up. Silty deposits 307-8 sealed what had been the northern end of Structure M (Period 6.1). Post-holes (277, 279, 285 and 337 (with post-pad 270)) cut into 310 (Fig. 60, Period 6.1) and 308 were fairly regularly spaced and possibly mark a reconstruction or replacement of part of Structure M.

The compacted cobbles and rubble (312, 314 and 382) with post-hole 365 replaced some earlier external surfaces of Period 6, while others were retained. This suggests either that the period of time between Periods 6.1 and 7.3 may not have been long, or that the repairs and resurfacing to the north were possibly rather earlier - perhaps contemporary with Structure J rather than the vicarage. These surfaces would have provided access either to Structure J and structures to the west on Site 77 or around the north wall of Structure K, to its rear door and to Structures M and L (see below).

Period 7.4: Structure L and other activity to the rear of Structure K (18th century) (Fig. 64)

Following the clearance at the rear of the vicarage (Period 7.3), level and compacted surfaces (351; 408 not illustrated) were laid outside the back door and to the north (350, shown in section only, Fig. 50, S.42). A dump of loose chalk (75) sloping down to the north and up to 0.4m thick was laid against the back of the west wall, probably acting as a soakaway to reduce dampness from accumulating deposits of hillwash. A narrow gully (301) cut into this may also have related to damp control or

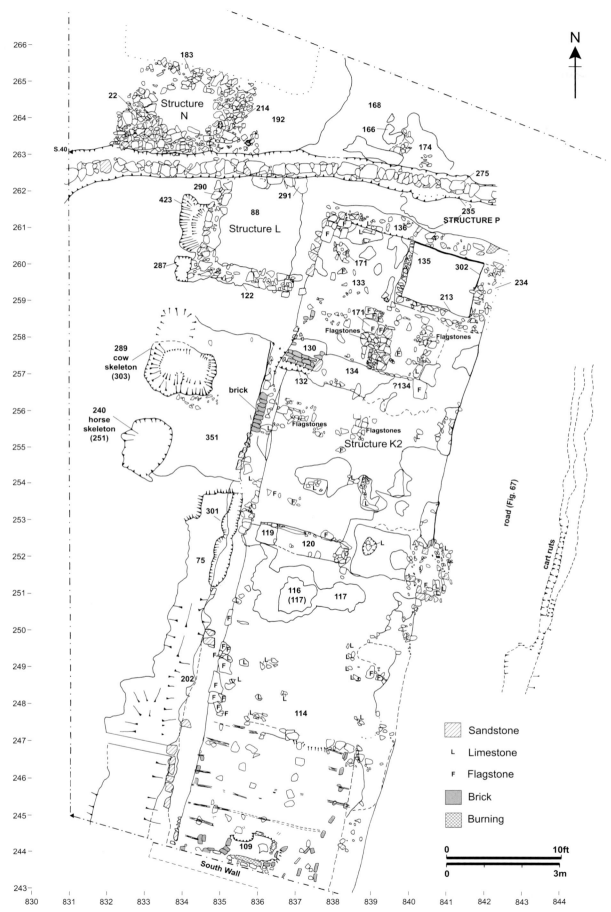

N

266 –
265 –
264 –
263 –
262 –
261 –
260 –
259 –
258 –
257 –
256 –
255 –
254 –
253 –
252 –
251 –
250 –
249 –
248 –
247 –
246 –
245 –
244 –
243 –

183
22   Structure
N
214
192
168
166
174
S.40
275
290
291
423   88   235
Structure L   STRUCTURE P
136
F   F   L
287   135   302
F   234
171   213
122   133
171   F   F
289   Flagstones   F   F   Flagstones
cow   130   134
skeleton   132   ?134   F
(303)   brick
240   Flagstones
horse   Flagstones
skeleton   351
(251)   Structure K2

road (Fig. 67)

cart ruts

301
119
75   120
L
116   117
(117)

202

114

F   Sandstone
L   Limestone
F   Flagstone
Brick
Burning

109
South Wall

0   10ft
0   3m

830 831 832 833 834 835 836 837 838 839 840 841 842 843 844

Fig. 64. Site 54: Period 7.2 plan. (E. Marlow-Mann)

111

possibly to the rebuilding of the wall itself, perhaps at the time of internal alterations to the north wall of Room 2 (see Period 7.2).

Two of the three large pits (240 and 289) cut into the edge of surface 351 contained animal burials including a cow (303), but it is difficult to suggest why these burials should have taken place so close to the house; however, it is worth noting that the backfill of Structure J would have made this area much easier to dig than the natural chalk. It is likely that stabling (see Periods 6.1, 7.3 and 7.5) was close by to the north (see also Site 73) and some of the ephemeral structures on Site 26 (Periods 6 and 7) might also have been for livestock and for stabling (Site 26 Period 6.2).

Walls/footings 122 and 290, one to two courses high, of large chalk, grey stone sandstone and burnt sandstone facing a core of small and medium mixed rubble bonded with yellow-brown silty clay formed the south and west walls of Structure L. The east wall of this building would have been the west wall (101) of the vicarage, Structure K (Period 7.1). Slabs of limestone (291) appear to have served as a threshold for a northern entrance but the rest of any north wall had been removed, apparently by the conduit trench (Period 7.6). Cuts 423 and 287 may relate to the construction of the walls. From the frequency of the coal fragments included in trampled clay surface 88 this structure had clearly been used at some stage for the storage of coal, and was presumably in contemporary use with the vicarage. Overall internal dimensions would have been 2.2m east to west by 2.4m north to south. There was no evidence that wall 290 had continued further north. Pottery from the wall footings of Structure L provided a *terminus post quem* in the first half of the 18th century.

To the north of the vicarage and Structure L was a series of external surfaces (226, 231, 269 and 272; 315 and 316 not illustrated), mostly compacted small chalk cobbles, mixed stone and brick. Cutting through the north-west side of deposit 269 was a rectangular feature (284) of unknown function. This may have been part of an ephemeral structure which also included mortar pad 166 (Period 7.5). On the surface of 231 was a dump of coal and burnt wood (230) which had burnt through to the cobbles beneath. These surfaces may relate to the vicarage or to the farmyard (Sites 73, 49) to the north.

Period 7.5: External surfaces and Structure N (18th century) (Fig. 64)

Deposits of clay with various inclusions sealed the external area at the rear (west) of the vicarage. Although the silty clay layer 202 appeared homogeneous the presence of patches of limestone and lenses of charcoal with burnt nails (283) suggest that it had accumulated over time. These external surfaces would have been subject to intermittent deposition of hillwash from the hillside to the west.

Overlying make-up and levelling deposits (250 and 261, not illustrated) just to the north of Structure L was an extensive area of collapsed rubble, parts of which clearly represented wall footings; 22, 183 and probably 214 formed three sides of a small structure, Structure N. The north side was cut away by a modern intrusion. Stake-holes (189, 193 and 282, not illustrated) were possibly associated with its construction. The disturbed nature of the surviving rubble makes the actual wall lines difficult to define, but a usable internal floor surface, at least 1.6m square, would have been formed. The function of this small structure which may have been open to the west (or the north) is not known; possible uses include storage or animal shelter. There was no obvious associated internal flooring but 272 (Period 7.4) could have served as a good surface although it was not particularly worn. Pottery from wall footing 22 provided a *terminus post quem* of the early 18th century for its construction.

Contemporary external clay and cobbled surfaces (192 and 168) lay to the east of Structure N. Two patches of hard pale brown mortar (166) may represent a robbed floor bedding or perhaps an eroded wall footing and was possibly related to 174 which included patches of mortar and regularly set larger rubble. Although these might have had a possible structural function, as some sort of lean-to structure against the north wall of the vicarage, they may equally have been debris from repairs and alterations to the northern rooms of the vicarage (Rooms 4 and 4A) which were remodelled more than once (Period 7.2).

As with features in Period 7.4 there was no direct evidence of contemporaneity between the surfaces to the rear of the vicarage and structures and surfaces further north because of the intrusion of the conduit (Period 7.6).

Period 7.6: Structure P: the conduit, (18th century) (Fig. 64)

A major linear feature (235, Fig. 51), up to 1m wide and 1.2m deep, was cut for the construction of a freshwater conduit channel (275, Fig. 51), Structure P, which brought water from a spring on the hillside south of the church presumably to the farmhouse (Site 74) north-east of the vicarage. This feature has been identified previously in excavations in the churchyard (Sites 52, 68 and the west end of the church) as well as on adjacent Site 26 (cut 11, channel 84, Fig. 65, Site 26 Period 7.1) and Site 77 (Period 5.1) where its construction was identical. Its depth increases to the north and east with the rise in ground level.

The upper surface of the fills (170, not illustrated; 184, shown only in section, Fig. 51) was heavily compacted. The pottery from these fills was primarily Ryedale Ware, but with some late 18th and early 19th-century material in each. The general debris of the fill and the wide variety of inclusions may relate to the destruction of features noted to the north (Structures M and N, Periods 6.1, 7.3 and 7.5 above), to the south (Structure L, Period 7.4), or to the west (Site 77).

The area above and around the conduit was consolidated with further deposits of rubble (167, not illustrated) and demolition debris (34, 186 and 233, not illustrated) from Structure N, the southern side of which

S. 64

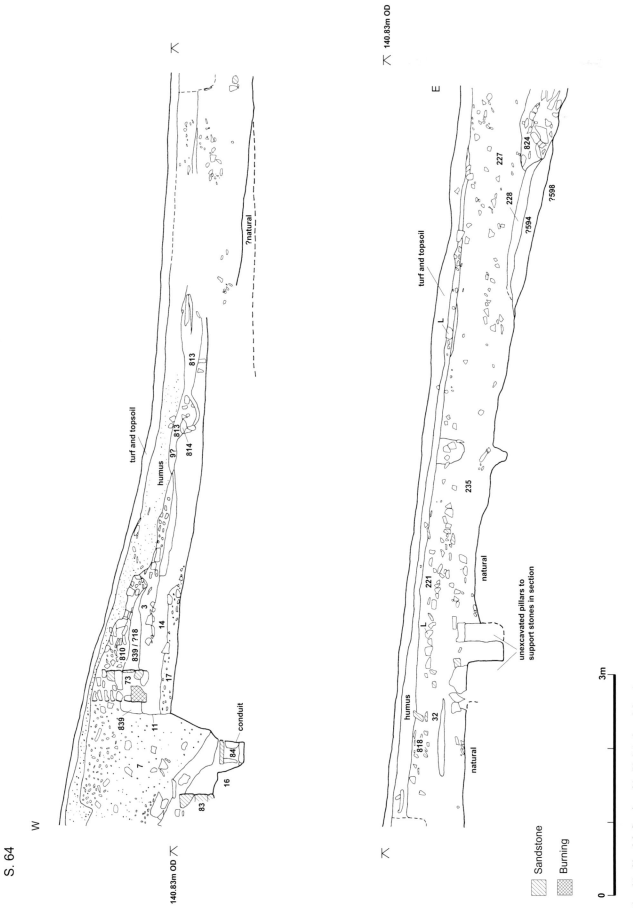

Fig. 65. Site 26: Section 64. (E. Marlow-Mann)

113

Plate 25. Site 54: general view of site looking south.

was clearly damaged by the insertion of the conduit. Deposit 248 comprised 'bonding'-type material and appears to represent part of the reconstructed north 'wall' line of Structure L (Period 7.4) however, its alignment is skew to the rest of the structure and it is likely that it either represents original wall material redeposited or a replacement 'footing' in the form of pad-stones.

Period 7.7: Structure Q (18th century) (Fig. 66)
At the western edge of the excavation was wall footing 19. It was 0.35m wide and constructed mostly of large chalk and limestone with occasional large sandstone and flint; it survived for one course, aligned north to south. Directly abutting the eastern side of 19 was wall 20, with very large to medium limestone and chalk in a single course, in a continuous U-shape forming the southern part of Structure Q1, the northern half destroyed by a modern intrusion (Period 8.4). A possible construction cut (18) into the steep hillside on the outer face of 19 may have been necessary to 'terrace' in the wall-footing. The relationship of cut 18 and wall footing 19 to wall 20 is unclear. Wall 19 may have been part of an earlier phase, or may have been constructed as a deliberate revetment against the steep hillside slope to the west, perhaps added immediately after the initial construction of wall 20. Alternatively, wall 20 may have replaced other parts of Q1 of which no trace was otherwise evident. This structure (Structure Q1-2) replaced Structure N (Period 7.5).

To the south, debris from Structure L (Period 7.4) (197; 86, 87, 191 and 196, not illustrated) was concentrated over the site of the structure and up the slope

to the west. It is not known whether the disuse of this outbuilding was directly contemporary with the construction of Structure Q.

Hillwash deposits (97/91/106) concentrated at the bottom of the slope west of the vicarage. The 'bowl' effect into which these deposits were formed suggests either that the rear entrance of Structure K was still in use, or that this represents sinkage into Structure J as its backfill settled. Sealing these was a more weathered surface (98 and 99, not illustrated).

Cobbled surface 21 (not illustrated) was laid along the line of the conduit (Period 7.6) providing further consolidation as a path/external surface together with deposits 72 and 74 (not illustrated). A sub-rectangular rubbish pit (165) was cut into surface 74.

Period 7.8: Structure R (18th century) (Fig. 67)
To the east of the vicarage (Structure K), an extensive area (16) of compacted small rounded packed chalk cobbles formed a fairly level surface sloping down to the east, merging to the north and west with similar contemporary cobbled surfaces (e.g. in Periods 7.3-7.5) lying against the north wall of the vicarage. Although there was no evidence of a particular repair to the surface following the construction of the conduit (Period 7.6), resurfacing and patching must have been undertaken fairly regularly. Extending the entire north-south length of the excavation and beyond, this surface was up to 6m wide, of which only the western 4m was particularly worn, with ruts along the surface. It merged into the threshold of the front entrance to the vicarage (Period

Fig. 66. Site 54: Period 7.7 plan. (E. Marlow-Mann)

7.1). This feature, a well-worn and wheel-rutted road, is known from other excavated sites to have extended south into the churchyard (Site 26 Period 7.2; *Wharram XI*, 55, fig. 45) and north at least as far as the courtyard farm (Site 49, see above, Period 2). Deposits 10, 15 and 27 were only variations or repairs to the road surface. Context 110 lay right up against the east wall of the vicarage with the result that the chalk was not particularly worn, the linear depression on its surface possibly the result of 'eaves drip'. A silty deposit (70) against the north end of the east wall, and a similar deposit (104) at the south end of 110, probably represented rain-washed silt accumulated against the wall-line.

The eastern edge of the most worn area of the road surface was marked by a line of post and stake-holes (63, 52, 54, 56, 65, 80, and 89), fairly regularly spaced 2.5-2.6m apart, forming a fence line. Deposits of burning (83 and 50) probably marked 'one-off' rubbish disposal while pit 26

represented longer term use. Cut 1132, although irregular, appears to have served as a drainage channel, the nails and friable composition of the fill suggesting a possible decayed (?burnt) timber lining. The drain was capped on the north side by a line of regularly-laid sandstone (12).

Although the latest surface was clearly laid after the construction of the conduit, the laying out of this road or trackway is likely to be contemporary with the original construction of the vicarage. Its good quality upper surfaces may represent upgrading at the time of the construction of the farmhouse (Sites 49 and 74) to the north. As the road was left *in situ* its period of use can only be estimated from Site 26 to the south where it was removed and appeared to have been laid down in the 18th century, sealing a sequence of 17th-century external yard surfaces and outbuildings (Site 26 Period 6.2). Detailed discussion of the conflicting evidence of the excavated sequence and the 1836 and 1851 estate maps has been

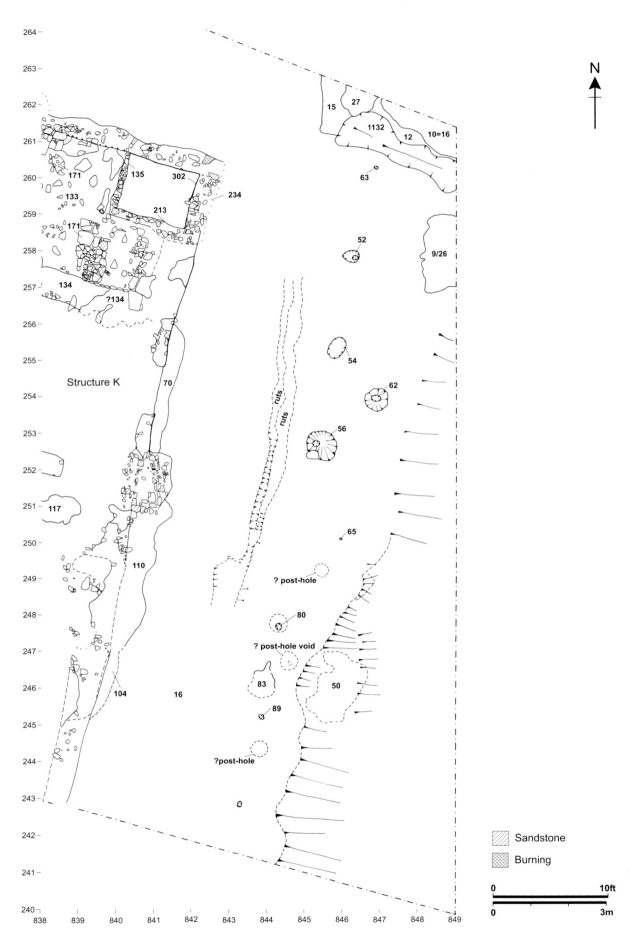

Fig. 67. Site 54: Period 7.8 plan. (E. Marlow-Mann)

included in the Churchyard report (*Wharram XI*). The earlier map shows a track crossing the site of the former vicarage towards the north door of the church only a year after the building was 'taken away', although no evidence of such a track was found here or on Site 26 to the south.

Period 8.1 (19th century to late 20th century) (not illustrated)

Spreads of building debris (5 and 28) across the western half of the site mark the robbing and destruction of Structure K (Period 7.1). Deposit 111 had settled between the remains of floor joists (199) and joist supports (198), which suggests that the floorboards had been removed from Room 1 rather than left to decay. Plaster was noted as a component of both 111 and 113 in Rooms 1 and 2 and from the lobby area. Lime-wash on bare walls might have served the kitchen area, whereas plaster would have been more likely in the parlour (Room 1). At least five separate layers of plaster were noted on the fragments from Room 1, many of which were still attached to fragments of lathes. Patterned plaster in a diamond pane design in applied lattice strips (at least two layers, with the pattern at different angles) was included here. Each diamond pane measured 260 x 180mm. In general there was an absence of roof-tile which supports documentary evidence that the building was thatched (see Period 7).

Period 8.2 (19th century to late 20th century) (not illustrated)

Pit 94, cut into robber trench 92 (Period 8.1), contained an ox skeleton: the last in a sequence of animal burials (see Periods 6.3 and 7.4) although it is easier to explain in the context of an abandoned area. Deposit 77 indicates the final abandonment of the vicarage and the accumulation of rain-washed silts and topsoil.

The spread of debris (5 etc) over the western edge of the road (Period 7.8) suggests that with the disuse of the vicarage use of the road declined. Mixed rubble (7) appears to have been laid to reinstate the road surface but in terms of quality and width it would have demoted it from a fairly good road to a trackway and was not particularly worn or compacted. It may be equated with a track shown on an estate survey of 1855 and is possibly the continuation of similar deposits recorded on Site 26 to the south (*Wharram XI*, Period 4.4). The apparent inconsistencies between the archaeological record and the 1836/1855 estate surveys have been discussed above (Period 7.8 and also ref to *Wharram XI*). Deposits of rain-washed topsoil (11, 13 and 14, not illustrated) accumulated beside the trackway washing down the very steep hillside slope along the eastern edge of the terrace.

Period 8.3 (19th century to late 20th century) (not illustrated)

A sub-rectangular cut (30) with five substantial posts (44, 48 and 1133-5) and possibly contemporary post/stake-holes (38, 40-42 and 51) formed a structure of comparatively recent date. This has been identified from photographs of this area in the 1950s as the site of a timber hen-house.

Period 8.4 (19th century to late 20th century) (not illustrated)

A linear bank of rubble (8) lay along the edge of the terrace forming a revetment; it included finds of mid-19th-century date and was probably the result of dumping or 20th-century garden clearance.

General discussion

The specific aims of the excavation were obviously not realised: no definable pre-conquest occupation was identified - merely hints - nor was any structural northern boundary of the churchyard located - merely the absence of further burials. On the positive side however was the unexpected survival and identification of the complete plan of the last vicarage as well as the expected fragments of earlier vicarages with clear evidence of a complex and continuous process of terracing and levelling. Inevitably the interpretation of features and structures here is linked to adjacent sites 26 and 77.

Period 1-2 (Romano-British to early medieval)

Dating these levels is problematic: although there is little help from finds the contrast with comparable features to the south on Site 26 Period 1 (*Wharram XI*, 31-6) is marked and puzzling. The aceramic nature of Site 54 Period 1 is in contrast to adjacent levels on Site 26 where Romano-British ceramics and animal bone were plentiful in the features cut directly into natural, and suggests either that on Site 54 some (or all) of these features have been truncated and are from a later date or that they are in a completely different functional zone. The Period 2 post-holes and fragmentary surfaces are also characterised by few finds with the exception of fragments of slag in several of the post-hole fills. The post-holes were in form quite different from those to the south (Period 2 Site 26, *Wharram XI*, 34-6) and clearly represent some sort of substantial structure requiring tall posts. The arrangement of four post-holes in a trench (954, Period 2.1 and 740, Period 2.3) was also recorded on Site 41 in a Romano-British level (Period 2: *Wharram XI*, 34-6). It is of note that Period 2 (early medieval) on Site 26, was also virtually aceramic. The function of all these early remains will be discussed in *Wharram XIII*, in the context of Iron Age, Romano-British and Anglo-Saxon activity throughout the valley.

Period 3

The process of terracing whereby the lower levels (i.e. down slope to the east) survive and those uphill do not was very clear in this period. Walls D and E (Periods 3.1 and 3.3) were on slightly different alignments but similarly truncated confirming the regular and repetitive nature of this process. As it appears that whole phases of building have been removed almost totally leaving isolated odd wall stubs, opportunities for linkage with the adjacent sites and interpretation are obviously limited. Deposits contemporary with Period 3 may survive north of Site 54 but comparative levels were not reached on Site 77.

It was clearly established that the medieval cemetery had never extended further north than Site 26 to the south (see *Wharram XI*, 332, fig. 158) and equally that it is unlikely that it had ever had a formal northern boundary. A ditch would have survived the terracing and if there had been a wall it had obviously been totally robbed, unless Structure D, for example, was its only surviving fragment. To the south following the disuse and contraction of this area of the graveyard the Site 26 Period 4.1 building (*Wharram XI*, 39-42) may be contemporary with this phase.

Pit 465 (Period 3.3) was clearly associated with some form of metalworking which would be quite consistent with agricultural or even domestic activity. The new ordination of the vicarage in 1440 and the probable move from the North Manor down to the valley may have been the context for the construction of these buildings.

Period 4

In contrast with Period 3, deposits of this phase survived against the hillside. Whether there were other intervening phases of occupation completely removed by terracing we cannot say. The surviving evidence of these structures was their distinctive flooring - none of their external walls survived on this site. Fragments of Period 4.1 masonry apparently represented the stubs of possible partition features e.g. 529, 626 and 726. This pattern was mirrored in Structure H2, a later building on this alignment. The frequent charcoal in Structure F (Period 4.1) clay surfaces seems typical of domestic/kitchen flooring although there were surprisingly few finds, while the burnt timber slots and post-holes of Structure G (Periods 4.2-4.3) suggest a raised floor, consistent with use as a grain store or possibly a hen-house. We have no evidence of the westward extent of these structures as any comparable levels did not appear to survive on Site 77 where they had been destroyed by later walls and major intrusions.

Period 5

Further buildings (Structures H and H2) occupied the level terraced area of Structures F and G but extended further east onto the compact external surfacing of Period 3. The construction trench 1139, for the western end of wall 254, (section Fig. 51) cut into earlier deposits up the slope (on Site 77), where it is presumed to have joined wall 591/358, Fig. 43, the west wall of Structure H and/or H2. As with Structures F and G, Structures H and H2 were characterised by patchy clay floors with few finds and evidence of stub walls/partitions against the western wall.

It has been suggested that the path through the Site 26 Period 5 boundary wall approached a vicarage building aligned west-east across the terrace; it is clearly not aligned on Structure H. It could have led to Structures F/G but on balance it would seem more likely to have served an earlier structure on the alignment of Structure D or E which has been terraced away and whose existence can only be inferred.

Period 6

The survival of the cool-room or cellar, Structure J was another surprise. The quality of its neatly coursed construction and the composition of the masonry stand out from earlier and later buildings in this area. The contrast with the barn and boundary walls on Sites 77 and 26 (predominantly of chalk blocks) and the walls of Structures H/H2 of mixed rubble and a rough build, is very marked. It may have reused sandstone building material from the church aisles or perhaps the later manor house. Its disuse is also interesting in that it was clearly carefully demolished leaving only smaller building rubble in the fill. This is another example of a structural fragment isolated by subsequent terracing (for Period 7) and for which we must assume that there were originally other building elements. Contemporary floors (and presumably structures) evidently continued northwards towards the farmhouse while the only other comparative surviving masonry was on Site 26 (Period 6.6, *Wharram XI*, 54). The absolute level of the floor gives a good idea of the overall depth of material removed by terracing for Structure K, some 45-50cms.

Periods 7-8

The survival and identification of this structure as the latest of the Wharram vicarages was an unexpected bonus. The contrast between this modest timber-framed structure and neighbouring and previous buildings of brick and stone says much about the relative poverty and status of the rural clergy in this part of England in the 18th century before agricultural improvement. This is illustrated by comparing it with the floor plan and size of the later Improvement farmhouse, while noting similarities to the earlier farmhouse in plan etc. It is interesting that there was no apparent access from the vicarage to the conduit supplying freshwater to the farmhouse (Period 7.6, Structure P).

A snapshot of the lifestyle and living standards of the incumbent and his family is provided by the range of contemporary finds. Some of the outbuildings (e.g. Structures M, N and Q) to the north of the vicarage extended towards the farmhouse and yard in front of it and it is possible that they belong with the farm and not the vicarage – representing encroachment by the farmer into the glebe, as in earlier periods the vicar had encroached into the churchyard. Outbuildings contemporary with this building lay to the south, on Site 26 (Period 7).

The removal of the vicarage in 1835 was complete: it was 'taken away', with the timbers and stone being reused elsewhere; no clue was left in the landscape, in contrast to the wall alignments of the peasant houses up on the plateau. A north-south bank (Period 8) proved to be a modern 'lynchet' formed of garden and other rubbish as a revetment at the top of the steep slope down to the stream. The final structure on this site was a chicken shed, raised above the ground as is customary, and whose existence was confirmed by oral tradition (Miss Myrtle Milner) as well as by a photograph from the 1950s.

Part Four
The Pottery

11 The Iron Age and Romano-British Pottery
by P. Didsbury

Introduction and methodology

Small amounts of Iron Age and Roman pottery, amounting to 122 sherds, weighing 2407 grams and having an average sherd weight (ASW) of 19.7 grams, were recovered from various sites in the North Glebe Area, viz. from Sites 21, 54, 49, 51, 73, 74, 77 and 79. The methodology employed is the same as that outlined for the post-medieval assemblages (below) and the material is recorded on the same databases. The distribution of the pottery by sherd count and weight according to fabric is shown in Tables 3 and 4. Fabric codes follow those used in Didsbury 2004.

Discussion

Most of the material tabulated below is unstratified, redeposited or residual in its context. A small number of deposits from Sites 49 and 54 do, however, deserve to be mentioned, and have yielded illustratable vessels.

Site 49 (Farmstead)
Period 1 layer 508, a buried soil overlying the natural chalk bedrock, contained five scrap sherds (22 grams) of CG4. A much larger assemblage of the same material (48 sherds, 1445 grams) was recovered from Period 2 context 30, the number designating both the cut and fill of a shallow curvilinear gully. The pottery from this gully gives the appearance of being a chronologically homogeneous assemblage. Three vessels were represented by rim sherds (Nos 1-3) but an uncertain number of others was undoubtedly present. All the vessels appear to find their best parallels among vessels from the ditches of the so-called 'early fortlet' at Langton Villa, cf. Corder and Kirk 1932, fig. 7, nos 19, 22, 34, 36 etc. Other broad parallels may be found in the Hawling Road, Market Weighton assemblages (Evans with Creighton, 1999). There seems little doubt that these vessels belong to the same 'peri-Conquest' phase of Late Iron Age occupation which produced the large assemblages from the North Manor (Didsbury 2004).

A residual Roman vessel from Period 3 post-hole fill 81 is illustrated (No. 4) for its intrinsic interest.

Site 54 (Vicarage)
The illustrated vessels (Nos 5-8) come from a variety of deposits, and are residual or redeposited in each case. The relevant contexts are: 5, a Period 8.1 vicarage demolition deposit; 244, a Period 7.1 padstone deposit for Structure K; 208, a Period 5.2 dump, possibly redeposited natural; and 272 or 300, reflecting the fact that the sherd in question bears different marking on the sherd and the packaging - the former number is a Period 7.4 external surface, and the latter designates unstratified finds from the 1983 excavations.

Once again, the vessels probably derive from the same late phase of occupation noted above. Particular attention may be drawn to No. 6, the slashed rim decoration probably reflecting that 'specifically late Iron Age horizon of plastic decoration' north of the Humber which was noted by Challis and Harding (1975, 95).

Table 3. Number of Iron Age and Romano-British sherds per site.

	Farmstead					Vicarage		
Site	74	51	49	73	79	21	77	54
Fabric								
CG1	1	2					1	3
CG4	2	2	16	6	1		6	33
CG1/4		2		1				10
RG		1					5	11
RG1		3	2				4	3
RS						1		2
RO			1				1	
RW		1						
RW1A		1						
Total	3	12	19	7	1	1	17	62

Table 4. Weight of Iron Age and Romano-British sherds per site (grams).

	Farmstead					Vicarage		
Site	74	51	49	73	79	21	77	54
Fabric								
CG1	20	22					5	51
CG4	11	15	1579	33	5		40	437
CG1/4		8		3				52
RG		7					17	64
RG1		86	13				38	12
RS						1		7
RO			8				8	
RW		4						
RW1A		16						
Total	31	158	1600	36	5	1	108	623

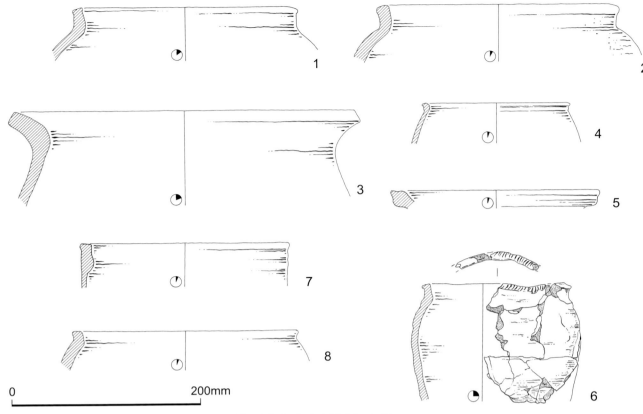

Fig. 68. Iron Age and Romano-British pottery Nos 1-8. Scale 1:4 (C. Marshall)

Illustration catalogue (Fig. 68)

Site 49

1*   CG4. Jar with almost upright rim, with bevelled edge. Abundant ill-sorted calcite, mainly fine but up to *c.* 5mm. Dark grey with darker exterior and patchy light brown interior. Exterior carbonised deposits. *49/30; Period 2*

2*   CG4. Large jar with flaring rim with bevelled edge. Moderate ill-sorted calcite, much of it *c.* 2-4mm, but several examples 7-15mm. Very dark grey with red exterior margin in places; light pinkish grey exterior and upper part of the inside of the rim. Cf. Evans with Creighton 1999, fig. 7.18, G32-J01 and cited parallels. *49/30; Period 2*

3*   CG4. Jar with fairly upright, square-cut rim. Abundant well-sorted chalk and calcite, *c.* 1-2mm. Dark grey with light pinkish grey surfaces. Cf. Evans with Creighton 1999, fig. 7.18, G01-J07 and cited parallels. *49/30; Period 2*

4*   RO (RO7?). Bag-shaped beaker with cornice rim. Hard, dense, light red fabric with well finished surfaces. York form KC4 (Monaghan 1997) but in oxidised, not colour-coated, ware. Probably *c.* AD 160-225. *49A/81; Period 3*

Site 54 (Vicarage)

5*   CG4. Everted, thickened, square-cut rim fragment. Abundant ill-sorted calcite, to *c.* 5mm. Patchy dark grey and light pinkish grey core and surfaces. *54/5; Period 8.1*

6*   CG4. Small jar with upright, flat-topped, slash-decorated rim. Abundant ill-sorted calcite, several *c.* 4-8mm. Dark grey with patchy grey and pinkish brown surfaces. External carbonised deposits. For other late slash-decorated vessels in the North Manor assemblage, cf. Didsbury 2004, nos 22, 49, 50. *54/208; Period 5.2*

7*   CG4. Jar. Upright flat-topped rim with internal thickening. Abundant ill-sorted calcite to *c.* 4mm. Dark grey with patchy red and grey exterior, and light brown interior. *54/244; Period 7.1*

8*   CG4. Jar. Short, upright, flat-topped rim. Common ill-sorted calcareous fragments to *c.* 5mm. Patchy mid to dark grey throughout. Some external carbonised deposits. *54/272 or 300; Period 7.4 or unstratified*

12 The Medieval Pottery
by A.M. Slowikowski

Methodology

The medieval pottery assemblage totalled 5271 vessels, which were made up of 6270 sherds, weighing 68.255kg with an Estimated Vessel Equivalence of 26.28. The pottery was recorded and analysed following the methods described in *Wharram VIII* (Slowikowski 2000, 60). Sites with large medieval assemblages, Sites 51, 54 and 77, are described separately; the others are summarised only (Table 5) and their record may be consulted in the archive. The pottery descriptions below, however, relate to all the sites of the North Glebe Terrace, as do the illustrations.

Pottery descriptions

Pottery types are coded according to the Wharram ceramic type series, as published for the South Manor, where all major types are described (Slowikowski 2000,

Table 5. Pottery totals from each site.

Site	Vessels	Sherds	Weight (g)
Farmstead			
74	91	120	1220
51	1240	1299	10337
11	29	33	423
49	38	43	399
73	132	140	1278
79	14	14	266
Total		1649	13923
Vicarage			
20	1	1	13
77	2374	3044	39602
54	1352	1576	14717
Total		4621	54332

60-81). New types previously unpublished in the Wharram series are described fully below.

The pottery has been grouped into broadly similar chronological groupings, based on the dates used in the bibliographic database of the Medieval Pottery Research Group. In summary, they are:

Ceramic Group 1 - Prehistoric and Roman pottery
Ceramic Group 2 - Anglo-Saxon AD 450-850
Ceramic Group 3 - 'Anglo-Scandinavian'/Saxo-Norman AD 850-1150
Ceramic Group 4 - Early medieval AD 1150-1250
Ceramic Group 5 - High medieval AD 1250-1400
Ceramic Group 6 - Late medieval AD 1400-1500
Ceramic Group 7 - Late medieval/post-medieval transitional AD 1500-1750

The type code and description are followed by the quantification by vessel:sherds:weight in brackets. Each type description is followed by a catalogue of illustrated pottery of that type (Figs 69-74), each entry containing the following information: catalogue number; description of vessel/sherd; (sherd count:weight (in grams) ratio); site code/context number; phase.

Ceramic Group 2 (Anglo-Saxon)

A small quantity of Anglo-Saxon pottery was recovered, all single abraded sherds, residual in later contexts. The following fabric types were found:

A01a Organic-tempered (3:3:5) 0.04% of total site assemblage
A02a Whitby-type (with mica) (2:2:7) 0.03% of total site assemblage
A02b Whitby-type (without mica) (1:1:8) 0.01% of total site assemblage
A04a Sandstone (with calcareous inclusions) (1:1:4) 0.01% of total site assemblage

A04b Sandstone-tempered (5:5:28) 0.07% of total site assemblage
A05 Quartz-tempered (1:1:2) 0.01% of total site assemblage

Site 51 produced a reused sherd in fabric type A04a, from a mixed assemblage within surface 51/377. It is a body sherd, reshaped into a disc 30mm in diameter (see Chapter 17, No. 2 for more details).

Ceramic Group 3 ('Anglo-Scandinavian'/Saxo-Norman)

B01 York type A (16:24:162) 0.38% of total site assemblage
Fig. 69, No. 1
Only jars were recognisable, most of which were sooted on their exteriors. Among them are a small lid-seated jar and a jar with an inturned rim (No. 1).

1* Jar with inturned rim. (1:11g) *54/594; Period 2.4*

B03 York type D (12:16:59) 0.25% of total site assemblage
No illustrations
Small jars with everted rims.

B05 Stamford-type ware (8:8:60) 0.12% of total site assemblage
Fig. 69, No. 2
Two jars, one of which is sooted externally, a body sherd with spots of light yellow-green glaze which may be from a spouted pitcher, and a possible fragment from a bottle (No. 2). The bottle fragment is from a narrow neck and has a thick, glossy lemon-yellow glaze.

2* Bottle in a buff-white fabric with thick glossy lemon yellow glaze. (1:4g) *51/1036; Period 1*

Ceramic Group 4 (Early Medieval)

B07 Pimply ware (84:91:481) 1.45% of total site assemblage
Fig. 69, No. 3
Only jars were recognised, two of which were reduced to a light grey colour.

3* Jar with unusual undercut rim. (1:5g) *54/203; Period 7.1*

B08 Pimply ware variant (27:28:103) 0.44% of total site assemblage
No illustrations
Three jar rims, one the usual rectangular type, the others slightly rounded; the rest are body sherds.

B09 Glazed Pimply (7:8:35) 0.12% of total site assemblage
No illustrations
Five small body sherds from jugs and a single body sherd with internal glaze, possibly a bowl.

B10 Splash Glazed ware (Splashed Pimply) (23:23:159) 0.36% of total site assemblage
No illustrations
Body sherds only, all probably from jugs.

B12 Staxton ware (2188:2254:17483) 35.94% of total site assemblage

Fig. 69 , No. 4-8

Jars are the commonest form, although peat pots, bowls and a curfew are also present. 'Peat pots' are shallow vessels with bases with a wider diameter than the rim, said to have been used on peat fires. They were not all necessarily used in this way, and indeed, many of the bases found have no signs of sooting. The term 'peat pot', however, has been retained for vessels of this shape. Rims are mainly developed, a possible late medieval characteristic. A possible spout or socket from a spouted or socketed bowl was also found (No. 7); these are rare in this fabric type. Decoration is sparse: incised horizontal lines on one body sherd; applied thumbed strips on a curfew and three other body sherds; combed wavy lines on a jar rim and one other body sherd; square notch rouletting on a body sherd; and stabbed and wavy line decoration on the shoulder of a jar. One body sherd has been reshaped into a roughly rounded disc, with a diameter varying between 32 and 40mm (see Chapter 17, No. 3).

4*   Full profile of peat pot with simple everted rim, slightly sooted exterior but clean base. (1:51g) *51/508; unphased*

5*   Jar with rectangular, lid-seated rim. (1:21g) *77/85; Period 5.2*

6*   Jar with triangular rim, stabbed and wavy line decoration. (1:19g) *51/1036; Period 1*

7*   Spouted or socketed bowl, abraded. (1:26g) *73/1; Period 3*

8*   Body sherd with lines of square notch rouletting, a rare decorative motif on Staxton wares. (1:28g) *51/1052; Period 1*

B13 Glazed Staxton ware (32:34:706) 0.54% of total site assemblage

Fig. 69, No. 9-11

A relatively large quantity of glazed Staxton vessels was found. Most are likely to be jugs although there is a single internally-glazed base which may be a bowl, and two developed-rim jars, one of which has glaze restricted to a band beneath the rim (No. 9). Overall, the glazes are poorly applied and sometimes unfluxed, as that on No. 10. There is no attempt to improve the quality of the potting. Indeed, the unglazed utilitarian jars and bowls are better made than the glazed jugs. There is one exception to this, a jug with incised lines decorating the handle and a relatively good glaze (No. 11).

9*   Jar with developed rim and band of yellow glaze beneath the rim. (1:8g) *77/84; Period 5.1/5.2*

10*   Jug with poorly fluxed glaze. (1:72g) *77/219; Period 5.2*

11*   Jug handle with incised decoration; well made with good quality glaze. (1:106g) *77/234; Period 5.1*

B14 Reduced Chalky ware (19:20:103) 0.31% of total site assemblage

No illustrations

Two small rectangular jar rims; the rest are body sherds.

B16 Beverley 1 (2:2:25) 0.03% of total site assemblage

No illustrations

Two sherds, both probably from jugs.

B18 York Glazed (88:94:445) 1.50% of total site assemblage

No illustrations

The fabric is similar to C01 Hambleton ware (see below), however, it does not have frequently occurring clay/grog lumps, and when they do occur, they are very sparse. Red iron ore is usually more frequent. Quartz is also frequent, sub-angular and approx. 0.5mm.

Body and base sherds, all probably from jugs. Decoration occurs in the form of applied strips, combed wavy lines and combed zig-zags on the body. One jug fragment from 77/50 is low fired, soft and powdery to the touch with barely fluxed glaze. A similar poorly-fired jug in the same fabric, identifiable as a York seal jug, was found on Site 30 (Slowikowski 2005, 75).

B18U Unglazed whiteware (20:28:375) 0.44% of total site assemblage

Fig. 69, No. 12

Only jars were recognised, with very sparse spots of light brown glaze on the body, possibly accidental. These jars are comparable in form and glazing to examples found in the Churchyard (Site 26), and dated to the 12 to 13th centuries (Slowikowski 2007, 253, fig. 132, nos 6-7).

12*   Jar with random spots of light brown glaze, and external sooting. (7.85g) *54/643; Period 2.3.* (2.79g) *54/458; Period 3.3*

B27 Splash glazed orange (1:1:6) 0.01% of total site assemblage

No illustrations

A single body sherd from a jug.

B28 Beverley 1 type (Splash glazed chalky) (14:16:45) 0.25% of total site assemblage

Fig. 69, No 13

Body sherds only, all probably from jugs. Decoration is present in the form of combed wavy lines and incised decoration.

13*   Jug in a reduced fabric with incised decoration. (1:5g) *77/494; Period 3.2*

B32 Developed Stamford ware (3:3:33) 0.04% of total site assemblage

No illustrations

One jug, the rest are body sherds.

Ceramic Group 5 (High Medieval)

B17 Scarborough (91:116:1277) 1.85% of total site assemblage

Fig. 69, Nos 14-18

Two rare Scarborough ware forms were recognised: a chafing dish rim with the scar of a knob (No. 17), and a lamp (No. 18). The remaining sherds are handles and body sherds from jugs. The majority are in the fine,

Fig. 69. Medieval pottery Ceramic Groups 3, 4 and 5: Nos 1-26. Scale 1:4 (C. Marshall)

0   200mm

powdery orange-pink Scarborough fabric although there are instances of sherds in the creamy white variant. Decoration includes vertical lines of small applied scales alternating with applied strips; vertical lines of applied pellets, glazed either green or red; and double incised or combed vertical lines. Decorative schemes are often combinations of these motifs. Handles are rod-sectioned with ribbing and there is one instance of a small twisted subsidiary handle (No. 16). Base angles are pinched, and there is one example of a base sherd with many random fingernail impressions on the interior.

14*   Jug with vertical applied strips and combed decoration. (8:147g) *51/47; unphased*

15*   Jug. (1:11g) *77/324; Period 3-5*

16*   Twisted subsidiary handle with all-over greenish-brown glaze. (1:7g) *77/85; Period 5.2*

17*   Rim of chafing dish with scar of knob and handle; very glossy green glaze. (1:6g) *77/235; Period 1-5*

18*   Stem of pedestal lamp; glazed bright green. (1:145) *51/1036; Period 1*

B17v Scarborough variant (59:62:705) 0.98% of total site assemblage
Fig. 69, Nos 19 and 20
Pink fabric with occasional darker orange-pink surfaces and a buff, or sometimes light grey, core. Hard, gritty, with many tiny voids, mainly 0.1mm or less. Quartz is moderate, well sorted, sub-rounded or sub-angular, 0.3-0.5mm. Iron ore is small, 0.1-0.3mm, and varies from sparse to moderate. Most vessels appear to be jugs, with rod handles, largely unglazed although there is one body sherd with sparse spots of yellow glaze, a handle with a sparse copper-speckled glaze (No. 19), and a base with internal barely-fluxed yellow glaze. The latter sherd may be from a bowl. A single decorated fragment was found: a stamped rosette and combed wavy lines (No. 20). One jug has knife trimming facets on the exterior of the lower body.

The fabric has similarities to B17 Scarborough ware, and has been coded as a variant of it, although the fabric is grittier. The quantities occurring in late medieval contexts on the North Glebe Terrace suggest this type is of a later date than B17 Scarborough ware. It has not been defined separately in previously published assemblages from Wharram, although small sherds may have occurred and been coded as B17 Scarborough ware. As this is the first major late medieval assemblage to be examined from Wharram and most of the pottery from previous sites is of an earlier date, large quantities are unlikely elsewhere in the village.

19*   Jug with rod handle, sparse copper-speckled glaze. (1:54g) *77/426; Period 5.1*

20*   Jug with rosette stamp and combed wavy line decoration. (1:5g) *77/682; Period 4*

B19 Gritty (13:15:131) 0.23% of total site assemblage
No illustrations
Two jug handles were found, both strap handles with a thumbed groove along the length. The rest are body sherds, probably from jugs. One has a dribble of purple glaze and may be of late medieval date.

B20 Brandsby-type (306:356:2853) 5.68% of total site assemblage
Fig. 69, Nos 21-26
Grittier in feel than either B18 York Glazed ware or C01 Hambleton ware. Most frequent inclusion is common sub-angular quartz, 0.2-0.7mm. Occasional black patches and voids where organic matter has imperfectly fired out.

Jugs are the most common form recognised although a single skillet handle (No. 26) also occurred. Jug handles are rod-sectioned, as is one small subsidiary handle. Decoration includes rectangular-notch, triangular-notch and complex herringbone rouletting, as well as one instance each of applied red pellets and applied vertical strips. There is a single example of a face mask (No. 25) which has come away from either the neck or shoulder of a jug. These are rare; a single example from York is published by Jennings (1992, 49, no.106).

21*   Jug with rouletted decoration. (1:4g) *77/549; Period 4*

22*   Jug with herringbone rouletted decoration. (1:3g) *77/78; Period 5.2. (1:4g) 77/181; Period 5.1. (1:3g) 77/426; Period 5.1*

23*   Jug with herringbone rouletted decoration. (1:6g) *77/50; Period 5.1/5.2*

24*   Jug with complex herringbone rouletted decoration. (1:6g) *54/13; Period 8.2*

25*   Face mask from jug. (1:10g) *54/546; SF1623; unstratified*

26*   Skillet handle. (1:64) *77/85; Period 5.2*

B21 Hard Sandy (6:11:49) 0.17% total site assemblage
No illustrations
Body sherds only, probably from jugs. There is a single example of patchy yellow-green external glaze.

B22 Hard orange (224:250:1900) 3.98% of total site assemblage
No illustrations
All sherds appear to be from jugs. Handles are oval or rod-sectioned, occasionally ribbed. There is one example of an indentation from a small finger which has been pushed into the interior wall of the upper handle join. This indicates the possibility of children or women working on the pottery, either as part of the potter's family or employed from outside. Evidence of this occurs elsewhere, for example documentary references from the Midlands and on the pottery from Cheam, Surrey (Le Patourel 1968, 116; Marshal 1924, 88).

Decoration is mainly combed wavy or vertical lines although one example of applied rows of scales occurred. Glaze is speckled with copper, although there are

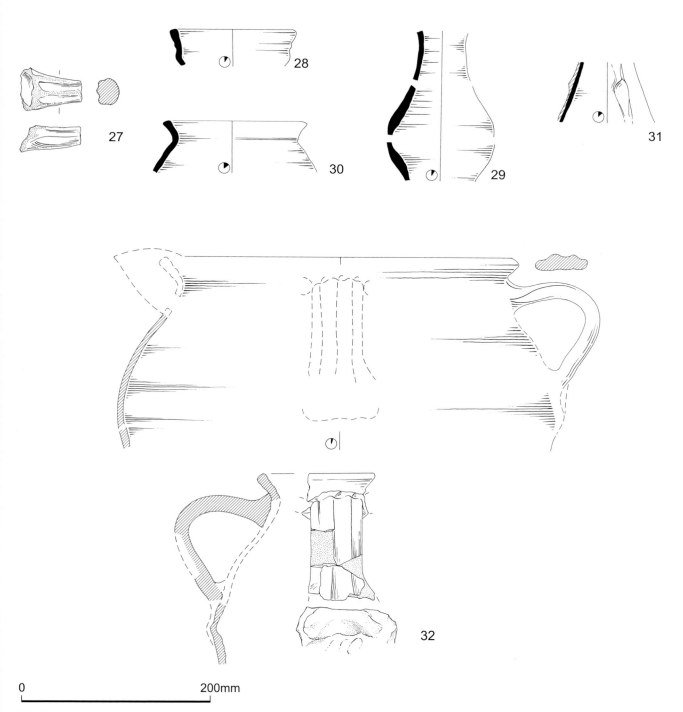

Fig. 70. Medieval pottery Ceramic Group 5: Nos 27-32. Scale 1:4 (C. Marshall)

examples of a matt olive-green glaze. This fabric type is said to occur in 14th-century contexts in York, but not in large quantities (Ailsa Mainman pers. comm.).

B22v Hard orange variant (5:5:132) 0.08% of total site assemblage
Fig. 70, No. 27
Although calcareous inclusions do occasionally occur in Hard orange ware (B22), some sherds were particularly heavily tempered with chalky inclusions. The inclusions are large and obvious to the naked eye, up to 2.0mm.

27* Skillet handle. (1:58g) *73/1; Period 3*

B23 Yorkshire Red ware (1:1:12) 0.01% of total site assemblage
No illustrations
A single sherd, glazed internally but not externally, may be from a bowl.

B26 Lightly Gritted (83:96:512) 1.53% of total site assemblage
Fig. 70, No. 28
Fragments of three rod handles were found; the rest are body and base sherds, probably all from jugs. Decoration is sparse but there is one example each of combed wavy lines, incised lines and applied strips. One example has

125

applied vertical strips in green, the same colour as the glaze on the body of the vessel, and applied pellets in brown on the shoulder.

28* Jug. (1:26g) *77/50; Period 5.1/5.2*

B30a Fine micaceous (19:36:451) 0.57% of total site assemblage
No illustrations
First recognised on the North Manor, in which publication it is described (*Wharram IX*, 189). Further finds of a fine micaceous fabric have led to this type being subdivided, with subsequent variations coded B30b and B30c. Body sherds only. Both glazed and unglazed examples were found; the glazed sherds may be from jugs.

B30a, b and c all appear in column B30 in the tables.

B30b Fine micaceous (1:12:177) 0.19% of total site assemblage
Fig. 70, No. 29
Soft powdery fabric, pale pink throughout except where wall is thickest, when there is a thin buff core. Unglazed with a heavily abraded external surface. Very micaceous, quite obvious to the naked eye. Fabric is very fine with frequent small quartz measuring 0.1-0.5mm, most being at the lower end of the scale. Red iron ore is common, ranging from 0.1-1.0mm. A single jug was found. A source for this type has not been identified but might be France.

29* Jug: possible French import. (12:177) *77/191; Period 1-5*

B30c Fine micaceous (1:5:74) 0.08% of total site assemblage
Fig. 70, No. 30
Hard, with very fine, smooth surfaces. Pale orange-pink throughout. Very finely micaceous, particularly obvious on the external surface. Background of fine rounded quartz and red iron ore, both 0.1mm or less, giving a speckled appearance. Hard white round lumps, sparse but large, 0.5-1.5mm, although may be up to 5.0mm, only visible in the break as surfaces are well smoothed. A single vessel was found.

30* Jar with upright rim and sparse tiny spots of yellow glaze which may be accidental. (5:74g) *77/209; Period 5.1*

B31 Coarse micaceous (4:6:126) 0.09% of total site assemblage
No illustrations
Body sherds only.

B33a Saintonge green-glazed (2:2:18) 0.3% of total site assemblage
Fig. 70, No. 31
Fine white micaceous fabric described and discussed by Brown (2002, 26). A single jug was found, with an applied vertical strip with wide thumbing.

The presence of imported green-glazed pottery from the Saintonge area of south-west France was recorded in the South Glebe area and coded B33 (*Wharram X*, 81). Subsequently, unglazed pottery from Saintonge has been recognised, leading to a subdivision of the original code into a and b.

31* Jug with vertical applied thumbed strip. (1:2g) *54/371; Period 5.3.* (1:15g) *54/557; Period 3.3*

B33b Saintonge (1:8:364) 0.13% of total site assemblage
Fig. 70, No. 32
Off-white, unglazed fabric, with mid-grey core throughout. Fairly soft-fired, easily scratched with fingernail and powdery to the touch. The fabric is fine micaceous with moderate amounts of small red (or, where reduced, black) inclusions, probably iron ore, varying from 0.1-0.4mm although there are larger examples up to 1.5mm or even 2.0mm. A characteristic inclusion is large white lumps rounded, 0.3-1.5mm. They are quite hard and unlike limestone or grog and most will not be scratched with the fingernail, although some disintegrate and flake when pressure is put on them. A single 'pegau' (as defined in the Classification of Medieval Ceramic Forms, MPRG 1998, 3.1.1b) was found, the only instance of this form at Wharram.

32* 'Pegau' or three-handled pitcher with parrot-beak spout. Heavily abraded with several sherds split. (2:248g) *77/226; Period 5.1.* (6:116g) *77/253; Period 5.1*

B34 Tees Valley ware (44:64:445) 1.02% of total site assemblage
Fig. 71, Nos 33-8
The quantity of sherds in this type has increased dramatically since they were first identified at Wharram, and a clearer picture is emerging of the types of vessels reaching the village. The North Glebe Terrace produced two jars with bi-fid rims; the rest are body sherds or handles from jugs. Most are glazed in varying shades of yellow, and at least nine sherds have a white slip underlying the glaze. A single sherd is white-slipped but unglazed. Decoration is varied: applied strips in red or green; applied pellets, also in red or green; combed lines, either vertical or horizontal, and comb impressions. Strap handles have deep thumbing down their length while rod handles are either plain or ribbed.

33* Jar with bi-fid rim. (1:17g) *77/200; Period 5.1. 77/250;* (1:30g) *unstratified*

34* Jug with applied red strip and comb impressions. (1:12g) *77/85; Period 5.2*

35* Jug with vertical combed lines alternating with green pellets. (3:25g) *77/180; Period 5.1.* (2:3g) *77/181; Period 5.1*

36* Jug with white slip beneath glaze. (4:18g) *77/323; Period 5.1*

37* Jug with alternating green strip and red pellets. (1:4g) *77/605; Period 4*

38* Ribbed rod handle from a jug. (1:92g) *77/1; Period 6*

B35 Light Red ware (11:11:139) 0.17% of total site assemblage
No illustrations
One abraded rod handle and one thin strap handle; the rest are body sherds. All are probably from jugs.

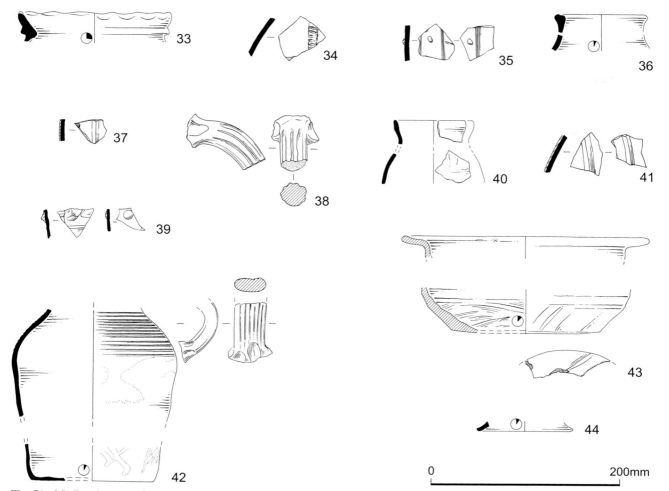

Fig. 71. Medieval pottery Ceramic Group 5: Nos 33-44. Scale 1:4 (C. Marshall)

B38 Rouen ware (1:2:6) 0.03% of total site assemblage
Fig. 71, No. 39

Very hard, fine fabric, off-white throughout. Frequent well-sorted, sub-rounded quartz, 0.1-0.2mm; sparse small black inclusions and slightly more common red inclusions, possibly iron ore, both approx. 0.1mm, the black inclusions standing out clearly against the white fabric. Two sherds from a single jug were found, the only examples of Rouen pottery from Wharram. These jugs are usually highly decorated with slip decoration in panels. They were imported into this country from the mid-13th to mid-14th centuries.

39* Thin walled jug decorated with applied white pellets over a red slip. (1:4g) *77/494; Period 3.2.* (1:2g) *77/559; Period 2*

B39 Flemish Highly Decorated ware (1:2:12g) 0.03% of total site assemblage
Fig. 71, No. 40

A bright orange, fine sandy fabric with a bright green glaze over a white slip. Fully described by Trimpe Burger (1962-3, 12-13), Dunning (1976, 184), and Janssen (1983, 137) when it was called 'Aardenburg' ware. A single jug was identified (Koen de Groote pers. comm.)

These vessels are found mainly in the south and east of the country, particularly in coastal regions, and only occasionally further inland. The bulk of the vessels in this type appear to be imported into this country in the late 13th century, but they continued in use into the 14th century (Dunning 1976, 186).

40* Jug. *77/226; Period 5.1* (2:12g)

Unrecognised wares

A relatively large number of unrecognised fabric types were found. Most were allocated to Ceramic Group 5 (coded B Unrecognised medieval wares (13:22:144) 0.35% of total site assemblage) or Ceramic Group 6/7 (coded C Unrecognised late medieval wares (5:9:238) 0.14% of total site assemblage). As on other Wharram sites, most are single sherds, and each has its own description in the archive. Twelve sherds were so small and abraded that they could not be allocated either codes B or C.

There are instances, however, where more than one sherd occurs in the same fabric type, or enough survives for a vessel to be illustrated. In those cases, a letter has been allocated to the fabric code and a separate description is given below.

BA (2:4:15) 0.06% of total site assemblage
No illustrations

Very fine buff-pink fabric. Quartz is moderate, sub-rounded 0.3-0.5mm; black inclusions, possibly iron ore, are rounded 0.1-0.3mm, also in moderate amounts. Mica

127

is quite clear in the break, as are rare red inclusions. In some examples the red inclusions are more frequent, replacing the black inclusions, and varying in size from 0.1-1.0mm. Sherds are glazed internally and externally, possibly from a bowl or lobed cup. Interior is yellow with copper speckles, exterior is more even green, although on some sherds the exterior glaze is thin, matt and dull yellow in colour with less copper. Possibly all are from a single vessel, unevenly glazed.

BB (1:4:19) 0.06% of total site assemblage
Fig. 71, No. 41
Very fine, smooth pale grey surface with darker mid-grey core and white margin beneath a good cover of dark green glaze with darker green copper streaks. The main body of the vessel has mainly common sub-rounded quartz, 0.3-0.5mm, and red iron inclusions, 0.1-0.3mm. Very fine mica is visible in the break and on the surfaces. Exterior is decorated with vertical applied strips in black. The fabric of the applied strips is rich in black possible iron filings. All sherds are from a single jug.

41* Jug, possible import. (1:8g) *77/168; Period 5.1.* (1:6g) *77/185; Period 5.1.* (2:5g) *77/522; Period 4*

BC (1:38:247) 0.60% of total site assemblage
Fig. 71, No 42
Very hard fine slightly gritty fabric, bright pinkish-orange, with occasional light blue-grey core. Inclusions are mainly sub-rounded quartz, 0.2-0.5mm, in moderate amounts and well sorted. Occasional rounded soft white calcareous inclusions, 0.5-1.5mm. Background of very fine mica. Occasional red or black iron ore approximately 0.3mm. Exterior is patchily glazed with a light apple-green colour. Decoration is thin incised lines running down the oval handle and horizontal on the shoulder. All sherds are from a single jug.

42* Jug. (1:3g) *77/209; Period 5.1.* (2:14g) *77/250; unstratified.* (6:55g) *77/255; Period 5.2.* (1:4g) *77/335; Period 5.1.* (1:4g) *77/371; Period 5.1.* (4:34g) *77/400; Period 3-5.* (1:10g) *77/403; unstratified.* (1:6g) *77/429; Period 3-5.* (8:30g) *77/456; Period 3-5.* (13:87g) *77/483; Period 3-5*

BD (2:2:111) 0.03% of total site assemblage
No illustrations
Hard orange-pink fabric, harsh to the touch, and slightly 'brick-like' in appearance and feel. Occasional off-white-buff core. Abundant quartz grains that give it the harsh feel, well sorted and sub-angular, 0.3-0.5mm, or sub-rounded when they are larger up to 0.7mm. Sparse red iron ore approximately 0.2mm. External glaze is patchy and a rich yellow colour. Only one sherd, a jug handle with a deep thumbed groove down the centre.

BE (3:10:166) 0.16% of total site assemblage
Fig. 71, No. 43
Hard fabric, smooth but lumpy and very micaceous. Pinky-buff with a light buff core. Surfaces have been smoothed out, although the exterior surface has flaked off revealing the coarse inclusions. Small splashes of yellow glaze on exterior. Characterised by very common red iron ore inclusions and white rounded possible limestone. Iron ore varies from less than 0.1-0.5mm with occasional larger inclusions at approximately 1.5mm. The limestone lumps vary from 0.2-0.5 with occasional larger inclusions at 1.5-2.0mm. All sherds may be from the same vessel, but only those that are certainly so have been illustrated as such. Two sherds from different contexts are too abraded to be certain.

43* Bowl, possibly handmade. Base has been roughly shaved with a knife above and below the base angle. (1:95g) *77/354; Period 5.1.* (1:9g) *77/375; Period 3.2.* (6:46g) *77/380; Period 5.1*

BH (2:3:14) 0.04% of total site assemblage
No illustrations
Very hard dense fabric, grey-white throughout. Fairly lumpy where quartz pokes through the surface. Slightly micaceous. Quartz is not common but quite large, 0.5-1.0mm, sub-rounded and poorly sorted. Sparse black iron ore, 0.1-0.4mm. External glaze is thick olive green with brown spots and streaks. Applied dark red (black) strip made up of the body clay with a mixture of possible iron filings.

This type has some similarities to Rawmarsh-type pottery (C11, see *Wharram VI* and *X*) particularly in the presence of black iron ore. All sherds are from a single possible jug.

BI (12:14:288) 0.22% of total site assemblage
No illustrations
Hard, orange to brick-red fabric packed full of quartz to give a coarse, harsh appearance. Quartz is abundant and sub-rounded, although some can be well rounded, generally well sorted, 0.2-0.4mm. Occasional red iron ore, approx. 0.3mm. Glaze is patchy and a purple-brown colour, sometimes over a sparse light slip or wash. Only two handles are diagnostic of form and these are either from jugs or cisterns. One is a rod handle and the other is a strap handle with ribbing down its length.

There are similarities with Brick-red Sandy ware found in West Yorkshire, dated to the late 15th-16th centuries, although this type is localised in its distribution and is unlikely to have reached so far north (Slowikowski 1991, 77).

BL (2:2:12) 0.03% of total site assemblage
No illustrations
Hard and finely gritted, like very fine emery board. Off-white interior with orange-pink exterior; surfaces wear away easily. Fabric is distinctive under the microscope in that it is full of small red inclusions, rounded iron ore, 0.1-0.5mm. Quartz is sub-angular, small and moderately frequent, 0.1-0.3mm. Occasional rare rounded white chalky inclusions, 0.2-0.5mm. All sherds are from a single vessel, of unrecognisable form.

BQ (1:1:2) 0.01% of total site assemblage
Fig. 71, No.44

Very smooth, fine, light grey fabric. Sub-angular quartz and red iron ore are both frequent, 0.1-0.3mm. Occasional small, calcareous inclusions, 0.2-0.3mm. A single lid was found in this fabric; medieval ceramic lids are rare at Wharram.

44* Small fragment of a lid with thick, good quality bright green glaze externally. (1:2g) *51/501; Period 2.1*

BR (1:1:19) 0.01% of total site assemblage
No illustrations

Very hard, buff-orange surfaces, light blue-grey core with lighter buff margins. Gritty in texture but well-smoothed surfaces. Surfaces are finely micaceous. Moderate quartz, sub-rounded, 0.3-0.5mm. Sparse but large rounded red-iron ore approx. 0.7mm.

Jug with small applied pellet, 7mm in diameter, applied 20mm below the rim. This could be accidental or it might be deliberately applied to look like a metal rivet, possibly as part of a decorative scheme.

Ceramic Group 6/7 (Late Medieval/Post-medieval Transitional)

C01 Hambleton ware (435:657:12583) 10.47% of total site assemblage
Fig. 72, Nos 45-53

There are some differences in the various published descriptions for this type. For example, Le Patourel (1979, 93) describes it as 'normally reduced and very dark grey', while Jennings (1992, 53) says it is a fine fabric, white to pale pink and very similar to York Glazed ware (see B18 above).

The type, as defined at Wharram, is as follows. The fabric is smooth, hard-fired and off-white or light to mid-grey. It is characterised by relatively large sub-rounded lumps of clay pellets or grog, which can make the surface lumpy. These vary in size from quite small, at approximately 0.2mm, to quite large, at approximately 0.8mm. They are common and poorly sorted, with most occurring within the 0.5-1.0mm range. Their colour is either off-white or mid-grey, when they can appear as dark speckles clearly visible to the naked eye. Other inclusions are sparse, sub-rounded to sub-angular quartz, approximately 0.5mm. Tiny fragments of red iron ore may also be seen, 0.1-0.2mm, but are generally quite rare.

Forms are mainly jugs but there are also bowls possibly lobed, chafing dishes, cisterns and a skillet handle. The jugs have applied vertical strips and horizontal combing, and are invariably poorly glazed, often with bubbles clearly visible in the glaze. The possible lobed bowl sherds were identified from the thinness of the walls and the internal glazing. A number of possible cisterns were identified on the basis of particularly heavy bases, 10-15mm thick; at least one is 20mm thick. Two cisterns have heavy thumbed strips rather clumsily applied below the rim, two have internal white residues, and one has a circular wear mark all the way around the underside of the base, about 10mm in from the base angle. A possible handle (No. 51) is decorated with combed wavy lines and comb stabbing. A body sherd reshaped to form an implement is described in Chapter 17 (No. 4).

There is a group of sherds which have characteristics of both C01 Hambleton and the earlier B18 York Glazed ware. The fabric is fine and smooth, but lumpy. Often a pinky-buff colour with light pink core in patches, although some sherds are reduced to a light grey colour. Glaze is greenish yellow with copper speckles, very like the glazes of B18 York Glazed ware. The surfaces may be slightly micaceous, although not excessively so. This group of sherds is characterised by large, but not very common, rounded, red iron ore inclusions which may be up to 5.0mm and clearly visible to the naked eye. Background fabric has more abundant smaller red inclusions, 0.3-0.5mm, and some sub-rounded or sub-angular white grog-like inclusions, varying in size from 0.2-2.0mm. These white inclusions are also characteristically found in the more usual Hambleton ware (C01). Quartz is small 0.3-0.5mm, poorly sorted and not very common. All sherds appear to be from jugs.

A second group of sherds has the same characteristics as the usual Hambleton ware (C01), but was distinguishable by its heavily micaceous fabric. Most sherds appear to be from jugs, although there is a fragment from an internally glazed vessel, possibly a lobed bowl. One thick strap handle is decorated with an applied strip running down the centre.

A large part of the assemblage comprises sherds of Hambleton ware, which, together with the Humber wares, is ubiquitous in the late medieval period. The differing fabrics within this type, often difficult to tell apart, suggest more than one source within the same wide-ranging area.

45* Jug with applied curved decoration in B18 York Glazed style. It has been suggested that this might be late Brandsby ware (Judith Roebuck pers. comm.), but the fabric is micaceous C01 Hambleton ware. (3:109g) *77/433; Period 5.1*. (5:71g) *77/479; Period 4*. (11:286g) *77/560; Period 5.1*

46* Jug with clumsily applied strip impressed with a double-toothed comb. (1:13g) *77/381; Period 5.1*. (3:115) *77/426; Period 5.1*

47* Jug with deeply-thumbed handle attachment; the central thumbing is a common feature on these jugs. (5:40g) *77/225; Period 5.1*. (10:93g) *77/400; Period 3-5*. (5:25g) *77/403; unstratified*. (1:220g) *77/421; Period 3-5*

48* Jug with applied flower decoration on shoulder, comparable to a jug in the Yorkshire Museum, described as Late Brandsby-type ware (Jennings 1992, 25, fig. 32). (4:67g) *77/191; Period 1-5*

49* Jug. (5:249g) *77/250; unstratified*

50* Vessel with narrow neck, lid seating and scar of handle. Recorded as a jug but possibly a handled jar or pipkin. (1:9g) *77/341; Period 5.2*. (1:16g) *77/357; Period 5.1*

51* Possible handle. Decorated with combed wavy lines and comb stabbing. (1:23g) *54/516; Period 6.3*

52* Skillet handle. (1:49g) *77/253; Period 5.1*

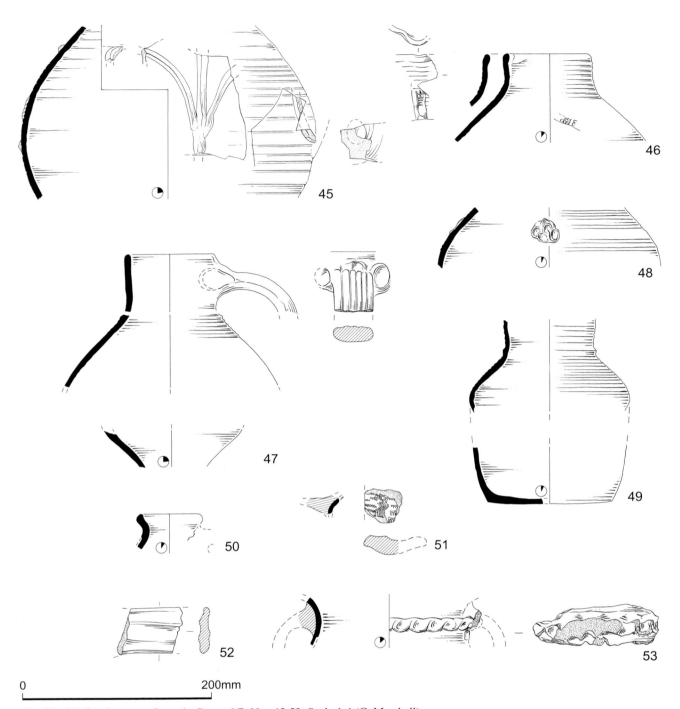

Fig. 72. Medieval pottery Ceramic Group 6/7: Nos 45-53. Scale 1:4 (C. Marshall)

53* Chafing dish fragment with pinched strip applied to the body. (1:49g) 77/324; Period 3-5. (1:59g) 54/5 Period 8.1

C01b Late Medieval/Transitional Reduced ware (248:454:5711) 7.24% of total site assemblage
Fig. 73, Nos 54-61

Very smooth, off-white or light grey fabric, with a dark grey, almost black, interior, and a thick, even, dark green external glaze. It is characterised by the consistently reduced black internal surface and distinctive green glaze. Oxidised patches may occur however, where oxygen has reached the interior, for example a cistern (No. 60) is reduced to the normal black interior except a patch inside the bung hole, which is a light buff-brown colour. There are examples of oxidised interiors, although these are not common. Inclusions are generally very fine and dense, with abundant quartz, mainly measuring approx. 0.1mm, but with rare examples of larger grains, 0.3-0.5mm. In the lighter areas of the break, moderate amounts of rounded black iron ore inclusions may be seen, approx 0.3mm. Mica is present in varying quantities, occasionally large, dense and clearly visible on the surfaces. On some rare examples the glaze is a lighter green and has the 'dimples' characteristic of Ryedale ware (see Chapter 13). The sherds are, nevertheless, in the usual smooth, black and often micaceous fabric.

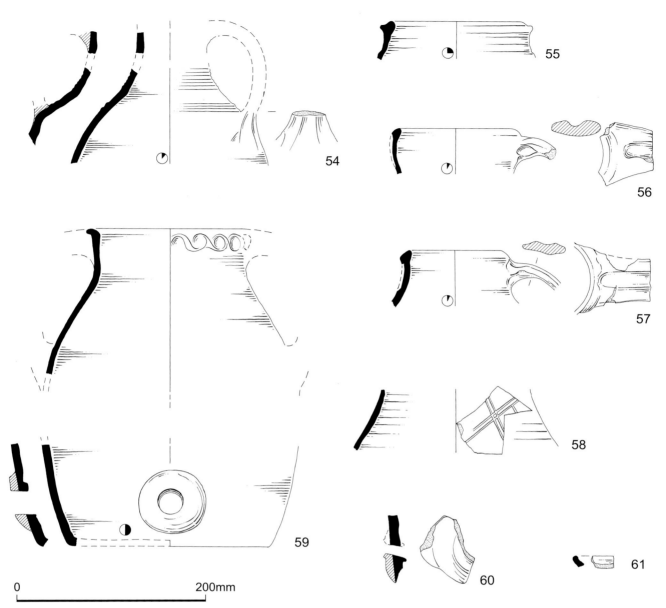

Fig. 73. Medieval pottery Ceramic Group 6/7: Nos 54-61. Scale 1:4 (C. Marshall)

Forms are more limited than those of either Hambleton ware (C01) or Humber ware (C02), with jugs predominating and cisterns making up a small proportion of the assemblage. A sherd with internal yellow-green glaze and an unglazed exterior suggests the presence of at least one possible bowl. Vessels are plain, and bung holes are equally undecorated. There are only five examples of body decoration: horizontal combing, horizontal incised lines, incised vertical lines, a lattice design, and a vertical strip in brown glaze. A characteristic of C01b-type vessels is glaze on the exterior surface of the base; there is usually a good, thick cover of dark green glaze which is so consistent that it must be deliberately applied, possibly as an attempt to waterproof the vessel.

This type appears to be contemporary with C01 Hambleton ware, and has many affinities with it. The limited repertoire of forms and the absence of decoration are characteristic of pottery of the 15th and 16th centuries, and the Ryedale-type glaze on some of the sherds suggests a possible overlap between the two types.

The appearance of this type is very consistent. It was recognised in the South Glebe and Churchyard areas but not in sufficient quantities to characterise it fully, and the sherds were recorded with the C01 Hambleton wares, albeit with a separate description in the archive record.

54* Jug. (5:310g) *77/226; Period 5.1.* (1:21g) *77/234; Period 5.1*

55* Jug in heavily micaceous fabric, with 'dimpled' Ryedale-type glaze. (1:49g) *77/114; Period 6*

56* Jug with central groove running down handle, and scar on rim. (1:99g) *54/33; Period 8.4*

57* Jug with central groove running down handle, and scar on rim; Ryedale-type glaze. (3:161g) *54/13; Period 8.2*

58* Jug with incised lattice design on the body. (3:32g) *54/357; Period 7.3*

59* Cistern with plain bung hole. (17:248g) *77/180; Period 5.1.* (31:433g) *77/193; Period 1-5*

60* Plain bung hole from a cistern, with oxidised patch on interior of hole. (1:53g) *77/479; Period 4*

61* Fragment of rim from a small bowl or salt with yellow-green internal glaze. (1:2g) *54/471; Period 6.3*

C02 Humber ware (889:1048:14971) 16.71% of total site assemblage
Fig. 74, Nos 62-68

A large quantity of Humber ware was recovered, mainly jugs, but jars, bowls, cisterns and chafing dishes are among the identifiable sherds. Jars are a rare occurrence at Wharram but at least one is a handled jar. Sherds with internal glaze are mainly identified as bowls, but glazing also occurs on the interior of some jars, and at least one internally-glazed sherd may be from a chafing dish. Only one cistern (No. 68) was positively identified, although some of the heavier base sherds may be from others.

Decoration is rare: there is one instance each of combed wavy lines, very indistinct incised decoration, a possible face mask, and a raspberry stamp (No. 66). Handles may be deeply ribbed and some, especially those from cisterns, are thick and wide. One is decorated with fine stabbing. Bases have knife-trimmed angles and those of jugs are often pinched, either consecutively or in groups. Scars on bases and rims, as well as reduced rings on bases, are common. One such scar is on a vessel with a small rim diameter of 60mm. One jug has three small fingerprints inside the lower handle join, suggesting that the handle was attached by a child.

There is little sooting, as one might expect from a group of vessels consisting mainly of jugs, but the presence of internal white residues suggests that some vessels were used for long-term storage of water. One jug has an internal black residue. Of the eight jars, only one has signs of sooting on the exterior suggesting they were used for storage rather than cooking. By the late medieval period, ceramic cooking pots were replaced by metal cauldrons, even in poorer households. Number 64, a jar with a heavily worn rim, either had a lid or was itself used as a lid.

62* Jar with spots of dark brown glaze on exterior. (1:18g) *77/127; unphased.* (2:11g) *77/132; Period 5.2*

63* Jar in a slightly grittier fabric than usual. (1:19g) *77/180, Period 5.1*

64* Jar with very worn rim, possibly used as a lid or with a lid. (1:64g) *51/986; Period 1*

65* Jug with unusual rounded profile; scar and reduced ring on base; internal white residue. (1:51g) *77/226; Period 5.1*

66* Jug with raspberry stamp, characteristic decoration occurring early in the Humber tradition, 14th century. (8:47g) *77/200; Period 5.1*

67* Jug with hole and exterior scar from handle attachment. (2:22g) *54/59; Period 7.8*

68* A particularly thick body sherd from a cistern, oxidised orange throughout, unglazed, with a plain hole instead of a pierced bung hole. (1:117g) *54/5; Period 8.1*

C03 Chalky Humber ware (88:103:1413) 1.64% of total site assemblage
No illustrations

Mainly body and base sherds, the latter are often pinched. One base has been clearly pinched with the left hand. Most appear to be from jugs, although there are a number of thicker bases which may be from cisterns. A thin-walled round-bodied sherd with external sooting may be from a pipkin, and there is a single jar rim. In some cases, particularly where the sherd is small, it can be difficult to distinguish this type from the chalky version of B22.

C04 Humber ware spoutless jugs ('Skipton-on-Swale type') (77:115:1767) 1.83% of total site assemblage
No illustrations

There is some variety in the fabric, including sherds that are softer and pinker than the usual orange-brown, others that are particularly hard-fired, and examples with blue-grey cores. This variation suggests a number of different sources and firing techniques, but all are producing the same small drinking jugs. Two rod handles have spots of orange-brown glaze. These jugs are generally unglazed so the two jugs were probably fired in the same kiln as glazed wares.

C10 Green glazed (5:5:55) 0.07% of total site assemblage
No illustrations

A small number of body sherds, three of which have an internal glaze and may be from bowls. Le Patourel originally identified it as a separate type and recorded it in her site notes as '15th-century green-glazed ware'. Glaze is generally a patchy green-brown colour, although there is one example of a light brown honey-coloured glaze. Very few sherds of this type have been recovered, and, as they are largely undiagnostic body sherds, it is difficult to characterise satisfactorily.

C11 Rawmarsh ware (2:2:15) 0.03% of total site assemblage
No illustrations

Two body sherds from either jugs or cisterns. The source for this type is the production sites at Rawmarsh and Firsby in South Yorkshire. Very few vessels from there reach as far north as Wharram, but the large part of a jug was found in the north end of Building 5, Area 5 (Slowikowski 1989, 37)

C14 White-slipped ware (2:2:18) 0.03% of total site assemblage
No illustrations

This type was described by Moorhouse and Slowiskowski (1987, 64) in the Kirkstall Abbey assemblage as 'White-slipped Humber ware'. White slip, either as an overall cover or as decoration, is not a characteristic of the Humber ware tradition and this type is therefore unlikely to be a Humber ware, although it is contemporary with it. A jug and a chafing dish were found.

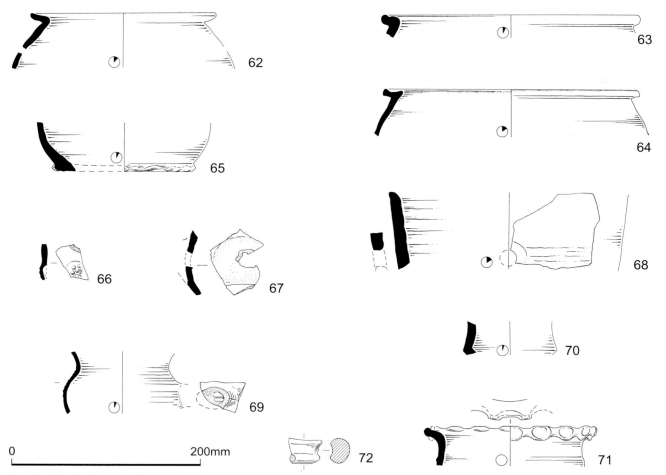

Fig. 74. Medieval pottery Ceramic Group 6/7: Nos 62-72. Scale 1:4 (C. Marshall)

C15 Low Countries Redware (2:4:35) 0.06% of total site assemblage
Fig. 74, No. 69

Dark orange–brown throughout, hard, fairly fine and micaceous. Sub-rounded quartz is common, well sorted, 0.1-0.3mm. Mica is visible on the surfaces but not in the break, although there is a background of tiny inclusions less than 0.1mm. Sparse red iron ore, also very small, 0.1-0.3mm. No decoration, but a distinctive glossy orange glaze. A single pipkin and some unrecognisable body sherds were found, the only occurrence of the type at Wharram so far. Imported from the Low Countries in the 14th-16th centuries, they are more commonly found in eastern coastal areas.

69* Pipkin, sooted externally. (1:31g) *77/226; Period 5.1*

C19 Archaic Pisan Maiolica (1:1:8) 0.01% of total site assemblage
Fig. 74, No. 70

Described by Thomson and Brown (1992, 179) as having a dense red fabric, with tin-glaze on one surface and lead glaze on the other. A single fragment of the body carination from an albarello was found. This pottery was imported into Britain in the 15th century.

70* Albarello or drug jar with decayed exterior glaze but still lustrous interior glaze. (1:8g) *77/209; Period 5.1*

C20 French import, possibly Beauvais
A sherd from a chafing dish is described and illustrated in Chapter 13 (Fig. 82, No. 70).

C05 Purple-glazed Humber ware (34:42:791) 0.67% of total site assemblage
Fig. 74, No. 71

Mainly jugs, but cisterns also occur as evidenced from at least one massive strap handle, which has the body wall pushed into the handle and the resulting hollow very clumsily plugged with a pad of clay. Jars occur rarely; one has spots of purple glaze on the interior but no sign of any glaze on the exterior. Glaze is invariably dark purple in colour, sometimes with metallic sheen but at other times a dull matt finish. Decoration is rare although there is one jug with horizontal combed wavy lines on the body.

71* Jar with thumbed rim. (2:36g) *51/377; Period ER-2*

Unrecognised wares
See Group 5 for discussion (p. 127).

CJ (7:12:154) 0.16% of total site assemblage
Fig. 74, No. 72

Very hard, almost vitrified, reduced fabric with brown surfaces, orangey-brown margins and a grey core.

Abundant sub-rounded quartz giving a coarse appearance as for type BI, but characterised by the hard firing which is unlikely to be accidental. Glaze is purple. Two fragments from pipkins or skillets and one base, 10mm thick, possibly from a cistern; the rest are body sherds.

72* Pipkin or skillet handle. (1:21g) *77/185; Period 5.1*

Quantification and discussion of pottery by site, phase and context

Farmstead sites
Site 74
Period 1 contained a small assemblage of late medieval pottery, dating to the 15th century, from sub-floor layer (341). There was no medieval pottery from Period 2, while Period 3 contexts produced a mixed assemblage dating throughout the medieval period.

Site 51
Not all the phased contexts in Site 51 could be related to the structures discussed in Chapter 5, but all the pottery from phased contexts is included in the tables. Much of this site remains unphased, and pottery from these contexts, and unstratified ones, is listed in the archive.

In the discussion of each range of the farmyard buildings, and within each period, the contexts discussed in Chapter 5 are followed by a summary of the other phased contexts.

West Range (Tables 6 and 7)
Period 1
Medieval pottery associated with the possible cruck-built peasant dwelling was recovered from three stratified contexts. Pottery from the rubble of wall 1040 is very fragmentary and dates from the 12th to the 14th centuries. The burnt layer 1044 contained a small amount of pottery, the latest of which is three sherds of 13th to 14th-century Brandsby ware (B20), however none of it shows signs of burning. Surface 1054 contained a small sherd of 15th-century Humber ware, but at only 1g this could be intrusive.

Pottery from other Period 1 contexts is generally fragmentary, although some relatively large sherds were found, up to 81g in weight. It ranges in date from 11th-century Stamford ware (B05) to 15th-century Humber ware (C02), including a lid, No. 64, in layer 986. No Hambleton ware (C01) was found, although there was one sherd of Late Medieval/Transitional Reduced ware (C01b). Among the vessels of note are two Staxton sherds (B12), a triangular-rim jar with stabbed and wavy line decoration on the rim (No. 6) in rubble layer 1036, and a body sherd with rows of square-notch rouletting (No. 8) in the fill of linear feature 1052. Both these types of decoration are rare on Staxton ware. Rubble layer 1036 also contained two forms rare at Wharram: a possible bottle (No. 2) in Stamford ware (B05), and a Scarborough ware (B17) lamp (No. 18).

Period 2.1
Period 2.1 contexts produced a small assemblage of pottery, the largest coming from the fill (501) of foundation trench 500. The latest sherds date to the 13th to 14th centuries. Among them are a Tees Valley (B34) jug comprising five sherds, and a tiny fragment of a lid in unrecognised fabric BQ (No. 44). The rest of the pottery in this period is fragmentary, mainly Staxton ware with some Pimply (B07), York Glazed (B18), Brandsby-type (B20), and Hambleton (C01b), and Humber (C02 and C03) wares.

Period 2.2
Large quantities of medieval pottery were recovered from the make-up layer of floor 471 in Room 2. Although it is all redeposited and mainly single sherds from individual vessels, the sherds are not particularly abraded and some are relatively large; nearly all weigh over 10g, unusual for Wharram, with some up to 51g. The bulk of it is Staxton ware (B12) but it includes some sherds from Groups 3, 4, 5, 6 and 7, the latest being Hambleton ware (C01), Humber wares (C02 and C03) and Purple-glazed Humber ware (C05), all 15th to 16th-century in date. The pottery in floor level 563 was again mainly Staxton ware, with the latest sherds being Humber ware. The remaining pottery has a date range similar to that in Period 2.1, but with some large sherds weighing up to 49g.

Periods 2.3 and 2.4
Context 470, the make-up level of the floors in Rooms 1 and 2, produced a small amount of medieval pottery, the latest of which is a Brandsby ware (B20) jug sherd and two sherds of Lightly Gritted ware (B26), 13th to 14th-century in date. Pottery from other contexts is mainly Staxton ware and Hard orange ware (B22), with occasional sherds of other types, the latest being a single sherd of Late Medieval/Transitional Reduced ware (C01b).

North Range (Table 8)
Period 1
Only one phased context from the North Range, the black humic layer 547, produced medieval pottery, a small sherd of possible Humber ware (C02).

Period 2.1
Layers/surfaces 513 and 540 contained only small amounts of medieval pottery. The assemblage from layer 548 was larger, but of mixed date, ranging from the 12th to the 16th centuries.

Period 2.2
Pottery recovered from rubble layer 539 was very fragmentary and mixed, with a wide date range from the 13th to 15th centuries.

East Range (Table 9)
Period 1
Small amounts of pottery of mixed date, ranging from the 10th-11th centuries to the 15th-16th centuries, were

Table 6. Site 51: medieval pottery from the West Range, Ceramic Groups 3 and 4 (phased contexts only).

Period	Ctx	Interpretation	Saxo-Norman		Early medieval										
---	---	---	B01	B05	B07	B08	B10	B12	B13	B14	B16	B18	B18U	B27	B28
1	225	Unexcavated – rubble layer						2:2:35							
1	233	Rough surfacing layer						1:1:18		1:1:8		2:2:1			
1	237	Post-hole fill						1:1:4							
1	986	Clay & chalk layer			2:2:12			16:16:90				2:2:9			
1	1031	Make up layer						12:12:111							
1	1036	Rubble deposit		1:1:4				26:26:118			1:1:7		3:3:12		
1	1040	Wall tumble/rubble						21:21:104		1:1:3					
1	1044	Burnt surface layer						5:5:40							
1	1052	Linear feature fill						1:1:28							
1	1054	Possible chalk surface						2:2:4							
1	1056	Linear feature fill			1:1:2			1:1:4							1:1:3
2.1	228	Chalky loam deposit						2:2:8							
2.1	229	Chalky loam deposit			1:1:1			1:1:4				1:1:11			
2.1	500	Cut of foundation trench						1:1:5							
2.1	501	Foundation trench fill				1:1:7		17:17:196				1:1:7		1:1:6	
2.1	566	Fill of wall trench						1:1:6							
2.1	589	Sandstone flagging						1:1:3							
2.1	609	Gully fill			1:1:2			7:7:32					1:1:22		
2.1	622	Floor repair						1:1:2							
2.1	701	Gully fill						1:1:10							
2.1	739	Gully fill						1:1:6							
2.1	905	Stake-hole fill						1:1:6							
2.1	923	Post-hole fill													
2.1	933	Foundation trench fill				1:1:2		5:5:26	1:1:13			1:1:2			
2.1	984	Clay & chalk pebble surface			3:3:5			2:2:7							
2.1	1034	Foundation trench fill			1:1:1			9:9:53							
2.1	1062	Robber trench fill						3:3:27				1:1:1			
2.2	471	Make-up layer	1:1:4		2:2:20		3:3:15	265:266:2296		5:5:17		3:3:32	3:3:32		1:1:1
2.2	563	Floor level				1:1:1		17:17:53				1:1:3			
2.2	587	Wall core						1:1:2							
2.2	1042	Foundation trench fill						1:1:14							
2.3	470	Make-up layer			1:1:10			4:4:54							
2.3	800	Floor make-up						4:4:13							
2.4	467	Topsoil					1:1:2	15:15:88							
2.4	469	Buried soil layer				1:1:4	3:3:44	26:26:196				1:1:2	1:1:6		

Table 7. Site 51: medieval pottery from the West Range, Ceramic Groups 5 and 6/7 (phased contexts only).

Period	Ctx	Interpretation	High medieval										Late medieval/Post-medieval transitional				
			B17	B17v	B20	B22	B26	B30	B31	B34	BI	BQ	C01	C01b	C02	C03	C05
1	233	Rough surfacing layer	2:2:28		1:1:1	3:3:16								1:1:23	2:2:2		
1	986	Clay & chalk layer			1:1:10	2:4:79	1:4:13								1:1:64		
1	1031	Make up layer								1:1:3							
1	1036	Rubble deposit	2:2:153		3:8:213		1:1:2		1:1:10						1:1:42	1:4:36	
1	1040	Wall tumble / rubble			2:2:7		1:1:3										
1	1044	Burnt surface layer			3:3:18												
1	1054	Possible chalk surface													1:1:1		
1	1061	Chalk rubble fill					1:1:6										
2.1	228	Chalky loam deposit													1:1:1		
2.1	229	Chalky loam deposit													3:3:4		
2.1	501	Foundation trench fill	1:1:48							1:5:32		1:1:2					
2.1	534	Roadside drainage ditch				1:1:1											
2.1	584	Foundation trench fill												1:1:58			
2.1	609	Gully fill					1:1:11								1:1:1		
2.1	933	Foundation trench fill													1:1:2		
2.1	984	Clay & chalk pebble surface			1:1:1	2:2:8											
2.1	1034	Foundation trench fill														2:2:23	
2.1	1062	Robber trench fill			1:3:11												
2.2	471	Make-up layer	2:2:7	4:4:26	11:11:78	12:12:201	5:5:23	2:2:13			1:1:8		4:4:18		25:25:312	1:1:39	1:1:14
2.2	563	Floor level					1:1:1								2:5:20		
2.3	470	Make-up layer			1:1:2		2:2:43										
2.3	586	Gully fill			1:1:10												
2.4	466	Road surfacing/make-up				1:1:8											
2.4	467	Topsoil				2:2:3											
2.4	469	Buried soil layer			3:3:11	7:8:77	1:1:2							1:1:2			

Table 8. Site 51: medieval pottery from the North Range, Ceramic Groups 3-6/7 (phased contexts only).

Period	Ctx	Interpretation	Early medieval					High medieval					Late medieval/Post-medieval transitional				
			B07	B08	B12	B13	B18	B17	B17v	B20	B22	B34	C01	C01b	C02	C03	C11
1	547	Soil layer													1:1:2		
2.1	513	Clay loam deposit			4:5:38										1:1:32		
2.1	540	Chalk pebble surface											1:1:1		1:1:10		
2.1	548	Silty loam deposit	1:1:9	2:2:6	28:28:156	2:2:32	2:2:5	2:2:15	1:1:36	4:4:33	4:4:13			7:7:41	2:4:31		
2.2	539	Rubble layer?			10:10:53					3:3:6		1:1:3				1:1:38	1:1:1

Table 9. Site 51: medieval pottery from the East Range, Ceramic Groups 2-6/7 (phased contexts only).

Period	Cxt	Interpretation	Anglo-Saxon	Saxo-Norman	Early medieval						High medieval						Late medieval/Post-medieval transitional			
			A04B	B05	B07	B08	B09	B10	B12	B16	B17v	B19	B20	B22	B26	B34	C01	C01b	C02	C05
1	410	Floor make-up															1:1:6	1:1:16		
1	411	Backfilling to support wall? Or floor levelling?		2:2:44			1:1:7		15:15:96	1:1:18						0:1:9 CC51				
1	420	Layer?							6:6:38		1:2:10	1:1:4								
2	34	Cobble surface						1:1:9	2:2:4								1:1:38		1:1:19	
2	281	Post-hole fill						1:1:2	1:1:2											
2	303	Post-hole							1:1:5											
2	323	Floor level							7:7:50				1:1:2						1:1:21	
2	335	Post-hole fill							1:1:3											
2	368	Pit fill							5:5:34		1:1:1						1:1:4			
2	377	Surface?	1:1:8	1:1:4					17:17:114		1:1:3		1:1:6		1:1:1		1:1:6			1:2:36
2	383	Shallow scoop											1:1:5	1:1:2						
2	384	Fill of shallow scoop				1:1:2			1:1:2											
2	407	Foundation trench							3:3:11											
3	263	Bank			1:1:8										1:1:3					
3	264	Demolition debris/make-up						2:2:2	4:4:50				1:1:2						1:1:25	

recovered from Period 1 contexts. The two sherds from the floor make-up layer, 410, are both late medieval.

Period 2

Pottery was recovered from a number of Period 2 contexts, mainly post-holes. Post-holes 334, 303 and 280 contained only early medieval sherds. The sherd from post-hole 303 is, however, marked 303/312 so there is some doubt about its provenance. The chalk rubble surface 153 produced two sherds of late medieval pottery, while floor level 323 and the fill of pit 367 both produced mixed assemblages dating from the 12th to 15th centuries.

Most of the pottery from other Period 2 contexts comes from a possible surface 377. The pottery is fragmentary, with a wide date range, the latest sherd being a rim from a 15th to 16th-century Purple Humber ware jar (C05, No. 71). Jars in Humber ware are not a common find at Wharram.

Period 3

The small amount of pottery from Period 3 contexts is fragmentary and of mixed date, from the 12th to 15th centuries.

Site 51, unphased contexts

The pottery from totally unphased contexts was mainly single, quite large sherds, of the full range of pottery dating from the 12th to the 16th centuries. In this assemblage is a Scarborough ware jug (No. 14), made up of eight sherds weighing 147g, and decorated with vertical applied strips and combed decoration; it was found in rubble, context 47. Post-hole fill 508 produced a relatively large assemblage of pottery for a post-hole, 37 sherds all dating to the 12th or 13th centuries, among which was a complete profile of a Staxton (B12) 'peat pot' (No. 4). Modern garden soil produced a mixed group of fragmentary sherds, but included a small fragment of Humber ware with incised decoration (C02). The design is very indistinct but could be part of a face mask. Another face mask (No. 25) was found in an unphased context on Site 54, but in the earlier Brandsby ware (B20).

Sites 11 and 49

Pottery recovered from the initial phase of trenching in Site 11 was of mixed date, ranging from the 12th to 15th centuries, and, in addition to the ubiquitous Staxton ware (B12), comprised Pimply ware (B07), York glazed (B18), Brandsby type (B20), Hard orange (B22), Coarse micaeous (B31), Tees Valley (B35), Humber wares (C02 and C03), and Hambleton ware (C01). A small assemblage in an unnumbered modern cess pit, was made up of three sherds of Coarse micaceous ware, a jar with a bi-fid rim in Tees Valley ware, three sherds of Humber ware and a sherd from a Late Medieval/Transitional Reduced ware jug (C01b).

Three phases were defined on Site 49. The only Period 1 context containing medieval pottery is infill 31, used to repair depressions in the road; the pottery dates from the 12th-13th centuries to the 14th-15th centuries. The same date range pertains to the medieval pottery from Periods 2 and 3. The site assemblage is made up of single redeposited sherds.

Site 73

The medieval pottery recovered from contexts in Periods 2 and 3, dates from the 12th-13th centuries to the 14th-15th centuries. It is made up of single redeposited sherds although some are quite large, weighing up to 58g. There was no difference in the date ranges of the pottery from the two phases. The topsoil contained sherds from two notable vessels: a spouted or socketed bowl (No. 7) in Staxton ware (B12), an unusual form in that ware, and a skillet handle (No. 27) in Hard orange variant (B22v).

Site 79

The medieval pottery comprises a small assemblage dating from the 12th-13th centuries to the 14th-15th centuries. Vessels are made up of single sherds, but these are large when compared to the majority of sherds at Wharram. Their average sherd to weight ratio is 1:19.0, compared to 1:7.8 on other sites. All contexts, however, are unphased.

Vicarage sites
Site 77
Period 1 (Table 10)
Pottery relating to the barn structure mainly dated from the 12th to 14th centuries, with the exception of 15th-century sherds within bonding material 704 beneath the eastern wall. All the sherds are small and fragmentary. Pottery recovered from the interior of the barn, from floor 716=660, was again a mixed assemblage ranging in date

Table 10. Site 77: medieval pottery from Period 1 contexts.

Period	Context	Interpretation	Early medieval		High medieval			Late medieval/Post-medieval transitional		
			B08	B12	B17	B20	B22	C01	C01b	C02
1	589	Wall		1:1:7						
1	641	Wall		1:1:6		1:1:3				
1	642	Wall/division		3:3:24		1:2:4	2:3:6			
1	704	Rubble dump	1:1:2	1:1:4	1:4:18	4:6:61		1:1:7		1:3:39
1	716=660	Barn floor		1:1:6		1:1:9	2:5:32	1:1:18	1:1:3	1:7:36

Table 11. Site 77: medieval pottery from Period 2 contexts.

Period	Context	Interpretation	Early medieval			High medieval		Late medieval/Post-medieval transitional			
			B07	B08	B12	B38	BA	C01	C02	C04	C
2	204	Levelling deposit			1:1:2			2:2:18	2:2:39		
2	320	Destruction debris							1:1:184		
2	545	Rubble & hillwash / levelling deposit		1:1:3				1:1:5	1:1:6	1:1:5	1:1:1
2	553	Demolition debris & hillwash/ levelling deposit	1:1:1		2:2:13		0:2:5 CC3	1:1:7	2:3:201		1:1:1
2	559	Burnt deposit			1:1:3	1:1:2		2:2:34			
2	561	Demolition debris			2:2:14			2:4:69 CC46, 47	2:2:6		
2	617	Wall tumble						0:1:3 CC46			

Table 12. Site 77: medieval pottery from Period 3 contexts.

Period	Cxt	Interpretation	Early medieval	High medieval							Late medieval/Post-medieval transitional		
			B12	B17	B19	B22	B28	B38	BE		C01	C02	C04
3.1	182	Wall	6:6:28								3:3:28	1:1:6	
3.1	220	Wall		0:1:3 CC14							1:1:165		
3.1	435	Robber trench fill/ bedding material?											1:1:13 CC8
3.1	461	Structure	1:1:2										
3.2	375	Wall collapse/? dumping							0:1:9 CC12			2:2:26	1:1:15
3.2	377	Wall tumble/? dumping	1:1:9									1:1:10	
3.2	494	Robber trench backfill	5:5:35		1:1:20	2:4:55	2:4:15	1:1:4 CC1			4:8:134	1:1:93	

Table 13. Site 77: medieval pottery from Period 4 contexts.

Period	Context	Interpretation	Early medieval	High medieval	Late medieval/Post-medieval transitional	
			B12	B20	C02	C04
4	358	Wall			1:1:23	
4	446	Chalk block Structure	2:2:22	1:1:3	1:1:3	1:1:11
4	575	Foundation layer	5:6:78			

from the 12th century to the 15th century, but including seven sherds from a Humber ware jug (C02). Wall fragment 589, a later addition to the barn, contained a single sherd of 12th to 13th-century Staxton ware (B12).

Period 2 (Table 11)
A small amount of pottery, associated with the fire and subsequent demolition and levelling, was of mixed medieval date, but mostly dating to the 15th century. It is

Table 14. Site 77: Early medieval and High medieval pottery from Period 5 contexts.

Period	Context	Interpretation	Early medieval					High medieval													
			B07	B11	B12	B13	B18	B17	B17v	B19	B20	B22	B26	B30	B34	B35	B	BA	BB	BH	BL
5.1	117	Wall											2:2:4								
5.1	144=168=185	Surface		2:2:20	37:37:37:320	1:1:3	1:1:1	4:5:130 CC14	2:2:48	1:1:2	8:8:115	14:15:123	5:5:11	1:2:8 CC30	1:1:1	1:1:2	1:1:8	1:1:7 CC3	1:2:14 CC4	1:1:3 CC26	
5.1	200	Hillwash			39:39:310			4:4:9			3:3:5	5:5:88	1:1:4		1:2:19 CC44						
5.1	339	Robber trench fill				1:1:12															
5.1	364	?Yard surface	1:1:6		2:2:33																
5.1	478	?Structure			2:2:43																
5.1/5.2	203	Hillwash			12:12:130				4:4:41		3:3:15	4:4:73	1:1:4								
5.1/5.2	50	Hillwash			4:7:169		1:1:21	1:3:49			1:1:6	2:3:65	1:1:26		1:1:5						
5.2	105	Upper fill of conduit			11:11:124		2:2:4				2:2:11					1:1:22					1:1:7 CC34
5.1	181	Surface deposit			9:9:49	2:2:23	1:1:2				0:1:4	2:2:2	1:2:115		0:2:3 CC31						

Table 15. Site 77: Late medieval/post-medieval transitional pottery from Period 5 contexts.

Period	Context	Interpretation	Late medieval/post-medieval transitional							
			C01	C01b	C02	C03	C04	C05	C10	CJ
5.1	117	Wall	1:1:26	1:1:3						
5.1	144=168=185	Surface	35:44:480 CC28	15:30:356	51:60:718	6:7:70	6:7:102	1:1:12		2:2:28
5.1	200	Hillwash	8:9:113	1:3:18	8:19:158	1:1:3				
5.1	478	?Structure			1:1:37					
5.1/5.2	203	Hillwash	7:8:225		8:16:415	2:2:17	3:4:51			
5.1/5.2	50	Hillwash	2:2:96		1:1:12					
5.2	105	Upper fill of conduit	5:6:222	5:8:167	4:4:191	1:1:5			1:1:2	
5.1	181	Surface deposit	6:14:313		22:22:203		1:1:6			

notable that none of the pottery showed any signs of burning. Vessels with sherds from different phases indicate how much disturbance there was in this area. For example, sherds from a possible lobed bowl in unknown fabric type BA were found in Period 2 destruction debris, context 553, as well as in context 552 in Period 4. Other vessels had sherds scattered across various destruction dumps, for example sherds from a Hambleton ware (C01) jug in contexts 561 and 617. Fragments from a Rouen ware jug (B38; No. 39) were in both the barn, context 559, and the backfill (494) of a robbing trench in Period 3.2.

Period 3 (Table 12)

Pottery from the Period 3.1 structure south of the Period 1 barn comprises single sherds dating from the 14th to 15th centuries, and, in the adjacent room, a tiny sherd of Staxton ware found in wall 461.

Pottery from within the collapsed Period 3.2 walls, 375 and 377, dates from the 12th-15th centuries, and includes sherds from a bowl in an unknown fabric (BE; No. 43), sherds of which were also found in Period 5.1 contexts. Although the backfill of the robbing trench 494 contained a mixed assemblage, the sherds dating to the 15th and 16th centuries are noticeably larger. Among these late medieval vessels is a body sherd from a Humber ware (C02) jug weighing 93g and four sherds from a Hambleton (C01) jug, whose weight totals 91g.

Period 4 (Table 13)

The medieval pottery recovered from wall 358 and its foundation layers is all small, fragmentary and of mixed date, with the latest sherd dating to the 15th century. Other contexts within Period 4 contained parts of vessels worthy of illustration in a range of pottery types: Figs 69, 71-3, Nos 20, 21, 37, 41, 45 and 60.

Period 5 (Tables 14 and 15)

An assemblage, wide ranging in both fabric type and date, was recovered from the Period 5.1 make-up levels 144, 168 and 185. The earliest pottery within it is 12th to 13th-century Pimply ware (B07), whilst the latest is Purple Glazed Humber ware (C05), dating to the 15th to 16th centuries; it also included two sherds from vessel No. 41, see Period 4.

Period 5.1 walls 117, from the major structure in the south-west of the site, and 478, from the northerly structure, both had pottery within them with a latest date of the 15th century, and yard surface 364 contained small quantities of 12th to 13th-century pottery.

The pottery in the hillwash deposits 50, 200 and 203 is only slightly less varied than that in the make-up levels, but its dates are as wide ranging.

Also among the Period 5.2 contexts, medieval pottery was found in the upper fill (105) of the 18th-century conduit, including a fragment from a Staxton ware (B12) curfew, a large ribbed rod handle from a Humber ware jug (C02), and two particularly thick bases in Hambleton ware (C01) and Late Medieval/Transitional Reduced ware (C01b), both probably cisterns. The large fragments

of pottery may have been deliberately used as part of the filling. A wide variety of vessels, dating throughout the medieval period, were recovered from floor/surface 181.

A large number of the illustrated vessels, in a wide range of fabrics, came from contexts within this period: twenty jugs (Nos 10, 11, 16, 19, 22-23, 28, 30, 34-36, 40, 42, 46-47, 54, 65 and 66), five jars (Nos 5, 9, 33, 62 and 63), and single examples of a Scarborough ware handle (No. 16), a pegau (No. 32), a skillet (No. 52), a cistern (No. 59), a pipkin (No. 69) and an albarello (No. 70).

Period 6

Two illustrated vessels, both jugs (Nos 38 and 55) came from Period 6 contexts that are not discussed in the excavation text, and a further four jugs (Nos 15, 29 and 49) and a chafing dish (No. 17) from unstratified contexts.

Site 54

Period 1 (Table 16)

Most of the Period 1 post-holes and pits did not contain medieval pottery, the exception being the fill of shallow quarry 920, from which three very small sherds of 13th to 14th-century date were recovered. Post-hole 962 (only tentatively placed within this period) also contained a single small sherd of similar date.

Table 16. Site 54: medieval pottery from Period 1 contexts.

Period	Context	Interpretation	High medieval		
			B17	B20	B22
1	920	Scoop fill	1:2:2		1:1:2
1	961	Post-hole fill		1:1:1	

Period 2 (Table 17)

Two post or stake-holes in Period 2.1 contained pottery. The four sherds of Late Medieval/Transitional Reduced ware (C01b) from stake-hole 798 may be intrusive, but, with a total weight of 68g, they are relatively large. The Staxton ware (B12) from 947, the fill of post-hole 948, could date from the 12th or 13th centuries.

Staxton ware (B12) was also recovered from Period 2.2 features, one sherd each from surface 637 and the fill (652) of scoop 653.

Pottery from Period 2.3 features is largely 12th or 13th-century in date. The majority came from the fill (643) of the rubbish pit 644, a fragmentary assemblage, but which includes seven sherds from an Unglazed whiteware jar (B18U; No. 12), two sherds from which were also found in dump 458 (Period 3.3). The features making up Structure C contained sherds of comparable date to the rest of Period 2.3. Sherds from the same vessel were found in post-holes 670 and 739 (fill 738), as well as in post-hole 666 in Period 3.1, and in the fill of scoop 515 in Period 3.3.

Table 17. Site 54: medieval pottery from Period 2 contexts.

Period	Cxt	Interpretation	Saxo-Norman	Early medieval					Late medieval/Post-medieval transitional	
			B01	B07	B08	B12	B14	B18U	C01	C01b
2.1	798	Stake-hole (cut and fill)								4:4:68
2.1	947	Post-hole fill				2:3:15				
2.2	637	Surface				1:1:6				
2.2	652	Scoop fill				1:1:22				
2.3	628	Gully fill				2:2:4				
2.3	638	Surface				4:4:16				
2.3	643	Rubbish pit fill		2:2:13	1:1:4	42:43:338	1:1:10	1:7:85 CC57		
2.3	645	Scoop fill		1:1:6						
2.3	670	Post-hole	0:1:12 CC55							
2.3	696	Post-hole fill				1:1:3				
2.3	738	Post-hole fill	1:1:6 CC55							
2.4	594	Post-pit fill	2:2:13							
2.4	689	Pit/post-hole fill				1:1:18			1:1:128	

Post-hole fills 594 and 689 (Period 2.4) contained 12th or 13th-century pottery, including a York type A jar (B01; No. 1), although 689 also contained a large, possibly intrusive, rim fragment from a Hambleton (C01) cistern.

Period 3 (Tables 18 and 19)
In Period 3.1, pottery from the levelling deposit 650 and dump 649 is sparse, and 12th to 13th-century in date. Surface 598 and the burnt area 574 within it, contained the same widely-dated pottery, and wall footing 599 (Structure D) contained a relatively large assemblage of pottery of mixed date, ranging from the 12th century to the 15th-16th centuries. Pit 579 contained two fills, 576 and 577, both with small amounts of pottery: 12th and 13th-century pottery was recorded from both the cut 579 and the fill 577, whilst 13th to 14th-century sherds were also recovered from 576.

The destruction material from Structure D and levelling deposits in Period 3.2 contained fragmentary pottery, most of which came from make-up layer 578, including four sherds from a 12th to 13th-century Pimply (B07) jar, weighing 47g. None of it is dated later than the 14th century.

Layers 480, 557 and 558 (Period 3.3) accumulated to form a surface which contained fragmentary pottery, including a sherd from a Saintonge (B33a) jug decorated with an applied vertical strip (No. 31); another sherd from this jug came from the Structure H wall footing, context 371, in Period 5.3. Scoop 542 and the fills (522, 524 and 527) of scoops 515, 523 and 526 respectively, contained no pottery later than the 13th to 14th centuries. The sherd

in the fill (522) of 515, from a York-type (B01) jar, sherds of which also occurred in features of Periods 2.3 and 3.1, is clearly residual by Period 3.3. Post-hole 552 (fill 549) contained mainly late medieval pottery which may have got into the hole on removal of the post. Deposit 416 sealed the shallow scoops and contained a large deposit of animal bone, but only tiny sherds of pottery were recovered, the latest being a crumb of Hambleton ware (C01). Although deposits 468 and 466, associated with hearth 472, appeared to have been burnt in situ, the pottery showed no signs of having been burnt.

Surfaces and dumps 458, 459, 478, 491 and 885 (Period 3.3) contained small amounts of predominantly early medieval pottery, the only late sherd being a tiny fragment of Humber ware (C02) in surface 491. Among the sherds in dump 458 were two fragments of rim from the same Unglazed Whiteware (B18U) jar as was found in the fill (643) of the Period 2.3 rubbish pit 644 (see Table 17).

Surface 1015 (Period 3.4) contained pottery dating to the 13th to 14th centuries. It was sealed by a dump of redeposited debris 755, which contained an assemblage of mixed date ranging from the 13th to the 15th-16th centuries.

Period 4 (Table 20)
Dump 603, a possible surface in Period 4.1 associated with Structure F, contained a thick strap handle of residual 12th to 13th-century pottery and a small sherd of 14th to 15th-century Humber ware (C02). Surface 528 contained a single small sherd of 15th to 16th-century date, the sparseness of the ceramic assemblage

Table 18. Site 54: medieval pottery from Period 3 contexts, Ceramic Groups 3-5 (phased contexts only).

Period	Cxt	Interpretation	Saxo-Norman		Early medieval								High medieval							
			B01	B03	B05	B07	B08	B10	B12	B14	B18	B18U	B17	B20	B21	B22	B26	B30	B33a	B34
3.1	574	Area of *in situ* burning				2:3:19			8:8:62									1:1:2		
3.1	576	Rubbish pit fill							6:6:19				1:1:1			2:2:7		1:1:3		
3.1	577/579	Cut and fill of pit			1:1:3				2:2:15											
3.1	598	Surface or hill-wash	3:4:16	1:1:2		24:24:98	3:3:10	1:1:2	58:59:359	2:2:5		1:1:11	1:1:2							
3.1	599	Wall footing							18:18:104		2:2:12						2:2:7			
3.1	649	Silty loam deposit							1:1:6											
3.1	650	Levelling/make-up surface									1:1:6									
3.1	651	Surface							1:1:2											
3.1	666	Post-hole	0:1:2 CC55																	
3.2	560	Surface		1:2:4		1:1:2			8:8:42											
3.2	575	Clay & chalk deposit							1:1:8				1:1:7							
3.2	578	Make-up deposit		1:1:5		8:14:75	3:3:8		7:7:46	1:1:3				1:1:24						
3.3	416	Surface				1:1:4														
3.3	458	Deposit		1:2:7		1:1:13			9:9:52			0:2:79 CC57								
3.3	459	Surface/repair							1:1:6											
3.3	466	Post-hole fill/hearth deposit							3:3:18											
3.3	468	Post-hole fill							2:2:14											
3.3	472	Hearth							2:2:33											
3.3	478	Post-pit fill	1:1:6																	
3.3	480	Surface		1:1:8					4:4:7											
3.3	522	Fill of scoop 515	0:1:6 CC55			4:4:10			9:10:64			1:1:1		1:1:2		2:2:2				
3.3	524	Fill of scoop 523				1:1:20			34:37:186						1:4:12					
3.3	527	Fill of scoop 526		1:1:2		1:1:1														
3.3	542	Cut of scoop				1:1:1			4:4:15											
3.3	557	Surface				3:3:15			67:71:529	1:1:2				2:3:9		6:6:80			1:1:15 CC58	1:4:23
3.3	558	Surface				1:1:2				1:1:4										
3.3	559	Fill of 552																		1:1:2
3.3	885	Surface								1:1:6										
3.4	755	Topsoil and demolition debris							8:8:18					1:30:157		1:1:3				1:1:1
3.4	1015	Surface							1:1:9											

Table 19. Site 54: medieval pottery from Period 3 contexts, Ceramic Groups 6-7.

Period	Cxt	Interpretation	Late medieval/Post-medieval transitional					
			C01	C01b	C02	C04	C05	CJ
3.1	599	Wall footing	1:1:9					
3.3	416	Surface	1:1:1					
3.3	466	Post-hole fill / hearth deposit			1:1:4			
3.3	491	Surface repair deposit			1:1:2			
3.3	527	Scoop fill				1:1:15		
3.3	549	Fill of 552			1:1:2			
3.3	557	Surface					1:2:32	
3.3	559	Fill of 552		1:1:7	3:3:4			
3.4	755	Topsoil and demolition debris	1:1:84		11:11:86	1:8:34		1:3:8

Table 20. Site 54: medieval pottery from Period 4 contexts.

Period	Context	Interpretation	Saxo-Norman		Early medieval					High medieval		Late medieval/Post-medieval transitional				
			B01	B03	B09	B12	B14	B18	B18U	B17v	B20	C01	C01b	C02	C03	C04
4.1	436	Make-up deposit									1:1:1					
4.1	528	Surface										1:1:6				1:1:37
4.1	603	Clay & chalk deposit											1:2:4			
4.1	770	Hillwash				1:1:8		1:1:40				1:1:2				
4.2	760	Terracing cut												1:1:59		
4.3	589	Pit	3:7:32	1:1:2		7:7:50	1:1:3		2:2:9							
4.3	600	Clay & chalk deposit										1:1:1				
4.3	616	Make-up deposit				2:2:15					2:2:9	1:1:11	1:1:38	2:2:4		
4.3	745	Post-hole fill										1:1:2				
4.3	761	Fill of hearth 960				1:1:3										
4.3	937	Surface			1:1:12	2:2:1					1:1:2		1:2:6	1:1:3		
4.3	963	Surface									1:1:5					
4.3	964	Clay & mortar deposit								1:1:8						
4.3	988	Silt & chalk deposit													1:1:9	
4.3	1050	Post-hole fill									1:1:1					

Table 21. Site 54: medieval pottery from Period 5 contexts.

Period	Ctx	Interpretation	Saxo-Norman	Early medieval					High medieval											Late medieval/Post-medieval transitional				
			B03	B08	B10	B12	B13	B18	B17	B17v	B20	B21	B22	B26	B33a	B34	B	BD	BR	C01	C01bC02	C04	C15	C05
5.2	138	Cobbled surface						1:1:1											1:1:48		2:2:26	1:1:1		1:2:16
5.2	209	Clay surface	1:1:1			1:2:5																		
5.2	215	Cobbled surface																			1:1:132			
5.2	216	Cobbled surface				2:2:32	1:1:13																3:3:25	
5.2	220	Cobbled surface																		1:1:150	1:1:2			
5.2	222	Cobbled surface																			1:1:2			
5.2	254	Wall																						
5.2	271	Dump of burnt material				2:2:12	1:1:7											1:1:19			1:1:5	2:3:56		
5.2	399	Surface	1:3:17	1:1:2	1:1:5	15:15:147					4:4:25	2:3:23	2:2:1											
5.2	406	Post-hole fill				1:1:6																		
5.2	413	Surface				1:1:4		2:2:3														1:1:2		
5.2	419	Construction debris				1:1:2																		
5.2	443	Surface							1:1:8												1:1:1			
5.2	452	Make-up deposit									2:3:23											1:1:3		
5.2	484	?Pit fill															1:1:2							
5.2	521	Clay & coal deposit									1:1:10													
5.2	570	Surface															1:2:5				1:1:5		1:3:4	
5.3	322	Hillwash				1:1:16		1:1:4	1:1:2		1:1:10		1:1:2							1:1:3	2:18:140			
5.3	334	Wall footing/deposit																		1:1:24				
5.3	342	Clay & chalk deposit				1:1:2					2:2:3		4:4:7	3:4:16		1:1:5				5:5:49	1:1:2	1:2:11		
5.3	371	Wall footing													1:1:2 CC58									
5.3	393	Surface																		1:1:26				
5.3	394	Wall footing				1:1:11					1:1:2													
5.3	396	Wall footing				1:1:21							1:1:7							2:5:19				
5.3	451	Surface																			2:2:10			
5.4	810	Pit fill																			1:1:1			
5.4	836	Clay surface				5:5:18					1:1:21													
5.4	837	Clay surface																			1:1:33			
5.4	838	Clay surface																		1:1:2	1:1:3			
5.4	860	Pit fill																						
5.4	882	Demolition debris				2:2:1					1:1:3													
5.4	922	Demolition debris				1:1:2														1:1:2				

Table 22. Site 54: medieval pottery from Period 6 contexts Ceramic Groups 3-5 (phased contexts only).

Period	Ctx	Interpretation	Saxo-Norman		Early medieval							High medieval										
			B01	B05	B07	B12	B13	B14	B18	B18U	B28	B17	B17v	B19	B20	B22	B26	B30	B31	B34	B35	B
6.1	23	? Hillwash													1:1:9							
6.1	377	Rubble filled feature				1:1:1																
6.1	389	Make-up deposit				1:1:3									1:1:4					1:1:16		
6.1	409	Surface				7:7:92	1:1:2					1:1:2				6:8:30		1:1:4				
6.1	431	Surface				1:1:1			1:1:2						1:1:1					1:1:13		
6.1	433	Clay & chalk deposit													4:4:11							
6.1	757	Silt & rubble deposit				6:6:27				1:1:10	1:1:2			1:1:7	1:1:5							
6.1	791	Pit fill				1:1:12									1:1:12	1:1:3						
6.3	241	Demolition debris				3:3:15						1:1:24										
6.3	243	Demolition debris				3:3:9										1:1:1					2:2:29	
6.3	245	Demolition debris				1:1:2			1:1:6													
6.3	264	Demolition debris				1:1:15										1:1:11						
6.3	266	Demolition debris				1:1:3						1:3:21										
6.3	320	Surface			1:1:114	1:1:12		1:1:6	2:2:7											1:1:2		
6.3	341	Demolition debris				1:1:2							1:2:12		1:1:12							
6.3	367	Demolition debris				1:1:2													1:1:8			
6.3	369	Demolition debris				5:5:90									1:5:42							
6.3	390	Structure J backfill		1:1:1		20:20:70			1:4:20		3:3:11	1:1:5			21:21:45	5:5:3						1:1:3
6.3	391	Structure J backfill				2:2:2					1:1:1				3:3:14							
6.3	412	Demolition debris																		1:1:3		
6.3	424	Surface				1:1:2									1:1:3		1:1:4					
6.3	437	Rubbish pit fill																				
6.3	455	Structure J backfill				1:1:4									2:2:24					1:1:1		
6.3	456	Structure J backfill				1:1:1																
6.3	462	Structure J backfill				7:7:19									2:2:5	2:2:2						
6.3	471	Structure J backfill				2:2:28																
6.3	481	Structure J backfill	1:1:1			1:1:5																
6.3	516	Structure J backfill				4:4:68						1:1:3			2:2:25					1:1:6		
6.3	520	Structure J backfill				4:4:12						1:1:2										
6.3	612	Structure J backfill											1:1:5									

confirming the interpretation of 528 as an interior surface in Structure F. Make-up layer 436 may have abutted a removed wall footing and the single tiny sherd of 13th to 14th-century pottery is likely to be residual.

The Period 4.2 terrace cut 760 contained a single but large sherd of Humber ware (C02), dating to the 14th to 15th centuries.

In Period 4.3 the surfaces over Structure F, 616 and 600, contained a mixed assemblage of small sherds, the latest and largest being a fragment from a Humberware 'Skipton-on-Swale-type' (C04) drinking jug, of 14th to 15th-century date. Surface 937 and the fill (1050) of post-hole 1051, possibly associated with the construction of Structure G, both contained early medieval pottery, but surface 937 also contained late medieval pottery, albeit only as small fragments. The fill (761) of hearth pit 960 contained only a small sherd of Staxton ware (B12).

Other features in this period contained small fragments of mixed date. Although only weighing a total of 26g, the earliest and largest number of fragments, from pit fill 589, are from a jar in York-type ware (B01) dating to the 11th to 12th centuries. The latest sherds, Chalky Humber ware and Hambleton ware (C03 and C01 respectively), come from dump 988 and post-hole fill 745.

Period 5 (Table 21)

There is no medieval pottery from features in Period 5.1.

Period 5.2 surfaces 209 and 399 contained pottery with a date range of 12th to 14th centuries, but nothing later, whilst the cobbled surfaces, 138, 215, 216 and 220, contained mainly late medieval pottery with some residual earlier material. Compacted deposits 452 and 570 sealed the remnants of Structures F and G; they contained small quantities of late medieval pottery, including tiny fragments of a Low Countries Redware (C15) vessel, possibly a pipkin or skillet. In Structure H, the wall footing 254 contained a single tiny sherd of Humber ware (C02), while construction material 419 contained a fragment of Staxton ware (B12). Its only floor surface to contain pottery was 443, in which a tiny sherd of late medieval date was found. The fill of pit 485, context 484, included a small 15th to 16th-century sherd.

The resurfacing of Structure H1 in Period 5.3 is represented by surface 451, the only one of the repair surfaces to contain medieval pottery; it is of 14th to 15th-century date. The second phase of Structure H, designated H2, is marked by wall footing 371 and deposits 342 and 322, dumped against the exterior of wall 254. Pottery from these features dates throughout the medieval period, but with Hambleton ware (C01) and Late Medieval/Transitional Reduced ware (C01b) being the latest. Pottery of a similar date was recovered from the robbed footings 394 and 396. The gap between walls 254/78 and 371 was blocked by 334, from which only 13th to 14th-century sherds were recovered.

The dumps and surfaces of Period 5.4 contained pottery with a wide date range, but included late medieval sherds of the 15th to 16th centuries.

Period 6 (Tables 22 and 23)

The make-up layers and surfaces of Period 6.1 contained a mixed assemblage of sherds ranging from 12th-13th-century Staxton ware (B12) to 15th-16th-century Late Medieval/Transitional Reduced ware (C01B). The possible internal surfaces contained no medieval pottery, but the rubble-filled feature cutting into them, 377/388, contained small quantities of both early and late medieval pottery.

In Period 6.2 the floor bedding of Structure J, context 625, contained a small sherd of Hambleton ware (C01), dating to the 15th or 16th century.

Among the residual medieval pottery from Period 6.3 are a fragment of decorated Scarborough ware (B17) with applied red pellets and vertical two-prong combing; a possible Hambleton ware (C01) handle decorated with combed wavy lines and comb stabbing, an uncommon form of decoration on this type of pottery (No. 51); and part of a bowl (No. 61) in Late Medieval/Transitional Reduced ware (C01b).

Period 7 (Tables 24 and 25)

The residual medieval pottery from Period 7.1 includes part of a Pimply ware (B07) jar with an undercut rim (No. 3), from the fill (203) of rubbish pit 207 and a sherd of Late Medieval/Transitional Reduced ware (C01b) from the wall footing of Structure K, 205; the latter joins another found in the Period 7.4 soakaway, context 75.

The only medieval pottery of note in Period 7.2 is a massive strap handle from a Purple-glazed Humber ware (C05) cistern, with the interior body of the vessel pushed into the handle and then clumsily plugged with a pad of clay.

An insignificant quantity of residual medieval pottery was recovered from Period 7.3 contexts, including, in the large mainly post-medieval assemblage in robber trench fill 357, a sherd of 15th or 16th-century Late Medieval/Transitional Reduced ware (C01b) with an unusual lattice design (No. 58).

Although there was little medieval pottery of note among that recovered from contexts in Periods 7.4 to 7.8, two sherds from a Humber ware jug, from the fill (59) of post-hole 58, are illustrated (No. 67).

Period 8 (Table 26)

Only small amounts of medieval pottery were recovered from Period 8 contexts but included some worth illustrating. Among the sherds from Period 8.1 was part of a Hambleton ware chafing dish, found in the demolition debris from Structure K (context 5); another fragment from the same dish came from an undated context in Site 77. In Period 8.2, context 13 contained a Brandsby-type (B20) sherd with complex decoration (No. 24), and three sherds from a Late Medieval/Transitional Reduced ware (C01b) jug (No. 57). A sherd from another jug in the same fabric was in the fill of pit 32 (No. 56), and another Brandsby-type sherd (No. 25), a face mask from a jug, was recovered from an unstratified layer, 546.

Table 23. Site 54: medieval pottery from Period 6 contexts, Ceramic Groups 6-7 (phased contexts only).

Period	Cxt	Interpretation	Late medieval/Post-medieval transitional					
			C01	C01b	C02	C03	C04	C05
6.1	23	? Hillwash			3:4:84			
6.1	323	Make-up/deposit		1:1:2				
6.1	377	Rubble filled feature			2:2:2			
6.1	389	Make-up deposit			3:3:10			
6.1	409	Surface			3:3:82			
6.1	431	Surface		2:2:16	4:4:21	1:2:69		
6.1	444	Silt & sandstone deposit			1:1:14			
6.1	756	Make-up deposit	1:1:8				1:2:55	
6.1	757	Silt & rubble deposit		3:3:66				
6.2	625	Make-up deposit		1:1:3				
6.3	241	Demolition debris		1:1:38				
6.3	245	Demolition debris						1:2:89
6.3	260	Demolition debris	1:1:3					
6.3	266	Demolition debris		2:2:16				2:2:34
6.3	320	Surface	1:1:42		5:5:159		1:2:30	1:1:10
6.3	360	Demolition debris						
6.3	367	Demolition debris	3:5:13	1:1:20				
6.3	369	Demolition debris		3:19:223				
6.3	390	Structure J backfill	3:3:79	1:1:4	10:11:53			
6.3	410	Surface		1:1:5				
6.3	424	Surface				1:1:3		
6.3	455	Structure J backfill			1:1:3			
6.3	461	Structure J backfill				1:1:7		1:1:36
6.3	462	Structure J backfill			1:1:10	1:1:3		
6.3	471	Structure J backfill		1:1:2		1:1:8		
6.3	516	Structure J backfill	4:4:33	11:15:228	4:4:22			
6.3	612	Structure J backfill						1:1:17

Table 24. Site 54: medieval pottery from Period 7 contexts Ceramic Groups 3-5 (phased contexts only).

Period	Ctx	Interpretation	Early medieval					High medieval								
			B07	B08	B09	B12	B18	B17	B17v	B20	B21	B22	B26	B30	B34	B
7.1	100	Make-up deposit										1:1:4				1:8:17
7.1	112	Partition base					1:1:2					1:1:2				
7.1	118	Wall footing				1:1:8	1:1:2									
7.1	125	Make-up deposit				1:1:1										
7.1	203	fill of rubbish pit 207	1:1:5													
7.1	255	Wall footing								1:1:1						
7.1	352	Slot					1:1:3									
7.2	133	Make-up deposit									1:2:8				1:1:2	
7.2	171	Floor bedding				1:1:4										
7.2	212	Make-up deposit				6:6:28	1:1:2			7:7:47			1:1:2		1:1:2	
7.3	308	Surface				4:4:27										
7.3	314	Surface						2:2:4								
7.4	75	Soak-away deposit				1:1:2			1:1:3	1:1:1					1:1:3	
7.4	123	Construction debris								1:1:2					1:1:2	1:1:3
7.4	226	Surface				3:3:19										
7.4	247	Fill of pit 240				1:1:7										
7.4	272	Surface						1:1:3		1:1:7		1:1:2			1:1:2	
7.4	350	Surface				1:1:6										
7.4	351	Surface								1:1:3		2:2:2		1:1:14		
7.4	408	Silt & chalk deposit			1:2:6	3:3:23		1:1:13	2:2:24			2:2:12				
7.4	422	Rubbish pit fill					1:1:1									
7.5	22	Wall footing								1:1:6						
7.5	124	Surface accumulation				2:2:19	1:1:2					2:2:110			1:1:2	
7.5	169	Fill of 284/wall footing				1:1:13										
7.5	202	Hillwash	1:1:6		1:1:2	13:13:65	4:4:5	3:3:8				1:1:1	1:1:8			1:1:30
7.6	167	Surface/path										1:2:4	1:1:3			
7.6	170	Conduit trench fill				2:2:9	1:1:1									
7.6	184	Compacted conduit fill				1:1:6		2:2:3							1:1:3	
7.7	21	Cobbled surface		1:2:24		6:7:86				1:1:1						1:1:30
7.7	97	Hillwash deposit				2:2:6										
7.7	98	Surface/deposit				2:2:57	1:1:5									
7.8	12	Drain fill					1:1:3									
7.8	57	Post-hole fill				1:1:2										
7.8	104	Silt deposit				4:4:14										

149

Table 25. Site 54: medieval pottery from Period 7 contexts Ceramic Groups 6-7 (phased contexts only).

Period	Ctx	Interpretation	Late medieval/Post-medieval transitional							
			C01	C01b	C02	C03	C04	C05	C	CJ
7.1	101	Wall footing	1:1:15							
7.1	112	Partition base	1:1:3							
7.1	118	Wall footing		1:1:3	1:1:3					
7.1	121	Threshold Kerb			1:1:6					
7.1	125	Make-up deposit			10:18:79					
7.1	159	Wall footing			1:1:2					
7.1	199	Wall footing	1:1:8							
7.1	200	Floor bedding						1:2:18		
7.1	203	Rubbish pit fill	2:3:11							
7.1	205	Wall footing		0:1:3 CC53						
7.1	210	Wall footing			1:1:29					
7.1	237	Clay & chalk deposit					1:1:1			
7.1	252	Wall footing			1:1:61					
7.1	273	Wall bonding			1:1:2					
7.1	305	Wall			1:1:1					
7.2	117	Hearth					1:7:18			
7.2	120	Wall bonding			1:1:9					
7.2	135	Wall		1:1:2	1:1:7					
7.2	212	Make-up deposit			5:5:19			1:1:6		
7.3	357	Robber trench fill		1:3:32						
7.3	364	Post-hole fill	1:1:2							
7.4	75	Soak-away deposit	1:1:321	2:3:53 CC53				1:1:35	1:3:26	
7.4	88	Surface deposit			1:1:16					
7.4	226	Surface		1:1:8						
7.4	240	Pit for animal burial			1:1:20					
7.4	247	Fill of pit 240			4:4:21					
7.4	269	Surface		1:2:60	1:2:12					
7.4	350	Surface			2:2:21					
7.4	408	Silt & chalk deposit		2:3:23	3:3:59					
7.5	124	Surface accumulation	1:1:28	1:1:1	1:1:3			1:1:5		
7.5	202	Hillwash	4:4:170	11:12:94	11:12:74	4:4:48				1:2:37
7.6	167	Surface/path			3:3:27					
7.6	170	Conduit trench fill		1:1:6	5:5:66					
7.6	184	Compacted conduit fill			15:15:120					
7.7	21	Cobbled surface	2:2:110		3:4:50	1:2:27	1:1:4			
7.7	97	Hillwash deposit	3:3:29		1:1:2					
7.7	98	Surface/deposit			3:3:42			2:2:179		
7.7	99	Surface/deposit	1:1:18					1:1:45		
7.7	158	Rubbish pit fill			1:1:1					
7.8	9	Pit fill		1:1:22						
7.8	16	Cobbled road surface			1:1:92					
7.8	59	Fill of post-hole 58			1:2:22					
7.8	96	Drainage gully fill	2:2:7							
7.8	104	Silt deposit	1:1:12							
7.8	110	Surface/deposit	3:3:16		2:2:35					

Table 26. Site 54: medieval pottery from Period 8 contexts.

Period	Ctx	Interpretation	Anglo-Saxon	Early medieval				High medieval							Late medieval/Post-medieval transitional					
			A02B	B07	B12	B13	B18	B17	B17v	B19	B20	B22	B26	B30	C01	C01b	C02	C04	C05	C
8.1	5	Demolition debris		1:1:4	4:4:101		1:1:2	3:3:19	2:2:32		4:4:225	1:1:10	1:1:6		3:3:90	1:4:56	12:12:240			1:1:12
8.1	17	Topsoil deposit			2:2:12												1:1:66			
8.1	85	Clay & chalk deposit			1:1:7												3:3:37			1:3:68
8.1	93	Robber trench fill															1:1:17			
8.1	102	Robber trench		1:1:7												2:2:12				
8.1	111	Demolition debris			1:1:9												1:1:8			
8.1	113	Demolition debris			1:1:1	1:1:10					1:1:20						5:15:213	2:4:26		
8.1	141	Surface deposit					1:1:3													1:1:25
8.1	150	Rubbish pit fill									1:1:8					1:1:6				
8.1	154	Rubbish pit	1:1:8																	
8.1	162	Demolition debris															1:1:4			
8.2	7	Surface deposit														1:1:6				
8.2	11	Silt deposit				1:1:8					1:1:3					1:1:4				
8.2	13	Topsoil deposit									2:2:13				1:1:30	2:4:165	5:9:257		1:1:14	
8.2	14	Rubble deposit															1:1:52			
8.3	29	Post-hole fill															1:1:3			
8.4	1	Topsoil		1:1:2	14:14:124		9:9:88				3:3:13	2:2:3		1:1:7	6:6:44	6:6:84	26:26:556	2:2:17	3:3:20	1:1:85
8.4	2	Demolition debris														1:1:3				
8.4	3	Demolition debris								1:1:25							1:1:3			
8.4	4	Demolition debris			3:3:17						1:1:2	1:1:6								
8.4	33	Rubbish pit fill														1:1:99				

151

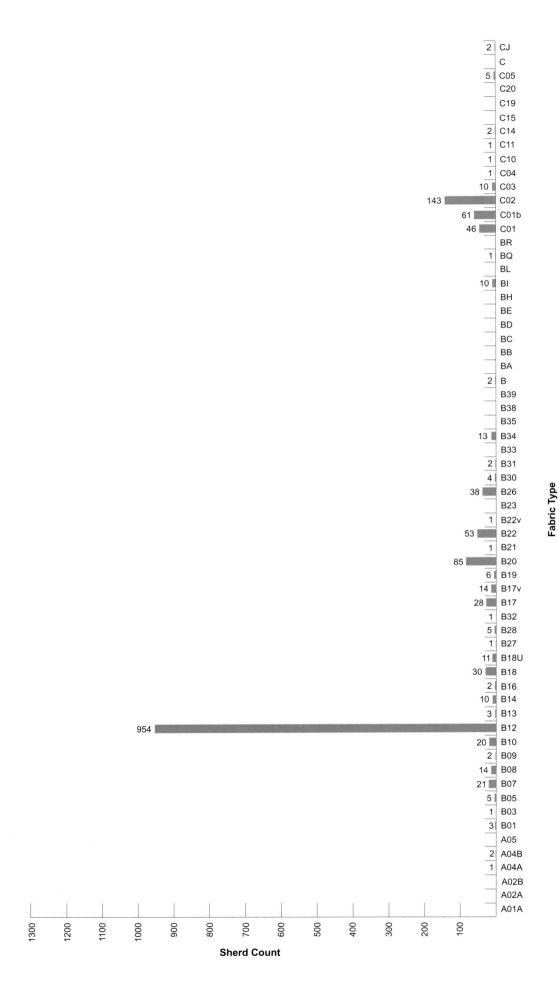

Fig. 75. Histogram of the quantification of fabric types by sherd count: farmstead sites. (E. Marlow-Mann)

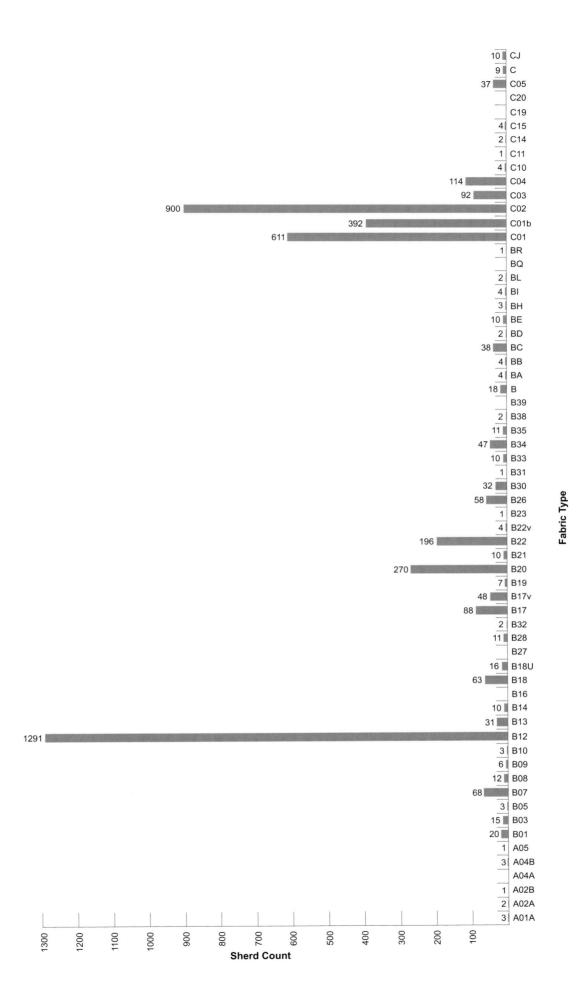

Fig. 76. Histogram of the quantification of fabric types by sherd count: vicarage sites. (E. Marlow-Mann)

Pottery discussion

Although much of the pottery was redeposited and residual, some comments can be made.

The assemblage from the vicarage area was larger than that from around the farmhouse, suggesting greater use of this area in the medieval period. Despite this the overall pattern of fabric use is similar in many ways (Figs 75-6).

Staxton ware, as elsewhere at Wharram, was the largest component on both sites but on the farmhouse sites it made up a noticeably larger proportion. Minor peaks occur with Pimply ware (B07) in Ceramic Group 4, Brandsby-type ware (B20) and Hard orange ware (B22) in Ceramic Group 5, and Hambleton ware (C01), Late Medieval/ Transitional Reduced ware (C01B) and Humber ware (C02) in Ceramic Group 6/7; these are the same for both areas. The main difference in these peaks is the large quantity of Hambleton, Late Medieval/ Transitional Reduced and Humber wares which occur on the vicarage sites. This is unlikely to be due to chronology as the same fabrics occur in both areas, and may indicate less reliance on organic materials, such as wood for tubs and barrels, in the vicarage area. It could also be the result of the function, and possibly status, to which the pottery was put. Staxton ware, although largely an early medieval type, continued in use well into the 14th, and possibly 15th, centuries (Le Patourel 1979, 84). Its function as a ceramic cooking pot was dominant in the early medieval period but by the 14th century, metal cooking pots were available to households which had not been able to afford them a hundred years before. The quantity of Staxton sherds which are sooted, indicating use as cooking pots, is noticeably smaller on these sites than in the early medieval assemblages elsewhere at Wharram. There are, however, more sooted sherds in the farmhouse than the vicarage area, 6.07% and 2.01% respectively, and, although there is only a difference of 4%, and the numbers of sooted sherds are generally very low, this could indicate that Staxton vessels were being used for cooking less frequently at the vicarage.

Although Humber and Hambleton wares form a peak on both sites, there are noticeably more of them from the vicarage sites. The forms in these fabrics tend to be for liquids, either long-term storage, such as cisterns, or short-term storage and pouring, such as jugs. All households would have had a need for storage facilities for liquid, whether in ceramic or organic materials, but it appears that ceramics were used to a greater extent in the vicarage.

The most noticeable difference in the fabrics occurring on these sites is the absence of Continental wares and unrecognised non-local vessels from the farmhouse sites. The source of these imported wares found in the vicarage sites is not confined to one country, and pottery from France, Holland and Italy is present. The pottery of France is best represented: there is a green-glazed jug, a 'pegau' and a possible jar from the Saintonge area in south-west France (B33a, B33b), a jug from Rouen (B38), and a chafing dish possibly from Beauvais (C20; Chapter 13, No. 70). There are also two vessels from the Low Countries: a jug in Flemish Highly Decorated ('Aardenburg') ware (B39) and a pipkin in Low Countries Redware (C15). A single albarello was found in Archaic Pisan Maiolica (C19). The dating of these vessels is wide ranging. The Rouen and the Flemish Highly Decorated jugs and the pottery from Saintonge are the earliest of the imports, and date from the mid-13th century. These could be either residual or long lived vessels perhaps kept as heirlooms, although they are very fragmentary and only a few sherds survive. The Rouen sherds were found in the burnt remains of the barn (77/559) and the Period 3.2 backfill of a robbing cut (77/494).

The other imports date to the late medieval/transitional period, 15th and 16th centuries, and are likely to be contemporary with the local pottery in Ceramic Group 6/7 fabrics.

With the exception of the pottery from Saintonge, which also occurs on Site 10 and in the South Glebe area (*Wharram I*, 94; *Wharram X*, 81), imported pottery is rare at Wharram. It is uncertain, however, whether this is due to the bias of excavation, with this assemblage being the largest late medieval group analysed so far, or whether it is a genuine result of a difference in status of the households. The same situation pertains to the post-medieval imports (see Chapter 13).

The Archaic Pisan Maiolica, in particular, is a rare commodity inland. It usually occurs as decorated plates, bowls and jugs, whose function was display as much as the serving of food (Thomson and Brown 1992, 183). The albarello found at Wharram appears to be plain, but as only a small fragment of the shoulder survives, it cannot be certain that there was no decoration further down the body. The main function of the albarello, however, is as a container and it is the contents that were important not the vessel itself. Although it is not possible to determine what the contents might have been, as an Italian import, it would have been recognised as a luxury.

The most common vessel forms on both sites are bowls, jugs and jars. The number of bowls and jugs from each area is comparable (Table 27), but there are twice as many jars from the farmhouse sites. Most are in Staxton ware and suggest that these continued in use as cooking vessels here for a longer period (see above). Only one fragment of a drinking vessel occurs in the farmhouse area, suggesting that other materials were being used; in the vicarage sites they make up 3.4% of the total site assemblage.

Vessels which are restricted to one of the sites only are the albarello, curfew, handled jar, lobed cup, pegau and pipkin from the vicarage sites, and the bottle, lamp, lid, and socketed bowl from around the farmhouse. The latter are in earlier fabrics (B05, B17, BQ and B12 respectively) and at least three of them are from the area of the medieval building on Site 51. They are not, therefore, directly comparable. With the exception of the curfew from an earlier period, the vessel forms which only occur around the vicarage, do indicate a difference in status, if not necessarily in function.

Table 27. Comparison of identifiable forms on the farmhouse and vicarage sites, as a percentage of the total individual site assemblages. Figures in brackets indicate only possible identification (see text).

Form	Farmstead		Vicarage	
	Vessels	% Farmhouse total	Vessels	% Vicarage total
Albarello			1	0.04
Bottle	1	0.18		
Bowl	4	0.72	19	0.86
Chafing dish	1	0.18	7	0.31
Cistern	(8)	(1.42)	23	1.04
Curfew			1	0.04
Jar	81	14.59	148	6.72
Handled jar			1	0.04
Jug	452	76.57	1904	86.46
Drinking jug	1	0.18	75	3.41
Lamp	1	0.18		
Lid	1	0.18		
lobed cup			1	0.04
Pegau			1	0.04
Pipkin			4	0.18
Peat pot	11	1.98	15	0.68
Socketed bowl	1	0.18		
Skillet	1	0.18	2	0.09
Total	555		2202	

Cisterns were identified on the vicarage sites by the characteristic rims, handles and bung holes. These diagnostic elements were missing from the farmhouse assemblage, and therefore no cisterns were definitely identified. A number of particularly thick bases were found, measuring 10mm or more, which might be from cisterns; if these are included in the figures (Table 27 figures in brackets), then the numbers on both sites are comparable. It would have been unusual to find that this basic liquid storage container was absent from a domestic assemblage.

13 The Post-medieval Pottery
by P. Didsbury

Introduction and methodology

The pottery considered here totals 20,165 sherds, weighing 230,539 grams and having an average sherd weight (hereafter ASW) of 11.4 grams. It comprises all the post-medieval pottery from the farm and vicarage sites, together with a small amount of material from the

plateau. The relative amounts and distribution by site are shown in Table 28, below. The North Glebe Terrace assemblages constitute the vast majority, though not all, of the post-medieval pottery from the village. Some material was published by Peter Brears in *Wharram III* (text and fiche), and it should be noted that relatively small amounts from other areas (notably Sites 26 and 30) are not included here, though they have been catalogued in the archive, however, two vessels, worthy of illustration, have been included.

All material was quantified by the two measures of sherd count and sherd weight, according to fabric type (see below) within archaeological context. These data, together with supplementary observations of various kinds, were entered onto a series of Access databases. These now form part of the site archive and have been interrogated in the interests of producing this report. The Hambleton wares discussed in this chapter have been quantified in Chapter 12.

Table 28. Amounts and relative distribution of post-medieval pottery by site (weights in grams).

Site	sherds	wt (g)	ASW (g)	% sherds	% wt
Farmstead sites:					
74	4002	36271	9.1	19.8	15.7
51	2033	21203	10.4	10.1	9.2
11	42	492	11.7	0.2	0.2
49	1024	19131	18.9	5.1	8.3
49/51	62	1371	22.1	0.3	0.6
15	117	5175	44.2	0.6	2.2
73	539	10193	18.9	2.7	4.4
79*	9	869	96.6	0.04	0.4
97*	9	282	31.3	0.04	0.1
Cottages/US	519	5484	10.6	2.6	2.4
Farmstead : totals	8356	100471	12.0		
Vicarage sites:					
77	402	7093	17.6	2.0	3.1
54	11373	122743	10.8	56.4	53.2
20/21	13	62	4.8	0.1	0.02
75	7	55	7.9	0.03	0.02
Vicarage : totals	11795	129953	11.0		
Plateau	14	115	8.2	0.06	0.04
Total	20165	230539	1.4	100.1	99.9

* Sites 79 and 97 relate to a cesspit and the clearance of the spring, and produced only small unstratified assemblages, included here for the sake of completeness.

Aims, potential and constraints

At the outset of this investigation, a number of factors suggested a greater degree of research potential in these assemblages than has, perhaps, proved to be the case. As virtually the only site of this date and character between the Humber and Tees in which the post-medieval deposits have been almost totally excavated, and being a rural, rather than an urban site, Wharram Percy seemed to offer the opportunity of relating the pottery to the structures in which it had been used with a greater degree of certainty than is usually possible. Theoretically, all the material consumed on site had remained on site, in contrast with urban centres like York, where rubbish disposal from early in the post-medieval period has resulted in a present dearth of ceramics of this date. The village provides, in effect, a single, large, 'closed' assemblage and thus constitutes a unique body of evidence for the range of ceramics in use on such a site, in a continuous sequence from the 16th to the mid-20th century. Unfortunately, the evidential value of the data is constrained by a number of interrelated factors. Perhaps most importantly, the funding process required an assessment of potential to be undertaken at a point when post-excavation work, including the generation of much necessary site data, was insufficiently advanced to make such assessment worthwhile, and at which the limited usefulness of parts of the excavation record had not yet become apparent. The extent to which the site assemblage lacked chronologically discrete closed groups, but was, conversely, dominated by large open groups exhibiting a high degree of redeposition and residuality, was thus severely underestimated. The high levels of brokenness and dispersal within the assemblage are reflected by the low ASWs for many of the sites (Table 28). In the event, it proved almost impossible to relate assemblages to the structures in which they had been used, and thus to explore, for example, differences between the ceramic repertoires of the farm and the vicarage throughout the period. On the contrary, the research came to be dominated by the complex taphonomy of the site and on the need to establish as accurate a chronology as possible for the various farm and vicarage buildings. This approach has made valuable contributions to our understanding of the structural sequence, particularly in relation to the successive farmhouses (Site 74, below), but it has been time-consuming. All these factors have influenced the shape of the present report, the remainder of which comprises: the site fabric series; an account of the assemblages from the farm and vicarage groups of sites; an illustration catalogue; and a concluding discussion. The illustrations are arranged in site and phase order; the material did not lend itself to arrangement as a corpus of fabrics, though it will be seen that the majority of the illustrated Ryedale Ware, for example, falls together in a limited number of contexts from Site 54 and should be relatively easy to view and consult as a whole.

The post-medieval fabric series

This section presents the fabric terminology used to categorise the post-medieval pottery from Wharram Percy. Fabrics and wares are listed in alphabetical order, according to the alphanumeric codes used to identify them in the archive databases. Each is briefly described, and references for further reading are given where appropriate. Many of the components are well-defined fabrics with agreed common names, and known production centres; others are more generic types, *e.g.* the ubiquitous glazed red coarse earthenwares (GRE, below) of northern and eastern England. The structure of the fabric series has been heavily influenced by those already published for Hull (Watkins 1987) and Norwich (Jennings 1981) and it is hoped that cross-referencing between all three will prove to be both instructive and straightforward. In the following, the code precedes the common name and any comments.

BLAK1
Blackware. The 17th-century 'Midlands Blackwares' defined by Brears (1971, 37-9). The form repertoire (Brears 1971, 37-9) comprised a range of beakers, cups and mugs, with costrels and jugs also being produced. Small body sherds can be difficult to distinguish from later varieties (see below).

BLAK2
Late Blackware. 18th and 19th-century coarsewares in red fabrics with iron-rich glazes, manufactured at a large number of locations in Yorkshire and elsewhere. Jugs and pancheons are particularly common, but almost impossible to date closely within the period. For Yorkshire manufacturers, see Lawrence 1974, *passim.*

BLAK3
Jackfield ware. The code is applied, for convenience, to a single possible example. 'Jackfield' is a generic term applied to a later 18th-century fineware with red body and brilliant black glaze, often highly decorated, first produced at Jackfield in Shropshire, and subsequently at some Staffordshire potteries. Hughes and Hughes 1968, 91; Charles 1974, 131.

BORD
Border ware, cf. Pearce 1992. Light-firing 16th- and 17th-century coarsewares from the Surrey-Hampshire border. Only a single possible occurrence was noted. Previously widely referred to as 'Surrey Whiteware', cf. Jennings 1981, 129-133.

CEROBJ
Ceramic object. This small category includes a small number of figurine and fairing fragments, ceramic bottle-stoppers and furniture castors, as well as a modern handmade mug of 'evening class' type.

CIST

Cistercian ware. Brears 1971, 18-23. Moorhouse and Roberts 1992. Fabric C08 in the Wharram fabric series.

CISTR

Reversed Cistercian ware. Brears 1971, 18-23.

CREAM

Creamware. As commonly used in the literature. Developed by Josiah Wedgwood from 1759, and in wide production in Staffordshire, Yorkshire and other locations from the 1770s. The ware continued in various forms into late Victorian times, but, in the sense employed here, was largely superseded by factory-produced 'white' earthenwares in the second quarter of the 19th century. Most, if not all, of the Wharram material undoubtedly comes from Yorkshire manufacturers. The ware has not been subdivided (but see WHIEL, below). Towner 1957; Kybalová 1989.

ES

English stonewares. These have been subdivided into eight categories, of varying degrees of specificity, as below:

ES0

General English stoneware. Assorted 'modern' stoneware, including bottles, kitchen wares, preserve jars etc., as well as undatable brown stoneware fragments. Most of the material is likely to be of late 18th to early 20th-century date, and to come from regional potteries in Yorkshire and Derbyshire. Hildyard 1985, 86-123.

ES1

White English salt-glazed stoneware. The Staffordshire products of the 1720s to 1770s. See also ES5. Edwards and Hampson 2005; Jennings 1981, 222-226.

ES2

Red English stonewares. The small amounts which occur belong to the mid-18th-century re-establishment of red stoneware production in England, not to the earlier phase associated particularly with the Elers Brothers in the 1690s. Price 1963; Elliott 1998.

ES3

Nottingham-type 18th-century brown stonewares. Oswald et al. 1982; Jennings 1981, 219-221.

ES4a

White felspathic stonewares of 'Castleford' type. The fabric was used for fine teawares at many production centres in the period from the 1780s to the 1820s. Roussel 1982.

ES4b

Black fine stoneware of 'Castleford' type. Closely linked with the above. Also known as 'basalt' ware, or, confusingly, as 'blackware'. Roussel 1982.

ES5

Staffordshire white-dipped stoneware tankards. Widely distributed c. 1710-1760. The vessels are a thicker and heavier product than their ES1 equivalents, in off-white to grey-buff clay. They are dipped in a white engobe slip, with the rim usually banded in a brown ferruginous wash. Kelly 1973; Kelly and Greaves 1974; Jennings 1981, 221-222; Edwards and Hampson 2005.

ES6

Brown stonewares which cannot be grouped with the essentially 19th-century products of ES0, or the Nottingham types of ES3. The category consists mainly, though not entirely, of tankard and bottle fragments. Hildyard 1985, passim; Oswald et al. 1982, passim; Green 1999.

FRE

Frechen stoneware. 16th and 17th-century. Hurst et al. 1986; Reineking-von Bock 1976; Gaimster 1997.

GRE

Glazed Red Earthenwares. This is the staple category of post-medieval coarseware made from the iron-rich clays which cover much of eastern and northern England. The wares were widely produced from the first half of the 16th century until the early 20th century. Brown, orange and reddish glazes are normal on oxidised wares, green glazes on reduced wares. Bichromes also occur. The wares are notoriously difficult to date within the period, especially in the case of undiagnostic body sherds. At Wharram, the category has been broadly subdivided according to dominant glaze colour, as below. Jennings 1981, 157-185.

GREB

GRE with brown glaze.

GREG

GRE with green glaze.

GREP

GRE with purple glaze. This type tends to be most common in the 16th and 17th centuries in the region.

HAMB

Hambleton ware. Late 14th and 15th-century regional fineware, successor to York Glazed and Brandsby wares, and precursor to Ryedale ware. Fabric C01 in the Wharram medieval fabric series (Slowikowski 2000, 80). A further fabric, possibly related, has been designated C01b (pp 130-31).

HUMPM

Post-medieval Humberware. Humberware (Fabric C02 in the Wharram fabric series) was the dominant regional fabric in East Yorkshire throughout the 14th and 15th centuries, and continued to supply a large proportion of the area's domestic pottery (in Hull, for example) until the late 16th century. From the later 15th century, it developed new forms of decoration, and internal glazing became much more common. It is this variety which is under consideration here, equivalent to 'Humber (5)' in the Hull fabric series (Watkins 1987, 106). The ware is hard, close-knit, and often sandy, and is fairly easy to distinguish from the softer fabrics of the green-glazed GREs mentioned above. Unfortunately, this distinction was not noted when the Hull fabric series was constructed, and the term was applied to all post-medieval green-glazed coarsewares.

LFP

Late factory products. These are the industrial products of the later 19th and 20th centuries, principally white earthenwares from manufactories in both Yorkshire and Staffordshire. All may be considered as belonging to a 'post-Pearlware' phase of industrial production, and may therefore be dated after *c.* 1830-1850. They occur in very large amounts in certain parts of the site, for example on Site 54, where they account for *c.* 62%, by number of sherds, of the entire pottery assemblage. The amount of attention which could be given to such wares was constrained by considerations of time and funding, and they were therefore subdivided into nine more or less specific categories, as below. Detailed information on manufacturers, patterns, and provenance, where it could be ascertained, is recorded in the archive database.

LFP1
Transfer-printed white earthenwares. Coysh 1972; Coysh and Henrywood 1982; Roberts 1998; Griffin 2001; 2005.

LFP2
Plain white earthenwares with little or no decoration or ornament. Fragments from the undecorated areas of otherwise decorated (*e.g.* transfer-printed) vessels will clearly have been included.

LFP3
Factory products with red/brown bodies and/or glazes. A broad range of 'teapot-type' wares.

LFP4
Earthenwares with coloured glazes and/or extravagant decoration on white or coloured bodies.

LFP5
Yellow-glazed earthenwares with white or pale yellow bodies.

LFP6
Banded slipware. Utilitarian wares, *e.g.* bowls, mugs and chamberpots, with coloured (blue, brown, white, green) slip bands, often on a yellow ground, in which case they are banded variants of LFP5. 'Mocha' decoration is common on such wares. They were produced at many centres, *e.g.* the Don Pottery under Barker ownership (Griffin 2001, who refers to 'banded' decoration).

LFP7
Sponged ware. Another cheap, utilitarian white earthenware in which the decoration, in garish colours, is applied with a 'loose' or a 'cut' sponge. The former produces an amorphous, watery effect, such products being referred to as 'spatter ware' in the United States of America. The latter can be used to produce more rigid designs, usually geometric or floral. Both types occur at Wharram Percy. The ware was produced at many centres in England and Scotland from *c.* 1820 onwards. Davey 1999, 287 provides a useful introduction to the ware.

LFP8
Lustreware. Hughes and Hughes 1968,103-106; Shaw 1973; Baker 1984; Gibson 1999.

LFP9
Commemorative mugs.

MCAMP

Martincamp flasks. These are flattened flasks in both earthenware and stoneware produced in the region of Martincamp in Normandy, exported to Britain between the late 15th century and the 17th century. Hurst *et al.* (1986, 102-104) distinguish three types (I-III) with different date-ranges, but it is often in practice almost impossible to apply their ware, form and colour definitions to individual sherds.

MYEL

Midland Yellow ware. A range of cups, bowls, handled cooking vessels and other forms, such as candlesticks and ointment pots, in light-firing clay with egg-yolk yellow glazes. Production began on a small scale in the second half of the 16th century. The ware was widely distributed in the first half of the 17th century, and on the decline in many areas thereafter, being superseded by the superior yellow-glazed Staffordshire Slipwares. Woodfield 1963-4; Brears 1971, 31-37.

PEARL

Pearlware. A fine, blue-tinted white earthenware first developed by Josiah Wedgwood in 1779 and produced widely until the second quarter of the 19th century. The heyday of Pearlware was probably over by *c.* 1830 but the ware was produced for many years afterwards. The type has been subdivided into six varieties. Hume (1991, 128-133) provides a useful introductory account and suggests a broad dating scheme, though this should not be applied too rigidly. The ware was produced at most of the main Yorkshire potteries of the period, *e.g.* Castleford (Roussel 1982), Don (Griffin 2001), Leeds (Griffin 2005).

PEARL1
Underglaze hand-painted in blue.

PEARL2
Underglaze hand-painted with polychrome enamels.

PEARL2a
As PEARL2, but with overglaze enamelling.

PEARL3
Transfer-printed.

PEARL4
With engine-turned (chequer-band) decoration.

PEARL5
Other, including plain fragments, blue shell-edged vessels etc.

PMLOC
Post-medieval local coarsewares. A small number of vessels which could not be attributed to Ryedale, Glazed Red Earthenware, or other named fabrics, has been gathered together under this head.

PORC
Porcelains and bone china. Constraints upon time and funding dictated that this category was neither subdivided nor studied in detail. Specialist opinion was sought only in regard to two sherds of suspected Chinese porcelain (see discussion of the assemblage from Site 54, Structure J, below). Thanks are due to Mr Ben Cooper for kindly identifiying these.

PURP
Purple-glazed earthenwares. This category includes a very small number of sherds which could not be accommodated in GREP. They were generally harder, and the group possibly includes fragments from theHumberware and Midland Purple fabric spectra.

RAER
Raeren stoneware. Late 15th and 16th-century. Hurst *et al.* 1986; Reineking-von Bock 1976; Gaimster 1997.

RYED
Ryedale ware. This is the dominant '17th-century' regional coarseware, manufactured at a number of centres in the Howardian Hills, south of the river Rye. These include Coxwold, Gilling East, Grimstone Manor Farm and Stearsby. The ware first appears in Hull in later 16th-century groups and occurs throughout the 17th century. Jennings and Boyles (1995, 228) suggest an early 18th-century end for the industry. Useful accounts occur in Jennings and Boyles (1995); Hayes 1978; Earnshaw and Watkins 1984; Watkins 1987, 113-14.

STAFS
Staffordshire slipwares. These have been subdivided into the following three categories:

STAFS1
A general category embracing most varieties of the familiar late 17th and 18th-century Staffordshire product, including vessels with combed, jewelled, feathered and trailed decoration, as well as press-moulded flatwares. Celoria and Kelly 1973; Jennings 1981, 104ff; Kelly and Greaves 1974; Wondrausch 1986.

STAFS2
Staffordshire Black-dipped ware. A slipware in which the exterior surface is glazed 'black' or very dark brown, upon which white slip decoration is then applied. Watkins 1987, 123 (Decorated Black-Dipped Ware); Jennings 1981, 106 ('hollow-wares with brown slip').

STAFS3
Staffordshire manganese mottled wares. Jennings 1981, 106 ('Staffordshire mottled ware'); Kelly and Greaves 1974 ('lead/manganese glazed ware').

SYG
South Yorkshire gritty ware. Late medieval to early post-medieval South Yorkshire Coal Measure fabrics of the type made, for example, at Rawmarsh and Firsby in the 14th to 16th centuries. Hayfield and Buckland 1989; Watkins 1987. Fabric C11 in the Wharram fabric series.

TIN
Tin-glazed earthenwares ('Delftware'). English and Netherlandish, 17th and 18th-century. The category has not been subdivided, though probable sources of some vessels, as well as decorative and form details, are recorded in the database. The terms 'majolica' and 'faience' are used to distinguish, respectively, (flatware) vessels with tin-glaze on the upper surface only (and lead-glaze on the underside), and vessels with overall tin-glaze (cf. Bartels 1999, 418-19). Jennings 1981, 187-216; Korf 1968; 1973; Garner and Archer 1972; Archer 1997. Fabric C13 in the Wharram fabric series.

TRSL
Trailed slipwares of essentially 17th-century date and 'metropolitan' type, though undoubtedly from more local sources. They are essentially slip-decorated variants of GRE. Cf. Watkins 1987, 117.

UCD
Unattributed chafing dish. Only a single vessel falls into this category. See Fig. 82, No. 70.

UGRE
Unglazed red earthenwares. The category is restricted to flowerpots and occasional other forms in similar fabrics.

UNAT
Unattributed to fabric and/or period.

UNATSLIP
Unattributed post-medieval slipware. A small amount of material which could not be assigned to the major named slipware categories (STAFS1-3, TRSL, WHDIP) has been gathered together under this head.

WESER

Weser slipware, made at several centres in the region of the river Weser, in Germany, the main export period being c. 1590-1620. Hurst *et al.* 1986, 250-59.

WEST

Westerwald stoneware. Hurst *et al.* 1986; Reineking-von Bock 1976; Gaimster 1997.

WHDIP

White-dipped wares. These are usually GRE open forms (particularly large bowls/pancheons) in which the interior has been coated with white slip before glazing, producing a yellow colour. Such vessels were made at a large number of potteries in Yorkshire, Staffordshire and elsewhere from the later 18th century to earlier 20th century. Watkins 1987, 123.

WHIEL

Whieldon-type wares. Following common practice, the term is used here to denote cream-coloured bodies with multi-coloured 'tortoiseshell' glazes, produced during the second half of the 18th, and early 19th, centuries, particularly in Staffordshire. In fact, Thomas Whieldon made many other kinds of ware, while tortoiseshell wares were produced by many other potters. Hughes and Hughes 1968, 157; Jennings 1981, 228-229.

The farmstead sites

Site 74

Study of the pottery from Site 74 has led to significant changes in the previously published interpretation and dating of the farmhouse sequence (Beresford and Hurst 1990, 110ff). The idea of a 16th-century farmhouse is not supported by the ceramic evidence. Not only are there no deposits in which the latest pottery is of this date, but the entire site assemblage, including unstratified material, contains almost no definitively 16th-century pottery; there is, for example, only a single sherd of Cistercian Ware. This is inconsistent with what one might expect to have been redeposited in the vicinity if a farmhouse of this date had been sited here.

This assumed building was held to have been succeeded by a 17th-century farmhouse, and then by one dated to the 18th and early 19th centuries. This is now seen to have been erroneous. The Period 2/3 farmhouse must probably be seen as having been founded before the end of the 17th century but with most of its occupation in the 18th; while the Period 4/5 farmhouse must have been built in the opening years of the 19th century. This interpretation receives a great deal of support from a re-examination of the documentary evidence.

The following sections marshal the principal evidence in phase order. A simplified fabric profile of the whole site assemblage is presented in Table 29.

Table 29. Site 74: simplified fabric profile.

Fabric	% no. sherds	% weight
BLAK1/BLAK2	0.04	0.02
BLAK2	3.8	6.1
CEROBJ	0.2	0.2
CIST	0.02	0.1
CREAM	9.1	7.5
ES0	5.1	7.8
ES1	1.4	0.6
ES2	0.04	-
ES3	0.2	0.1
ES4b	0.02	0.01
ES5	0.1	0.2
ES6	0.9	1.5
FRE	0.02	0.02
GREB	3.9	6.2
GREG	5.5	16.0
GREP	0.4	0.2
HAMB	0.1	0.2
HUMPM	0.02	0.3
LFPs	32.4	12.5
MYEL	0.02	0.1
PEARLs	16.1	5.8
PMLOC	0.6	4.6
PORC	2.9	1.1
RAER/WEST	0.02	0.01
RYED	8.3	22.7
STAFS1-3	3.1	1.6
TIN	2.8	1.5
TRSL	0.1	0.1
UGRE	0.5	0.4
UNAT	0.1	0.03
WESER	0.02	0.04
WEST	0.1	0.02
WHDIP	1.1	2.5
WHIEL	0.3	0.1
TOTAL	99.3	100.2

Period 1

Only two pottery-bearing contexts occur in Period 1. Not only do these not support the idea of a 16th-century farmhouse, but each poses serious dating problems, as will be evident below.

Layer 360, *possibly* situated beneath the tiled floor of the Period 2 building, contained a small, poor quality assemblage of three body sherds. The largest (22 grams) was Ryedale Ware or Green-Glazed Red Earthenware, broadly of 17th-century date. Two further fragments (2 grams each) were Staffordshire Slipware and Creamware. Creamware of the type represented (Queen's Shape) first occurs in the period *c.* 1760-1780 and is probably best dated to the last third of the 18th century, which provides a broad *terminus post quem* for emplacement of this deposit. Unfortunately, some doubt attaches to the provenance of this sherd – it is clearly marked '360', though had been mis-bagged. Even if this sherd is discounted, the Staffordshire Slipware remains to provide a very late 17th or earlier 18th-century *terminus post quem*.

Layer 341, interpreted as a sub-base for the floor of the Period 2 farmhouse, is even more obviously problematical. It contained eight residual medieval sherds and 73 post-medieval. The earliest post-medieval material is probably 17th-century Ryedale Ware, but there are also 18th-century Tin-Glazed Earthenwares (Fig. 78, No. 1) and Staffordshire Slipwares and late 18th to early 19th-century Creamware (Fig. 78, No. 2), porcelains and Pearlware. A date in the period *c.* 1790-1820 seems to be indicated for most of the finer wares, though the associated coarsewares (Glazed Red Earthenwares and White-Dipped Ware) probably take the deposit even further into the 19th century. Two clay tobacco pipe fragments from the layer are dated 1800-1880 (Chapter 18, No. 46 and not illustrated).

Period 2

This is held to be the construction phase of a 17th-century farmhouse, possibly the one known from the will of William Botterell to have been in existence in 1699.

Internal deposits containing pottery were mainly floor bedding layers etc.: 323, 342, 344, 345 and 363.

The most important deposit in this group is 323, the sand bedding for the flagstone floor in Room B. It contained twelve sherds (89 grams) deriving from two different Staffordshire Slipware handled hollow forms (Fig. 78, Nos 3 and 4) and sherds of plain white Tin-Glazed Earthenware. The latter are not closely datable. The Staffordshire-type vessels probably date to the very late 17th or early 18th century, an opinion based on the fact that the handles are press-moulded 'ear' types resembling those on Tin-Glazed porringers of the period. Staffordshire vessels equipped with such handles, as well as moulds for producing them, are associated with the Albion Square kiln in Hanley, Stoke-on-Trent, Staffordshire, for which a date of *c.* 1690-1714 might be appropriate (Celoria and Kelly 1973, 3).

The remaining internal layers typically contain small assemblages consisting of Ryedale and Brown-Glazed or Green-Glazed Red Earthenwares (Fig. 78, No. 5). The latter are essentially undatable. Ryedale, which occurs in all of these deposits except 363, is usually taken as a 17th-century type-fossil, but has a probable overall date-range from the last quarter of the 16th century to the first quarter of the 18th century. A possible flowerpot rim in Unglazed Red Earthenware also occurs, in 344, but the dating implications of this sherd are uncertain.

Ash-pit 319, in Room B, poses a more defined problem, in that its fill 320 contains a single sherd of heavily burned plain white earthenware, either PEARL5 or LFP2, but almost certainly of 19th-century date.

In summary, all these layers could have been emplaced in the 17th or early 18th century, though this must probably be narrowed in the case of 323 to the *very late* 17th or early 18th century. All are probably acceptable in a house known to have been in existence in 1699. If these are the *original* floor bedding deposits, the house may have been of quite recent build when mentioned in the will of that date.

Various external deposits have also been allocated to this period: 219, 271, 278, 300 and 321.

In yard 219 (22 sherds, 119 grams) Ryedale is completely absent, and all the diagnostic products are 18th and early 19th-century in date. The latest products are Creamware and Pearlware, suggesting a closing date for the assemblage of *c.* 1800 or somewhat later.

Surface 278 contained eight sherds, ranging in date from the 17th century (Ryedale) probably to the later 19th century (Transfer-Printed Whiteware and modern brown stonewares).

Chalk bank 300 has 24 sherds, perhaps ranging in date from the 16th century, through the 17th and 18th, to the mid/late 19th: Late Humberware, Ryedale, White English Salt-Glazed Stoneware (Fig. 78, Nos 6 and 7), Modern Stoneware, Pearlware, Late Blackware, Factory-Produced Whitewares, and the usual Green-Glazed and Brown-Glazed Red Earthenwares.

Wall tumble or surface 321 had 25 sherds. With the exception of a residual medieval sherd, and examples of 18th-century Staffordshire Slipware and White English Salt-Glazed Stoneware, the assemblage consists of 19th-century material, almost certainly extending into the middle or second half of the century (Pearlware, Modern Stoneware, Porcelain, Sponged Ware, Late Blackware, Banded Slipware and Transfer-Printed Whitewares). A clay tobacco pipe fragment was dated 1660-1690 (Chapter 18, No. 19).

It will be noted that the external deposits are consistently different, in containing 19th-century material, from the internal ones.

Period 3

The Period is held to represent occupation of the Period 2 farmhouse, though the evidential value of the pottery assemblage is limited, since the pottery-bearing contexts, listed below, are almost entirely external deposits. These include levelling layers, downwash deposits, and garden soils: 106*, 165*, 230*, 238*, 255*, 263*, 264*, 277*, 287, 299*, 301, 320*, 362, 374, and 376.

Period 3 contexts clearly consistently end around the beginning of the 19th century, or even later. Asterisked contexts in the list above all have Creamware and/or Pearlware as their latest diagnostic contents. In some cases, coarsewares which might take the closing date further into the 19th century are also present, while chalk

161

gravel layers 106 and 165 may be noted as probably also containing earlier 20th-century material.

Context 374, described as 'worn chalk and sandstone blocks overlying threshold flags', presumably of the Period 2 farmhouse, produced a small assemblage apparently entirely of 17th-century date, comprising seven sherds of Ryedale Ware and two of Tin-Glazed Earthenware.

Two contexts appear to contain only 17th and 18th-century material: soil 287 (Fig. 78, No. 8), and area of burning (?) 362 (Fig. 78, No. 9), the former containing clay tobacco pipe fragments of 1640-1660 (Chapter 18, Nos 4 and 7).

The large assemblages from chalk gravel layers 106 and 165 (with 354 and 134 sherds respectively) contain a wide chronological range of material, including products which are of interest in casting light on the range and quality of products reaching Wharram in the 17th and 18th centuries, including Tin-Glazed Earthenwares, Weser Slipware and Red English Stoneware. Cf. from these layers, Fig. 78, Nos 10-20. For other illustrated material from Period 3, see Fig. 79, Nos 21 and 22. Four of the five clay tobacco pipe fragments from 106 had a maximum date-range of 1630-1690 (Chapter 18, Nos 2, 5, 12 and one not illustrated).

Periods 4 and 5

The Period 4/5 farmhouse appears to be that known to have been built after 1806 and demolished at some time between 1830 and 1850-1851. Period 4 represents the construction stage and Period 5 the building's use, though there is little ceramic evidence relating to the latter.

Evidence for the date of construction comes from fills 259, 284, 335 and 347 of the building's wall foundation cuts. The evidence is relatively poor and much of the material very small and fragmentary.

The largest assemblage (22 sherds) is from 284, which has 17th and 18th-century material (including clay tobacco pipes of 1640-1660, Chapter 18) but ends with Late Blackware fragments of the late 18th or 19th century.

The remaining contexts contained Transfer-Printed Whitewares (early to mid-19th century onwards) or stonewares of apparently 19th-century date.

The fabric of wall 130 contained a single small fragment of very late 18th or early 19th-century Pearlware (PEARL3) or Transfer-Printed Whiteware.

The fabric of wall 154 contained a single fragment of Lustre Ware (LFP8) and two of transfer-printed Pearlware (PEARL3). The former is Purple ('Gold') lustre, which seems to have been produced from *c.* 1807 (Gibson 1999, 7-8); it thus provides a *terminus post quem* for incorporation into the build. The ware was manufactured in large quantities throughout the 19th century, though particularly in the first third.

Both walls contained residual clay tobacco pipe fragments of 1660-1680 (Chapter 18, No. 15 and others not illustrated).

Room 1

The Room 1 floor was made up of layer 199 surfaced by layer 232. The lower deposit had two sherds of residual 17th-century Ryedale Ware, and twelve Creamware, Pearlware and Late Blackware. The Pearlware includes a *standard* Willow Pattern print, providing a *terminus post quem* for emplacement in the period *c.* 1800-1810 (Coysh and Henrywood 1982, 402). The upper layer contained a further three sherds of Pearlware (PEARL3) and an undatable Green-Glazed Red Earthenware.

Fill 181 of Period 4 ash-pit 196 contained a single tiny burned fragment of Pearlware or Transfer-Printed Whiteware, and clay pipe fragments dated 1800-1840 (Chapter 18, No. 29) and 1800-1900 (not illustrated). (Cf. fill 320 of earlier Period 2 ash-pit 319, which also contained a single small burned fragment of 19th-century whiteware).

Oven 228 was situated over a layer of pea grit (237). An assemblage of eight sherds, the latest material in which is certainly of at least early 19th-century date, is marked '237'; unfortunately, a note on the packaging queries whether the pottery has been attributed to the right context, and the material cannot therefore be relied on.

Room 2

Partition wall 104 incorporated three small fragments of Pearlware and porcelain in its build.

Deposit 102, described as a floor or floor make-up layer, produced a large deposit of 89 sherds, ranging in date from the 16th century to the later 19th or early 20th century. It includes at least twenty late 18th or early 19th-century Creamware sherds and White Salt-Glazed English Stoneware (Fig. 79, No. 23) but Late Blackware, White-Dipped Ware and, particularly late stonewares (ES0), take the deposit much later ('Bristol'-type glazes and possibly a fragment of 'marmalade jar'). This at least suggests contamination after demolition of the building, in which regard it is appropriate to note a cross-contextual join with Period 6 context 156.

Room 6

Deposits 339 and 340 are interpreted as bedding layers for the farmhouse foundations.

The lower deposit, 339, contained eight sherds, the majority once again comprising Creamware, Pearlware/Transfer Printed Whiteware, Late Blackware and Glazed Red Earthenwares, providing a *terminus post quem* in the early 19th century.

The higher deposit, 340, had a single sherd of Creamware.

Room 3

Ash-pit 223 produced two sherds from a Pearlware (PEARL3) cup or tea-bowl. Since these are attributed to the cut number, rather than to a fill, they were presumably incorporated into the build, for which a *terminus post quem* centred on *c.* 1800 is therefore indicated. It may be noted that a sherd with the same pattern (vermicelli border with stylised floral designs) occurs in the Period 5 floor-packing material (context 211). The uppermost fill of the ash pit, supposed to consist of demolition rubble, was 224. This contained a handled bowl (LFP4) which is certainly of later 19th and possibly of 20th-century date. It may be noted that the pit is described as having had a 'slate' base. If Welsh slate is meant, then the base probably could not have been installed before the 1840s at the earliest. Its presence therefore suggests construction, or refurbishment, of this feature towards the end of the farmhouse's life.

Deposit 242, in the northern part of the room, is one of a series described as either demolition material or floor make-up. It contained two sherds, an undatable Green-Glazed Red Earthenware and, once again, a Pearlware (PEARL 3) saucer.

Layer 310 (Period 5) was on the outside of the east wall of this room and is interpreted as a possible path. Its 21 sherds are all of late 18th and 19th-century date, comprising Creamware, Pearlware, Porcelain, Late Blackware, Modern Stoneware, and Green-Glazed Red Earthenwares. The Modern Stoneware provides a possible cross-contextual join with floor-base 314 in Room 5 (q.v., below).

Room 4

Layers 211 and 244 are interpreted as make-up for the floor. They produced between them 29 sherds. An early 19th-century component is represented by Creamware and Pearlware (PEARL2 and PEARL3) while 'modern' rouletted brown stoneware (ES0) and Banded Slipware (LFP6) probably take the deposit into the second half of the 19th century. At least three *possible* joins between upper surface 211 and other contexts were noted: a Creamware plate from floor-base 314 in Room 5 (Fig. 79, No. 24); Pearlware (PEARL2) in the fill of construction cut 334 for partition wall 141 (Fig. 79, No. 25); and Pearlware (PEARL3) in ash pit 223.

Room 5

Deposit 267, a raised layer in one corner of the room, has been interpreted as possible demolition material, presumably of the Period 2/3 farmhouse, used as make-up. The pottery assemblage was, however, heavily dominated by early 19th-century Creamware and Pearlware, while Glazed Red Earthenwares, Late Blackware and modern stoneware (ES0) may take the deposit even later.

Floor base 314 provided a large assemblage of 137 sherds. Once again, the majority consisted of Creamware and Pearlware (74 and 37 sherds respectively; Fig. 79, No. 40), a clay tobacco pipe fragment dated 1770-1800 being broadly contemporary (not illustrated). Other, and possibly somewhat later, '19th-century' wares included Porcelain, Modern Stoneware and White-Dipped Ware. There is only a small 17th/18th-century component of thirteen sherds, comprising Ryedale, Tin-Glazes, White English Salt-Glazed Stoneware and Staffordshire Slipware. There are cross-contextual joins to Period 4 context 339, and probably to 321 (Period 2), 211 (Period 5) and 226 (Period 6).

Room 7

Deposit 267, which extends from Room 5, has already been considered.

For other illustrated vessels from these periods see Figs 79 and 80, Nos 33 and 41.

Period 6

Pottery was recovered from some sixty contexts in this phase, considered to represent the demolition phase of the Period 4/5 farmhouse and its subsequent use as gardens and for rubbish disposal. The area was considered too disturbed to warrant treatment in the excavation narrative, though all pottery is fully quantified and described in the site archive. As might be expected, a wide range of material was recovered, much of it of 19th-century date. Clay tobacco pipes from the phase were also almost entirely of 19th-century date, a majority of these from the period 1800-1840 (see Chapter 18). Vessels of intrinsic or representative interest have been illustrated, including No. 31 from an unstratified context (Figs 79 and 80, Nos 26-32, 34-39 and 42).

Site 51

A simplified site fabric profile is presented in Table 30. N.B. the illustrated pottery from this site is all essentially unstratified. Fig. 80, Nos 43-54.

Table 30. Site 51: simplified fabric profile.

Fabric	% no. sherds	% weight
BLAK2	3.8	7.0
CEROBJ	0.1	0.4
CIST	0.1	–
CREAM	3.4	1.5
ES0	11.8	21.5
GREB	2.9	3.2
GREG	0.8	3.1
HAMB	0.1	0.2
LFPs	56.2	41.1
PEARLs	2.6	1.2
PORC	11.2	5.6
RYED	1.2	1.5
STAFS1-2	0.1	0.01
TIN	0.04	0.03
UGRE	2.0	2.3
UNAT	0.2	0.1
WHDIP	3.4	11.4
TOTAL	99.9	100.1

West Range

Period 1

The chalk rubble footings of wall 1043 were cut by linear feature 1059, fill 1060 of which contained a single body sherd of Glazed Red Earthenware (GREB). The sherd has no chronologically diagnostic features and does no more than provide a c. 16th-century *terminus post quem* for the fill.

Period 2.1

Small amounts of post-medieval pottery were found in Rooms 1-3, and in an external deposit.

Room 1

The only post-medieval pottery from any of the rooms in this period/phase was a single one-gram fragment of later 18th or early 19th-century Creamware from floor-raising chalk surface 565.

Room 2

A small assemblage (eleven sherds) of mainly medieval pottery from slot 690 (fill 609) contained a single sherd of Glazed Red Earthenware (GREB) of late (possibly 19th-century) appearance.

Room 3

Fill 923 of post-hole 922 contained a residual medieval sherd and three joining fragments of late 18th or early 19th-century Creamware.

The only post-medieval pottery from external deposits accorded to this period was a minute fragment of *c.* 17th-century Ryedale Ware, from flint and sandstone surface 606.

Period 2.3 and 2.4

This encompasses the final phase of building modifications followed by demolition and post-demolition events.

Room 1
Period 2.3

Chalk make-up layer 470 had eight residual medieval and three residual early 19th-century sherds: Pearlware (PEARL3), Creamware and 'modern' brown stoneware (ES0).

Period 2.4

West Range demolition layer 558 produced a large assemblage of 48 sherds, mainly from at least four later 19th-century yellow-glazed earthenware (LFP5) open forms. Transfer-printed and plain white earthenwares (LFP1 and LFP2) were also present.

Post-demolition cart rut 544 contained a late 19th or early 20th-century assemblage of five sherds: printed and plain white earthenwares (LFP1 and LFP2) and Late Blackware.

Rooms 2-4 amalgamated
Period 2.3

For floor-raising sand and chalk gravel deposit 470 see above (Room 1). A similar deposit, 800, contained only medieval material.

Period 2.4

Hillwash 528, which partially overlay the external trackway, produced five fragments of post-medieval pottery. The earliest was 17th-century Ryedale Ware, the remainder late 19th or early 20th-century factory products (LFP2 and LFP3) and a plain white porcelain fragment.

North Range

No post-medieval pottery was recovered.

East Range

Period 2 - ER

Hard-packed clay and chalk layer 323, which extended to the north of the building produced a fairly large assemblage of 33 sherds, ranging in date from the Roman period to the late 19th or earlier 20th century. Of the 21 post-medieval sherds, the earliest were single fragments of Ryedale Ware and Staffordshire Black-Dipped Ware (STAFS 2), but the remainder was late, ranging from Creamware and Pearlware through to Late Factory Products.

Several post-holes were cut into this surface, only one of which (367, fill 368) contained post-medieval pottery, a sherd from a late 19th or early 20th-century Banded Slipware (LFP6) bowl.

The cottages

Some 436 unstratified post-medieval sherds were specifically identified as having come from the topsoil in front of and behind the cottages. The opportunity has been taken to illustrate some of these: Figs 80-81, Nos 54-57.

Site 11

Post-medieval pottery was recovered from disturbed upper layers 3 and 6, and from a 'cesspit' (no context number, but apparently a rubbish pit from the 1958 excavations). The range was from the 17th century (Ryedale Ware) to the later 19th century (ES0 stonewares with Bristol/lead glazes). A single vessel is illustrated (Fig. 81, No. 58).

Site 15

This code was given to unstratified material found around the village; objects from areas adjacent to the cottages are published in this volume. Four vessels are illustrated, Fig. 81, Nos 59-62.

Site 49

A simplified fabric profile of the site assemblage is presented in Table 31.

Period 1

No post-medieval pottery was recovered. For the Iron Age pottery from this and subsequent periods, see Chapter 11.

Period 2

Stone deposit 23, which overlay probable destruction material used to level the area west of the farmhouse, contained a small, low-weight assemblage (five sherds, 14 grams) consisting of a single sherd of residual Ryedale Ware and small fragments of assorted late factory products (LFP1, LFP2 and LFP5).

Table 31. Site 49: simplified fabric profile.

Fabric	% no. sherds	% weight
BLAK2	7.0	4.8
CEROBJ	0.3	2.1
CREAM	0.6	0.2
ES0	4.1	4.3
ES6	0.1	-
FRE?	0.1	0.04
GREB	1.6	2.0
GREG	0.4	0.9
LFPs	66.3	70.7
PEARLs	1.6	0.2
PORC	13.8	9.4
RYED	1.7	2.6
STAFS1	0.1	0.1
TIN	0.1	0.02
UGRE	0.3	0.2
UNAT	0.2	0.1
WHDIP	1.9	2.3
TOTAL	100.2	100.0

Deposits 3 and 5 are identified as road repairs to a trackway running to the west of the western farmhouse wall. These contained, respectively, a sherd from a Glazed Red Earthenware (GREB) flatware vessel, possibly of 17th-century date; and an assemblage of sixteen sherds of mixed 17th and late 19th-century date.

The aforementioned trackway was overlain by humic deposits 26 and 32. Both produced assemblages of mixed 17th, 18th and late 19th-century date.

Chalk deposit 75, interpreted as a pathway, produced nine small fragments of transfer-printed and plain white earthenwares (LFP1 and LFP2). There was also half a ceramic chair castor, made of black-glazed red stoneware. Part of this object probably also occurred in Period 3 overburden deposit 2.

In the southern trench extension, chalk rubble layer 523, overlying road surface 524, produced three small 19th-century sherds, comprising Pearlware (PEARL1) and Late Blackware.

Period 3
The only post-medieval pottery came from topsoil 1, overburden 2, and various 'modern' pits. Contexts 1 and 2 produced a combined assemblage of 529 sherds, or 52% of the entire site assemblage, by sherd count. A further 27% came from a single pit (502). Apart from a few sherds of 17th to early 19th-century material (Ryedale, Tin-Glazed Earthenware, Staffordshire Slipware and Creamware) this assemblage is dominated by later 19th and 20th-century pottery. A single vessel is illustrated (Fig. 81, No. 63); another with uncertain provenance may belong here or be from Site 51 (Fig. 81, No. 64).

As the excavation narrative indicates, the remaining Period 3 contexts are associated with use of the area as a garden and yard for the cottages, for rubbish disposal, and for activities associated with the archaeological excavations. They have therefore been regarded as 'too recent and disturbed to warrant further discussion'. Since they will not, of course, remain 'recent' forever, they have been catalogued in some detail in the database. It has, moreover, in light of the fact that the excavations form an intrinsically interesting part of the whole archaeological artefact which is 'Wharram', been thought appropriate to offer here a brief discussion of the contents of rubbish pit 502 (fill 503). A large, rectangular feature, it appears to date from the 1950s excavations and, at least in part, to represent material brought onto the site by its temporary residents and abandoned at the end of the excavation season. It produced an assemblage of 273 sherds, weighing 12629 grams (ASW 46.3 grams). A minimum of 76 individual vessels was recognised, many of them substantially complete, with sherds from an unknown further number. The material consisted almost entirely of Late Factory Products (LFP1, 2, 4, 6 and 9) and porcelain, the only exceptions being a sherd from a brown stoneware (ES0) bottle and an almost complete amateur ('evening class') handled mug. The latter has the initials 'MM' incised on the base, and it is interesting to speculate that it might have been made by Maureen Milner, a member of the last family to inhabit the Wharram Percy cottages. Association of at least one vessel with the first excavators is proved by documentation: a thick-walled plain white 'Vitrified' bowl made by Ridgway (not illustrated) is accompanied by a card bearing a pencil sketch of the vessel, its dimensions, and the note 'Bought in Leeds Market 1954 for 6d'. A note in biro in a different hand notes that this was 'info from digger of 1950s' and Peter Brears (pers. comm, 2006) recalls that the vessel is supposed to have been purchased by Maurice Beresford. The form and fabric composition of 74 vessels is given below (Table 32).

Table 32. Form and fabric composition of 74 vessels from Pit 502.

Fabric/ form		LFP1	LFP2	LFP4	LFP6	LFP9	PORC
cup	(10)	1	4	5			
mug	(11)		4	2	3	2	
beaker	(5)			3	1		1
jug	(1)		1				
saucer	(3)		1				2
dish/ bowl	(12)	2	4	1	1		4
plate	(22)	1	12	7	1		1
soup/ dessert plate	(10)		9				1
TOTALS	(74)	4	35	18	6	2	9

The form composition of the pit assemblage, with its concentration on handled drinking vessels (largely unaccompanied by saucers) and a range of plates and bowls, is what might well be expected from a short-lived camping community. Very few of the vessels belong to 'sets' from the same manufacturer, with the possible exception of some of the blue-banded LFP6 wares. The assemblage is made up largely of oddments, perhaps those which wives or mothers were willing to regard as dispensable as well as those bought, like Beresford's bowl, as cheap singles for the specific occasion. This impression is reinforced by the date-range of the wares. There are several vessels which bear the mark ENGLAND, often, though not exclusively, indicative of a very late 19th-century date (post-1891, Godden 1968, 10), and at least two vessels which can be shown to be from the first half of the 20th century: a plate by W.H. Grindley of Tunstall, bearing a printed mark of the period 1914-1925 (Cushion 1976, 250-51); and a dish bearing the name WOOD & SONS, with the date 1938. Two commemorative mugs celebrating the coronation of Queen Elizabeth II in June 1953 are among the latest vessels present, and, far from being destined for the patriotic china cabinet, were obviously considered as being quite appropriate for this kind of rough duty. One, by Burgess and Leigh of Burslem, probably belongs at the cheaper end of the spectrum of such wares; the other is of far superior quality, and bears the basal legend OFFICIAL DESIGN, BRITISH POTTERY MANUFACTURERS FEDERATION, and ENGLAND 23. The very latest vessel in the assemblage may be a saucer by Barratt's of Tunstall, backstamped in grey with the legend BARRATT'S DELPHATIC WHITE TABLEWARE E. The name Delphatic was first used in 1957 according to Cushion (1976, 250).

A full list of manufacturers (with ware and pattern names) in this assemblage is as follows:

Adams, of Tunstall ('Royal Ivory', 'Titian Ware'); 'Alma Ware'; Ashworth and Bros, of Hanley ('Paynsley Pattern'); Barratt's, of Tunstall ('Delphatic'); Bishop and Stonier, of Hanley ('Bisto'); Burgess and Leigh, of Burslem ('Burleigh Ware'); Cartwright and Edwards, of Langton; W.H. Grindley and Co., of Tunstall ('The Marquis'); Johnson Bros, of Hanley ('Goldendawn', 'Pareek'); Keele Street Pottery, Tunstall; Alfred Meakin, of Tunstall ('Old Willow'); PPC; Ridgway, of Hanley; Wade Heath, of Burslem; Wood and Sons ('Royal Ivory').

Site 73

A simplified fabric profile of the site assemblage is presented in Table 33.

Period 1

No pottery was found.

Period 2

A small amount of material was recovered, of little evidential value. None was associated with either of the two structures in the excavated area.

Table 33. Site 73: simplified fabric profile.

Fabric	% no. sherds	% weight
BLAK2	5.9	5.3
CIST	0.4	0.1
CREAM	0.2	0.03
ES0	11.7	12.4
FRE	0.2	0.1
GREB	1.7	2.2
GREG	1.9	1.5
HAMB	0.4	0.06
HUMPM	0.2	0.2
LFPs	49.2	60.4
PEARLs	3.7	0.6
PORC	10.8	8.9
RYED	9.3	6.4
STAFS1	2.6	0.2
TRSL	0.2	0.2
UGRE	0.6	0.2
WEST	0.2	0.01
WHDIP	1.1	1.2
TOTAL	100.3	100.0

Only two of the chalk rubble or cobble surfaces produced any pottery: two small sherds of late 18th or early 19th-century Late Blackware came from 51, and a rim sherd from a 17th-century Ryedale open form from 98.

Possible yard surface 55 produced a small, fragmentary pottery assemblage (thirteen sherds, ASW 1.5 grams). The earliest material was 15th or 16th-century Hambleton Ware, the largest and latest component 18th-century Staffordshire Slipware.

Post-pit 125 contained three sherds (ASW 3.0 grams), comprising one Hambleton and two Ryedale Ware.

In the extension trench, hillwash deposit 104 produced a small sherd of 17th-century Ryedale Ware and two undiagnostic fragments of unglazed red earthenware (UGRE).

The fill (106) of pit 105 contained two sherds of Ryedale Ware and one Late Blackware, the latter of late 18th or 19th-century date.

Period 3

Possible road surface 100 produced ten sherds. With the exception of four small fragments of Ryedale Ware, these were all 19th or early 20th-century factory products.

A number of modern rubbish pits (10, 12, 13, 17 and 19) produced an aggregated assemblage of 111 sherds, weighing 3204 grams, representing 20.1% or 31.4% of the entire site assemblage (by count and weight, respectively). The assemblage was dominated (84 sherds) by Late Factory Products, mainly transfer-printed and highly decorated white tablewares (LFP1 and LFP4).

Some of these have cross-contextual joins in the large topsoil assemblage (context 1). Trademarks on the pottery suggest a chronological range of *c.* 1875 to after *c.* 1955 for the bulk of the material. All these are noted in the database and referenced to Cushion 1976. They include the following: Cartwright and Edwards, of Longton; Dunn, Bennett and Co., Ltd, of Burslem; Lovatts of Langley Mill, Nottingham; Maddocks, of Burslem; Alfred Meakin, of Tunstall; Ridgway, of Hanley; and Tams, of Longton. These late assemblages cannot be discussed in detail, but two vessels from fill 18 of pit 17 may be mentioned for their intrinsic interest.

The first is a complete pub ashtray bearing the words 'King's Ale' and ROSE'S MALTON, on either side of a stylised barrel in a green floral border. Rose's was a Malton brewery, founded *c.* 1767 and taken over by Tetley's in 1970. It had half a dozen pubs in the town. The tray is backstamped WADE'S/Regency/LONDON/ENGLAND.

The second is an octagonal drinking mug with pedestal base, angular handle, and decoration of broad, vertical, grey-blue stripes. It is backstamped with the Gresley's church mark in a rounded triangular cartouche above the word 'England', and the following legend, in green: SPECTRA/ASCOT WHITE /IRONSTONE/ COLOURS ENTIRELY /UNDERGLAZE/DESIGNED BY/TOM ARNOLD/DES RCA MSIA/ "ELEGANTE". Tom Arnold was one of a group of leading designers who graduated from the Royal College of Art after 1948. Most of his designs were for Ridgway and Adderley (McLaren 1997, 18).

The vicarage sites

Site 77
A simplified fabric profile of the site assemblage is presented in Table 34.

Period 4
The stratigraphically earliest post-medieval pottery comes from 522, a deposit of loose yellow/brown soil with frequent chalk pebble inclusions. It appears to be stratigraphically later than deposit 591, and runs along the east side of the wall line (591 and 506). The material in question is a single body sherd from an internally glazed open form, in a hard, slightly sandy pinkish buff fabric. The glaze is greenish yellow and pitted. The fabric may be related to, or a variant of, Ryedale Ware. It has been recorded as 'post-medieval local' (PMLOC).

Period 5
South of wall 117 (Period 5.1), surface chalk rubble deposit 165=181 extended to the edge of the excavation. Component 181 contained a large assemblage of 60 sherds, of which 59 were medieval. The latest was a sherd from a Cistercian cup, belonging to the very late 15th or 16th century (post-*c.* 1485).

Conduit 106 contained pottery in upper fills 105 and 333, and secondary fill 154. Lower fill 155 was aceramic. The secondary fill contained an entirely medieval assemblage of nineteen sherds. The upper fills produced a large assemblage of mainly medieval material and undatable post-medieval coarsewares (Fig. 82, No. 65); several sherds of Ryedale, in both contexts, point to a late 16th to early 18th-century *terminus post quem.* In the case of 105, a sherd of Westerwald stoneware refines this date-range somewhat. It is from the simple, slightly insloping rim of a closed form and has a cordon a little way below the rim edge, cf. Gaimster 1997, nos 111 (tankard), 121 and 122 (globular mugs and tankards etc.) Similar rims may date from *c.* 1620 into at least the earlier 18th century, depending on form. Further support for these broad dates comes from context 132, which is stated to be equivalent to both lower fill 155 and secondary fill 154. The post-medieval material in this context contained a range of material from the 16th century (Cistercian Ware) to the first half of the 18th century (Fig. 82, No. 66). Fill 333 has later material still, in the shape of a sherd of 18th-century Staffordshire Slipware (STAFS1).

Table 34. Site 77: simplified fabric profile.

Fabric	% no. sherds	% weight
BLAK1	0.8	0.2
BLAK2	7.8	10.9
BORD?	0.3	0.01
CIST	2.8	2.0
CISTR	0.3	0.1
CREAM	2.3	0.5
ES0	4.5	6.7
ES1	0.3	0.1
ES3	0.8	0.2
ES6	1.3	3.6
GREB	6.0	3.1
GREG	5.8	10.7
LFPs	7.8	5.8
MCAMP	0.8	0.1
MYEL	0.5	0.1
PEARLs	4.0	0.6
PMLOC	1.5	2.9
PORC	0.8	0.4
RAER	0.3	0.04
RYED	43.9	45.4
STAFS1	2.0	0.5
SYG	1.0	1.7
TIN	0.5	0.2
UCD	1.0	1.6
UGRE	1.5	2.5
UNAT	0.8	0.2
WEST	0.8	0.2
WHDIP	0.5	0.5
TOTAL	100.7	100.9

Two vessels from Periods 5.1 and 5.2 deposits not discussed in the excavation narrative are illustrated for their intrinsic interest: Fig. 82, Nos 67-8. For other illustrated vessels from Period 5.1, see Fig. 82, Nos 69-71.

Deposit 297 contained a large assemblage of 19th or early 20th-century material, together with a clay tobacco pipe fragment of c. 1800-1880 (Chapter 18).

Road surface 85 contained pottery of at least the first half of the 19th-century, together with clay tobacco pipe of c. 1800-1840 (not illustrated).

Period 6
Pottery came from various 'modern' deposits: topsoil (1), old archaeological spoil dumps (114 and 625), demolition rubble (104) and hillwash (538). For illustrated material from these deposits, as well as from unstratified or unphased deposits, see: Fig. 82, Nos 72-74.

Site 54
A simplified fabric profile is given in Table 35.

Period 3.1 (Structure D)
The stratigraphically earliest post-medieval pottery from the site is from levelling layer 650, accorded to this phase. It consists, however, of a minute (< 1-gram) fragment of 19th-century transfer-printed white earthenware of pearlware (LFP1/PEARL3), and is best regarded as an intrusion or contamination during excavation.

Period 4.1 (Structure F)
Late to post-medieval pottery comes from only two contexts, both of them layers/surfaces. They are of little evidential value in respect of the date of the structure itself.

Context 528 was a cobbled surface between rubble wall footings 529 and 530. It incorporated two small sherds, one possibly 15th or early 16th-century Hambleton Ware, and the other fabric C01b. The latter is possibly a fully reduced variant of Hambleton Ware (Chapter 12).

Context 386 was an external cobbled surface. It contained a single sherd of 15th or early 16th-century Hambleton Ware.

Period 4.2
The only pottery recovered came from terracing cut 760. It contained a sherd of Humberware (which has a 14th to 16th-century date range) and a sherd of Ryedale Ware (late 16th to early 18th-century).

Period 4.3 (Structure G)
North of the structural slots were several 'fragmentary surfaces', only one of which (937) produced pottery. This was a small, chronologically mixed assemblage. The earliest post-medieval pottery was two sherds of 15th or 16th-century fabric C01b (see above), and the latest a handle from a later 19th or 20th-century plain white earthenware (LFP2) cup. Sherds of coarseware (GREB) may be contemporary with the latter.

Table 35. Site 54: simplified fabric profile.

Fabric	% no. sherds	% weight
BLAK1	0.03	
BLAK2	5.1	9.8
BLAK3	-	-
C01b	0.7	1.0
CEROBJ	-	-
CIST	0.2	0.1
CIST/BLAK1	0.1	0.2
CREAM	9.5	5.3
ES0	2.7	4.3
ES1	0.6	0.2
ES2	-	-
ES3	0.1	0.1
ES4a?	0.2	0.3
ES4b	0.03	0.01
ES5	0.1	0.1
ES6	0.1	0.1
FRE	0.1	0.2
GRE	0.2	0.1
GREB	5.5	10.1
GREG	1.6	4.6
GREP	0.1	0.1
HAMB	0.9	1.3
HUMPM	1.1	2.3
LFPs	4.3	4.0
MCAMP	0.1	0.1
MYEL	-	-
PEARLs	8.1	2.1
PMLOC	0.1	0.1
PORC	0.9	0.3
PURP	0.03	0.01
RAER	0.04	0.3
RYED	47.2	48.3
STAFS1-3	2.3	0.9
TIN	5.9	1.6
TRSL	-	-
UGRE	0.8	0.7
UNAT	0.4	0.1
UNATSLIP	0.2	0.2
WEST	0.5	0.4
WHDIP	0.3	0.9
WHIEL		
TOTAL	100.1	100.2

In the same area, slot 1043 (fill 1042) contained a single one-gram flake of ceramic, possibly '17th-century' Ryedale Ware.

Hill-wash 989 produced a single small sherd of 18th-century Staffordshire Slipware.

Pit 589, held to be associated with Structure G, contained residual medieval sherds and six large sherds of Ryedale ware.

Dump 1049 contained a single small body sherd, possibly 15th/16th-century Hambleton ware.

Period 5.2 (Structure H1)
External surfaces in the south-east of the site are interpreted as re-structuring of the area after the Period 3 structures. Deposit 399 produced medieval sherds, the latest apparently 15th or early 16th-century Hambleton Ware. Deposit 209, which lay above it, produced eight sherds, of which five were post-medieval. These ranged from '17th-century' Ryedale Ware to 19th-century transfer-printed Pearlware (PEARL3) and White-Dipped Ware. If the deposits are correctly phased, this late material must be assumed to be intrusive.

A series of cobbled surfaces to the north produced mainly medieval and late medieval pottery. Definite post-medieval material came from 138, which produced two sherds of Cistercian Ware and, once again, sherds of 19th-century transfer-printed tea wares (PEARL3 or LFP1). In addition, a minute fragment of possible Ryedale Ware came from 221.

Two of the compacted clay surfaces still further to the north produced small amounts of post-medieval pottery: a Ryedale open form from 259, and a fragment of Cistercian Ware from 361. The Ryedale from 259 provides a cross-contextual join with Period 7.5 deposit 202.

Also to the north of Structure H was dump 521. It produced three sherds of Ryedale ware.

To the south, the remnants of Structures F and G were sealed by demolition debris deposits. One of these, 452, produced an assemblage of eleven sherds, the largest and latest component in which was '17th-century' Ryedale Ware.

Stakehole 514, which was cut through 452, contained 18th-century slipware and stoneware (STAFS3 and ES3), as well as residual Ryedale Ware. The stoneware sherd (Fig. 82, No. 75) provides a cross-contextual join with Period 6.3, context 516, one of the backfills of Structure J. The stakehole presumably relates to post-Period 5.2 activity.

A sequence of clay floor surfaces and a hearth to the north of wall footing 254 produced small amounts of post-medieval pottery: 413 had sherds of late 15th and/or 16th-century Cistercian and Hambleton Wares, and 443 a sherd of post-medieval Humberware; single sherds of Cistercian Ware came from 489 and hearth 448, while 517 contained two sherds of '17th-century' Ryedale Ware.

Period 5.3 (Structure H2)
A sequence of clay surfaces, mainly within the area of Structure H1, is interpreted as marking resurfacing or repair in preparation for the rebuilding or alteration of the structure. Two of these deposits produced pottery: 414 contained a single fragment of unidentified and undated dark brown stoneware (ES6) with sprigged decoration, possibly from a straight-sided tankard; 451 produced a small assemblage of Humberware, possible Ryedale Ware and 18th-century Staffordshire Slipware. The latter is a minute fragment.

These surfaces all respected wall 371 of structure H2, the build of which incorporated a sherd of post-medieval, but not closely datable, coarseware (GREB).

Deposits 394-7 were interpreted as 'collapsed/robbed footings of stub or partition walls at right angles to the main axis of the structure'. Two of them produced post-medieval pottery. Deposit 395 contained a virtually complete 16th or 17th-century Cistercian or Blackware costrel and the base of a tripod-footed vessel in Glazed Red Earthenware (Fig. 82, Nos 76 and 77), while 396 contained six sherds of fabric C01b.

Period 5.4
Post-medieval pottery came only from exterior clay surfaces 837 and 838, the former producing two large body sherds from the same Ryedale open form, and the latter a sherd of unattributed, but Ryedale-like, pottery (catalogued as PMLOC).

Period 6.1 (Structure M)
Deposits 815, 409 and 431 (the former possibly make-up for the two latter) all contained post-medieval pottery. Deposit 815 had five sherds of Ryedale and 409 a further three, though in that case the majority of the assemblage was redeposited medieval material. In 431, which contained ten sherds, a very late 15th to 16th-century component is represented by Cistercian and Raeren wares (Fig. 82, No. 78), while the latest is Ryedale and a fragment of Tin-Glazed Earthenware (not illustrated). The latter is a majolica, with a mauve-tinted lead-glazed back, the design on the interior comprising *schaakbord motief* and concentric circles in blue (cf. for decoration Korf 1963, fig. 47 and *passim*; Bartels 1999, no. 925 and *passim*). The sherd is almost certainly Netherlandish, and *c.* the first quarter of the 17th century.

Deposits 323 and 389 are interpreted as redeposited demolition material. Some vessels are probably represented in both assemblages. Deposit 323 contained 21 post-medieval sherds. The most diagnostic material was Ryedale Ware and Tin-Glazed Earthenware, the latter a plain white eared handle of 'porringer' type, of 17th or 18th-century date; also present was a small fragment from the grooved base of a brown stoneware (ES6) tankard, and a slipware resembling Staffordshire (STAFS1) but probably of more local manufacture. Deposit 389 contained 55 sherds, most of it Ryedale, but with four sherds of the same local slipware present in 323. The possibility of 18th-century material in these demolition deposits cannot be discounted.

Fill 768 of post-hole 769 contained a minute (one-gram) chip of post-medieval coarseware (GREB), not closely datable.

Period 6.2 (Structure J)

The only pottery from this period was a small assemblage of six sherds (70 grams) from 625, interpreted as a make-up layer for a non-extant flagged floor. The largest component (4 sherds, 65 grams) was Ryedale Ware, the remaining sherds being Westerwald (4 grams) and an unattributed fine brown stoneware (ES0). The Westerwald is a fragment with manganese-coloured panels between grouped incised lines. The conventionally accepted date for the introduction of manganese purple at Westerwald is 1665 (Hurst *et al.* 1986, 222) though Hume (2001, 91-94) has recently suggested a somewhat earlier date, in the 1630s, for its first known occurrence. The sherd should therefore provide a *terminus post quem* for emplacement of this surface and installation of the flagged floor, assuming the sherd was present when the material was laid down. Unfortunately, the remaining sherd in the assemblage poses certain problems of interpretation. This is a one-gram fragment from the bead rim of a small, thin-walled vessel, probably a cup or small bowl, in an unidentified brown stoneware. Although categorised as ES0, the fabric bears a strong resemblance to that of Fig. 82, No. 75, a *possible* Nottingham stoneware (ES3?) product, which would imply a very late 17th or early 18th-century *terminus post quem*. The sherd from 625 joins another from the same vessel in Period 6.3 context 612, which is interpreted as demolition rubble from Structure J used to backfill the cellar. Given this inter-contextual join, it seems much more probable that this small assemblage is also part of the backfill deposits, and connected with demolition of the structure rather than with its construction.

Period 6.3

Several deposits described as 'demolition debris and domestic rubbish' were used to backfill Structure J. This is interpreted as essentially a single event, rather than a gradual accumulation. Many of these fills contained pottery assemblages, as follows: 390, 391, 455, 456, 461, 462, 471, 481, 516, 520, 591 and 612. The aggregated backfill assemblage (post-medieval pottery only) amounted to 1477 sherds, weighing 21190 grams (ASW 14.3 grams). The largest single contributing context assemblage was 516, which yielded 1053 sherds, weighing 17288 grams (ASW 16.4 grams). This represents 71.0% by number of sherds, or 81.1% by weight. A fabric profile of the whole assemblage is presented in Table 36.

The chronological range of the post-medieval pottery is from the late 15th or 16th century (*e.g.* CIST, C01b, HAMB, HUMPM and RAER) through to at least the mid-18th century (ES1 and 3, PORC and STAFS1-3), though the overwhelming majority was '17th-century' Ryedale Ware. It is appropriate to mention here the presence of two sherds of Chinese porcelain (neither illustrated). The first is a fragment of *famille verte* of the periods *c.* 1690-1750 (fill 516), and the second a sherd from a 'Chinese export' tea-bowl dating from *c.* 1730 to the end of the 18th century (from fill 612). The broad dating of the

Table 36. Site 54: fabric profile of the Structure J backfill deposits.

Fabric	% no. sherds (n = 1477)	% wt (grams) (n = 21190)
BLAK2	0.2	0.01
C01b	1.1	1.1
CIST	0.1	0.01
CIST/BLAK1	0.1	0.2
CIST?	0.1	-
ES0	0.5	0.2
ES1	0.4	0.4
ES3	0.1	-
ES3?	0.3	0.1
FRE	0.4	0.6
GREB	4.1	3.9
GREP	0.1	0.2
HAMB	0.2	0.2
HUMPM	0.1	0.2
MCAMP	0.5	0.3
MYEL	0.1	0.01
PORC	0.1	0.01
RAER	0.1	-
RYED	85.2	90.4
STAFS1	0.4	0.1
STAFS2	0.1	0.2
STAFS3	0.2	0.01
TIN	3.6	0.9
TRSL	0.1	-
UGRE	1.1	0.3
UNAT	0.2	-
UNATSLIP	0.1	0.04
WEST	0.7	0.6
TOTAL	100.3	100.0

whole pottery assemblage is consonant with the dates of the three clay tobacco pipes from the assemblage; these, all from fill 516, comprised single examples of the periods 1680-1710, 1710-1740, and 1700-1770 (Chapter 18, Nos 22-3, others not illustrated).

Numerous definite or probable cross-contextual joins were noted (Table 37):

Unfortunately, these joins do little to elucidate the taphonomy of the infill deposits. Only two of the joining contexts are from earlier periods, and it has been suggested above that one of these (625) is probably better interpreted as being itself part of these infill deposits. The other (514) was a stake-hole containing a small 18th-century assemblage. It has probably been wrongly attributed to Period 5.2. The largest number of vessels

Table 37. Site 54: Structure J backfill deposits, cross-contextual joins.

Fill	Joins context	Period	Context type
462	437 (?)	6.3	Fill of rubbish pit
462	351 (?)	7.4	Exterior surface
516	514	5.2	Stake-hole
516	99	7.7	Surface deposit
516	247	7.4	Fill of animal burial pit
516	269	7.4	Exterior surface
516	288 (?)	7.4	Fill of animal burial pit
516	350	7.4	Exterior surface
516	202	7.5	Clay deposit
612	625	6.2	Interior make-up deposit

with extra-contextual links comes from 516, with at least fourteen such vessels. Among the contemporary or later joining contexts most joins are with 202. It will be suggested below that the backfilling of Structure J and the *initial* emplacement of external deposit 202 might have been broadly contemporary events. If the excavator is correct in suggesting that these backfills were deposited as a single event, and not as a gradual process, then the pottery and clay tobacco pipes suggest at least an early to mid-18th-century *terminus post quem* for that event.

Although the Structure J backfill deposits produced such a large pottery assemblage and contributed so many vessels to the illustrated catalogue (Figs 82-5, Nos 79-117), their evidential value in terms of furthering our understanding of pottery usage at Wharram Percy is rather limited. It is impossible to be certain of the sources from which the pottery ultimately derives and, given the date-range of the assemblage, which components should be considered as contemporary. The major component in the assemblage, Ryedale Ware, has a long period of use, as noted several times in this report, and it need not, therefore, represent a single, chronologically discrete component. It would certainly be possible to see much of this assemblage as representing the clearance of a late 17th to mid-18th-century kitchen, but this can not be demonstrated. Its principal worth, therefore, may consist simply in the very size of the Ryedale assemblage, and the range of vessels which it has added to the published *corpus* of this ware.

The south wall of the cellar was overlain by deposit 519. It contained a sherd of Ryedale Ware and a one-gram fragment of Tin-Glazed Earthenware.

A further deposit composed of probable building debris, was 454. This produced 25 sherds of post-medieval pottery, weighing 174 grams; the particularly 'scrappy' nature of the assemblage is reflected in a very low ASW of 7.2 grams. Chronologically, the material cannot be distinguished from Structure J backfill deposits such as 516, the most diagnostic components being

Ryedale, Westerwald, and Staffordshire Slipware (STAFS1). Indeed, although the deposit does not form part of the cellar backfill, it clearly derives from some of the same deposits which contributed to that event, as witness a cross-contextual join with context 516 (cf. No. 116).

Cut into the building debris over the now backfilled Structure J were three rubbish pits/animal burials – 321, 438 and 447 – all of which contained pottery. Fill 326 of pit 321 yielded a single sherd of Ryedale Ware, while fill 445 of pit 447 produced tiny fragments (three sherds, five grams) of probable Ryedale Ware and an 18th-century Staffordshire manganese-mottled (STAFS3) tankard. Fill 437 of cut 438 produced a fairly large assemblage (29 sherds, 304 grams) of post-medieval pottery; the largest component (23 sherds) was Ryedale Ware, but fragments of 18th-century Staffordshire Slipware (STAFS1), Westerwald stoneware with *possible* manganese decoration, and plain white Tin-Glazed Earthenware were also present. It will be seen that 18th-century *termini post qous* are demonstrable for the fills of two of these pits.

Mortar surface 320, to the north of Structure J, produced a small assemblage of seventeen sherds. These were all medieval, the latest being three sherds of 15th or early 16th-century Hambleton Ware.

Several deposits are interpreted as demolition debris derived from Structure H and other features to the west: 241, 243, 245, 249, 260, 264, 266, 341, 367, 369 and 412. These produced a large aggregated assemblage of 193 sherds, weighing 4750 grams. The vast majority of these assemblages (69% by number, 81% by weight) consisted of Ryedale Ware. Eighteenth-century Staffordshire Slipware occurs in small amounts in deposits 266 and 369. It may be noted that many of the deposits contain either specifically early 19th-century wares (LFP2 and 5, and PEARL3) or coarsewares which could be of this date (BLAK2 and GREs). Whatever the date of the deposit's emplacement, it clearly continued to receive small amounts of material at least as late as the mid-19th century. Two vessels from these deposits are illustrated (Fig. 85, Nos 118 and 119).

Period 7.1 (Primary construction of Structure K)
Parts of the west and east walls of this structure incorporated post-medieval pottery.

The contexts making up the west wall (101, 118, 252 and 255) produced a combined assemblage of 22 sherds, of which six were medieval. Context 255 contained only medieval pottery. The latest material in each of the other wall sections was of early 19th-century date. This consisted of Pearlware in each case: PEARL2 in 101 (Fig. 85, No. 120), PEARL5 in 118 (with possible Creamware), and PEARL3 (or LFP1) in 252.

The east wall (205, 210 and 234) incorporated fewer sherds, of rather less evidential value. Context 210 contained only medieval material, while 205 produced a single sherd of Cistercian Ware and two Ryedale Ware bodies. Context 234 contained a sherd of Staffordshire Slipware, a fragment of green-glazed and brown-glazed

Creamware, and a sherd of unglazed red earthenware (UGRE). A late 18th-century *terminus post quem* is indicated for construction of this section.

Centrally placed in this eastern wall was stone threshold 121, which produced two sherds of post-medieval pottery, each weighing less than one gram. One was Pearlware (too small to be attributed to a sub-variety) and the other a transfer-printed fragment, either PEARL3 or LFP1. An early 19th-century *terminus post quem* is indicated. Unfortunately, the relationship of the pottery to the threshold itself is not recorded. The threshold make-up deposit (211) produced a small assemblage (seven sherds, 25 grams) of mixed 15th to 16th and 18th to 19th-century date (HAMB, RAER, PEARL3/LFP1 and ES0).

Towards the southern end of Structure K, rubble and clay deposit 112 and post-holes 156 and 181 (fills 157 and 182) formed the base of a partition. Deposit 112 contained only a single sherd of coarseware (GREB), not closely datable. Post-hole 157 produced a small, low-weight assemblage (twelve sherds, 37 grams) of 18th and early 19th-century pottery, consisting of Creamware, White English Salt-Glazed Stoneware, Porcelain, Tin-Glazed Earthenware and transfer-printed Pearlware (PEARL3). The latter, possibly the latest vessel in the group, is a saucer/dish with scalloped rim and an external offset, the internal blue decoration floral/geometric and the rim greenish gilt (not illustrated). Post-hole 179, which may also have been associated with this partition, had two sherds of Creamware in its fill (180). Wall deposit 199, into which the joist supports were set, produced a further sherd of transfer-printed Pearlware, a fragment from a flatware rim.

In Room 2, floor deposit 200 produced a small residual assemblage consisting of late medieval Humberware, with flakes of Cistercian and Ryedale wares. One of the latter (Fig. 85, No. 118) provides a cross-contextual join with Period 6.3 deposit 266, interpreted as demolition débris from Structure H. From part of the north wall footing (265) of Room 2 came single small sherds of Ryedale Ware and coarseware (GREB), the latter also possibly indicating a cross-contextual join with deposit 266. Surface 125, possibly part of the lobby entrance, incorporated a mixed assemblage of medieval (nineteen sherds) and post-medieval (seven sherds) pottery. The latter comprised 15th to 16th-century Hambleton, 17th-century Ryedale, and undated coarseware (GREB).

In Room 3, deposit 100 is interpreted as a floor bedding or make-up. This produced two sherds of coarseware (GREG and GREB), not closely datable; a sherd of thick-walled plain white porcelain, and a sherd of white earthenware with pinkish-yellow overall glaze (LFP5). This sherd belongs to a dish/bowl with everted rim, which also occurs in demolition deposits 2 and 5 (Periods 8.4 and 8.1). Although not closely datable, the porcelain and LFP5 have a decidedly later appearance than the Pearlwares etc. of the construction deposits, and it may be that they found their way into this layer during the demolition process, perhaps after the removal of a flagged floor (103), or even during the machine-stripping of the top-soil for excavation (see Chapter 10). Flagstone bedding 195 produced a single sherd of post-medieval coarseware (GREB), not closely datable but of 'late' appearance.

Brick hearth setting 137 incorporated a single sherd of late medieval or post-medieval Humberware.

In the north-west corner of Room 4, fill 203 of possible rubbish pit 207 produced a sherd of 19th-century Banded Slipware (LFP6) and a fragment of handmade Iron Age pottery (CG4). Deposit 237, which lay beneath the remnants of a flagstone floor, incorporated a one-gram flake of Tin-Glazed Earthenware and a fragment of coarseware (GREB) of 18th or 19th-century appearance. Below 237, compacted coal dust deposit 335 contained a one-gram fragment of Ryedale ware.

In Room 4a, pottery was recovered from wall 258 and return 305. This was residual in each case, comprising Roman greyware (RG) from the former and late medieval Humberware from the latter.

Period 7.2 (Alterations and repairs to Structure K)
In Room 2, new hearth area 117 produced an assemblage of 27 post-medieval sherds. The earliest were late 18th and early 19th-century Creamware and transfer-printed Pearlware (PEARL3); the remainder comprises transfer-printed Pearlware/White Earthenware (PEARL3/LFP1) and Banded Slipware (LFP6). The PEARL3 (not illustrated) is a one-gram fragment from a vessel which is also represented, by larger sherds, in Phase 8.1 demolition deposits 5, 113, and 143. The largest sherd (from 113) shows the vessel to have been a slop bowl with deep internal vermicelli band, and on the exterior a ruined castle scene in an oval cartouche on a vermicelli ground. Details of the border on the rim interior, and that surrounding the cartouche, as well as of the vermicelli itself (which has dots on both sides of the line) are identical to those on Don Pottery products, cf. Coysh and Henrywood 1982, 111, photograph at lower left; Griffin 2001, 112 and figs 65, 67-68. The vessel would have been manufactured before 1839. The LFP6 vessels (Fig. 85, Nos 121 and 122) are a chamberpot, of a type produced from the first half of the 19th century into the 20th century, and a bowl. Both vessels could easily be broadly contemporary with the Don Pearlware.

Period 7.3 (further robbing of Structure J and disuse/alterations Structure M)
To the north, deposit 314, interpreted as resurfacing of Period 6.1 deposits, produced a small assemblage of four sherds, the latest an 18th-century White English Salt-Glazed Stoneware. No doubt all are residual, as are the two small sherds of plain white Tin-Glazed earthenware from surface 312.

Silty deposit 308, which sealed what had been the north end of Structure M, produced fourteen sherds, most of them (nine sherds) Ryedale Ware, but also including undatable coarseware (GREB) and 18th-century White English Salt-Glazed Stoneware. The latter, the latest material in the group, included a sherd from a small jug (Fig. 85, No. 123) which also appears in Period 7.5 deposit 202, a context which furnishes several cross-contextual joins with material from the Structure J infill deposits.

Post-pad 270 in post-hole/depression 285 produced a single sherd of undatable post-medieval coarseware (GREB) and an unattributed flake.

Fill 281 of post-hole 277 contained single sherds of Ryedale and later 17th or 18th-century Tin-Glazed Earthenware.

Fill 364 of post-hole 365 contained a detached flake of glaze from a Tin-Glazed Earthenware vessel.

Fill 357 of robber trench cut 370 (Structure J) produced a large group of 152 sherds, ranging in date from the 15th and 16th centuries (Hambleton, C01b and Cistercian) to at least the 17th century. The majority is Ryedale Ware, and there is no other material (plain white Tin-Glazed Earthenware and GREB) which is necessarily of 18th-century date.

Period 7.4 (Structure L and other activity to the rear of Structure K)

Exterior surfaces 351 (outside the back door of the vicarage), 350 (to the north) and 408 all produced post-medieval pottery assemblages. The former contained eight sherds, of which the latest were 18th-century Staffordshire products (STAFS1 and STAFS3); 350, with 38 sherds, consisted almost entirely of Ryedale Ware, one vessel of which provided a cross-contextual join with Structure J backfill deposit 516 (Fig. 84, No. 115); 408 produced ten sherds of post-medieval pottery weighing 10 grams, with a maximum possible date-range from the late 15th to the early 18th centuries (C01b, CIST, HAMB, RYED and TIN).

Probable chalk soak-away 75, laid against the west wall, had 32 post-medieval sherds. The largest component was, once again, Ryedale Ware, with the latest diagnostic material present being Staffordshire Slipwares (STAFS1 and STAFS2). See Fig. 85, Nos 124-6.

Two animal burials also produced post-medieval pottery. Fill 247 of cut 240 for animal burial 251 had a large assemblage of 81 sherds, mainly later 17th and 18th-century in date. The latest is Staffordshire Slipware (STAFS1), and possibly Frechen, the remainder including Ryedale, Westerwald with manganese decoration, and Tin-Glazed Earthenware with 'Chinaman among rocks and grasses' decoration, particularly popular during the 1680s. The assemblage contains vessels which also occur in Structure J backfill deposit 516 and Period 7.5 deposit 202. See Figs 84-5 Nos 113, 114, 117, 127 and 128.

Fill 288 of cut 289 for cow burial 303 produced a large assemblage of 128 sherds. Once again, the majority (103 sherds) was Ryedale (Fig. 85, No. 119). The latest was Staffordshire manganese-mottled ware (STAFS3).

Wall/footing 290, the west wall of Structure L, incorporated a one-gram fragment of Ryedale Ware.

The stone blocks of threshold 291 of Structure L produced a single sherd of Tin-Glazed Earthenware, a fragment from a faience flatware with polychrome geometric/floral decoration of c. the first half of the 18th century.

Cuts 423 and 287 (fills 422 and 286), both of which may relate to the construction of the walls of Structure L, produced further small assemblages of post-medieval pottery. In the case of 423, this consisted of single sherds of Ryedale Ware and Creamware, the latter providing a late 18th or early 19th-century *terminus post quem* for the fill. The small tin-glazed ointment or dispensing pot which formed the sole content of 287 probably dates from the first half of the 18th century (Fig. 86, No. 129).

Floor 88 contained three sherds, the earliest being 14th to 16th-century Humberware; the other sherds were 16th and 17th-century Cistercian and Ryedale wares.

A number of external surfaces to the north produced pottery. These contexts (226, 231, 269, 272, 315, 316, dump 230, and 355 in Period 7.5) produced an aggregated assemblage of 154 sherds. Most of these groups are dominated by Ryedale Ware but end with Staffordshire Slipwares or other 18th-century products; 226 contained, in addition, a ceramic hair curler of the first half of the 18th century (Chapter 17) and 315 a possible sherd of Tin-Glazed Earthenware with overglaze enamels, possibly a mid-18th-century Liverpool product. Context 269 has a sherd of late 18th or early 19th-century Creamware, while 231 and 355 appear to contain some typical 19th-century products (BLAK2 and WHDIP).

Deposit 123, which may have been debris left over from the construction of Structure L, produced fourteen sherds, weighing 153 grams (Fig. 86, Nos 130, 131 and 132). The only closely diagnostic material was 18th-century Staffordshire Slipware (STAFS1).

Period 7.5 (external surfaces and Structure N)

West of the vicarage, silty clay deposit 202 produced an extremely large pottery assemblage; after the exclusion of Iron Age and medieval pottery (one and six sherds, respectively) this consisted of 2715 sherds, weighing 12300 grams, and having an ASW of 4.5 grams. The material ranges in date from the 15th or 16th century to the 19th century and has provided a considerable number of illustrations for this report: Figs 84-86, Nos 108, 110-114, 116, 123, 126, 128 and 133-141. A slightly simplified fabric profile is given in Table 38, below.

As will be noted, the overwhelming majority is '17th-century' Ryedale Ware, with small amounts of both earlier and later material. The 18th century is most visible in the form of STAFS1-3 and ES1-2, while the late 18th and 19th centuries are represented by CREAM, PEARL5, BLAK1-2 and LFP6. The datable clay tobacco pipes from the context comprise two examples from c. 1660-1680, one from c. 1710-1740, and one of '18th-century' date (Chapter 18, Nos 14 and 24, two unillustrated). The deposit was probably derived from more than one source and subject to intermittent augmentation from sources such as hillwash, as the excavation narrative suggests. The large number of cross-contextual joins may be noted in this regard. There was a minimum of 29 such joins, involving fifteen other contexts (Table 39).

Table 38. Site 54: deposit 202 fabric profile.

Fabric	% no. sherds (n = 2715)	% wt (n = 12300 g.)	ASW (grams)
BLAK1/BLAK2	0.1	0.02	1.5
CIST	0.1	0.1	5.7
CREAM	0.03	0.01	1.0
ES1	0.4	0.3	4.2
ES2	0.3	0.01	12.0
FRE	0.1	0.4	23.0
GREs	2.4	11.2	20.9
HAMB	0.4	1.2	12.7
HUMPM	0.03	0.1	14.0
LFP6	0.1	0.1	7.0
MCAMP	0.1	0.2	11.0
PEARL5	0.03	0.01	1.0
PMLOC	0.1	0.6	17.5
RYED	88.0	81.4	4.2
STAFS1-3	1.7	1.2	3.2
TIN	6.3	2.5	1.8
UNATSLIP	0.03	0.3	33.0
WEST	0.1	0.2	9.3
TOTAL	100.3	99.9	

Table 39. Site 54: deposit 202, cross-contextual joins.

Context	Period	No. of vessels	Context type
259	5.2	1	compacted clay surface
454	6.3	1	demolition débris in vicinity of Structure J
516	6.3	7	backfill of cool room (Structure J)
98	7.7	2	surface deposit
75	7.4	1	soakaway fill
123	7.4	2	construction débris from coal cellar (Structure L)
247	7.4	1	fill of horse burial cut 240
288	7.4	1	fill of cow burial cut 289
124	7.5	6	surface accumulation
173	7.5	1	exterior surface
201	7.5	1	exterior surface
97	7.7	1	rain washed silt deposit
106	7.7	2	rain washed silt deposit
141	8.1	1	surface deposit
1	8.4	1	topsoil

The table points to a complex taphonomy of deposition and redeposition. Ten of the 'join contexts' (with twenty-two vessels) belong to Period 7.5 or earlier. Very noticeable is the large number of joins (eight) with vessels first noted in the Structure J backfill deposits. A common source for much of this material must be envisaged. The same sources also appear to have contributed material to other, similar, external surfaces of this Period, *i.e.* 124, 173 and 201. These deposits produced further assemblages (of 246, 16 and 36 sherds, respectively) of similar composition to 202, the latest material in deposit 124 being 19th-century PEARL1 and 3, and BLAK2. As might be expected, the layer appears to have continued to receive ceramic material from, or contributed it to, other contexts in later phases (Figs 85-86, Nos 125, 139 and 141). Indeed, the attribution of such a deposit to a single site phase is probably in itself misleading.

Wall footings 22 and 183, of Structure N, both incorporated small pottery assemblages. Staffordshire slipware and a sherd from a Westerwald jug with rilled neck and manganese colouration, cf. Jennings 1981, 852-853, probably provide an early 18th-century *terminus post quem* for the construction of 22, while 183 produced three sherds of Ryedale Ware.

External clay and cobbled surfaces 192 and 168, which lay to the east of Structure N, are interpreted as being contemporary with this structure, and surface 174 may also be related. The combined assemblage from these contexts was 49 sherds, of which 32 were Ryedale. A fragment of White English Salt-Glazed Stoneware occurred in 192, while 168 contains 19th-century WHDIP and ES6. A sherd of Ryedale from 192 provides a cross-contextual join with fill 82 of a Period 8.2 rubbish pit.

Deposit 250, interpreted as make-up/levelling material for the construction of Structure N, contained a single sherd of 18th-century Staffordshire Slipware (STAFS1).

Fill 268 of post-hole 282, which may have been associated with the construction of N, contained two scrap fragments of ceramic, weighing 6 grams. These are difficult to attribute to fabric, though one is possibly a post-medieval coarseware (GREB).

Period 7.6 (Structure P: the conduit)

Deposit 186, interpreted as demolition debris from Structure N, contained seven sherds, comprising Staffordshire Slipwares (STAFS1 and STAFS3), coarseware (GREB) of 'late' appearance and plain white factory earthenware (LFP2). The latest contents presumably date to at least the middle of the 19th century.

Contexts 170 and 184, the compacted upper fills of conduit 235 both produced pottery. The aggregated post-medieval component amounted to 36 sherds, weighing 879 grams. The date-range of the pottery was from the late 15th or 16th century onwards. Both assemblages were dominated by Ryedale Ware but there were late 18th or early 19th-century inclusions in each. In 170, this was a Creamware plate with Bath edge; in 184, porcelain fragments with blue underglaze enamelling of 'cottage among trees' and other patterns.

Deposit 34, possibly a surface or make-up layer for a later surface or structure, contained fourteen sherds, weighing 60 grams. The earliest diagnostic type was 18th-century Staffordshire Slipware (STAFS1), but the latest types present (PEARL3, LFP1) take the deposit into at least the early to mid-19th century.

Deposit 167, probably a consolidation of the surface above the conduit, produced eleven post-medieval sherds, weighing 98 grams. These ranged in date from the 17th century (RYED) to the early 19th century (ES4a?, cf. Fig. 86, No. 142).

Period 7.7 (Structure Q)
None of the pottery from this period related to Structure Q, all deriving from 'debris' associated with Structure L, with hillwash deposits, or with a path/external surface.

Material from 86, 87, 191 and 197 is interpreted as coming from Structure L. They produced a combined assemblage of 23 sherds. The latest material comprises Staffordshire slipwares (STAFS1 and STAFS3), White English Salt-Glazed Stoneware and brown stonewares (ES6). Nothing need postdate the 18th century (Fig. 86, No. 143).

Rain-washed silt deposits 97 and 106 produced a combined assemblage of 46 sherds (Fig. 86, No. 144). It consisted mainly of material of 17th and 18th-century date, including Westerwald, Ryedale, and Staffordshire Slipware; the latest material, however, includes fragments of plain white earthenware, brown stonewares and brown earthenwares (LFP2, ES0 and GREB) which probably take the group some considerable way into the 19th century. Two sherds in the group, from Westerwald and Unattributed Slipware vessels, provide cross-contextual joins with various other assemblages of Periods 7.4 to 8.1: 1, 75, 97, 124, 164, 173, 202 and 247. Details of all these contexts are given in Table 39.

The above deposits were sealed by weathered surfaces 98 and 99, which produced an aggregated assemblage of 35 sherds of post-medieval pottery, weighing 493 grams. The chronologically diagnostic wares were Ryedale, 18th-century Staffordshire Slipwares (STAFS1 and 3) and Late Blackware of probable 19th-century date. A cross-contextual link with Period 7.4 context 123 was established by a coarseware bowl (Fig. 86, No. 131).

Cobbled surface 21 and associated surface 72 produced a combined assemblage of 49 sherds of post-medieval pottery, of widely differing dates. The latest material was of late 18th and 19th-century date (CREAM, PEARL2 and 3 and LFP6).

Deposit 196, interpreted as demolition debris from Structure L, produced four sherds of Ryedale ware.

Period 7.8 (Structure R)
Surface 16, to the east of the vicarage, produced an assemblage of seven sherds, all but one of them from a 19th-century Late Blackware vessel; the remaining sherd was residual 14th to 16th-century Humberware. Associated surface 110, against the east wall, produced a single small fragment of 19th-century transfer-printed Pearlware or white earthenware (PEARL3/LFP1). Deposit 104, taken to be rain-washed silt along the wall line, produced five sherds of medieval pottery and three post-medieval, the latter consisting of transfer-printed Pearlware (PEARL3) fragments, and a sherd of modern stoneware (ES0).

Pottery was also recovered from the following fence-line features: post-hole fills 57 and 59 (of post-holes 56 and 58) and post-pipe 62 (of post-hole 58). These produced a combined assemblage of 26 sherds (22 of which were from fill 57). The latest material is 19th-century in each case, including BLAK2, CREAM, LFP2/5/6, PEARL3 and PORC.

Fill 9 of pit 26 produced a large assemblage of 88 sherds of post-medieval pottery, weighing 1788 grams. The largest component consisted of GRE coarsewares, the more chronologically diagnostic wares ranging from the 17th and 18th centuries (RYED, TIN and STAFS1) to the late 18th and 19th centuries (CREAM, PEARL3, PORC, LFP1 and 5). The Creamware included a footring base with the impressed mark 'W T & Co 3'. The mark might be associated with either William Tomlinson or William Taylor who, between them, were associated with the Rothwell, Castleford and Swillington Bridge potteries, in the period 1780-1804 (cf. Lawrence 1974, 256-257, mark 155). It may also be noted that the deposit contained a clay tobacco pipe bowl of 1820-1880 (Chapter 18, No. 36). For illustrated vessels from this deposit, see Figs 86-7, Nos 145-148.

Fill 96, of possible drainage channel 1132, produced 70 sherds, weighing 361 grams. With the exception of a few fragments of 17th and 18th-century material (TIN and STAFS3) this is essentially a 19th-century assemblage. Two joining sherds, from a stoneware bottle with greenish glaze, bear part of a type-impressed legend: [-]ichd Gr[—]. Richard Gray is listed as a Wines and Spirits dealer in Malton in Baines' 1823 Trades Directory. Others of his products appear in the topsoil (cf. Fig. 89, Nos 177 and 184). A clay tobacco pipe of 1800-1840 may also be mentioned (Chapter 18, No. 31). The only illustrated vessel from 96 is No. 149 (Fig. 87).

The north side of the drainage channel was capped with sandstone blocks (12), which produced 28 sherds of post-medieval pottery, weighing 237 grams. As far as can be judged, these are almost entirely of 19th-century date. Cf. Fig. 87, No. 150.

Period 8.1
The great majority of the pottery assemblage from this period comes from contexts interpreted as demolition debris from Structure K. Other contributing contexts include hillwash, dumps, and pit/post-hole fills. The post-medieval assemblage amounted to 876 sherds, weighing 17341 grams (ASW 19.8 grams). A simplified fabric profile of the pottery assemblage is given in Table 40. The possible maximum date-range is from the 16th to 19th centuries. The high proportion of iron-glazed and lead-glazed coarsewares (BLAK2 and GREs) may be noted. Together with what may be broadly contemporary Pearlwares, these fabrics account for 66.9% of the whole Period assemblage by number of sherds. See Figs 87-8, Nos 151-159 and 161-167.

Table 40. Site 54: Period 8.1 fabric profile.

Fabric	% no. sherds (n = 876)	% wt (n = 17341 g.)
BLAK2	27.2	35.2
CIST/BLAK1	0.5	0.1
CREAM	14.0	4.5
ES0	1.8	3.5
ES1	1.0	0.4
ES4a?	0.1	0.04
GREs	27.4	41.6
LFPs	5.4	5.1
PEARLs	12.3	2.4
PORC	1.7	0.5
PURP	0.1	0.03
RYED	5.3	5.9
STAFS1-3	1.0	0.1
TIN	0.1	-
UGRE	1.4	0.4
UNAT	0.3	0.2
WEST	0.1	0.1
WHDIP	0.2	0.1
TOTAL	99.9	100.2

Period 8.2

Fill 95 of animal burial pit 94 produced 46 sherds, ranging in date from the 17th (RYED) to the 19th centuries (BLAK2, PEARL2, LFP1 and LFP6). Vessel joins to the following contexts were noted: 5 (Period 8.1); 82 and 7 (Period 8.2).

Deposit 77 indicates the final abandonment of the vicarage and the accumulation of rain-washed silts and topsoil. It produced a small pottery assemblage (fourteen sherds, 337 grams), principally composed of Ryedale ware but ending with late 18th to 19th-century products: Creamware, porcelain and possibly felspathic stoneware (ES4a).

Context 82 was a dump of charcoal and burnt loam representing a consolidating deposit in the area of pit 94. It produced an assemblage of 43 sherds, weighing 582 grams. The date-range was from the 17th century (Ryedale) to at least the late 18th or 19th century. See Figs 86 and 88, Nos 142, 168 and 169, the latter of which reflects a number of cross-contextual joins with other late deposits.

Rubble layer 7, perhaps intended as a reinstatement of the road surface, produced an assemblage of 170 sherds (2453 grams). Its composition and chronological emphasis was very similar to that of Period 8.1 as a whole (Table 40), though there was a much greater representation of tablewares, mainly in the form of Creamware and Pearlware (60% of the assemblage by sherd count). See Fig. 88, Nos 170-172.

Deposits of rain-washed topsoil (11, 13 and 14) produced an aggregated assemblage of 66 sherds (663 grams) of post-medieval pottery, ranging in date from the late 15th or 16th century to at least the 19th century. See Fig. 88, No. 173.

Period 8.3

The period produced a small assemblage of 21 sherds (380 grams). All the material came from post-holes etc. associated with the 20th-century hen-house and all was of 17th to 19th-century date.

Period 8.4

The period produced a large assemblage of 1458 sherds (17462 grams). Much of this came from the topsoil and from dumps and debris deposits, including those connected with the demolition of the 20th-century hen house. Linear bank of rubble 8 (257 sherds, 2498 grams) contained material of 17th to at least mid-19th-century date. See Figs 88-89, Nos 174-179.

Numbers 180-186, Figure 89 are unmarked vessels of intrinsic interest but uncertain provenance.

Concluding discussion

The most difficult period to discern in the ceramic record from these sites at Wharram Percy is the very late 15th and 16th centuries. It is most visible in the type fossils Cistercian Ware and Raeren stoneware, though these are both poorly represented (Figs 82 and 89, Nos 67, 76, 78 and 185). Cistercian Ware occurs on several sites, with a total of 42 sherds (322 grams), while Raeren contributes a meagre six sherds (91 grams) to the village assemblage. As proportions of the excavated assemblage, these figures equate to < 0.2% for Cistercian, and < 0.03% for Raeren. It is possible that three fragments (7 grams) of Martincamp stoneware from Site 77 derive from a Type II flask, and could therefore be of 16th-century date (Hurst *et al.* 1986, 102-4).

The principal coarsewares in the 16th century are hard to determine. If the conventional dating of Ryedale Ware, which dominates the record throughout a 'long' 17th century, is correct then the likelihood is that Hambleton Ware (and fabric C01b?) continued to provide the coarsewares until supplanted by Ryedale at some point in the later 16th century. Hambleton may have been supplemented by post-medieval Humberware, some early examples of the Glazed Red Earthenwares, and perhaps the occasional purple-glazed product, though none of this can actually be demonstrated.

The bulk of the Cistercian occurs on Vicarage Sites 54 and 77 (with 22 and eleven sherds respectively), but it is really only on Site 54 (where it occurs as early as Period 4.1) that any 16th-century component is really discernible; and even there, the combination of Hambleton, C01b, (Late) Humberware, Cistercian and Raeren amounts to no more than 3-4% of the site assemblage. The available evidence would seem to suggest that ceramic supply to Wharram Percy at this period consisted largely of coarseware from relatively local sources, supplemented by Cistercian cups and Raeren globular drinking mugs. Both these latter types were widely distributed and occur commonly on rural sites. That European products of finer quality, or from other sources, occasionally reached Wharram is shown by a Raeren cavalier panel jug (Fig. 89, No. 185) and by an unattributed, but probably French, chafing dish (Fig. 82, No. 70). The wares are most likely to have been imported through Hull.

The most obvious fact about the 17th-century assemblage is that it is dominated by Ryedale Ware (Figs 79-87, Nos 33, 54-5, 58, 68, 71, 79-102, 108-113, 115, 118-19, 124, 133-6 and 161). The type accounts for 28-29% of the entire village assemblage. Its share of the contemporary ceramic repertoire at Wharram is difficult to calculate accurately; but the small quantities of such other 17th-century wares as can be discerned (see below) suggest that Ryedale may have accounted for c. 93-97%.

The known Ryedale production centres are all to the west of Malton, in and around the Howardian Hills (Jennings and Boyles 1995, fig. 20.1). From which of them Wharram was drawing its supplies is unknown, though some material appears similar to fabric samples from Stearsby held in the Humber Archaeology Partnership fabric reference collection. Petrological and chemical analysis has perhaps the potential to link the Wharram material to known production centres, but this was beyond the scope of the present enquiry. It may be mentioned that the ware displays much more variable characteristics than is sometimes suggested in published descriptions; in particular, oxidisation is quite common, and a large but unquantified proportion of the material may have bright, smooth or even metallic green glazes rather than the pitted 'orange peel' surface which is often regarded as typical (Jennings and Boyles 1995, 228-229). Some of the colour variations probably reflect the season at which the pots were fired, rather than different production centres (Peter Brears, pers. comm.). No proportional form analysis could sensibly be undertaken, given the constraints noted earlier, though the form range seems essentially similar to that in other large Ryedale assemblages. Attention may, however, be drawn to at least two examples of dripping-pans (Fig. 81, No. 58 and Fig. 83, No. 89), a form which to Jennings and Boyles (1995, 230) seemed generally absent from the Ryedale industry. Sooting and other use characteristics are noted in the illustration catalogue.

Other English products of 17th-century date are difficult to isolate. There are only four possible fragments of Blackware of this period (BLAK1), and only five examples of Trailed Slipware, some of which could be of 18th-century date. Midland Yellow is represented by up to four sherds of more or less dubious scrap, and Border Ware by a single possible fragment. Once again, it is possible that some of the Glazed Red Earthenwares might be of this date, but the overwhelming impression is that this tradition only begins to contribute largely to the Wharram assemblage after the demise of Ryedale Ware, in the 18th and 19th centuries.

Imported vessels of the period comprise Frechen and Westerwald stonewares, Martincamp flasks, Weser slipware and Netherlandish Tin-glazed earthenware. All these are, however, sparsely represented. Frechen has twelve sherds (228 grams), all from Bellarmine-type bottles. The only illustrated example (Fig. 84, No. 114) is of late 17th or even early 18th-century date. Westerwald contributed 64 sherds (453 grams) to the village assemblage, from an uncertain number of vessels. Much of the material has manganese colouration, and must therefore date to the last third of the century, or later (Fig. 87, No. 151). The range of vessels is well represented by the illustrated examples (Figs 84-7, Nos 107, 117, 137 and 151). Once again, the concentration (60 sherds) is in Site 54. Turning to Martincamp flasks, nine sherds (76 grams) from Site 54 appear to derive from a single 17th-century Type III vessel (Hurst et al. 1986, 102-4). Weser slipware is represented by two sherds (18 grams) from Site 74, and could belong to the very end of the 16th or first quarter of the 17th century (Fig. 78, No. 10). Finally, a proportion of the site's Tin-glazed assemblage is of 17th-century date, though this is difficult to quantify. Early 17th-century vessels which are almost certainly Low Countries products occur (Fig. 84, Nos 103 and 104); other 17th-century candidates are Figs 78, 85, 86 and 88, Nos 12, 14, 127 and, possibly, 145 and 162.

In most respects the 17th-century assemblage is similar to that from the previous century, in that it is dominated by local pottery and shows scarcely more impact from national and international sources. Such imports as do occur were probably once again acquired via Hull. It is only in the 18th century that non-local products begin to be slightly more obvious, and in this the site typifies a national trend. The national distribution of Staffordshire products such as Slipwares and Salt-Glazed Stonewares gathered momentum from the 1730s onwards; those eventually reaching Wharram Percy would have travelled from North Staffordshire via a short overland route to Willington Ferry and then via the Trent and Humber to Hull, at which point some of the material would have been redistributed northwards via the coastal trade, to ports such as Bridlington, Scarborough, Whitby and Stockton (Weatherill 1971, 76-95, and Maps 5 and 6). Hull had a dedicated retail outlet for pottery and glassware at least as early as 1787 (Bennett 2005, 82-85) and pottery warehouses which could have supplied pottery to retail outlets in other towns may already have existed in Hull for some decades.

Staffordshire Slipwares contributed 413 sherds (1771 grams) to the village assemblage, and the main Staffordshire stoneware varieties (ES1 and ES5) a further 136 sherds (636 grams). Together they account for 1-3% of the entire village assemblage. The wares are concentrated on Sites 54 and 74; the slipwares display a ratio of c. 2:1 in favour of Site 54, while the stonewares are almost equally distributed. The Slipwares cover a typical range of open forms, cups, chamber-pots and press-moulded flatwares (Figs 78, 85-6 and 88, Nos 3, 4, 126, 128, 130, 139 and 174). The White English Salt-

Glazed Stoneware (ES1) is mainly very fragmentary, but a range of plates, saucers, bowls, a jug, and possibly a teapot and a tea-canister was noted (Figs 78-9, 84-5 and 87-8, Nos 6, 7, 11, 15, 16, 21, 23, 38, 39, 105, 123, 152 and 167). As indicated above, it is impossible to link these wares to either the farm or the vicarage, and the most that may be observed is that the staple fineware products of the Georgian tea table were not unfamiliar to the inhabitants of Wharram Percy. Even Chinese porcelain tewares could find their way here, as already noted. The brown-dipped stonewares (ES5) are represented by mugs and a capuchin (Figs 78 and 87-8, Nos 17, 160 and 175). It is perhaps worth noticing that one of the mugs bears an AR excise mark and that the optimum date for the capuchin would appear to be in the first quarter of the 18th century.

As indicated above, coarsewares after the demise of Ryedale must have been supplied by the regional Glazed Red Earthenware industries. These were widely distributed over much of Yorkshire (Lawrence 1974, *passim*) and Peter Brears suggests (pers. comm.) that some of the material found at Wharram could have travelled by water from the West Riding to Malton, as return loads for the grain which was being shipped to Leeds and other centres from at least the middle of the 18th century.

From the late 18th century onwards, the finer wares reflect the usual national pattern of Creamware, followed by Pearlware, and then a number of what are here called Late Factory Products. The large quantities of these products, and their very low ASWs, will be noted from the various site fabric profiles, and it was not possible to pay them more than scant attention, and to note the most salient facts.

Creamware appears to consist almost entirely of flatwares, with a single closed form. A representative sample is illustrated (Figs 78-80, 86-88, Nos 1, 24, 30, 34, 35, 56, 144, 158, 165, 169 and 170). Several sherds bore impressed marks. Most of these were fragmentary, or simple circles, crosses and numbers, though a few are more informative and can be linked to individual potteries, as below:

WT & CO 3 cf. Lawrence 1974, 166 and 256-7, mark 155. The main possibilities are William Tomlinson & Co. of the Ferrybridge Pottery (1801-1804) and William Taylor of the Rothwell, Castleford and Swillington Bridge potteries (1780-1795).

CASTLEFORD POTTERY (below a cross) cf. Lawrence 1974, mark 175. Used by David Dunderdale and Co. (1790-1820).

FERRY[ ] cf. Lawrence 1974, mark 156. Used by the successive occupants of the Ferrybridge Pottery (1801-1870).

In addition to the above, there are some suggestions that products of the Don Pottery may be present, cf. the numerous examples of flatwares with 'Bath' edge, and Fig. 80, No. 56, though the latter might also be a Castleford product. For other possible Castleford vessels cf. Figs 86-88, Nos 142, 150 and 165.

Pearlware is the last fabric group which has been illustrated in any quantity: Figs 79-80, 85 and 87-8, Nos 40 and 166 (PEARL1); 25, 120, 153 and 154 (PEARL2); 171 (PEARL2a); 159 (PEARL4); 46 (PEARL5). No transfer-printed Pearlwares (PEARL3) have been illustrated, partly because of the difficulty of representing them satisfactorily, and partly because of the very fragmentary nature of the material and the difficulty of attributing designs to known centres. Patterns are more or less fully described in the databases, and where the same design occurs in more than one context this is noted. It would theoretically be possible, given sufficient time, funding and expertise, to reconstitute some of the pattern 'sets' of this kind of ware (as also of the later LFP1 transfer-printed vessels), but this was beyond the scope of the present exercise. Even so, a small number of the printed Pearlwares, including named patterns, can be attributed to two particular potteries. Castleford yielded fragments of the following patterns: 'Two Farmers and a Church', 'Long Bridge' variant of Willow Pattern (possible), 'Manor House', 'Castle and Fisherman'. These are four of the seven printed patterns known to Roussel at the time of her survey (Roussel 1982, Plates 48-49, 53 and 54). Interestingly, 'Buffalo and Ruins', very distinctive and apparently produced in far larger amounts than the other patterns, was not noted here. Pearlware which almost certainly comes from the Don Pottery has already been alluded to above (Site 54, Period 8.1, context 113).

The very large amount of material which dates from *c.* the mid-19th century onwards is not discussed here, though all is recorded in the databases, and a representative sample, together with some vessels of intrinsic interest, is illustrated.

Key to colours

black/dark brown (also dark blue where shapes too small to hatch)

white (where coloured background)

dark blue

light blue

red

yellow/gold

orange/light brown

green

Fig. 77. Key to colour conventions used in the post-medieval pottery figures. (C. Marshall)

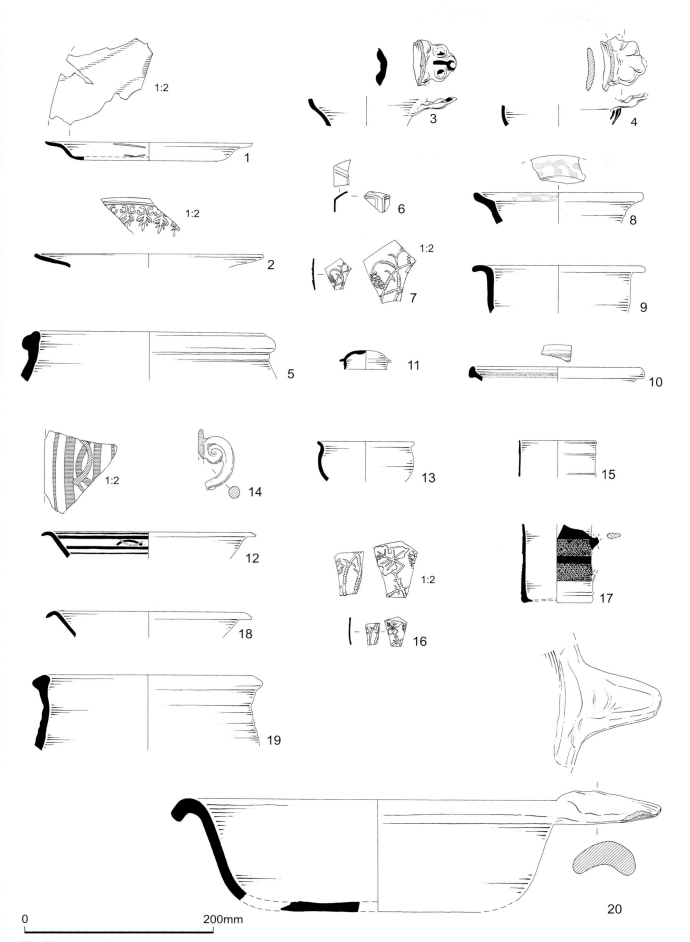

Fig. 78. Post-medieval pottery Nos 1-20. Scale 1:4 (C. Marshall)

1:2

1:2

1:2

1:2

1:2

1:2

1:2

0   200mm

Illustration catalogue

The farmstead sites

Site 74

1*   TIN. Faience. Plate. Blue curvilinear decoration on eggshell-blue ground. Eighteenth-century? *74/341; Period 1*

2*   CREAM. Plate rim with border of fronds below opposed C-scrolls. *74/341; Period 1*

3*   STAFS1. Press-moulded 'ear' handle of hollow ware form, possibly similar to Celoria and Kelly 1973, nos 126, 262 *et al*. Dark brown trailed slip decoration on three applied roundels on the upper face. The roundels are in an iron-rich clay, different from that of the white-firing body. Usual lead glaze firing yellow. *74/323; Period 2*

4*   STAFS1. As No. 3, but the 'ear' is plain, with dark brown slip decoration only on the exterior body below it. Handles of this type occur on a number of different vessel forms. For a useful range, both of vessels forms and decorative treatment, see Celoria and Kelly 1973; Kelly and Greaves 1974. *74/323; Period 2*

5*   GREG. Closed form. Sandy light red fabric with rich, lustrous very dark green glaze overall. *74/342; Period 2*

6*   ES1. Sherd from vessel with polyhedral panelled body. It is drawn here as if from a shoulder, though orientation is not entirely certain. The most likely form would be a teapot or tea-canister, though it is difficult to match this fragment to published examples. *74/300; Period 2*

7*   ES1. Sherd with grape and vine-leaf decoration. The pattern closely resembles that of a slip-cast teapot of *c*. 1740-1760 in Northampton Museum (Draper 1977b, no. 43). Vine decoration was used on a number of wares in the mid-18th century, and can be found on white salt-glazed stoneware from at least *c*.1740. *74/300; Period 2*

8*   TRSL. Bowl with everted rim flange, dished internally. Red earthenware with clear lead glaze, firing to a rich reddish brown, slightly iron flecked. Trailed scrollwork in white slip has fired yellow beneath the lead glaze. *74/287; Period 3*

9*   GREB. Bowl with horizontally outbent rim. Pale red sandy fabric. Iron-rich reddish brown glaze overall. *74/362; Period 3?*

10*   WESER. Bowl with hammer-head rim. Pinkish white fabric covered in white slip, with thick and thin encircling reddish brown bands on the interior. The background fires yellow under a clear lead glaze, the glazed area extending over the vertical exterior face of the rim. Probably from a Wavy Bands dish, though similar borders were employed also on slipware 'bird bowls' (cf. Hurst *et al.* 1986, nos 375 and 377, and colour plate XV). *c*.1590-1620. *74/106; Period 3*

11*   ES1. Cover. The size and shape suggest it might belong to a small teapot, though other forms are possible. Cf. Edwards and Hampson 2005, figs 171, 196 and 218 (left-hand example) for a range of similar examples *c*. 1720-1770, Jennings 1981, fig. 102, no. 1607. *74/106; Period 3*

12*   TIN. Bowl with curved outbent rim. For form, cf. Orton 1988, fig.132, nos 1287 and 1288. Interior decoration of blue bands and blue and red 'chain'. Slightly blue-tinged faience, pale yellow body. The chain motif occurs on various forms from at least the second quarter of the 17th century and continues into the 18th. At Mark Brown's Wharf, London, vessels with this motif fall into 'decorative group D', attributed broadly to the second half of the 17th century (Orton 1988, 327). *74/106; Period 3*

13*   TIN. Jar. Plain, slightly blue-tinged, white faience, pale yellow body. A similar vessel, with manganese-mottled exterior, occurs in 54/124. *74/106; Period 3. 74/165; Period 3*

14*   TIN. Plain white, pink-tinged, faience. Simple upright rim with rolled handle. The handle type occurs on a number of forms in the late 17th century, particularly possets, cups and bowls (cf. Archer 1997, D12-13, F2; Orton 1988, fig. 133, no. 1328). A date in the last third of the century might be most appropriate. *74/106; Period 3*

15*   ES1. Closed form with broad turned band below the rim. *74/106; Period 3*

16*   ES1. Two sherds with grape and vine-leaf decoration. See No. 7. *74/106; Period 3*

17*   ES5. Mug. Two bands of rouletted decoration within a brown-dipped area which probably extended as far as the (missing) rim. For similar vessels, cf. Edwards and Hampson 2005, colour pl. 192; Kelly and Greaves 1974, fig. 6, nos 30, 31; Baker and Hassall 1979, fig. 142, no. 902. The latter bears an AR capacity excise mark. Probably from the first quarter of the 18th century, though the first of the cited examples is thought to be *c*. 1750. *74/106; Period 3*

18*   TIN. Bowl, cf. No. 12. Plain white faience, pale yellow body. *74/165; Period 3*

19*   GREG. Closed form. Fine sandy light grey core, light red margins and core in places. Light red unglazed exterior. Lustrous green internal glaze with large brown iron-rich area. Glaze spills over onto the external rim bevel. *74/165; Period 3*

20*   PMLOC. Handled large bowl (pancheon). Hard sandy fabric with dark grey core, pale exterior margin and reddish orange surfaces. Areas of a pale green glaze, reminiscent of some Ryedale wares, on the exterior below the handle and on the inside of the rim. *74/165; Period 3*, possibly also represented in *54/106 and 79/10*

21*   ES1. Plate. 'Queen's' shape with 'seed' or 'barley(corn)' pattern. Hume (1991, 115) dates this pattern to *c*. 1740 and later, though a *floruit* of *c*. 1760-1780, based upon references in inventories, has more recently been suggested by Edwards and Hampson (2005, 41, caption to fig. 60, and indexed references). *74/255; Period 3*

22*   BLAK2. Small bowl with outbent rim. Fabric dark red and white-flecked. Overall, even, rich black glaze. *74/255; Period 3*

23*   ES1. Sherd with vine-leaf decoration. See No. 7. *74/102; Period 4*

24*   CREAM. Plate. White earthenware with yellowish cream glaze. Feathered edge. *74/211; Period 5*

25*   PEARL2. Bowl. Underglaze enamels. Pattern of sprays tipped with three leaves or berries in cobalt blue on the exterior, with an encircling band of greenish yellow and brown below. The inside of the rim has a band of dark blue dots on a lighter blue ground, framed between greenish yellow bands. First quarter of 19th century? *74/334; Period 4*

26*   PORC. Saucer with hand-painted underglaze lustre and enamel decoration. Purple lustre bands at the rim and in the well enclose fronds and leaves in pink, purple and gold lustre, and deep red enamel. A date in the first third of the 19th century seems likely, but this kind of simple decoration, and lustre-decorated pottery in general, continued for many years afterwards. *74/101; Period 6*

27*   LFP6. Bowl with footring base. Factory white earthenware with clear lead glaze; pairs of dark brown slip bands below the rim and on the lower body, enclose a linear 'Mocha' ropework motif in blues and browns. A mug in the Northampton Museum with similar 'rope' decoration is described as a possible Staffordshire product and dated to *c*. 1800-1820 (Draper 1977a, no. 58). Hughes and Hughes (1968, 112-113) suggest *c*. 1830 for the beginning of 'Mocha' decoration on white earthenware bodies, and a jug of this type from excavations at Hanley is dated to *c*. 1835-1840 (Kelly and Greaves 1974, fig. 5, no. 6). *74/101; Period 6*

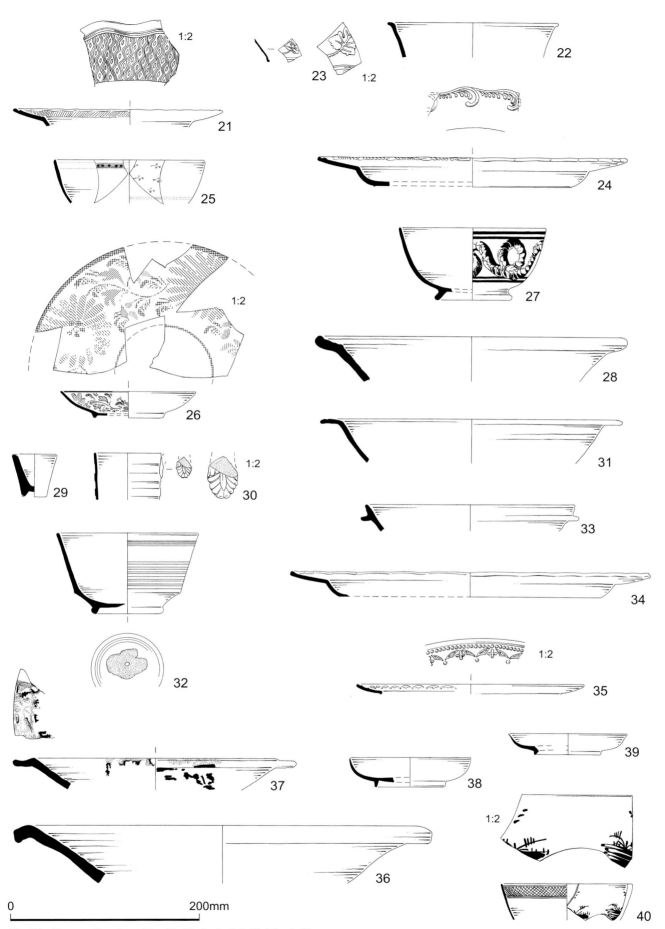

Fig. 79. Post-medieval pot Nos 21-40. Scale 1:4 (C. Marshall)

28* GREG. Shallow bowl with long outbent rim flange. Sandy redware with buff margins and darker red exterior. Dark olive-green lead glaze over whole interior. Apparent sooting marks below rim on exterior, but the sherd has also been burned post-fracture. The form would allow a 17th or 18th-century date. *74/112; Period 6*

29* ES0. Boot-blacking pot. As No. 64 but with richer and darker brown glaze. *74/125; Period 6*

30* CREAM. Handled closed form. Engine-turned to leave decorative raised bands. *74/126; Period 6. 74/150; unstratified. 74/9000; unstratified*

31* ES0. Bowl with everted rim flange. Light grey stoneware with pale margins. Dark brown dip overall. Undecorated in extant portion. *74/150; unstratified*

32* LFP6. Carinated ('London' shape) bowl. Body as Nos 121 and 182. Pale blue band below rim, with six white slip bands above the carination. A deliberate perforation of *c.* 4mm diameter has been made (post-firing) in the centre of the base. The form was common throughout most of the 19th century, and was, for example, produced in quantity at the Don Pottery during the Barker period of ownership, 1839-1893 (Didsbury 2000). *74/182; Period 6*

33* RYED. Straight-sided flanged bowl. Fairly fine pinkish buff fabric with dark brown to reddish brown exterior. Lustrous, slightly pitted, dark olive-green glaze on interior with splashes on exterior. Interior groove below rim edge. Extensive carbonised deposits and dark staining on the exterior of the rim and both sides of the flange. *74/262; Period 4*

34* CREAM. Plate. Fabric as that of No. 56. *74/272; Period 6*

35* CREAM. Plate. Fabric as that of No. 56. Bead row with pendent leaf and berry motifs, separated by quatrefoils. *74/272; Period 6*

36* GREB. Bowl with square-cut outbent rim. Hard, light red fabric with greenish brown glaze on outer edge and top of rim, and whole of interior. *74/272; Period 6*

37* WHDIP. Bowl with internally dished everted rim. Slightly sandy brick-red paste, with white slip under clear lead glaze on interior, firing pale yellow. Deliberate brown iron mottling on the rim flange. Traces of external sooting (?) on the exterior. *74/272; Period 6*

38* ES1. Saucer. *74/275; Period 6*

39* ES1. Saucer. *74/275; Period 6*

40* PEARL1. Bowl. Underglaze hand-painted cobalt blue decoration, consisting of a lattice border on the inside of the rim, and clumps of vegetation on the exterior. Very late 18th or early 19th-century, *c.* 1780-1810? *74/314; Period 4*

41* GREG. Closed form. Jar? Hard, Humberware-like, fabric, light grey with dark grey core, and light red exterior. Dull green pitted glaze over the whole exterior, lapping over the exterior of the rim. Brown-edged green glaze splashes on the exterior. Triple girth groove at the base of the neck. Light-coloured interior deposits. The fabric and glaze have many points in common with Ryedale Ware, and this vessel illustrates the difficulties encountered in trying adequately to categorise some post-medieval coarsewares in the region. *74/337; Period 4*

42* LFP. Small white earthenware jar for 'Poor Man's Friend' with blue transfer-printed inscription. 'Poor Man's Friend' was a proprietary medicine invented by Dr G.L. Roberts (1766-1834), of Bridport. It was widely advertised in newspapers of the period, described as a salve for piles, cuts, burns and leg ulcers 'which should be found on every dressing table'. After Dr Roberts' death, it was produced by Messrs Beach and Barnicott and was manufactured until at least the end of the 19th century. A typical legend reads:
Poor Mans Friend
Price 1/1½
Prepared only by

Beach and Barnicott
Successors to the late
Dr Roberts
Bridport

A second fragment (from 51/100) bears part of the last three lines of the legend and is in the same blue printing, suggesting that both are post-1834. Black-printed examples also occur, but the dating of these is uncertain. At the time of writing, a complete example dresses a shop window display at the Ryedale Folk Museum, Hutton-le-Hole, North Yorkshire, and there are apparently several examples in Bridport Museum. *74/9000; unstratified*

Site 51

43* WHDIP. Large bowl (pancheon) with externally expanded rim. Brick-red earthenware with white slip under clear lead glaze, firing yellow, on the interior. A reddish brown band on top of the rim, where the slip and glaze have been wiped away. Runs and splashes of white slip and glaze on the exterior. *51/264; Period ER-3*

44* LFP2. Conical pot with strung rim. Creamy glaze with greenish pooling under the base, but not Creamware *sensu stricto*. Later 19th or 20th-century. *51/264; Period ER-3*

45* ES0. Complete preserve jar. Off-white body with grey liquid glaze inside and out. Later 19th or 20th-century. *74/264; Period ER-3*

46* PEARL5. Plate. Moulded and coloured blue shell-edge. *51/264; Period ER-3 or 54/1; Period 8.4*

47* BLAK2. Large bowl. Red paste with common white flecks. Square-cut rim, grooved on the exterior leading edge. A thick purplish internal glaze begins 10-15mm below the rim. *51/72; unphased*

48* ES0. Preserve jar. Yellowish white stoneware with overall very light buff lead or Bristol glaze. The exterior as far as the shoulder is dipped in dark brown, and this extends onto the inside of the rim in an irregular line. The base is unglazed. A band of beaded rouletting runs around the shoulder carination. There is what appears to be a small impressed circle (*c.* 6mm diam.) just above the basal angle. Later 19th or earlier 20th-century. *51/100; unphased*

49* LFP7. Bowl with outbent rim. Factory white earthenware with 'cut sponged' rosettes on the rim, with pendent leaf motifs below, all in a mauve blue. The edge of similar decoration is visible above the fracture on the exterior. *51/100; unphased*

50* LFP7. Dish/bowl with out-turned rim. Factory white earthenware with decoration of 'cut sponged' rosettes in blue, both inside and out. *51/9000; unphased*

51* PORC. Inkwell. Plain white porcellanous body. Perhaps from a school desk. Nineteenth or 20th-century. *51/469; Period 2.4*

52* LFP8. Mug. Lead-glazed white earthenware with bands of purple lustre below rim and above base on exterior, and on the inside of the rim. The name 'Isabel' is done in thick dark red overglaze paint below the upper lustre band; fragments of two letters (perhaps an accompanying surname?) occur on the lower body. The second quarter of the 19th century was the heyday of lustreware, though it continued into the later part of the century. *51/-; unstratified*

53* LFP4. Salt cruet. Glazed white earthenware hollow ware in the form of a bird. Deep blue underglaze dots on the body, the eyes with a deep blue centre in a pale blue-grey surround; the remains of the damaged beak (open in song) in underglaze yellow. There is a single pouring hole in the top of the head, and a filling hole in the centre of the base, surrounded by an oblong footring (damaged).The words PLICHTA LONDON are done in underglaze black, in two lines, on the base. Jan Plichta was an immigrant Czech who traded novelty wares (such as piggy banks, models, cruets *et al.*), out of London, mainly stamping the products of the Bovey Pottery (Wemyss) between 1930 and the second half of the 1950s (Internet sources). *51/-; unstratified*

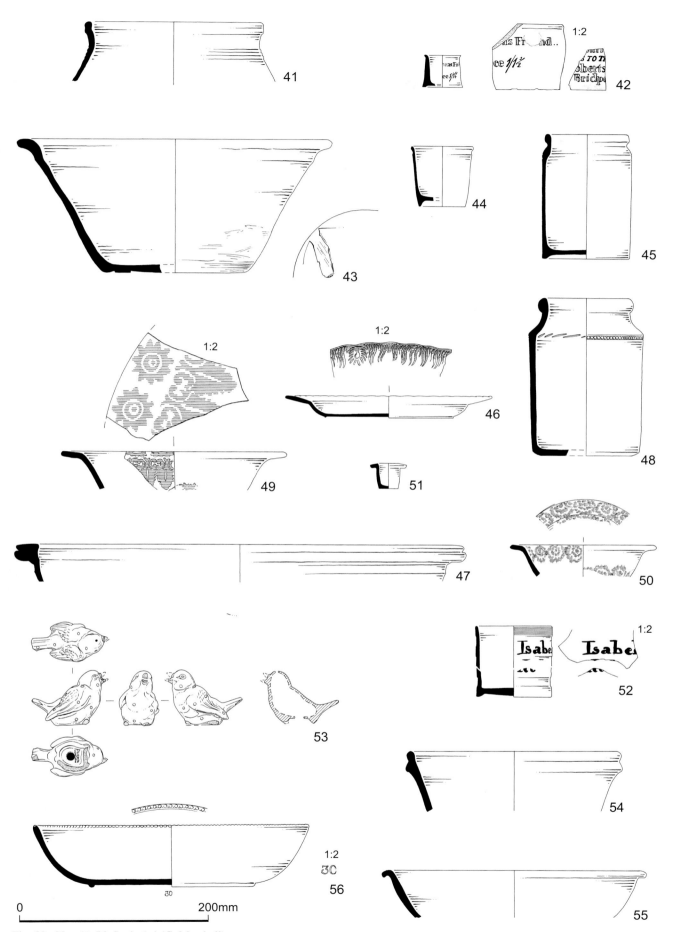

Fig. 80. Nos 41-56. Scale 1:4 (C. Marshall)

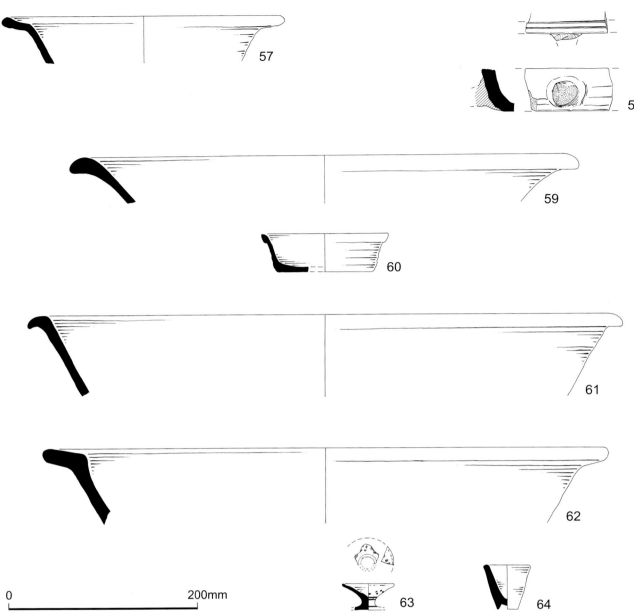

Fig. 81. Nos 57-64. Scale 1:4 (C. Marshall)

The Cottages

54* RYED. Straight-sided flanged bowl. Sandy very pale grey fabric with light red exterior margin and surface. Lustrous, almost metallic, dark apple green glaze over whole interior, with runs and splashes on the exterior. The top and inside edge of the rim are heavily worn. *Unstratified, from the area of the cottages*

55* RYED. Lipped bowl. Very pale grey, with variable pinkish core in parts of the fracture. Dark apple-green glaze over whole exterior and patchily on top of the rim, with a single long iron-rich, dark brown streak. Unglazed light reddish brown interior. *Unstratified, in the area of the cottages*

56* CREAM. Dish. Substantially complete. White earthenware with cream-coloured glaze. Greenish glaze pooling on the interior edge of the footring. The underside of the base has the number '30' impressed. The rim has beaded decoration; an almost identical form is referred to as a 'beaded nappy' in the 1807 Don Pottery Pattern Book (Doncaster Library Service 1983, no. 67). In David Dunderdale's 1796 Castleford Pottery Pattern Book (reproduced in Roussel 1982), which was intended for French and Spanish-speaking customers, the same form (Roussel 1982 nos 94, 95) is annotated 'pour cuire les mets au four'/'para cocer los manjares en horno'. *Unstratified, from the area of the cottages*

57* WHDIP. Bowl with internally dished everted rim. Brick-red paste, with thin white slip under a clear lead glaze internally, firing to a rich reddish-yellow dark 'egg yolk' colour. There is a fine brown iron speckling over the whole interior, with occasional larger patches of the same colour. *Unstratified, from the area of the cottages*

Site 11

58* RYED. Sherd from the wall of a dripping pan, with the stump of a lateral handle. Sandy pinkish buff fabric with pinkish red unglazed exterior. Dull green glaze over most of the interior, with orange areas below the rim and over the whole top face of the rim. The rim has two parallel grooves. Unusually, there are what appear to be traces of light sooting below the handle and along the basal angle. See also No. 89. *11/3; unstratified*

Site 15

59* BLAK2. Large bowl with rounded rim. Fabric as that of No. 172. Black glaze, as on No. 74. *15/6; unstratified*

184

60* UGRE. Small dish with externally thickened rim. Fine red fabric, the interior smoothed for *c.* 18mm below the rim. Perhaps horticultural, *e.g.* a tray for seeds or cuttings. *15/6; unstratified*

61* UGRE. Bowl. Unglazed, fairly coarse, brick-red 'flowerpot' fabric. *15/6; unstratified*

62* BLAK2. Large bowl with out-turned rim. Fabric as that of No. 172. Internal black glaze extends to underside of rim, though it has pulled away from most of the leading edge. *15/EP4; unstratified*

Site 49

63* TIN. Faience. Pedestal-based form? Pale blue-tinged ground with blue decoration. The two sherds, from different sites and contexts, do not join but are almost certainly from the same or a similar vessel. *49/92; Period 3. 54/462; Period 6.3*

64* ES0. Boot-blacking pot. Grey stoneware with light yellowish brown salt-glaze. The form is referred to by Oswald *et al.* (1982, 62), who note that, while the form is regularly mistaken for a spirit measure, examples still containing blacking were found on the site of Day and Martin's Blacking Factory in Holborn. The authors hold (Oswald *et al.* 1982, 62) that the form was discontinued during the first half of the 19th century, while Green (1999, 171, fig. 139, no. 427) suggests that the form may have been introduced at Fulham before 1865. See No. 29 for another example. *49/-; unstratified or 51/1; unstratified*

The vicarage sites
Site 77

65* GREG. Closed form (jug?). Hard fine, light red fabric with thick grey inner margin. Apple green interior glaze with fine darker green mottling. A single splash of yellow brown glaze on the interior. *77/333; Period 5.2*

66* TIN. Chamber pot with ridge below rim. Plain white faience, light yellow body. Probably first half of the 18th century, cf. Amis 1968, illus. nos 17-18; Hume 1991, fig. 56 (right); Orton 1988, fig. 131, no. 1270. Hume (1991, 147) suggests that the shoulder ridge on these vessels had disappeared by *c.* 1735. *77/132 = 154, 155; Period 5.2*

67* CIST. Three-handled cup (Brears 1971, Type 2). Very dark purplish brown, almost black, glaze on a dark red body. Applied dots of greenish yellow in pairs between the handles. Fine mortar accretions over all fractures and underneath the base. *77/144; Period 5.1*

68* RYED. Large diameter form with applied thumbed strip below the rim. Grey fabric, dull green internal glaze with pitting and iron flecking, and light red exterior with greenish yellow glaze splash. Applied thumbed strips occur on jugs/cisterns (cf. Jennings and Boyles 1995, fig. 20.2, nos 5 and 6), but the diameter of this vessel would perhaps be more appropriate to a large jar. *77/85; Period 5.2*

69* SYG. Jug. Pale pinkish white fabric with abundant polychrome quartz and other grits. Yellowish surfaces, with splashes of purplish brown, light green and orange glaze. Later 15th or 16th-century? *77/91; Period 5.1*

70* UCD. Frilled base of a chafing dish, unattributed to source, though possibly French. Fine, slightly sandy and micaceous, light-firing fabric, off-white with extensive pink laminae. Yellowish-brown external glaze, and light red unglazed areas. Fractured through the remains of a single extant perforation. *77/209; Period 5.1*

71* RYED. Jar with lid-seated rim, the exterior face of which is slightly hollowed. Pale grey-buff fabric with reddish unglazed exterior, the outside of the rim and the whole of the interior with a dull olive-green glaze with brown iron pitting. There are extensive areas of sooting on the exterior. *77/304; Period 5.1*

72* ES6? Bottle. Pale grey stoneware with mottled rich brown glaze on exterior, and unglazed yellowish interior. Eighteenth or 19th-century? *77/250; unstratified*

73* GREG. Bowl. Fabric and glaze as No. 147. *77/114; Period 6*

74* BLAK2. Large bowl with out-turned rim. Fabric as that of No. 172. Black glaze on interior and on both sides of rim (partial and smeared on the underside). *77/14; Period 1-5*

Site 54
Period 5

75* ES3? Small, shallow, near complete, straight-sided vessel. Fine pinkish stoneware with thin white margins and rather lustrous reddish brown overall glaze, patchy under the base. The form is presumably a glass-stand, cf. similar items in Creamware at a rather later date (*e.g.* Doncaster Library Service 1983, no. 170). A Nottingham attribution is by no means certain. Joining sherds from *54/514; Period 5.2. 54/516; Period 6.3*

76* CIST/BLAK1. Costrel. Complete except for edge of rim. Hard red fabric, with brownish purple glaze to *c.* 15mm above the base. Dribbles of glaze inside the neck. The sides parallel to the suspension lugs are both flattened. The vessel has been removed from the wheel with a single pull from a straight wire, which at the major production centre at Wrenthorpe, near Wakefield, is a technique associated with Blackware, a looped wire usually being employed in the case of Cistercian wares (Moorhouse and Slowikowski 1992, 91, 96-97). On the other hand, the body profile and general fabric and colouration is nearer that of Cistercian wares at Wrenthorpe (Moorhouse and Slowikowski 1992, fig. 57, nos 129-31, as opposed to fig. 63, nos 233-4). The difficulty of distinguishing between Blackware and Cistercian costrels is remarked upon (Moorhouse and Slowikowski 1992, 95),and the vessel need not, in any case, be a Wrenthorpe product. Seventeenth-century. *54/395; Period 5.3*

77* GREG. Tripod-footed base, probably of pipkin. Sandy and slightly chalky light red fabric. Variably yellow and green iron-flecked internal glaze, with runs and splashes on the exterior. *54/395; Period 5.3*

Period 6.1

78* RAER. Neck and shoulder of globular drinking jug. Mid- grey stoneware with glassy rich brown glaze over the exterior and on the inside of the neck, below which the interior is matt. The form is widespread in eastern England in the period *c.* 1475-1550. *54/431; Period 6.1*

Period 6.3: Context 516

79* RYED. Bowl with externally grooved rim. Pale grey fabric with thick light red exterior core margin and surface. A dark coppery green glaze over the outside of the rim and the whole interior. Externally sooted in patches, with thick carbonised accretions in the rim groove. *54/516; Period 6.3*

80* RYED. Bowl with hollowed rim. Light grey fabric with pinkish buff margins in places, and core in thickest parts of rim. Dark coppery green glaze on interior, patches of thin apple-green glaze on exterior. The whole of the rim component is uniformly sooted. *54/516; Period 6.3*

81* RYED. Bowl with hollowed rim. Grey core with light red exterior margin and surface. Pitted and iron-flecked dull olive-green glaze on interior. The glaze overlaps the rim edge in places and is orange. Orange glaze dips and runs on the exterior body. *54/516; Period 6.3*

82* RYED. Bowl with hollowed rim. Grey core, light grey interior margin, light red exterior margin and surface. Dull olive-green interior glaze, pitted and iron-flecked. *54/516; Period 6.3*

83* RYED. Bowl with hollowed rim. Light red with fairly dark apple-green glaze on interior. Neat band of sooting on the exterior of the rim and for a short distance on the underside of the rim flange. *54/516; Period 6.3*

84* RYED. Bowl with slightly hollowed rim. Pinkish buff with pale red exterior. Quite lustrous apple-green interior glaze, lapping over the rim edge in places. *54/516; Period 6.3*

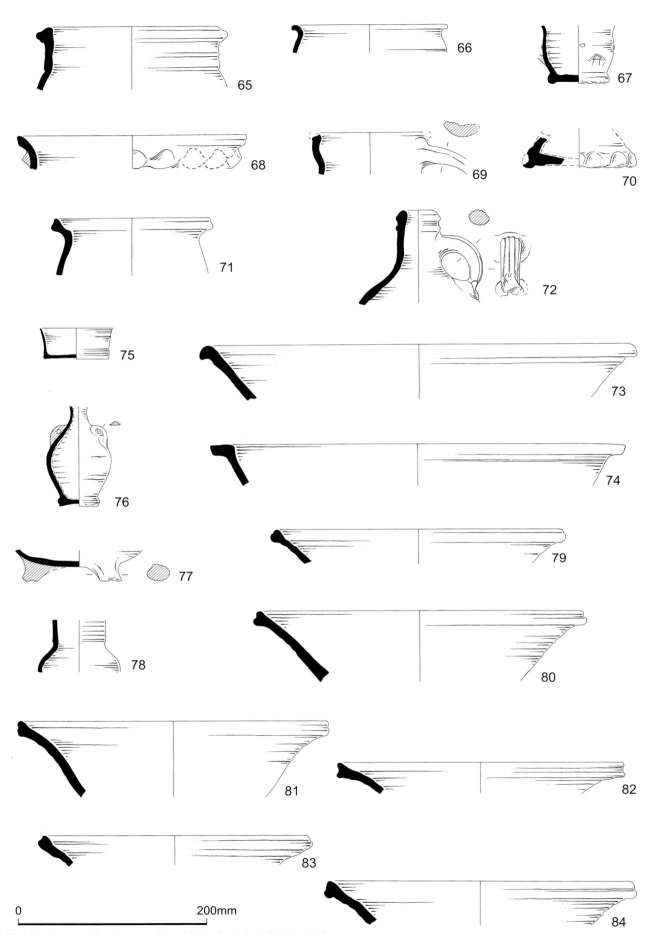

Fig. 82. Post-medieval pottery Nos 65-84. Scale 1:4 (C. Marshall)

0   200mm

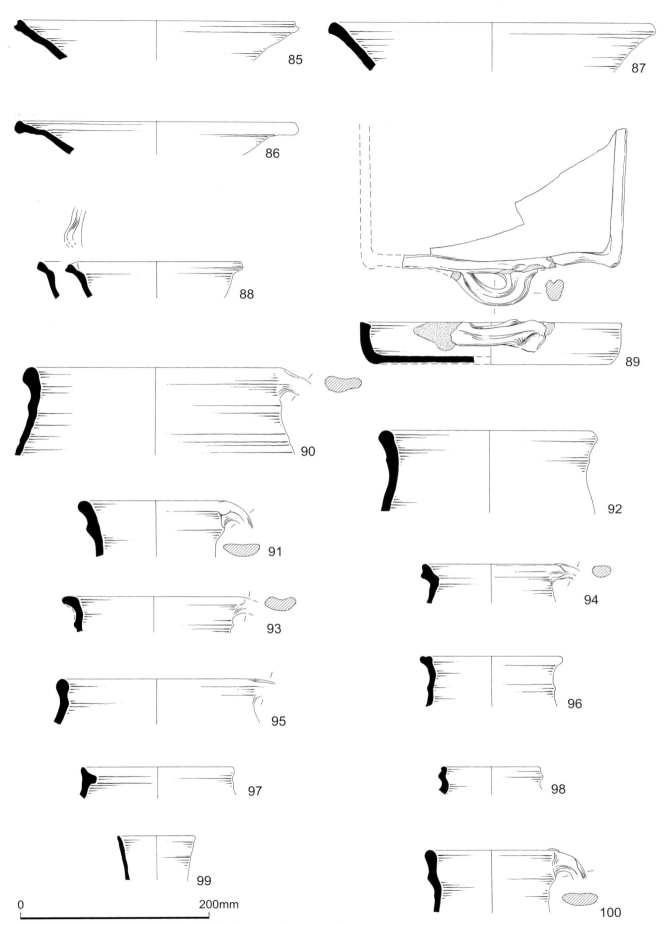

Fig. 83. Post-medieval potterty Nos 85-100. Scale 1:4 (C. Marshall)

85* RYED. Bowl with slightly hollowed rim. Light red body and interior, lustrous brownish green interior glaze. Extensive carbonised deposits on the outer edge of the rim. *54/516; Period 6.3*

86* RYED. Bowl. Pinkish fabric with light grey interior margin, and light red exterior surface. Dark coppery green glaze, with darker iron mottling, on interior. Extensive but light sooting on the rim edge and underside of the rim flange. *54/516; Period 6.3*

87* RYED. Bowl. Light buff with light brown exterior, lustrous apple-green glaze on interior, and overlapping the rim. *54/516; Period 6.3*

88* RYED. Bowl (?) with internally dished rim and pulled spout. Pinkish buff fabric with light red exterior and lustrous, slightly iron-spotted, apple-green glaze on interior. There are extensive sooting deposits on the exterior surface. *54/516; Period 6.3*

89* RYED. Dripping pan. Pale grey fabric with slightly pitted and iron-flecked dull green glaze on interior and top of handle. The glaze runs patchily onto the exterior walls of the vessel. These are light red where unglazed. There is a lateral handle on the extant long side; this was presumably centrally placed, allowing the original length to be estimated. There is an area of dark discolouration inside and below the curve of the handle. This is unlikely to be sooting and may be the result of cooking residues transferred by the user's hand (cf. No. 89). *54/516; Period 6.3*

90* RYED. Handled jar. Pale grey with light red exterior margin and reddish grey exterior. Lightly pitted and iron-flecked apple-green glaze over whole interior. *54/516; Period 6.3*

91* RYED. Handled jar. Light pinkish buff with browner exterior. Rich coppery green glaze on interior. *54/516; Period 6.3*

92* RYED. Jar, probably handled. Pinkish buff with thick, light grey inner margin. Light reddish brown exterior. Very finely and abundantly pitted apple-green glaze on interior, spilling over onto the outer edge of the rim. *54/516; Period 6.3*

93* RYED. Handled jar? Variably light grey and pink body with lustrous iron-streaked green glaze on all surfaces. *54/516; Period 6.3*

94* RYED. Handled closed form with internally dished (lid-seated?) rim. Pinkish with thick light grey core in the thicker parts of the rim. Light red exterior. Dark apple-green glaze on interior. *54/516; Period 6.3*

95* RYED. Handled closed form with internally dished (lid-seated?) rim. Light grey with pinkish exterior margin and reddish brown exterior surface. Heavily pitted dull olive-green glaze on interior. *54/516; Period 6.3*

96* RYED. Closed form with neck cordon. Orange buff with light grey core and inner margin in places, and red exterior where unglazed. Lustrous dark iron-streaked apple-green glaze on interior, patchily extending over and underneath the rim. Handle attachment scar on rim. *54/516; Period 6.3*

97* RYED. Closed form. Dished rim with internal bead. Pinkish fabric with thin worn brownish green glaze on all surfaces. *54/516; Period 6.3*

98* RYED. Closed form. Cordoned rim, hollowed on interior. Pale fabric with light buff inner margin and dark reddish grey interior where unglazed. Dull green iron-flecked glaze on exterior, extending unevenly over the inside of the rim. *54/516; Period 6.3*

99* RYED. Closed form. Pinkish buff, light grey in parts. Overall dull dark green glaze, thin and patchy on parts of interior. *54/516; Period 6.3*

100* RYED. Jug/cistern? Pinkish red with dark green glaze over all surfaces, including handle. *54/516; Period 6.3*

101* RYED. Pipkin handle. Light-coloured fabric with pale buff unglazed exterior. Slightly iron-flecked apple-green glaze on interior, with splashes on handle. The handle is discoloured on the underside, possibly from cooking residues left by the user's hand cf. No. 89. *54/516; Period 6.3*

102* RYED. Form uncertain. Flat outbent rim with internal bead. Light grey throughout, with overall dull green glaze, iron-flecked. *54/516; Period 6.3*

103* TIN. Majolica. Open form with cobalt-blue decoration on tin-glazed interior, faintly mauve lead-glazed exterior. The chequer pattern (*schaakbordmotief*) derives from Italian majolicas and was widely employed on Dutch majolicas of the first quarter of the 17th century, though it does not appear to have been used by English manufacturers. On Dutch open forms, it is often accompanied by a blue-dashed rim, as here, cf. Bartels 1999, catalogue nos 925, 953-955; Korf 1973, illus. nos 39-40, 47; Korf 1968, illus. nos 64-72. The latter are Haarlem products, and Haarlem is probably the most likely source for this vessel. *54/516; Period 6.3*

104* TIN. Majolica. Plate. Cobalt blue foliage on lighter slate-blue undulating stems, and encircling slate-blue bands. The ground on the tin-glazed interior is off-white and rather matt, the lead-glazed back a greyish cream colour. Like No. 103, this is probably a Low Countries product. Broadly similar decoration appears to occur throughout the first three quarters of the 17th century, cf. Bartels 1999, catalogue nos 912, 921. *54/516; Period 6.3*

105* ES1. Bowl with slightly flared rim, footring base and turned double groove on the upper body. *54/516; Period 6.3*

106* GREB. Base of tripod-footed vessel, with one extant foot and scar of another. Sandy orange fabric with rich reddish brown glaze over whole interior, with splashes and runs on the exterior and the underside of the base. The exterior is dark red where unglazed and there are patches of sooting. The vessel appears to have been burned post-fracture. *54/516; Period 6.3*

107* WEST. Rim of mug (*Humpen*)? Cobalt blue and manganese purple infill colouration. Manganese purple was added to Westerwald products from *c.* 1665, and continued into the 18th century. There is a wide variety of decoration on *Humpen* of this period. Almost identical rims of similar diameter can appear on contemporary globular and other jugs, so attribution to form is not entirely certain. *54/516; Period 6.3*

108* RYED. Bowl with hollowed rim. Pinkish buff outer margin and surface, pale grey inner margin. Apple-green interior glaze, with light red surface on unglazed patches. The outer edge of the rim, the underside of the rim flange, and an area of the upper body are extensively sooted. *54/516; Period 6.3. 54/202; Period 7.5*

109* RYED. Bowl with hollowed rim. Grey core with light red exterior margin, and surface patches where unglazed. Dull olive-green internal glaze, pitted and iron-flecked. Extensive lighter green glaze patches on exterior. *54/516; Period 6.3. 54/202; Period 7.5*

110* RYED. Bowl with deeply hollowed rim. Pale grey fabric with very light red exterior and thin core margin in places. Light apple-green glaze over whole interior and parts of rim on exterior, lightly pitted and iron-flecked. *54/516; Period 6.3. 54/202; Period 7.5*

111* RYED. Bowl with deeply hollowed rim. Very pale pink fabric with pale grey margins and light pinkish buff exterior. Lightly pitted and iron-streaked apple-green glaze on interior. *54/516; Period 6.3. 54/202; Period 7.5*

112* RYED. Closed form with neck cordon. Brownish grey with light red margins in places. Dark reddish grey exterior with brown glaze splashes, overall brownish green glaze on interior. *54/516; Period 6.3. 54/202; Period 7.5*

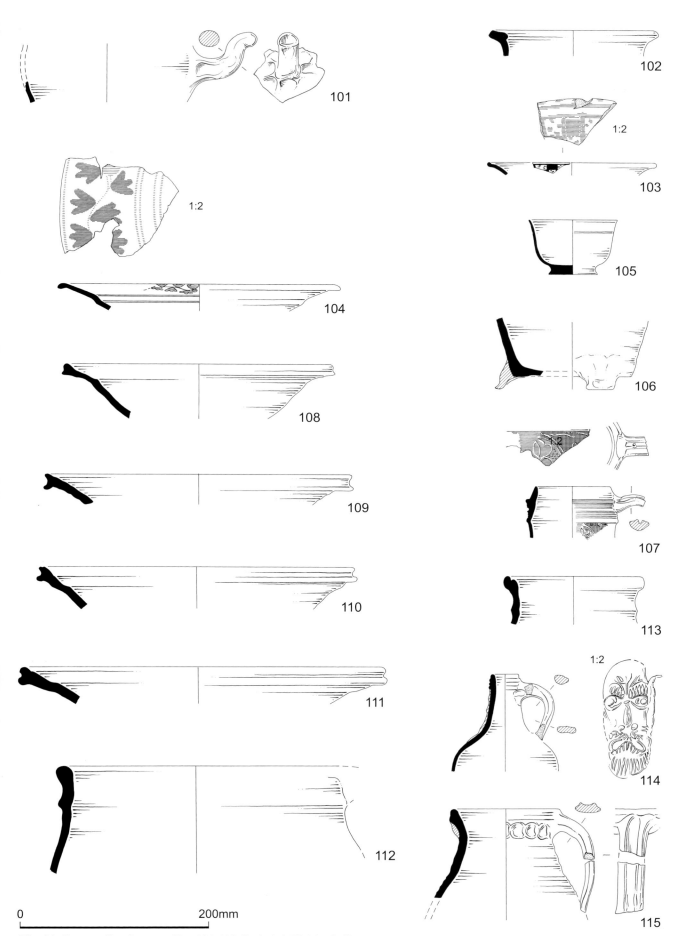

Fig. 84. Post-medieval pottery Nos 101-115. Scale 1:4 (C. Marshall)

113* RYED. Closed form with lid-seating groove on interior of rim.Patchy light grey and pinkish buff, with overall dull green glaze. *54/516; Period 6.3. 54/202; Period 7.5. 54/247; Period 7.4*

114* FRE. Bellarmine. Grey with pinkish grey interior. Freckled rich brown glaze over whole exterior, with glaze runs into interior. Anthony Thwaite suggests (pers. comm.) a late 17th or even early 18th-century date for this example. *54/516; Period 6.3. 54/202; Period 7.5. 54/247; Period 7.4*

115* RYED. Jug with applied thumbed strip below the rim. Light grey with dark grey interior margin and variable light red and grey unglazed interior. The exterior has a patchy pitted and iron-flecked dull green glaze, with light red unglazed areas. *54/516; Period 6.3. 54/350; Period 7.4*

116* GREB. Lid. Hard red sandy fabric with occasional splashes of reddish brown glaze on the interior and the edges of the rim and handle. The vessel was thrown as a bowl, and the handle shows that it was removed from the wheel with a straight wire. *54/516; Period 6.3. 54/202; Period 7.5. 54/454; Period 6.3*

117* WEST. Base of jug (*Krug*). Decoration of dot-infilled flower buds on combed stalks. Manganese purple between the various floral elements, the centre of the buds in cobalt blue, which also covers the cordon above the base. The decoration is widespread on various forms in the late 17th century and the first half of the 18th, cf. Seewaldt 1990, plates 371 (*Humpen*) and 392b (*Kanne*); Reineking-von Bock 1976, plates 535 (*Krug*) and 577 (*Humpen*). Joining sherds from *54/516; Period 6.3, 54/164; Period 8.1 and 54/462; Period 6.3*. Other sherds which might belong to this vessel or to No. 107 occur in *54/247; Period 7.4, 54/351; Period 7.4 and 54/1173; unstratified*

Period 6.3: other contexts
118* RYED. Bowl with externally hollowed rim. Sandy very pale grey fabric with common ferrous inclusions. Light red exterior margin in places. Dark-olive green glaze with brown iron mottling and abundant pits over whole interior. Light red exterior with similar apple-green glaze runs and patches. *54/266; Period 6.3. 54/200; Period 7.1*

119* RYED?. Jar? Sandy light-firing fabric with reddish external margin in places. Lustrous dark apple-green glaze with occasionaliron streaks and some pitting internally. The glaze extends over the rim and there are runs, streaks and splashes of brownish green glaze externally. The unglazed areas of the exterior are patchy dark red. Extensive light-coloured residues on the interior, as far as the rim. *54/241; Period 6.3. 54/266; Period 6.3. 54/288; Period 7.4*

Period 7.1
120* PEARL2. Saucer. Hand-painted underglaze decoration on the interior only, consisting of a border of dark brown leaves separated by sprays tipped in cobalt blue. There is a dark brown line in the well, and traces of colour suggest that the main motif may have been repeated in the centre of the base. A date in the first third of the 19th century would be appropriate. *54/101; Period 7.1. 54/95; Period 8.2*. Also unstratified and unmarked sherds

Period 7.2
121* LFP6. Chamberpot. Clear lead glaze over white body, firing yellow. Pairs of dark brown slip bands flank a broader band of white slip, upon which are dendritic 'Mocha' patterns in blue. The type was produced from the first half of the 19th century, lasting into the early 20th century. Cf. Amis 1968, no. 48. *54/117; Period 7.2. 54/5; Period 8.1. 54/1; Period 8.4*. Also unmarked sherds

122* LFP6. Bowl with footring. Off-white body with yellow-firing glaze, paler on the exterior than the interior. Three zones of thick white slip banding on the exterior. *54/131; Period 7.2. 54/5; Period 8.1*

Period 7.3
123* ES1. Small jug with side pouring spout. Turned bands at rim and on shoulder. For general form cf. Edwards and Hampson 2005, fig. 63. *54/308; Period 7.3. 54/202; Period 7.5*

Period 7.4
124* RYED. Chafing dish. Pale grey core, with thick whitish margins; iron-flecked dull green glaze overall. The rim and carination are decorated with short oblique slashes, and there is a group of three stamped rosettes at the base of the only extant knob. The left-hand fracture of the sherd runs through a small perforation, placed just above the carination. Glaze has run into this aperture, which was clearly made before firing. The stumps of a vertically orientated handle are in line with the knob. A Ryedale chafing dish from Aldgate, York, has similar rim slashing, but a lateral handle and no stamps (Brooks 1987, fig. 77, no. 810). An identical vessel was found in excavations at Blanket Row, Hull (Didsbury forthcoming, illus. no. 116). *54/75; Period 7.4*

125* TIN. Footring base and lower body of (?) chamber pot. Plain white, slightly mauve-tinged, faience, on light yellow body. *54/75; Period 7.4. 54/124; Period 7.5*

126* STAFS2. Press-moulded dish with pie-crust rim. Very dark brown slip over whole interior. Dark red slip runs and splashes on unglazed exterior. *54/75; Period 7.4. 54/1; Period 8.4. 54/97?; Period 7.7. 54/125; Period 7.1. 54/202; Period 7.5*

127* TIN. Dish/plate. Decoration in purple (manganese). Slightly blue-tinged faience, pale yellow body. Closely similar borders occur on the 'Chinaman-in-grasses' plates of. *c*. 1680-1700, cf. Archer 1997, catalogue nos B.191-193. *54/247; Period 7.4*

128* TIN. Cup. Dark brown trailed slip lines on a yellow ground, with dark brown pellets below the rim. Probably *c*. 1700-1720. Cf. Jennings 1981, fig. 44, nos 716-717. *54/247; Period 7.4. 54/202; Period 7.5*

129* .TIN. Small dispensing or ointment pot. Plain, slightly pink-tinged, white faience, light yellow body. Perhaps first half of the 18th century, cf. Archer 1997, catalogue nos J13-14. *54/286; Period 7.4*

130* STAFS1. Oval press-moulded dish with pie-crust edge. Feathered decoration in light brown and dark brown slips on a yellow ground, on interior only. Early to mid-18th century, or slightly later. C. 65% of vessel extant. *54/123; Period 7.4*

131* GREG. Straight-sided bowl with heavy externally thickened rim. Fairly coarse pinkish red fabric with white-firing *laminae*. Lustrous green glaze on rim and interior only. Dark reddish brown unglazed exterior, with band of shallow grooves/ridges at mid-body. Seventeenth or 18th-century? *54/123; Period 7.4. 54/93; Period 8.1. 54/98; Period 7.7*

132* GREG? Bowl with heavily thickened rim, and encircling grooves above lower fracture. Pinkish red fabric with pale buff outer margin. Lustrous brownish green, slightly iron-flecked glaze over rim and whole of interior. Dark reddish brown unglazed exterior. *54/123; Period 7.4*

Period 7.5
133* RYED. Bowl similar to No. 118, but with more deeply hollowed rim. Fabric similar, but the interior glaze is more finely pitted and mottled, and there are no glazed areas on the exterior. *54/202; Period 7.5*

134* RYED. Straight-sided flanged bowl. Very pale grey fabric with light red exterior margin in some small areas. Bright, lustrous, apple-green glaze with abundant pitting and brown mottling over whole interior. Similar glaze areas on exterior, with thin green and orange patches. *54/202; Period 7.5*

135* RYED. Closed form. Pale red fabric with light grey core in the thickest parts of the rim. Pitted orange glaze over whole exterior, with some green patches towards the rim. The exterior is very abraded, but may have had overall orange glaze. The glaze survives in the rim hollow and in patches elsewhere on the exterior. There is a girth groove above the lower fracture. *54/202; Period 7.5*

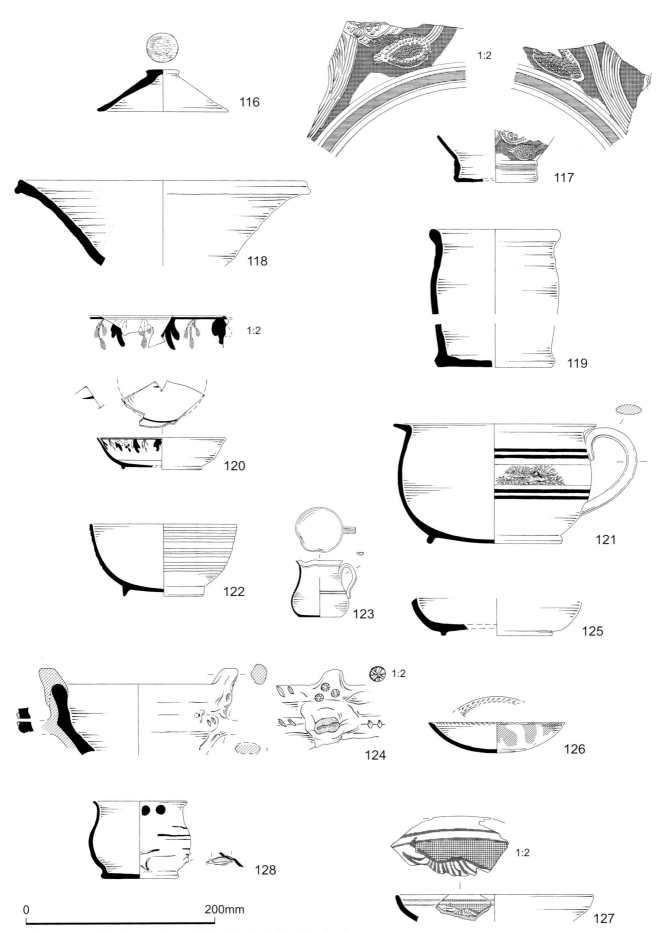

116

117

118

119

1:2

120

121

122

123

125

124

126

128

127

1:2

1:2

1:2

0   200mm

Fig. 85. Post-medieval pottery Nos 116-128. Scale 1:4 (C. Marshall)

191

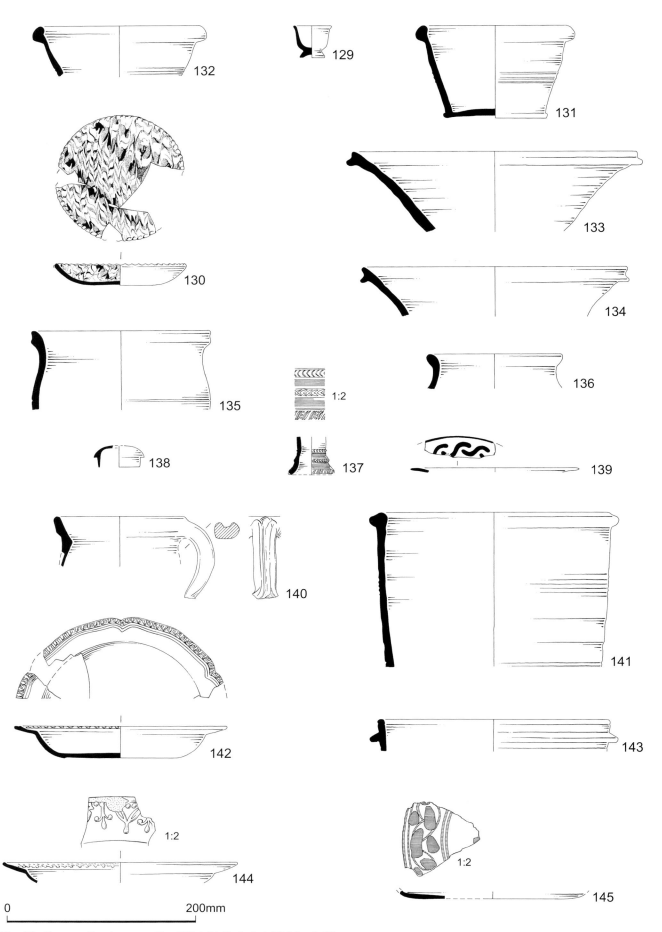

Fig. 86. Post-medieval pottery Nos 129-145. Scale 1:4 (C. Marshall)

192

136* RYED. Jar? Light grey fabric with pitted and iron-stained apple-green glaze overall. *54/202; Period 7.5*

137* WEST. Fragment, possibly from the pedestal base of a jug. Three cordons, the uppermost two of which are notched with chevrons, the lowest having groups of oblique strokes separated by three dots. The cordons are separated by cobalt blue bands. Their treatment might suggest a date in the very late 16th or earlier 17th century, cf. Gaimster 1997, plates 114-115. *54/202; Period 7.5*

138* ES2. Turned cover, possibly from a coffee pot. Dark red stoneware. *54/202; Period 7.5*

139* STAFS2. Chamberpot (?) rim. Dark brown slip over whole of exterior, with S-scrolls in dark brown slip on yellow ground on inner face. *54/202; Period 7.5. 54/124; Period 7.5*

140* GREB. Jug with deeply grooved handle, joining straight to rim. Hard light red ware. Brownish and patchy olive green internal glaze on interior, almost completely obscured by off-white (lime-scale, urine?) residues. The glaze continues on the exterior to *c.* 10mm below the rim edge, and there are patches of thin reddish brown glaze over much of the exterior. *54/202; Period 7.5*

141* GREG. Storage jar. Fairly fine, hard, light grey ware. Dull, dark green glaze overall. The thickened rim is slightly hollowed on the exterior. A band of girth grooves on the upper body, and the edge of another above the extant lower edge. *54/202; Period 7.5. 54/124; Period 7.5*

Period 7.6

142* ES4a? Plate, 'Queen's Shape' with gadrooned rim edge. Very hard, fine white fabric with, in its present state, yellowish surfaces. Traces of what appears to be a smeared glaze. It is possible that this vessel should be regarded as a mis-fired Creamware 'second', rather than ES4a. For the latter, cf. Roussel 1982, 29-30. *54/167; Period 7.6. 54/5; Period 8.1. 54/31; Period 8.1. 54/82; Period 8.2. 54/93; Period 8.1. 54/95; Period 8.2*

Period 7.7

143* GREG. Straight-sided flanged bowl. Sandy pinkish red fabric with pale buff core margins. Dirty green glaze internally, on outer edge of the rim, and in patches externally. Dull red exterior where unglazed. The form suggests a 17th or 18th-century date, and the fabric might just fall within the Ryedale spectrum. *54/87; Period 7.7*

144* CREAM. Plate. Fabric as that of No. 56. Bead row with alternating pendent trefoil and 'winged seed' motifs. *54/97 = context 91; Period 7.7*

Period 7.8

145* TIN. Faience. Base of plate with decorative band in well, cobalt blue on a light blue band. Light yellow paste with slightly blue- and pink-tinged white background glaze. Late 17th or 18th-century. For the same motif on the rim of a London plate with a portrait of Queen Anne (1702-1714) cf. Archer 1997, catalogue no. B.4. *54/9; Period 7.8*

146* GREB. Bowl. Fabric and glaze as No. 157. *54/9; Period 7.8*

147* GREG. Bowl. Hard light red ware with dull olive-green glaze on outer face of rim and over whole interior. *54/9; Period 7.8*

148* GREG. Handled jar. Hard, fine, variably light red or light grey fabric, with dull green glaze over whole extant interior. Light red unglazed exterior. *54/9; Period 7.8*

149* UGRE. Dish with bead rim. Hard, light red earthenware with slightly darker surfaces. Cf. No. 60. *54/96; Period 7.8*

150* ES4b. Sherd from a stoneware teapot gallery, with moulded rosettes above leaf motifs. The sherd has been burned post- fracture; in its present state it has a black body with very dark red surfaces. The design of the gallery can not be matched precisely at Castleford, though it is generically very similar. *c.* 1800-1815. *54/12; Period 7.8*

Period 8.1

151* WEST. 'GR' medallion from a straight-sided tankard ('Humpen'). Light grey stoneware. The medallion stands out on a cobalt ground, and the letters are also picked out in cobalt. A cordon above the medallion, and curvilinear incised decoration to the right (as viewed). 1714-1760. *54/5; Period 8.1*

152* ES1. Small bowl with rolled-over rim. Near complete. There are extensive areas of purplish brown 'flashing' on the interior, and patches on the exterior. A date of '*c.* 1745+' is claimed for a similar example from Norwich (Jennings 1981, fig. 102, no. 1617). *54/5; Period 8.1*

153* PEARL2. Saucer. Underglaze enamels. Decoration as No. 154. Brown encircling line in the well. *54/5; Period 8.1*

154* PEARL2. Tea-bowl. Underglaze enamels. Blue rim edge. On the exterior, a band of decoration consisting of blue dots and ochre 'berries' on brown stalks, attached to a dark brown zig-zag line. First quarter of 19th century? *54/5; Period 8.1. 54/111; Period 8.1*

155* LFP6. Chamberpot. Yellowish-white paste, firing to a dark yellow under a clear lead glaze. Dark brown rim edge, and multiple dark brown slip banding on the body. *54/5; Period 8.1*

156* GREB. Storage jar. Hard, fine redware, with reduced core inplaces. Rich, lustrous, reddish brown glaze inside and out. Although coded GREB, the vessel is actually a bichrome, since there is a broad band of lime green *c.*35mm deep immediately below the rim on the interior. The exterior grooves have perhaps been treated with a thin white slip, since they have fired to a pale yellow. *54/5; Period 8.1*

157* GREB. Bowl. Turned-over rim. Light red earthenware. Internal reddish orange glaze, with runs below the rim on the exterior. *54/31; Period 8.1*

158* CREAM. Plate. Fabric as that of No. 56. Bath edge. *54/111; Period 8.1*

159* PEARL4. Bowl. Engine-turned chequer-pattern border consisting of dark brown and white rectangles, this above a zone of eggshell-blue. Hume (1991, 131 and fig. 48) suggests a date-range of *c.* 1795-1815 for this kind of ware. For a similar bowl in a group dated to *c.* 1780-1800 at Oyster Street, Portsmouth, see Fox and Barton 1986, fig. 100, no. 3. *54/113; Period 8.1*

160* ES5. Capuchin. Iron-dipped band both sides of the rim. The optimum date is *c.* 1700-1725. Cf. Edwards and Hampson 2005, colour plates 34 and 172, though neither of these examples is brown-dipped. *54/11; Period 8.2*

161* RYED. Storage jar. Light grey fabric, with thin, even, lime-green glaze over the whole interior. Light pitting and iron flecking in the basal area. Glaze runs and splashes under the base and around the basal angle. The neck ridge is a common feature of large jars in this ware, cf. Jennings and Boyles 1995, fig. 20.2, no. 14. *54/150; Period 8.1*

162* TIN. Faience. Slightly pink-tinged underside. Base of flatware with part of building and fence (?). Blue with linear elements in brown. Later 17th or 18th-century. *54/150; Period 8.1*

163* TIN. Base and lower body of mug. Plain white pink-tinged faience, the underside of the base unglazed. Light yellow body. Early 18th-century? *54/150; Period 8.1*

164* TIN. Base of dispensing pot. Plain, pink-tinged, white faience, pale yellow body. Underside slightly concave. Pots in the Victoria and Albert Museum with this profile are dated *c.* 1700-1770 by Archer (1997, cat. nos J.15-17). *54/150; Period 8.1*

165* CREAM. Plate. As No. 142, except that the outer half of the rim flange is washed in a vivid green. Shell-edged plates wiped in green are known from Castleford, and this might be contemporary (cf. Roussel 1982, plate 25, dated *c.* 1800-1820). *54/150; Period 8.1*

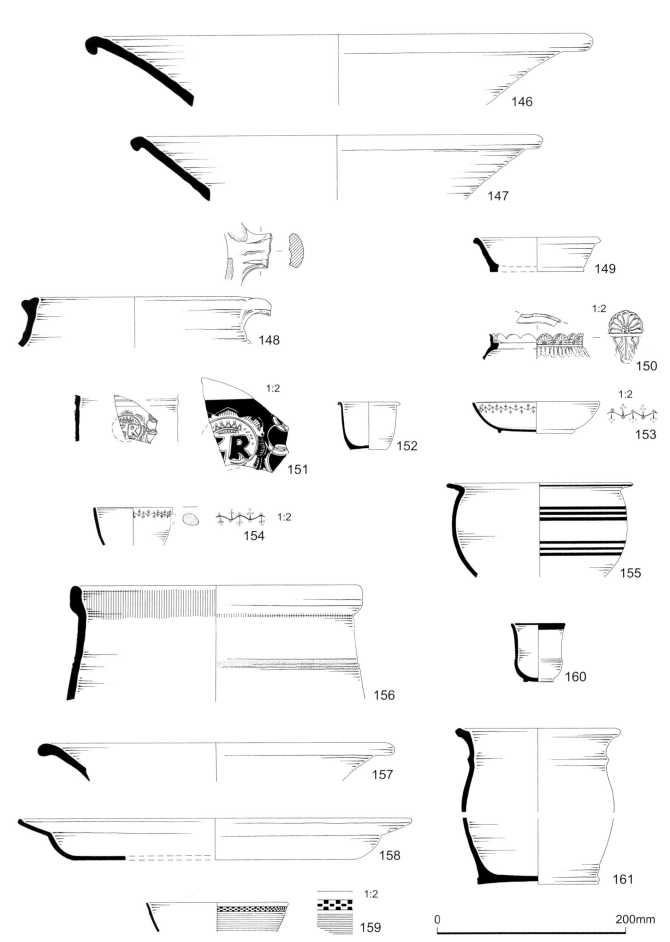

1:2

1:2

1:2

1:2

1:2

1:2

0   200mm

Fig. 87. Post-medieval pottery Nos 146-161. Scale 1:4 (C. Marshall)

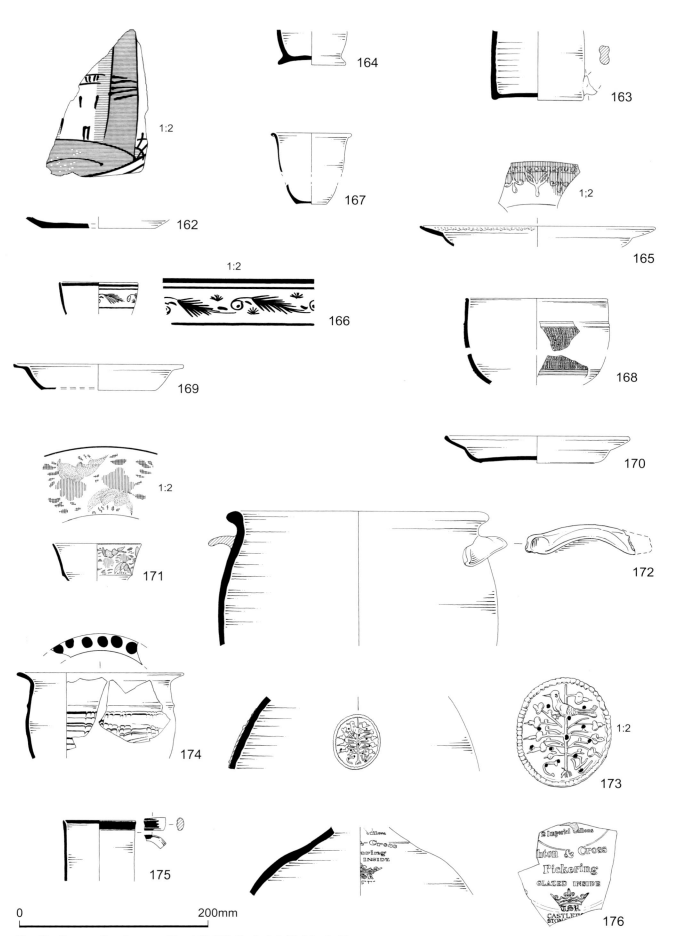

Fig. 88. Post-medieval pottery Nos 162-176. Scale 1:4 (C. Marshall)

166* PEARL1. Bowl. Underglaze hand-painted blue decoration, consisting of a band on the inside of the rim and a border of stylised fronds on the exterior. Very late 18th or early 19th-century, *c.* 1780-1810? *54/1; Period 8.4. 54/113; Period 8.1; 54/162; Period 8.1.* Also unmarked sherds

167* ES1. Small bowl, in all respects as No. 152. *54/1; Period 8.4. 54/141; Period 8.1. 54/150; Period 8.1*

Period 8.2

168* ES3? Bowl with bead rim and central band of rouletting demarcated by grooves. The fabric is light grey with fine white margins in the upper part of the fracture, pinkish buff lower down. Lustrous mid-brown metallic finish overall. Bowls and punch bowls of this same general form, which resembles the Roman samian ware form 37, were made at Nottingham and other centres throughout most of the 18th-century and possibly later, cf. Hildyard 1985, nos 231-232, 238 and 256. *54/82; Period 8.2*

169* CREAM. Dish/deep plate. Rim with 'Bath' edge. *54/82; Period 8.2*

170* CREAM. Plate. Fabric as that of No. 56. Rims of this form, with a raised bead at the edge, are referred to as 'Bath' types in the 1807 Don Pottery Pattern Book (Doncaster Library Service 1983, *passim). 54/7; Period 8.2*

171* PEARL2a. 'London-shape' cup. There is a band of dark purplish brown overglaze paint covering the rim; faint watery overglaze mauve bands occur below the rim and above the carination on the exterior, and there is an overall background of irregular elongated 'droplets' in the same colour. Dark orange red overglaze motifs in thicker paint were applied over this background. These are reminiscent of autumn leaves, and were perhaps intended to be so. A date *c.* 1815-1825 seems the most appropriate. *54/7; Period 8.2*

172* BLAK2. Large jar with externally thickened rim and applied lateral 'shell' handles. Light red paste with fine white flecking, very dark reddish brown glaze on both surfaces. The lower edge of the glazed area on the exterior is just visible above the fracture. *54/7; Period 8.2*

173* ES6? Bottle body with applied medallion in relief. 'Sandwich' fabric, with light red inner and light grey outer layers, pinkish grey interior. Rather mottled brown salt-glaze on exterior. The medallion shows a bird sitting in the upper branches of a bush, with the initials 'CW' flanking the base of the stem. Twelve small holes show where the medallion has been pegged onto the body during firing. It is possible that the image refers to a tavern sign ('The Bird in the Bush' or similar). Applied medallions from late 17th-century vessels made by John Dwight at Fulham include examples with depictions of tavern signs, accompanied by the tavern-keeper's initials (Green 1999, Appendix 4). In this respect it is of some interest that the Wentworth Woodhouse Muniments Schedule mentions a 'Bird in the Bush' as having existed in Appletongate, Malton (present-day Wheelgate) in 1714 (quoted in Hudleston 1962) *54/14; Period 8.2*

Period 8.4

174* STAFS1. Chamberpot. Dark brown trailed and combed decoration on a yellow ground, with applied dark brown roundels on top of the rim. Probably *c.* 1700-1720. *54/1; Period 8.4*

175* ES5. Mug rim and upper body. Rich dark brown iron dip on the rim, neatly demarcated by a groove on the exterior and by the change of angle on the interior. Faint light brown mottling for some distance below. Conventionally dated *c.* 1700-1725, excavations on Staffordshire production sites suggest that the type may have been produced at least as late as 1750-1770, cf. Edwards and Hampson 2005, colour plates 8, 141, 142, 176 and 192. *54/1; Period 8.4*

176* ES0. Sherd from shoulder of spirit bottle. Light yellowish grey stoneware, glazed both sides. The exterior and upper part of the interior are dipped in a rich brown wash, the remainder of the interior has a yellowish lead or Bristol glaze. The sherd bears the following impressed legends: '2 Imperial Gallons/[As]hton & Cross/Pickering/GLAZED INSIDE/ (A crown) /TSR/ CASTLEF[ORD]/STON[E POTTERY]. Expansions are based upon the sources named below. Early 19th-century Trades Directories (Baines 1823; Pigot 1829; 1834; White 1840) list Ashton and Cross as Wine and Spirit Merchants, or as Porter and Spirit Merchants, in Hallgarth, Pickering. For an almost identical sherd, in respect of the rest of the legend, cf. Northern Ceramic Society 1997, no. 125, which indicates that 'TSR' was Thomas Stephen Russell, who had been manager of the coarseware manufacturing side of the Castleford Pottery under David Dunderdale, before the latter's business failure in 1821. Russell subsequently ran that section as an independent concern at Whitwood Mere, from *c.* 1821 to the late 1830s. The only differences between the legends on the two vessels are that the Wharram Percy example has the word 'Imperial' before 'Gallons', and 'GLAZED INSIDE' instead of 'WARRANTED GLAZED INSIDE'. At the time of publication, the cited vessel was believed to be the only known marked piece from this pottery. *54/1; Period 8.4*

177* ES0. Bottle shoulder. Light grey stoneware with pale brown salt-glazed exterior and pinkish grey unglazed interior. Part of a type-impressed legend reads: 'Grays' (cf. No. 184). *54/1; Period 8.4*

178* ES0. Bowl with everted rim flange. Grey stoneware with lustrous reddish brown exterior and matt, darker brown, interior. Undulating lines of rouletting on the exterior. *54/1; Period 8.4*

179* HAMB? Jug rim. Hard, slightly gritty, light-firing fabric with reduced core and pale margins. Dark coppery suspension glaze on exterior. Fifteenth-century? *54/2; Period 8.4*

Unmarked sherds

180* TIN. Sherd with part of inscription. Faience, yellowish white paste with eggshell-blue glaze both sides. The inscription, in very dark brown, appears to include the name '[W]alke[?]r'. *54/-; unmarked sherd*

181* PORC. Bone china cup. London-shape, with moulded basket-weave moulding enclosing plain scroll-bordered cartouches. 'Dresden'-type handle (?). The cartouches contain faint traces of fine floral (?) decoration in overglaze gold, red and blue enamels. Cf. Berthoud 1982, plates 399, and 483-4; the latter are particularly close in overall design and are attributed to New Hall. For other New Hall vessels employing very similar basket-weave, cf. de Saye Hutton 1990, plates 186, 188, 199, 201, 213, and 326. A date *c.* 1812-1825 would be appropriate. *54/-, unmarked sherds*

182* LFP6. Chamberpot. Similar to No. 121, but the dark brown pairs of bands each enclose a narrow white slip band; the central white slip panel consists of two bands in some places, three in others; and the blue decoration consists of pale watery patches rather than typical 'Mocha' designs. *54/-, unmarked sherd*

183* PORC. Bone china saucer. Basket-weave moulding and scroll-bordered panels, cf. No. 181, which clearly belongs to the same service. Once again, there are the remains of fine floral decoration in the cartouches and on the interior base. *54/-, unmarked sherds*

184* ES0. Sherd from shoulder of spirit bottle. Yellowish white stoneware with mottled brown salt-glazed exterior. The sherd bears part of a type-impressed legend: 'Gray & [.....]/Spirit M[........]/M[.....]. Early 19th-century Trades Directories (Baines 1823; Pigot 1829; 1834) list Richard Gray, and later Margaret Gray, as Wine and Spirit Merchants (and Confectioners) in the Market Place, Malton. *54 or 51a, context uncertain*

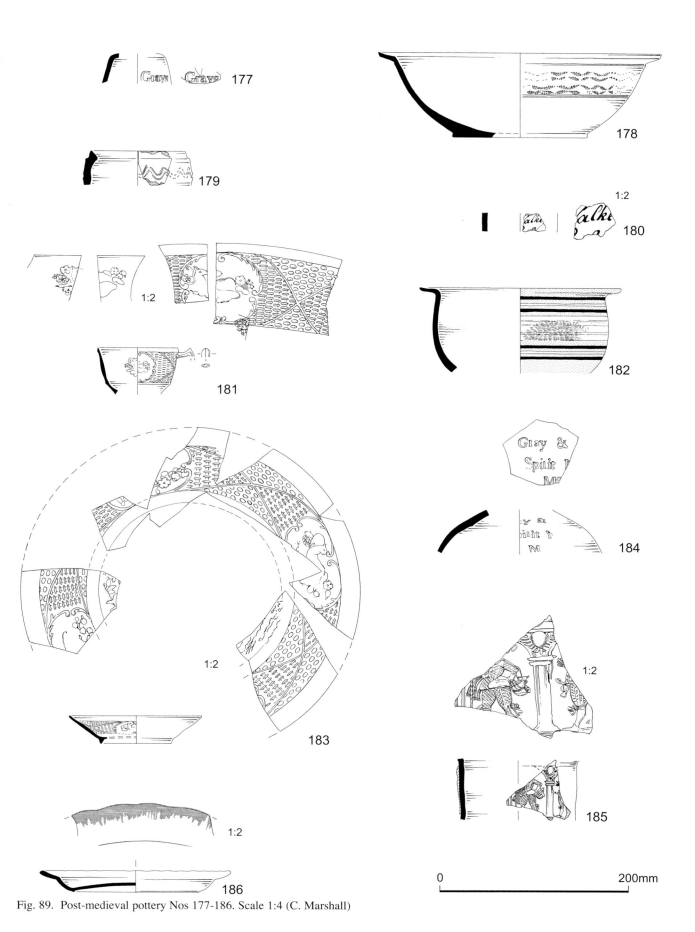

Fig. 89. Post-medieval pottery Nos 177-186. Scale 1:4 (C. Marshall)

197

The Plateau Sites

185* RAER. Body sherd from the vertical central section of a 'Cavalier' panel jug. Dark grey stoneware with glossy, finely mottled brown glaze, and light yellowish-brown interior. The arcaded panels are separated by columns surmounted by winged masks. Each panel, of which two are partially extant, would have contained a different kind of *Landsknecht* soldier (musketeeer, standard bearer, swordsman etc.). The left-hand figure in this example is holding a vertical stave in his right hand, probably a musket stand, cf. Hurst *et al.* 1987, fig. 98.315, dated 1576-1600. *Plateau. Site 33/-; unstratified*

Site unknown

186* PEARL5. Plate. The blue grass-edge is coloured only, not moulded. *Unmarked sherd*

Part Five
The Small Finds
edited by E.A. Clark

14 Introduction
by E.A. Clark

The finds assemblage from the North Glebe Terrace Sites is by far the most extensive collection of objects from the Wharram excavations. It includes large numbers of post-medieval artefacts, all of which were either brought into the village, or made or reworked there, for the use of Wharram's inhabitants. We can say with a fair measure of confidence that these objects are a reasonably accurate reflection of the more durable part of the material culture of a small rural community. Moreover, despite the gaps and inconsistencies in the documentary record, we can characterise that community as one which, from the late 16th to early 19th centuries, comprised a vicar and his immediate family (if any) and servants, and a farmer and his family along with domestic servants and agricultural labourers, both male and female.

The Wharram assemblage is, therefore, a 'closed' assemblage in the sense that very few items will have been brought into the settlement once they ceased to serve their function – that is, as discarded objects redeposited there. Thus it stands in marked contrast with many other assemblages of post-medieval artefacts, particularly from sites in urban contexts, where redeposited objects, brought into a site during cutting and filling operations associated with redevelopment, will form a significant but not readily quantifiable element of most assemblages.

A second important aspect of the Wharram assemblage is that it has provided an opportunity to compare objects recovered in archaeological contexts (in some cases broadly datable ones) with similar or identical artefacts in both public and private collections. More than one specialist reporter has commented on the fact that working with these post-medieval groups of artefacts has brought the world of the archaeological finds researcher and that of the museum curator and antiquarian collector much closer together. Recent years have seen a growing interest in, and recognition of post-medieval objects, and collaborative research on excavated artefacts and objects in collections has much to offer both areas of interest.

The sites included in the catalogues for this volume are those discussed in earlier chapters: Sites 49, 51, 73 and 74 covering the farmstead area, and Sites 54, 20 and 21, and 77 (with its extensions, Site 99 and Site 100) exploring the area of the vicarage. (Site 99 contexts are part of the Site 77 series of context numbers.) Also included are finds from other small sites associated with these areas of

the village. Site Code 11 was allocated to finds from a small part of the garden on the south side of the cottages. Finds from a series of trenches dug for electricity pylons in the valley east of the cottages were given Site Code 15. Site 97 is a spring on the slope immediately east of the cottages. The vicarage orchard and a series of cess pits dug into the valley floor were allocated Site Codes 75 and 79 respectively. Site Code 55 was given to objects found within the village but not as part of any excavation; those of any significance have been published with finds from the nearest site, and therefore appear among finds from both the farmstead and vicarage sites.

All the sites in this volume were recorded using the recording system current at Wharram between 1976 and 1990; it is fully discussed, and the need for it explained, in the introduction to *Wharram II*.

Apart from the soil samples taken from the floor of the vicarage barn (Chapter 9), all the material was recovered by hand during excavation. Unless otherwise stated, objects have been examined by eye during the post-excavation process, with limited amounts of radiography, cleaning, conservation and other techniques as appropriate. The reports include discussion and select catalogues; the full catalogues, including lithological and scientific reports, form part of the Archive. In each chapter, the published objects are recorded in a single sequence of illustrated and unillustrated material; the archive catalogues continue the same numerical sequence so references to unpublished items appear thus: 'Archive 208'.

The order in which finds are reported is determined by the material from which they were manufactured, and it is the same order as that used in previous Wharram volumes. Finds of the same material are catalogued together whether they came from the farmstead sites or from those of the vicarage; but within each chapter, those from the farmstead area are followed by those from the vicarage area. The words 'farmstead' and 'vicarage' are used for the whole of these socio-economic units, and do not necessarily indicate that a particular find came from either of the dwellings. The importance of finds to a specific context is in some cases discussed in the finds report, but in others it is dealt with in the relevant section of the excavation chapters; a more general discussion of the contribution of finds to our understanding of these sites is included in Chapter 28.

The opportunity has been taken in this volume to review the post-medieval material from other parts of the village – see for example the clay pipe and coin chapters.

15 Stone Objects

by E.A. Clark and G.D. Gaunt, with milling stones by S.R. Watts

Introduction

Although over 1500 stones were recovered from all the sites discussed in this volume, the vast majority are building stones from the vicarage and barn (Sites 54 and 77). The smaller number from the farmstead buildings reflects a different collection policy on sites where much of the material being recovered was of very recent date and where a policy of selection during excavation was therefore followed. It is worth noting that twice as many small stone objects survive from the vicarage sites as from the farmstead (122:64), perhaps indicating the value of the more total collection policy adopted on other areas of excavation.

All the stone has been identified and its lithology examined by G.D. Gaunt using a hand lens and low power microscope in reflected light. The limestone mortar No. 24 and a possible fragment of Tournai 'Marble' (Archive 173) add to the rock types previously identified at Wharram. Further discussion of stone sources can be found in previous volumes, and the full lithological and descriptive catalogues form part of the Site Archive. Measurements, where given, are the maximum possible and usually approximate.

The small stone objects will be deposited with other finds at Hull Museum and the large worked stones in the English Heritage store at Helmsley. As alternative storage, some of these stones, of a repetitive and/or non-diagnostic nature, will be considered for reburial on site, subject to meeting English Heritage's criteria.

Objects used for decorative and leisure purposes

Two small stones with perforations (Nos 1 and 3), one of siltstone and one of chalk, both show evidence of use and may have been used as pendants, although the latter is very crude. A fragment of siltstone with a polished surface (No. 4) and a fragment of jet (No. 5) may have had a decorative or possibly functional use. Pebbles with ?discoid shapes and flat surfaces (Archive 41-68), found on Site 54, may, like others from the village, have been used as counters, as may a small chalk 'disc' formed from a fossil (No. 2).

Farmstead

1   Fragment of siltstone. Lower Palaeozoic of southern Scotland or Cumbria. Although the tapering shape is similar to small hones, the perforation is too small and this rock type would not make a satisfactory hone. It may be the remains of a pendant or touchstone. L. 15mm. *51/469; SF554; Period 2.4*

2   Fragment, chalk. Welton Chalk Formation of Chalk Group. Section of tubular 'trace fossil', probably a burrow-fill. Possibly a curiosity or used as a disc. Diam. *c.*15mm. *49/10; SF70; Period 3*

Vicarage

3   Perforated stone, chalk. Chalk Group. The perforation through one of the natural erosion hollows is probably artificial and the slight bevelling at one end of the hole certainly is, suggesting possible use as a pendant. Natural and very irregular shape. L. 47mm. *77/646/B; SF1777; Period 1-5*

4   Fragment, siltstone/silty mudstone. Pre-Carboniferous. One curving surface is highly polished. Possibly part of an ornamental item. Max. remaining l. 83mm. *54/14; SF1642; Period 8.2*

5   Fragment, jet. Jet Rock sequence of Lower Jurassic of north-eastern Yorkshire. Good quality. A very irregular fragment but some polished areas suggest it has been artificially shaped. 14 x 11mm. *77/9000; SF1627; unstratified*

Objects used for functional purposes (Figs 90 and 91)

Only a small group of stone objects relate to life within the post-medieval farm and vicarage buildings.

Gun shot

Sixteen small limestone spheres, 13-18mm in diameter and weighing from 3-10g, were found in the farmhouse (Site 74, Archive 75-84) and vicarage (Site 54, Archive 69-74). Spherical stones of this size range are known to have been used as gun shot, and their presence within the domestic buildings may reflect measures for security in both households. In the vicarage the earliest context containing shot is in Period 6.1, but four are from Period 8.1, context 111. Six of those from the farmhouse were recovered from Period 1, context 341, having fallen through gaps in the floor of the room above. Other stone gun shot has been found during fieldwalking.

Writing slates

Fragments of school-type writing slates (Nos 6, 8 and Archive 85) and the 'slate' pencils with which to write on them (Nos 7, 9 and Archive 86-100) were found around both sets of buildings. Slates framed in wood and 'slate' pencils were made at factories in Wales from the 18th century. Most of the 'slate' pencils are hand-finished but a few perfectly cylindrical ones are machine made, and two retain 'grip' marks along the sides.

Farmstead

6   Fragment, slate. Probably North Wales or abroad. Bevelled edge to fit into wooden frame and two lightly incised parallel lines suggest a writing slate. L. of bevel 47mm. *51/513; SF40; Period 2.1*

7   'Slate' pencil, slate. Source unknown but probably Lower Palaeozoic slates in north Wales and/or Cumbria or abroad. Pointed at one end. L. 43mm; diam. 6mm. *51/469; SF332; Period 2.4*

Vicarage

8   Fragment, slate. Probably Lower Palaeozoic of Cumbria. Bevelled edge and two thin parallel scored lines as No. 6. L. of bevel 40mm. *77/93/P2; SF2329; Period 5.1/5.2*

9   'Slate' pencil. Lithology as No. 7. Pointed at one end. L. 41mm; diam. 4mm. *54/5; SF22; Period 8.1*

Medieval, or earlier, objects of types already known from the village include spindlewhorls (Nos 10 and 11),

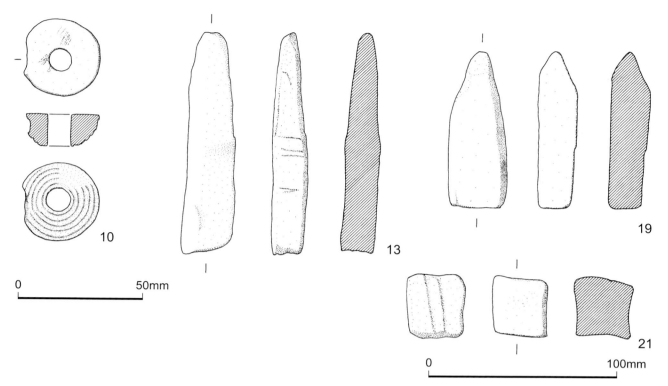

Fig. 90. Stone objects Nos 10 (Scale 2:3), 13, 19 and 21 (Scale 1:2) (E. Marlow-Mann)

hone stones (Nos 12-22 and Archive 104-106), a stone weight (No. 23), mortars (Nos 24-27) and fragments of milling stones (Nos 28-31 and Archive 107-167). The stone bearing (No. 32) from a mill is discussed in *Wharram X*.

Spindlewhorls
These are both from contexts formed from hillwash and may originate from buildings on the plateau above the terrace.

Vicarage
10* Spindlewhorl, chalk. Ferriby Chalk Formation. Parallel incised lines around the sides. Diam. of upper surface 32mm; diam. of spindle hole 9mm. Form A1. *54/598; SF1454; Period 3.1*

11 Spindlewhorl, chalk. Chalk Group. Heat-reddened and heat-cracked. Very fragmentary but one flat surface is apparent. Diam. of upper surface *c.* 25mm; diam. of spindle hole 9-10mm. Form A?1. *54/770; SF1526; Period 4.1*

Hones
Although many of the hones are of types known to have been used in the medieval village, some may have been used in later periods. Some reused architectural stones show evidence of use as hones or point-sharpening stones. (Archive 104-106).

Farmstead
12 Hone, schist. Eidsborg Schist. Part of one surface and part of possible end. Max. l. 50mm. *51/211; SF5; unphased*

13* Hone, schist. Eidsborg Schist. Rectangular section, 25 x 15mm. Tapering to point at one end; other end broken. Max. l. 120mm. *51/508; SF30; unphased*

14 Fragment, schist. Eidsborg Schist. Irregular surfaces but sub-rectangular section suggests rough-out for hone. Max. l. 220mm. *74/210; SF1663; Period 6*

15 Fragment, phyllite. Purple Phyllite. No surfaces remain but probably originally from a hone. Max. l. 65mm. *51/1031; SF569; Period 1*

16 Hone, sandstone. Closely comparable to Wharram Type A. Oval section, w. 31mm. Broken both ends. Max. l. 50mm. *51/469; SF341; Period 2.4*

Vicarage
17 Hone, schist. Eidsborg Schist. Incomplete section, remaining w. 15mm. Possible rough end. Max. l. 54mm. *54/202; SF1659; Period 7.5*

18 Hone, schist. Eidsborg Schist. Part of two faces. Remaining width suggests it was unusually large. Max. l. 60mm. *77/451; SF1752; Period 3.2*

19* Hone, sandstone. Comparable to Wharram Type A. Rectangular section, 28 x 18mm. End tapering to irregular point. Four flat very smooth surfaces. *54/598; SF1639; Period 3.1*

20 Hone, sandstone. Upper Carboniferous, or Middle or Upper Jurassic. Squarish section, w. 28mm. Tapering to rough end; other end broken. Max. l. 65mm. *54/13; SF1641; Period 8.2*

21* Hone, sandstone. Middle Jurassic. Lithologically identical to an architectural fragment reused for sharpening, but square section of this hone suggests it has been purposefully made. 26mm square. Three honed surfaces, fourth has point sharpening grooves. One end slightly bulbous; other end broken. Max. l. 30mm. *77/104/E1; SF62; Period 6*

22 Hone fragment, sandstone. Lower Palaeozoic. Erratic. One concave area has been used for honing. Max. l. 57mm. *77/191; SF1776; Period 1-5*

201

Weight

Farmstead

23 Erratic cobble, probably from beach, chalk. Chalk Group. Heavy. Broken at artificial perforation. Possibly used as a weight. Max. remaining l. 150mm. *49/29: SF1; Period 2*

Mortars

Fragments from four mortars, all probably reused as building stone, add to the series already known from the village.

Vicarage

24* Mortar, limestone. White ('weathering' to pale yellowish brown), fine to (mainly) medium and (slightly) coarse grained, poorly sorted with (for a limestone) an unusually granular appearance due to mainly bioclastic/pelletal texture. The source of this stone type is uncertain but could be the Broken Shell Limestone from the Portland-Purbeck area of Dorset (also known locally as burr-stone). The suggestion of a Portland/Purbeck origin is strengthened by the bulbous shape which is very similar to Dunning's Type 2 mortars in 'burr-stone' from Northolt and elsewhere (Dunning 1961). Section through rim, wall and base of four-lobed mortar. *54/254; SF1066; Period 5.2*

25* Mortar, limestone. Permian Lower Magnesian Limestone. This stone type forms a narrow outcrop from the Knaresborough area almost to Nottingham. Short section of rectangular-sectioned rim, offset from side, and part of body. Shallow and slightly rounded channel in lug; short triangular rib. *55/26; SF19; unphased*

26* Mortar, limestone. Basal part of Lower Magnesian Limestone. Rectangular-sectioned rim, offset from side, and part of body. Rough outer surface with vertical tooling on the rim. Inner surface well-made and smooth. *77/600/J; SF1602; Period 1-3*

27* Mortar, limestone. Upper part of Lower Magnesian Limestone. Short section of vertical rim and part of body. Shallow channel in triangular-shaped lug. Lug undercut and forming a triangular-shaped rib, broken at lower end. *77/9000; SF1717; unstratified*

Milling stones

by S. Watts

Excavations on the North Glebe Terrace recovered 91 fragments of querns and milling stones. Joining fragments or those that were found together have been recorded as a single entry and this report, therefore, is based on a catalogue of 65 entries (Nos 28-31 and Archive 107-167).

More than half the fragments are of Crinoid Grit-type sandstone (57%), with Mayen lava and Millstone-Grit sandstone accounting for 20% and 17% respectively. There are also single fragments of igneous rock, oolitic limestone and Middle or Upper Jurassic sandstone.

Most of the fragments are comparatively small, the largest piece representing less than 25% of a stone. Although a grinding surface survives on 34 of the fragments, few retain any diagnostic features and it is rarely possible to state whether they derive from upper or lower stones or what their original diameter may have been. The remaining 29 fragments show no features at all and are only identified as milling stones by the fact that the stone from which they were manufactured is not known to have been brought to the village for any other purpose. Only one fragment (No. 28) has the definite remains of a central eye or spindle hole, the original diameter of which was *c.* 50mm. The slight lip around the surviving portion indicates that the fragment derived from a lower stone.

The extant grinding surfaces are predominantly randomly pecked, with a number showing evidence of wear with glazed high spots. Two joining fragments of lava (No. 29), from the edge of a stone originally *c.* 600mm in diameter, are dressed with pecked furrows in a harp-shaped pattern which indicates that it was intended for clockwise rotation. The furrows are unevenly spaced and it is noticeable that some are slightly curved. A fragment of lava quern with slightly curved dressing was also found in the Churchyard (Watts in *Wharram XI*) and it was suggested that stones with particular forms of dressing may have had specific uses such as malt milling. The mixture of straight and curved furrows seen on this stone from the North Glebe Terrace may point to inexpert dressing rather than a special use.

All the fragments represent material brought to the terrace for reuse and although all the fragments were recovered from medieval contexts, some, in fact, may be considerably older. A large fragment from the lower stone of a saddle quern of Crinoid Grit (No. 30), with a pecked, slightly concave grinding surface, was reused within a wall footing, and a piece of igneous rock (No. 31) with a very worn grinding surface, which may derive from a saddle quern or rubbing stone, was found within the make up of an extension to the terrace. Such stones potentially date from the earliest occupation of the site. The querns and milling stones found on the North Glebe Terrace, together with those from the Church and Churchyard (Watts in *Wharram XI*), clearly show, therefore, how material, having been brought onto the site, was subsequently reused and redeposited within the village.

Farmstead

28 Fragment, lava. Fragment of lower stone. Worn grinding surface. The remains of the spindle hole survive as a smooth curved area on one side, originally *c.* 50mm diameter. Slight lip around spindle hole. L. 58mm; w. 47mm; th. 26mm. *51/644; SF289; unphased*

Vicarage

29* Two joining fragments, lava. From edge of stone. Grinding surface dressed with pecked furrows in a harp-shaped pattern in a clockwise direction. The furrows are unevenly spaced with centres varying from *c.* 19-39mm. Some are slightly curved. Worn with evidence of glazing. Stone appears to narrow in thickness towards the centre. Possibly an upper stone. Original diam. *c.* 600mm. L. 345mm; w. 140mm; th. 46mm. *77/498; SF1711, SF1712; Period 1-3*

30 Fragment, sandstone. Crinoid Grit. Pecked, worn grinding surface with very slight concavity. Remains of pointed hole in grinding surface, *c.* 36mm deep and originally *c.* 25mm diameter. Wrong shape for a spindle hole. It is possibly a fragment of saddle quern that has been reused. Mortar on one surface suggests reuse. L. 235mm; w. 155mm; th. 104mm. *54/101; SF1736; Period 7.1*

31 Fragment. Igneous rock. Worn, pecked grinding surface with evidence of glazing. Possibly from a saddle quern or rubber. L. 100mm; w. 92mm; th. 87mm. *77/101/H4; SF1715; Period 5.1*

Stone bearing

32 Stone bearing, sandstone (almost othoquartzite). Upper Carboniferous or Middle Jurassic, if latter possibly Moor Grit. Erratic. Heavy. Slightly heat-reddened. Top of stone *c.* 180 x 160mm; the base is uneven suggesting that it was sunk into something in use. Rotary-drilled hole with 'shiny' base, diam. *c.* 60mm; depth *c.* 20mm. Likely to have been used for a vertical shaft or spindle in the mill. See *Wharram X*, 224, for further discussion. *54/249; SF2285; Period 6.3*

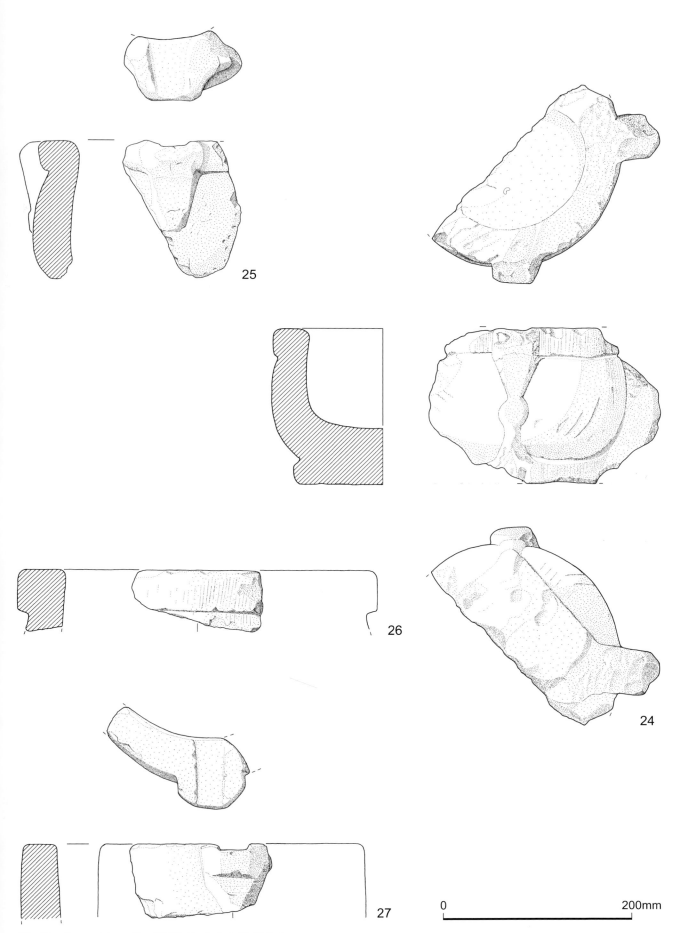

25

26

24

27

Fig. 91. Stone objects Nos 24-27. Scale 1:4 (C. Philo)

0   200mm

Stones related to burial and memorial

Another group of stones, all reused within the vicarage buildings, originate from memorials within the church. Although no wording remains, the fragments making up No. 33 are almost certainly part of a limestone tablet. The flat and polished surfaces of three of the eight fragments of Purbeck 'Marble' (Nos 34-36 and Archive 168-172) suggest it too might have formed a memorial tablet, although, as with the small fragment of possible Tournai 'Marble' (Archive 173), other forms are possible. Purbeck 'Marble' fragments were also found near the pond and in the churchyard (*Wharram X*, 128; *Wharram XI*, 298). The Coral Rag sarcophagus fragment (No. 37) is one of a number recovered around the village; they are discussed and illustrated, with the lids to which they relate, in *Wharram X*, 271-87. Stone from the Coral Rag and Malton Oolite outcrops near Malton was extensively used as building material from the Roman period onwards and building stone of this type was recovered at Wharram in the North Manor area along with other Roman stones. The only other use of it identified is for 19th and 20th-century repairs to the church. It is therefore likely the other small, usually worn, fragments found on both farmstead and vicarage sites (Archive 174-9) originate from the sarcophagi.

Vicarage

33 Fragments, limestone. North Grimston Cementstone. Nineteen worked, some joining, and another 22 fragments found with them. Some flat and well-smoothed surfaces; two different types of moulded edge. Another fragment (SF1717) which has weathered very differently but having an identical moulded edge, is almost certainly from the same object. Probably part of a memorial. Largest piece 120 x 100mm. *54/8; SF1666; Period 8.4, 54/211; SF1748 and SF1717; Period 7.1*

34 Fragment, limestone. Purbeck 'Marble'. Degraded cut and polished surface 115mm x 75mm, th. 20mm. *54/75; SF1667; Period 7.4*

35 Fragment, limestone. Purbeck 'Marble'. Cut and polished surface 15mm x 13mm, th. 7mm. *54/357; SF1722; Period 7.3*

36 Fragment, limestone. Purbeck 'Marble'. Cut and polished surface 105mm x 60mm; th. 90mm. *54/9000; SF2286; unstratified*

37 Sarcophagus fragment, limestone. Coral Rag. Length of sides 70mm, 240mm; w. 180mm; th. 70mm. *54/254; SF1066; Period 5.2*

Stone used for building

Some of the stones found within the walls of the farmstead and vicarage buildings are carved and in some cases are identical to others found in the church from where they are likely to have originated. Frequent tooling and other evidence of reuse, including patches of mortar, on other stones from both areas suggest that they too came from the same source. A mason's mark in the form of a cross is on a block from Site 49 (Archive 198), and a block from Site 77 bears a possible, V-shaped, mason's mark (Archive 472).

Part of a flat and worked stone (No. 38) found on Site 77, which has been subjected to severe heating, may have been used in a fireplace.

Traces of white-washed plaster and paint on four stones found in the barn (Site 77) in 16th and 17th-century contexts (Archive 451, 483, 502 and 548) may

reflect decoration but whether from the church or the later buildings cannot be known as they are all reused. A block from a Period 7.5 context in the vicarage has a black surface which has not been caused by fire.

As is normal at Wharram, the majority of building stone is Birdsall Calcareous Grit (Archive 187-570), a stone which has constantly been reused throughout the village, although a few fragments of other sandstones were also recovered (Archive 571-589).

North Grimston Cementstone, a locally available limestone, has been found in most areas of the village, usually as unshaped blocks. Among those from the farmstead and vicarage sites, however, are a number of regularly formed, and sometimes tooled, blocks, some in the form of flat flagstones with neatly worked edges (No. 39).

Brandsby Roadstone, an excellent roofing stone which outcrops in the Hambleton and Howardian Hills, was used on the church at Wharram, but has been recovered only in small quantities on most excavated areas as it was removed for reuse. Large quantities of mainly small fragments were recovered from the North Glebe sites (Archive 746-1484). Of these some 800 fragments were found in the barn (Site 77) mainly from contexts dating to Period 5, and, to a lesser extent, from Periods 4 and 3 (Archive 938-1484). Only one almost complete roofing stone (No. 40) was among them, and many fragments are small. The greatest concentration of roofing stone fragments in the barn was in context 380, Period 5.1, where it might have been used as levelling material.

A fragment of Elland Flags type sandstone (Site 49, Archive 1485) is comparable to other fragments from the North Manor where a Roman origin was suggested (*Wharram IX*, 229).

The arrival of the railway in the 19th century enabled two types of slate, Burlington Slate and slate from the Borrowdale Volcanic Group, to be safely transported from the Lake District as roofing material. Small fragments (Archive 1486-1558) were recovered from both groups of buildings.

Vicarage

38* Fragments, sandstone. Birdsall Calcareous Grit. A large minority are fire-blackened, several severely so, and a large majority are heat-reddened. Some are obviously heat-cracked. There are at least twelve joining fragments forming one corner of a slab and another four joining fragments which do not join the slab but are from the same object. Another 30+ fragments, none of which join but some with tooled surfaces, are also likely to originate from it.

Both pieces have one rebated side with neat, broad tooling. The other side of the corner slab has a short length of smooth concave depression on the underside. The top is roughly dressed. A cross with one longer arm is incised in the corner. A fragment of window tracery reused as part of a fireplace. L. *c.* 530+mm; w. *c.* 220+mm; th. *c.* 76mm. *77/598/G; SF2509; Period 3.1*

39 Block, limestone. North Grimston Cementstone-type. Flag from floor surface. One tooled side. 200 x 180; th. 90mm. *54/114; SF2621; Period 7.2*

40 Roof tile. Sandstone, Brandsby Roadstone. Almost complete. L. *c.* 455mm; w. across base *c.* 300mm, tapering to other end. Perforation for attachment at narrower end. *77/182E; SF2254; Period 3.1*

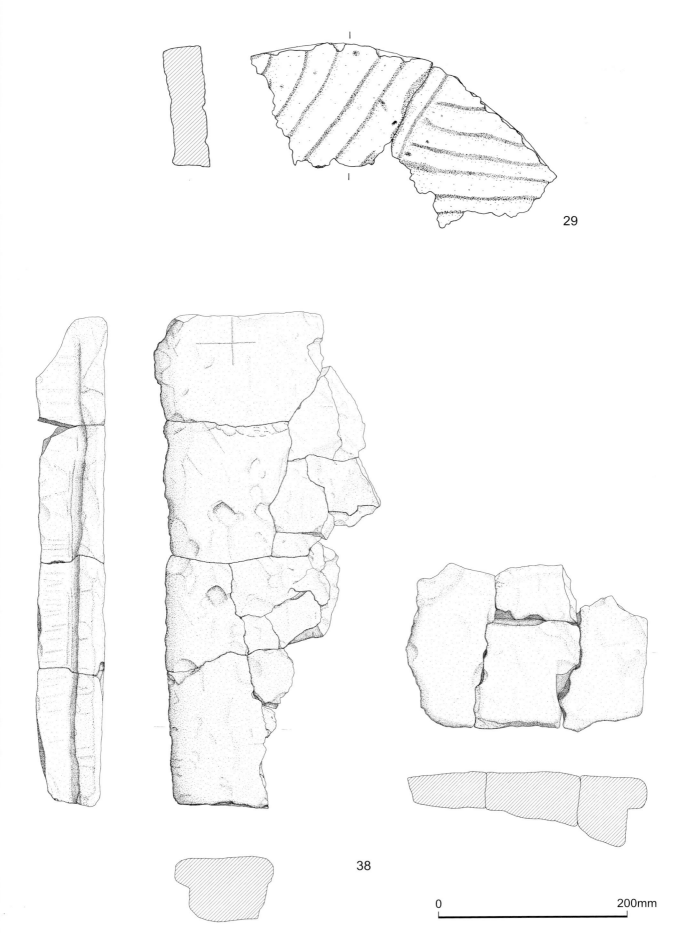

Fig. 92. Stone objects Nos 29 and 38. Scale 1:4 (M. Chisnall)

16 Ceramic Building Material

Introduction

Ceramic building material from Wharram consists of brick, roof tile, small quantities of other tile types, and burnt clay, some of which is daub. Non-roof tile and burnt clay have been listed and discussed in each volume, but the bricks and roof tiles were all examined at the same time and are discussed in this chapter.

Only small amounts of brick have been recovered on any sites other than those discussed in this volume.

Ceramic tile is found across the whole village. The small quantities of Roman box tile probably all originate from the North Manor area (*Wharram IX*, 231). Fragments of flat tiles and pantiles have been found in almost all the excavations throughout the village, although it is unlikely to have originated from all the sites.

The flat tile recovered from both Houses 6 and 10 (*Wharram I*, 66 and 131-2) suggests that tile was being used there, perhaps in hearths and on the ridges of the roofs. Most of the tile from these sites was disposed of after the report was written, but the descriptions and the tile that remains both from these areas and the adjacent South Manor sites (*Wharram VIII*, 119-121) suggest that it was flat tile of type and form similar to the flat tiles discussed below.

The small quantities of tile recovered in and around the church support Bell's suggestion (*Wharram III*, 169) that they originate from elsewhere in the village.

The main assemblages of both brick and tile were found around the vicarage and farm buildings, and these are discussed below.

Ceramic tile

by J. Tibbles and S. Watts

Introduction

The ceramic building material assemblage from the North Glebe Terrace sites includes more than 5727 fragments of ceramic tile. This consists of 5615 fragments of roof tile; the remaining material being floor tile, hearth tile, chimney pot, drainage tiles and unidentifiable fragments (Table 41). The initial classification by Siobhan Watts was used in this report. It should be noted, as with brick manufacture (see below), that the diversity of size and colour within tiles caused during the manufacturing process must be taken into consideration when comparing examples within collected assemblages and local typologies. The varying sizes and colours can be attributed to the variation in the clays used, shrinkage during drying, firing within the kiln or clamp, and the location of the tile within the kiln.

Because of their reusable nature, tiles alone cannot provide a firm date for an excavated feature, but it has been possible to date types of roof tile by their earliest occurrence within dated contexts.

Ceramic roof tile

Four types of ceramic roof tile were identified, representing 98% of the total tile assemblage, but of these only ten fragments could be equated with near-parallels within the regional tile typology (Tibbles in prep.).

Diagnostic qualities include the varying methods of suspension, and length, width and thickness of the tile. Width and/or thickness alone suggest multiple possibilities within the flat roof tile typology and it was not therefore possible to attempt identification of the remaining fragments. Some fragments of flat and pan tiles showed suspension methods, whilst mortar adhesions on many examples indicate a primary structural use prior to demolition. Manufacturing techniques are still evident on many fragments including moulding sand and residual moulding lips.

Positions of the nibs and peg holes are usually described from the nib side of the tile, i.e. the underside as hung, not necessarily as made. Demand normally dictated the size and quality of flat roof tile which often varied until a statute was instigated in 1477 (17 Edward IV, c iv) that dictated the size. A flat tile was fixed at 10in by 6in by $^{5}/_{8}$in (255mm x 153mm x 16mm), a ridge tile 13in long by $^{1}/_{2}$ inch thick, and a hip tile 10in in length with a convenient width and thickness (Celoria and West

Table 41. Tile types.

| Tile types | Farmstead sites | | | | | | Vicarage sites | | | | Total |
	74	51	11	49	73	79	77	54	99	100	
Flat	8	13	-	6	7	1	1149	637	-	1	1822
Hip	-	1	-	-	-	-	2	-	-	-	3
Ridge	-	1	-	-	-	-	22	3	1	-	27
Pantile	2018	910	4	110	50	1	163	478	2	27	3763
Hearth	-	1	-	firebrick	-	-	-	-	-	-	2
Floor	-	-	-	-	-	-	3	-	-	-	3
Chimney	-	6	-	3	-	-	-	-	-	-	9
Drain	1	48	3	31	-	-	3	-	-	-	86
Unidentified	2	-	-	10	-	-	-	-	-	-	12
Total	2029	980	7	161	57	2	1342	1118	3	28	5727

Table 42. Flat tile type description.

Tile type	Description
1a	Single pulled nib usually semi-circular and centrally placed on the top edge of the underside
1b	As above but pressed bevelled nib
7	Single small tapering round peg hole centrally placed. Hole tapers from 13mm to 10mm and is generally made from the underside
11	Square peg holes *c*. 10mm square. 100mm apart and 20-30mm from upper edge. Punched from the underside

1967, 218). Early flat roof-tiles were suspended by projecting nibs or by peg/nails. Alternatively, flat tiles were often secured by iron nails, as were ridge and hip tiles. Each layer of tiles overlapped the layer below and was bedded on moss to make the roof weatherproof. The lowest layers, and sometimes all the layers, were often pointed or rendered with mortar (Salzman 1952, 233). In 1725 parliament legislated that the size of a pantile must be a minimum of 13¹/₂in long by 9¹/₂in by ¹/₂in thick.

Flat tiles (Table 42)
There is clear evidence to show that clay roof tiles were in use within the Hull valley and the surrounding regions by the late 12th century (Armstrong and Armstrong 1992; Armstrong 1991), and had become common roofing material by the 13th century, with Types 1a and 1b being the most prevalent. Types 1a, 1b and 7 have been identified within 12th-century and later deposits within the region, whilst Type 11 has been identified from 13th and 14th-century contexts (Tibbles 2003, 32; Armstrong 1991, 206).

These types continued to be manufactured in the region until the early 18th century.

Although there is little material for comparative analysis, the fragments from Wharram displaying suspension methods were identified as Types 1a, 1b, 7(?) and 11(?).

The small assemblage of brown-glazed flat roof tile fragments present in the assemblage suggests that the building or buildings from which they originated, may have incorporated glazed tiles along the eaves and/or surrounding a smoke vent or 'chimney'. Glazed roof tiles have previously been recorded within 13th-century deposits at Beverley (Tibbles 2001a) and early 14th-century deposits at Hull (Armstrong and Ayers 1987).

Hip tile
Three small fragments of hip tiles were identified from both the farmhouse and vicarage buildings. Hip tiles were, and still are, generally used to cover the external angle of adjoining slopes and valleys of tiled roofs and are held by a single nail at their apex. They have been recorded within 12th to 13th-century deposits within the region (Armstrong 1991, 205).

Ridge tiles
Within the relatively small assemblage of ridge tiles (27 fragments), the majority were identified as knife-cut

crested, each displaying a fragment of a prominent '*fan*'-shaped crest, the rest being plain ridge tile. As there are no complete or near complete tiles, fragments were mainly identified only by thickness and manufacturing characteristics; the assemblage must therefore be treated with caution.

Plain ridge tiles have been recorded from late 12th-century and 13th-century deposits within the region (Tibbles 2001a; Armstrong and Ayers 1987). The ridge tile was custom-made to facilitate joining the two sides of a roof along its crest or ridge. Held in place by mortar and/or nails, they overlapped the adjacent tile, although some were butted end to end.

Fan-shaped knife-cut crested tiles have been recorded within late 13th-century deposits at Beverley (Armstrong and Armstrong 1992, 224), from the late 15th century at Lyveden (Steane 1975, 95), from 13th to 14th-century deposits at York (Spall and Troop 2005, 295), and were present in unstratified contexts at Howden (Tibbles 2001b).

Pantile
Diagnostic traits of the pantile tend to suggest that the longer nibs, generally associated with long rounded corners, are of an earlier date than tiles displaying shorter rectangular nibs. None of the nibs from this assemblage bore impressed letters, common within Holderness and denoting the manufacturer. Three fragments of glazed pantile were present.

Within Holderness, pantile is generally a reddish-orange colour with occurrences of green, yellow, brown and black/blue glaze, the latter being the most common, although still rare. Areas within southern Holderness (i.e. Hedon, Hull, Holme-on-Spalding-Moor, Warter and Beverley) have produced assemblages of blue glazed pantile.

Although pantiles were imported into Britain by the 16th century, there is no evidence for their manufacture in this country before 1700 (Neave 1991). The use of pantile, with its single overlap, significantly decreased the number of tiles needed to roof a building, therefore decreasing the amount of timber required to support it. Also, the pitch of the roof needed was much less than required for flat tiles, altogether making pantile a more economic roofing material.

Manufacture and use
Roofing tiles were much thinner than bricks (*c*. 10-20mm) and needed to be made from a finer clay as any

remaining stones might explode during firing and damage the tile. Wherever possible tiles would be fired in structural kilns to enable more control over firing although both clamp and kiln structures were recorded at the Beverley tileries (Atkins 1986). It is therefore unlikely that the tiles from Wharram were manufactured on site but are likely to have been imported from the larger surrounding settlements.

Flat roof tile was still a common roofing material by the late post-medieval period but due to economics and architectural styles during the 17th and 18th centuries, it began to be relegated to lesser areas, often the rear roofs. The presence of both pantile and flat tile within the same context is therefore not unusual. By the 18th century, pantiles became more fashionable, they became far more common, replacing the traditional flat tile. It is difficult without fabric analysis to differentiate between the imported Dutch tiles (*Dakpannen*) and English pantiles manufactured locally.

Non-roof tile

Three fragments of thicker tile, between 20mm to 22mm thick, were tentatively identified as floor tiles, as they displayed the manufacturing characteristics of paving tiles or quarries. These generally ranged in size; between 6 and 12in square, and were usually 1in thick (Rivington 1910). A few fragments of chimney pot and possible hearth tiles were also identified.

Land drains/service drains

Eighty-six fragments of 19th to 20th-century land drain and service pipe were within the assemblage. It should be noted that by the early 19th century, the land drain had evolved from a horseshoe form into a cylindrical type, and became widespread after the removal of the tile tax in 1850. No stamp impressions were observed on any of the fragments, suggesting a post-1850 date of manufacture.

Roof tile discussion

Although much of the roofing material is from dumps and refuse tipping and therefore has only minimal interpretational value for the site, the appearance of glazed medieval tile does indicate the presence of an earlier building of high status within the village.

Of the total roof tile fragments recovered from both areas, 67% are pantiles and 32% are flat tiles. The vast majority of the pantiles (82%) were from the farmstead buildings and mainly from the farmhouse itself, where they occurred in contexts of all periods. Another 29% were found on Site 51, where some of the courtyard buildings may have had tiled roofs. Only 35 fragments of flat tile were identified from the farmstead sites.

This contrasts with the vicarage sites where the majority of the tile (72%) is flat tile. Most of it had been used as levelling material in the barn and may have originated from anywhere in the village. The vicarage (Site 54), however, produced almost equal proportions of flat (57%) and pantiles (43%), suggesting repair and/or the insertion of new roofs.

The range of roof tiles recorded showed at least four different flat roof tile types in addition to ridge tile, hip tile and pantile. The earlier flat tiles, Types 1a, 1b and 7, may have been reclaimed and incorporated into a new roof or used as repairs. The presence of fifteen different types of roof tile at County Hall, Beverley, (Tibbles 2001a) and at least fourteen different types at Lurk Lane, Beverley, (Armstrong 1991), suggests this may have been a common practice within medieval structures.

Numerous examples of poor quality tiles, such as abraded, under-fired and over-fired fragments, make a local manufacturing source, or sources, likely.

Brick
by J. Tibbles

Introduction

The assemblage of over 1600 brick fragments from the North Glebe sites was subjected to a visual detailed examination of all the retained material using a 15x-magnification lens. Information regarding the dimensions, shape and fabric of the material was recorded and catalogued accordingly within the database. Where possible, the identified material was compared with the existing regional typologies. It should be noted that the diversity of size and colour within the brick caused during the manufacturing process, must be taken into consideration when comparing examples within collected assemblages and local typologies. This diversity can be attributed to the use of different clays, to shrinkage during drying, to firing within the kiln or clamp and the location of the brick within them.

Background

The term brick, probably derived from the French *brique*, was not commonly used in this country until the mid-15th century (Salzman 1952), although it was used at Windsor in 1340 (Kaner 1980, 4). The general term used in England at this time was either *tegula murali*, *walltyle* or *walteghell* (Kaner 1980, 4). By 1357 they were generally called *Flaunderdrestiell*, an indication of their introduction from Flanders.

One of the earliest references to wall-tiles (*tegulae murales*) in England is in 1335 during the construction of a new chamber at Ely (Salzman 1952). The earliest reference to *Waltighel* in Hull is in 1353 (Bilson 1896), although the Hull Corporation were paying rent for a *tegularia* in 1303.

Manufacture

The manufacture of brick and tile varied little from the 13th century until the introduction of mechanised brick-making in the mid-19th century.

Dobson (1850, 9) postulates that variations in the clay, even in the same district, lead to corresponding variations in the same brickyard, so the variable fabrics recorded within an assemblage are likely to be from the same sources. The raw clays common in Northern England are generally from the Middle and Upper Pleistocene (Glacial clays and sands, boulder clays) or the Holocene periods (Alluvial clays). Pockets of suitable clays for brick-making are found within the Yorkshire Wolds, and have been successfully exploited from the 17th century.

The raw material was dug in the autumn or early winter and left to allow the elements to break it down ready for use early in the following year. A statute of 1477 (17 Edward IV, c iv), relating to tile manufacturing, stated that the clay was not to be dug before the 1st November and that tempering or puddling was to be undertaken before the 1st February. It was then left until the 1st March before it was used (Celoria and West 1967, 217). Tempering or puddling, to remove small stones that would explode the brick when fired, involved mixing the clay with water using shovels or bare feet, and later by horse-drawn puddling machines.

A wad of clay was pressed into a bottomless wooden mould, previously wetted and often sanded, and the surplus clay struck off. The slight lip which might inadvertently be formed around the arris of the brick, was, if too extant, pressed down by the edge of the wooden mould, leaving a narrow linear indent along one or more sides of the brick. Alternatively the lip was pared with a sharp knife.

Once moulded, the green tiles were laid out on specially prepared smooth areas of ground known as *hacksteads*, over which straw or sand had been spread to prevent the bricks from sticking to the ground (Smith 1985, 48). After two to three days, they had dried to a semi-biscuit-like state, and were then stood on edge to allow the air to circulate across more surface areas until they were hard enough to be stacked in the kiln.

From the medieval period to the mid-19th century, stakes, faggots, turves, logs, green wood and coal have all been used successfully to fire kilns in different places. The location of the brick within the kiln or clamp accounted for the quality of the fired brick, those closest to the heat being reduced to a stone-like hardness. In some cases the brick vitrified, or partially vitrified, resulting in wasters, or, conversely, the bricks furthest away might only be partially fired (*samels*). In both cases the less severely distorted bricks could be sold at a reduced price as '*seconds*'.

By the early to mid-19th century, machines were capable of producing vast quantities of brick and tile at a cheap price for the new market which grew up following the withdrawal of brick tax. Bricks became cheap and plentiful, particularly with the introduction of Staffordshire Blues whose self-burning properties made them much cheaper to manufacture, and the coming of the railway in the mid-19th century allowed easy distribution at a cheaper price.

The bricks recorded at Wharram are all handmade with the odd exception, suggesting a pre-mid-19th-century date of manufacture at a source possibly within a few miles of the site or even on the site itself. The Buck building accounts indicate that one source of bricks in 1776 was Old Malton (NYCRO ZQG XIII/11/2), and nearby Norton was producing bricks in the early 19th century. Prior to the railways, bricks were transported by horse and cart if the cheaper alternative of water transport was not available, and Woodeforde (1976, 136) refers to a horse and cart being limited to carrying a maximum of 800 bricks at any one time over bad roads. Blair and Ramsey (1991, 229) noted that, in the Low Countries, transporting bricks by cart doubled their costs making road transport uneconomic over any great distances, and by the mid-18th century most parishes had their own brickyard in operation (Woodeforde 1976, 60). Even the cheapest railway rates would also have doubled their costs (Dobson 1850, 114), and therefore it made sense to obtain bricks from as near as possible.

Brick types

The North Glebe assemblage has been categorised, on a best-fit policy, into six different site types with subdivisions (Table 43). Part bricks are more difficult to

Table 43. Site brick typology.

Site type	Length mm	Width mm	Thickness mm	Comments
1	?	110	42(?)	Handmade
2	220-225	100-110	48-55	Handmade
2b	240	115-125	50-53	Handmade
3a	?	100	58	Handmade
3b	?	110-115	55-58	Handmade
3c	?	125-132	56-57	Handmade
4a	215-220	95-103	60-62	Handmade
4b	220-230	105-111	60-62	Handmade
4c		112-115	60-62	Handmade
4d	?	125-128	60	Handmade
5a	225-250	100-105	65	Handmade
6a	?	115	65	Firebrick. Machine-made
6b	220	102-110	70	Firebrick. Machine-made

categorise as the width and thickness may correspond to more than one category. Identification of a large proportion of fragments was not possible due to their small size and/or degraded or abraded surfaces.

Farmhouse (Site 74)

The earliest presence of brick is within the sub-floor or base in Period 1. The small non-diagnostic fragment (15g) has substantial mortar over its surfaces suggesting a probable filler piece or wall-coursing leveller.

From within the general demolition dumps of Period 2, foot-worn fragments were identified with residual dimensions of ?mm x 105-110mm x 50-53mm, slightly smaller in width than the worn bricks identified within the vicarage. The worn nature of this group prevents them being securely typed, but a provisional classification of Type 2 may be assigned, suggesting a late 17th-century date of manufacture. Most fragments were found to be non-diagnostic, but displayed mortar suggesting non-reusable fragments probably from wall cores or foundations.

The trample, rubble and make-up layers are mainly non-diagnostic with only a few fragments displaying diagnostic qualities. Once again, the presence of underfired material suggests local firing. The under-fired material is similar to that identified from the vicarage. A modern brick recorded within Period 3 is likely to be intrusive.

A single complete Type 2 brick, identified within the floor make-up, measuring 220 x 102 x 50mm (8³/₄in x 4in x 2in), is late 17th-century. Foot-worn fragments within the floor make-up material, may represent residual elements of the floor. One fragment, displaying mortar over the foot-worn surface, had already been reused within structural coursing.

Very little information was obtained from the mostly non-diagnostic fragments of demolition material recorded within the Period 4 floor surfaces and trample. Despite heavy abrasion, mortar adhesions were still evident. Excluding the modern brick intrusion, a late medieval and early post-medieval date of manufacture is suggested.

The majority of the material recorded within Period 5 is from demolition, and includes two complete Type 2 bricks, 225mm x 106mm x 55mm (9in x 4¹/₄in x 2¹/₄in), and two part-bricks, 105mm x 50mm, 120mm x 40mm (4³/₄in x 1¹/₂in). The latter are residual late medieval and post-medieval fragments, whilst the complete bricks, still retaining substantial white render adhesions, may be attributed to a late 18th or early 19th-century date of manufacture, with the render more recently applied prior to demolition.

The assemblage from Period 6 contains substantial residual elements, including examples of foot-worn, lime-washed and underfired fragments with mortar adhesions. Little additional information can be gleaned from this latest phase.

Vicarage (Site 54)

Of the small number of complete bricks recovered, 47% (9 examples) are from the vicarage. They range in size between 220 and 225mm x 102 and 108mm x 60 and 70mm (8³/₄-9in x 4-4¹/₄in x 2³/₈-2³/₄in) and are generally of a late 17th to 18th-century date of manufacture. Although fragments of 19th to 20th-century firebricks were identified (Types 6), the brick samples from the hearth (129) may be of a slightly earlier date suggesting reuse of material. The bricks showed both slop and sand moulding characteristics suggesting different manufacturing techniques, possibly from different sources or at least different makers.

The earliest presence of brick was in Period 2.2 stake-hole 933, however, the small size of the fragment (2g) may be attributed to animal activity. Similarly, the small fragment (3g) within the Period 3.1 hillwash is likely to be of casual deposition.

The terrace cut within Period 4 has a small assemblage displaying burning over breaks and surfaces, suggesting either fragments from hearths or fireplaces, or material burnt during demolition. The diagnostic elements suggest Type 4d of early 16th-century date. Evidence of casual deposition is frequent throughout this phase with fragments showing typical abrasion, whilst mortar indicates demolition material incorporated into surfaces and their associated make-up dumps.

Similar characteristics of brick type and deposition continue through Period 5, with the addition of fragments of footworn bricks from internal floors and thresholds. The presence of underfired bricks (samels) and wasters from this phase onwards suggests the clamp firing of bricks on site or nearby.

Approximately 10% of the brick fragments were recovered from within the Period 6 dumps and make-up layers, mainly of Type 5a (17th to 18th-century) and Types 3a, 4a and 4b (late 17th to 18th-century), although the occasional intrusive modern fragment was also present. More hearth fragments were identified within the dumps, as well as further examples of footworn, underfired and waster bricks.

The demolition rubble associated with Structure J, the cellar, contained typical characteristics of demolition i.e. burning over broken edges, mortar adhesions and smooth surfaced floor bricks. The presence of two different mortars on several fragments showed reclamation or reuse of material. Abrasion suggests casual deposition and/or wear within roads or surfaces. Fragments of under-fired seconds and other wasters were identified, implying local manufacture.

The continuing presence of Types 3a, 4a and 4b was noted within the make-up dumps and surfaces within Period 7, in association with fragments of slightly earlier material (16th to 17th-century), this latter type also being associated with the joists within the vicarage. The presence of 16th to 17th-century material and seconds may indicate a slow down in the settlement economy, resulting in the reuse of old material and purchase of brick of lesser quality. The threshold bricks are all of Type 4b (17th to 18th-century). The surfaces and make-up dumps continued to have demolition material incorporated within their make-up. The majority of fragments within these contexts were generally non-diagnostic.

The presence of bricks displaying well-worn upper surfaces represents residual elements of earlier floors, hearths or thresholds. The partial floor or surface within Room 4 of Structure K (Period 7) may have been constructed from already-worn bricks reused from earlier buildings. Other foot-worn bricks from this area were of similar fabric, width and thickness (Type 4b) to the only complete brick from within surface/floor 130 (228mm x 108mm x 60mm), although thickness should be treated with caution due to the inconsistent wear on individual bricks. Wear was also identified on bricks recovered from the hearth (137) which are likely to have been worn *in situ*; their sizes are comparable to Types 4a, 4b and 3b, and of a similar date to floor 130. The presence of plaster adhering to bricks from the rear of the fireplace suggests a decisive decoration rather than the rendering over blemished bricks.

The only presence of 'special' bricks is from the threshold assemblage, context 126, where a part 'Bullnose' brick was recorded. The header was round-moulded, possibly originating from a windowsill as two mortars were evident from reuse.

Unseen bricks incorporated within floors and walls could be reused numerous times and would be far cheaper than new. Fresh plaster, render or limewash was an easier and cheaper method to cover blemishes or broken exposed brick surfaces, particularly within cowsheds, barns and outbuildings.

Among the standard bricks identified from the fireplace within the vicarage, were some fragments of firebricks. All these are machine-made, indicating a mid-19th to 20th-century date of manufacture. During the 19th and 20th centuries, most houses had stoves or fireplaces containing firebricks (Douglas and Oglethorpe 1993). The remnant of a stamp '..LEY', distinguishable on one fragment, suggests its source as Wortley at Leeds.

Discussion

Although only a small percentage of the brick assemblage contained diagnostic traits, it was possible to create a site typology based upon those which survived. Six broad types were identified, with broadly spread subdivisions. None of the bricks examined could be attributed to earlier than the late medieval period.

The source of bricks can be attributed either to multiple firing of clamps on or near the site, or to importation by road from larger towns with brick-making facilities, of which Norton, 7km to the north-west, is a prime example. There is substantial evidence for both cases to be considered. The documentary record indicates bricks coming from the Norton/Malton area in the late 18th century, though the presence of brick wasters and 'seconds' suggests local clamp firing.

There is substantial reuse of material throughout most periods in both the vicarage and the farmstead buildings, and, although the diagnostic material does not confirm the interchange or movement of demolished material from one site to another, it would be reasonable to suggest that this action was frequently undertaken, particularly in times of economic depression when necessity dictated reuse. Within the demolition dumps, the frequency of late medieval bricks may be attributed to the demolition of pre-farmhouse structures.

17 Clay Objects
by E.A. Clark, P. Didsbury, A.M. Slowikowski and S. White

Three discs (Nos 1-3), all formed from pottery sherds and likely to have been used as counters, are further examples of these objects from Wharram. Another sherd (No. 4) has been reshaped for use as an implement.

Clay spheres (Nos 5-7), all from the farmstead, have similar diameters to stone spheres identified as shot (Chapter 15). They and the 18th-century hair curler (No. 8) relate to life in the farmhouse and vicarage, as may a decorative object (No. 9). Three fragments of clay (Nos 10-12), whose function is unknown, were found in Period 5 and 6 contexts.

Other objects (A13-32), including a porcelain brooch in the shape of flowers and various fragments from dolls and other fairings, probably relate to the 19th and 20th-century occupation of the cottages.

Discs (Fig. 93)
Farmstead

1 Possibly reshaped body sherd. Two straight sections but otherwise neatly rounded. Diam. *c*. 18mm. *49/10; SF104; Period 3*

2 Reshaped body sherd from an Anglo-Saxon sandstone-tempered vessel (A04). Neatly rounded. The sherd is sooted on the interior; this is likely to have occurred while the vessel was complete and in use, rather than as a result of its secondary use as a disc. The sherd could have been reshaped at any time after the vessel was discarded. The fabric is very hard, which may be the reason it was reused. Max. diam. 30mm. *51/377; SF668; Period ER-2*

Vicarage

3 Reshaped body sherd from Staxton ware vessel (B12). Roughly rounded. Diam. 32-40mm. *77/192; SF2406; Period 1-5*

4* Body sherd from Hambleton jug (CO1) with spalled surface, reshaped to make a right-angled implement. Sherd weighs 1.9g. Similar sherds have been found on late medieval kilns sites in the South Midlands; they may have had several functions (Slowikowski forthcoming). *77/209; SF2507; Period 5.1*

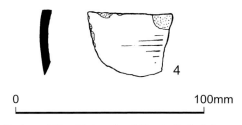

0   100mm

Fig. 93. Reshaped Hambleton sherd No. 4. Scale 1:2
(C. Marshall)

Clay spheres

Farmstead

5 Clay sphere. Diam. 13mm. *51/264; SF648; Period ER-3*

6 Clay sphere. Diam. 12mm. 1gr. *51/411; SF18; Period ER-1*

7 Clay sphere. Diam. 15mm. 2gr. *74/112; SF1799; Period 6*

Miscellaneous objects (Fig. 94)

Vicarage

8* One end of a hair curler stamped WB in a circular frame with a single dot above and below; first half of the 18th century (Le Cheminant 1982, 348, fig. 1, nos 8 and 9; also see White 2004, 254, fig. 40, no. 9, for a similar stamp). Max. remaining l. 24+mm. *54/226; SF476; Period 7.4*

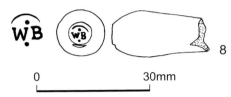

Fig. 94. Hair curler No. 8. Scale 1:1 (S. White)

9 Fragments of possibly circular object made from clay. Decorated with circles and dots, the circles filled with what is probably coloured glass. *54/471; SF1081; Period 6.3*

10 Short oval cylinder, probably clay. Roughly made. Max. l. 22mm; diam. 20mm. *54/443; SF1030; Period 5.2*

11 Fragment of clay with remains of pre-firing perforation on broken edge. Probably not roof tile. Max. l. 19mm. *54/516; SF2278; Period 6.3*

12 Fragment of clay as No. 11. Max. l. 40mm. *54/516; SF2279; Period 6.3*

18 The Clay Tobacco Pipes from Wharram Percy

by P. Davey and S. White

Introduction

Between 1964 and 1989 the excavations at Wharram Percy produced a total of 840 fragments of clay tobacco pipe and one pipe clay hair curler (Chapter 17, No. 8) from 218 contexts in eighteen separate sites, including two stray finds from the area of the farmhouse recorded under site code 55 (Fig. 95; Table 44).

The following report is divided into two main sections. First, the evidence provided by the pipes is considered in relation to the archaeological contexts in which they were found. Secondly, all the marked and decorated pipes are discussed as individual products and the evidence provided by the Wharram assemblage is placed in the context of pipe studies in Yorkshire and beyond.

The methodology and recording system employed for this study are described in full in Appendix 1. The archive consists of the pipes themselves, a set of data tables as Excel files, record sketches and drawings carried out by both authors, and copies of related correspondence. The pipe stamps have been recorded as part of the National Catalogue of Clay Pipe Stamps held in the national Clay Pipe Archive at the Department of Archaeology at the University of Liverpool.

Throughout this chapter, measurements of stem bores are shown as 64ths of an inch, e.g. 6/64" equals six sixty-fourths of an inch.

Table 44. Clay tobacco pipe fragments by site.

Site	Stems	Bowls	Mouthpieces	Fragments	Burnished	Total	Contexts
12			1			1	1
14	24	6		3	2	33	26
15	10					10	4
26	57		2		13	59	9
30	11	1				12	7
44	3					3	2
49	46	6		3	1	55	9
51	38	4	1	1	1	44	17
52	1					1	1
54	170	12	2	8	9	192	47
55	2					2	2
59	1					1	1
70	1					1	1
71	2					2	2
73	23			1	1	24	4
74	319	23	9	11	8	362	69
77	33	3			2	36	15
78	2					2	1
Total	743	55	15	27	37	840	218

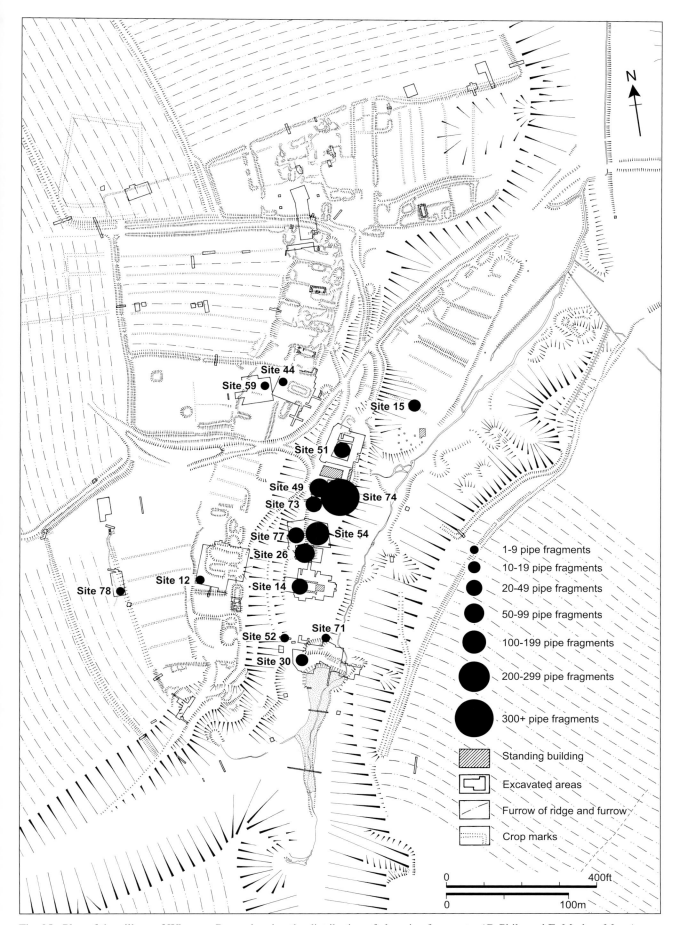

Site 44

Site 59

Site 15

Site 51

Site 49

Site 73   Site 74

Site 77   Site 54

Site 26

Site 12

Site 14

Site 78

Site 71

Site 52

Site 30

● 1-9 pipe fragments

● 10-19 pipe fragments

● 20-49 pipe fragments

● 50-99 pipe fragments

● 100-199 pipe fragments

● 200-299 pipe fragments

● 300+ pipe fragments

Standing building

Excavated areas

Furrow of ridge and furrow

Crop marks

N

0   400ft

0   100m

Fig. 95. Plan of the village of Wharram Percy showing the distribution of clay pipe fragments. (C. Philo and E. Marlow-Mann)

The pipes in context - general overview of the evidence

Sample size and type

Although a total of 840 fragments represents a significant collection of pipe fragments, especially deriving as it does from a rural site, when considered in relation to the archaeological contexts from which they were recovered (Table 45) the assemblage can be seen to contain two major problems: sample size and context type.

The numbers of fragments occurring in any one context are generally very low with an average of 3.85 fragments per context. Looked at more closely this figure actually tends to exaggerate even this degree of 'richness' in the deposits. Half of all the contexts contain single pieces and only 39 exceed four fragments, of which the two largest with 93 and 49 fragments respectively are from topsoil or unstratified deposits.

If the pipes from all similar topsoil and unstratified contexts throughout the Wharram assemblage are discounted, the number of stratified pipes and the average number of fragments per context is reduced further (Table 46).

The second underlying problem is that of the stratified contexts themselves. Quite apart from the numbers of contexts that are unstratified or from topsoil deposits, the overwhelming majority are from layers, rather than discrete features. These layers are often spreads of

Table 45. Number of fragments by site and context.

Site	Number of fragments																						No. of contexts	Total frags	Average per context
	1	2	3	4	5	6	7	8	9	10	11	13	14	15	16	20	21	23	26	30	49	93			
G	9	2																					11	13	1.18
14	22	2	1	1																			26	33	1.27
15	1		3																				4	10	2.50
26	5			1								1	1					1					9	59	6.56
30	4	2		1																			7	12	1.71
49	3		1	2	1										1	1							9	55	6.11
51	8	4		1	2		2																17	44	2.59
54	22	10	3	3	2	2	1					1		1				1			1		47	192	4.08
73	3																1						4	24	6.00
74	26	9	10	6	5	1	3	1	1	2	1		1						1	1		1	69	362	5.25
77	6	4	2	1	1		1																15	36	2.40
Total	109	33	20	16	11	3	7	1	1	2	1	2	2	1	1	1	1	2	1	1	1	1	218	840	3.85

G includes all of the sites which produced fewer than ten pipe fragments: 12, 44, 52, 55, 59, 70, 71 and 78.

Table 46. Number of fragments by site and context, excluding topsoil and unstratified deposits.

Site	Number of fragments																	No. of contexts	Total frags	Average per context
	1	2	3	4	5	6	7	8	9	10	11	13	14	15	23	26	30			
G	3	2																5	7	1.40
14	17	2	1	1														21	28	1.33
15			1															1	3	3.00
26	3			1									1					5	21	4.25
30	4	2																6	8	1.33
49	1		1	1	1													4	13	3.25
51	4	2		1														7	12	1.71
54	22	10	3	3	2	2	1					1		1	1			46	143	3.11
73	1																	1	1	1.00
74	26	9	10	6	5	1	3	1	1	2	1		1			1	1	68	269	3.96
77	6	3	1	1	1													12	24	2.00
Total	87	30	17	14	9	3	4	1	1	2	1	1	2	1	1	1	1	176	529	3.01

Table 47. Fragment type by site.

Site	9	8	7	6	5	4	S	B	M	U	T^1	T^2	T^3	Con.
12				1					1			1	1	1
14	1	2	8(1)	9(1)	3	7	24	6		3	2	30	33	26
15		3(3)			6	1	10					10	10	4
26		1	2	1(1)	30(5)	25(7)	57		2		13	59	59	9
30		1	4	2	2	3	11	1				12	12	7
44		1				2	3					3	3	2
49		2(1)	8	5	18	19	46	6		3	1	52	55	9
51		1	1(1)	2	23	16	38	4	1	1	1	43	44	17
52		1					1					1	1	1
54		15(8)	17	18(2)	77	57	170	12	2	8	9	184	192	47
55					2		2					2	2	2
59		1					1					1	1	1
70				1			1					1	1	1
71				1	1		2					2	2	2
73		1(1)		3	10	9	23			1	1	23	24	4
74	1	20(2)	36(1)	30(5)	145	119	319	23	9	11	8	351	362	69
77		11(1)	1(1)	1	5	18	33	3			2	36	36	15
78					2		2					2	2	1
Total	2	58(16)	79(4)	73(9)	325(5)	276(7)	743	55	15	27	37	813	840	218

(Numerals = stem-bore diameters in /64"; S = total number of measured stem fragments; B = total number of measured bowl fragments; M = total number of measured mouthpiece fragments; U = number of unmeasurable fragments; T^1 = total number of burnished fragments; T^2 = total number of measured fragments; T^3 = total number of fragments in each context. Con. = total number of contexts. NB numbers in brackets record the quantity of burnished fragments.)

material that contain mixed and redeposited finds which cannot be used to give any reliable indication of absolute date. Examples of the problems caused by the very small sample size and the 'generalised' context types at Wharram will become apparent when individual excavated sites and groups are considered.

Dating

The use of clay pipes for dating archaeological deposits has been discussed extensively elsewhere, and alternative and sometimes competitive systems are lauded. The most reliable dating tool remains the bowl form, with any attendant stamp or decoration that may also occur. Stem-bore analysis retains some validity, if used with caution. White, using all the available data from the county has shown that, despite some significant inter-regional variation, Yorkshire follows the broad trend of southern Britain, and that for the period up to c. 1750 the bore data provide a reasonable indication of absolute date (White 2004, 57-65). For most bowls a date range of between 20 and 40 years is usually possible, although this becomes more difficult in later 19th-century products. In order that the bowl range evidence can be used with confidence, at least twelve datable bowl fragments in a given context are needed. At Wharram the largest number of bowls in a context is five, in 74/106. The average numbers of bowls per context is 0.38. Thus the dating of contexts by pipe

bowl range is liable to be hazardous. Where lower numbers are involved, analysis of the stem-bore analysis of context groups of around twenty and above has been shown to give a good indication of the overall date range of the deposit. It also provides an assessment of the quantities of intrusive material, and for groups dating before around 1740, a reasonable indication of the absolute date. As the ratio of bowls to stems recovered is often between 1:5 and 1:10, depending on ground conditions, the numbers of bowl fragments present for dating may be very small. In the case of the Wharram assemblage only 55 out of 840 pieces are identifiable bowls, a ratio of just over 1:15; if the 29 bowl fragments, including bowl/stem junction, are used this becomes around 1:10 (Table 47).

Thus for dating purposes neither the numbers of bowls or stem fragments per context present at Wharram is sufficient for confident chronological assessment to be made.

Despite these problems it is possible, using the two techniques together, to provide an overview of pipe use and loss for the excavations at Wharram as a whole. There are in total 74 identifiable bowl fragments together with marked and/or decorated pieces that can be assigned with confidence to a production date range of between twenty and eighty years (a further eleven bowl fragments could not be assigned to a date range with this degree of

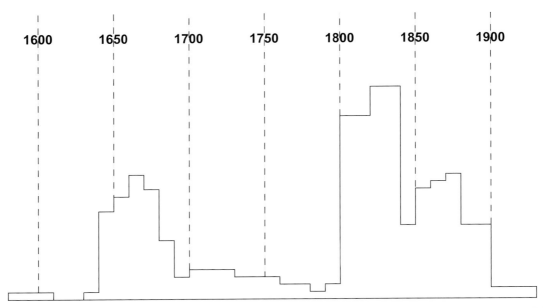

Fig. 96. Accumulated date ranges, by decade, for all the identifiable bowl forms and decorated fragments for the whole Wharram clay pipe assemblage. (P. Davey and S. White)

precision). If these ranges are tabulated accumulatively, using each decade of range for each fragment, a general indication of the major periods of activity can be obtained (Fig. 96). Three distinct phases can be discerned: 1640 to 1690, 1690 to 1800, and 1800 to 1900. With the exception of one earlier fragment, the 17th-century pipe evidence reaches a maximum around 1660. Far fewer 18th-century pipes were recovered. The largest grouping of pipes belongs to the 19th century, with a peak around 1830 and another around 1880. The height of the latter part of the diagram will be slightly exaggerated because of the wider ranges applied to pipes of that period. Whilst the 19th century is represented by 35 pieces, the 17th and 18th centuries combined, nevertheless, produced 39 datable fragments.

A histogram showing the stem-bore data provides some confirmation of this overall picture (Fig. 97). Even though individual stem-bore values cannot be precisely

dated they do give some chronological information. Thus bores of 9, 8 and 7/64" are unlikely to belong to the period after 1700, and values of 4/64" almost certainly belong to later 18th or 19th-century pipes. The histogram has two elements; an initial '17th-century' phase up to 1690, represented by one quarter of the collection, and a much larger 18/19th-century block covering the remaining three-quarters. The ratio of bowls to stems for the first phase is 32 to 212 or 1:6.3. In contrast the ratio for the 18th and 19th-century material is 42 to 701 or 1:16. The difference between these two ratios is almost certainly explained by the varying stem lengths and bowl wall thicknesses of pipes at different periods. The 17th-century bowl is smaller, more compact and much thicker walled than its 18th or 19th-century successors so that, although longer in the ground, it is much less likely to break down into very small pieces and so is much more likely to be recovered. In addition, later periods of pipe production saw a much bigger variation in stem length, including some much longer examples, so that on average a single later pipe will produce a greater number of separate stem fragments.

Overall the Wharram clay-pipe evidence indicates an important phase of activity during the middle of the 17th century and another in the 19th century. (Fig. 98)

Geography of the sites

While clay-pipe fragments were recovered from eighteen of the separate excavations at Wharram, the only significant concentrations were derived from sites in the Glebe Terrace (North and South), including the Church, with only occasional finds on the Plateau or elsewhere. Given the very small numbers outside the terrace, it is not possible to discern any chronological or distributional pattern for most of the village (Fig. 95). The following

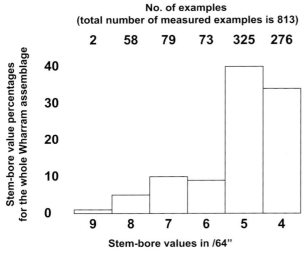

No. of examples
(total number of measured examples is 813)

Fig. 97. Stem-bore values for the whole Wharram clay pipe assemblage. (P. Davey and S. White)

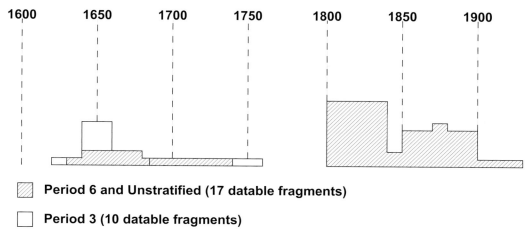

| | | | | | |
|1600|1650|1700|1750|1800|1850|1900|

▨ **Period 6 and Unstratified (17 datable fragments)**

☐ **Period 3 (10 datable fragments)**

Fig. 98. Accumulated date ranges, by decade, for all the identifiable bowl forms and decorated fragments from Site 74. (P. Davey and S. White)

text provides a discussion of the pipe evidence from each of the areas of the excavation. Inevitably, the main focus of detailed attention will be on those sites on the Northern Glebe Terrace that produce the overwhelming majority of pipe fragments from reliable archaeological deposits.

Plateau sites

No pipe fragments were derived from the North Manor and only four fragments from two sites on the South Manor (Sites 44 and 59). The single probable 17th-century stem fragment from Site 59 was from a medieval context and must therefore be considered as intrusive. The three pieces from Site 44 are of mixed 17th and 19th-century date. There were also no pipes from the peasant houses (Sites 3, 6, 8 and 9) with the exception of a single mouthpiece from Site 12. Further to the west a total of three stem fragments of probable 18th or 19th-century date were found in Sites 70 and 78. Given the significant areas excavated this negative evidence strongly suggests that the plateau sites were not being ploughed, gardened or otherwise disturbed at least from the 17th to the 20th centuries.

Southern Glebe Terrace sites

The church and graveyard (Sites 14, 26 and 52; Wharram III and Wharram XI)
The 33 fragments of clay pipe from the church (*Wharram III*, 167-8 and fiche) and the 60 from the graveyard provide an interesting contrast. Whilst, on the basis of stem-bore, stem thickness and fabric, together with bowl form range, possibly as much as two-thirds of the material from the church (Site 14) is of 17th-century date, over 90% of finds from the graveyard are of 19th-century type. In the case of the church the earlier phase of activity seems to be associated with reflooring and refitting of the nave and burials within the nave prior to the 1829 restoration. The later finds which concentrate in the period 1850 to 1900 probably relate to the 1847 restoration and later 19th-century repairs (*Wharram III*,

52). In the graveyard (Sites 26 and 52) the numbers of later pipe finds, whilst insufficient to imply the kind of ritual smoking and destruction of pipes that took place at Irish funerals, does suggest regular use of the area for smoking, possibly as a respite from the agricultural work environment.

The mill dam and its environs (Sites 30 and 71; Wharram X)
A total of fourteen fragments was recovered from these two excavations, the majority from Site 30. The forms and stem-bore values present indicate an even spread - a 'light rain' - of deposition over time from the mid-17th century to the end of the 19th century.

Northern Glebe Terrace sites

The farmstead and vicarage sites, with totals of 497 and 228 clay pipe fragments respectively, provide the major clay-pipe assemblages from Wharram, representing some 86% of the total collection from the village.

The farmstead (Sites 74, 51, 49, 73 and 55)
Site 74
The site of the farmhouse itself produced a total of 362 clay-pipe fragments from 69 contexts and six identified phases. This assemblage amounts to 43% of the whole from Wharram and is only approached by the vicarage (Site 54) with 23% of the total. Thus the two post-medieval domestic sites can boast two-thirds of all the pipes from the village between them. In order to make sense of the large number of relevant contexts the pipes from the area will be discussed in phase order.

Period 1 (Table 48)
The structural remains beneath the 17th-century farmhouse have been assigned to Period 1 (74/341 and 74/361/2). The presence of eleven fragments of clay-pipe stem fragments, seven of which are of 19th-century type, poses a problem. Even if the remaining three measured stems could be assigned to a period early in the 17th

Table 48. Clay-pipe fragments from Site 74 Period 1.

Context	8	7	6	5	4	S	U	T²	T³	Period 1 contexts
341	1				6	7	1	7	8	Sub-floor base
361/2		1	1		1	3		3	3	Wall under floor
Total	1	1	1		7	10	1	10	11	

(Numerals = stem-bore diameters in /64"; S = total number of measured stem fragments; B = total number of measured bowl fragments; M = total number of measured mouthpiece fragments; U = number of unmeasurable fragments; T¹ = total number of burnished fragments; T² = total number of measured fragments; T³ = total number of fragments in each context. NB numbers in brackets record the quantity of burnished fragments.)

Table 49. Clay-pipe fragments from Site 74 Period 2.

Context	8	7	6	5	4	S	B	M	T²	T³	Period 2 contexts
219		1		1	3	4		1	5	5	Yard surface
271		1				1			1	1	Surface outside
300			1			1			1	1	Bank of chalk
321		1	1			1	1		2	2	Wall tumble
323			1					1	1	1	Floor bedding
345	1					1			1	1	Below construction
Total	1	3	3	1	3	8	1	2	11	11	

(Numerals = stem-bore diameters in /64"; S = total number of measured stem fragments; B = total number of measured bowl fragments; M = total number of measured mouthpiece fragments; U = number of unmeasurable fragments; T¹ = total number of burnished fragments; T² = total number of measured fragments; T³ = total number of fragments in each context. NB numbers in brackets record the quantity of burnished fragments.)

century, before the construction of the farmhouse, a clear majority of the finds would appear to be intrusive. They do not represent contamination of earlier deposits during the construction of the farmhouse, as they are far too late, but some much later set of activities, possibly as late as mid-20th-century archaeological excavation.

Period 2 (Table 49)

A further eleven pipe fragments were associated with the construction of the farmhouse. The five fragments from the yard surface (74/219) to the west of the house represent deposition from the 17th until the 19th centuries. The finds had presumably been forced into the surface of the yard during use and do not argue necessarily for a later date for the construction of the surface itself. The six fragments from the five remaining deposits are all of 17th-century type. On the basis of the single bowl (Fig. 100, No. 19) assigned to the phase, the floor bedding in Room B (74/323) is unlikely to pre-date 1660, whilst the majority of the remaining stems cannot be dated more precisely. The exception is the thick-walled and wide-bored crude stem from rubble (74/345) below the construction layer (74/344) in Room D which is likely to date from the first half of the 17th century.

Period 3 (Table 50)

Fifty-seven fragments of clay pipe were recovered from occupation deposits relating to the 17th-century farmhouse. The two largest groups with a total of 36 pieces were derived from superimposed contexts, interpreted as garden levelling layers, to the west of the house (74/106 and 74/299). Fragments from six surviving bowls are all datable to the period 1630 to 1680 (Fig. 99, Nos 2-5 and 7). The majority of the stems are also 17th-century in type. There are certainly a number of later finds, in particular the mid-18th-century stem by Isaac Hodgson of Leeds (Fig. 100, No. 27) and a few small narrow-bored late 18th or 19th-century stem fragments, mostly from the higher of the two layers (74/106). This garden area was built over by Room 6 of the 19th-century farmhouse. The pipe finds from these two layers confirm the pottery and documentary evidence, that the later farmhouse was not constructed until the early 19th century.

Three other layers (74/165, 74/230 and 74/255), also located to the west of the 17th-century farmhouse and beneath Rooms 1 and 6 of the later house, tend to confirm this picture. The surface (74/165) produced two wide-bore and two narrow-bore stems; the downwash (74/230) and the demolition material (74/255) both produced

Table 50. Clay-pipe fragments from Site 74 Period 3.

Context	9	8	7	6	5	4	S	B	M	U	T¹	T²	T³	Period 3 contexts
106		6	15	4(4)	2	3	25	5			4	30	30	? Layer
165		2				3	5					5	5	Earlier surface
230						1	1			1		1	2	Down wash
238					1	1	2			1		2	3	Bank
255						1	1					1	1	Demolition
264			1(1)		1	1	2		1		1	3	3	Floor
277				3			3					3	3	? Layer
287			4				2	2				4	4	Area of soil
299	1		1	1	1	2	4	1	1			6	6	Garden
Total	1	8	21(1)	8(4)	5	12	45	8	2	2	5	55	57	

(Numerals = stem-bore diameters in /64"; S = total number of measured stem fragments; B = total number of measured bowl fragments; M = total number of measured mouthpiece fragments; U = number of unmeasurable fragments; T¹ = total number of burnished fragments; T² = total number of measured fragments; T³ = total number of fragments in each context. NB numbers in brackets record the quantity of burnished fragments.)

Table 51. Clay-pipe fragments from Site 74 Period 4.

Context	8	7	6	5	4	S	B	M	U	T1	T2	T3	Period 4 contexts
100			1			1					1	1	Sandy loam within S and W walls
105			1	1		2					2	2	Demolition layer
115				1		1					1	1	Sandy gravel, compacted chalk
130		1					1				1	1	Sandstone wall
154		1					1				1	1	Chalk block wall
169				1		1					1	1	Compacted black silty layer
237			1	2		3					3	3	Pea grit silt with demolition
244			1			1					1	1	Mortar rich surface of floor R4
245		1				1					1	1	Brown silt with brick
267				1		1					1	1	Mortar and rubble demolition floor
269		1				1					1	1	Orange silty sand
284	1(1)	1	2			3	1			1	4	4	Fill of construction trench R1
286		2				1	1				2	2	Crumbly sand with brick and tile
314			3		10	12	1		1		13	14	Grey plaster rich layer R5
334					1	1					1	1	Sand with chalk, flint and pea grit
337	1(1)				1	2				1	2	2	Cut for construction trench
339					1	1					1	1	Sand with chalk, flint and pea grit
349		1				1					1	1	Brick and chalk construction
Total	2(2)	5	5	7	19	32	5	1	1	2	38	39	

(Numerals = stem-bore diameters in /64"; S = total number of measured stem fragments; B = total number of measured bowl fragments; M = total number of measured mouthpiece fragments; U = number of unmeasurable fragments; T¹ = total number of burnished fragments; T² = total number of measured fragments; T³ = total number of fragments in each context. NB numbers in brackets record the quantity of burnished fragments.)

single late stem fragments. The floor surface in Room C (74/264) and the bank in Room D that lay beneath Room 3 of the later farmhouse reflect a similar situation. All these layers suggest that the occupation of the 17th-century farmhouse continued until late in the 18th century. Only two areas of soil (74/277 and 74/287) included solely 17th-century finds, and then only seven pieces in all.

Period 4 (Table 51)
A further 39 clay-pipe fragments were associated with the construction of the 18th-century farmhouse. A small group of pipes were recovered from within the structure of the walls (74/100, 74/105, 74/130 and 74/154). These cannot be closely dated except to say that they must date from the late 18th century at the earliest. Interestingly, the fill of the construction trench for wall 130 (74/284)

Table 52. Clay-pipe fragments from Site 74 Period 5.

Context	5	4	S	B	U	T²	T³	Period 5 contexts
181	6		5	1	1	6	7	Pit fill
224	3	1	4			4	4	Silt and chalk
310		3	3			3	3	Sand/mortar fill
Total	9	4	12	1	1	13	14	

(Numerals = stem-bore diameters in /64"; S = total number of measured stem fragments; B = total number of measured bowl fragments; M = total number of measured mouthpiece fragments; U = number of unmeasurable fragments; T¹ = total number of burnished fragments; T² = total number of measured fragments; T³ = total number of fragments in each context. NB numbers in brackets record the quantity of burnished fragments.)

Table 53. Clay-pipe fragments from Site 74 Period 6 and unphased contexts.

Period	8	7	6	5	4	S	B	M	U	T¹	T²	T³
6	4	2	6(1)	58	51	114	5	2	5	1	121	126
U/S	4	4	7	65	23	98	3	2			103	103
Total	8	6	13(1)	123	74	212	8	4	5	1	224	229

(Numerals = stem-bore diameters in /64"; S = total number of measured stem fragments; B = total number of measured bowl fragments; M = total number of measured mouthpiece fragments; U = number of unmeasurable fragments; T¹ = total number of burnished fragments; T² = total number of measured fragments; T³ = total number of fragments in each context. NB numbers in brackets record the quantity of burnished fragments.)

contained entirely 17th-century material including two mid-century bowl fragments (Fig. 99, No. 6). In contrast the main floor make-up deposits lack such derived material. In particular, the loose whitish grey plaster-rich layer within Room 5 (74/314), which is interpreted by the excavator as the preparation layer for a flagged floor, contains only late 18th or early 19th-century finds. The only specifically datable piece is the fragment of a fine quality fluted bowl from the generalised period 1770 to 1800. These finds are compatible with a construction date for the latest farmhouse of around 1800.

Period 5 (Table 52)
Only fourteen pipe finds could be associated with the demolition of the Period 4 farmhouse. Seven of these were from the fill of a stone-lined ash pit (74/181) within Room 1, including a Britannia bowl dating from c. 1800 to 1840 (Fig. 101, No. 29). The remaining two demolition layers (74/224 and 74/310) also contained stem fragments of late 18th-century or 19th-century date. On the evidence of the pipes the farmhouse must have been demolished by around 1840 to 1850, especially considering the quantities of later pipes that occur in Period 6.

Period 6 (Table 53)
The largest group of pipes from Site 74, 126 pieces in all, were derived from Period 6 which represented both the Period 4 farmhouse demolition and all subsequent activity on the site. The excavator has described this phase as 'so disturbed that further interpretation is of little use'. If the contexts which were not ascribed to a phase

are added, a total of 229 pipe fragments, almost two-thirds (some 63%) of the whole collection from the site, has to be described as effectively unstratified.

An accumulated date-range graph for the sixteen datable bowl and single stem fragment demonstrates that the quantity of 17th-century residual material in these contexts is much lower than that for the ten datable pieces in Period 3, for example (Fig. 98). Whilst the latest occupation of the 17th-century farmhouse appears to be around 1800, only a handful of stems and one stamped stem reflect this date. The remainder of the pipe finds are firmly of 17th-century date. In contrast, the Period 6 graph shows only a trace of residual finds from the 17th century (Fig. 99, No. 13), while the later pipes appear to form two blocks. One focuses on the earlier part of the 19th century (Fig. 101, Nos 33 and 37), presumably representing the occupation and demolition of the farmhouse. The other which peaks in the 1880s and continues well into the 20th century (Fig. 101, No. 52) is the product of the post-farmhouse occupation and use of the site.

Site 51 (Table 54)
Forty-four pipe fragments from seventeen contexts were recovered from Site 51. Of these, 32 pieces from ten of the contexts are from topsoil or modern disturbance and rubbish deposits (unphased) and are almost entirely of 19th-century or later date. This only leaves twelve fragments from seven contexts which can be regarded as stratified; most are from layers or area spreads rather than features.

Only two pieces each from disturbed contexts 51/1 and 51/202 may derive from earlier activity on the site.

Table 54. Clay-pipe fragments from Site 51.

Context	8	7	6	5	4	S	B	M	U	T^1	T^2	T^3	Bowl date range	Context type/period
539				1		1					1	1		2.2
593				1		1					1	1		2.2
264				1		1					1	1		ER-P3
467				3	1	4					4	4		2.4
469					2	2					2	2		2.4
558				1		1					1	1		2.4
569					2	2					2	2		2.4
1	1	(1)		3	2	5	1	1		1	7	7	1860-1880	U/P
2				1			1				1	1	1850-1900	U/P
72				1	1	2					2	2		U/P
100				2	3	3	2				5	5	1850-1900	U/P
104				1		1					1	1		U/P
201				1		1					1	1		U/P
202			2	4		6			1		6	7	1800-1840	U/P
204					1	1					1	1		U/P
209					2	2					2	2		U/P
211				3	2	5					5	5		U/P-CRT
Total	1	1(1)	2	23	16	38	4	1	1	1	43	44		

(Numerals = stem-bore diameters in /64"; S = total number of measured stem fragments; B = total number of measured bowl fragments; M = total number of measured mouthpiece fragments; U = number of unmeasurable fragments; T^1 = total number of burnished fragments; T^2 = total number of measured fragments; T^3 = total number of fragments in each context. NB numbers in brackets record the quantity of burnished fragments.) ER = East Range

Table 55. Clay-pipe fragments from Site 49.

Context	8	7	6	5	4	S	B	U	T^1	T^2	T^3	Bowl date range	Context period
21		1		2	2	5				5	5		2
26	(1)	2			1	3	1		1	4	4	1660-1690	2
1	1	2		8	7	16	2	2		18	20	1800-1900	3
2		2	2	6	6	13	3			16	16	1660-1840	3
6		1	3			4				4	4		3
11				1	2	3				3	3		3
76				1		1				1	1		3
500					1	1				1	1		3
78								1			1	1880-1920	U/P
Total	2(1)	8	5	18	19	46	6	3	1	52	55		

(Numerals = stem-bore diameters in /64"; S = total number of measured stem fragments; B = total number of measured bowl fragments; M = total number of measured mouthpiece fragments; U = number of unmeasurable fragments; T^1 = total number of burnished fragments; T^2 = total number of measured fragments; T^3 = total number of fragments in each context. NB numbers in brackets record the quantity of burnished fragments.)

Site 49 (Table 55)
A total of 55 clay-pipe fragments was recovered from nine contexts to the west of the farmhouse. Six of the contexts, containing 43 of the finds, were topsoils or debris from the 1958 archaeological excavations (Period 3 and unphased). All but one of the bowls from these deposits and almost all the stems indicate 19th-century activity; only one bowl of 1660-90 (Fig. 100, No. 20) and between six and eleven fragments appear to derive from earlier phases of occupation in the 17th century. A further stratified layer (49/11) also within Period 3 contained three late stem fragments. The two Period 2 contexts, 49/21 and 49/26, with a total of eight pipe fragments, represent the bed of a road overlain by an apparent turf-

Table 56. Clay-pipe fragments from Site 73.

Context	8	7	6	5	4	S	U	T¹	T²	T³	Type	Period
55	1(1)					1		1	1	1	Yard surface	2
1			3	10	7	20	1		20	21	Layer	3
15				1		1			1	1	Pit fill	3
16				1		1			1	1	Pit fill	3
Total	1(1)		3	10	9	23	1	1	23	24		

(Numerals = stem-bore diameters in /64"; S = total number of measured stem fragments; B = total number of measured bowl fragments; M = total number of measured mouthpiece fragments; U = number of unmeasurable fragments; T¹ = total number of burnished fragments; T² = total number of measured fragments; T³ = total number of fragments in each context. NB numbers in brackets record the quantity of burnished fragments.)

Table 57. Clay-pipe fragments from Site 77.

Context	8	7	6	5	4	S	B	T¹	T²	T³	Type	Period
14					1	1			1	1	Layer	1-5
304	3					2	1		3	3	Fill of feature	5.1
136			1			1			1	1	Robber trench	5.1
335	2	1(1)				3		1	3	3	Buried soil	5.1
344	1					1			1	1	Layer	5.1
374					2	2			2	2	Compacted layer	5.1
50					1	1			1	1	Hillwash	5.1/5.2
84				1		1			1	1	Hillwash	5.1/5.2
85				1			1		1	1	Road surface	5.2
86				1	3	4			4	4	19th-century surface	5.2
132	2(1)					2		1	2	2	Conduit backfill	5.2
297					2	1	1		2	2	Layer	5.2
114	2			1	2	5			5	5	Arch dump	6
250					2	2			2	2		U/S
9000	1			2	4	7			7	7		U/S
Total	11(1)	1(1)	1	5	18	33	3	2	36	36		

(Numerals = stem-bore diameters in /64"; S = total number of measured stem fragments; B = total number of measured bowl fragments; M = total number of measured mouthpiece fragments; U = number of unmeasurable fragments; T¹ = total number of burnished fragments; T² = total number of measured fragments; T³ = total number of fragments in each context. NB numbers in brackets record the quantity of burnished fragments.)

line. Although the later of these layers produced a bowl fragment dating from c. 1660 to 1690 (Fig. 100, No. 20) both contexts produced stem fragments typical of the 19th century. It seems unlikely, therefore, that any of the pipe producing layers are earlier than 1800.

Site 73 (Table 56)
The southerly extension of Site 49 produced 24 pipe fragments from four contexts. All but three of the pieces are from topsoil and spoil from previous excavations (73/1). There are no bowl fragments and the majority of the stems are clearly of 19th-century type, with a few that may be a little earlier. Two further 19th-century stems were recovered from modern rubbish pits (73/15 and 73/16). All of this material has been placed by the excavator in Period 3. A single burnished, wide-bored,

stem from a yard surface (73/55) in the upper part of Period 2 provides a *terminus post quem* for the feature of c.1600 to 1650.

Site 55
The two stem fragments are probably of 19th-century date.

The vicarage (Sites 77 and 54)
Site 77 (Table 57)
A sequence of buildings situated to the west of the 18th-century structure and interpreted as earlier vicarage sites provided a further 36 clay pipe fragments, all from the latest phases of occupation (Periods 5 and 6). A group of three pieces from a Period 5.1 robbed feature (77/304), included a bowl of c. 1660 to 1680 (Fig. 99, No. 16) and

222

Table 58. Clay-pipe fragments from Site 54 Period 6.

Context	8	7	6	5	4	S	B	M	U	T¹	T²	T³	Period
323		1				1					1	1	6.1
625				1		1					1	1	6.2
241		1				1					1	1	6.3
245	1(1)	1				2					2	2	6.3
298	1					1					1	1	6.3
456				1		1					1	1	6.3
462	1(1)			1		2			1		2	2	6.3
516	1(1)		1	3		3	2		1	1	5	6	6.3
Total	4(3)	3	1	6		12	2		1	2	14	15	

(Numerals = stem-bore diameters in /64"; S = total number of measured stem fragments; B = total number of measured bowl fragments; M = total number of measured mouthpiece fragments; U = number of unmeasurable fragments; T¹ = total number of burnished fragments; T² = total number of measured fragments; T³ = total number of fragments in each context. NB numbers in brackets record the quantity of burnished fragments.)

two early stems. This might well represent later 17th-century activity on the site. Within Period 5 the majority of all the pipe stems are of later 18th or 19th-century type. The main exceptions are the buried soil (77/335) and the backfill of the late 18th-century conduit (77/132), which appear to contain entirely 17th-century material. The numbers involved in these contexts are so small that it is difficult to make a precise estimate of date with any confidence. The same applies to the Period 6 and unstratified material which is the product of 20th-century activities, many of them archaeological.

Site 54
The site of the 18th and early 19th-century vicarage produced a total of 192 clay-pipe fragments, almost a quarter of the assemblage from the village, from Periods 6 to 8.

Period 6 (Table 58)
Fifteen pipe fragments were recovered from the eight layers associated with the cellared Structure J that preceded the vicarage. The presence of wider stem bores in a number of the contexts suggest 17th-century activity. This dating is confirmed by the three bowl fragments from the largest of the contexts (54/516) which fall into the combined range of 1680 to 1770 (Fig. 100, Nos 22 and 23). The only stem directly derived from the floor of the building (54/625) is likely to be an 18th-century product, and probably therefore derived from the backfill. Given the presence of the vicarage in the 1764 terrier, the pipes suggest that Structure J may have been constructed at any time after 1700. The lack of very narrow bores also suggests an 18th-century date for this assemblage.

Period 7 (Table 59)
Five pipe-stem fragments were recovered from the first structural phase (Period 7.1) of the 18th-century vicarage (Structure K), from wall footings (54/252), from post-pits associated with a dividing wall towards the southern end of the building (54/157 and 54/182), and from a worn threshold (54/121). Although difficult to date, these pieces suggest a date not much earlier than the middle of the 18th century.

Four further stems, indistinguishable in date, were found in a new hearth to the north of the building (Period 7.2; 54/117) and a single stem from a surface associated with the robbing of Structure J (Period 7.3; 54/308).

The building of Structure L and other activities to the rear of the vicarage (Period 7.4) produced a further nine stems. These included 18th-century types from a construction layer for a coal cellar (54/123), surfaces (54/226 and 54/308), a rubbish pit (54/422) and an animal burial (54/288), together with 17th-century types from a coal cellar (54/75) and another animal burial (54/247).

Yard surfaces to the east of the vicarage contained domestic occupation material including rather more pipe finds (Period 7.5; 54/124, 54/168, 54/202 and 54/250). They are described by the excavator either as 'hillwash' or 'surface accumulation'. The most important deposit (54/202) produced some early 17th-century burnished stems and bowls dating from c. 1660 to 1680 (e.g. Fig. 99, No. 14) and c. 1710 to 1740 (Fig. 100, No. 24). The clearly mixed nature of these finds rather confirms the idea that the deposits had accumulated over a period of time and were derived from elsewhere. Two stems were found in the floor bedding for Structure N. These too appear to be of mixed 17th and 18th-century type.

Stratigraphically, the latest activity on the site prior to the demolition of the vicarage is represented by a single 18th or 19th-century stem fragment from hillwash associated with the use of Structure Q (Period 7.7; 54/97) and four fragments (two bowls and two stems) from the fill of pits and gullies related to the cobbled road surfaces to the east of the site (Period 7.8; 54/9, 54/56 and 54/96). One of the bowls is a Masonic type dating from c. 1800 to 1840 (Fig. 101, No. 31) and the other is a fluted example dating from c. 1820 to 1880 (Fig. 101, No. 36). These finds indicate that this phase dates to sometime after 1820 and, presumably before the demolition of the vicarage in 1834.

Table 59. Clay-pipe fragments from Site 54 Period 7.

Context	8	7	6	5	4	S	B	U	T¹	T²	T³	Period
121				1	1	2				2	2	7.1
157					1	1				1	1	7.1
182					1	1				1	1	7.1
252					1	1				1	1	7.1
117				4		4				4	4	7.2
308				1		1				1	1	7.3
75			1(1)			1			1	1	1	7.4
123				1		1				1	1	7.4
226			1			1				1	1	7.4
247		1		1		2				2	2	7.4
288				2		2				2	2	7.4
422				1		1				1	1	7.4
124	3(1)			2		5			1	5	5	7.5
168	1					1				1	1	7.5
192		1	1			2				2	2	7.5
202	2(2)	4		5	1	9	3	1	2	12	13	7.5
250				1		1				1	1	7.5
97					1	1				1	1	7.7
9					1		1			1	1	7.8
59				1		1				1	1	7.8
96				1	1	1	1			2	2	7.8
Total	6(3)	6	3(1)	21	8	39	5	1	4	44	45	

(Numerals = stem-bore diameters in /64"; S = total number of measured stem fragments; B = total number of measured bowl fragments; M = total number of measured mouthpiece fragments; U = number of unmeasurable fragments; T¹ = total number of burnished fragments; T² = total number of measured fragments; T³ = total number of fragments in each context. NB numbers in brackets record the quantity of burnished fragments.)

Period 8 (Table 60)

The final phase of activity on Site 54, as identified by the excavations, produced a total of 132 clay-pipe fragments, more than two thirds (69%) of the collection from the site. The first major group, consisting of 52 pieces, was associated with the demolition and robbing of the vicarage itself (Period 8.1; 54/5, 54/93, 54/111, 54/113, 54/150 and 54/162). This sequence of finds included a bowl fragment of c. 1660 to 1680, as well as some clearly 17th-century stems, an 18th-century rim fragment and a bowl of c. 1750 to 1780 (Fig. 100, No. 25), together with a considerable number of late 18th and 19th-century stem fragments. In contrast, the rain-washed dump within this phase (54/17) provided the earliest bowl from the whole village, dating from c. 1580 to 1610 (Fig. 99, No. 1).

The rather more quiescent deposits of Period 8.2 (54/7, 54/11 and 54/14) contained only later pipe stems as did the construction trench for the 20th-century henhouse (54/29). The topsoil itself (54/1) produced a further 49 pipe fragments covering the whole range from the 17th to the 19th centuries and including bowls of c. 1800 to 1840 (Fig. 101, No. 32) and c. 1820 to 1880 (Fig. 101, No. 35).

The demolition of the henhouse (54/3 and 54/4) and the latest dumping on the site (54/2) also appeared to include residual material but did provide a small fragment of a probable 20th-century bowl (54/3).

Discussion of the pipes as archaeological evidence

Dating

Despite the difficulties inherent in the Wharram assemblage referred to earlier, the pipe evidence has provided a number of clear dating indications. First, tobacco smoking begins in the late 16th century and develops quickly by the middle of the 17th century. In this there is no suggestion that the inhabitants of the village were isolated or especially conservative compared with the rest of the country. As elsewhere clay pipes continued to be smoked into the 20th century.

Secondly, the pipes clearly show that there was a significant occupation of the village during the 17th century, albeit the evidence is derived from extensive

Table 60. Clay-pipe fragments from Site 54 Period 8.

Context	8	7	6	5	4	S	B	M	U	T¹	T²	T³	Type	Period
5	1	3		7	12	22	1				23	23	Demolition of K	8.1
17	1		2				2	1			3	3	Rain washed dump	8.1
31				1		1					1	1	Hillwash	8.1
93				2		2					2	2	Robber trench K	8.1
111				7	8	15					15	15	Demolition debris (K)	8.1
113				2	3	5					5	5	Demolition debris (K)	8.1
141		4	1	1	1	7					7	7	Rain washed	8.1
150			2			2			1		2	3	Fill of rubbish pit	8.1
162					4	4					4	4	Demolition debris (K)	8.1
7					3	3					3	3	Surface deposit	8.2
11				2		2					2	2	Dump	8.2
14				1		1					1	1	Dump	8.2
29					1	1					1	1	Post-hole fill	8.3
1	3(2)	1	6(1)	20	15	42	2	1	4	3	45	49	Topsoil	8.4
2				2		2					2	2	Modern demolition	8.4
3									1			1	Modern demolition	8.4
4			2	1	1	4					4	4	Demolition of S	8.4
8			1	4	1	6					6	6	Dump	8.4
Total	5(2)	8	14(1)	50	49	119	5	2	6	3	126	132		

(Numerals = stem-bore diameters in /64"; S = total number of measured stem fragments; B = total number of measured bowl fragments; M = total number of measured mouthpiece fragments; U = number of unmeasurable fragments; T¹ = total number of burnished fragments; T² = total number of measured fragments; T³ = total number of fragments in each context. NB numbers in brackets record the quantity of burnished fragments.)

residual deposits and not from contemporary structures. This was followed by a further intense phase of pipe smoking activity during the end of the 18th century and early 19th century, and again during the latter part of the century.

Thirdly, the pipes have provided specific and clear confirmation of the construction of the 17th-century farmhouse between *c.* 1660 and 1690, its use in the 18th century, the construction of its replacement around 1800 and its destruction around 1840. The pipes place the construction of the latest vicarage somewhere between 1690 and 1770 and its demolition, also by 1840.

The archaeological deposits

The pipes are especially interesting in the light they throw upon the nature of the deposits from which they derived. Differing classes of deposit seem to exhibit differing degrees of residuality. For example, almost all topsoil layers (e.g. 49/1, 51/1, 54/1, 74/9000 and 77/9000) include the full range of bore sizes and datable material. The same applies to archaeological dumps such as 77/114 and also to some layers that have clearly accumulated over time, such as those described by the excavators as rain-wash and hillwash (e.g. 54/17, 54/124, 54/141 and 54/202) and buried soils such as 74/299 and 77/2. Where later 18th or 19th-century demolition or construction involves intrusive activity, the pipes again reflect this by including residual 17th-century elements. Good examples of this are the fills of construction trenches in the Period 4 farmhouse (74/284 and 74/337) and the conduit backfill 77/132. In contrast, lack of residual material in a number of deposits may suggest shorter periods of accumulation, less intrusive activity, or both. For example, some hillwash (74/230, 54/31, 777/50 and 77/84), construction (54/121, 54/157, 54/182 and 54/252) and demolition (54/111, 54/113, 54/162 and 74/255) deposits include later material only. Given the small size of the samples such differences should be treated with caution.

Pipe fragments derived from actual structures also exhibit the same ambivalence. Some, such as the 'bed of a road' (49/21 and 49/26), yard surfaces (74/219 and 74/271) and the floor surfaces (74/165 and 74/264) include pipes from the 17th to 19th centuries. These surfaces appear to have had material crushed into them over a long period of use. In contrast, the finds from other structures, such as those from within the walls of the 18th-century farmhouse (74/100, 74/105, 74/130 and 74/154), from the bedding layer for its floor (74/314) and from the first structural phases of the 18th-century vicarage (54/121, 54/157, 54/182, 54/252 and 54/117), appear to provide reliable dating for a short phase of activity.

Burnishing and milling

A large number of burnished pipes from a site might well suggest high status occupation as the work involved in polishing the bowls and stems increased the price significantly. Unfortunately, burnishing ratios vary greatly between different production centres and until the results of detailed regional studies are available it is difficult to generalise. In the case of Yorkshire, however, White has shown that even within one county there is significant local variation. For example in the East Riding and West Yorkshire about 10% of all pipes dating up to about 1800 are burnished; in Hull this value is nearer 5%. In contrast, in the York area and West Yorkshire something like half of all pipes from 1580 to 1800 are burnished. In addition, in York there is considerable variation between sites (White 2004, 75-82), possibly due to differences in status between them. In the case of Wharram, of 80 identifiable bowls, four are burnished (5%); if only the 32 bowls dating from c. 1580 to 1800 are considered, then around 9% are burnished. If all the fragments are used, 41 out of 840 pieces are burnished (4.9%); if the values of 4/64" bore are removed, then 34 out of 573 pipe fragments are burnished, almost exactly 6%. Thus the burnishing ratio for the Wharram pipe assemblage is consistent with what is known from much larger collections in Hull and the rest of the East Riding. It may be socially significant that three out of the four burnished 17th and 18th-century bowls were recovered from the vicarage sites (Sites 54 and 77) - 37.5% of the collection, and only one from a much larger collection derived from the farmstead sites (49, 51, 74 etc.) - 5.3% of the whole. This difference is also apparent if the burnished stems are included. Twelve burnished pieces were recovered from the vicarage sites out of a total of 228 fragments (8.7%), and eleven from the farmstead sites out of a total of 487 (2.3%). These figures suggest that, even with a low general burnishing ratio, it is possible to distinguish class differences between sites using this attribute.

Only 47 out of 80 bowl fragments have enough of the rim surviving for milling to be recorded. Out of these only nine bowls (11%) are milled. If only 17th and early 18th-century bowls are considered four out of twenty bowls (25%) are milled. While both these figures are somewhat lower than those recorded by White for the eastern part of Yorkshire, given the very small numbers involved it is difficult to say whether this is significant (White 2004, 66-8).

Comparative material

Published excavated assemblages of clay pipes from rural sites in the British Isles are not common, and finds are often few in number, not clearly related to archaeological contexts and, when they are, there is rarely any discussion of the evidence they provide for stratigraphic interpretation. For example, while a small group of six 17th-century bowls was recorded from 'upper levels' at the deserted village of Cowlam and single finds from a number of 'lower levels' (Brewster and Hayfield 1988),

there is no adequate quantification of the pipes and no discussion of them. In contrast, for perhaps the largest group from a rural excavation, the 1,899 fragments from Llanmaes in South Glamorgan, there is a very useful analysis of the sources of the pipes, but no account of their archaeological contexts (Newman 1996). Perhaps the most interesting group published to date is still the relatively small assemblage from the deserted village of West Whelpington in Northumberland (Jarrett 1970; Belcher and Jarrett 1971) which, on the basis of a final date for the occupation of the village of 1719 to 1721, provided a means of testing stem-bore analysis against independent 'historical' dating.

The Wharram Percy clay pipe assemblage which is both sufficiently large and derived from many specific archaeological deposits, provides a range of important archaeological and sociological evidence on a scale and of a complexity that has not been achieved on any other rural site in the British Isles. The long-term significance of these finds will await equivalent rural assemblages from other areas.

The pipes themselves

This section of the report describes the range of bowl forms, decorative motifs, and the marked and decorated stems recovered from the excavations at Wharram Percy.

Seventeenth-century pipes, including those from the late 16th century c. 1580 to 1610

Of the 85 bowls recovered from the excavations 31, or 36%, can be dated to the 17th century. A selection of the bowl forms has been illustrated in Figures 99-100 (Nos 1 to 20). These illustrations have been arranged chronologically to show the development of the bowl form from c. 1580 to 1610 (No. 1) through to c. 1660 to 1690 (No. 20).

From the inception of pipe smoking in England at the end of the 16th century until about 1640, it was London that set the fashion throughout the rest of the country. Pipes from almost anywhere in England during the period c. 1580 to 1610 are virtually indistinguishable from those produced in London. Pipes from this period are extremely rare with only ten examples known from the whole of Yorkshire. The single example from Wharram (Fig. 99, No. 1) was recovered from 54/17 and is a fine example of one of these earliest bowl forms.

The Civil War marked a turning point in English history and saw an unprecedented level of upheaval and disruption to all aspects of life, including pipe production. It was during the Civil War years that the beginnings of regional diversity in the bowl form were seen. Heel types dominate the bowl forms of the Civil War period in all parts of Yorkshire, and in some regions within the county, including the north-east, this trend continues throughout the remaining years of the 17th century. It is interesting to note that all thirteen of the Civil War period bowls recovered from Wharram are heel forms (Fig. 99, Nos 2-7).

By the period 1660 to 1690 the first truly regional bowl form in Yorkshire emerges – the 'Yorkshire bulbous'. There are hints of the origins of a bulbous form during the Civil War period but it is not until the period 1650-1670 that a true bulbous form appears. The assemblage from Wharram includes at least three of these early bulbous forms (Fig. 99, Nos 8-10). The actual height of these bowls has changed very little from the earlier Civil War period bowls, but the actual body of the bowl is much fuller giving the 'bulbous' appearance.

The most pronounced 'bulbous' forms of the period 1660 to 1690 can be found in York and Hull, although the form does occur in centres throughout the county at this period. Typical of this form is the large circular heel suitable for the application of a circular stamped mark, which is also typical of the county. See below for a discussion of the marks.

The excavations at Wharram produced fragments from sixteen 'bulbous' bowl forms, ten of which have been illustrated (Figs 99-100, Nos 11-20). Although this is a relatively small group of bulbous forms they include a range of interesting features relating to workshop practises. Number 11 (Fig. 99) illustrates a bulbous bowl with a damaged rim recovered from the church. There is a small indentation in the rim away from the smoker that has clearly occurred after the pipe was moulded but prior to firing, possibly the result of the pipe being knocked or pressed against something during the manufacturing process. A pipe from the farmhouse (Fig. 99, No. 12) is slightly deformed on the seam facing the smoker giving the pipe a rather lumpy profile. This is the result of the rather over zealous trimming of the seam prior to firing. A problem with a poorly fitting mould can be seen in No. 14 (Fig. 99) from the vicarage. A marked step in the two halves of the mould is clearly visible in the heel plan indicating that the two halves of the mould did not fit together properly.

In a recent survey of Yorkshire pipes, an analysis of the chronological and geographical distribution of marked pipes was carried out (White 2004, 102). This analysis suggested that in the north-east of the county 23% of all the pipes from the period *c.* 1660 to 1690 were stamped with a maker's mark. It is interesting to note that from the Wharram Percy group, which had a total of 30 pipes from this period, only four (13%) were marked. Having said that however, the arbitrary divisions in the county used in this analysis would place Wharram Percy very close to the border with east Yorkshire, an area in which only 18% were marked.

The excavations at Wharram Percy produced a total of five pipes from the period *c.* 1660 to 1690 with stamped heel marks. One of these, from 54/5, is so damaged that it is impossible to say what the original mark may have looked like. Of the remaining four pipes one had the initials IG and three had the initials RB.

The IG bowl was recovered from 74/275, and is a nicely produced bowl with a well-burnished surface (Fig. 99, No. 13). The mark, comprising the letters IG flanking a central motif, which may represent a stylised tobacco plant, can be attributed to Judith Gill of Wakefield who is known to have been working at Potovens, near Wakefield *c.* 1692/3 to 1709 (White 2004, 170). This mark has been recorded for the National Clay Tobacco Pipe Stamp Record, which is housed within the Department of Archaeology at the University of Liverpool, and has been allocated Die No. 1846. This particular maker and her mark are interesting as both were the subject of a case recorded in the Wakefield Quarter Sessions for 1692/93 when Judith Gill claimed that other pipemakers were copying her mark in order to improve their sales (Brears 1967, 42). The implication, therefore, is that not every pipe bearing this mark was actually produced by Judith Gill herself. A further two examples of this mark are known, the first comes from Pontefract Castle (Acc. No. PC82087) and is currently held by the Wakefield Museum and Art Gallery (cf. White 2004, fig. 8.8). The second appears on a Yorkshire bulbous bowl recovered from St Elphin's Rectory, Warrington (Davey and Pierce 1977, fig. 41 no. 26).

The remaining three marked bowls from this period are stamped with the initials RB either side of a more elaborate floral motif, which may also represent a tobacco plant (see *Wharram III*, fig. 182, no. 4). This RB mark has also been recorded for the National Clay Tobacco Pipe Stamp Catalogue and has been allocated Die No. 1469, and is attributed to Robert Burrill of Hull who is recorded as working from *c.* 1675 to 1725 (White 2004, 166). Robert Burrill appears to have been a successful pipemaker in Hull employing no less that seven apprentices between 1685 and 1727.

All three RB pipes from Wharram appear on bowls made from the same mould. The pipes are finely burnished and stamped using the same die. At least nineteen other examples of this die have been recorded in Yorkshire, one from Acaster Malbis, one from Thorne, four from Beverley, five from Hull and eight from York,

Eighteenth-century pipes, including those from the Transitional Period *c.* 1690 to 1720

Of the 85 bowls recovered from the excavations ten, or 12%, can be dated to the 18th century, these include three bowls from the Transitional Period (*c.* 1690 to 1710). A selection of the bowl forms has been illustrated (Fig. 100, Nos 21-26) together with two marked stem fragments (Fig. 100, Nos 27 and 28).

The end of the 17th century saw a dramatic change in the form of some of the pipes produced in Yorkshire with the heavy bulbous forms of the period 1660-1690 being replaced with an elongated form, leaning away from the smoker, of the Transitional Period (1690-1720). In the east of the county, particularly around Hull, this lean became very pronounced (White 2004, 49). By the early 1700s the bowl forms become more upright, as seen with the three illustrated examples from Wharram Percy (Fig. 100, Nos 23-25).

Very few 18th-century pipe bowls survive in the archaeological record due to two major factors. First is the fact that the bowl walls are much thinner than had previously been the case with the result that they often break into small fragments making them difficult to recover. The second factor is the introduction of snuff as the preferred method of taking tobacco in the 18th century. In a recent survey of clay tobacco pipes from Yorkshire only 12% of some 7,000 bowls recorded in the county dated to the 18th century.

This late 17th and 18th-century group includes five marked fragments, two heel stamps, two stem stamps and a bowl with moulded initials. The earliest of the two heel stamps comprises an AB mark on a heel fragment recovered from 77/15. To date, no documented makers with the initials AB and working in Yorkshire at this time, have been discovered. This particular mark has been recorded for the National Clay Tobacco Pipe Stamp Catalogue and allocated Die No. 1899. At least four other examples of the mark are known, three from Acaster Malbis and one from York. Attribution of the AB marks from the period c. 1690-1720 to a documented maker presents a problem. In his study of York pipemakers, Lawrence identified two pipemakers called Abrahams Boyes, and attributed all the 1690 to 1710 AB marks to a second Abraham Boyes who was working as a trunk maker in 1711 (1979, 80). There is evidence, however, to suggest that the 1711 reference may be a misreading of the document and in fact there was no second Abraham Boyes (White 2004, 119). It has, therefore, been suggested that it was in fact Frances Boyes, the widow of the first Abraham Boyes who died in 1681, who produced the transitional period AB pipes, including the example from Wharram Percy. It was not unusual for a widow to continue to use the moulds and stamps formerly used by their deceased husband or indeed for them to commission new moulds and marks themselves (White 2004, 120).

The second stamped fragment, from an unstratified context around the farmhouse is a finely burnished heel that appears to be Dutch in origin (Fig. 100, No. 26). The heel mark on this fragment is rather poorly impressed but appears to be a crowned tobacco roll. Duco has identified a similar mark as that of a maker from Gouda, Johannes Jansz. De Presser, who was working c. 1681 to 1682 (Duco 2003, 139).

Both the stamped stem fragments date to the mid-18th century, c. 1740 to 1780. The first (Fig. 100, No. 27) was recovered from 74/106 and bears the incuse lettering ISAAC HODGSON MAKER IN LEEDS in two lines around the stem. The Wharram Percy fragment is the only example of this particular mark so far recorded in Yorkshire. It is also the only evidence for a maker by the name of Isaac Hodgson from Leeds that survives, as this particular maker has not yet been identified in the documentary records.

The second stem fragment was recovered from the churchyard (Site 26) and bears a rather elaborate stem stamp comprising the lettering RIH.SCORA ROMARSH in two lines, above and below which is a frieze of running animals, possibly foxes (Fig. 100, No. 28). To date, a total of 50 stem marks attributed to Richard Scora (or Scorah) of Rawmarsh have been recorded from Yorkshire with at least four different dies being identified. The example

from Wharram Percy has been identified by the National Clay Tobacco Pipe Stamp Catalogue as Die No. 1508 and a further 31 examples of this particular die are known from Yorkshire, four from Pontefract, five from Wood Hall Moated Manor, three from Doncaster and nineteen from Beverley. There are two Richard Scorah's known from the documentary records. The first was working from c. 1718 to at least 1767 with the second working from c. 1783 to 1793 (White 2004, 180). On stylistic grounds it is most likely that these stems can be attributed to the first Richard Scorah.

The final marked 18th-century fragment is a bowl with the maker's initials RW moulded on to the sides of the heel (Fig. 100, No. 25). This particular bowl fragment was recovered from 54/5 and dates from c. 1750 to 1780. Moulded heel marks are a form of marking that was introduced in the 18th century and continued in use into the 20th century. This type of mark was created during the moulding process as the mould itself was engraved with the maker's initials, his name, or an abstract motif such as a flower or star. This particular method of marking had the advantage that the pipe was marked as part of the moulding process rather than having to be separately stamped as an additional task.

During a recent survey of Yorkshire clay tobacco pipes, a total of 441 18th-century bowls with moulded maker's initials was recorded, only three of which bear the initials RW, and all recovered from sites in York (White 2004). To date there are no known makers with the initials RW recorded in York, or for that matter from anywhere in Yorkshire, from the 18th century.

Late 18th-century and later pipes, including all the mould-decorated pipes (Table 61)

This final group comprises 43, or 51%, of the total bowl fragments recovered from the excavations. These include three decorated bowls that date from the end of the 18th or early 19th century, two decorated with Masonic motifs, one of which is illustrated (Fig. 101, No. 30), and one decorated with a series of enclosed flutes. It is interesting to note that of these 43 bowl fragments only ten are plain, the rest being mould decorated.

The majority of the plain bowls, comprising ten fragments, are very fragmentary but include the remains of two Irish bowls (Fig. 101, Nos 49 and 50). Both examples have thick walls with a cut rim and moulded milling around the rim, distinctive features of these Irish-style bowls. Only one (No. 50) has traces of an incuse mark stamped onto the bowl facing the smoker. This mark would originally have read CORK but only the K and part of a shamrock wreath, which would have appeared below the lettering, survive. These rather heavy Irish-style bowls and bowls with Irish motifs were common in the 19th century and can be found countrywide. They were a style of pipe that was favoured by navvies and other manual labourers (Flood 1976, 19). The use of Irish motifs and marks such as DUBLIN and CORK, may well have been intended to make the pipes more appealing to Irish immigrant workers (Taylor and Gault 1979, 292).

Table 61. Details of each of the mould-decorated bowl fragments recovered from the excavations.

Site	Cxt	SF	Date	CN	SN	Other	Dec/Modification	Cat. No.	Comments
49	1	188	19th				Acorn?	48	Small bowl fragment with only faint traces of moulded decoration, possibly originally an acorn.
49	1	189	1800-1880				Pearl/Beaded cutty/ French Com. Cutty	43	cf. Davidson of Glasgow, Pattern No. 85 known as 'Pearl'/Holland of Manchester, Pattern No. 34/6 known as a 'Beaded Cutty'/Pollock of Manchester, Pattern No. 159 known as a 'French Com. Cutty' (Jung 2003, 289).
51	1	980	*c.* 1860	TOM	S...		Boxers	42	Commemorates a famous bout between Tom Sayers and John C. Heenan; two examples in the Ryedale Folk Museum, Hutton-le-Hole and one in Craven Museum, Skipton (White 2004).
77	297		1800-1880				Britannia		Part of a Britannia bowl (see No. 29); unusual internal bowl mark.
74	181	370	1800-1840	TJ	M		Britannia + leaf decorated seams	29	Initials placed ambiguously.
74	125		1800-1840	T	M		Britannia + leaf decorated seams		Rim damaged and spur missing.
74	9000		1800-1840				Britannia + leaf decorated seams		Bowl fragment only; same as the other Britannia bowls from Site 74.
74	9000		1800-1840				Britannia + leaf decorated seams		Britannia bowl, the same as the others from Site 74.
74	85/N5		1800-1840				Britannia + leaf decorated seams		Bowl fragment but appears to be the same as the other Britannia bowls from Site 74; unusual markings inside the bowl cavity made by the stopper.
54	1		1800-1840				Britannia + leaf decorated seams		Small bowl fragment only; appears to be part of a Britannia bowl as those from Site 74.
74	314		1770-1800				Enclosed flutes		Very fine quality moulding.
74	125	2094	1800-1840	W	H	Flower*	Fluted	33	Bowl made up of four joining fragments; spur fragment almost certainly from a similar bowl but does not join. Spur has a moulded flower motif on each side.
74	134		1800-1840			Flower	Fluted		Spur fragment only, but almost certainly same as No. 33.
49	2	190	1800-1840				Fluted	38	Probably spurless.
74	125	2092	1800-1840				Fluted	37	
74	123		1800-1840				Fluted		Fluted bowl fragment; spur missing.
54	9	2648	1820-1880				Fluted	36	Flutes on lower part of bowl only.
54	1	2649	1820-1880				Flutes and swags	35	Line just below rim suggests that the mould has been modified or repaired. Underneath the swags are traces of flutes extending up to the rim, again suggesting that mould has been modified. Spur missing.

Table 61 continued.

Site	Cxt	SF	Date	CN	SN	Other	Dec/Modification	Cat. No.	Comments
51	100	979	1800-1880				Fluted?	44	Traces of possible flutes; spur is also fluted.
74	153	2093	1800-1840				Griffin	34	Poorly fitting mould; traces of a griffin visible on smoker's right; beaded seams.
51	202	978	1800-1840				Hand	47	Very small bowl fragment.
51	2	982	1850-1900				large rib mould seam	40	cf. Davidson's 'Baltic' design.
51	100	981	1850-1900				large rib mould seam	41	cf. Davidson's 'Baltic' design.
74	9000	2091	1850-1900				large rib mould seam	39	cf. Davidson's 'Baltic' design.
54	1		1800-1840				Leaf decorated seams (?Britannia bowl)		Almost certainly part of a Britannia bowl as the examples from Site 74.
54	1	4	1800-1840	I	H		Leeds Arms/Bird	32	
49	1		1800-1840				Masonic		Fragment from a Masonic bowl.
14	-		1790-1830				Masonic + leaf	30	Three joining fragments; Davey 1987, Fig 182.7; line around rim indicating mould has been repaired. Same mould as the fragment from Site 44.
54	1		1790-1840				Masonic + leaf decorated seams		Small fragment only.
49	1		1800-1840				Masonic + leaf decorated seams		Fragment only; spur missing; Same mould as No. 30.
54	96	2650	1800-1840				Masonic + leaf decorated seams	31	Spur broken.
74	102		1800-1880				Shield?		Very small fragment (extracted from pottery).
74	341	2090	1800-1880				Star	46	Rim fragment only.

A number of these mould-decorated bowls are rather fragmentary and only traces of their original decorative scheme survive. These include a fragment with what appears to be a griffin or dragon and which also has a series of raised dots running up the seam (Fig. 101, No. 34); a possible acorn design where the bowl itself is in the form of an acorn (Fig. 101, No. 48); a hand on the side of the bowl, where just the four fingers survive (Fig. 101, No. 47); a star motif, also on the side of the bowl, (Fig. 101, No. 46); and part of a shield (not illustrated), although this is too small to be able to identify what the shield may represent.

All the major pipe-producing firms in England and Scotland were producing similar products during the 19th century. The fragment No. 43 (Fig. 101) is a good example of how difficult it is to identify the source of some of these 19th-century mould-decorated pipes, particularly in the absence of a pattern number or maker's mark. This particular fragment is similar to a spurless cutty that was recovered from 44/1. A similar example, recovered from the excavations at Speke Hall, Merseyside, was from a securely dated deposit of c. 1867/8 (Higgins 1992, 68). Both fragments are examples of a pattern that Pollocks of Manchester illustrated in their catalogue of c. 1906 as pattern number 159 the 'French Com Cutty', which was being produced into the early part of the 20th century. A similar design was being produced by Joseph Holland, also of Manchester, and Turpins of Macclesfield under the name of 'Beaded Cutty', pattern numbers 34/6 and 15 respectively, and by Thomas Davidson Jnr. & Co of Glasgow as pattern number 85 under the name 'Pearl', where it appears in their catalogue of c. 1880 (Gallagher and Price 1987, 126).

A similar situation exists with three other fragments from the excavations at Wharram (Fig. 101, Nos 39-41). All three examples are rather small and fragmentary but have a distinct rib along both seams. In Davidson's

Plate 26. The Sayers-Heenan fight of 1860 from a print based on a photograph by G. Bonnier (after Chesney 1970, facing page 272).

catalogue of *c*. 1880 this particular design appears as pattern number 33 which is known as the 'Baltic' although a very similar design produced by the same company is referred to as 'Keel Balm' (Pattern number 62). To add to the confusion, in McDougall's catalogue of *c*. 1880 this design appears as pattern number 44 and is referred to as the 'Keel Baltic'.

All these rather small scrappy fragments of 19th-century material represent designs that are commonly found nationwide, such as the acorns and Irish motifs. Some of the other fragments, however, are much more commonly encountered in the north of England and Scotland, such as the star motifs, the hand and the pipes with the ribbed seams – Keel/Baltic types. The lack of any identifying pattern numbers, or makers' marks, make it difficult to pin down the source of these pipes. There is no reason why Scottish material shouldn't turn up on the site at Wharram, but perhaps the major pipe producing firms in the north of England are more likely suppliers.

The excavations did, however, produce a small group of more complete and highly decorated bowls that are worthy of fuller discussion. These are the boxers, Britannia, the fluted bowls, the pipe bearing the arms of Leeds and those with Masonic motifs. These are discussed in more detail in alphabetical order below, followed by fragments bearing moulded or stamped marks.

Boxers

A single pipe bowl with a mould decorated design comprising a boxer on either side of the bowl was recovered from 51/1 (Fig. 101, No. 42). On the smoker's right is the lettering TOM S... in relief. This is Tom Sayers, a famous British bare-knuckle fighter from the mid to late 19th century. The lettering on the smoker's left is missing, but would have read Heenan.

This pipe bowl commemorates the famous boxing match between John C. Heenan from America and the British heavyweight champion, Tom Sayers, which took place in Farnborough, Hampshire on 17 April 1860. The match roused a lot of national interest and lasted 37 rounds. It was reported as being a 'vicious fight ... only broken off when both men were in an appalling condition' (Chesney 1970, 278). Although officially a draw, Heenan was later acclaimed as the world champion. After the match a public subscription was made for Sayers' benefit raising £3000 that was paid to him on condition that he retired. He died five years later, in 1865, of diabetes and tuberculosis, and aged just 39. He was buried in Highgate Cemetery and his funeral was attended by an estimated 10,000 people. A print, based on a photograph taken at the time of the match by G. Bonnier, is very similar to the design on the pipe and may well have been the inspiration for the mould maker (Plate 26).

Four other examples of this pipe are known, two in the collections of the Ryedale Folk Museum, Hutton le Hole (Acc. Nos. C6646 and C6639), one in the museum of Yorkshire Dales Lead Mining and one in the Craven Museum, Skipton (White 2004, fig. 81.2). It is clear that this design commemorates a particular bout in Sayer's career but it could have been produced either shortly after the actual bout in 1860, or at the time of his death in 1865, which ever is the case it provides a tight date range of *c*. 1860 to 1865 for this particular design.

Britannia
A total of eight bowl fragments with the Britannia motif were recovered from the excavations - two from Site 54, five from Site 74 and one from Site 77 (Fig. 101, No. 29). All these bowl fragments appear to be from the same mould and all date from *c*. 1800 to 1840. Two of the examples, from 74/297 and 74/85, have an unusual internal bowl mark, which takes the form of two concentric rings in the base of the bowl cavity. Similar examples have been noted in a George and Dragon bowl from Doncaster (White 2005a) and a Masonic bowl from Sheffield (White 2005b). Although no systematic survey of internal bowl marks has been carried out nationally it does appear that there may be some regional variation, for example bowl crosses with a distinctive double bar have only been noted from a number of sites in Sheffield. It is possible that the concentric rings represent another regional type of internal bowl marking.

The decorative motif itself represents Britannia, on the smoker's right, with a trident in her right hand and a shield in her left, surrounded by three initials T, J and M. Both seams are decorated with simple leaves and around the rim there is a single row of raised dots. On the smoker's left is a coat of arms with two human supporters. It has not been possible to identify the arms. (see below for a discussion of the mark).

Fluted bowls
One of the most common forms of decoration on bowls of the late 18th and 19th centuries were flutes and scallops. Broader flutes or scallops, that were thicker at the top tapering to a pointed tail, were common at the end of the 18th century. These were sometimes enclosed within a row of dots or a loop. In contrast, flutes tended to be of a more uniform thickness and narrow flutes became more common during the course of the 19th century. A total of nine bowls with fluted designs, including one with flutes and swags, were recovered from the excavations.

The earliest of the fluted bowl fragments was recovered from 74/314. This fragment is part of a rim from a bowl decorated with enclosed flutes or scallops and dates from *c*. 1770-1800 (not illustrated). The design appears to comprise a series of broad flutes or scallops each of which is enclosed within a row of dots. The tallest flute, or scallop, appears on the seam away from the smoker. The other flutes then become shorter as they come closer to the smoker. Bowls of this type are known from sites across Yorkshire including Sheffield and

Doncaster. Occasionally these bowls have additional decorative motifs on the seam facing the smoker, for example the Prussian Eagle (White 2003, fig. 1) or more commonly, a stag's head (White 2003, figs 2-4; White 2004, 32, fig. 5.1 1). Raphaël, in a late 18th-century French publication (1991, 10), illustrates a pipe with scallops and a stag's head, which was considered to be a typical English form.

The remaining fluted bowl fragments date from the 19th century. Two of these, from 74/125 (Fig. 101, No. 33) and 74/134 (not illustrated), have a moulded flower motif on either side of the spur. These two fragments are almost certainly from the same mould. The example from 74/125 is more complete and has the initials WH incorporated into the mould-decorated band that runs around the rim (see below for a discussion of the mark).

The only other fluted bowl of interest is the fragment recovered from 54/1 (Fig. 101, No. 35). This particular bowl fragment, which dates from *c*.1820 to 1880, is a rather crude example of a flutes and swags design. The lower half of the bowl is decorated with crisply executed fine flutes; the upper part of the bowl however is rather more crudely decorated. There are clearly traces of swags, but underneath the swags there are also traces of more widely spaced flutes that extend up to the rim, suggesting that the mould has been modified. This particular fragment also has traces of a mould line running around the rim, which again suggests modification to the mould, this time in the form of a repair. During the manufacturing process a knife was pushed across the top of the pipe, whilst it was still in the mould, in a slot specially designed for this purpose. This process gave the pipe its clean-cut rim, but the continual action of the knife in the slot itself eventually caused the mould to become slightly dished at this point. This wear was repaired by inserting a new piece of metal into the mould, but the new insert left a tell-tale line around the top of any pipes that were subsequently produced from it.

Leeds arms
The excavations produced a single example of a bowl decorated with the Leeds city arms (Fig. 101, No. 32). This particular bowl was recovered from 54/1, and dates from *c*. 1800 to 1840. The Leeds arms appear on the smoker's right, and on the smoker's left there is a rather crude depiction of a bird within a floral wreath. The rim shows signs of being repaired at some time during its life, but this has been partly disguised by swags that appear to have been either recut or freshly cut into the mould after the repair. The seam facing the smoker is decorated with simple leaves, whilst that away from the smoker is more elaborately decorated. Either side of the seam facing the smoker are the maker's initials IH (see below for a discussion of the mark).

Masonic motifs
A total of five bowls decorated with Masonic motifs were recovered from the excavations at Wharram Percy, all dating from the late 18th or early 19th century, *c*. 1790 to

1840, and representing three different designs. The fragments from 14/- (Fig. 101, No. 30) and 49/1 (not illustrated) are certainly from the same mould. The illustrated fragment has a clear mould line running around the rim suggesting that the mould for this pipe had been repaired during the course of its life. It is possible that another very small fragment, from 49/1, is also from the same mould.

The second design is represented by a substantially complete bowl dating from *c*. 1800 to 1840, from 54/96 (Fig. 101, No. 31). Although the basic elements of the design are the same as No. 30, they are clearly from different moulds. The third and final design is represented by a very small fragment from 54/1 (not illustrated). This particular fragment is part of the seam that would have been away from the smoker. The seam is decorated with simple leaves but on the smoker's left there is the image of a trowel.

Bowls with a wide range of designs comprising Masonic motifs were circulating in Yorkshire during the 19th century indicating that this was a popular regional design.

Marked fragments
The clay tobacco pipe fragments recovered from the excavations include a single stem with a stamped mark, a stamped bowl mark reading CORK (already discussed and illustrated as Fig. 101, No. 50) and nine fragments with moulded bowl or stem marks. These are discussed in alphabetical order below.

Hall Ripon
A single stem fragment, *c*. 1860 to 1900, with a partial incuse stamped mark that would have read HALL RIPON was recovered from 30/1 (Fig. 101, No. 51). This particular mark is identical to an example recovered from excavations in Ripon (Davey forthcoming). The marks from both examples have been recorded for the National Clay Tobacco Pipe Stamp Catalogue with the resulting composite die drawing being allocated Die No. 1282. Oswald recorded a similar mark on a pipe from Bowes Museum, found in the fireplace of a house near Harrogate, which he attributes to Peter Hall of Ripon *c*. 1822 (1975, 100). Lawrence (1973, 191) lists a James Hall working in Ripon *c*. 1867 to 1893 which is perhaps a more likely candidate given that the fragment itself appears to be more mid to late 19th-century in date. At the time of the 1881 census James Hall, then aged 53, was living at 4 Robinsons Yard, Ripon, with his wife Hannah and their five children. James's occupation is given as a 'pipe manufacturer (Artiz)'. His son Albert, aged 17, is also listed as a 'pipe manufacturer'.

IH
A single mould-decorated bowl, *c*.1800 to 1840, with the moulded initials IH either side of the seam facing the smoker was recovered from 54/1 (Fig. 101, No. 32). The bowl is decorated with the arms of Leeds on the smoker's right and a bird with a wreath on the smoker's left (see

above for a discussion of the bowl). Makers with the initials IH are difficult to pin down, as they were such common initials. In West Yorkshire alone there are at least ten 19th-century makers with the initials IH (Lawrence 1973). Given that the initials on the pipe from Wharram Percy appear on a bowl decorated with the arms of Leeds, it is not unreasonable to suggest that this may be a Leeds maker. Lawrence lists three makers with the initials IH working in Leeds in the first half of the 19th century: John Hayes *c*. 1798 to 1835; John Hayes (Senior) *c*.1817 and John Hammond *c*.1853. In addition, White's Trade Directory of 1853, lists a fourth candidate, Joseph Hayes, at 1 Cross Glue Street.

WH
A fluted bowl with the moulded lettering WH on either side of the bowl, close to the rim, was recovered from 74/125, and dates from *c*.1800 to 1840 (Fig. 101, No. 33). This particular bowl also has a moulded flower motif on the sides of the spur. The initials WH are very neatly executed and enclosed within a curl of foliage that decorates a band beneath the line of moulded milling round the rim. The style of the bowl and the decorative motifs are reminiscent of pipes from Whitby and there is certainly a maker with the surname Hilton, working in Whitby in the 19th century. It is however, doubtful that the initial W on this particular pipe stands for Whitby, but is much more likely that it is a Christian name initial. There are currently no known makers with the initials WH working in or around Wharram in the first half of the 19th century, this may, therefore, represent a previously unrecorded maker.

TJM or TM
Two moulded bowl fragments, *c*.1800 to 1840, with the moulded lettering TJM or TM on the sides of the bowl were recovered from 74/181 and 74/125 respectively. The bowls are decorated with Britannia on the smoker's right and a coat of arms with supporters on the smoker's left (see above for a discussion of the bowl). In addition to the two marked fragments there are a further six bowl fragments that were almost certainly made in the same mould, but none of the fragments that survive is a part that would have been marked. The letters T and J are in relief on either side of Britannia and towards the rim. The relief letter M is placed in front of Britannia. The T and J are in a position where the Christian name and surname initials of 19th-century makers are occasionally placed, although there are no known makers with these initials from Yorkshire. The position of the letter M, however, is more unusual. It is possible that this is a place name initial.

Ben Nevis
A single stem fragment with the incuse moulded letter 257 BEN NE[VIS] / [C]UTTY was recovered from 74/9000. Many of the English and Scottish pipe manufacturing firms of the 19th century were producing short stemmed (cutty) pipes with the pattern name BEN

NEVIS. The 257 denotes the mould number, made by Waldie of Glasgow between 1870 and 1929 and described in the catalogue as 'Ben Nevis Basket' (Gallagher 1987, 161, fig. 19; Martin 1987, 350).

T Penn Leeds

A single stem fragment, recovered from 14/1238, marked with the incuse moulded lettering T.PENN.LEEDS (Fig. 101, No. 53). This mark can be attributed to Thomas Penn of Leeds who is known to have been working *c.*1853 to 1893 (Lawrence 1973, 192).

RW

A single bowl, dating from *c.* 1750 to 1780 and marked with the relief moulded letters RW on the sides of the heel, was recovered from 54/5 (Fig. 100, No. 25). This particular bowl form, and style of marking, is typical of Hull. There are currently no known makers in Hull with the initials RW. There were, however a number of members of the Westerdale family working in Hull during the 18th century, including Michael Westerdale, *c.* 1714 to 1757, William Westerdale *c.* 1754 to 1774 and Thomas Westerdale *c.* 1790 to 1806 (White 2004, 184-5). The initials RW may, therefore, belong to another member of this highly successful pipe making family from Hull.

Summary

The pipe assemblage from Wharram Percy represents a good group of pipes from the early 17th century right through to the 19th and early 20th centuries. This mix of material in itself is not unusual from urban sites, but the excavation at Wharram Percy provides a rare opportunity to examine a pipe assemblage from a rural site. A high proportion of these pipes are marked or decorated and can therefore be, more easily, sourced to their point of origin. The presence of pipes at Wharram Percy from Leeds, Rawmarsh, Wakefield, Ripon, Hull and York give an indication of the towns and cities that would have been providing, not only the pipes, but other goods and services as well.

In terms of the pipes themselves, this assemblage is important on a number of counts. First, it includes a late 16th-century pipe, dating from *c.* 1580 to 1610, which is rare nationally. Although there are only a small number of marked pipes among the assemblage there are examples from three previously unrecorded makers. The first, and earliest, fragment is the stem stamped with the lettering ISAAC HOGESON MAKER IN LEEDS. This fragment is the only known example of this particular stamp and of a maker that has not yet been traced in the documentary record. Rather unusually, it provides us with the full name maker as well as the place of manufacture. Other unidentified maker's marks include the RW moulded spur mark, which may represent a member of the Westerdale family from Hull, and the WH moulded bowl mark on a decorated bowl that has parallels with material from Whitby.

This assemblage is also interesting in that it includes a high proportion of mould-decorated pipes from the 19th and early 20th centuries. Some of the designs represented in the group are found nationally, but there are one or two examples, such as those decorated with the Masonic motif and Leeds arms, that are clearly decorative motifs that were popular more locally. A small number of the pipes in the assemblage have the added interest of exhibiting signs of two different workshop practices. The first is the mould-line caused by a repaired mould and the second is a rather unusual internal bowl marking that may well represent a new regional type.

In summary, the Wharram Percy clay pipe assemblage provides a range of important archaeological and sociological evidence on a scale and of a complexity that has not been achieved on any other rural site in the British Isles. The long-term significance of these finds will await the study of equivalent rural assemblages from other areas.

Catalogue of illustrated clay pipes

1* Small bowl, tailed heel; 7/64"; [AK; 23539]; 1580-1610. *54/17; SF1654; Period 8.1*

2* Heeled bowl, finely milled, but rim damaged; 7/64"; [23528]; 1630-50. *74/106; SF2105; Period 3*

3* Heeled bowl, milled; 7/64"; [23522]; 1640-60. *74/299; SF1276; Period 3*

4* Heeled bowl, milled, but rim damaged; two joining fragments; 6/64"; [23533]; 1640-60. *74/287; SF32104; Period 3*

5* Heeled bowl, milled; 8/64"; [23527]; 1640-60. *74/106; SF2103; Period 3*

6* Heeled bowl, milled; 7/64"; [23519]; 1640-60. *74/284; SF2102; Period 4*

7* Heeled bowl, incomplete profile; groove round half the rim rather than milling; 7/64"; [23532]; 1640-60. *74/287; SF2101; Period 3*

8* Heeled bowl, partly milled; 7/64"; [23520]; 1650-70. *74/286; SF2100; Period 4*

9* Heeled bowl, poor quality mould and partially crudely milled; 7/64"; [23516]; 1650-70. *74/349; SF2099; Period 4?*

10* Bowl with slightly tailed heel; milled; 7/64"; [U; P0283]; 1650-70; LN790045. *14/-; C1879; unstratified, west of tower (Wharram III, fig. 182, no. 1)*

11* Heeled bowl, partly milled, damaged before firing; 7/64"; [O; P0284]; 1660-80; LN790007. *14/-; C537; Phase VI (?), chancel and N.E. chapel (Wharram III, fig. 182, no. 2)*

12* Heeled bowl, mould seams clumsily trimmed on the front; 7/64"; [23529]; 1660-80. *74/106; SF2698; Period 3*

13* Heeled bowl; IG heel stamp; burnished; 7/64"; [23534]; 1660-80; possibly one of the Gills of Wakefield. *74/275; SF1184; Period 6*

14* Heeled bowl; the two halves of the mould have not fully registered; 7/64"; [AI; 23538]; 1660-80. *54/202; SF2653; Period 7.5*

15* Damaged heeled bowl; pink external fuming; 7/64" [23526]; 1660-80. *74/130; SF2097; Period 4*

16* Fine quality heeled bowl; RB heel stamp; burnished; 7/64"; [AH; 20964]; 1660-80; probably Robert Burrell of Hull. *77/304; SF2526; Period 5.1*

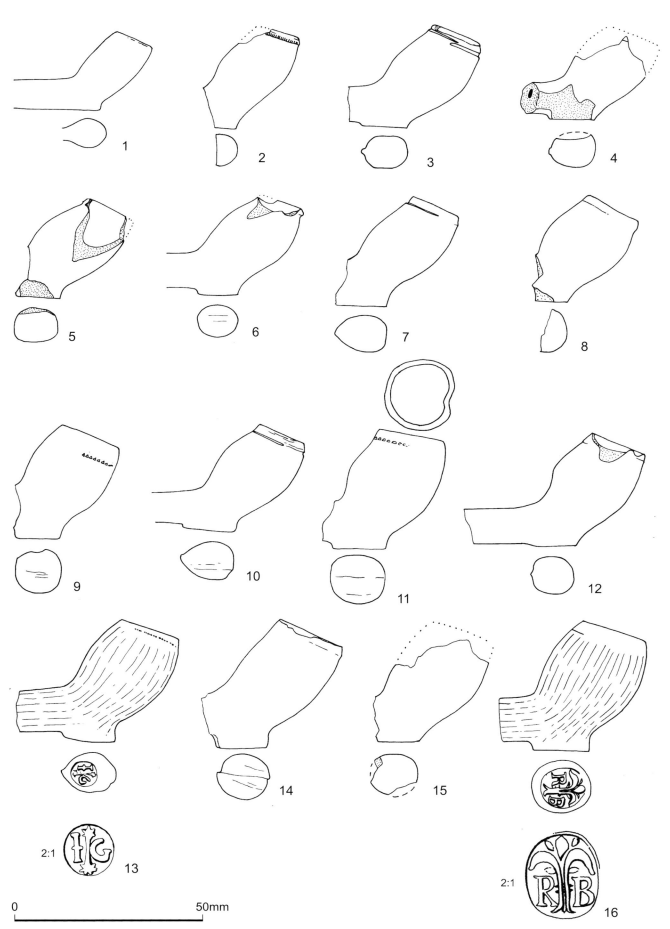

0   50mm

Fig. 99. Clay pipes Nos 1-16. Scale 1:1 (S. White)

17* Heeled bowl; single line cut across base of heel; partly and crudely milled; very glossy surface but no obvious burnishing lines; broken into three pieces since first excavated 7/64"; [N; 23513]; 1660-90. (*Wharram X, 68, 129 and 228*) *30/25; SF1029; Phase 4.2*

18* Part of heeled bowl; 7/64"; [P: P0286]; LN790013. *14/-; C721; Phase IX-XI, north aisle (Wharram III, fig. 182, no. 3)*

19* Part of heeled bowl; milling on base of heel; 6/64"; [23521]; 1660-90. *74/321; SF950; Period 2*

20* Part of heeled bowl; 7/64"; [AD; 23515]; 1660-90. *49/26; SF191; Period 2*

21* Heel and stem fragment; AB heel stamp; 6/64"; [AEF; 20963]; 1680-1710. (*Wharram X, 129 and 228*), *71/15; SF186; Phase 6*

22* Small-heeled bowl; 5/64"; [23510]; 1680-1710. *54/516; SF1340; Period 6.3*

23* Small-heeled bowl; 5/64"; [23509]; 1710-40. *54/516; SF1168; Period 6.3*

24* Small-heeled bowl; damaged; in three pieces, now glued together; 4/64"; [AG; 23537]; 1710-40. *54/202; SF2652; Period 7.5*

25* Small-heeled bowl with the letters W and R moulded on either side of the heel; very thin bowl and stem; two joining fragments; 4/64"; [AJ; 23536]; 1750-80. *54/5; SF2651; Period 8.1*

26* Burnished stem and heel; crowned tobacco roll stamped on the underneath of the heel; 5/64"; probably Dutch and 18th-century. *74/9000; SF2096; unstratified*

27* Roller-stamped stem; (I)SAAC HODGSON/MAKER IN LEEDS; 5/64"; [Y; 23535]; 1740-60. *74/106; SF2095; Period 3*

28* Roller-stamped stem; RIH SCORA(H)/(R)OMARSH in an animal freeze; 4/64"; [V; 20962]; 1740-60. (*Wharram XI, 299*). *26/7; SF199; Period 7, Phase 1*

29* Mould decorated and spurred bowl; Britannia on one side with the letters T, J and M placed ambiguously above and alongside; coat of arms and bearers on the other side; 5/64"; 1800-1840. *74/181; SF370; Period 5*

30* Mould decorated bowl with Masonic symbols and leaf moulded seams; line around rim indicating mould has been repaired; three joining fragments; same mould as the fragment from Site 49/1; 5/64"; [Q]; 1790-1830; LN790014. *14/-; SF743; Phase IX-XI, north aisle (Wharram III, fig. 182, no. 7)*

31* Masonic bowl with leaf decorated seams; spur broken; different mould from No. 30; 5/64"; [AL]; 1800-1840. *54/96; SF2650; Period 7.8*

32* Mould decorated bowl with letters H and I on either side of the seam; Leeds coat of arms on the right side, bird perched on branch on the left; 5/64"; [E]; 1800-1840. *54/1; SF4; Period 8.4*

33* Mould decorated bowl in four fragments, fluted design; floral border just below the top of the rim with the letters W and H within the border on the left and right sides respectively; spur fragment almost certainly from a similar bowl but does not join; spur has a moulded flower motif on each side; 5/64"; 1800-1840. *74/125; 2094; Period 6*

34* Mould decorated bowl fragment, beaded seams; traces of a griffin on smoker's right; poorly fitting mould; 1800-1840. *74/153; SF2093; Period 6*

35* Mould decorated spurred bowl, lower half fluted, upper part with swags; line just below rim suggests that the mould has been modified or repaired; underneath the swags are traces of flutes extending up to the rim, again suggesting that the mould has been modified; spur missing; 4/64"; [D]; 1820-80. *54/1; SF2649; Period 8.4*

36* Mould decorated spurred bowl, lower half only fluted; very similar mould to No. 35; 4/64"; [A]; 1820-80. *54/9; SF2648; Period 7.8*

37* Mould decorated bowl fragment, lower part missing; broad fluting, apparently all over; 1800-1840. *74/125; SF2092; Period 6*

38* Mould decorated base of bowl and stem fragment, narrow fluting; probably spurless; 4/64"; [AA]; 1800-1840. *49/2; SF190; Period 3*

39* Base of spur-less bowl and stem fragment with exaggerated ribs on the mould seams front and back; 5/64"; cf. Davidson's 'Baltic' design (Gallagher and Price 1987, 120, fig. 4, no. 33; Gallagher 1987, 154, fig. 12); 1850-1900. *74/9000; SF2091; unstratified*

40* Base of bowl and stem fragment similar to No. 39; 5/64"; [I]; 1850-1900. *51/2; SF982; unphased*

41* Base of bowl and stem fragment similar to No. 39; 5/64"; 1850-1900. *51/100; SF981; ER-unphased*

42* Mould decorated bowl, damaged; boxer on the right side with letters TOM..S.. above; legs of ?boxer on left side; commemorates a famous bout between Tom Sayers and John C. Heenan; two examples in the Ryedale Folk Museum, Hutton-le-Hole, and one in Craven Museum, Skipton; 5/64"; [H]; *c.* 1860; (cf. White 2004, 312-13, fig. 81.02). *51/1; SF980; unstratified*

43* Base of mould decorated, spur-less bowl with zones of alternating lines of dots and horizontal hatching; 4/64"; [W]; an example of a 'beaded cutty' (cf. Holland's *Catalogue*, nos 34 to 36) 1800-1880. *49/1; SF189; Period 3*

44* Base of ?fluted bowl, spur and stem fragment; spur is decorated with a spray device on each side; 4/64"; [J]; 1800-1880. *51/100; SF979; ER-unphased*

45* Pointed spur and stem fragment, with double circle moulded decoration on both sides; 4/64"; [S]; 1800-1850. *14/-; C1356; Phase XII-XIII, nave (Wharram III, fig. 182, no. 6)*

46* Very small mould decorated bowl rim fragment; part of a five-pointed star design on a plain background; 1800-1880. *74/341; SF2090; Period 1*

47* Small decorated bowl rim fragment, with four fingers of a hand design remaining; [L]; 1800-1840. *51/202; SF978; unphased*

48* Small bowl rim fragment with faint traces of moulded decoration, possibly depicting an acorn; [X]; 1800-1840. *49/1; SF188; Period 3*

49* Part of a plain-walled, Irish-style bowl; heavy rouletting around the rim; 5/64"; [AB]; late 19th or early 20th-century. *49/2; SF187; Period 3*

50* Part of a plain thick-walled, Irish-style bowl; heavy rouletting around rim; traces of a stamped mark probably reading CORK [AE]; late 19th or 20th-century. *49/78; SF186; unphased*

51* Stem roller-stamped ..IPO... in a double circular frame; 5/64"; [Y]; late 19th century; this is part of mark attributed to James Hall who is recorded in Ripon from *c.* 1867-93 (Lawrence 1973, 191); NSC die no. 1282. *49/1; SF185; Period 3*

52* Stem fragment stamped 157 BEN NE(VIS) on one side and (C)UTTY on the other; 4/64"; the 257 is the mould number, made by Waldie of Glasgow between 1870 and 1929 and described in the catalogue as 'Ben Nevis Basket'(Gallagher 1987, 161, fig. 19; Davey 1987, 350). *74/9000; SF2089; unstratified*

53* Stem fragment stamped T.PENN.LEEDS on one side; 5/64"; Thomas Penn working *c.*1853-93. *14/-; C1354; Phase XII-XIII, nave (Wharram III, fig. 182, no. 8)*

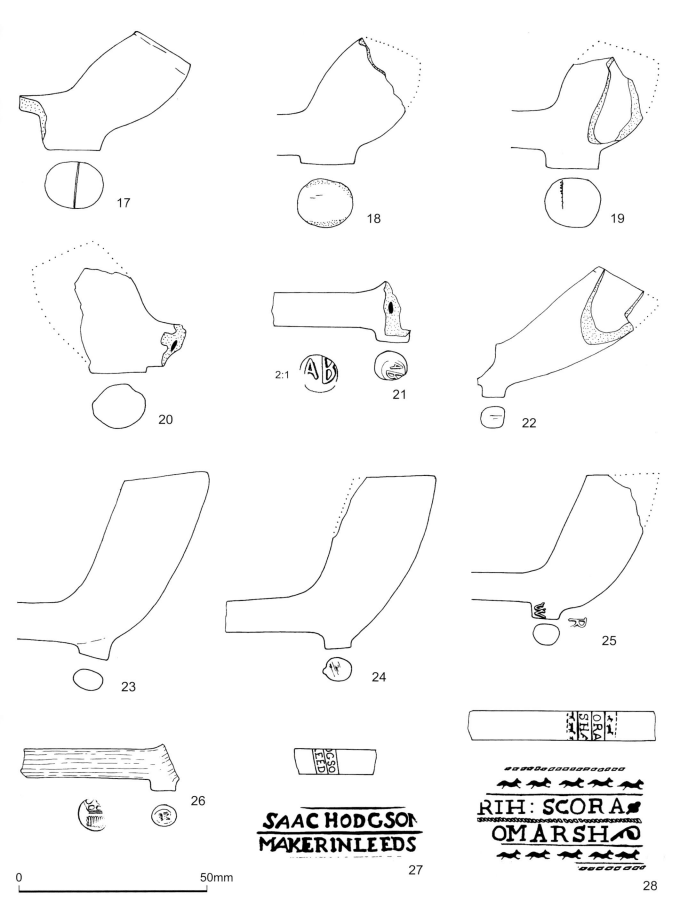

17

18

19

20

2:1

21

22

23

24

25

26

27

SAAC HODGSON
MAKERINLEEDS

28

RIH: SCORA
OMARSH

0   50mm

Fig. 100. Clay pipes Nos 17-28. Scale 1:1 (S. White)

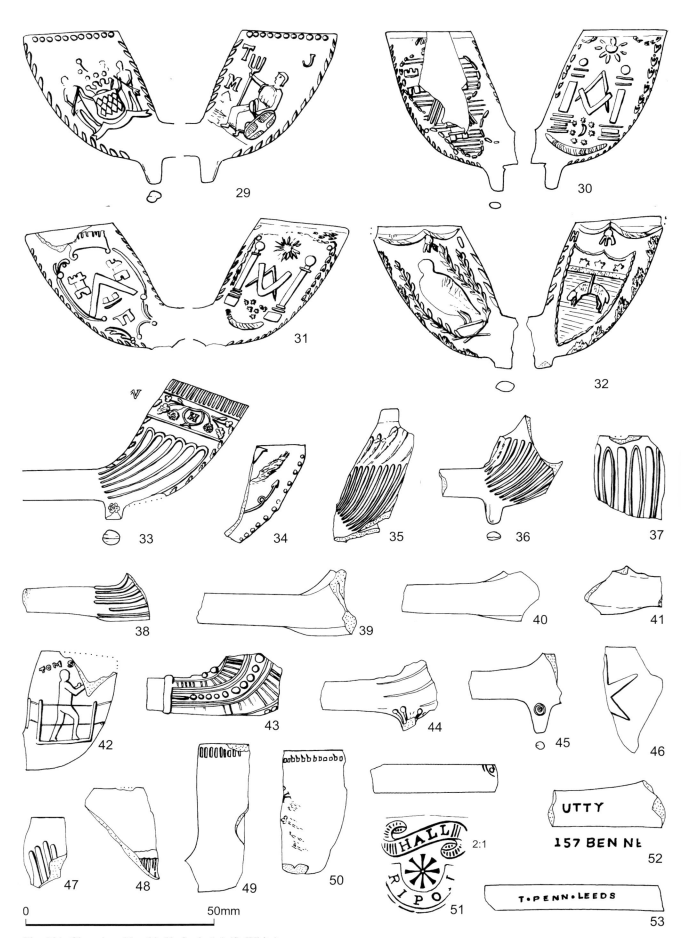

Fig. 101. Clay pipes Nos 29-53. Scale 1:1 (S. White)

238

19 The Glass

The vessel glass
by H. Willmott

Introduction

Excavations on the North Glebe of Wharram Percy have produced the largest collection of vessel glass ever to have been recovered from an English rural site. In total 3174 fragments were found (summarised in Table 62), over double the amount to have been recovered from the Shapwick Project in Somerset for example (Willmott 2007a). Of these, 1405 came from eight areas (Sites 11, 15, 49, 51, 73, 75, 77 and 79), and the vast majority from these sites is very late, dating to the end of the 19th and 20th centuries. Of the few earlier pieces none merited any special attention. The glass from these sites can be viewed either as occasional occupational debris, or in the case of most of the later fragments, intrusive after the disuse of the vicarage and farmhouse buildings. Consequently, only brief summaries have been produced for the Archive.

Table 62. Total numbers of vessel glass fragments.

Site	Total
Farmstead sites	
74	158
51	961
11	3
49	229
73	140
15	4
Vicarage sites	
77	63
54	1,611
75	2
79	3
	3,174

Two areas did produce more interesting assemblages. The largest was the vicarage (Site 54), where a total of 1611 fragments was recovered. Whilst the majority were again very late in date or too small for positive identification, 277 fragments (forming a minimum vessel count of 121) were earlier and sufficiently diagnostic. The second assemblage, numbering 158 fragments, came from the farmhouse (Site 74), where 100 of these (forming a minimum vessel count of 46) were sufficiently interesting to merit full reporting.

In both areas the glass was generally highly fragmented and found in a large variety of contexts with a wide date range. Some was clearly intrusive into earlier contexts, whilst other pieces were found in later phases and had clearly been disturbed at a subsequent date.

Given this, and the relatively small numbers of identifiable vessels, a detailed and contextualised intra-site analysis was not possible. It seems likely that, given that earlier vessel glass was largely absent in most other areas, the material found at the vicarage and farmhouse sites derived from activities taking place there, rather than representing dumping from other areas of the village. Therefore a more meaningful intra-site comparison between the assemblages was possible and appears at the end of this report.

The farmhouse (Site 74)

Although a much smaller assemblage than that from the vicarage, the glass found at the farmhouse is equally diverse. A range of tablewares and containers was recovered, although here all the material is late 17th or 18th-century in date.

Tablewares (Fig. 102)

A number of tablewares, all made in lead glass, were found, and three of these are fragments from wine glasses. The first (No. 1) is a rim and upper bowl, and this is decorated with the remnants of a wheel-engraved vine and foliage design dating to the first half of the 18th century, although it is too incomplete to reconstruct fully. There is also the complete profile of a small mid-18th-century ogee-shaped wine glass bowl (No. 2) although this is plain. A third small fragment is from a different rim (No. 3), but it is too small to allow more specific identification.

1*   Six fragments of rim and bowl from a wine glass, decorated with wheel-engraved vine and foliage design. Clear lead glass with little weathering. Early to mid-18th-century. Rim diam. 80mm. *74/314; Period 4*

2*   Two fragments of rim and ogee-shaped bowl from a wine glass. Clear lead glass with little weathering. Mid-18th-century. Rim diam. 50mm. *74/276; Period 6*

3*   Fragment of rim from a wine glass. Clear lead glass with little weathering. 18th-century. Rim diam. uncertain. *74/334; Period 4*

Three other tablewares came from this area. The first is a small portion of vertical rim from a tumbler (No. 4), whilst there is also a complete base (No. 5) from a comparable vessel. Both are apparently undecorated. The final vessel (No. 6) is harder to identify. It is a solid applied pad base made in a deep (possibly cobalt) blue glass. The rest of its form is unclear, but is possibly from a footed cup or even a small shallow bowl. Although difficult to parallel, the style of its manufacture suggests a date in the first half of the 18th century.

4*   Fragment of rim from a tumbler. Clear lead glass with little weathering. 18th to early 19th-century. Rim diam. 82mm. *74/115; Period 4*

5*   Complete thick base from a tumbler. Clear lead glass with virtually no weathering. Late 18th-century. Base diam. 48mm. *74/272; Period 6*

6*   Fragment of solid pad base possibly from a cup or small bowl. Deep blue glass with little weathering. 18th-century. Base diam. 56mm. *74/102; Period 4*

Case bottles and phials (Fig. 102)

A lesser, but interesting, assemblage of smaller glass containers was recovered. Amongst this was only one example of a case bottle, but unlike those from the vicarage, this is rectangular in cross-section, and dates to the late 17th or very early 18th century (No. 7). The remaining small containers are all phials and, like the vicarage site, they are all either of the broad or tall cylindrical varieties. One of the broad cylindrical phials (No. 8) is perhaps a little earlier, but the remaining four (Nos 9-12) belong to the first half of the 18th century. The remaining two phials are of the taller type, and are 18th-century in date.

7*   Eight joining fragments of base from a rectangular case bottle. Green glass with medium weathering. Late 17th to early 18th-century. Base diam. 75 x 88mm. *74/360; Period 1*

8*   Complete base from a cylindrical phial. Green glass with medium weathering. Late 17th-century. Base diam. 32mm. *74/362; Period 3*

9   Fragment of base with a high kick from a broad cylindrical phial. Blue/green glass with light weathering. Early to mid 18th-century. Base diam. uncertain. *74/299; Period 3*

10* Two joining fragments of base with a high kick from a broad cylindrical phial. Blue/green glass with light weathering. Early to mid-18th-century. Base diam. 50mm. *74/154; Period 4*

11   Fragment of base with a high kick from a broad cylindrical phial. Blue/green glass with light weathering. Early to mid-18th-century. Base diam. uncertain. *74/165; Period 3*

12   Fragment of shoulder from a broad cylindrical phial. Blue/green glass with light weathering. Early to mid-18th-century. *74/275; Period 6*

13   Fragment of base from a tall cylindrical phial. Blue/green glass with light weathering. 18th-century. Base diam. 25mm. *74/103; Period 6*

14* Fragment of rim and neck from a tall cylindrical phial. Blue/green glass with light weathering. 18th-century. Rim diam. 22mm. *74/9000; unstratified*

Wine bottles (Fig. 102)

The majority of the glass from the farmhouse derives from wine bottles. There is a minimum vessel count of 32, although as is usual with wine bottles this is a significant underestimation of the original number discarded. Twenty-five of these bottles are of the onion/mallet type. One example (No. 15) has a stamped seal decorated with an armorial shield displaying originally six fleur-de-lys, flanked by *cornucopia* and surmounted by a feathered and crested helm. The remaining onion/mallet bottles (Nos 16-39) are more ordinary plain types.

15* Fragment of decorative stamped seal from an onion or mallet wine bottle. Decorated with an armorial shield. Green glass with heavy weathering. Late 17th to early 18th-century. *74/106; Period 3*

16* Fragment of rim and neck from an onion or mallet wine bottle. Green glass with medium weathering. Late 17th to early 18th-century. Rim diam. 27mm. *74/9000; unstratified*

17* Fragment of rim and neck from an onion or mallet wine bottle. Green glass with medium weathering. Late 17th to early 18th-century. Rim diam. 26mm. *74/165; Period 3*

18   Fragment of rim and neck from an onion or mallet wine bottle. Green glass with medium weathering. Late 17th to early 18th-century. Rim diam. 24mm. *74/106; Period 3*

19   Fragment of rim and neck from an onion or mallet wine bottle. Green glass with heavy weathering. Late 17th to early 18th-century. Rim diam. 25mm. *74/258; Period 6*

20   Fragment of rim and neck from an onion wine bottle. Green glass with heavy weathering. Late 17th to early 18th-century. Rim diam. 25mm. *74/165; Period 3*

21   Fragment of rim from an onion or mallet wine bottle. Green glass with medium weathering. Late 17th to early 18th-century. Rim diam. 27mm. *74/165; Period 3*

22   Fragment of rim from an onion or mallet wine bottle. Green glass with medium weathering. Late 17th to early 18th-century. Rim diam. 27mm. *74/102; Period 4*

23   Fragment of rim from an onion or mallet wine bottle. Green glass with medium weathering. Late 17th to early 18th-century. Rim diam. uncertain. *74/156; Period 6*

24   Fragment of rim from an onion or mallet wine bottle. Green glass with heavy weathering. Late 17th to early 18th-century. Rim diam. uncertain. *74/299; Period 3*

25   Fragment of rim from an onion or mallet wine bottle. Green glass with medium weathering. Late 17th to early 18th-century. Rim diam. uncertain. *74/9000; unstratified*

26   Fragment of base from a shaft and globe wine bottle. Green glass with light weathering. 1650-80. Base diam. 65mm. *74/106; Period 3*

27   Fragment of base and side from a small mallet wine bottle. Green glass with heavy weathering. Early 18th-century. Base diam. 76mm. *74/165; Period 3*

28* Seven fragments of base and side from an onion wine bottle. Green glass with heavy weathering. Late 17th to early 18th-century. Base diam. 105mm. *74/158; Period 6*

29   Three fragments of base from an onion wine bottle. Green glass with heavy weathering. Late 17th to early 18th-century. Base diam. 110mm. *74/165; Period 3*

30   Fragment of base from an onion wine bottle. Green glass with heavy weathering. Late 17th to early 18th-century. Base diam. uncertain. *74/165; Period 3*

31   Five fragments of base from an onion or mallet wine bottle. Green glass with medium weathering. Late 17th to early 18th-century. Base diam. uncertain. *74/165; Period 3*

32   Fragment of base from an onion or mallet wine bottle. Green glass with medium weathering. Late 17th to early 18th-century. Base diam. 100mm. *74/165; Period 3*

33   Two fragments of base from an onion or mallet wine bottle. Green glass with medium weathering. Late 17th to early 18th-century. Base 110mm. *74/287; Period 3*

34   Three fragments of base from an onion or mallet wine bottle. Green glass with medium weathering. Late 17th to early 18th-century. Base diam. uncertain. *74/165, Period 3*

35   Two fragments of base from an onion or mallet wine bottle. Green glass with medium weathering. Late 17th to early 18th-century. Base diam. uncertain. *74/245, Period 4*

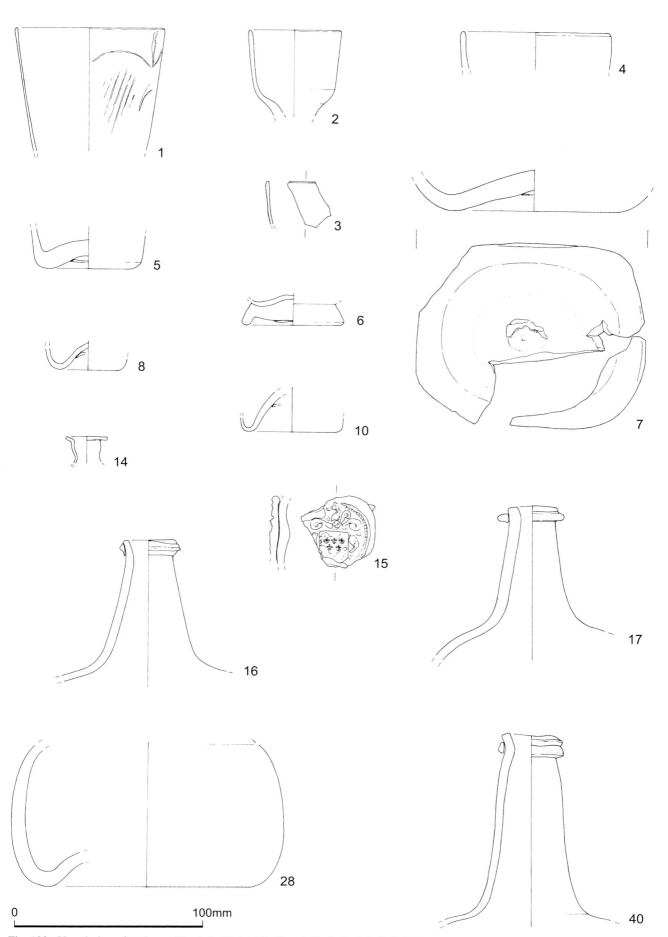

Fig. 102. Vessel glass: farmhouse Nos 1-8, 10, 14-17, 28 and 40. Scale 1:2 (J. Kobe)

36 Fragment of base from an onion or mallet wine bottle. Green glass with medium weathering. Late 17th to early 18th-century. Base diam. uncertain. *74/245; Period 4*

37 Fragment of base from an onion or mallet wine bottle. Green glass with medium weathering. Late 17th to early 18th-century. Base diam. uncertain. *74/9000; unstratified*

38 Four fragments of base from an onion or mallet wine bottle. Green glass with medium weathering. Late 17th to early 18th-century. Base diam. uncertain. *74/9000; unstratified*

39 Four fragments of base from an onion or mallet wine bottle. Green glass with medium weathering. Late 17th to early 18th-century. Base diam. uncertain. *74/284; Period 4*

The remaining seven wine bottles are all of the slighter later squat cylindrical form. As at the vicarage, these are relatively fewer in number than their earlier counterparts, and this again probably indicates a change in use of the area.

40* Six fragments of rim and neck from a squat cylindrical wine bottle. Green glass with very little weathering. Mid to late 18th-century. Rim diam. 26mm. *74/272; Period 6*

41 Fragment of rim from a squat cylindrical wine bottle. Green glass with medium weathering. Mid to late 18th-century. Rim diam. uncertain. *74/165; Period 3*

42 Fragment of rim from a squat cylindrical wine bottle. Green glass with medium weathering. Mid to late 18th-century. Rim diam. 24mm. *74/165; Period 3*

43 Three fragments of base from a small squat cylindrical wine bottle. Green glass with medium weathering. Mid-18th-century. Base diam. 95mm. *74/9000; unstratified*

44 Fragment of base from a squat cylindrical wine bottle. Green glass with medium weathering. Mid to late 18th-century. Base diam. uncertain. *74/135; Period 6*

45 Five fragments of shoulder from a squat cylindrical wine bottle. Green glass with medium weathering. Mid to late 18th-century. *74/284; Period 4*

46 Six fragments of shoulder from a squat cylindrical wine bottle. Green glass with medium weathering. Mid to late 18th-century. *74/158; Period 6*

The vicarage (Site 54)
As well as being the largest assemblage from Wharram, the glass from the vicarage is the most diverse. There is a wide range of tablewares present, and there is a comprehensive range of containers which includes flasks, case bottles, phials and wine bottles.

Tablewares (Fig. 103)
Fragments from only three medieval vessels were recovered from the vicarage site and, given that all are totally devitrified, it is possible that others discarded have simply not survived in Wharram's soil conditions. The first (No. 47) is just a small section of everted rim from a green potash glass jug. Such vessels are a relatively common medieval form, however this example is more unusual as it is decorated with three opaque red trails. A similar, but much more complete example of such a flask was excavated in a pit dated 1300-1350 at High Street C, Southampton (Charleston 1975, 216 no. 1489), and it is

probable that the vicarage example is of similar date. Another, but much smaller fragment of body (No. 48) decorated with green horizontal trailing was also recovered. This might be from a similar jug, although it could come from a beaker or similar tableware. The final fragment of medieval glass (No. 49) is the basal push-in from a small green potash flask. Such vessels were quite common and changed little in form from the 13th to the early 16th centuries.

47* Two fragments of rim and neck from a jug. Rim is pinched to form a pouring lip and decorated with three horizontal opaque red trails. Green potash glass with heavy weathering. 14th-century. Rim diam. uncertain. *54/254; Period 5.2*

48 Four joining small fragments of body, possibly from a jug or beaker, decorated with three bands of horizontal trailing. Green potash glass with heavy weathering. Late medieval. *54/641; Period 3.3*

49* Fragment of basal push-in with a distinct pontil mark, probably from a small flask. Green potash glass with heavy weathering. 13th to early 16th-century. *54/516; Period 6.3*

Some small fragments of goblets dating to the 16th and early 17th centuries were recovered. The most diagnostic (No. 50) is a small inverted baluster stem, a form typical of English production in the second half of the 16th century (Willmott 2002, 59). The remaining fragments are less typologically distinct, although the style of their manufacture and the quality of the glass indicates that they must date to the 16th or first half of the 17th century. There is a fine everted rim (No. 51) and the lower bowl merese (No. 52) from two different goblets, whilst there are five different goblet bases with characteristic under-folds (Nos 53-57), again typical for products of the later 16th and 17th centuries.

50* Fragment of a small inverted baluster knop from a goblet. Clear, slightly tinted glass, with some weathering. Mid to late 16th-century. *54/124; Period 7.5*

51* Fragment of very fine everted rim from a goblet bowl. Clear fine glass with medium weathering. 16th-century. Rim diam. 180mm. *54/157; Period 7.1*

52 Fragment of lower stem merese and upper flaring base from a goblet. Clear fine glass with medium weathering. Late 16th/early 17th-century. *54/794; U/S*

53 Fragment of fine flaring base with under-fold from a goblet. Clear glass with medium weathering. Late 16th to early 17th century. Base diameter uncertain. *54/157; Period 7.1*

54* Fragment of fine flaring base with very slight under-fold from a goblet. Clear glass with no weathering. 17th-century. Base diam. 70mm. *54/1; Period 8.4*

55 Fragment of flaring base with under-fold from a goblet. Clear glass with no weathering. 17th-century. Base diam. uncertain. *54/516; Period 6.3*

56 Fragment of flaring base with under-fold from a goblet. Clear glass with little weathering. 17th-century. Base diam. uncertain. *54/269; Period 7.4*

57* Four joining fragments of flaring base with large under-fold from a goblet. Clear glass with no weathering. 17th-century. Base diam. 78mm. *54/157; Period 7.1*

Goblets were not the only drinking vessels of 16th or early 17th-century date recovered. Fragments from two almost identical but different clear glass beakers were found. One is a base (No. 58) decorated with a rigaree base-ring as well as rigaree trailing on its body, whilst the other (No. 59) is just a fragment of trail-decorated body. These are a relatively common English form and are now viewed as a typical product of the Mansell era monopoly in the first half of the 17th century, as numerous fragments and wasters were recovered from the waste associated with his Broad Street furnace in London (Willmott 2005, 99-100). Two fragments (No. 60) are from a more elaborate vessel. It is a vertical-sided footed cup which originally had two applied decorative handles (of which only one survives). The body of the vessel, but not the handle itself, is decorated with fine bands of marvered opaque white and red *vetro a fili* trails. These footed cups are relatively rare finds, and seem to date to the later 17th century. A number of similar examples, but with varying forms of decoration, are known from a variety of art historical collections, such as the Veste Coburg (Theuerkauff-Liederwald 1994, 133), although archaeological examples are rather rarer. The remaining drinking vessels from this period are less unusual. The first (No. 61) is a very small fragment of inverted rim from a potash-rich pedestal beaker, decorated with wrythen ribbing. These vessels are typical English products of the late 16th and early 17th centuries and are found on almost all types of site of that date (Willmott 2002, 46-7). The second fragment (No. 62), although heat distorted, can still be identified as a portion of body from a larger cylindrical beaker decorated with a pinched diamond or mesh-work pattern. Whilst not a common find in England, this form of beaker is often found in the Low Countries where they were produced (e.g. Henkes 1994, 144 no. 32.3).

58* Two joining fragments of base and lower side from a small cylindrical beaker. Decorated with 1 horizontal rigaree trail and a rigaree base-ring. Clear slightly tinted glass with light weathering. Late 16th to early 17th-century. Base diam. 42mm. *54/175; Period 7.6*

59 Fragment of side from a small cylindrical beaker. Decorated with two horizontal rigaree trails. Clear slightly tinted glass with light weathering. Late 16th to early 17th-century. *54/431; Period 6.1*

60* Two fragments of rim and decorative handle from a small pedestal cup. Decorated with fine spiral opaque white and red *vetro a fili* trails. Clear glass, very slight weathering. Mid-17th-century. Rim diam. approx. 120mm. *54/226 and 520; Periods 7.4 and 6.3*

61 Fragment of slightly inverted rim from a pedestal beaker. Decorated with optic-blown wrythen ribbing. Green glass with very slight weathering. Late 16th to early 17th-century. Rim diam. uncertain. *54/921; Period 5.4*

62 Fragment of body from a cylindrical beaker. Decorated with pinched diamond or mesh-work pattern. Clear glass, quite heat distorted and slightly weathered. 17th-century. *54/202; Period 7.5*

Two other tablewares dating to the late 16th or early 17th century were also recovered from the vicarage area. One (No. 63) is the base and spout from a small clear glass jug or cruet, probably used to hold vinegar or oil at the table. This type of small jug was a common Italian form, although some examples have been found in England, such as several fragments from the Old Hall, Temple Balsall (Gooder 1984, 228-9). The other tableware (No. 64) is the rim from a small potash bowl with an out-turned edge. These bowls are not particularly common, but a couple of similar examples were found in a Civil War dump deposit at Eccleshall Castle, Staffordshire (Willmott 2002, 95).

63* Two fragments of simple pushed-in base and spout from a small spouted jug. Clear slightly tinted glass with no weathering. Late 16th to mid-17th-century. Base diam. 45mm. *54/150; Period 8.1*

64* Fragment of folded-out rim from a vertical sided bowl. Green glass with quite heavy weathering. Early 17th-century? Rim diam. 100mm. *54/184; Period 7.6*

The remaining tablewares from the vicarage date to the later 17th and 18th centuries, and all are made in a lead glass. After its initial development in the Low Countries and England in the 1670s, lead glass rapidly became the preferred choice for drinking glasses. The greater viscosity of the glass when molten resulted in new designs becoming fashionable and new decorative techniques, such as wheel-engraving, being developed. Probably the earliest fragment of lead glass is a solid handle (No. 65) from a tankard. This dates to the late 17th or early 18th century, and is similar to several examples from the Old Hall Temple Balsall (Gooder 1984, 228).

65* Fragment of thick solid oval-sectioned handle, possibly from a tankard. Clear heavy glass with no weathering. Very late 17th or 18th-century. *54/612; Period 6.3*

Amongst the later tablewares recovered is a small, but still important group of wheel-engraved glasses. This relatively crude technique was achieved by holding the finished glass against a fast-rotating wheel which created cut and abraded patterns on the surface. Wheel-engraved glass of the type found at Wharram is not uncommon archaeologically, but it has been largely ignored by traditional art-historical studies as it appears fairly crude compared to the finer decoration that survives on glasses favoured for curation in museums. This imbalance has only just started to be addressed, such as the recent study of a group of similar glass from Lisbon (Almeida Ferreira 2005). As the decoration was only applied to the body areas of the vessel, when fragmentary the final form of wheel-engraved glasses can be difficult to reconstruct. At Wharram where sufficient portions of the vessels survive, all wheel-engraved examples appear to be on the bowls of wine glasses, although some of the smaller fragments might have come from tumblers which were also decorated in this way. Although dating of these vessels is far from precise, at present the type of wheel-engraving found on most of the Wharram examples appears to be from the first half of the 18th century.

The most complete example (No. 66) forms the majority of a wine glass bowl. Just below the rim is a

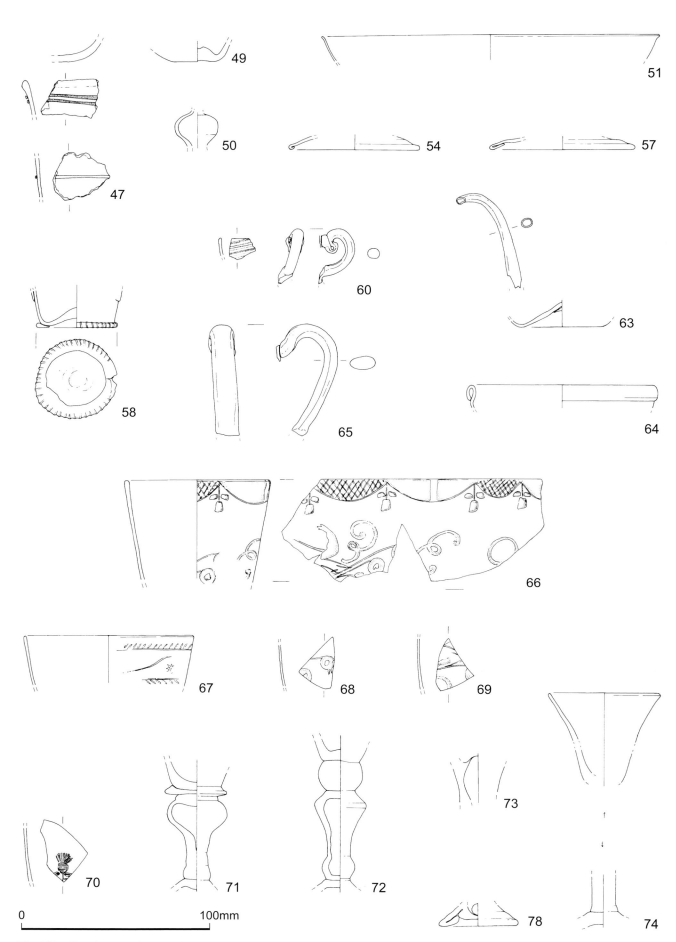

Fig. 103. Vessel glass: vicarage sites Nos 47, 49-51, 54, 57-8, 60, 63-74 and 78. Scale 1:2 (J. Kobe).

running border consisting of alternating panels of hashing and inverted tulips. The remaining portion of the goblet bowl is decorated with engraved scrollwork. The second goblet bowl in this category (No. 67) is decorated differently, having a panel formed from feathered borders engraved below the rim. Within this panel is engraved a scroll and star design, although insufficient remains to reconstruct it further. Two other fragments (Nos 68 and 69) are decorated in the same manner as No. 66, and it is possible that they are from the same glass, but they cannot be joined to the surviving pieces. The final fragment (No. 70) is different, and contains an upstanding thistle, probably from a lower decorative border on a wine glass bowl or tumbler.

66* Three joining fragments of rim and upper body from a wine glass. Clear heavy glass, decorated with wheel-engraved panels of hashes, inverted tulips and scrolls. First half of the 18th-century. Rim diam. 78mm. *54/75, 454 and 516; Periods 7.4 and 6.3*

67* Fragment of rim from a wine glass. Clear heavy glass, decorated with a wheel-engraved panel with a feathered border. Late 18th-century. Rim diam. 90mm. *54/126; Period 7.1*

68* Fragment of body from a wine glass. Clear glass, decorated with a wheel-engraved scroll. Same vessel as No. 66? First half of the 18th-century. *54/75; Period 7.4*

69* Fragment of body from a wine glass. Clear glass, decorated with a wheel-engraved scroll. Same vessel as No. 66? First half of the 18th-century. *54/519; Period 6.3*

70* Fragment of body from a wine glass or tumbler. Clear glass, decorated with a wheel-engraved upstanding thistle. First half of the 18th century. *54/516; Period 6.3*

Fragments from four different wine glass stems were recovered, and whether any of these were originally attached to the engraved bowls is uncertain, but at least possible. The earliest (No. 71) dates to the very end of the 17th century or early 18th century and is a simple rounded inverted baluster stem. Similar is a more sharply shouldered version (No. 72), which is early 18th-century in date. A smaller fragment, (No. 73) that probably comes from a stem similar to No. 72 was also recovered. The remaining wine glass (No. 74) is probably mid-18th-century in date. It has a small trumpet-shaped bowl and the lower portion of a solid rod stem also survives. These relatively simple stems are typical of styles common in the 18th century, and, whilst relatively understudied archaeologically, have been found in numerous excavations, particularly in urban contexts (e.g. Charleston 1986, 46).

71* Fragment of complete balustroid stem and lower bowl from a wine glass. Clear lead glass with very little weathering. Very late 17th or early 18th-century. *54/1; Period 8.4*

72* Fragment of complete balustroid stem and lower bowl from a wine glass. Clear lead glass with virtually no weathering. Early 18th-century. *54/471; Period 6.3*

73* Fragment of the upper portion of a balustroid stem from a wine glass. Clear lead glass with slight weathering. Early 18th-century. *54/612; Period 6.3*

74* Three fragments of lower plain rod stem, and trumpet-shaped bowl from a wine glass. Clear lead glass with slight weathering. Mid-18th-century. Rim diam. 60mm. *54/113; Period 8.1*

Three further fragments (Nos 75-77) can be identified as coming from 18th-century wine or cordial glasses, although they are less typologically distinctive. All are the upper portions of thick bases, but beyond being typically 18th-century in style, little more can be said about them. The remaining piece of tableware (No. 78) from the vicarage assemblage is a small portion of thick folded base from a mid-18th-century jelly glass.

75 Fragment of lower stem and upper base from a wine glass. Clear lead glass with slight weathering. 18th-century. *54/1; Period 8.4*

76 Fragment of thick base from a wine or cordial glass. Clear lead glass with slight weathering. 18th-century. Base diam. 80mm. *54/1; Period 8.4*

77 Fragment of thick base from a wine or cordial glass. Clear lead glass with slight weathering. 18th-century. Base diam. uncertain. *54/162; Period 8.1*

78* Fragment of pedestal base from a jelly glass. Clear lead glass with virtually no weathering. Mid-18th-century. Base diam. 45mm. *54/4; Period 8.4*

Flasks, case bottles and phials (Fig. 104)
As is typical for a post-medieval assemblage, the vicarage excavations produced numerous smaller glass containers which would have been used for all manner of ordinary domestic purposes. The earliest are bases from two small plain potash flasks (Nos 79 and 80). Although hard to date precisely, the quality of the glass suggests they belong to the 16th century.

79* Complete base with a low push-in from a small oval flask. Green potash glass with quite heavy weathering. 16th-century? Base diam. 45 x 50mm. *54/245; Period 6.3*

80 Fragment of base with a low push-in from a small spherical flask. Green potash glass with heavy weathering. 16th-century. Base diam. 44mm. *54/1; Period 8.4*

Fragments from four larger storage, or case bottles, were found. These are so-called as there is both documentary and pictorial evidence to suggest that they were sometimes packed and transported in wooden crates (Willmott 2002, 86-7). Three of the vicarage examples (Nos 81-83) are typical case bottles with a square cross-section, to facilitate packing. On two of these the neck survives showing that they had everted glass rims, as opposed to a pewter cap more typical on Continental examples. The remaining example (No. 84) is similar, but is slightly smaller and appears to have a circular cross-section.

81* Fragment of rim and neck from a case bottle. Green glass with heavy weathering. Late 16th to early 17th-century. Rim diam. 24mm. *54/57; Period 7.8*

82* Near complete base from a small square-section case bottle. Green glass with quite heavy weathering. Late 16th to early 17th-century. Base 65 x 65mm. *54/31 and 97; Periods 8.1 and 7.7*

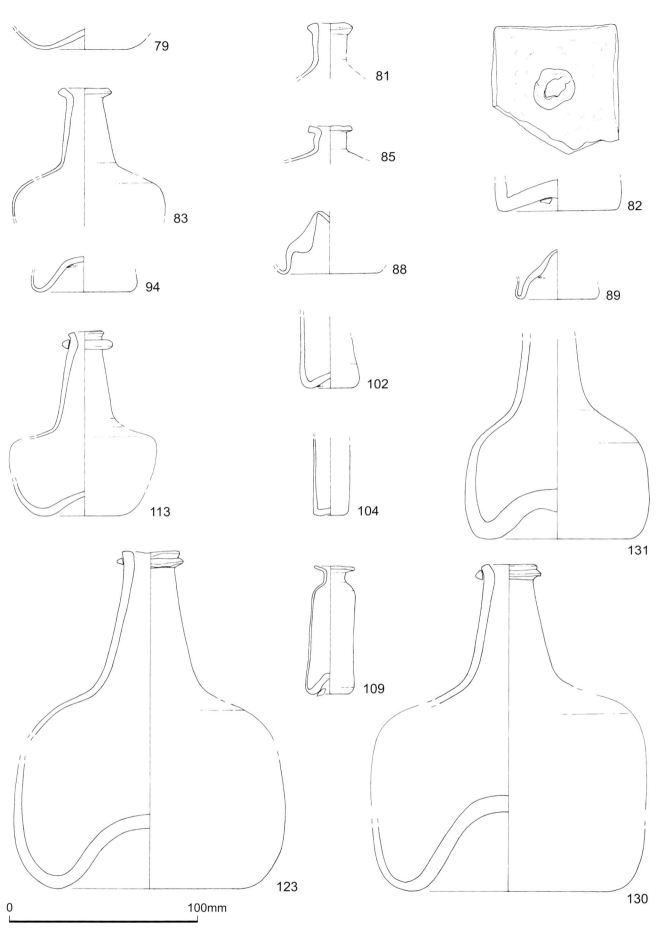

Fig. 104. Vessel glass: vicarage Nos 79, 81-83, 85, 88-9, 94, 102, 104, 109, 113, 123 and 130-131. Scale 1:2 (J. Kobe).

83* Three fragments of rim, neck and shoulder from a small square-section case bottle. Green glass with medium weathering. Late 16th to early 17th-century. Rim diam. 25mm. *54/264; Period 6.3*

84 Complete low base from a small cylindrical bottle. Green potash glass with medium weathering. Early to mid-17th-century. Base diam. 42mm. *54/202; Period 7.5*

A large number of fragments of phials were found. Phials first occurred in the late 16th century, but did not become a common form until the 18th century, and they are found on virtually every post-medieval site (Willmott 2002, 89-91). Phials were used to hold all types of liquids, perfumes and medicines, and therefore no specific functions can be assigned to them. Variations in size and shape do occur. On the vicarage site two types are present. The first is the broad cylindrical phial (Nos 85-100), of which sixteen examples were found. This has a base with a typically high-kicked and pointed push-in kick, broad cylindrical sides and a short neck with everted rim. Interestingly the glass this type of phial is made from often has a distinct aquamarine tint to it, although why this is the case is unclear. The broad cylindrical phial primarily dates to the first half of the 18th century, although a few earlier examples are occasionally found.

85* Rim and neck from a broad cylindrical phial. Blue/green glass with little weathering. Early to mid-18th-century. Rim diam. 24mm. *54/1; Period 8.4*

86 Complete base from a broad cylindrical phial. Blue/green glass with little weathering. Early to mid-18th-century. Base diam. 32mm. *54/1; Period 8.4*

87 Complete base with a high kick from a broad cylindrical phial. Green glass with little weathering. Early to mid-18th-century. Base diam. uncertain. *54/5; Period 8.1*

88* Fragment of base with a high kick from a broad cylindrical phial. Blue/green glass with little weathering. Early to mid-18th-century. Base diam. 48mm. *54/5; Period 8.1*

89* Complete base with a high kick from a broad cylindrical phial. Blue/green glass with little weathering. Early to mid-18th-century. Base diam. 40mm. *54/5; Period 8.1*

90 Fragment of base with a high kick from a broad cylindrical phial. Clear glass with medium weathering. Early to mid-18th-century. Base diam. uncertain. *54/9; Period 7.8*

91 Fragment of base with a high kick from a broad cylindrical phial. Blue/green glass with little weathering. Early to mid-18th-century. Base diam. uncertain. *54/13-14; Period 8.2*

92 Two fragments of base with a high kick from a broad cylindrical phial. Blue/green glass with little weathering. Early to mid-18th century. Base diam. 50mm. *54/17; Period 8.1*

93 Fragment of base with a high kick from a broad cylindrical phial. Blue/green glass with little weathering. Early to mid-18th-century. Base diam. 48mm. *54/29; Period 8.3*

94* Fragment of base with a high kick from a broad cylindrical phial. Blue/green glass with little weathering. Early to mid-18th-century. Base diam. 45mm. *54/48; Period 8.3*

95 Fragment of base with a high kick from a broad cylindrical phial. Blue/green glass with little weathering. Early to mid-18th-century. Base diam. uncertain. *54/96; Period 7.8*

96 Fragment of base with a high kick from a broad cylindrical phial. Blue/green glass with little weathering. Early to mid-18th-century. Base diam. uncertain. *54/113; Period 8.1*

97 Fragment of base with a high kick from a broad cylindrical phial. Blue/green glass with little weathering. Early to mid-18th-century. Base diam. uncertain. *54/136; Period 7.1*

98 Fragment of rim and neck from a broad cylindrical phial. Blue/green glass with little weathering. Early to mid-18th-century. Rim diam. 21mm. *54/288; Period 7.4*

99 Two fragments of base with a quite low kick from a broad cylindrical phial. Blue/green glass with little weathering. Early to mid-18th-century. Base diam. 50mm. *54/351; Period 7.4*

100 Fragment of base from a broad cylindrical phial. Blue/green glass with little weathering. Early to mid-18th-century. Base diam. uncertain. *54/390; Period 6.3*

The second type of phial found on the vicarage site is the tall cylindrical phial, of which twelve examples were recovered (Nos 101-112). This is typically smaller than the broad variety and is much narrower proportionally to its height. Tall cylindrical phials first appear in the second half of the 17th century and continue to be produced into the 19th century. Given the quality and colour of the glass, all the vicarage examples are 18th-century in date.

101 Fragment of rim and neck from a tall cylindrical phial. Blue/green glass with little weathering. 18th-century. Rim diam. 23mm. *54/1; Period 8.4*

102* Two fragments of base and lower side from a tall cylindrical phial. Blue/green glass with little weathering. 18th-century. Base diam. 20mm. *54/5; Period 8.1*

103 Fragment of base and lower side from a tall cylindrical phial. Blue/green glass with little weathering. 18th-century. Base diam. 20mm. *54/5; Period 8.1*

104* Fragment of base and lower side from a very narrow tall cylindrical phial. Blue/green glass with little weathering. 18th-century. Base diam. 18mm. *54/5; Period 8.1*

105 Fragment of rim and neck from a tall cylindrical phial. Blue/green glass with little weathering. 18th-century. Rim diam. uncertain. *54/93; Period 8.1*

106 Fourteen fragments of rim, neck and body from a tall cylindrical phial. Blue/green glass with little weathering. 18th-century. Rim diam. uncertain. *54/111; Period 8.1*

107 Four fragments of rim, neck and body from a tall cylindrical phial. Blue/green glass with little weathering. 18th-century. Rim diam. uncertain. *54/113; Period 8.1*

108 Fragment of base from a tall cylindrical phial. Blue/green glass with little weathering. 18th-century. Base diam. 26mm. *54/141; Period 8.1*

109* Complete tall cylindrical phial. Blue/green glass with little weathering. 18th-century. Rim diam. 22mm, base diam. 20mm, ht 72mm. *54/202; Period 7.5*

110 Two fragments of rim, neck and upper body from a tall cylindrical phial. Blue/green glass with little weathering. 18th-century. Rim diam. 28mm. *54/202; Period 7.5*

111 Fragment of rim, neck and upper body from a tall cylindrical phial. Blue/green glass with little weathering. 18th-century. Rim diam. 23mm. *54/202; Period 7.5*

112 Fragment of rim, neck and upper body from a tall cylindrical phial. Blue/green glass with little weathering. 18th-century. Rim diam. 24mm. *54/202; Period 7.5*

Wine bottles (Figs 104 and 105)

By far the most common vessel found on the vicarage site is the wine bottle. This is typical for a post-medieval site, as from the late 17th century onwards wine bottles were produced in huge numbers in regional centres all over England (see Willmott 2005, 108-44). The form was primarily manufactured for the temporary storage and serving of wine; they were used more as decanters than the disposable storage container that they have become today. Furthermore it is probable that they were also used in many households to store other liquids too. For both these reasons they had a very long lifespan, and it is common to find wine bottles deposited in contexts some decades later than their date of manufacture. Wine bottles have received quite a considerable amount of study by archaeologists and collectors alike. There has been the tendency by many scholars to over categorise and ascribe very tight dating to the different forms based on very subtle nuances of design. It is clear that wine bottles were produced quickly, cheaply and often very roughly, and when fully reconstructed a single example might possess the characteristics of several supposedly distinctive types, depending on which aspect of its profile is selected for illustration.

At Wharram three broad designs of wine bottle were found. The earliest, dating to between 1650 and 1680, is known as a shaft and globe, as it has a bulbous body and long slightly tapering neck. Only one example (No. 113) is sufficiently complete for the form to be fully reconstructed, and this particular example is unusually small. Two further bottles of this form (Nos 114-115) are represented by neck fragments only.

113* Three fragments of low pushed-in base, neck and rim from a miniature shaft and globe wine bottle. Green glass with quite heavy weathering. *c.* 1650-1680. Rim diam. 18mm, base diam. 37mm. *54/150; Period 8.1*

114 Fragment of long neck and rim from a shaft and globe wine bottle. Green glass with medium weathering. *c.* 1650-1680. Rim diam. 34mm. *54/516; Period 6.3*

115 Fragment of base from a shaft and globe wine bottle. Green glass with medium weathering. *c.* 1650-1680. Base diam. uncertain. *54/1; Period 8.4*

The most common type of wine bottle from the vicarage is the onion or mallet variety. A minimum of 45 were found (Nos 116-160), although this is certainly a significant underestimation of the original total. Traditionally this category is divided into two or more groups, with the onion bottle having a rounded body and the mallet a more flattened one (similar to the woodworking tool from which it derives its name). In a number of cases at Wharram, as elsewhere, bottles might have one side that is rounded, but the other which is more flattened, so they are categorised together here. Their bases are usually quite wide and have a large domed kick,

whilst their necks are shorter than those of the shaft and globe variety. Onion/mallet bottles date to the last decades of the 17th century and continued until the 1740s, although there is chronological overlap with both the earlier shaft and globe and the later short cylindrical bottle.

116 Five fragments of complete base and lower side from an onion wine bottle. Green glass with heavy weathering. Late 17th to early 18th-century. Base diam. 85mm. *54/1; Period 8.4*

117 Fragment of rim and neck from an onion or mallet wine bottle. Green glass with heavy weathering. Late 17th to early 18th-century. Rim diam. 26mm. *54/1; Period 8.4*

118 Fragment of rim and neck from an onion or mallet wine bottle. Green glass with heavy weathering. Late 17th to early 18th-century. Rim diam. uncertain. *54/1; Period 8.4*

119 Three fragments of neck from an onion or mallet wine bottle. Green glass with heavy weathering. Late 17th to early 18th-century. *54/1; Period 8.4*

120 Fragment of rim and neck from an onion or mallet wine bottle. Green glass with heavy weathering. Late 17th to early 18th-century. Rim diam. uncertain. *Site 54/1; Period 8.4*

121 Fragment of base and lower side from an onion wine bottle. Green glass with heavy weathering. Late 17th to early 18th-century. Base diam. uncertain. *54/1; Period 8.4*

122 Nine fragments of neck and body from a mallet wine bottle. Green glass with heavy weathering. Early 18th-century. *54/4; Period 8.4*

123* Nineteen fragments of rim, neck, body and base from a mallet wine bottle. Green glass with heavy weathering. Early 18th-century. Rim diam. 28mm, base diam. 100mm. *54/5; Period 8.1*

124 Fragment of rim and neck from an onion or mallet wine bottle. Green glass with heavy weathering. Late 17th to early 18th-century. Rim diam. 28mm. *54/5; Period 8.1*

125 Fragment of base and lower side from an onion wine bottle. Green glass with heavy weathering. Late 17th to early 18th-century. Base diam. 120mm. *54/5; Period 8.1*

126 Three fragments of base and lower side from an onion wine bottle. Green glass with heavy weathering. Late 17th to early 18th-century. Base diam. 105mm. *54/8; Period 8.4*

127 Fragment of rim and neck from an onion or mallet wine bottle. Green glass with heavy weathering. Late 17th to early 18th-century. Rim diam. 27mm. *54/22; Period 7.5*

128 Fragment of rim and neck from a mallet wine bottle. Green glass with heavy weathering. Early 18th-century. Rim diam. 26mm. *54/82; Period 8.2*

129 Fragment of base from an onion wine bottle. Green glass with heavy weathering. Late 17th to early 18th-century. Base diam. uncertain. *54/87; Period 7.7*

130* Four fragments of rim, neck, body and base from a mallet wine bottle. Green glass with heavy weathering. Early 18th-century. Rim diam. 30mm, base diam. 105mm. *54/95; Period 8.2*

131* Seven fragments of neck, body and base from a tiny mallet wine bottle. Early 18th-century. Base diam. 76mm. *54/123; Period 7.4*

132 Fragment of rim and neck from a mallet wine bottle. Green glass with heavy weathering. Early 18th-century. Rim diam. 25mm. *54/124; Period 7.5*

133 Four fragments of base from an onion or mallet wine bottle. Green glass with heavy weathering. Late 17th to early 18th-century. Base diam. uncertain. *54/124; Period 7.5*

134 Complete base from an onion wine bottle. Green glass with heavy weathering. Late 17th to early 18th-century. Base diam. 105mm. *54/141; Period 8.1*

135 Eleven fragments of base from an onion or mallet wine bottle. Green glass with heavy weathering. Late 17th to early 18th-century. Base diam. uncertain. *54/141; Period 8.1*

136* Four fragments of rim, neck, body and base from a mallet wine bottle. Green glass with heavy weathering. Late 17th to early 18th-century. Base diam. 85mm. *54/150; Period 8.1*

137 Five fragments of base and lower side from an onion or mallet wine bottle. Green glass with heavy weathering. Late 17th to early 18th-century. Base diam. uncertain. *54/150; Period 8.1*

138 Fragment of rim and upper neck from an early onion bottle. Green glass with heavy weathering. Late 17th-century. Rim diam. 25mm. *54/150; Period 8.1*

139 Four fragments of rim and base from an onion wine bottle. Green glass with heavy weathering. Late 17th-century. Rim diam. 25mm. *54/158. Period 7.7*

140* Fragment of rim and neck from an onion bottle. Green glass with heavy weathering. Late 17th to early 18th-century. Rim diam. 25mm. *54/170; Period 7.6*

141 Fragment of rim and neck from an onion wine bottle. Green glass with heavy weathering. Late 17th to early 18th-century. Rim diam. 25mm. *54/184; Period 7.6*

142* Fragment of rim, neck and shoulder from an onion or mallet wine bottle. Green glass with heavy weathering. Late 17th to early 18th-century. Rim diam. 26mm. *54/202; Period 7.5*

143 Fragment of rim and neck from an onion or mallet wine bottle. Green glass with heavy weathering. Late 17th to early 18th-century. Rim diam. 28mm. *54/202; Period 7.5*

144 Fragment of rim and neck from an onion or mallet wine bottle. Green glass with heavy weathering. Late 17th to early 18th-century. Rim diam. 24mm. *54/202; Period 7.5*

145 Fragment of rim from an onion or mallet wine bottle. Green glass with heavy weathering. Late 17th to early 18th-century. Rim diam. 27mm. *54/231; Period 7.4*

146 Four fragments of rim and neck from an early onion wine bottle. Green glass with heavy weathering. Late 17th-century. Rim diam. 28mm. *54/316; Period 7.4*

147 Complete base from an onion or mallet wine bottle. Green glass with heavy weathering. Late 17th to early 18th-century. Base diam. 90mm. *54/323; Period 6.1*

148 Fragment of rim and neck from a mallet wine bottle. Green glass with heavy weathering. Early 18th-century. Rim diam. 27mm. *54/516; Period 6.3*

149 Two fragments of base and lower side from a mallet wine bottle. Green glass with heavy weathering. Late 17th to early 18th-century. Base diam. uncertain. *54/516; Period 6.3*

150 Fragment of base and lower side from a mallet wine bottle. Green glass with heavy weathering. Early 18th-century. Base diam. 110mm. *54/516; Period 6.3*

151 Two fragments of base and lower side from a mallet wine bottle. Green glass with heavy weathering. Early 18th-century. Base diam. uncertain. *54/516; Period 6.3*

152 Complete base and lower side from a mallet wine bottle. Green glass with heavy weathering. Early 18th-century. Base diam. 110mm. *54/516; Period 6.3*

153 Fragment of rim and neck from an early onion wine bottle. Green glass with heavy weathering. Late 17th-century. Rim diam. 32mm. *54/316; Period 7.4*

154 Two fragments of rim and neck from a mallet wine bottle. Green glass with heavy weathering. Early 18th-century. Rim diam. uncertain. *54/316; Period 7.4*

155* Six fragments of rim, neck, body and base from a mallet wine bottle. Green glass with heavy weathering. Early 18th-century. Rim diam. 32mm, base 107mm. *54/612; Period 6.3*

156 Fragment of rim and neck from a mallet wine bottle. Green glass with heavy weathering. Early 18th-century. Rim diam. 30mm. *54/612; Period 6.3*

157 Fragment of rim and neck from a mallet wine bottle. Green glass with heavy weathering. Early 18th-century. Rim diam. 28mm. *54/612; Period 6.3*

158 Twenty-eight fragments of base and lower side from a mallet wine bottle. Green glass with heavy weathering. Early 18th-century. Base diam. 120mm. *54/516; Period 6.3*

159* Fifteen fragments of rim, neck, body and base from a mallet wine bottle. Green glass with heavy weathering. Early 18th-century. Rim diam. 28mm, base diam. 120mm, ht 164mm. *54/516; Period 6.3*

160 Complete base from an onion wine bottle. Green glass with heavy weathering. Early 18th-century. Base diam. 98mm. *54/516; Period 6.3*

The final type of bottle found is the short cylindrical bottle. By the mid-18th century, wine was being stored for longer in the bottle, so a style that allowed stacking was required. As a result a new bottle which was broadly cylindrical in body was developed, although it was still considerably shorter than the later style it was to develop into, and which is still in use today. The neck was also shorter and usually had a better finished rim and string course than the earlier varieties of bottle. Again the dating of the form must be treated with some degree of flexibility, although they were most popular between 1740 and 1780. Only seven examples were found on the vicarage site, and this reflects a site specific change, rather than the wine bottle becoming less popular generally at this time. Interestingly one example (No.167) has a thus far unidentified green (copper-based?) residue inside, again confirming that wine bottles were used to contain things other than wine.

161 Fragment of rim and neck from a squat cylindrical wine bottle. Green glass with little weathering. Mid to late 18th-century. Rim diam. 23mm. *54/1; Period 8.4*

162 Fragment of rim and neck from a squat cylindrical wine bottle. Green glass with little weathering. Mid to late 18th-century. Rim diam. 23mm. *54/5; Period 8.1*

163* Fragment of base and lower side from a small squat cylindrical wine bottle. Green glass with heavy weathering. Mid-18th-century. Base diam. 65mm. *54/5; Period 8.1*

164 Fragment of base from a small squat cylindrical wine bottle. Green glass with heavy weathering. Mid-18th-century. Base diam. 90mm. *54/5; Period 8.1*

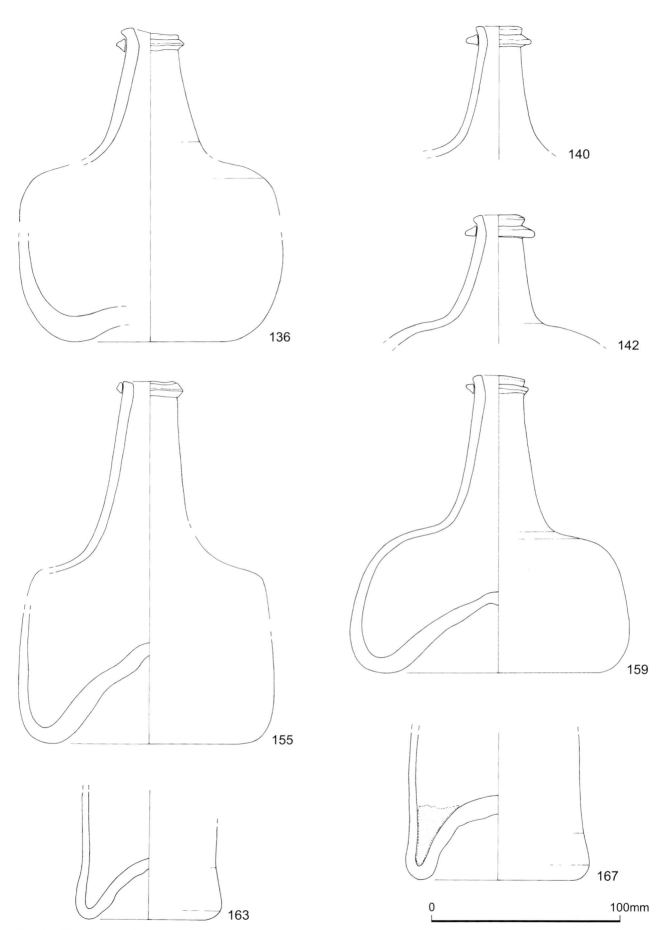

Fig. 105. Vessel glass: vicarage Nos 136, 140, 142, 155, 159, 163 and 167. Scale 1:2 (J. Kobe).

165 Fragment of base and lower side from a small squat cylindrical wine bottle. Green glass with heavy weathering. Mid-18th-century. Base diam. 75mm. *54/5; Period 8.1*

166 Fragment of rim from a squat cylindrical wine bottle. Green glass with little weathering. Mid to late 18th-century. Rim diam. 26mm. *54/5; Period 8.1*

167*Fragment of base and lower side from a small squat cylindrical wine bottle. Emerald green powdery deposit in base. Green glass with heavy weathering. Mid-18th-century. Base diam. 85mm. *54/99; Period 7.7*

Discussion

The vessel glass from the North Glebe Terrace sites is important for two reasons. First, with the exception of Shapwick (Gerrard with Aston 2007), there have been few studies of the material culture, and vessel glass in particular, from the very late medieval and early post-medieval village. Few groups have been excavated, let alone published, for these periods so the assemblages from Wharram are crucial in building a picture of glass consumption in the rural environment. Second, as well as being important in providing further information about the vessels being used, the presence of at least two larger assemblages allows for a certain degree of inter-site comparison.

The range of vessels

As might be expected, the range of glass found at Wharram is rather different to assemblages of the same date excavated in urban areas or on high status rural sites, particularly those belonging to the later medieval period. Nonetheless, the presence of at least one or maybe two medieval jugs (Nos 47-48) from the vicarage is interesting. Medieval vessel glass is extremely rare on deserted village sites, and is usually restricted to the occasional urinal, as at Thrislington (Austin 1989, 147) or the two examples from the North Manor area at Wharram (Willmott 2004, 234). These two new fragments, and the flask (No. 49) coupled with the two 14th-century opaque red glass vessels from the Churchyard at Wharram (Willmott 2007b, 300), start to add to the growing impression that glass use was not entirely restricted to urban or high status sites in the medieval period, although admittedly the numbers of fragments found thus far are low.

The quantity of 16th and early 17th-century glass is also relatively limited, and interestingly this was a period when glass was being used by an increasing sector of society. William Harrison's observation in 1587 that 'the poorest also will have glass if they may' might be a slight exaggeration (Edelen 1994, 128), but excavations in towns have repeatedly demonstrated that glass was used by all sectors of urban society. Interestingly, there is a virtual absence of the cheaper potash-rich drinking vessels (with the exception of No. 61) and almost the only tablewares from this period are the more expensive soda-rich goblets (Nos 50-57), beakers and cup (Nos 58-60 and 62) and jug (No. 63). Why more potash-based glasses were not found is uncertain, but it might be that this more unstable glass has simply not survived as well in the particular soil conditions at Wharram.

Whilst there is a relatively limited range of earlier tablewares, later 18th-century styles are well represented amongst the farmhouse and vicarage assemblages. The plain stems and bowls (Nos 2-3 and 71-4) are typical English products of the early to mid-18th century, and demonstrate that inhabitants in these areas had access to, and an appreciation of, the latest fashions of glassware. Furthermore, the presence of a number of wheel-engraved examples (Nos 1 and 66-70) is important in highlighting the popularity of this decorative technique. The increased consumption of fine tablewares in the 18th century seems to contrast with the preceding two centuries and, as already noted, the types found are closely mirrored in contemporary urban contexts.

As might be expected both the farmhouse and vicarage produced a diverse range of small utilitarian containers, primarily case bottles (Nos 7 and 81-84) and phials (Nos 8-14 and 85-112). These are ubiquitous on 17th and 18th-century sites, and represent items essential for the storage of all manner of every-day liquids and semi-solids. As such these types of vessel are found on all types of site, from peasant to elite, rural to urban.

The final general category of glass found was the wine bottle (Nos 15-46 and 113-167). Generally recognised as the most common non-ceramic find on post-medieval sites in general, it is no surprise that the same is the case at both the farmhouse and vicarage. Nonetheless, this is still an important assemblage, as most other rural excavations, such as Seacourt, Berks (Biddle 1961/2) and Thrislington, Co. Durham (Austin 1989) amongst many others, have tended to concentrate on villages that were totally deserted by the 17th century, so have failed to produce comparable sequences. The material from the North Glebe Terrace sites confirms an emerging pattern from other village sites which were only partially or not at all deserted, such as Shapwick. This shows that wine bottles were as popular in many rural contexts as they were urban ones.

Inter-site comparisons

As the glass from the North Glebe Terrace is derived from two separate sites there is some scope for inter-site comparison. As has already been noted, nine other sites in addition to the farmhouse and vicarage produced glass (Table 62), however, the vast majority was modern, and the relative lack of earlier glass in these areas is indicative of their desertion prior to the post-medieval period.

If the vessels found at the farmhouse and vicarage are divided into three broad groups some similarities and differences between the two assemblages can be observed (Table 63). As the vicarage assemblage is considerably larger, direct comparison of estimated minimum numbers is difficult, but when relative proportions are considered it is easier to evaluate the two assemblages. The most obvious similarity that the two groups share is that the numbers of both tablewares and small storage vessels (primarily phials) are broadly proportional in each area. This might well be coincidental, as it is unlikely that the consumption of tablewares was directly related to the consumption of these small storage containers.

Table 63. Minimum numbers and percentages of glass vessels from both sites.

Site	Tablewares	Small storage	Wine bottles	Total
Farmhouse	6	8	32	46
Vicarage	32	34	55	121
Farmhouse	13%	17%	70%	100%
Vicarage	26%	28%	46%	100%

Perhaps what is more striking is the rather large percentage of the farmhouse assemblage comprising wine bottles. It might be assumed, with its much larger number of wine glasses, that the vicarage would have had considerably more wine bottles than the farmhouse. Although, in actual numbers there are more from the vicarage, the total from the farmhouse is not significantly smaller. There are two possible reasons for this larger than expected number. First, it is likely that the bottles were being used for a wider range of domestic uses at the farmhouse than at the vicarage. Second, it might be that the occupants of the farmhouse were less inclined to discard wine bottles unnecessarily. Indeed, the presence of a bottle stamped with a complex armorial device (which was most unlikely to have belonged to any inhabitant of the farmhouse), might suggest that occupants were intentionally gathering wine bottles from elsewhere.

Conclusion
The glass assemblage from the North Glebe of Wharram is the largest excavated from a rural context in England. Until recently, knowledge of post-medieval glass use has been restricted to the assemblages found in urban environments or from specific elite sites such as castles and moated manors. The Wharram assemblage is therefore key to developing a more sophisticated appreciation of material culture consumption by rural communities.

Whilst the quantity of glass found dating to before the 18th century was relatively limited, the presence of three medieval vessels, as well as some good quality 16th to 17th-century tablewares, suggests that there was a market for these products in Wharram. The 18th-century assemblages are perhaps more informative. The group from the vicarage, as might be expected, demonstrated that the occupants of this area had a taste for the most fashionable tablewares of their day, as well as the resources to purchase them. They were also clearly enthusiastic consumers of wine. It is also interesting that a similar pattern was being partially followed by the occupants of the farmhouse. Whilst being found in rather smaller quantities, they too had access to some fine tablewares, as well as other utilitarian storage bottles and phials. More interestingly, during the 18th century the tenants of the farmhouse were also using a considerable number of wine bottles, and possibly for a wide variety of purposes.

The glass objects
by J. Price and E.A. Clark

Fifty-two glass objects were recovered from the North Glebe Terrace sites, mainly from the farmstead area, and all have been examined by Professor J. Price. Among sixteen beads from the farmstead area and five from the vicarage (Nos 168, 169 and Archive 171-189), only two, both from Site 54 might be datable, one (No. 168) could be Saxon and another (No. 169) is possibly from the 11th century; the remainder are of varying shapes, colours and sizes, and could be of any date. Their contexts suggest that a post-medieval date is most likely.

Eight post-medieval glass buttons (Archive 190-97) from the farmhouse and from Site 51 add to the variety of buttons in other materials found in this part of the village.

Like the other glass objects, the fifteen glass marbles (Archive 198-212) were found mainly in and around the farm buildings.

A collar stud was amongst three miscellaneous items (Archive 213-15). Five droplets of molten glass (No. 170 and Archive 216-19) include one from the vicarage that might be Roman in origin.

168 Glass bead. Dark green/blue. Cylindrical. Could be Saxon or later. L. 13mm. *54/4; SF2282; Period 8.4*

169 Fragment of glass bead. Bright turquoise. Annular and ribbed with deep grooves. Some wear. Large aperture. Possibly 11th-century. Ht 6mm. *54/576; SF2283; Period 3.1*

170 Melted blob of green glass, tear-drop shaped. Possibly Roman. *54/4; SF2281; Period 8.4*

20 The Coins

Note on the Roman and medieval coins
by E.A. Clark, B. Sitch and C. Barclay

One Roman and six medieval coins and jetons were recovered from the North Glebe Terrace sites, and have all been published with those from all the excavated sites: the Roman coins by Bryan Sitch (2004) in *Wharram IX* and the medieval ones by Craig Barclay (2007) in *Wharram XI*. These volumes were published before all the phasing for the North Glebe Terrace sites had been finalised; the coins are therefore listed here under their original catalogue numbers, with the phasing added or verified.

The Roman coin (No. 19) was found in the garden area behind the cottages, and is residual.

The discovery of a Henry I penny (No. 9) and other medieval objects in the north-west corner of Site 51, suggests significant activity in the vicinity during that period. The 12th-century Stephen penny (No. 10) from the vicarage was found in a later context. Barclay (2007, 301-2) writes that both are 'scarce coins … worthy of note even if found in an urban context'. He comments that 'significantly, no later medieval coins' came from any of these sites.

The four jetons (Nos 32-35) are all imports of 16th to early 17th-century date. Three other imports of similar date, as well as a late 13th-century English jeton, have been recovered around the village. Although their primary purpose was as counters in arithmetical calculations, they may also have served as unofficial 'small change'. Either function might have been appropriate at Wharram.

Roman coin

19   Constantine I; copy; AD 341-6
       Rev.: Urbs Roma. Perforated
       51/23; SF1; unphased

Medieval coins

9   Henry I; penny
      Quadrilateral on cross fleury type; 1125-35
      BMC xv
      rev) [ ] ON [ ]
      1.19g, as struck, contemporary loss
      51/1034; SF422; Period 2.1

10   Stephen; penny
      Watford type; 1136-45
      BMC i
      1.08g, as struck, contemporary loss
      54/209; SF753; Period 5.2

32   Jeton; Nuremberg
      Rose and orb type; Hans Krauwinckel II; 1586-1635
      rev) ***GLVCK BECHERT IST IN GWERTT
      cf. Mitchiner (1988) 1508-11
      1.82g, light wear, contemporary loss
      74/300; SF1123; Period 2

33   Jeton; Nuremberg
      Rose and orb type; 16th to early 17th-century
      1.22g, light wear, contemporary loss
      54/369; SF680; Period 6.3

34   Jeton; Nuremberg
      Rose and orb type; 16th to early 17th-century
      1.40g, moderate wear, contemporary loss
      54/516; SF1385; Period 6.3

35   Jeton; Nuremberg
      Rose and orb type; 16th to early 17th-century
      1.22g; pierced, moderate wear, contemporary loss
      54/990; SF1603; Period 5.4

A review of the post-medieval coins from Wharram Percy

by C. Barclay

Introduction

This review covers only those coins and related items struck between 1600 and 1900, earlier material having been covered in depth elsewhere (Roman coins: *Wharram IX*, 234-40; medieval coins: *Wharram XI*, 301-4). A late medieval coin, a half groat of Elizabeth I (fifth issue 1582-1600), from an unstratified context in Site 74 and identified after the publication of the medieval coin list, has been added to the archive. Twentieth-century material is only listed in the archive. The post-medieval numismatic archive is made up primarily of well-worn low-value coins, many of which had enjoyed a very long period in circulation prior to being lost. This is particularly true of the halfpenny issues of the 17th and 18th centuries, which frequently remained in circulation until the late 1790s.

Discussion

Although the site has produced a number of jetons that may have been struck as late as the early 1600s, only a single 17th-century piece, a 'Richmond' token farthing (No. 50) of definite pre-Restoration date has been recovered. Later 17th-century material is primarily of low value and includes a Scottish turner of Charles II (No. 46) which probably circulated as a farthing. Numerous similar coins have been recovered by detectorists on sites across northern Yorkshire. A local trade token, issued in Malton in 1666, was also found (No. 51). Well-worn Charles II farthings have been recovered from the Church (Nos 1 and 2), North Glebe Terrace (Nos 3 and 5) and from the North Manor (No. 4), whilst a range of later 17th-century copper pieces have been recovered from across the village. Many of these are very worn, and were probably lost in the 18th century. An unusual 17th-century find is an unworn Irish 'gunmoney' crown of James II dated 1690 (No. 47). This coin, which is of a short-lived base-metal emergency issue, would not have enjoyed any formal currency status in England. The only precious-metal coin of 17th-century date recovered is a well-worn sixpence of William III (No. 7), struck in Chester in 1696-7 and almost certainly a mid to late 18th-century loss.

The 18th-century material from the village comprises the accustomed accumulation of halfpennies, ranging from the relatively freshly struck to the severely worn, and including a counterfeit one (No. 54). The assemblage includes two Irish halfpennies (Nos 48 and 49). High-value coins are noticeably absent, although this to a large extent mirrors a national phenomenon. Issues of the late 18th to early 19th centuries are common, and include freshly struck pennies of 1797 from Matthew Boulton's Soho mint. Later 19th-century material is again restricted to coins of low face-value.

Number 55 is an unidentified white metal medal of the early 19th century.

Area summaries

Church and Churchyard (Wharram III and XI)
A well-preserved Charles II farthing and two worn William III halfpennies (Nos 2, 11 and 13) were recovered from the northern part of the churchyard. A lightly-worn farthing of 1672 and a third worn William III halfpenny (Nos 1 and 8) were found beneath the Victorian floor of the nave. All have been published previously (*Wharram III*, 175).

North Manor Area (Wharram IX)
Only two post-medieval coins were recovered from this area: a Charles II farthing and an illegible heavily worn halfpenny (Nos 4 and 24).

North Glebe Terrace – Post-medieval Farmstead and Vicarage (this volume)

This area produced numerous low-value coins of the 17th century, including one Scottish coin (No. 46), one Irish coin (No. 47) and a local trade token of 1666 (No. 51). Eighteenth-century halfpennies are likewise well represented, including several well-worn pieces. Three unworn specimens of Boulton's 'cartwheel' penny issue of 1797 were recovered (Nos 30-32), together with several slightly later products of the Soho mint. The site also produced well-worn coins of Victorian date.

South Glebe Terrace – Pond and Dam Area
(Wharram X)

The South Glebe Terrace produced three well-worn Georgian halfpennies (Nos 15-17) and a heavily circulated token of later 18th-century date (No. 53).

Catalogue
English/British coins

1 Charles II; copper farthing; 1672
6.63g, light wear, late 17th-century loss
(Wharram III, 175) Church, middle of nave: 14/-; C1203, R18; Phases VI-XI

2 Charles II; copper farthing; 1673
5.11g, light wear, late 17th-century loss
(Wharram III, 175) North Churchyard: Site 14/-; C694A, M29; Phase XIII

3 Charles II; copper farthing; 1672-79
5.63g, light wear, late 17th-century loss
North Glebe Terrace, Farmhouse: *74/313; SF1444; Period 6*

4 Charles II; copper farthing; 1672-79
4.66g, moderate wear, late 17th to early 18th-century loss
North Manor Area: 43/1; SF442; Period 6

5 Charles II; copper farthing; 1672-79
4.99g, heavy wear, probably early 18th-century loss
North Glebe Terrace, Vicarage Buildings: *77/85; SF36; Period 5.2*

6 Corroded tin (?) disc possibly farthing; 1684-92
North Glebe Terrace, Vicarage: *54/9; SF2020; Period 7.8*

7 William III; sixpence; 1696-97
Chester
2.80g, heavy wear, mid to late 18th-century loss
North Glebe Terrace, Vicarage: *54/202; SF451; Period 7.5*

8 William III; halfpenny; 1698(?)
10.19g, moderate/heavy wear, early 18th-century loss
(Wharram III, 175) Church, middle of nave: Site 14/-; C1174, R17; Phase XI

9 William III; halfpenny; 1700
10.10g, moderate wear, mid-18th-century loss
North Glebe Terrace, Farm Buildings: *51/1; SF3; unphased*

10 William III; halfpenny; 1695-98
8.48g, moderate wear, early 18th-century loss
North Glebe Terrace, Vicarage: *54/111; SF77; Period 8.1*

11 William III; halfpenny; 1695-1701
9.13g, heavy wear, mid-18th-century loss
(Wharram III, 175) North Churchyard: Site 14/-; C695A, K27; Phase XIII

12 William III; halfpenny; 1695-1701
7.97g, heavy wear, mid to late 18th-century loss
North Glebe Terrace, Farmhouse: *74/314; SF931; Period 4*

13 William III; halfpenny; 1699-1701
9.65g, very heavy wear, late 18th-century loss
(Wharram III, 175) North Churchyard: Site 14/-; C753, V29; Phases XI-XII

14 George II; halfpenny; 1734
10.26g, unworn, contemporary loss
North Glebe Terrace, Vicarage: *54/100; SF15; Period 7.1*

15 George II; halfpenny; 1729-39
young bust
8.69g, moderate wear, mid to late 18th-century loss
South Glebe Terrace: 30/1251; SF70; Phase 3

16 George II; halfpenny; 1729-39
young bust
7.27g heavy wear, late 18th-century loss
South Glebe Terrace: 30/1; SF306; topsoil

17 George II; halfpenny; 1729-39
young bust
8.26g, heavy wear, late 18th-century
South Glebe Terrace: 30/16; SF309; Phase 8

18 George II; halfpenny; 1740-54
old bust
7.20g, heavy wear, late 18th-century loss
North Glebe Terrace, Farmhouse: *74/9000; SF2087; unstratified*

19 George III; halfpenny; 1774
6.86g, light wear, contemporary loss
North Glebe Terrace, Farm Buildings: *51/6; SF1; unphased*

20 George III; halfpenny; 1774
7.29g, moderate wear, late 18th-century loss
North Glebe Terrace, Farmhouse: *74/255; SF632; Period 3*

21 George III; halfpenny; 1775
6.62g; moderate to heavy wear, late 18th-century loss
North Glebe Terrace, Farmhouse: *74/198; SF353; Period 6*

22 George III; halfpenny; 1770-75
6.50g, heavy wear, late 18th-century loss
North Glebe Terrace, Vicarage: *54/4; SF12; Period 8.4*

23 George III; halfpenny; 1770-75
8.55g, heavy wear, late 18th-century loss
North Glebe Terrace, Vicarage: *54/111; SF57; Period 8.1*

24 Copper halfpenny; *c.* 1672-1775
6.69g, worn flat, 18th-century loss
North Manor Area: 602/-; SF96; unstratified

25 Copper halfpenny; *c.* 1672-1775
9.54g, worn flat, 18th-century loss
North Glebe Terrace, Vicarage: *54/9; SF2020; Period 7.8*

26 Copper halfpenny; *c.* 1672-1775
7.36g, worn flat, 18th-century loss
North Glebe Terrace, Farmhouse: *74/9000; SF1660; unstratified*

27 Copper halfpenny; *c.* 1672-1775
7.45g, worn flat, 18th-century loss
North Glebe Terrace, Farmhouse: *74/314; SF945; Period 4*

28 Copper halfpenny; *c.* 1672-1775
8.45g, worn flat, 18th-century loss
North Glebe Terrace, Vicarage: *54/191; SF280; Period 7.7*

29 Heavily encrusted copper-alloy disc probably halfpenny, *c.* 1672-1775
North Glebe Terrace, Farmhouse: *74/349; SF1425; Period 4?*

30 George III; penny; 1797
27.33g, light wear, contemporary loss
North Glebe Terrace, Vicarage Buildings: 77/85; SF1; Period 5.2

31 George III; penny; 1797
27.60g, light wear, contemporary loss
North Glebe Terrace, Farmhouse: 74/157; SF213; Period 6

32 George III; penny; 1797
28.16g, unworn, contemporary loss
North Glebe Terrace, Farm Buildings: 51/540; SF162; Period 2.1

33 George III; halfpenny; 1799
12.07g, unworn, contemporary loss
North Glebe Terrace, Vicarage: 54/5; SF14; Period 8.1

34 George III; halfpenny; 1799
13.60g, light wear, contemporary loss
North Glebe Terrace, Vicarage: 54/113; SF199; Period 8.1

35 George III; halfpenny; 1799
12.17g, light wear, contemporary loss
North Glebe Terrace, Vicarage: 54/113; SF221; Period 8.1

36 George III; halfpenny; 1799
11.97g, moderate wear, early 19th-century loss
North Glebe Terrace, Vicarage: 54/113; SF157; Period 8.1

37 George III; halfpenny; 1806
9.10g, light wear, contemporary loss
North Glebe Terrace, Vicarage: 54/95; SF13; Period 8.2

38 George III; farthing; 1806-7
3.46g, moderate wear, early 19th-century loss
North Glebe Terrace, Vicarage: 54/182; SF351; Period 7.1

39 Victoria; farthing; 1860
2.79g, unworn, contemporary loss
North Glebe Terrace, Vicarage: 54/1; SF2017; Period 8.4

40 Victoria; penny; 1867
9.35g, unworn, contemporary loss
North Glebe Terrace, Farmhouse: 74/9000; SF2088; unstratified

41 Victoria; penny; 1878
8.65g, moderate wear, early 20th-century loss
North Glebe Terrace, Farm Buildings: 51/466; SF33; Period 2.4

42 Victoria; halfpenny; 1883
5.19g, moderate wear, early 20th-century loss
North Glebe Terrace, Vicarage: 54/1; SF2016; Period 8.4

43 Victoria; penny; 1860-95
6.80g, worn flat, 20th-century loss
North Glebe Terrace, Farmhouse: 74/314; SF1237; Period 4

44 Victoria; halfpenny; 1899
5.36g, heavy wear, mid-20th-century loss
North Glebe Terrace, Farm Buildings: 51/4; SF4; unphased

45 Heavily encrusted copper-alloy disc probably penny, post-1860
North Glebe Terrace, Farmhouse: 74/349; SF1746; Period 4?

Scottish coin
46 Scotland; Charles II; turner coinage of 1663
cf. Seaby and Purvey 1984, 5625
2.60g, heavy wear, probably late 17th-century loss
North Glebe Terrace, Vicarage: 54/374; SF689; Period 6.1

Irish coins
47 Ireland; James II; gunmoney crown; 1690
cf. Seaby and Purvey 1984, 6578
13.50g, unworn, perhaps contemporary loss
North Glebe Terrace, Vicarage Buildings: 77/101; SF5; Period 5.1

48 Ireland; George I; halfpenny; 1723
William Wood's coinage
cf. Seaby and Purvey 1984, 6601
8.00g, light wear, contemporary loss
North Glebe Terrace, Farmhouse: 74/158; SF221; Period 6

49 Ireland; George III; halfpenny; 1782
cf. Seaby and Purvey 1984, 6614
8.20g, moderate wear, contemporary loss
North Glebe Terrace, Farmhouse: 74/140; SF227; Period 4

Tokens
50 Charles I; farthing token
Richmond type, class 1b; 1625-34
0.49g, unworn, contemporary loss
North Glebe Terrace, Farm Buildings: 49/26; SF2; Period 2

51 Token; farthing; 1666
Malton; William Pennock
cf. Dickinson 1992, 224
2.02g, light wear, contemporary loss
North Glebe Terrace, Farm Buildings: 49/26; SF3; Period 2

52 Token; halfpenny; 1812
Sheffield; Roscoe Mills
cf. Davis 1904, 150
9.16g, pierced, unworn, contemporary loss
North Glebe Terrace, Vicarage: 54/5; SF10; Period 8.1

53 Copper halfpenny token; late 18th-century
engrailed edge
6.83g, worn flat, perhaps early 19th-century loss
South Glebe Terrace: 30/584; SF310; Phase 7.1

Counterfeit coin
54 George II; halfpenny (counterfeit)
old bust; brockage; prototype 1746-54
5.97g, moderate wear, late 18th-century loss
North Glebe Terrace, Vicarage: 54/162; SF261; Period 8.1

Medal
55 Commemorative medal; 1813
white metal; unidentified
15.97g, corroded; possibly contemporary loss
North Glebe Terrace, Vicarage: 54/14; SF2647; Period 8.2

21 Non-ferrous Metal Objects
by A.R. Goodall and E.A. Clark, with identification of No. 28 by C. Barclay and Nos 62-85 by R. McNeill Alexander

Introduction

More than 1050 identifiable non-ferrous metal objects were found in and around the vicarage and farmhouse buildings. Although there was some residual material, most are from the post-medieval period. In view of the greater proportion and variety of alloys other than copper, all the non-ferrous metal objects are included in the same catalogue and report.

Most are later versions of types of object already known from earlier periods within the village, some however, the buttons and pins for example, occurring in far greater numbers; in fact buttons and pins form slightly over 50% of all the non-ferrous finds. The assemblage also includes a few entirely new types such as parts from clocks, watches and mouth organs, as well as a pocket sundial. These provide an insight into the lives of the occupants in the post-medieval phases of the site.

All the objects and fragments have been examined and described, but no conservation work has been done. The complete catalogue forms part of the site archive.

Dress and personal items (Fig. 106)

Although a few items in this group, for example two of the strap ends (Nos 1 and 2), are medieval, most relate to the dress and personal life of the inhabitants of the post-medieval farmhouses and vicarages. Among these are buckles (Nos 3-8 and 11-18), which include shoe and spur buckles (and see No. 13 for other possible uses). Some of the buckles would have had uses other than in dress: No. 18, for instance, is probably a harness buckle. Another D-shaped buckle similar to No. 18, a fragment of a possible lead buckle frame and two rectangular double-looped modern buckles, one in a light alloy, are listed in the full catalogue (Archive 128-131).

Farmstead
1* Strap end of copper alloy. Forked spacer with acorn knop onto which plates have been soldered. The front plate is decorated with two grooves running the length of the plate and lines of traced zig-zags forming a diamond pattern. Parts of very similar strap ends were found at Wharram on Site 12 (Goodall, A. 1979, fig. 55, nos 16-18; Goodall, A. 1989, fig. 31, no. 103) and also at York where, although unstratified, a date of mid-14th to early 15th-century was suggested (Ottaway and Rogers 2002, fig. 1476, 14711). A date in the second half of the 14th century is likely for the present example. L. 74mm. *49/31; SF12; Period 1*

2* Strap end or buckle plate of copper alloy, with traced decoration and possible gilding. Probably medieval. L. 43mm. *51/471; SF351; Period 2.2*

3* Double-looped buckle of copper alloy, decorated with fleur-de-lys motifs on the ends of the pin-bar and with rosettes and scrolls on the loops. The buckle has been cast in an open mould and is light in weight. Probably 17th or early 18th-century. Ht 33 mm; w. 48mm. *74/219; SF951; Period 2*

4* Incomplete double-looped buckle frame of copper alloy, with scroll decoration. There are remains of a socket which would have held a separate pin-bar. The buckle has the characteristic convex profile of a shoe buckle. 18th-century. L. 48mm. *74/314; SF1445; Period 4*

5 D-shaped loop or buckle frame of copper alloy. Ht 30mm; w. 25mm. *51/264; SF507; Period ER-3*

6 Large D-shaped loop of copper alloy. Made from a rectangular-sectioned strip, bent to a loop and with the ends butted. It could have been used as a simple buckle frame but may have had other uses. Ht 44mm; w. 49mm. *51/263; SF510; Period ER-3*

7 Possible rectangular buckle frame or belt slide of copper alloy. The central bar is rectangular in section and is unlikely to have supported a swivelling pin. Ht 33mm; w. 25mm. *73/15; SF185; Period 3*

8 Buckle frame or brooch of copper alloy. Irregularity probably due to wear or corrosion. Diam. 27mm. *74/312; SF918; Period 4*

Vicarage
9 Strip of copper alloy, with a rivet at one end and traces of solder close to the long edges. Possibly part of a strap end. L. 45mm; w. 9mm. *77/1; SF2288; Period 6*

10 Terminal from repoussé strap ornament of copper alloy. L. 8.5mm. *77/487; SF633; Period 5.1*

11* Double-looped buckle, probably of brass, thinly cast with transverse mouldings and shallow bosses. There would have been a separate pin bar, now missing. L. 33mm. *54/310; SF660; Period 6.1*

12 Double-looped buckle of copper alloy with iron pin bar. The D-sectioned frame is damaged and distorted and it is not clear whether it was cast or made from a strip that was bent round to form a loop. Ht 17mm; w. *c.* 28mm. *77/259; SF192; Period 5.1*

13* Oval buckle of copper alloy, with double pin swivelling on an iron spindle inserted into the frame. Small buckles date from the 18th century when they were used as knee or breeches buckles or on garters or boots (Hume 1970, 86; Whitehead 2003, 111 and 114). L. 19mm. *54/111; SF114; Period 8.1*

14* Shoe or spur buckle of copper alloy, with moulded frame and a broad pin; waisted plate with iron rivet for attachment to strap. L. 30mm. *54/202; SF408; Period 7.5*

15* Oval frame from shoe or breeches buckle of copper alloy; curved profile. It would have had a separate pin bar. 37 x 38mm. *54/233; SF403; Period 7.6*

16 ?Small shoe buckle of copper alloy. Oval ring, possibly split and thickening on one side. Greatest diam. 19.5mm. *54/412; SF868; Period 6.3*

17* Single-looped moulded buckle frame of copper-alloy, probably with white metal plating. 17th to early 18th-century type. L. 28.5mm. *54/1; SF1940; Period 8.4*

18* Rectangular buckle frame of copper alloy with recessed central pin bar, possibly a harness buckle. 26 x 33mm. *54/5; SF1947; Period 8.1*

The T-shaped loop, No. 19, is of uncertain date and function, but it could have been used as a belt fastening with a hoop on an opposing loop. The dress fastener, No. 20, similar to one from Area 6 and to examples from Norwich, is probably 17th-century.

Vicarage
19 T-shaped loop of copper alloy, possibly a belt fastener. L. 65mm. *54/1; SF2633; Period 8.4*

20* Dress hook of copper alloy. The plate has foliate decoration and a rectangular loop. Two hooks from Area 6 (Goodall, A. 1979, 111, no. 25, fig. 56) were less elongated in form and had a simpler type of decoration on the heads. They were joined by a chain, linking the loops on the heads, and evidently served as a garment fastening. Other examples were found at Norwich (Margeson 1993, 17, fig. 8, 71-75) in contexts of 17th-century date, except for one, with a similar decoration to the Wharram example, which comes from an 18th-century context. Number 20 may also date from the second half of the 17th century but see Egan (2005, 42-4) for an earlier dating. L. 41mm. *77/324; SF340; Period 3-5*

Jewellery is only sparsely represented. The only object definitely identifiable as a brooch is No. 22, very similar to a 19th-century brooch with hair in the centre illustrated by Luthie (2007, 13, fig. 24), although No. 8 might be a brooch rather than a buckle frame. Two possible finger-rings (Nos 21 and 23) are both very fragmentary; a third ring (No. 24) may be from a purse.

Farmstead
21 Possible finger ring of copper alloy. Four sections which may form complete ring. One section is thicker but it is not clear whether this is due to deliberate shaping or to corrosion. Diam. *c.* 22mm. *74/123; SF120; Period 6*

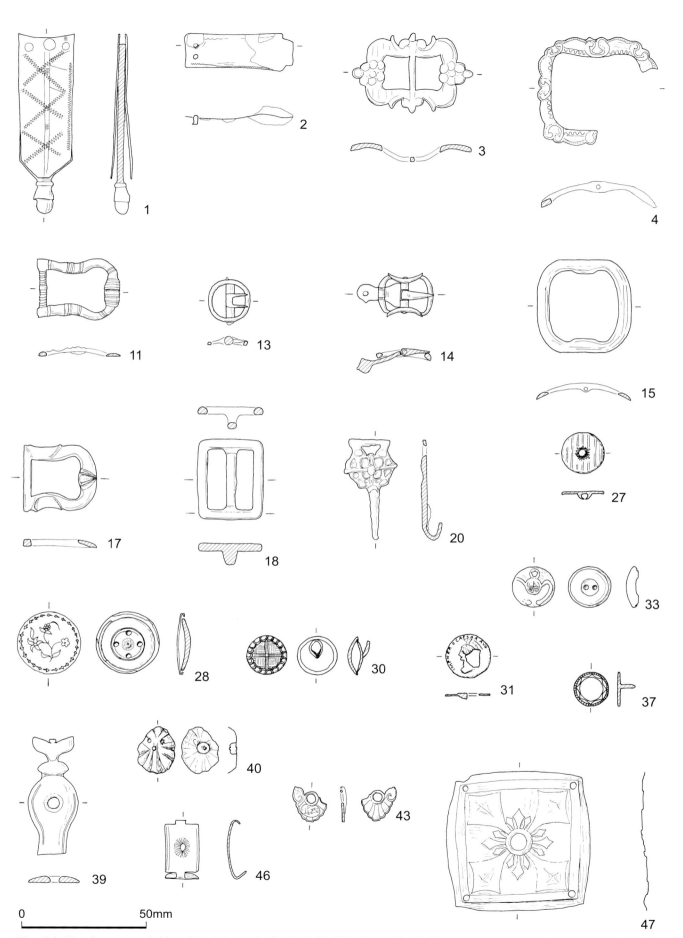

Fig. 106. Non-ferrous metal objects Nos 1-4, 11, 13-15, 17-18, 20, 27-8, 30-31, 33, 37, 39-40, 43 and 46-7. Scale 2:3 (E. Marlow-Mann)

Vicarage

22 Brooch. Pin missing, but marks of attachment remain. Shallow S-shape with pointed ends. Gold-coloured metal, with ?enamel in a cell which follows the shape of the brooch. *54/1; SF2021; Period 8.4*

23 Fragments of ring of copper alloy with what appears to be a pierced bezel. Although it looks like a finger ring, its size suggests it could have had a more functional use. Diam. *c.* 21mm. *54/705; SF1512; Period 2.3*

24 Ring of copper alloy. Flat, similar to chain mail. Could be from a 19th-century purse. Diam. 8mm. *54/1; SF2309; Period 8.4*

25 Tweezers of copper alloy. Small knop on end; broadens to spatulate blades. L. 53mm; max. w. of blades 8mm. *54/600; SF1398; Period 4.3*

The large assemblage of 106 buttons (Nos 28-38 and Archive 132-223) is a distinctive feature not seen on other sites at Wharram. Although a few were in 17th and 18th-century contexts, most were in late or unstratified ones.

Numbers 26 and 27 are examples of the type of buttons that make up the majority (65%) from both buildings. They are flat-topped with wire attachment loops, some (as No. 26) with shanks; they vary between 12-31mm in diameter, and while most are plain, some are gilded and a few have decorative features (as No. 27).

Among the remainder are composite and domed buttons. A disc (No. 31) purporting to be a Roman coin, and bearing a partially legible legend, may be from a button. Three livery buttons (Nos 32-4) have possible coats of arms although it has not been possible to distinguish any of them; they were all found in topsoil and unstratified contexts, so it is possible that they originate from the 20th-century occupation of the cottages. A small group of eight dished buttons (No. 36, Archive 132-5, 137, 143 and 176) were all found in late contexts in the cottage gardens, and are all modern. Another group, of four buttons, (No. 37, Archive 203, 204 and 214) was found at the vicarage: they have flat tops and milled edges, and are decorated with a raised field which has eight slightly concave sides. Number 38 is a pair of linked buttons, probably used as cuff-links; another, No. 35, attached to an elongated loop, may also be from a cuff-link. Four of the buttons are stamped with information such as 'BEST PLATED' and 'STANDARD ORANGE GILT', but only one of them (No. 36) identifies its maker, T. Allott of Scarborough.

The majority of the buttons are of types that can be dated to the 18th and 19th centuries (Bailey 2004). Many of the more decorative buttons came from the farmhouse and its outbuildings, whereas the vicarage produced mainly plain flat-topped ones.

Farmstead

26 Flat top, white metal plating or greyish alloy, with small cone shank and wire loop. Diam. 16mm. *74/341; SF1512; Period 1*

27* Copper alloy, flat top; loop may be pierced lug rather than wire. Top has cast or repoussé decoration with daisy-like design made up of small raised areas against background of strips done in a similar way. Diam. 17mm. *74/219; SF895; Period 2*

28* Composite. Bone back with four stitch holes, concave profile. Cap of copper-alloy foil decorated with flower motif. Diam. 26mm. *74/244; SF778; Period 4*

29 Composite. Bone back with four stitching holes. Front is conical, shiny metal, probably a zinc-rich alloy. Diam. 17mm; ht 9mm. *74/275; SF1836; Period 6*

30* Copper alloy, made in two parts, with convex repoussé cap, edge folded over concave back. Wire loop passes through back. The cap is decorated with a central cross with a hatched background. Round this is a border of 'U's. Diam. 16mm. *74/341; SF1621; Period 1*

31* Disc of copper alloy, purporting to be a coin of Nero, with the partial legend 'IMP NERO CAESAR AVG ….'. It appears to be machine-made, and is likely to be from a button. Diam. 18mm. *74/119; SF124; Period 6*

32 Livery button of copper alloy, made in two parts. Loop passes through two holes in back. Convex front with indecipherable heraldic badge, possibly the royal arms with lion and unicorn supporters. Diam. 24mm. *51/1; SF672; unphased*

33* Copper alloy, made from two discs. Back has two stitching holes. Front has repoussé coat of arms with crown above, supporters etc. Possibly regimental. Diam. 17mm. *74/9000; SF1718; unstratified*

34 Copper alloy, slightly convex surface with raised (rolled) edge and crown in relief against roughened ground. Loop at back. Diam. 21mm. *74/9000; SF1726; unstratified*

35 Flat top, shiny white, possibly plating or zinc. Possible geometric decoration (or accidental scratches) on front. Back appears to have some form of shank and an elongated loop suggesting this may have been a link button. Diam. 15mm. *74/102; SF863; Period 4*

36 Copper alloy, dished centre and four stitch holes. Flange stamped 'T.ALLOTT.SCARBORO'. Diam. 16mm. *51/100; SF674; unphased*

Vicarage

37* Copper alloy, flat top, decorated with milled edge and wire loop. Slightly raised octagonal shape with concave sides. Traces of a more gold colour in spaces between points of octagon. Diam. 14mm. *54/111; SF63; Period 8.1*

38 Linked buttons of non-ferrous metal, probably used as cuff fastenings. Octagonal shape with cast geometric decoration. Joined by an oval link. Diam. 17mm. *54/5; SF11; Period 8.1*

Thirty-one lace-ends (Archive 224-252), some fragmentary, were recovered. Two damaged examples were in a medieval context, the remainder were in contexts from the 16th century onwards. Twenty-three of them, varying in length between 21 and 32mm, were found in the vicarage buildings. Archive 251, also from the vicarage, is exceptionally long (79mm) and robust enough to have been used as a point or ferrule. The lace-ends from the farm buildings range from 18 to 32mm in length. Two eyelets also came from the vicarage: one of twisted wire was in an 18th-century context, the other, a disc with a central hole, from a context dated to the 16th or 17th centuries (Archive 253 and 254),

Among the many fragments of wire (see below) are some which could have been used on garments or for hairdressing. A large bodkin-like object (No. 105 below) may also be for use in the hair.

Decorative items and objects associated with literacy and leisure (Figs 106 and 107)

Although some of the decorative items included here (Nos 39-45 and 50-53) may have originated elsewhere, for example from items of dress or from caskets, a small

258

group of objects can be associated with reading and writing. Number 54 is a book clasp of a type already found at Wharram (Goodall, A. 1987, 173, fig.191, nos 38-9; Goodall, A. and Paterson 2000, fig. 61 no. 31; Goodall, A. 2007, 307, fig. 145, no. 28). A small clasp, No. 46, may also have been used on a book, as may the possible hinge (No. 55), a binding strip (No. 56), and a square mount (No. 47). Whilst the existence of books, such as copies of the Bible and other religious works with elaborate bindings, would be expected in the vicarage, the presence of the possible book clasp and decorative mount in the farmhouse must be noted.

Three possible lead pencils (Nos 48, 57 and 58) were recovered. They were used in medieval times, from the end of the 11th century, for writing notes on paper or parchment. Marginal notes written in lead are found in manuscripts of the 13th and 14th centuries. Objects identified as writing leads were found in the excavations at Winchester (Biddle and Brown 1990, 735-8, 743-6, figs 211-12, nos 2290-2316). These are of four different types, the example from Wharram Percy (No. 48) corresponding approximately to the Winchester Class II type. This type has also been found in York (Ottaway and Rogers 2002, 2934), in both medieval and post-medieval contexts, and in areas of the city which reflect Biddle and Brown's suggestion that Class II leads might have been used more by craftsmen than in book production, a suggestion that makes their presence at Wharram more likely.

A narrow section of wood with copper-alloy end, possibly from a ruler (No. 49), found around the farmhouse, and the dividers (No. 59) from an 18th-century context in the vicarage, are also likely to be associated with craftsmen.

Farmstead

39* Incomplete decorative mount of copper alloy, perforated in the middle and with a fish-tail terminal at one end; the other end is incomplete. L. 48mm. *74/270; SF706; Period 4*

40* Scallop-shaped repoussé mount of copper alloy with small rivet secured at the back by a rove. Possibly medieval. L. 19mm. *74/9000; SF1710; unstratified*

41 Possibly a decorative mount of copper alloy, convex, leaf-shaped but with no rivet for attachment. L. 23mm. *49/7; SF46; Period 3*

42 Leaf-shaped object of copper alloy, with central boss, and another smaller one each side of it in shiny material, possibly glass. L. 25mm. *74/106; SF9; Period 3*

43* Fragment of lead/tin ornament with central perforation. Cast in two-piece mould so that there is similar, but not identical, scalloped and scrolled decoration on both faces. L. 14mm. *49/500; SF58; Period 3*

44 Large circular boss of thin grey alloy with six-pointed star in relief. The central stud would have been screwed into something. Diam. 48mm. *73/1; SF236; Period 3*

45 Disc of copper alloy with central depression and decoration of radial ridges. Diam. 38mm. *97/10; SF1; unphased*

46* Small clasp of copper alloy, possibly from a book binding. The rectangular plate is decorated with a cast oval chrysanthemum motif between incised lines. One end is hooked, the other has a lunate projection. L. 24mm. *74/314; SF1110; Period 4*

47* Square mount of copper alloy with repoussé decoration. It is too large to have been a belt mount but may have come from a book binding. It has pin holes in each corner. 56mm square. *51/201; SF503; unphased*

48 Possibly a writing lead or pencil, round-sectioned, straight-sided. Sharpened to a point at one end, the other being cut off straight. L. 71mm. *74/272; SF1413; Period 6*

49 Possibly a fragment from a narrow wooden ruler with a copper-alloy end. No calibrations visible. Remaining l. 13+mm; w. 11.5mm. *74/153; SF2116; Period 6*

Vicarage

50* Flat mount or binding of copper alloy, expanded at each end and with a swelling in the middle. Rivet at each end within concentric ring mouldings. L. 58mm. *54/5; SF1946; Period 8.1*

51* Sheet of lead or lead alloy with decoration on both faces. L. 45mm. *54/162; SF239; Period 8.1*

52 Stud or rivet of copper alloy with ball-head and collar. Found with washer and tiny perforated strip, both of which may belong with it. L. of stud 11mm; diam. of washer 11mm. *77/578; SF804; Period 1-4*

53 Pair of small rectangular plates of copper alloy with central perforation. A fragment of thin ?leather remains between the plates. Plates such as these were used either as belt mounts or could be used as book fastenings, attached to the end of a strap and with the central perforation fitting over a small knop. L.16mm. *54/169; SF452; Period 7.5*

54* Book clasp of copper alloy with flared end, incised and traced decoration. Rivet and back plate probably of iron. The type dates from the 16th or 17th century. L.37mm. *54/431; SF911; Period 6.1*

55* Possibly a hinge from a book binding or casket of copper alloy, or a buckle plate. Ends cut to a point and there is an eccentrically placed dome-headed rivet; possible perforation in other section. Folded length 32mm. *54/97; SF1999; Period 7.7*

56 Fine binding strip of copper alloy, folded longitudinally to fit over an edge. One face has stamped or rouletted decoration and possibly decorative plating. L. *c.* 100mm. *54/113; SF41; Period 8.1*

57 Pointed lead object, possibly a stylus or pencil. L.70mm. *54/516; SF1220; Period 6.3*

58 Lead object, possibly used as a pencil or stylus. One end has been rolled to a point, the other is broader and flattened. L. 85mm. *77/668; SF1515; Period 1-5*

59* Probably the hinge and bow of a pair of dividers of copper alloy. L. 85mm. *54/247; SF2027; Period 7.4*

It is observed in *Opgravingen in Amsterdam* (1977, 476-7) that metal jews' harps are found in Europe from the end of the 12th century but that there is no typological development to be observed. This means that it is not possible to date individual examples. Number 60 was in an early 19th-century context, but others have been recovered from earlier contexts within the village, for example an iron one from Area 6 (Goodall, A. 1979, fig. 63, no. 83). Other examples in iron were recovered from the North Glebe Terrace, see Chapter 22.

Number 61 is a plate from a mouth organ. It consists of copper reeds of different lengths riveted onto alternate sides of a slotted plate; the varying lengths of the reeds give the different notes and having reeds on both sides of the plate means that the note sounds as air is either blown or sucked through the instrument. Archive 255, 258 and

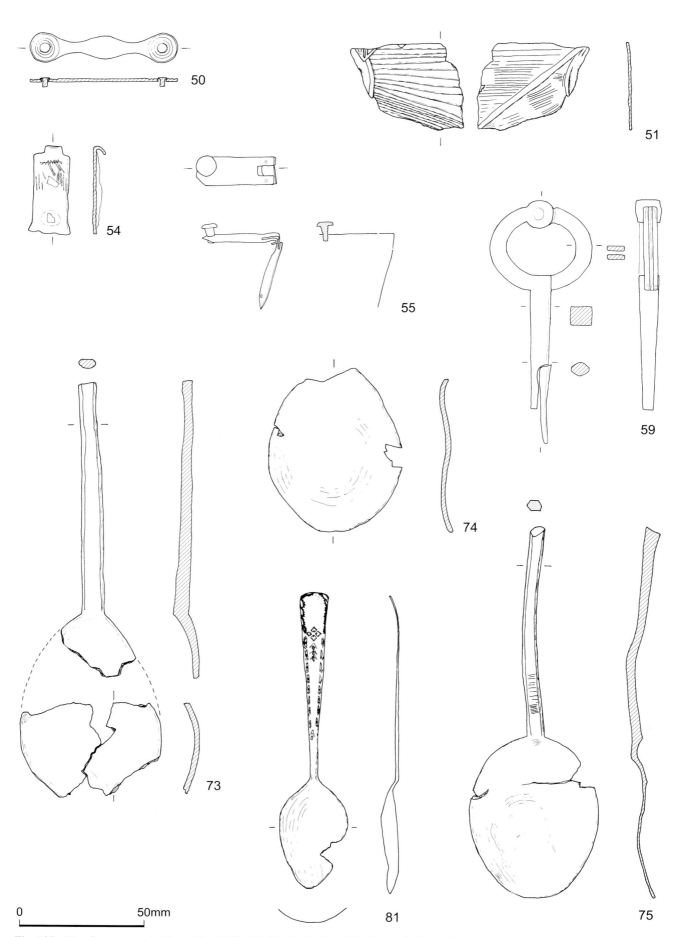

0   50mm

Fig. 107. Non-ferrous metal objects Nos 50-51, 54-55, 59, 73-5 and 81. Scale 2:3 (E. Marlow-Mann)

259 are all further fragments, at least one of which may be from the same instrument. The mouth organ was invented around 1825, but as these fragments were all in late contexts around the cottages, they may have been used at any period of occupation.

Two other plates (Archive 256 and 257) have, or have had, reeds on one side only and are more likely to be from a harmonium. These small keyboard instruments were frequently used instead of organs in churches; it is known that there was one in St Martin's Church in the late 19th century (*Wharram 1*, 37), a possible source for these fragments. They bring to mind the occasion in Thomas Hardy's novel, *Under the Greenwood Tree*, published in 1872, when a harmonium is introduced to Mellstock Church replacing the gallery Choir.

Farmstead

60   Jews' harp of copper alloy, iron reed missing. L. 54mm. *74/297; SF786; Period 4*

61   Plate of copper alloy from the inside of a mouth organ. *49A/78; SF181; unphased*

Objects associated with food preparation and consumption (Fig. 107 and 108)

The spoons and forks include pieces of late 19th and early to mid-20th-century electroplate, and nickel and Argentia silver. Some of these, especially those from late contexts around the cottages, were probably used by the inhabitants of the cottages or might be 'unfashionable' items brought to the site later in the 20th century for the excavators' personal use. Among those associated with the earlier vicarage are pewter spoons, of which some with fig-shaped bowls, (Nos 72-4), are likely to date from pre-1600. Number 75, with a slip-top and rounder bowl is of early or mid-17th-century date. Two silver spoons (Nos 79 and 80), presumably lost by accident, suggest some available wealth in the vicarage during the 18th century. The Sheffield plate teaspoons, together with the bone-handled fork No. 29 (Chapter 23), suggest a different picture. Sheffield plate, only available as sheet metal, was far from ideal for making spoons, resulting in an inferior product to those in silver. The fork is another cheap version of a high-quality object being made at an early stage in the history of forks. The authors are grateful to Professor McNeill Alexander for identifying these objects and for his comments which form the basis of this catalogue and discussion.

Farmstead

62   Sheffield plate teaspoon, *c.*1800. The handle is plain as on No. 82 (77/114/2412), not ornamented like No. 81 (54/5/18). L. 129mm. *74/9000; SF2083; unstratified*

63   Handle of electroplated Old English pattern dessertspoon marked T.Wilson/Sheffield. Thomas Wilson made electroplate from 1889 to 1910 (Matheau-Raven 1997) L. 90mm. *74/9000; SF1738; unstratified*

64   Fiddle pattern teaspoon, electroplated. Marks illegible but their format (a row of small punches resembling hallmarks) suggests the late 19th or 20th century. L. 135mm. *74/9000; SF1743; unstratified*

65   Electroplated Old English pattern teaspoon marked 'J Lodge Ltd EPNS/Sheffield England'. James Lodge made electroplate from 1900 to 1911 (Matheau-Raven 1997). L. 131mm. *51/201; SF969; unphased*

66   Electroplated dessertspoon, Hanoverian rat tail pattern. This is a revival of an early 18th-century pattern. It was available in electroplate at least from about 1885 (Silber and Fleming's catalogue) to 1936 (Army and Navy Stores' catalogue). Marked EPNS followed by indecipherable device in a shield. Engraved owner's initial 'R'. From the styles of the mark and engraved initial probably made between the two World Wars. L. 172mm. *49/500; SF57; Period 3*

67   Fiddle pattern dessert fork in nickel silver by William Page of Birmingham. Confusingly, the mark includes a crown (forbidden from 1897), but the mark is more like the one Page used on electroplate from 1897 than the one he had used previously. *Circa* 1890s. The front of the handle is marked with a name that seems to be W. HOL, once right way up and once inverted. L. 165mm. *51/1; SF970; unphased*

68   Nickel silver teaspoon, fiddle pattern with a shield instead of the usual drop on the back of the bowl. Marked 'Argentina silver', with a monogram JG in a shield. By John Gilbert of Birmingham, who was making 'Argentina silver' in the late 1890s or soon after. Late Victorian or Edwardian. L. 135mm. *74/9000; SF1739; unstratified*

69   Lower part of handle of fiddle pattern teaspoon. There are no marks on this fragment. Probably nickel silver, late 19th or early 20th-century. L. 52mm. *49/2; SF47; Period 3*

70   Bowl of nickel silver tablespoon. L. 77mm. *74/341; SF1507; Period 1*

71   Handle of dessertspoon or fork of copper alloy. Owner's initials TM or IM (Roman capitals with serifs). L. 77mm. *74/349; SF1428; Period 4?*

Vicarage

72   Fragment of fig-shaped pewter (?) spoon bowl. Probably pre-1600 as spoon bowls became progressively rounder and less fig-shaped. L. 54mm. *54/202; SF1867; Period 7.5*

73*   Pewter spoon with markedly fig-shaped bowl, which suggests 16th-century. Top end of handle damaged and shape not ascertainable. L. *c.* 170mm. *54/394; SF836; Period 5.3*

74*   Fig-shaped spoon bowl, probably pewter and before 1600. L. 67mm. *54/452; SF1082; Period 5.2*

75*   Pewter slip-top spoon with a near round bowl that suggests a late date (or has the severe flattening made it rounder than it was?). The earliest known silver slip-top spoon has a 1487 hall-mark, but most silver examples are 17th-century. Early or mid-17th-century. L. 153mm. *54/393; SF790; Period 5.3*

76   Pewter rod, possibly the handle of a spoon of the 17th century or earlier. L. 103mm. *54/394; SF837; Period 5.3*

77   End of handle of Dog-nosed tablespoon. Pewter (?). This pattern was fashionable around 1700-1720, but pewter spoons may perhaps have lagged behind the fashions. L. 73mm. *54/516; SF1298; Period 6.3*

78   Fragment of teaspoon-sized pewter spoon. Snodin (1974) suggests that some very small early spoons may be egg spoons; he quotes the mention of 'a little spoon for eggs' in Agnes Paston's inventory of 1479. L. 70mm. *54/111; SF81; Period 8.1*

79   Silver tablespoon, Hanoverian shell back. London, 1762, by Thompson Davis. Engraved initials FP on back. The shell on the back is little-worn and the spoon may have gone out of use before the fashion changed (in the late 18th and 19th centuries) from laying spoons on the table bowl-down, to laying them bowl-up. L. 207mm. *54/5; SF16; Period 8.1*

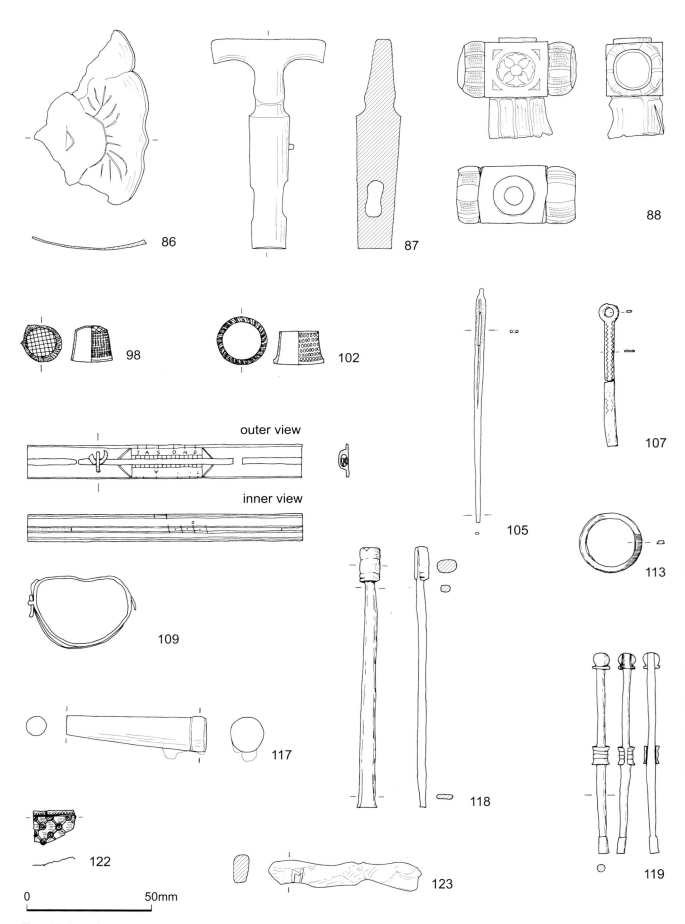

outer view

inner view

Fig. 108. Non-ferrous metal objects Nos 86-88, 98, 102, 105, 107, 109, 113, 117-119 and 122-3. Scale 2:3 (E. Marlow-Mann)

0   50mm

80 Silver teaspoon, Hanovarian scroll back. Bottom-marked with the lion passant and maker's mark only (no date letter). Mid-18th-century to about 1785 when the assay officers changed to top marking. The maker's mark is TW, probably either Thomas Wynne (mark entered 1754) or Thomas Wallis (entered 1778), both of London. Engraved initial F on back. L. 125mm. *54/5; SF17; Period 8.1*

81* Sheffield plate teaspoon, Old English pattern. Neo-classical ornament stamped on the handle. No marks. Most similarly ornamented silver teaspoons date from 1780 to 1800; this spoon is likely to have the same date range. Crudely constructed. L. 120mm. *54/5; SF18; Period 8.1*

82 Sheffield plate teaspoon, Old English pattern, probably made between 1780 and 1810. Undecorated handle. L. 120mm. *77/114; SF2412; Period 6*

83 Dessert fork, Old English pattern, nickel silver. Probably late 19th or early 20th-century. *54/1; SF2657; Period 8.4*

84 Fiddle pattern teaspoon, nickel silver (possibly EPNS) by William Page, Birmingham after 1897 when the inclusion of a crown in marks on electroplate was forbidden, and like other cutlery manufactures, Page was obliged to change his marks. L. 135mm. *77/1; SF2417; Period 6*

85 Handle fiddle pattern teaspoon, 'Argentina silver'. Late 19th-century. L.102mm. *77/86/K7; SF2416; Period 5.2*

Plates are only represented by a small section of a decorated pewter rim (No. 86), although other fragments of pewter sheet (Archive 260-63) may also be from them. The cooking vessel, No. 89, was found in a 16th-century and earlier context, and the other (No. 90) in a later context in the barn. Number 91 is a patch of a type used from the medieval period onwards. Tap No. 87 was recovered from a late 17th-century context; the possible tap fitting, No. 88, was found near a drinking trough at the north end of the cottage garden, but may have originated in the church.

Farmstead
86* Part of the rim of a pewter or tin plate. The edge is ornamentally shaped, and there is incised decoration on the upper surface. L. 73mm. *49/21; SF42; Period 2*

87* Heavy tap of copper alloy with T-shaped handle, probably from a barrel. The opening is dumb-bell shaped and there is a rivet above it which may have restricted the movement of the tap. L. 86mm. *74/294; SF921; Period 2*

88* Heavy cast fitting, possibly from a tap. Cube-shaped, decorated on two faces in 'Gothic' style with a cross 'flory' within a circle. The other faces have openings decorated with leaf and bark motifs. 45 x 42mm. *55/46; SF34; unstratified*

Vicarage
89 Possible rim fragment from a cast copper-alloy cooking vessel. L. 48mm. *54/588; SF1363: Period 4.1*

90 Rim fragment from a cast copper-alloy cooking vessel. The rim is everted and there is heavy sooting on the outer surface. W. 42mm; ht 35mm. *77/1; SF2290; Period 6*

91 Rivet of type used to patch and mend sheet metal vessels, made from folded sheet copper alloy. L. 31mm. *54/202; SF1983; Period 7.5*

Weights (Nos 92-97, Archive 271 and 272) are likely to have had uses other than in the kitchen.

Farmstead
92 Disc-shaped lead weight with chamfered edge. D.35mm. Weight <50g. *51/201; SF521; unphased*

93 Solid pointed object of copper alloy with two grooves cut round broader end. The narrow end is incomplete. Possibly a weight, or a handle. L. 65mm; diam. 8-11mm. *73/1; SF192; Period 3*

Vicarage
94 Lead oval, probably a weight. Possible traces of decoration or moulding. L. 40mm. *54/5; SF7; Period 8.1*

95 Pierced lead disc. Probably a weight. Diam. 22mm. *54/5; SF9; Period 8.1*

96 Lead weight or spindlewhorl. Slightly dome-shaped. Diam. 25-28mm; diam. of hole *c*.13mm. *54/202; SF455; Period 7.5*

97 Rectangular lead plate, probably a weight. 35 x 26mm. *54/516; SF1448; Period 6.3*

Objects associated with sewing (Fig. 108)

In the 17th century, English thimbles were tall and cylindrical and were usually made in two parts. The indentations on the sides and tops were arranged in patterns of small circles or waffles. Towards the end of the century thimbles became shorter and rounder (McConnel 1995, 25-27). In 1769 however, a machine was patented which allowed raised patterns to be formed on sheet metal by pressing it between dies. This meant that far more decorative thimbles could be produced. The thimbles from the farmhouse and vicarage (Nos 98-103 and Archive 273-281) appear to be of the earlier type and are likely to date from the 17th and 18th centuries. Thimbles similar to Nos 102 and 103, often referred to as tailors' thimbles, are illustrated by Rath (1979, 125-6), who dates them to *c*.1900, although No. 102 is from an 18th-century context; their presence suggests that some heavy sewing was undertaken.

Farmstead
98* Thimble of copper alloy. Small with very small regular indentations on the sides, hatched indentations on the crown. Thickened or rolled edge. Ht 14mm. *74/319; SF1443; Period 2*

99 Thimble of copper alloy. Rows of small regular indentations on sides, hatched indentations on crown. Thickened or rolled edge. Ht 20mm. *74/341; SF1626; Period 1*

Vicarage
100 Thimble of copper alloy. Small, child's size, with small regular indentations on sides and hatched indentations on crown. Thickened or rolled edge. Ht 14mm. *54/4; SF1941; Period 8.4*

101 Thimble of copper alloy. Machine-stamped indentations on sides, hatched indentations on top. Rebate between sides and top; plain strip around lower edge outlined by two raised ridges. Ht 24mm. *54/308; SF612; Period 7.3*

102* Open-topped tailor's thimble of copper alloy. Large indentations, thickened edge. Diam. 20mm. *54/127; SF44; Period 7.1*

103 Open-topped tailor's thimble of copper alloy. Made from thin metal, split down one side. Small indentations above a plain strip with two raised ridges. Ht 16.5mm. *54/300; SF427; unstratified*

More than 440 pins (Archive 282-679) were recovered from the North Glebe sites, just over 50% of them coming from the farmhouse.

With exception of No. 104 which might be medieval, the pins are of one type, having heads made from coils of fine wire which have been stamped in a die; this has the double effect of securing the head firmly to the shaft, and of creating a globular-shaped head. This method of manufacture was used widely throughout the post-medieval period, from the mid-17th century onwards. Many of the pins have white metal plating. Most of the complete pins are between 18 - 38mm long; five (Archive 285, 524, 567, 595 and 641) are longer, measuring between 42 and 51mm. It is noticeable that a few are more slender than is the norm.

Seventy-nine per cent of the pins found on Site 74 were in contexts 74/314 and 74/341, beneath the floor of the parlour area of the farmhouse, their distribution following the lines of the floorboards where they fell between the boards. This provides evidence for the ways in which different parts of the house were used, and suggests that the parlour was the room where the women sat sewing. Despite the large number of pins found in these contexts, no needles were found with them. The large bodkin-like object, No. 105, from a 17th-century context in the vicarage, may in fact have been used as a head-dress or hair pin (Margeson 1993, 8-9, pls II and III, fig. 4, nos 21-23) rather than for sewing. The smaller pins had many uses, for instance in costume, in dressmaking, or for holding papers together.

Farmstead

104 Coiled and stamped head. L. 86+mm. *74/208; SF360; Period 6*

Vicarage

105* Long needle or bodkin. Elongated eye set in a very long gutter containing traces of white metal plating. Transverse notched decoration on one face at upper end of head. Flattened cross section. L. 96mm. *54/516; SF1339; Period 6.3*

Objects associated with furniture and fittings to buildings (Fig. 108)

Another group of objects relate to the fittings and furniture within the buildings. As with other groups, many were found in late contexts and it is difficult to know which period of occupation they originate from; not all, therefore, are discussed here, although all have been catalogued.

The binding strip, No. 107, may be from a small box or casket from the vicarage; lock plates, handles, hinges, upholstery tacks (two of which appear to have fallen through the floorboards in the farmhouse parlour – see pins above) and a knob from a brass bedstead (Nos 106, 108, Archive 680 and 701-707) are reminders of the wide range of furnishings likely to have been present in both households. The only evidence for lighting the buildings is the decorated base of a metal, possibly tin, candlestick (Archive 710) and parts from four lamps (Archive 708, 709, 711 and 712); they were all found in the area around the cottages and likely to relate to 20th-century occupation.

Farmstead

106 Small keyhole escutcheon with rivet at top and bottom, copper-alloy. Probably from a drawer or other piece of furniture. Possibly 19th-century. L. 24mm. *74/9000; SF1716; unstratified*

Vicarage

107* Fragment of pewter or lead-alloy. Possibly a binding strip from a small box or casket. Ring terminal at one end. One face has a double row of raised zig-zag lines. L. 68mm. *54/113; SF192; Period 8.1*

108 Small ring handle from furniture, with attachment loop and remains of iron stud. Diam. of ring 30mm, overall L. 49mm. *54/11; SF2005; Period 8.2*

Cogwheels and parts of cases from clocks and watches (Archive 741-46), all from late contexts, indicate a society more aware of timekeeping than in earlier periods; see Chapter 22, No. 112 for a small iron key from a clock. The pocket sundial (No. 109) could date from as early as the late 17th century, but the type is known to have been used into the 18th century.

Farmstead

109* Pocket sundial. Annular with an iron suspension loop but now distorted. It operated by the sun's rays passing through a slot to fall on a calibrated scale on the inside of the ring. A number of ring dials of this type are known, including a metal detector find from Lincolnshire, found associated with late 17th-century pottery. D.38mm. *49/26; SF6; Period 2*

A fragment of metal grille and two door knobs (Archive 698-700) are from the cottages, as is a small knurled knob, Archive 747, which is likely to have come from a window fitting.

The presence of fragments of lead window cames (No. 110 and Archive 748-866) and lead ties (Nos 111 and 112), which held the panes in place, indicates glazed windows in both the vicarage and farmhouse (see Chapter 22 for iron fitments from windows). The fragments of H-sectioned window came fall broadly into two categories, although some of the pieces are too small or poorly preserved to be confident of the identification. Leads of the first type are made by casting, and the flanges which hold the glass in place are relatively narrow and plain. Cames of the second type are made by drawing the lead through a mill. The flanges of this latter type are broader and may have raised edges and ribs along the centre; the web between the flanges sometimes has transverse ridges. Many of those recovered from the vicarage are of this second post-medieval type. The process of manufacture is shown in Diderot (1772). Given the known movement of soil at Wharram, it is possible that some of the fragments, particularly those from around the vicarage area, originated from the church. The 118 fragments recovered, 29% from Site 74 and 58% from Site 54, were mainly in 17th-century and later contexts, making this less likely. In the farmhouse the cames were predominantly in Period 3; 19% were in Periods 1 and 2, and only a small amount found in later and unstratified contexts. On Site 54 virtually all the fragments were in Periods 6-8, with a very few in Period 5. It would appear that leaded windows, with rectangular or diamond-shaped panes, were introduced into both buildings sometime in the 17th century.

Farmstead

110 Fragment of lead cames and glass from diamond-paned window. L. of one side of pane *c*. 80mm (3ins). Another surrounding triangular pane, probably from edge of window, 45 x 55 x 40mm. Various other fragments of window lead and small fragments of glass. Width of leads 6mm. *74/299; SF926; Period 3*

Vicarage

111 Lead window tie, narrow, rectangular sectioned. It was used to tie the window onto the horizontal iron bars that supported it. *54/182; SF1856; Period 7.1*

112 Fragment of lead. Might be from window tie or window lead. *77/9000; SF761; unstratified*

A fragment of small-linked chain, and discs, washers and wire (Archive 681, 682-97 and 867-83) might have been used in various ways. A number of lengths of fine wire, some tightly coiled, others loosely folded and twisted, some of which were found with the pins and other objects under the floorboards of the farmhouse parlour, are likely to have had domestic use, possibly even in garments. Fine wire was also used in hair styling at some periods.

The rings (Archive 713-36) could have had many uses; Archive 716, from the farmhouse, might be a finger ring, and Archive 723, also from the farmhouse, a flat ring with broad section might be a decorative band. A group of twelve hexagonal-sectioned curtain rings (No. 113, Archive 727, 730A-E and 732-6) came from Period 7 and 8 contexts in Site 54, although two from the farmhouse (Archive 718 and 722) may have had the same use. They are similar to those found in a 17th-century well in Lincoln (Egan 2008, 25, no. 63).

113* Ring. Irregular and flattish section. File marks. Diam. 25mm. *54/111; SF35; Period 8.1*

Miscellaneous and unidentified objects

(Fig. 108)

The function of the two tubes, Nos 114 and 117, is uncertain, although the latter may be the handle to a tanged object. Most other objects of unknown use (Archive 884-918) are from pre-19th-century contexts; they include a lead bar (No. 115), and three copper-alloy objects of sufficient interest to be published (Nos 116, 118 and 119). The heavy, lead inside of a flat-iron (Archive 891), found in the garden north of the cottages, was probably used by the last inhabitants who left before electricity was installed.

Farmstead

114 Large tapering tube of copper alloy. L.41mm. *73/1; SF189; Period 3*

115 Round-sectioned lead bar. L. 57mm. *74/106; SF1832; Period 3*

116 Approximately T-shaped object resembling an angular jews' harp or a buckle frame. The incomplete prongs are square, rather than the diamond shape more usually found on a harp, and are not central to the frame. Fragmentary remains attached to it could represent the reed of a jews' harp or a buckle pin. W. 49mm. *74/360; SF1603; Period 1*

Vicarage

117* Possible handle. Tapering, cylinder of copper alloy. Broader end defined by a slight moulding and closed with a flat plate. Remains of iron tang at narrower end. L. 55mm. *54/21; SF2003; Period 7.7*

118* Incomplete spatula-like object of copper alloy. Cast with a collar (L. 14mm) at one end. The other end broadens out slightly but is broken. Total l. 107mm. *77/84; SF2287; Period 5.1/5.2*

119* Spindle-like object of copper alloy, with a knop at one end, and a collar in the middle made from a separate strip. A longitudinal seam suggests that the shaft may have been made by rolling or drawing a rectangular strip through a block. There may have been a second knop at the other end. L. 82mm. *77/324; SF339; Period 3-5*

Objects connected with shooting

Apart from two lead musket balls (No. 120), the only items representing shooting are numerous ends from the cartridge cases which are found all over the village.

Vicarage

120 Two lead musket balls, slightly irregular in form. Diam. 13mm and 10.5mm. *54/1; SF1888; Period 8.4*

Sheet, strip and other fragments (Fig. 108)

In addition to three decorated fragments (Nos 121, 122 and 124), pieces of sheet and strip, including lead, copper and other alloys, were found on both areas, and in all phases (Archive 946-1030). Two (Archive 953 and 954) have regular, circular shapes cut from them and may be the waste from making buttons or studs. Five fragments of strip, of which four are of lead, and some lead spillage fragments were found in medieval contexts in the vicarage and barn. Other fragments of metalworking waste (Archive 1031-1057), both lead and copper, were recovered from both sites, including No. 123 which appears to be a bar or ingot with the letter 'M' cast into it.

Farmstead

121 Sheet fragment. One edge is folded over and is decorated with fine ridges and a line of pellets or cable. L. 32mm. *49/26; SF52; Period 2*

122* Fragment of sheet with die-stamped decoration. Probably 19th or 20th-century. L. 17mm. *73/103; SF12; Period 2*

123* Irregular, rectangular/oval sectioned lead bar or ingot, partly fused at one end. At other end is what appears to be a letter 'M' cast into the bar. L. 60mm. *49A/75; SF59; Period 2*

Vicarage

124 Sheet fragment. Scored lines may be incidental or may be part of simple decoration. L. 35mm. *54/1; SF2637; Period 8.4*

22 Iron Objects
by E.A. Clark and I.H. Goodall, with a note on the nails by J.G. Watt

The iron recovered from the North Glebe Terrace sites forms the largest assemblage of iron objects from the village, some 1600 items excluding the nails. Not all have been X-rayed, but all have been catalogued, many by the late Ian Goodall who was part way through the work when he became ill. The authors are grateful to Professor R. McNeill Alexander for examining the cutlery; his comments are in italics after the catalogue entry. Some of the objects from the area around the farmhouse and cottages relate to the late 19th and 20th-century occupation of the latter, including occupation by the excavation team. The form of many iron objects changed little over long periods and, as residuality is high on these sites, dating individual objects is often difficult. Only selected objects are catalogued here, but the full catalogue forms part of the site archive.

Personal and leisure objects (Fig. 109)

Patten rings, found in unphased and 19th-century contexts around both buildings (Nos 1-4), are similar to others found in the village. These iron rings, used to keep the wearer's shoes and garments out of the mud, appear to have replaced pattens of wood and/or leather from about the 17th century. Fragments of iron used to protect the heels and toes of shoes and boots were frequent finds, especially around the farmhouse, the earliest being three from the vicarage in 18th-century contexts (Archive 117-150).

Farmstead
1   Patten ring. Near complete. Overall l. 207+mm; ring 122 x 104mm; section 4 x 9mm. *15/8; SF8; unphased*

2   Patten ring. Distorted oval. Two terminals. L. 145mm. *49/514; SF112; Period 3*

3   Patten ring. One fastening missing. L. of ring 134mm. *74/125; SF1926; Period 6*

Vicarage
4*   Patten ring. Oval, broken and distorted. One terminal has broken off and has narrow tail-like extension and one hole for attachment; the attached terminal may have had a similar extension and has two holes for attachment. Small, possibly for a child. Ring, oval *c.* 105 x 70mm. *54/1; SF2356; Period 8.4*

Footwear is otherwise only represented by the buckles that ornamented shoes and boots (Nos 5-11). Number 11 is similar to other small annular buckles in both iron and copper alloy found in the village and is likely to be medieval.

Two spur buckles (Nos 12 and 13) were found in 18th-century contexts in the vicarage, where a spur (Archive 1153) was also found.

Farmstead
5*   Shoe buckle. Thin, with C-section frame. Semi-circle forms D-shape with central bar which also forms one side of a square second section. Short integral tongue on curved side. W. 36mm; ht 33-28mm. *51/2; SF707; unphased*

6*   Shoe buckle, distorted. Two spikes and pitch-fork double tongue. 18th-century. W. 59mm; ht 53mm. *51/586; SF165; Period 2.3*

7   Shoe buckle. Square. Two pins on inserted centre bar. 16mm. *49/501; SF23; Period 3*

8   Shoe buckle. Rectangular. Thin metal. Bent. Sheet cylinder on frame. Pin, formed from sheet, on central bar. W. 30mm; ht 25-23mm. *51/100; SF696; unphased*

9   Shoe buckle. Circular. Fragment of pin. Diam. 17mm. *51/548; SF176; Period 2.1*

Vicarage
10*   Shoe buckle. Trumpet-shaped. Pin, broken, attached to narrow side. Narrow side ?rolled to take straight rod which projects each end. W. 24mm; ht 31-28mm. *54/269; SF508; Period 7.4*

11*   Shoe buckle. Annular. Probably medieval. Diam. 15mm. *54/415; SF902; Period 5.3*

12*   Buckle, possibly for spur. Post-medieval. Waisted at centre, ends wide and flattened. Central, very slender bar, h. 12mm, with narrow strap attached by two loops, one broken. W. 25mm; max. ht 16mm. *54/357; SF2558; Period 7.3*

13*   Buckle, from spur or strap. Rectangular. Pin on central bar. W. 31mm; ht 20mm. *54/357; SF2557; Period 7.3*

Among the other buckles recovered (Nos 14-18 and Archive 151-83), the earliest from 16th and 17th-century contexts, some will have had personal uses, although some of the larger ones, for example Nos 16 and 17, are likely to have been used on harness. The majority from both areas are square or rectangular, although there is at least one example each of annular and trapezoidal buckles. Many have central pin bars, and a few have rolling cylinders on one side of the frame. Archive 183 is a buckle pin and 165 is a strap fastener and probably modern. See Chapter 21 for buckles, including shoe buckles, in non-ferrous metals.

Farmstead
14*   Buckle. D-shaped. W. 40mm; ht 48-44mm. *51/264; SF7; Period ER-3*

15*   Buckle. Rectangular. W. 30mm; ht 40mm. *74/106; SF702; Period 3*

16   Buckle. Square. W. 47mm; ht 47mm; diam. of cross-section and bar 6mm. Centre bar set back from frame. *51/100; SF794; unphased*

Vicarage
17   Buckle frame. D-shaped. W. 45mm; ht *c.* 60mm. *54/170; SF2498; Period 7.6*

18*   Buckle. Rectangular. Broken. Possibly silvered. W. *c.* 40mm; ht 56-50mm. *54/96; SF2458; Period 7.8*

Other objects relating to the personal lives of the inhabitants are a thin ring (No. 19) of a suitable size to be a finger ring, found among the farm buildings, and, from the vicarage, a small button (No. 20) possibly late medieval in date, and an object which resembles a belt hook (No. 21). Number 22 may be a pair of dividers, the only iron object suggesting literacy. See Chapter 21, No. 59 for a pair of copper-alloy dividers.

Farmstead
19   Ring. Slight and broken. Possibly a finger ring. Diam. 12mm. *51/406; SF889; unphased*

Vicarage
20*   Fragment of spherical object with copper-alloy loop; probably a button. Remaining diam. 13mm. Possibly plated. *54/320; SF576; Period 6.3*

21*   Possible belt hook. Overall l. 55mm; h. of belt slit *c.*13mm. *77/132/G6; SF63; Period 5.2*

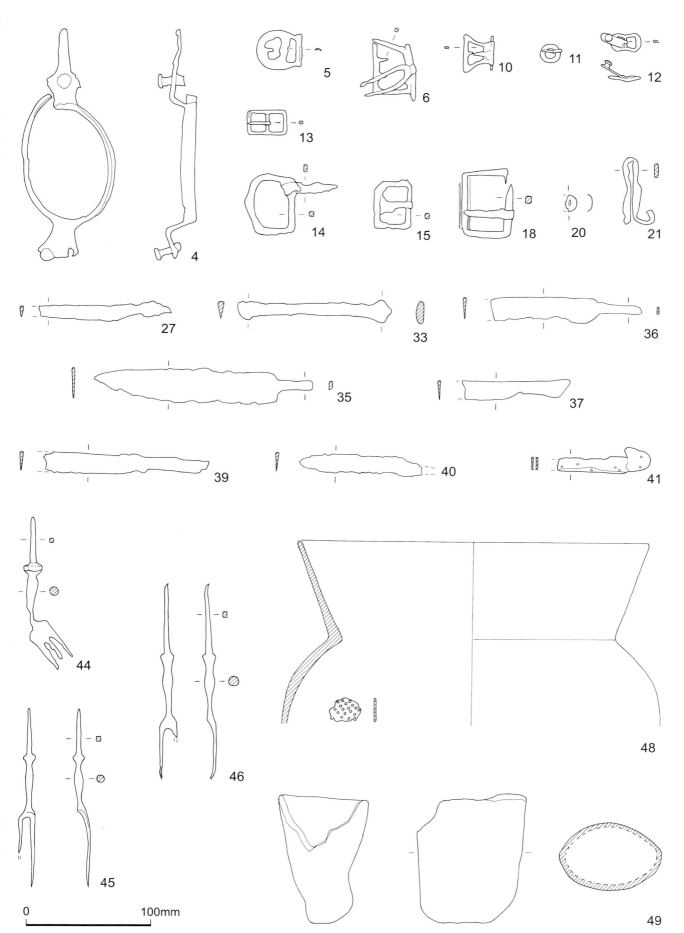

Fig. 109. Iron objects Nos 4-6, 10-15, 18, 20-21, 27, 33, 35-7, 39-41 44-6 and 48-9. Scale 1:3. (C. Philo)

22 Two arms, one pointed, at right angle; appear to be joined. Possibly a pair of dividers or could be part of staple. L. of arms 80+mm and 60+mm. *54/260; SF477; Period 6.3*

Jew's harps (Nos 23-6) are the only musical items found among the iron objects. A copper-alloy example was also found – see Chapter 21 for discussion of this type of instrument.

Farmstead
23 Jew's harp. Reed missing. Angular-shaped frame and section. L. 88; w. 52mm; section 9mm. *49/21; SF143; Period 2*

24 Probably a Jew's harp. Tongue missing L. 63mm. *51/438; SF19; Period ER-2*

25 Jew's harp. Tongue missing. L. 49mm; w. 30mm. *74/205; SF435; Period 4 or 6*

26 Possibly a Jew's harp. The arms are broken and the tongue missing but the diamond-shaped cross section suggests this is not a staple. *51/548; SF83; Period 2.1*

Objects relating to preparation and eating of food (Fig. 109)

Fifty-seven iron knives, or fragments of knives, were recovered, in addition to those which retain bone handles and are discussed in Chapter 23.

Two, possibly three, blades were recovered from medieval contexts, one from the medieval layers in the north-west corner of Site 51, and two fragments, found together and possibly from the same knife, in the north-west corner of Site 54 (Nos 27 and 34). The rest are from 16th-century and later contexts.

Around 50% of the knives and blades are so fragmentary that it is not possible to establish whether they had whittle or scale-tang handles (No. 34, Archive 193-205 and 217-27). Among those where differentiation is possible, sixteen have whittle tangs (Nos 27-31, 35, 36, Archive 184, 185 and 206-12) and fourteen have the scale-tangs (Nos 32, 37-40, Archive 186-90 and 213-16) which might be expected by the 16th and 17th centuries. A few of the knives have bolsters which became widespread in the second half of the 16th century. The whittle-tang knives without bolsters may be earlier, and see Chapter 23 for a discussion on early scale-tang knives. Number 33 has an integral handle of solid metal.

Folding knives were found in and around both the farmstead (Archive 191 and 192) and vicarage (No. 41) buildings; see Chapter 23, Nos 53-54 for other examples.

Farmstead
27* Knife blade and part of whittle tang. Medieval. L. 105+mm; max. w. of blade 14mm. *51/1036; SF432; Period 1*

28 Knife, with whittle-tang. L. 63+mm; w. of blade 8mm. *49/501; SF107; Period 3*

29 Knife, with substantial whittle tang. L. 133+mm. Blade: l. *c.* 75+mm; max. w. 25mm. *74/109; SF1894; Period 6*

30 Knife, with whittle tang. Fragments of handle remain. Overall l. *c.* 75+mm. Blade: l. mm; w. 20mm. *74/314; SF1059; Period 4*

31 Knife, with substantial whittle tang. *Symmetrical spear-pointed blade. Cowgill et al. (1987) illustrates similar blades from every century from the 12th to the 15th, and it seems likely that they were still made in the 16th century.* L. 143+mm. Blade: l. 72+mm; w. 25mm. *74/9000; SF1949; unstratified*

32 Knife, with bolster and scale tang. Rivet *in situ*. Broken both ends. Blade widens from bolster, straight back, tip tapers to point. L.of tang 27+mm; blade: l. 21+mm; w. at break *c.* 10mm. *74/102; SF760; Period 4*

33* Knife. Solid integral handle, splays at end, then tapers sharply to small knob. Blade broken. L. 122+mm; blade w. 15mm. *51/409; SF16; Period ER-2*

Vicarage
34 Knife blade fragment. L. 29+mm; w. 16mm. Another fragment of blade found with it (*54/603; SF2661*) many be part of the same blade. *54/603; SF2575; Period 4.1*

35* Knife, with whittle tang. *Spear-pointed blade (see No. 31).* Overall l. 172mm. Blade: l. 144mm; w. at shoulder 25mm. *54/31/97; SF2463; unphased*

36* Knife, with whittle tang. *Narrow blade. Late medieval or Tudor.* Overall l. 122+mm. Blade, bent and ?straight end: l. 86+mm; w. 20-18mm. *54/202; SF2521; Period 7.5*

37* Knife, with bolster and short scale tang. Broken. Overall l. 82+mm. Blade: l. 45+mm; w. 14mm. Tang: l. 31+mm; 1 hole. Archive 189 is a similar knife from an unphased context in the farmstead. *54/21; SF2428; Period 7.7*

38 Knife with scale tang. *?Long conical bolster. Very narrow blade. ?Late 16th or early 17th-century.* Overall l. 73+mm. Blade, ?straight end: l. 51mm; w. 11mm. *54/202; SF2523; Period 7.5*

39* Knife. *Scale-tang but no bolster. Slender tapering blade. Late medieval or Tudor.* L. 191+mm; max. w. of blade 14mm. *77/209; SF179; Period 5.1*

40* Knife. *?Scale tang but no bolster. Narrow blade with spear point. Late medieval or Tudor.* Overall l. 99+mm. Blade: l. 80mm; w. *c.* 15mm. *54/1; SF2614; Period 8.4*

41* ?Folding knife in two fragments. L. 75+mm; w. 12mm; th. 6mm. *54/323; SF599; Period 6.1*

42 Shaped object with rounded end and tapering; raised around edge. Part of identical and parallel surface remains. *Sheet iron, stamped with a very regular dimpled pattern and presumably machine made. Possibly the end of the hollow handle of a cheap knife, but not of a type seen before. 54/1; SF2329; Period 8.4*

The remains of forks and a spoon handle are further examples to add to those in non-ferrous alloys and those retaining bone handles (Chapters 21 and 23)

Farmstead
43 Fragment of three-pronged fork. One prong missing. *18th or 19th-century.* L. 60+mm; w. of tines 16mm. *49/78; SF150; unphased*

44* Three-pronged fork, with whittle tang. *Late 18th or 19th-century* L. 132mm; tine w. 19mm. *51/209; SF774; unphased*

Vicarage
45* Two-pronged fork, with whittle tang. *Earlier forks had straight prongs and most later ones had three prongs, so probably mid-18th-century.* Overall l. 149+mm; w. across base of prongs 13mm; l. of intact prong 65mm. *54/17; SF1923; Period 8.1*

46* Two-pronged fork, with whittle tang. *Probably mid-18th-century, as No. 45.* Overall l. 158+mm; tang l. 58+mm; Prongs l. 45+mm; w. 15mm across base of prongs. *54/111; SF58; Period 8.1*

47 Iron spoon handle. *Tinned iron spoons (but of different patterns) were offered (presumably for kitchen use) in Silber and Fleming's catalogue of c.1885 and the Army and Navy Stores one for 1935/6. 19th or 20th-century.* L. 136+mm. *54/1; SF2372; Period 8.4*

Among the twenty-three rim and body fragments from iron and cast-iron vessels recovered from both sites (twelve from the farmhouse, nine from the vicarage; No. 48, Archive 228-39 and 268-75), only No. 48, from a 17th-century context, is large enough to retain evidence of its shape and size. It was found together with fragments of perforated sheet which may have been used with it as some kind of strainer. A few vessel fragments came from 17th and 18th-century contexts. The vessels may have been used in or hung over the fire, or have been suspended by their necks in a furnace. Number 49 may be a distorted vessel; it was found in a post-hole.

Many of the numerous fragments of tins and bottle tops, tin openers and weights (Archive 240-67 and 276-87), including a very fine bull's head tin opener, all recovered from 19th-century and unphased contexts, probably originate from the excavation team's catering, although some may date to the occupation of the cottages.

Vicarage
48* Fragments of cauldron and perforated sheet found with it. W. of largest cauldron fragment 220mm; ht of neck 80mm; internal diam. at top of neck 272mm. *54/395; SF829; Period 5.3*

49* Hollow object. Possibly a vessel. Broken and distorted, oval mouth. 'Rectangular' bag-like body narrows to U or V-shaped base. Very corroded. Ht *c.* 100mm; w. 90 x 65mm. *54/706; SF1513; Period 2.2*

Sewing (Fig. 110)

The essential household task of sewing is represented by pin and/or needle shafts, a possible bodkin and scissors (Nos 50-54 and Archive 288-309). Found in contexts from the 16th to 20th centuries, these complement the copper-alloy pins and thimbles (Chapter 21), although needles seem to be notably absent from both sites. Scissors became more widely used by the mid-17th century. These examples, some of which were found in 16th-century contexts, vary in both size and blade-shape, probably reflecting different uses.

Farmstead
50 Needle shaft and start of eye. L. 20+mm; diam. 1mm. *74/230; SF592; Period 3*

Vicarage
51 Possible bodkin. Long, narrow object with two narrow slits, 10 and 6mm long, along length. L. 48+mm; w. 8mm. *54/111; SF2471; Period 8.1*

52* Scissors. Single blade and loop. L. 134+mm. Blade: l. 60mm; w. 12mm. *54/516; SF1204; Period 6.3*

53* Scissors. Single blade and loop. L. 155mm. Blade: l. 75mm; w. 14mm. Fragment of ?second blade in bag. *54/516; SF1228; Period 6.3*

54* Scissors. One loop missing. Blade l. 92mm; loop 25 x 20mm. *54/516; SF1288; Period 6.3*

Objects relating to heating and lighting
(Fig. 110)

Another small group of objects are those connected to heating and lighting the farm and vicarage buildings. Candlesticks and snuffers (Nos 55 and 56) must have been common household items until electricity was brought to the valley in the 20th century. Shovels and tongs (Nos 57-9 and Archive 327) were necessary pieces of equipment to keep the fires going in the grates which are represented by some 38 fragments of bars and plates (Archive 310-26 and 328-48). Among these, seventeen were recovered from the sites around the cottages in contexts no earlier than the 19th century. Only four are from the farmhouse itself (Site 74) and most probably originate from the later occupation of the cottages. A different picture emerges around the vicarage where almost 50% of the twenty fragments found are from 18th-century contexts and are likely to represent the final phase of the vicarage before demolition.

Farmstead
55 Conical object. ?Candle snuffer. H. 38mm; diam. at base 26mm. *49/2; SF164; Period 3*

Vicarage
56* Candlestick, tanged. L. 78mm; diam. at top of socket 19mm. *77/226; SF177; Period 5.1*

57 Shovel blade. Delicate. Tulip-shaped, with raised rim on both sides. L. 194mm; w. at lip 154mm. Decorative pierced oval in centre of base *c.* 75 x 60mm. *54/1; SF2320; Period 8.4*

58 Arm from pair of tongs. Overall l. 178+mm; cross-section of handle 15 x 6mm; end plate 26 x 21mm. *54/7; SF2314; Period 8.2*

59 Arm from pair of tongs. L. 578+mm; oval end plate 28 x 27mm. *77/86; SF2470; Period 5.2*

Tools relating to building and other crafts, including those of unknown function

The design of tools varies little over time, and although nearly all those found around the farm buildings (Nos 60, 61 and Archive 349-71) are in 19th-century or unphased contexts, some may be contemporary with their occupation rather than from later periods. Apart from a possible jemmy, a screwdriver likely to date from no earlier than the 19th century, and a spanner, these are all types which have been found elsewhere in the village and from earlier periods, including an awl, an axe head, chisels, a file, a leather worker's knife, saw blades, punches and a wedge. Chisel No. 60 is from a late 17th or 18th-century context. The function of four tool-like objects is uncertain, including a curved blade-like object (No. 61) from the farmhouse.

A similar but slightly more restricted range of tools was found in and around the vicarage, with a slightly greater number coming from 16th and 17th-century contexts (Nos 62-8 and Archive 372-86). Among other types of tools found in later contexts are an auger bit and a clamp, as well as a few probable tools of unknown use.

Farmstead

60 Probable chisel blade. One end flat and rounded, the other flattening but broken. L. 104+mm; cross-section in centre 5 x 5mm. *74/106; SF1854; Period 3*

61 Blade-like object. Curved. L. 268+mm; blade w. 18mm; back of blade w. 4mm. *74/103; SF1905; Period 6*

Vicarage

62 Bar, pointed at one end and probably at the other. Probably an awl. L. 80+mm. *77/209; SF181; Period 5.1*

63 Hacksaw. L. 251mm. Blade 6mm deep. *77/86; SF2485; Period 5.2*

64 Hammer, head with metal shaft, broken, through centre. Overall l. 134+mm. Head: one end circular, diam. 20mm; the other broad and flat with two prongs, w. 30mm, but very damaged. *54/452; SF1083; Period 5.2*

65 Saw blade fragment. Expanding at one end. Three teeth per cm. L. 49+mm; w. of blade 23mm. *77/85; SF2438; Period 5.2*

66 Spanner. L. 128mm; w. 32mm; th. 6mm. *77/86; SF2483; Period 5.2*

67 Wedge. L. 45mm; w. 18mm; th. 6mm. *100/2; SF3; unphased*

68 Wedge. L. 53mm; w. 24mm. *77/91; SF15; Period 5.1*

Objects relating to buildings and/or furniture and fittings (Fig. 110)

A large proportion of the iron objects could have been used either in the structure of the buildings and/or in the furniture and fittings within them.

Bars, collars, cramps, plates, spikes, bolts with their roves and nuts, washers and wire have many uses; they have been found in most excavations within the village and from all periods, although the quantities recovered from these sites are greater (Archive 387-425, 458-87, 488-90, 588-99, 634-56, 657-72, 979-88 and 989-1027). Three, a spike and a rove from Site 54 and a washer from Site 51, came from medieval contexts; of the rest, most types appear in contexts from the 16th century onwards.

Nineteen lengths or single links of chain (Archive 439-457) were found around the farm buildings and another six from the vicarage area; a single example (Archive 448) has circular, rather than oval, links. Archive 443 is still attached to a ring-headed staple; another two lengths (Archive 444 and 457) have an S-hook at one end, one with a loop and swivel attached to the hook and a ring at the other; all might have been used in agricultural machinery or to tether animals, although uses in the home, for example to suspend vessels, are also likely. Archive 441 is the chain from an animal trap.

Fourteen lengths of straight or slightly curved iron with circular sections have been catalogued as rods (Archive 619-633); a few have screw threads and/or collars, and one (Archive 621) has an acorn-shaped terminal. The majority of the 88 staples (Archive 673-739) in both areas are U-shaped but six ring-headed and ten rectangular ones were also found. Some of those from the farm area are modern.

Other objects relate more directly to the buildings. A length of cast iron (Archive 491), probably from a gutter, and a bracket (Archive 431) that might have held it, were found behind and in front of the cottages respectively, and are likely to have been used on those buildings.

A group of bars (Nos 69-74) found around the vicarage, with approximately square cross-section (4-8mm) and decorative terminals, the longest having a remaining length of *c*.440mm, are window bars. Another, 445mm long, found on Site 73 (Archive 426), may have originated in the vicarage. Archive 427-9 are terminals which have broken away from bars of this sort or from wall hooks with decorative terminals, such as Nos 74-80 also from the vicarage. Number 81 is a stay used to hold open a window; it is similar to others known to date from the 17th century. The strap with curled end, No. 82, may also have been part of a window fastening.

Vicarage

69 Bar. Oval terminal, with ?hole for attachment, at each end. L. 440mm; cross-section 5 x 4mm. *54/1; SF2597; Period 8.4*

70 Bar. One flattened and shaped end is pierced. L. 288+mm; cross-section 8 x 8mm. *54/5; SF2436; Period 8.1*

71 Bar. Flattened rectangular to oval terminal, with hole for attachment, at each end. L. 405mm; diam. 10mm. *54/5; SF2602; Period 8.1*

72 Bar. Flattened rectangular to shield-shaped terminal at each end with hole for attachment. L. *c*. 410mm; cross-section 5mm square. *54/7; SF2271; Period 8.2*

73 Bar. Distorted. Round terminal, with hole for attachment, at each end, both broken: diam. 30mm. Severe corrosion on section of stem. Overall l. 330+mm; cross-section 10mm square; centre section round, diam. 10mm. *54/9; SF1918; Period 7.8*

74 Bar. Terminal at one end, 16mm wide, expanded and flattened, with hole for attachment. Other end expands. Overall l. *c*. 100+mm; cross-section 6 x 3mm. *54/205; SF354; Period 7.1*

75 Wall hook. Pierced, leaf-shaped terminal at one end (broken). L. 348+mm; section 7 x 7mm. *54/1; SF2339; Period 8.4*

76 Wall hook. Pierced, leaf-shaped terminal at one end. L. 288+mm; section 5 x 5mm. Terminal l. *c*. 60mm; max. w. 20mm. *54/1; SF2340; Period 8.4*

77 Wall hook. Leaf-shaped plate, 27mm high, at right angle to one end. L. 225m; cross-section 9 x 6mm. *54/5; SF2437; Period 8.1*

78 Wall hook. Hooked at one end; bent in opposite direction to right-angle at other end, with ?heart-shaped terminal. L. 410mm; cross-section 8mm square. *54/8; SF2608; Period 8.4*

79 Wall hook. As No. 78. L. 415mm; cross-section 25 x 4mm. *54/8; SF2612; Period 8.4*

80 ?Wall hook. L. 298mm, with additional lower bar. Heart-shaped end plate, ht 34mm. *54/11; SF2485; Period 8.2*

81 Hooked window stay. Two joining fragments, overall l. 208+mm. Right-angled hook at one end, ht 34mm. Bar: cross-section 8 x 4mm, twisted over short section. Broken at fixing end. Similar examples in Hall 2005 (91, fig. 3.60) are dated to the 17th century. *54/462; SF1046; Period 6.3*

82* Strap. At intact end, continues at half the width and curls in on itself. Hole for attachment or turning in full width just before the terminal. Slight C-section. Possible door or window fastener. L. 85+mm; w. 23mm; th. at curled end 8mm. *54/1; SF2388; Period 8.4*

Although the wood from doors into and within the buildings, or from shutters and integral cupboards, has not survived, some items of door furniture have. Handles Nos 83 and 85 are probably both from exterior doors, No. 83 was found near the cottages and may have been used in the farmhouse or associated buildings. Number 85, from the vicarage, lacks its back plate. Latch fasteners such as Nos 86 and 87, may have been on either exterior or interior doors. Doors and shutters, as well as gates, might be hung on pivots (Archive 518-31), and a number of strap fragments (see below) retain, at one end, the curled hinges which may have pivoted on them (e.g. Nos 84 and 88-91). Both the hinge pivot Archive 520 and the strap hinge No. 84 are from a medieval context on Site 51.

Farmstead

83* Upright door handle with expanded ends. Top end is decorative but broken, lower end missing. Handle has round section at both ends, expanding to 16mm square in centre. Thumb plate broken; lifting bar *in situ*. L. 242+mm. Hall (2005, 56, fig. 2.82) illustrates a similar one from Yorkshire dated 1692. *15/6; SF5; unphased*

84* Strap hinge with curled hinge. Overall l. 66+mm; max w. 34mm; w. of hinge 12mm. *51/1040; SF402; Period 1*

Vicarage

85* Upright door handle. Substantial and probably for use with back plate. Centre expands and has three bands. Ends splay out, one flat, the other with short, 3mm, circular rod-like extension. Ht 102mm; d. 53mm. See Hall 2005 (57, fig. 2.83a) for similar handles. *54/1; SF2350; Period 8.4*

86 Latch fastener. L. 103mm; d. of latch 26mm. ?Missing lower bar or curl. See No. 87. *54/5; SF2422; Period 8.1*

87* Latch fastener with additional lower bar. L. 95mm; l. of lower bar *c.* 80mm; d. of latch 19mm. A similar example from Yorkshire in Hall 2005 (59, fig. 2.88) is dated 1654. *54/5; SF2423; Period 8.1*

88 Strap hinge. Curled hinge. L. 112+mm; w. 33mm; w. of hinge 15mm. *54/202; SF2524; Period 7.5*

89 Strap hinge. Possibly complete. Curled hinge. Two holes for attachment. L. 123mm; w. 28mm below hinge to 10mm at rounded end; w. of hinge 18mm. *54/448; SF1006; Period 5.2*

90 Strap hinge. Curled hinge. Shaped strap expands from hinge, narrows and expands again, but terminal is incomplete. Possibly 3 holes for attachment, one with stud remaining. L. 180+mm; max. w. 37mm; diam. of hinge 28mm. *77/86; SF2494; Period 5.2*

91 Strap hinge. Curled hinge. Strap broken. Leaf-shaped terminal expands to 60mm wide, then tapers to hinge. L. 780+mm; w. of strap, 25mm below terminal to 20mm; diam. of hinge 20mm. *77/522; SF834; Period 4*

Another group of objects may have been used on the doors and shutters of the buildings, but also had uses on movable items of furniture, such as chests and cupboards. Studs, straps and brackets, handles, hinges, hasps, and locks and keys, can all still be seen as part of extant furniture. As most of these iron objects were recovered from contexts relating to the demolition phases of the buildings, they are more likely to have come from items fixed within the rooms than from furniture which was probably moved out before demolition.

Twenty-four large studs (Archive 946-70), similar to others found within the village in medieval and later contexts, might have decorated and strengthened doors. They all have approximately square heads, the largest measuring 70mm. Archive 947 is from a medieval context on Site 51; the others, from contexts dating from the 16th century onwards, were found in the farmhouse, farm buildings and the vicarage.

Iron straps and strips make up a substantial proportion of the iron objects in both areas: 16% of all the objects found in the farm buildings (Nos 92, Archive 740-828 and 891-920), and 18% of those around the vicarage and barn (Nos 95-7, Archive 829-90 and 921-45). The largest are about 60mm wide, but most of the straps range between 25 and 40mm. Only very few are sufficiently complete to retain intact ends, but some taper, and a few rounded ends and circular to oval terminals can be identified, the latter being popular in the 17th and 18th centuries. Number 95 is a short but more elaborate strap fitting. Some over-lapping fragments are fastened together with metal studs. Curved examples may have been from barrels. Those less than 15mm wide have been identified as strips and, like the straps only very few retain any detail. Some are D-sectioned rather than flat, and others suggest the possibility of shaping. The brackets (Archive 430-38) are functional rather than decorative.

Handles (Archive 492-504) include both drop-handles and ones with terminals for fixing to a surface. The pinned hinges include three 17th to 18th-century butterfly hinges (Nos 93, 94, and 99) and one plate which might be from an H-hinge (No. 100). Used for lighter doors such as on cupboards and shutters, both the butterfly and H-hinge were common throughout the 17th and 18th centuries (Hall 2005, 53). Other pinned hinges (Archive 505-517) have rectangular plates ranging in height from 110-124mm.

Farmstead

92 Strap. Flat, circular head with hole for attachment, diam. 37mm. Overall l. 230+mm; w. 21 x 16mm. *51/468; SF744; unphased*

93 Butterfly hinge, pinned. One leaf only. Ht 80-45mm; w. 53mm. *51/470; SF768; Period 2.3*

94 Butterfly hinge. Pinned. L. 50mm. Plate: ht *c.* 75-50mm; w. 52mm. *74/210; SF487; Period 6*

Vicarage

95* Fitting. Short strap-type fitting with circular loop at one end; centre expands to circle with hole for attachment; arrow-shaped end also with hole for attachment. Looped end 30 x 25mm. Overall l. 124mm; max. w. 45mm. *54/1; SF2375; Period 8.4*

96 Strap. Expanded oval terminal is incomplete but retains a nail in the hole for attachment. Overall l. 120+mm; w. 25 to 15mm below head. *54/516; SF1338; Period 6.3*

97 Strap fragment. Fragmentary. Tapers to narrow round-ended terminal. One hole for attachment. L. 58+mm; max. w. 14+mm. *77/9000; SF851; unstratified*

98 Strip. Distorted. L. 45+mm; w. 15 but narrows before expanding to fish-tail shaped terminal. *54/260; SF461; Period 6.3*

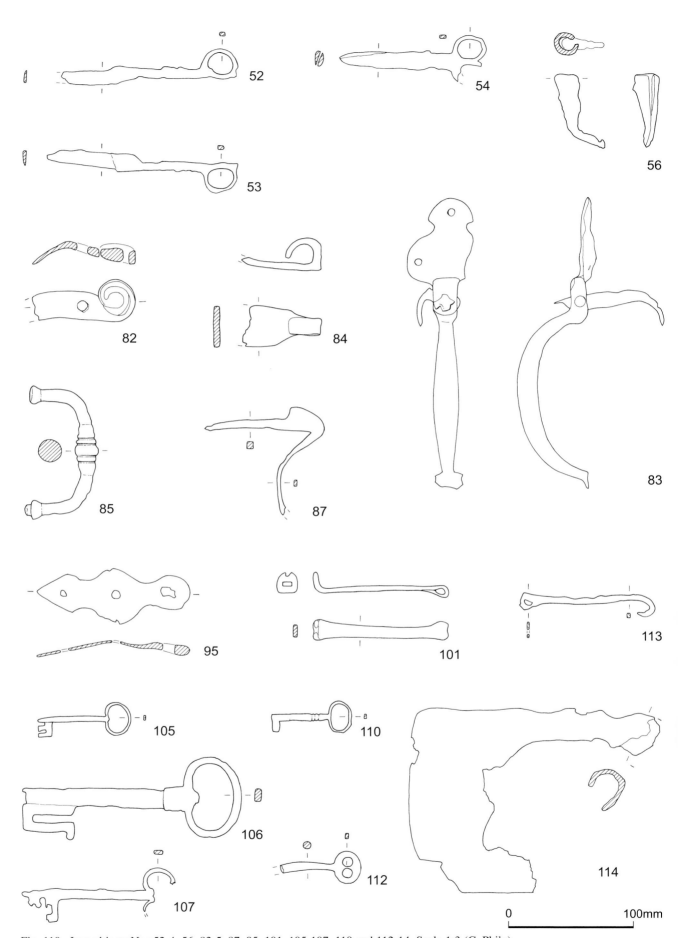

Fig. 110. Iron objects Nos 52-4, 56, 82-5, 87, 95, 101, 105-107, 110 and 112-14. Scale 1:3 (C. Philo)

99 ?Plate from butterfly hinge. Three nails *in situ* and two more holes. Ht 60+-41mm at pin end; w. 39mm. Fragment in same bag, 38+ x 32+mm, might be from second plate. *54/7; SF2041; Period 8.2*

100 Plate possibly from H-hinge. Strap, with nail holes and shaped terminal at one end. L. 190+mm; w. 23mm. 1mm. Rolled hinge on one long edge, l. 31mm; diam. 11mm. *54/1; SF2384; Period 8.4*

Security appears to have been an increasing concern in the post-medieval period as a greater number of locks and keys were found on these sites than elsewhere in the village. Hasps, which have been found throughout the village and in medieval contexts, were probably used on doors and gates as well as chests. Two were recovered from the barn (Nos 102 and 103) where they might have been used to secure enclosures or grain chests.

The earliest object among the locks and keys (Nos 101, 104-112 and Archive 565-83) is a padlock key from the medieval structure on Site 51 (No. 101). Two padlocks were found, one (No. 104) in a 17th to 18th-century context in Site 77, the other, Archive 566 from Site 51, may be modern. A number of the lock fragments come from fitted locks, perhaps from doors as well as chests. Among the nineteen keys, three are from Site 54, (Nos 105-107), and four from Site 77. Those with solid stems are likely to be from doors as they can be used from both sides, whilst those with hollow stems, which fit over a pin and can therefore only be used from one side, are probably for chests or cupboards. A clock key from Site 77 (No. 112) was among those from later and unstratified contexts.

Farmstead
101* Padlock key, complete. L. 407mm. *51/1040; SF404; Period 1*

Vicarage
102 Hasp. Rectangular section. L. 134mm; w. 31-25mm. *77/86; SF2478; Period 5.2*

103 Hasp. In two pieces. Long oval shape, clasped to form two unequal loops. Short tongue at end of longer loop. L. 120mm; max. w. 33mm. *77/653; SF986; Period 2*

104 Box padlock with shackle. Distorted and broken. Overall l. 105+mm; w. of shackle 61mm. *77/154; SF284; Period 5.2*

105* Key. L. 74mm. Solid stem; kidney-shaped bow. Overall l. 74mm; w. of bow 26mm. *54/292; SF512; Period 6.1*

106* Key. Large. Hollow stem; kidney-shaped bow; Overall l. 175mm; w. of bow 67mm. *54/323; SF581; Period 6.1*

107* Key. Solid stem; kidney-shaped bow broken. Overall l. 123+mm. *54/461; SF1026; Period 6.3*

108 Key. Hollow stem with long ward; ring bow. Overall l. 60mm; diam. of bow 19mm. *77/84; SF10; Period 5.2*

109 Key. Solid stem; bow broken. L. 57+mm. *77/233; SF204; Period 5.1*

110* Key. Solid stem with double knop; oval bow. Overall l. 66mm. *54/111; SF89; Period 8.1*

111 Key. Wide, hollow stem; lozenge-shaped bow; narrow ward. Overall l. 93mm. *77/341; SF298; Period 5.2*

112* Clock key. Stem broken. L. 64+mm. *77/9000; SF2477; unstratified*

Hooks might be used for a variety of purposes, both in the houses and farm buildings; seventeen were recovered from each area (Archive 532-564). Eight are simple L-shaped hooks used to fasten, for example, doors, gates and shutters. Number 113 is a more delicate version. Hooks for hanging objects can be divided into those with tangs and those with fixing plates, as well as S-hooks for suspension from a bar.

Swivels, and rings with diameters of 14-84mm, also had a wide variety of uses both in buildings and as part of domestic and agricultural equipment – see Chapter 21, for rings of copper alloy. The wheeled castors, found around the farmhouse (Archive 584 and 585), probably originated from chairs which were discarded when broken. Archive 587 is part of an iron bedstead from the vicarage; see Chapter 21 for the knob from a 'brass' bedstead found near the cottages.

A substantial tap (Archive 586), found near to a spring mouth close to the cottages, may have been part of the arrangements for collecting water. It is known that water was obtained there by the inhabitants of the cottages.

Vicarage
113* Hook. Long shank with expanded, triangular end, perforated for attachment. Delicate. Curled hook. L. 107mm; bar 5 x 2mm. *54/158; SF2510; Period 7.7*

Objects relating to crop and animal husbandry (Fig. 110)

The range of tools adds some new types to those previously recorded from the village. A plough share and nine parts from animal traps found around the farmhouse, are all modern, whilst a bill hook was recovered from 17th-century demolition rubble from vicarage Structure H.

All the objects from the farmstead area (Archive 1028-1045), including the plough and animal traps, are from 19th and 20th-century or unphased contexts. Two hoes, and blades from a spade and mattock, are all likely to be modern, whilst a clapper from a small animal bell and fragments of blades from a sickle, a weedhook and shears may be from earlier phases of activity.

A similar range of tools was recovered from the vicarage and barn areas (Archive 1046-1060), with the addition of the bill hook (No. 114) and a fish hook similar to others found elsewhere in the village. These and a sickle blade are all from 16th-century contexts. A hoe and a blade, possibly from shears, were in 17th or 18th-century contexts; another hoe, a further six parts of shears, another sickle blade and bell clapper, as well as parts of two animal traps, were all from later or unstratified contexts.

Vicarage
114* Bill hook. L. 215mm; w. across widest part *c.* 170mm. *54/369/393; SF775; unphased*

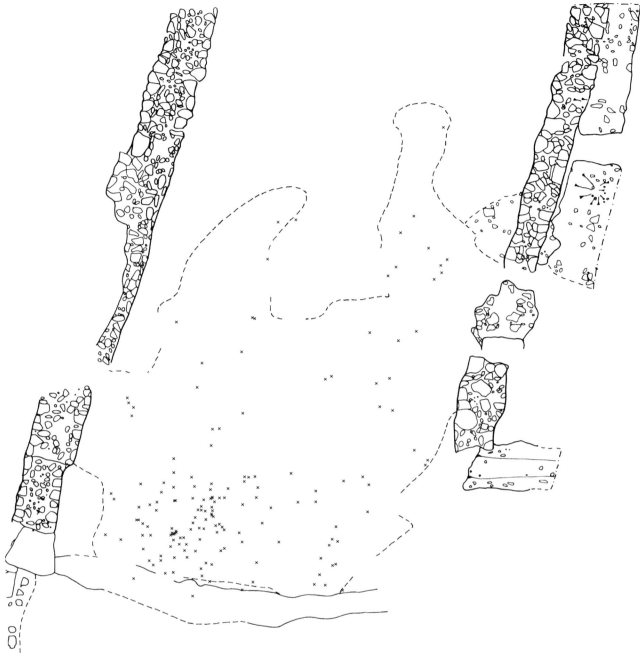

Fig. 111. Location of 'broddes' (nails) found in the barn area of Site 77 (E. Marlow-Mann).

Substantial numbers of horseshoe fragments have been found throughout the village (see Goodall 2005, 134-9 for discussion of types) and it is unsurprising that another 77 were found in and around the North Glebe Terrace sites (Archive 1061-1137). A small collection of horseshoes, which appear to have been collected from across the village and stored within the cottages (Site Code 55), and another three from Sites 73 and 74, are all complete and post-medieval in form, as are eight complete shoes from the vicarage. All the rest are from 16th-century and later contexts, but include some earlier fragments.

There is a striking contrast between the numbers of shoes and shoe fragments from the two excavated areas,

24 (2.7% of objects from those sites) from the farm and 45 (6.6% of objects from those sites) from the vicarage area. That only eighteen fragments came from Site 77 is consistent with the use of the barn for storing grain and not for sheltering animals. The contrast is even greater for ox shoes (Archive 1138-54), only 4 (0.45%) came from the farm, whilst thirteen (1.9%) were found around the vicarage and almost all from 16th to 18th-century contexts.

A curry comb and parts of bridles, stirrups and spurs (Archive 1155-67) add further examples to those already published from other parts of the village.

Weapons

Only two items of weaponry were found. The World War I German bayonet (No. 116) is an unusual find, possibly brought to the village by a 20th-century inhabitant of the cottages (identification by Jeffery Bates).

Farmstead
115 Possible arrowhead. L. 53+mm; w. 35mm. *51/1040; SF418; Period 1*

116 Bayonet. Blade broken, 'waisted' section. Broken guard; trace of wood remains on handle; shaped end. German 98/05 'Butcher Blade' bayonet, 1898-1918. This was a common type used by the German [army] during World War I and many were brought to Britain as souvenirs. L.310+mm; blade 27 x 6mm. *15/4; SF4; unphased*

Other iron objects

Another 75 iron objects, many obviously well and purposefully made, are either very modern or of uncertain and/or unknown use; they are described and listed in the archive (Archive 1168-1243). Archive 1244-1471 are fragments of sheet and cast iron. Some 220 small unidentifiable fragments, many of them burnt, were recovered from both the farmstead and vicarage areas; this is far more than has been usual on other sites at Wharram. While many were from contexts related to the fire in the vicarage barn, others probably originate from bonfires and fires within the grates of the houses.

Nails
by J.G. Watt

In view of the very large numbers of nails from these sites, many of them modern and from demolition levels, it was decided only to examine in detail two groups, both from the vicarage area – from Site 77 and from Context 516, the fill of Structure J on Site 54.

Site 77
Large numbers of nails were noticed during excavation on Site 77, especially within the barn itself, and this group was individually recorded in the hope of gaining information about the structure of the barn. Out of a total of 1917 nails from Site 77, together with Sites 99 and 100, only 23 are from horseshoes and two from ox shoes. The remaining 1892 are nail types used in building and construction work. Many show signs of burning.

All except one are types of nail that have been found on other sites within the village. The new type is a 'dog', a nail in the form of a large unused staple, used to join wood, and was recovered from Context 181, Period 5.1, a levelling layer in the barn. It has a central shank 70mm long with a cross-section of 10 x 4mm, and points at each end, one broken, 15mm long.

Thirty-seven per cent of the identifiable nails are 'broddes', a nail which rarely exceeds 38-51mm in length with a slender shank too light to be used in the construction of a building. They are more likely to be used on lighter wooden constructions and the presence of 173 of them in the burnt layer, context 559, suggests that the barn may have contained stalls, shelving and/or wooden bins. The concentration of broddes at one end of the barn (Fig. 111) suggests the possibility of an end loft.

Site 54, Structure J
Sixty-five nails were recovered from Structure J, covering most of the usual range of types previously found at Wharram. There is one horseshoe nail, the rest are from building activities and include one Roman type. Many have been extracted from wood, and they include a number of points broken at the clench.

23 Bone, Antler and Ivory Objects
by I. Riddler, with No. 12 by H. Leaf, and comments on the cutlery by R. McNeill Alexander

The North Glebe Terrace sites produced 70 objects of bone, antler and ivory, with Sites 54 and 74 providing the two largest assemblages. The objects have been separated into broad chronological bands of Anglo-Saxon and medieval, early post-medieval, and late post-medieval. The material of each period is discussed in turn, after which the spatial distributions are examined, and the possible social implications of the artefacts are discussed.

Anglo-Saxon and medieval objects (Fig. 112)

A small collection of twelve objects can be placed in this category. Most cannot be dated with any precision, although they can be assigned to this broad period. They include three bone needles, part of a flute, a perforated pig metapodial, a bone die, a stylus, two handles, and three mounts.

Needles
Farmstead
1 Fragment of a needle with the head cut from the proximal end of a pig fibula. Part of a knife-cut perforation survives. *74/106; SF1169; Period 3*

Vicarage
2* Head of a needle, cut from the unfused distal end of a pig fibula, with a large knife-cut oval perforation at the centre. The shaft has fractured just below the head. *54/404; SF773; Period 5.2*

3* Head and part of the shaft of a bone needle, probably produced from a pig fibula, with a knife-cut oval perforation at the head, which tapers towards a point, with a flat apex. The shaft is circular in section. *77/380; SF349; Period 5.1*

Three fragmentary needles, all made from pig fibulae, ably demonstrate the range of types available during the Anglo-Saxon and medieval periods. Number 2 is a common type with the head cut from the distal end of the pig fibula and the shaft trimmed to a straight or lightly curved form. The head often retains the unfused articular surface of the bone. Examples have been found elsewhere at Wharram, as is the case also with No. 1, where the head has been cut from the proximal end of the bone (MacGregor 1992, 58, fig. 30.15 and 17; 1989, 56, fig. 38.46. NB in MacGregor 1992, 46 the head of the needle has been cut from the proximal end of the bone and not from the distal end, as stated). The proximal end of the pig fibula was preferred as the head in around 5% of the needles produced from pig fibulae during the Anglo-Saxon period. The head was generally broader and thinner as a result and it could be damaged more easily, but, at the same time, the shaft could be cut to a straighter and slightly longer form.

The remaining object, No. 3, is clearly a needle and has a straight, tapering shaft of circular section and a head that narrows above the circular perforation to a flat apex. It is an equivalent to the type 3 needle from Ipswich, a type that cannot be closely dated and occurs in contexts of 7th to 13th-century date, as might be expected from an enduring object form (Riddler, Trzaska-Nartowski and Hatton forthcoming). The type is related to bone needles of Iron Age date where, however, the head is generally pointed and the perforation is elongated (Sellwood 1984, 380, fig. 7.32). Comparable Roman examples tend to be longer, with elongated perforations, and they are seldom made from pig fibulae (Crummy 1983, 65-7). The type, therefore, is distinctively post-Roman, its demise in the 13th century coinciding with a gradual movement away from the use of bone needles, in favour of those of metal (Walton Rogers 1997, 1783; Ottaway and Rogers 2002, 2739).

Perforated pig metapodial
Farmstead
4* An unfused pig metapodial (Metacarpus IV) pierced by a single knife cut perforation at the centre, otherwise unmodified. *51/1058; SF446; Period 1*

A detailed discussion of perforated pig metapodial from Wharram has been published recently (MacGregor and Riddler 2005, 143-5) and this example can be added to the group discussed there. It includes a single, central perforation and has been cut from a metacarpus IV, which was not a popular bone for this purpose, in comparison with the metatarsal III and IV bones, which produced a better sound when spun with a cord or strip of leather.

Bone die
Vicarage
5* Complete cubical die of bone or antler, the numerals arranged so that opposite sides add up to seven. Each side is stamped with double ring-and-dot motifs, set either at the centre or towards the edges. *77/553; SF750; Period 2*

This bone or antler die can be compared with two examples recovered from a late 15th to early 16th-century deposit within Area 10 at Wharram Percy, as well as a medieval example from Site 26 (Andrews 1979, 128, fig. 70.32; Riddler 2007b, no. 12). With this example the opposite sides add up to seven, which is the most common numerical arrangement to be found on cubical dice (Brown 1990, 692-3). The numbers are marked either at their edges or at the centre by double ring-and-dot motifs, suggesting that the die is of late medieval or early post-medieval date. Medieval dice use several numbering systems and tend to be marked with single ring-and-dot motifs, with double ring-and-dot motifs becoming more common from the 14th century onwards (Brown 1990, 694; Riddler in Egan 1998, 290-91; Riddler, Trzaska-Nartowski and Hatton forthcoming).

Bone dice were cut from prepared rods of square section, examples of which have come from Jarrow, Schleswig and Winchester, and possibly also from York (Riddler 2006, 280; Ulbricht 1984, 39-40 and taf 46.3; Biddle 1990, 261, fig. 56.352; MacGregor, Mainman and Rogers 1999, fig. 879.6776). Accordingly, it was possible to produce near-perfect cubes, and dice that would not roll preferentially to particular numbers. Rolling the die 100 times produced the following results:

1	23%	1 and 6 combined	39%
2	16%	2 and 5 combined	29%
3	22%	3 and 4 combined	32%
4	10%		
5	13%		
6	16%		

The numbers 1 and 6 are well represented, and they are set opposite each other on the die, but there does not appear to be any specific and deliberate tendency to roll towards them. This appears to be a straightforward die with no bias towards any particular number. These results can be contrasted with those obtained on a medieval cubical die from Launceston Castle, which rolled preferentially to even numbers, as well as a number of the medieval dice from Skiddy's Castle, Cork, which rolled to particular numbers (Riddler 2007a, 367-8; Hurley 1997a, 252). Several medieval dice are not perfectly cubical in shape and would also have rolled to particular numbers, including examples from Canterbury, Norwich and York (Riddler 2001, 280, fig. 211.44; Margeson 1993, 217; MacGregor 1995, 417). This particular example from Wharram Percy appears, however, to have been a reasonably honest gaming device.

Mounts
Farmstead
6 Small fragment of a mount, produced from an animal rib and of shallow plano-convex section. Fractured on three sides, with linear smoothing marks on the upper surface. From a comb or casket. *51/1038; SF533; Period 1*

Vicarage
7* Decorated bone mount, surviving in three conjoining pieces. Long and rectangular in shape with shallow plano-convex section and a continuous pattern of knife cut diagonal lines. Bevelled at the one surviving end. *54/389; SF1514; Period 6.1*

8* Fragment of a narrow bone strip for a mount, undecorated but highly polished. Shallow plano-convex section, fractured at both ends. *54/389; SF1515; Period 6.1*

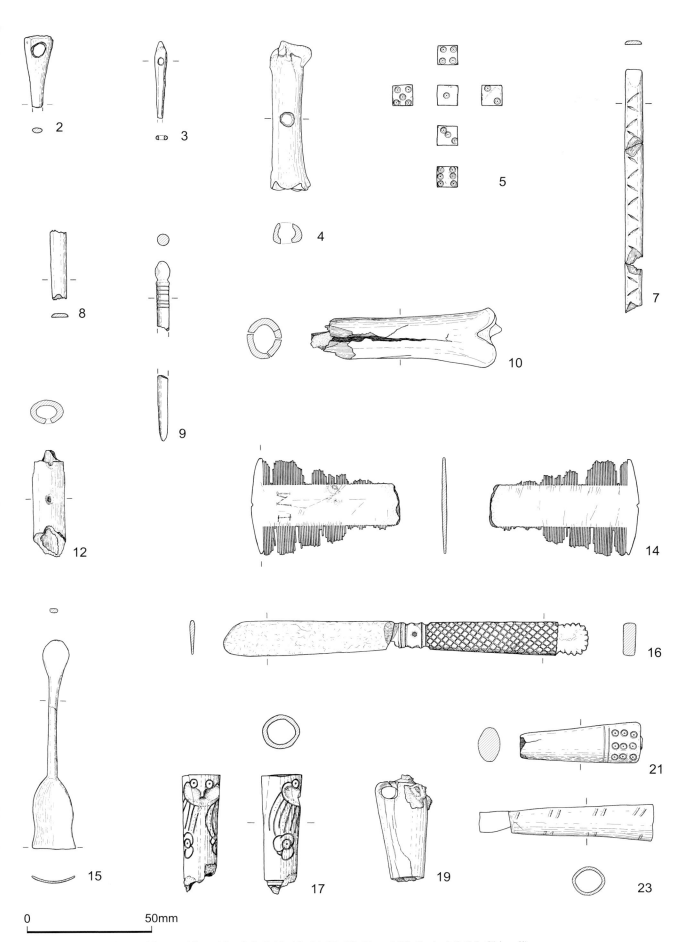

Fig. 112. Bone, antler and ivory objects Nos 2-5, 7-10, 12, 14-17, 19, 21 and 23. Scale 2:3 (M. Chisnall)

0   50mm

A small fragment of modified animal rib, No. 6, may stem from a comb or a casket. Two long and narrow bone mounts (Nos 7 and 8), both recovered from the same context, derive from the same casket. No rivet holes are present on either piece but both are fragmentary; however it has been noted that not all casket mounts include a provision for rivets (Biddle 1990, 782). It is also possible that they are unfinished. The majority of casket mounts are made of animal rib but examples of bone, antler and whalebone also occur. The simple chevron pattern seen on the decorated mount recalls the decoration on a casket lid from York (MacGregor, Mainman and Rogers 1999, fig. 913.6964). Casket mounts are usually decorated with ring-and-dot patterns but other designs are also found and where the caskets themselves survive to any extent, as at Dublin, Ipswich, Ludgershall Castle and York, they incorporate a variety of patterns and shapes (Waterman 1959, pl. XVII; MacGregor, Mainman and Rogers 1999, figs 913-14, 917 and 918; MacGregor 2000b, fig. 6.42; Riddler, Trzaska-Nartowski and Hatton forthcoming). Casket mounts are found in late Roman contexts and occur throughout the Anglo-Saxon period. It has been suggested that the latest examples come from contexts of 12th-century date (MacGregor 1985, 198; 1995, 420; 2000b, 162) but some appear to come from 13th-century contexts.

Styli

Vicarage

9* Two fragments of a bone stylus with an oval knop to the upper section and two thin lateral bands, each of three lines, at the top of the shaft. The lower piece is circular in section and tapers to a rounded, iron stained terminal, with the metal point now missing. Lathe-turned and polished. *54/12; SF1; Period 7.8*

A fragmentary stylus lacks its metal points and is now in two pieces. It can be compared with an example from the Churchyard (Riddler 2007b, Church no. 6). It is likely to be of medieval date, although recovered from a post-medieval context. As an indicator of literacy, the presence of a single example on Site 54 is of some interest in terms of the social standing of the structures there, and their proximity to the church.

Implement handles

Farmstead

10* Complete bone whittle-tang handle, made from the distal end of an unfused cattle tibia, with midshaft cut away and tapered crudely to form tang end. The handle is otherwise unmodified and accommodates tang of rectangular section. *74/219; SF1808; Period 2*

11 Fragment of a cattle tibia midshaft, perforated laterally towards the proximal end, from which the articulation has been removed. Also scored by knife along one edge. *74/105; SF1702; Period 6*

The simplest of all of the implement handles from Wharram Percy, No. 10, consists of the unfused distal end of a cattle tibia, which has been adopted as a handle without any modification beyond separating the midshaft from the remainder of the bone. A fragment of a cattle tibia from the same site, No. 11, has been perforated and partially worked, and may form part of an episode of local handle manufacture. The tradition of providing whittle-tang handles from largely unmodified bones is a distinctive trait of the medieval period. It can be seen with a knife from Winchester, which has a handle cut from a sheep metatarsus (Biddle 1990, 852, fig. 256.2804). A comparable example from Norwich, possibly cut from a sheep metacarpus, is also of early medieval date as is an example from York, produced from a sheep metatarsus (Margeson 1993, fig. 96.869; MacGregor, Mainman and Rogers 1999, 1972, fig. 927.7059). A further example from Galway has also been produced from a sheep metatarsus (Hurley 2004, fig. 6.9.10b). The Wharram example differs from these handles in the choice of cattle bone rather than sheep, but it retains the simplicity of the general design with little modification of the original bone, and it is also likely to be of medieval date.

Flute

by H. Leaf

Vicarage

12* Fragment of a bone flute, made from a sheep tibia, with one complete and two broken toneholes, all knife made. *77/101; SF4; Period 5.1*

In its complete state, this flute would typically have had a D-shaped window at its proximal end, and either three or four toneholes in the area between its centre and distal end. That the flute is broken across two of its toneholes allows the conical profile of the tonehole to be seen, consistent with having been made with the point of a knife. The surface has some longitudinal scrape marks, likely to have been made by knife during manufacture. Though its context is not closely dated, the flute can be compared to other sheep tibia flutes which are typically dated from the 12th to the 15th centuries

This flute is remarkably similar to the flute from Area 10 (Andrews 1979, 129, fig. 70.34), and can also be compared with the flute from the North Manor (Riddler 2004, 252-3, fig. 131.11). Another flute, from the South Manor area, is made from a goose ulna (MacGregor 2000a, 153, fig. 71.110).

Bone flutes appear to have been common in medieval times, with over 100 examples known in England alone. They have been found from both elite and non-elite sites, with the two most common types being those of sheep tibia and goose ulna (Leaf 2006), both of which are represented in the four flutes from Wharram.

Early post-medieval objects (Figs 112 and 113)

The post-medieval objects of bone, antler and ivory can be separated into those belonging to the earlier phase (16th to 18th centuries) and those of more recent date, essentially the 19th and 20th centuries. Whilst the modern objects are briefly described, more attention has been paid to the earlier post-medieval assemblage which includes ivory combs, a bone spoon and a bone knife, as well as a series of implement handles of bone, antler and ivory. The objects are considered within the two separate areas of the farmstead and the vicarage, and the two areas are compared and related to previous discoveries of post-medieval objects from Wharram.

Ivory double-sided simple combs

Farmstead

13   Fragmentary double-sided simple comb of elephant ivory with convex curve to one end and broad central area, with short, fine teeth to either side. Opposite end of comb missing. Teeth of similar length and fineness, with numerous wear marks on both sides of one set. *74/125; SF159; Period 6*

Vicarage

14* Fragmentary double-sided simple comb of elephant ivory with one curved end surviving and with most teeth now fractured. Initials IM carved into one side on broad space between two sets of teeth. Numerous wear marks at base of one set of teeth on each side. Small notch cut into centre of curve along back edge. *54/113; SF187; Period 8.1*

The two combs of elephant ivory have fine teeth (12–15 per cm) on both sides. Both have curved ends and broad central bands separating sets of relatively short teeth. They differ in these respects from the slightly earlier, 16th to 18th-century forms of ivory double-sided simple combs, which have straight backs and narrower central bands, with both fine and coarse teeth present. The differences are small but reflect changes in comb design at this period. Combs of the earlier type have been recovered from the Church and the North Manor at Wharram, and are well represented at numerous sites, including Norwich and London (MacGregor 1987, 176, fig. 195.2; Riddler 2004, 254; Margeson 1993, 66, figs 35-6; Egan 2005, 64-5). This later type represents a variant of that form, which can be seen also with combs from Galway, Plymouth and 's-Herogenbosch (Hurley 2004, 469, fig. 6.9.6; Fairclough 1979, 129, fig. 54.37; Janssen 1977, 299, fig. 11f). The type extends from the 18th century towards the modern period and is effectively a mass-produced product. The presence of both fine and coarse teeth on the same comb is abandoned at this time and the teeth are shortened in length, with the central area between them widened. By this time wooden combs were less fashionable and ivory combs were manufactured alongside those of horn, combs of the latter material continuing to be made well into the 20th century (Sahlberg 1960-61; van Vilsteren 1987, 41). One of the combs has the initials IM carved into it, a mark of possession that can be seen also on an apple corer from Oxford with the letters TP carved into it (Henig 1977, 163, fig. 38.30).

Spoon

Farmstead

15* Complete shovel-shaped bone spoon, now in two pieces, with an oval bowl curving inwards and splaying out to a flat end, and stem of oval section widening to a flat, rounded terminal. *74/341; SF1570; Period 1*

The customary form for small bone spoons utilises an oval bowl, as with an example from Hull or an earlier post-medieval spoon from Kings Lynn (Armstrong and Ayers 1987, 217, fig. 127.398; Clarke and Carter 1977, fig. 143.22). This spoon represents a later form, with sinuous sides to the bowl and a rounded terminal to the stem. Alexander notes 'Silver salts shovels of this size and distinctive shape were made in the second half of the 18th century. They were the earliest salt spoons, and soon gave way to the familiar ladle-shaped salt spoons. See fig. 344 in Pickford *Silver Flatware* and pl. 38 in Snodin *English Silver Spoons*.' MacGregor has also noted (1985, 182) that bone spoons reflect the design of a metal prototype, and on that basis this example belongs to the second half of the 18th century.

Bone knife

Farmstead

16* Near complete bone knife, now in two pieces, with highly decorated handle of rectangular section. Terminal rounded with knife cut notches around its edge. Main part of handle tapers gradually towards blade, with dense lattice decoration. Plain segment with three concave indentations on each side separates handle from blade; it includes a copper-alloy rivet through its centre. Blade has straight cutting edge and back, the latter widening before descending in a curve to rounded point. *55/31; SF22; unphased*

Knives made entirely of bone are a rare commodity in England, as noted by MacGregor, who summarised the slender evidence for their presence (1985, 183). They occur more commonly in post-medieval deposits in the low countries, where examples have been illustrated by Roes (1963, 50-51 and pl. LXII.1-8) and by van Vilsteren (1987, 42 no. 52 and 46 no. 67). Roes was unsure of the dating and function of post-medieval bone knives, but they have been catalogued and described by van Vilsteren (1988, 214-17) who has established that in Holland they are a 17th-century form of butter knife. Bone, antler and ivory produced no chemical reaction in contact with dairy products, unlike objects of some metals, and accordingly they were favoured for this purpose, as was horn. Bone knives remain a scarce commodity in England. Another possible example was found in a mid-16th to early 17th-century context at Norwich, and van Vilsteren has illustrated an example from London, comparable with a bone knife from an early 18th-century context at Aldgate (Margeson 1993, 121, fig. 86.762; van Vilsteren 1988, afb 6; Thompson *et al.* 1984, 98-9, fig. 50.31). Two examples have also come from Colchester (Crummy 1988, fig. 77.3105-6).

It is possible that the Wharram knife is later than the 17th century, but it is difficult to establish that and its typological dating is 17th-century. Alexander comments that silver butter knives as small as this do not seem to have been made until the later part of the 19th century.

Implement handles

Bone, antler and ivory implement handles form the largest category of objects of skeletal materials from the North Glebe Terrace sites, with 33 examples in total from this period (16th to 18th centuries). They occur in two basic forms, with whittle tangs or scale tangs, and in three materials, bone, antler and ivory. They are catalogued and discussed in order of site, material, and context, with the whittle tang handles preceding the scale tang examples. The discussion is centred on handles of 16th to 18th-century date, with later examples briefly described after the earlier post-medieval forms.

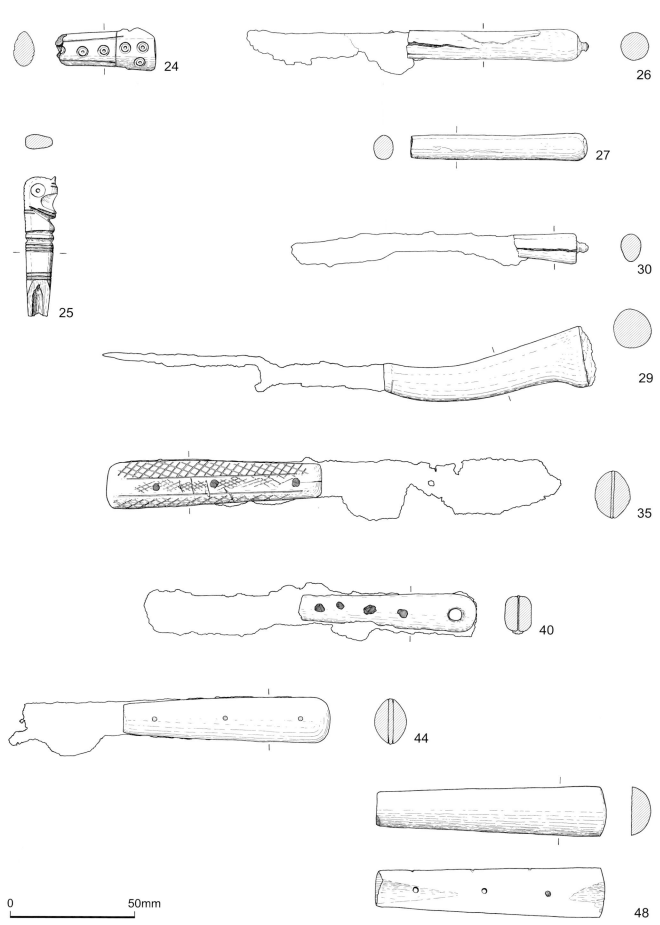

Fig. 113. Bone, antler and ivory objects Nos 24-27, 29-30, 35, 40, 44 and 48. Scale 2:3 (M.Chisnall).

Bone and ivory whittle-tang handles

Farmstead

17* Fragmentary handle produced from the midshaft of an ovicaprid metatarsus and decorated towards the terminal with a depiction of an owl, the beak formed from two concave depressions cut into the bone, the body and wings incised by knife, with the eyes and feet delineated by single ring-and-dot motifs. Probably 16th-century. *51/377; SF14; Period ER-2*

18 Complete bone whittle-tang handle, ovicaprid metacarpus, proximal end sawn away close to articular surface. Surface of the bone lightly trimmed by knife. Undecorated, apparently unfinished. *74/340; SF1310; Period 4*

19* Bone whittle-tang handle of oval section, widening from tang to flat terminal, with integral suspension loop. Loop lies above centre of terminal; lead washer accompanies one of a pair of iron rods set into tang area. Undecorated, with two areas of iron staining close to the lead washer. Probably Tudor. *74/106; SF1170; Period 3*

20 Near complete ivory whittle-tang handle for small implement, handle widening slightly to rounded, bulbous terminal. Undecorated and now in several pieces. *74/341; SF1435; Period 1*

21* Near complete bone whittle-tang handle, lacking part of narrow end. Handle is oval in section and widens to a flat terminal with a raised and perforated central stub. End of the handle decorated by three rows of single ring-and-dot motifs, set within paired lateral bounding lines. Probably Tudor. *55/5; SF3; unphased*

Vicarage

22 A small fragment of an elaborately decorated bone whittle-tang handle, produced from the midshaft of an ovicaprid metatarsus. Octagonal in section and tapering lightly towards one end, with a series of lateral mouldings, cut by knife. *54/1; SF1629; Period 8.4*

23* Whittle-tang handle made from an ovicaprid metatarsus, the proximal end sawn away and the midshaft cut and trimmed to shape, with the surface smoothed by knife and file. Tang placed into distal end of midshaft and handle widens to the terminal, which has been sawn laterally. There may originally have been a cover for this end, which does not survive. *54/98; SF1633; Period 7.7*

24* Fragmentary bone whittle-tang handle, oval in section with flat terminal. Handle widens towards terminal and is bevelled on one side, with a raised section opposite. Decorated on both sides by a single line of single ring-and-dot motifs, with an additional motif near to the terminal and a lateral line separating three of the motifs from the remainder. Two saw-cut framing lines are also present on each side. Probably Tudor. *54/124; SF1634; Period 7.5*

25* Near complete bone whittle-tang handle, elaborately decorated with profile head of an equine animal, possibly a sea horse, with raised stub at the apex, eyes formed of single ring-and-dot motifs and concave curves delineating muzzle, hatched mane along the back of head. Lateral moulding separates head from tapering shaft of rectangular section, with two bands of three saw-incised lines. Alexander comments that 'several much more sophisticated continental knives and forks in the Hollander Collection have ivory handles ending in an open-mouthed lion's head (#101, 16th-century; #145, 17th-century; #146, 18th-century, in van Trigt 2003). Compare a handle carved with a whale, judged to be 16th-century, on p.111 of Moore 1999. Probably 16th-century.' *54/243; SF759; Period 6.3*

26* Complete bone whittle-tang handle of circular section, cylindrical in profile, widening slightly towards terminal end, with carved bone stopper and knop securing that end. Undecorated, probably made from an ovicaprid metapodial. Alexander comments that 'silver knife handles of this shape (cannon handles) were made in the late 17th century (e.g. pl. 57 in Brown 2001). A German knife and fork of about 1700, with ivory cannon handles of exactly this shape, are in the Hollander Collection (Van Trigt 2003, pl. 148).' *54/200; SF342; Period 7.1*

27* Complete bone whittle-tang handle, midshaft of an ovicaprid metatarsus, widening to slightly bulbous terminal with bone stopper inserted at centre, which has flattened apex. Undecorated but possibly stained to produce a two-colour contrast along the handle. *54/247; SF1636; Period 7.4*

28 Fragment of lathe-turned bone whittle-tang handle with rounded terminal of circular section and a series of lateral mouldings above the lightly tapered main section, which is undecorated. *54/369; SF767; Period 6.3*

29* Near complete fork, lacking one prong, with whittle-tang antler handle, sawn from a tine and lightly curved, with exterior surface unmodified. Almost certainly red deer antler. Narrow end at stem bevelled on both sides, terminal has an iron plate securing the tang. Alexander comments that 'the prongs are of the early straight type. Late 17th or early 18th-century.' *54/516; SF1393; Period 6.3*

30* Fragmentary small knife with whittle-tang handle of elephant ivory, handle forming small part of the implement. Long stem separates handle from knife blade. Handle widens from stem to terminal and is circular in section, secured by an iron knop at the terminal. Alexander comments that 'it might have been tinned. The bone part of the handle is short, and there seems to have been a very long bolster. These features suggest a date between 1550 and 1650 (see for example plate 39a and c in Brown 2001).' *54/124; SF1635; Period 7.5*

Five distinct types can be identified within the bone, antler and ivory whittle tang-handles of 16th to 18th-century date:

I: Ovicaprid midshaft, proximal end removed: Nos 17, 18, 22 and 23
II: Rectangular section, solid end: Nos 19, 21, 24 and 25
III: Cylindrical, rounded terminal with stopper: Nos 26-28
IV: Largely unmodified, antler tine: No. 29
V: Ivory, partially hollowed, oval section: Nos 20 and 30

I   Ovicaprid midshaft, proximal end removed
Four handles (Nos 17, 18, 22 and 23) have been produced from ovicaprid metapodia, three from metatarsals and one from a metacarpus. The bones are likely to derive from sheep rather than goats. In each case the proximal end has been removed and the midshaft has been trimmed to provide a tapering cylinder, which is hollow throughout. In one instance the end retains porous tissue lying just below the proximal end. No end caps, which may have secured the terminals of the hollow handles, survive from them. Handles of this form are largely of mid-16th to 17th-century date. The simple handle (No. 23) can be compared with examples from Great Lynford and Norwich (Tyrell and Zeepvat 1991, fig. 94.309; Margeson 1993, fig. 87.767). A hollow handle from Colchester may represent a further example of this simple type (Crummy 1988, fig. 74.3069). An unfinished handle (No. 18) from the farmhouse is noticeably short, a characteristic it shares with another handle found near the farm buildings (No. 21), as well as a handle of elephant ivory from Site 30 (MacGregor and Riddler 2005, fig. 61.3). Short handles of this type are difficult to hold in the hand and might appear at first sight to have been used as delicate table implements. A further short handle described below (No. 30) is attached to a long knife

blade, forming a relatively large implement. A small fragment (No. 22) is octagonal in section with a series of lateral mouldings and stems from an elaborately decorated handle. The most impressive whittle-tang handle is undoubtedly the example from the East Range of Site 51, with a simple but elegant depiction of an owl incised into the bone, with light indentations forming the beak area (No. 17). Alexander suggests comparison 'with a handle carved with a whale, judged to be 16th-century, on p. 111 of Moore 1999.' A whittle-tang handle of the same bone type from Norwich includes elaborate scroll decoration and comes from a context of mid-16th to early 17th-century date (Margeson 1993, fig 87.766).

II Rectangular section, solid end

The skill seen in shaping hollow whittle-tang handles is evident also in the series produced from cattle bones with solid end sections leading to hollowed chambers for the tang. All four examples of this type (Nos 19, 21, 24 and 25) are decorated and one of them (No. 25) has a sculpted head at its terminal. It is representative of a group of bone handles of late 17th to early 18th-century date with similar characteristics, exemplified by examples from Exeter and Great Lynford (Allan 1984, fig. 195.34; Tyrell and Zeepvat 1991, 187, fig. 92.289). In each case relatively simple modelling of the handle is used to produce a bird or animal form. The simplified design seen on another handle (No. 21) is comparable with an unstratified example from Great Lynford (Tyrell and Zeepvat 1991, fig. 94.302) and is repeated with a further handle (No. 24) with ring-and-dot decoration and a notched edge close to its terminal. A longer, undecorated handle from Norwich is unfortunately unstratified, but a solid handle with a bifurcated terminal from Colchester is of 17th-century date (Margeson 1993, fig. 87.772; Crummy 1988, 75, fig. 75.3089). This variant of the type appears to be of 17th to early 18th-century date. The fourth handle (No. 19) is another short and delicate example, recalling those described above in the first group of handles. It may, however, be of an earlier date, its style suggesting that it can be set in the 16th century.

III Cylindrical, rounded terminal with stopper

Ovicaprid metapodia, and particularly the metatarsus, were also lathe-turned to produce handles of circular section (Nos 26, 27 and 28). Another example of this type came from the North Manor (Riddler 2004, 254). This is largely a late 17th to 18th-century handle form, with well-dated examples coming from London and Great Lynford, amongst other sites (Thompson *et al.* 1984, 103, fig. 52.46-7; Tyrell and Zeepvat 1991, 187, fig. 92.280-2). One example from Exeter, however, came from a context of *c.* 1660, and the type may first appear around the middle of that century (Allan 1984, 351, fig. 195.33). The elaborate handle (No. 28) with lateral mouldings can be compared with similar examples from Carisbrooke Castle, of 16th to 18th-century date, as well as Galway, where the handle was assigned a broad post-medieval date (Young 2000, fig. 54.81; Hurley 2004, fig. 6.9.8g). A

further handle from Galway provides a close parallel for a published handle from Wharram (Hurley 2004, fig. 6.9.8h; MacGregor and Riddler 2005, 143, fig. 61.3). The simple, undecorated handle (No. 27) with a rounded end is similar to examples from Chelmsford and Great Lynford, of late 16th to early 18th-century date (Cunningham 1985, fig. 36.9; Tyrell and Zeepvat 1991, fig. 94.307).

IV Largely unmodified antler handles

The single example of this type (No. 29) consists of the handle of a fork formed from a section of an antler tine. The original shape of the material has been retained and little has been done to transform it into a handle, beyond sawing away both ends. In that sense it resembles the medieval handle (No. 10) described above, and the concept of using a section of antler tine as a handle goes back at least to the medieval period. A 13th-century handle of antler was recovered from Southampton and a 15th-century example occurs on a glover's knife from London (Platt and Coleman-Smith 1975, 271, fig. 247.1919; Cowgill *et al.* 1987, fig. 68.304). This example continues that tradition but is later in date and probably belongs to the later 17th or 18th century. It can be compared with a similar antler handle of early 18th-century date from Aldgate and a longer post-medieval example from Southwark (Thompson *et al.* 1984, 105, fig. 52.52; Hinton 1988, fig. 188.246).

V Ivory partially-hollowed handles of oval section

The small and short handle with a rounded and slightly bulbous terminal (No. 30) is similar to an example from the North Manor (Riddler 2004, 254), and it can be compared with a handle from Norwich of late 17th-century date, as well as a handle from Winchester assigned to the period from the 18th to the 20th centuries (Margeson 1993, fig. 87.769; Biddle 1990, 868, fig. 261.2909). Ivory whittle-tang handles from Canterbury came from deposits of the mid-17th century to the mid-19th century, whilst an example from Poole came from a context of the mid-18th century (Driver, Rady and Sparks 1990, 190, fig. 68.109 and 111; Horsey 1992, 146 and fig. 85.31). Ivory handles from St Ebbe's Oxford, are also of a similar date, as are those from Aldgate (Hassall, Halpin and Mellor 1984, 229, fig. 40.6 and 8; Thompson *et al.* 1984, 101, fig. 51.37). The shape of the handle of the other ivory example (No. 20) is reflected in a handle from an 18th-century deposit at Hull (Armstrong 1977, 71, fig. 29.147).

Discussion

The bone, antler and ivory whittle-tang handles can therefore be divided into five types, spanning the period from the 16th to the 18th centuries, but with most examples attributable to the later part of that period. Interestingly, there are no pistol grip handles within the assemblage, which could be significant, given that they were particularly popular in the period from *c.* 1725-1750, and would be expected in assemblages of that date (Thompson *et al.* 1984, 100 and 103). The majority of the whittle-tang handles came from the vicarage (nine examples), with just five from the farmstead. Types III and IV were only found at the vicarage. The only unfinished example of a whittle-tang handle (No. 18) came from the farmhouse.

Bone and ivory scale-tang handles

Farmstead

31 Bone scale-tang implement handle, for which both plates survive. Poor condition and fragmentary, widening from blade end to fragmentary terminal. Iron tang flat and rectangular, secured by two iron rivets. Decorated by three framing lines on one side and five on the other, with hatched knife-cut lines in-between, set in a diagonal arrangement. *15/2; SF3; unphased*

32 Small fragment of part of a bone scale-tang handle, undecorated, fractured at either end and across a rivet hole. *49/501; SF 41; Period 3*

33 Near complete fork with two prongs of the early straight type. Two bone scale-tang plates, secured by two small iron rivets with iron pins also set through the lightly rounded terminal. Plates are D-shaped in section and decorated with dense lattice patterning, as well as a central panel of bands of triple diagonal lines, set within paired bounding lines. *51/2; SF 676; unphased*

34 Fragment of one side of a bone scale-tang knife handle, fractured at each end across a rivet hole, with traces of iron staining. Plano-convex section, undecorated. *51/469; SF340; Period 2.4*

35* Knife with scale-tang formed of two bone plates of shallow plano-convex section, one complete and the other near complete, widening slightly from blade to terminal, which has a rounded end. Both plates have raised central areas with a dense lattice mesh across their entire surfaces. They are secured by three iron rivets. Alexander comments that the 'bone handle, on this knife, decorated by hand with incised cross-hatched lines, matches a fork handle in the author's collection. 19th century.' *73/1; SF195; Period 3*

36 Fragmentary scale tang for iron implement, with two large bone plates, produced from a metapodial bone, probably cattle metatarsus. Both plates widen towards the flat terminal and are undecorated except for an arrangement of four small copper-alloy rivets, three of which are set in an arc beyond one of three iron rivets that secure the plates to the tang. Third copper-alloy rivet lies between two of the iron rivets. *74/106; SF1800; Period 3*

37 Degraded bone or antler scale-tang implement handle, secured by several small iron rivets, with no trace of decoration on the surviving fragments. *74/264; SF1163; Period 3*

38 Fragmentary iron knife with large scale-tang handle, the two bone plates undecorated and widening from blade to end of tang, with rounded end. Poor condition and fragile but with traces of three evenly spaced iron rivets, set in a line. *74/315; SF1009; Period 6*

39 Iron implement, probably a fork, with a complete bone scale-tang handle. Handle widens towards terminal, two bone plates fastened by two small rivets of iron, with flat tang extending entire length of handle. Bone plates undecorated, with square cut terminal. *74/316; SF1389; Period 6*

40* Knife with two complete bone scale-tang plates, both undecorated and of shallow plano-convex section. Sides widen to rounded terminal with large suspension hole nearby. Plates secured by four iron rivets, all located close to blade end. Alexander suggests it is probably 16th-century. *74/277; SF825; Period 3*

41 Two elephant ivory plates from a scale-tang handle, one complete and the other fragmentary, both with squared narrow ends and shallow plano-convex section, sides widening to bulbous terminal. Both decorated by groups of four perforations in a cruciform arrangement, with five groups on the complete plate. Four iron rivets arranged between decoration. Probably Tudor. *74/102; SF874; Period 4*

42 Fragmentary iron knife with scale-tang handle formed of two undecorated bone plates of shallow plano-convex section. Plates widen gradually from blade to end of tang, which is rounded. Fastened by three small iron rivets, lightly countersunk into the bone and arranged in a line. Dated by Alexander to the late 19th or early 20th century. *97/10; SF2; unstratified*

Vicarage

43 Fragment of an implement, probably a fork, with scale-tang plates for handle. Plates are bone and undecorated, widening gradually from implement to terminal, but with lower part fractured away. One iron rivet survives, with trace of a second. Alexander suggests it is probably 19th-century in date. *54/1; SF2086; Period 8.4*

44* Two complete bone scale-tang plates, forming handle for a knife, with narrow squared ends widening lightly to rounded terminal. Fastened by three copper-alloy rivets, not quite in line. Undecorated and of plano-convex section with bevel at stem end. Alexander comments: 'Knife with bone scales, as advertised, for example, in the Silber and Fleming catalogue of c.1885. Late 19th-century.' *54/1; SF1626; Period 8.4*

45 Two near complete bone scale-tang handle plates, both trapezoidal in section, sawn laterally at stem and widening lightly to rounded terminal. One plate complete, other lacks part of narrow end, where it has been lightly bevelled. Fastened by three iron rivets. Possibly 19th-century. *54/5; SF1631; Period 8.1*

46 Complete bone implement handle with two scale-tang plates, bevelled ends at stem widening lightly to rounded terminal, secured by two iron rivets. Traces of cortile tissue at terminal end with prominent file marks on both plates. *54/5; SF1632; Period 8.1*

47 Near complete knife with two short bone scale-tang handle plates, widening gradually from the blade to the terminal, which is rounded. Both decorated with a scored lattice of diagonal lines. Plates secured by several small iron rivets. *54/1; SF2347; Period 8.4*

48* Single bone plate from a scale-tang implement. Manufactured from a cattle-sized metapodial and plano-convex in section with cortile tissue visible on inner face at both ends. Handle widens to terminal, which is rounded, with three rivet holes on the inner face, one of which retains an iron rivet. None of these holes penetrates the outer face, however, indicating that the handle is unfinished. *54/5; SF1630; Period 8.1*

49 Fragment of bone scale-tang plate of plano-convex section, produced from a cattle-sized bone and fractured across rivet hole at one end. Decorated across entire surface by diagonal incised lines. *54/1; SF1628; Period 8.4*

The variety seen with the bone, antler and ivory whittle-tang handles is not matched by the scale-tang assemblage, which consists largely of undecorated bone handles of the same type. The nineteen examples of this handle form were used on both knives and forks. There are slight variations visible within the overall type. The terminals are either curved or flat, with rounded edges and with bevelled ends close to the blades in some cases. The use of copper-alloy rivets rather than those of iron occurs on one handle (No. 44), and the presence of just two rivets instead of three can be seen on two occasions (Nos 39 and 46). A knife with a scale-tang handle and two iron rivets also came from Site 30 (MacGregor and

Riddler 2005, 143, fig. 61.4). The basic form, however, remains the same across the assemblage, and includes one unfinished example from Site 54 (No. 48), for which the iron rivets do not penetrate through the outer surface of the bone.

One example (No. 47) has two flat plates with rounded ends, decorated with diagonal lattice patterns and fastened by a series of small iron rivets. This method of fastening the plates recalls a knife from Site 30 (MacGregor and Riddler 2005, 143, fig. 61.5). It occurs also on a fragmentary and degraded handle fragment (No. 37) from the farmhouse, and can be seen on a pistol-grip handle from Camber Castle (Biddle *et al.* 2001, fig. 7.3.59).

The phasing information for the implements with scale-tang handles is not overly useful, given that four examples came from topsoil on Site 54 and three more from a demolition deposit of Period 8.1 on the same site. A further two handles came from the demolition and subsequent garden use of Site 74 (Period 6). This tends to be a problem in general with post-medieval implements recovered from rural environments, which are often unstratified or occur in contexts disturbed by modern features. One handle came from Period 5 on Site 51, and another came from Period 3 on Site 74, of late 17th to 18th-century date.

Scale-tang handles occur in small numbers in the early Anglo-Saxon period, at a time when most knife handles were made of horn rather than bone or antler (Härke 1995, 75; Meaney and Hawkes 1970, fig. 13.8; Riddler and Trevarthen forthcoming). Thereafter they are found sporadically in England until the late medieval period, when they are first seen in some quantity (Cowgill *et al.* 1987, 26-7). It is often assumed that there were no scale-tang handles in England between the Roman period and the 14th century (e.g. Duncan 2002, 263) but they do occur in small numbers during the intervening centuries and they include a handle of 11th to 12th-century date from Wharram Site 30 (MacGregor and Riddler 2005, 143). Late medieval scale-tang handles tend to be relatively long and are fastened with numerous rivets. There is a series from London, however, fastened with just three or four rivets (Cowgill *et al.* 1987, figs 64-5). These differ from later scale-tang handles in the shape of the plates, which are more varied and tend not to have rounded terminals. In addition, the handles themselves are often longer than those of post-medieval date.

During the post-medieval period the design of the scale-tang handle is simplified and standardised, with fewer rivets used to fasten the plates to the tang. The particular type seen here can be matched by examples from a wide variety of sites, largely within contexts of 18th to late 19th-century date, although the dating evidence is not always precise. A fragmentary undecorated handle with a flat terminal came from the North Gate at Cork (Hurley 1997b, 147, fig. 43.13). A group of four bone scale-tang handle plates from Galway, each with three rivet holes, have been assigned to the 18th century (Hurley 2004, 470, fig. 6.9:8a-d). An undecorated

bone scale-tang handle of early 18th-century date with three iron rivets and four decorative copper-alloy pins came from Aldgate (Thompson *et al.* 1984, 105, fig. 52.51). Similarly, a bone scale-tang knife from Carisbrooke Castle with three iron rivets and ring-and-dot decoration between them came from a deposit of 17th to 18th-century date (Young 2000, fig. 54.83). An undecorated scale-tang knife with three iron rivets from Canterbury was recovered from a context of mid-16th-century or later date, whilst two further handles from St Augustine's Abbey, secured by three and four rivets, were not closely dated (Garrard and Elder 1988, 125 and fig. 21.59; Sherlock and Woods 1988, fig. 75.1-2). The scale-tang handle with decorative copper-alloy pins (No. 36) can be compared with two examples from Norwich of mid-18th to 19th-century date (Margeson 1993, 129, fig. 95.863-4). Simple undecorated scale-tang knife or fork handles, fastened by three rivets, could therefore be of 18th-century date, but the type does extend well into the 19th century and towards the 20th century. The simplicity of design inevitably means that it is the dating of contexts themselves that is of importance in determining the date of the implements in this case.

One handle (No. 40) differs from the remainder in the use of four rivets and the presence of a suspension hole near to the rounded terminal. It comes from a context of late 17th to 18th-century date, however, and appears to be contemporary with the remainder of the assemblage. A similar suspension hole can be seen on a whittle tang handle from Oxford (Hassall, Halpin and Mellor 1984, fig. 40.38).

The decorated examples also appear to be of the same date as the main type. The highly decorated scale-tang handles (Nos 31 and 35) and the smaller fragment (No. 49) with diagonal line decoration recall a fork handle from a late context at Site 71 (MacGregor and Riddler 2005, 143, fig. 61.6). A scale-tang knife handle with diagonal cut decoration along the entire plate came from Pontefract Castle, whilst another, with three iron rivets, was recovered from post-medieval garden soil at Ripon (O'Connor and Duncan 2002, 265, fig. 110.82; Whyman 1997, fig. 10.25). A handle with similar decoration came from a 'modern' context at Colchester (Crummy 1988, 36, fig. 40.1955) but better dating evidence is provided by a comparable handle with lattice decoration from an 18th-century phase at Hull (Armstrong 1977, 71, fig. 29.149). Another example was thought to come from an Anglo-Saxon context at Jarrow but is clearly part of this group and of late post-medieval date (Riddler 2007, 272, fig. 31.5.2.WB17). This type may also extend well into the 19th century. The bulbous end seen on the ivory scale-tang handle (No. 41) occurs in bone on a number of knives from Great Linford, and its decorative patterning and overall shape recall a scale-tang knife with bone plates from a 17th-century phase at Pontefract Castle (Tyrell and Zeepvat 1991, fig. 96.318, 321; Duncan 2002, fig. 110.81). The decorative alternation of iron rivets and groups of four small perforations is matched by a pistol-grip scale-tang handle from Southwark (Hinton 1988, fig. 188.244).

The majority of the scale-tang handles are made of bone and there is just one example of ivory (No. 41). Unlike the whittle-tang handles, which were largely clustered at the vicarage, there are more examples of scale-tang handles from the farmstead, with twelve examples from the farmstead and seven from the vicarage. There could be a simple explanation for this disparity in the distribution of the different types of handle. If the farmstead was not in operation before the mid to late 17th century, as the ceramics suggest, it would lack the earlier (mid-16th to 17th-century) forms of whittle tang, which are only present at the vicarage. Both sites were occupied during the 18th century, and correspondingly they show relatively even quantities of handles of that period, with slightly more from the farmstead than the vicarage.

No obvious social distinctions are apparent between the two sites. Ivory handles were found at both locations, as were decorated scale-tang handles. The slightly more elaborate, decorated bone whittle-tang handles (Nos 24 and 25) both came from the vicarage, but the splendid 'owl' handle (No. 17) came from the farmstead. It is noticeable that whittle-tang fork handles were only retrieved from the vicarage and this is a period at which the fork had not been in general use as a table implement for that long; but this is merely a small sample of the handles, rather than a representative sample of the implements themselves. Moreover, it is interesting to note that an unfinished whittle-tang handle (No. 18) came from the farmhouse and an unfinished scale-tang handle (No. 48) from the vicarage. This is useful testimony of the local post-medieval manufacture of bone handles, utilising bone from domestic sheep and cattle. The elephant ivory handles would not have been made locally and are more likely to have been manufactured in an urban centre like York, where there is evidence for an ivory comb workshop in the 18th century (MacGregor, Mainman and Rogers 1999, 1873).

Late post-medieval objects

Miscellaneous
Farmstead
50 Hollow lathe-turned handle, cattle metatarsus, with indented end and separate bone cap opposite, retaining circular iron loop of square section, which is likely to be a suspension loop. Probably 20th-century. *74/267; SF704; Period 4*

51 The terminal of a lathe-turned bone syringe, including a long, hollow tube with a lightly expanded terminal, pierced by several lateral perforations. The screw thread at the opposite end is heavily worn. *74/334; SF1250; Period 4*

52 An antler handle for a walking stick, with a screw thread cut into the beam and a short section of tine with incised crossing diagonal patterns for grip, cut into the upper and lower faces. *74/184; SF344; Period 6*

53 Scale-tang handles for two penknives, one made of antler with ridging of exterior surface clearly visible, the other smoothed and probably also made of antler. Both plates of shallow plano-convex section, widen to rounded terminal. Secured by three iron rivets. *74/9000; SF1701; unstratified*

Vicarage
54 A complete penknife with an iron blade set between two antler scale-tang plates, partially smoothed but with ridging of the exterior surface still visible. Secured by three iron rivets. *75/3; SF1; unphased*

55 Complete whittle-tang handle for a knife, rectangular in section, undecorated, widening slightly to squared terminal. Copper-alloy bolster lies between handle and blade. Alexander comments: A small knife, with a bolster of a form that was introduced in the mid-19th century. The handle (damaged by over-heating) is xylonite or similar imitation ivory, a material that was being used for cheap knife handles by the 1880s. The intended function of this knife is uncertain; the blade is as wide as on typical Victorian dessert knives, but the handle is much shorter. *54/1; SF1627; Period 8.4*

56 A lathe-turned bone finial from a composite object, with an indented screw thread at one end. *54/5; SF25; Period 8.1*

57 Two rectangular horn plates, secured by two iron rivets at one end and by a single iron rivet at the other end. The two plates retain a third sheet of horn, which tapers on its sides but is fragmentary and its original form is unclear. *54/5; SF21; Period 8.1*

A few handles of 19th to 20th-century date were retrieved from both sites. The bone-like handle (No. 55) is a typical product of the modern period, produced in an imitation ivory material. The form of bolster suggests a date of the mid-19th-century or later. An implement with horn plates (No. 57) is probably a pocket knife and was originally secured by two iron rivets at one end and one at the other, and retains a third horn sheet, set between the two outer plates. Three modern penknives (Nos 53 and 54) in contrast, have antler scale-tang plates. The lathe-turned hollow handle which includes an indented screw thread at one end (No. 56), has been produced from a cattle metatarsus, one of the most common bones to be utilised in bone working from the 8th century onwards, which formed the basis of most of the worked material encountered within the 19th-century assemblage at Launceston Castle (Riddler 2007a, 375-80). A rounded finial from a syringe (No. 51) has also been lathe-turned and the tube element is highly polished whilst the screw thread has worn away. Lateral perforations close to the end of the tube would allow liquids to disperse in several directions from the nozzle. Although described here for convenience as a syringe, it may not have been strictly for medical use. Doubtless it would have served well in syringing ears, for which it is well suited, but it may have had a variety of household and even garden functions. A similar but fragmentary example of the object type came from a post-medieval deposit at Worcester (Greep 2004, 501, fig. 270.79). Finally, a handle for a walking stick (No. 52) is a good example of the uses to which antler was put during the 20th century. It has a screw thread cut into the beam and a handle projecting from the inner section of the brow or bez tine, trimmed and smoothed on the outer surface and notched with crossing diagonal lines on the upper and lower faces for grip.

Buttons
Farmstead
58 Complete bone button, cut from both sides with a central circular perforation. Undecorated. *74/316; SF1432; Period 6*

59 Lathe turned plain button with separate suspension loop, now missing. Indented on the reverse to accommodate the loop. *74/9000; SF1700; unstratified*

60 Slightly unusual bone button of oval shape with flattened apex and reverse face, latter retaining part of a raised area to accommodate separate suspension loop. *74/109; SF20; Period 6*

61 Complete bone button with lightly indented centre and four perforations; rounded edge. *49/2; SF40; Period 3*

62 Complete bone button with lightly indented centre and four perforations; rounded edge. *51/74; SF531; unphased*

63 Complete bone button with indented centre on front face and four perforations. *51/469; SF532; Period 2.4*

64 Complete bone button with indented centre, four circular perforations, curved in profile. *74/127; SF1698; Period 6*

65 Fragmentary bone button with indented centre, two perforations surviving. *74/146; SF1699; Period 6*

Vicarage

66 Complete bone button, discoidal in shape and cut from both sides, with a central perforation. Undecorated. *54/113; SF179; Period 8.1*

67 Complete bone button of discoidal form with bevelled edges, cut from both sides, oval perforation at the centre. *Undecorated. 54/117; SF32; Period 7.2*

68 Incomplete bone button, lathe-turned with central perforation, dished front face. Copper-alloy suspension loop formed of wire of rectangular section, folded over on front face. *54/226; SF416; Period 7.4*

69 Complete button with indented centre, three perforations set in a line. Flat reverse. *54/162; SF242; Period 8.1*

70 Complete button with indented centre and three perforations in a line. Flat reverse. *54/111; SF40; Period 8.1*

The thirteen buttons occur in three distinct types. The first consists of flat discs with bevelled or rounded edges and a central perforation, and the second is similar but larger, with a concave, dished centre, also pierced by a single perforation but retaining a separate copper-alloy suspension loop, folded over on this side. The third type encompasses buttons with an indented, dished centre and either three or four perforations. Three buttons of the first type (Nos 58, 66 and 67) can be compared with similar examples from Castletown, Galway and Great Lynford (Davey, Freke and Higgins 1996, 123, fig. 64.1, 3 and 4; Hurley 2004, 468, fig. 6.9:5; Tyrell and Zeepvat 1991, 146, fig. 55.57-8). The majority of buttons of this discoidal type are of 18th-century date, and it has been persuasively argued that they formed the cores of cloth or thread covered buttons (Biddle 1990, 572; Hinks 1995, 11; Klippel and Schroedl 1999, 229-30). The second type (Nos 59, 60 and 68) is similar but generally larger in size, with a concave dished upper surface and narrow rim. In one case (No. 68) a copper-alloy wire suspension loop is still attached to the button, folded over on the front face, which would clearly have been covered to conceal the loop. The dished buttons with three or four perforations (Nos 61-65, 69 and 70) are essentially of 18th to 20th-century date, with the majority probably attributable to the 19th century. There are seven examples, all but two of which come from the farmstead. They are similar to examples from Castletown, Galway, Great Lynford and Norwich (Davey, Freke and Higgins 1996, 123, fig. 64.2; Hurley 2004, 468, fig. 6.9:5; Tyrell and Zeepvat 1991, 146, fig. 55.59; Margeson 1993, 22, fig. 11.107 and 109).

Part Six

The Environmental Evidence

edited by E.A. Clark

24 The Plant Remains

by W. Carruthers, with contributions by
M. van der Veen, A. Hall, C. Dyer,
J. Southey, R. Perry and S. Wrathmell

Introduction

This report primarily discusses the results from excavating the site of a barn (Site 77) burnt down in 1553. The barn was the earliest in a sequence of vicarage buildings excavated between 1984 and 1990. The excavated evidence consisted of two north-east to south-west parallel lengths of wall (see Chapter 9) constructed of chalk and sandstone blocks. The northern end of the barn was not excavated as it lay under a depth of overburden, and the south wall is thought to have been robbed out. The floor consisted of hard-packed chalky clay. A few spot samples and hand-picked charred plant remains from Sites 77 and 54 were also examined.

Because of the nature of preservation by charring, the majority of archaeobotanical samples recovered from archaeological sites come from mixed waste deposits such as rubbish pits, middens and hearths. As a result, the plant remains may have many origins and the charred assemblages are difficult to interpret with certainty. Therefore, the documented, accidental burning of stored crops in the barn at Wharram presented a unique opportunity to study an assemblage of charred plant remains in a primary context that had become preserved at a very specific point in time. It was hoped that, not only could the quality and range of crops being grown be determined, but also factors such as quantities of grain present might be linked to the documentary information. The main questions arising from the large deposit of burnt, stored grain in context 559 were:

Is there evidence of the building materials that were used for the barn, in particular, thatch?
What was the range of crops grown?
Does the distribution show where and how each crop was being stored?
How much grain was being stored in the barn at the time it was burnt down?
Does the weed ecology provide information about the location of the arable fields and the quality of crop husbandry being practised?

These questions are addressed in the discussion below.

Methods

During the excavations a thick layer of charred grain was observed across the floor of the barn, particularly within grid squares J and M, and the south-west corner of N. In order to examine the distribution of cereals across the barn floor, this charred deposit, context 559, was excavated in a metre square grid pattern, with the number of vertical spits depending on the depth of the deposit. Figure 114 shows the location of the samples across the deposit and the number of spits per metre square.

In 1998 a selection of the charred grain samples was processed and assessed in order to see whether any variation occurred across and through the deposit, and to determine how many samples should be analysed fully so as to recover the maximum information. Although only fifteen samples were examined for the assessment, it was clear that differences in composition existed from one end of the barn to the other, but that vertical differences through the thickness of the deposit were minimal. Each sample was found to contain large numbers of well-preserved cereal grains, so the assessment advised that subsamples of 200ml flot (measured after the large charcoal had been sieved off using a coarse (4mm) sieve) should be analysed per square. It was also recommended that each of the 31 squares across the barn should be included in the analysis, since examining any fewer might fail to detect patterning in the species composition. As the deposit was fairly uniform vertically, only one spit from each square was examined. As a check on uniformity, some of the samples were chosen from the top spit, while others were taken from the bottom or middle spits. The results are discussed below.

Table 64 presents the list of charred plant remains recovered from the barn samples. In Figure 115 the occurrences of the crop plants, bread-type wheat (*Triticum aestivum*-type), hulled barley (*Hordeum vulgare*), oats (*Avena* sp.) and cultivated vetch seeds (*Vicia sativa* ssp. *sativa*), have been plotted across the barn floor using pie charts; the unidentified large vetch seeds (*Vicia/Lathyrus* sp.) have been added to the cultivated vetch segments because the Canoco Correspondence Analysis and spatial plots indicated that they were probably one and the same item (see discussion below). Additional taxa have been plotted on schematic diagrams of the barn floor grid in Figures 120 to 121 and 123 to 125 so as to illustrate points made in the discussion below, e.g. crop/weed associations.

Table 64. The charred plant remains from context 559.

taxa	s.2	s.6	s.7	s.8	s.9	s.10	s.11	s.12	s.13	s.14	s.15	s.16	s.17	s.18	s.19	s.20
	cxt 321	cxt 559														
Grain																
Triticum aestivum/turgidum (free-threshing wheat grain)	1336	761	1778	1975	878	1048	2648	2919	1998	2212	743	581	1535	1390	2606	1858
Triticum sp. (wheat grain in ear)			1	11	2	1	12	9		4	4			1	1	
Hordeum sp. (hulled barley grain)	119	6	9	3	1	6	8	6		9	2	46	10	3	8	11
Avena sativa L. (cultivated oat grain + floret base)	5			3												
A. fatua L. (wild oat grain + floret base)				6												2
Avena sp.(wild/cultivated oat grain)	373	3	5	3	3	7	6	9	7	19	3	83	94	2	7	7
Secale cereale/Triticum sp. (rye/wheat grain)		1	1				1		2	2		2	cf.1		1	cf.3
indeterminate grain	558	341	1653	145	123	1465	308	198	418	335	283	240	330	223	280	190
Chaff																
Triticum aestivum-type (bread-type wheat rachis frag.)	2	15	33	186	13	25	91	68	22	39	19	11	9	14	44	18
Triticum turgium-type (rivet-type wheat rachis frag.)	cf.1		2	cf.6	cf.1	cf.1		cf.2		8	1	3	2	2		2
Triticum aestivum/turgidum (free-threshing wheat rachis frag.)	19	103	187	247	139	320	459	477	312	189	156	23	206	190	616	137
Triticum sp.(wheat collared rachis frag. from base of ear)	3	7	14	16	8	14	40	33	9	11	3	2	7	5	13	6
Triticum sp. (wheat apical spikelet)		2	1	1	1	1		4					1	3	3	
Hordeum sp. (barley rachis frag.)	1	7		1				1		6	5	5	3		1	
Avena fatua L. (wild oat floret base)					2						1					
A. fatua L.(wild oat rachilla)						1									1	
cereal-sized culm node	11	31	104	67	47	32	121	70	23	40	7	2	10	9	32	39
cereal-sized culm base			1	3		3		1	1	2	1		1	3	1	
Cultivated legumes																
legume tendril frag.	+	++	++	+		+	+	++	+	+	+	+	+	+	+	++
legume pod frag.	++	++	+++	+++	+	++	++	+	++	++	++	+	+++	+	+++	+++
Vicia sativa ssp. *sativa* (cultivated vetch seedwith hilum)	47	29	117	89	52	34	37	74	64	90	33	15	79	37	94	105
Vicia/Lathyrus sp. (probable cultivated vetch seed, no hilum, 3mm-4.5mm) (p=with pod frag)	21	70	168	12p	31	44	10	49	21	75	15	22	33	17	32	21
immature vetch seed (p=pod frags attached)	1	2	6	2	5	11	21	10	5	4	1	15	2	4	14	8p
Pisum sativum L. (pea)	cf.2											cf.2				
large legme frag (Pisum/Vicia/Lathyrus)		3			3		1			3	2	5	1		1	3

Table 64 continued.

taxa	s.21	s.22	s.23	s.24	s.25	s.26	s.27	s.28	s.29	s.30	s.31	s.32	s.33	s.34	s.35	Totals
Grain																
Triticum aestivum/turgidum (free-threshing wheat grain)	1533	2719	1863	1668	1348	551	758	1180	72	642	185	19	282	351	311	38412
Triticum sp. (wheat grain in ear)				2	1			1								50
Hordeum sp. (hulled barley grain)	21	21	37	90	91	42	23	28	26	105	295	54	95	107	216	1379
Avena sativa L. (cultivated oat grain + floret base)					cf.1	2										5
A. fatua L. (wild oat grain + floret base)																8
Avena sp.(wild/cultivated oat grain)	6	15	9	39	103	93	21	2	6	21	17	2	18	115	86	811
Secale cereale/Triticum sp. (rye/wheat grain)	cf.1	3	cf.4	cf.1	cf.1		cf.2		cf.1	cf.3						13
indeterminate grain	489	366	507	488	444	200	453	323	75	519	172	44	176	210	294	11292
Chaff																
Triticum aestivum-type (bread-type wheat rachis frag.)	16	24	34	31	27	11	12	9	2	1			2	4	3	783
Triticum turgium-type (rivet-type wheat rachis frag.)	cf.1		cf.2					1								
Triticum aestivum/turgidum (free-threshing wheat rachis frag.)	312	515	113	370	201	114	96	237	28	129	9	6	68	21	46	6026
Triticum sp.(wheat collared rachis frag. from base of ear)	18	19	11	14	14	4	4	13	1	7	1		4	7	3	308
Triticum sp. (wheat apical spikelet)		3		1	2	2		4		1						30
Hordeum sp. (barley rachis frag.)		1	3	1	1	5		2		2				1	2	47
Avena fatua L. (wild oat floret base)			1		1											
A. fatua L.(wild oat rachilla)																
cereal-sized culm node	40	85	56	38	25	15	9	19	2	10	6		5	14	8	966
cereal-sized culm base	1	5	1	1	1		1			1	1				1	30
Cultivated legumes																
legume tendril frag.	++	++	+	+	+	+	+	+			+	+	+	+		
legume pod frag.	+++	+++	+++	++	+	+		+		+	+		+		+	
Vicia sativa ssp. sativa (cultivated vetch seed with hilum)	100	224	56	94	38	31	26	88	2	19	11		17	17	16	1688
Vicia/Lathyrus sp. (probable cultivated vetch seed, no hilum, 3mm-4.5mm) (p=with pod frag)	103	36	47	41	26	12	14	103	13	88	23	6	4	11	16	1151
immature vetch seed (p=pod frags attached)	3	16	9	8	4	2	4	6		3	2		2			161
Pisum sativum L. (pea)		4+ cf.6	cf.19	1+ cf.1	1			6	1	3+ cf.7	2					10
large legme frag (Pisum/Vicia/Lathyrus)	2	16	16	5	5	1	2	12	7		37	3	4	4	1	137

Table 64 continued.

taxa	s.2	s.6	s.7	s.8	s.9	s.10	s.11	s.12	s.13	s.14	s.15	s.16	s.17	s.18	s.19	s.20
	Cxt 321	Cxt 559														

Weeds

taxa	s.2	s.6	s.7	s.8	s.9	s.10	s.11	s.12	s.13	s.14	s.15	s.16	s.17	s.18	s.19	s.20
Ranunculus repens/acris/bulbosus (buttercup achene) DG															1	
Atriplex patula/prostrata (orache seed) CDn			1	4	1	6	4	2	1	8	2	1	7	6	8	
Spergula arvensis L. (corn spurrey seed) Aa												1				
Agrostemma githago L. (corn cockle seed) A	13	11	12	23h	11	9	17	28	11	11	8	1	7	16	25	17h
Agrostemma githago L. (corn cockle capsule teeth) A					1				1	1	1	1			1	
Agrostemma githago L. (corn cockle capsule base) A				5					1	3			2		1	
Silene vulgaris Garke (bladder campion seed) Gdo																
Persicaria maculosa/lapathifolia (redshank/pale persicaria achene) CDo							1	1								
Polygonum aviculare (knotgrass achene) CD										2	1	1				
Fallopia convolvulus (L.)A.Love (black bindweedachene) CD																
Rumex acetosella L. (sheep's sorrel achene) EoGCas					2											
Rumex cf. *crispus* (cf. curled dock seed with valves) CD	2		1				2		2						5	
Rumex sp. (dock achene) CDG	3	3	4	5	6	26	7	42	11	8	5	1	2	12	9	19
Malva sp. (mallow nutlet) DG		1		1		cf.1	cf.1	cf.1								1
Brassica/Sinapis sp. (charlock, mustard etc. seed) CD*					1		1			11			3	1	1	1
Rosa sp. (rose seed) HSW*			cf.1													
cf. *Malus sylvestris* (cf. apple pip frag.) HSW*																
Vicia cf tetrasperma (L.) Schreb. (cf. smooth tare seed) G																
Vicia/Lathyrus sp. (small-seeded vetch/tare, 2-3mm)		6	60	1	4	3	5	6	2	7	16	8	10		4	
Medicago/Trifolium/Lotus sp. (medick/clover/trefoil seed) GD		1														
Scandix pecten-veneris L. (shepherds needle mericarp)			1		3		1		1	4	2	1	1		1	1
Aethusa cynapium L. (fool's parsley mericarp) CD			1			cf.1	7							2u		3
cf. *Conium maculatum* (cf. hemlock mericarp) Gw			1													
cf. *Bupleurum* sp. (cf. thorowax mericarp) Cc																
cf. *Daucus carota* (cf. carrot mericarp) Gc			1													

Table 64 continued.

taxa	s.21	s.22	s.23	s.24	s.25	s.26	s.27	s.28	s.29	s.30	s.31	s.32	s.33	s.34	s.35	Totals
Weeds																
Ranunculus repens/acris/bulbosus (buttercup achene) DG	1	1					1							1		
Atriplex patula/prostrata (orache seed) CDn	6	12	2	7	5		2	3		5				1		
Spergula arvensis L. (corn spurrey seed) Aa																
Agrostemma githago L. (corn cockle seed) A	5	9	16	7	7	5h	5	10	1	7			2	1	1	
Agrostemma githago L. (corn cockle capsule teeth) A		1	1											1		
Agrostemma githago L. (corn cockle capsule base) A		4														
Silene vulgaris Garke (bladder campion seed) Gdo	2	1								3	1					
Persicaria maculosa/lapathifolia (redshank/pale persicaria achene) CDo																
Polygonum aviculare (knotgrass achene) CD	1	2				1				1						
Fallopia convolvulus (L.) A.Love (black bindweedachene) CD											1					
Rumex acetosella L. (sheep's sorrel achene) EoGCas										1						
Rumex cf. crispus (cf. curled dock seed with valves) CD		3		7												
Rumex sp. (dock achene) CDG	27	30	3	5	4	7	9	8	2	16	2		3	6	4	
Malva sp. (mallow nutlet) DG																
Brassica/Sinapis sp. (charlock, mustard etc. seed) CD*	2	1	1	1	2			1		1						
Rosa sp. (rose seed) HSW*																
cf. Malus sylvestris (cf. apple pip frag.) HSW*	cf.1															
Vicia cf tetrasperma (L.) Schreb. (cf. smooth tare seed) G			2													
Vicia/Lathyrus sp. (small-seeded vetch/tare, 2-3mm)	7	4	7	14	7	2	2	6		4	1			4	4	194
Medicago/Trifolium/Lotus sp. (medick/clover/trefoil seed) GD		7	2h		1				1	3						
Scandix pecten-veneris L. (shepherds needle mericarp)	1	3		1				3		2	1		1			
Aethusa cynapium L. (fool's parsley mericarp) CD	1	2														
cf. Conium maculatum (cf. hemlock mericarp) Gw																
cf. Bupleurum sp. (cf. thorowax mericarp) Cc						1										
cf. Daucus carota (cf. carrot mericarp) Gc			1													

Table 64 continued.

taxa	s.2	s.6	s.7	s.8	s.9	s.10	s.11	s.12	s.13	s.14	s.15	s.16	s.17	s.18	s.19	s.20
	cxt	cxt														
	321	559														
Weeds continued																
Prunella vulgaris L. (selfheal nutlet) GDWo			1								1					
Plantago lanceolata L. (ribwort plantain seed) Go												1	1			
Odontites verna/Euphrasia sp. (red bartsia/eyebright seed) ADG					1											
Galium aparine L. (cleavers nutlet) CDSH	1				3	2		1			1				1	
Sambucus nigra L. (elderberry seed) DHSW													1u			
Knautia arvensis (L.) Coult. (field scabiousachene) GDl	2	6	1	1	2	6	5	2	1	1			2	1	2	
Centaurea sp. (cornflower, knapweed achene) CDG			1	2										2	3	
Lapsana communis L. (nipplewort achene) CD		6h	20h	2	14h	8	1	4	2	1			2	1		3
Anthemis cotula L. (stinking chamomile achene) ADhw		1					1						2			2
Chrysanthemum segetum L. (corn marigold achene) AD		1														
Tripleurospermum inodorum (L.) Schultz-Bip (scentless mayweed achene) AD		1h	4	3h	9	2	7	1	2			1	3	10	9	3h
Asteraceae NFI								1								1h
Carex sp. (trigonous sedge nutlet) MGw	1	6	4			1				7	3	2	9	1		1
Lolium temulentum L. (darnel caryopsis) AD	15	3	2	9	1	3	12		4	9	1	1	2	7	7	9
Lolium perenne/rigidum (rye-grass caryopsis) CDG								1								41
Bromus sect. *Bromus* (chess caryopsis) CD			1									cf.1				
Poaceae (various small-seeded grasses) CGD	2	2				1	3	2	2			1		1	4	1
cf. *Anguina tritici* (cf. wheat nematode gall)	5	5	10	22	9	8	28	35	4	14	7	2	3	6	20	18
Total remains	2540	1419	4188	2813	1352	3084	3867	4061	2929	3140	1329	1077	2378	1967	3857	2499
Volume of grain		50	90	101	45	62	130	130	90	90	45	37	76	50	100	89
Volume of >500 micons flot		60	50	44	60	60	35	30	50	50	78	85	69	25	50	51
volume of <500 microns flot		90	60	55	95	78	35	40	50	60	77	78	55	25	50	60
Volume of charcoal		150	100	175	200	50	10	200	200	33	200	100	25	20	50	16
vol. flot analysed (ml)		200	200	200	200	200	200	200	200	200	200	200	200	100	200	200
spit		3of4	3of4	2of5	7of7	1of1	4of5	6of7	2of4	5of5	1of2	2of3	1of3	2of2	3of4	2of2
remains per 100 ml flot		710	2098	1407	884	1542	1934	2029	1465	1570	664.5	538.5	1189	1967	1929	1250

(+ = occasional; ++ = several; +++ = frequent; h = seeds still embedded in seed head fragment; p = legume pod fragments still attached to seed; cf. = unconfirmed identification)

Table 64 continued.

taxa	s.21	s.22	s.23	s.24	s.25	s.26	s.27	s.28	s.29	s.30	s.31	s.32	s.33	s.34	s.35	Totals
Weeds continued																
Prunella vulgaris L. (selfheal nutlet) GDWo																
Plantago lanceolata L. (ribwort plantain seed) Go			1							1						
Odontites verna/Euphrasia sp. (red bartsia/eyebright seed) ADG		4								2						
Galium aparine L. (cleavers nutlet) CDSH	5	2		1	2			1		2	1					
Sambucus nigra L. (elderberry seed) DHSW																
Knautia arvensis (L.) Coult. (field scabiousachene) GDl	5	2	2	4	2		1	2	1	1	1				1	
Centaurea sp. (cornflower, knapweed achene) CDG	1				2											
Lapsana communis L. (nipplewort achene) CD	2	12h		2	1	2	1	1		1						
Anthemis cotula L. (stinking chamomile achene) ADhw		3								1						
Chrysanthemum segetum L. (corn marigold achene) AD									1							
Tripleurospermum inodorum (L.) Schultz-Bip (scentless mayweed achene) AD	9h	6	2	1	1	1		1	3							
Asteraceae NFI																
Carex sp. (trigonous sedge nutlet) MGw			1	5				1			1		1	1	1	
Lolium temulentum L. (darnel caryopsis) AD	5	17	4	15	10	2	7	8	3	13	52		1	5	6	
Lolium perenne/rigidum (rye-grass caryopsis) CDG	9	59	7					2		11	2					
Bromus sect. *Bromus* (chess caryopsis) CD																
Poaceae (various small-seeded grasses) CGD	1	2	2	2	3	5	4	1		2		2			1	
cf. *Anguina tritici* (cf. wheat nematode gall)	9	15	13	11	12	3	4	12		3				1	1	
Total remains	2734	4258	2827	2974	2392	1108	1460	2094	247	1628	824	136	685	881	1024	65232
Volume of grain	80	100	95	85	90	35	38	68	8	50	30	5	20	40	35	1964
Volume of >500 micons flot	56	43	63	58	70	87	55	62	8	80	30	8	70	85	90	
volume of <500 microns flot	64	57	42	57	40	78	37	70	12	70	20	8	35	75	75	
Volume of charcoal	40	25	100	60	200	100	40	80	15	80	20	0	75	200	200	
vol. flot analysed (ml)	200	200	200	200	200	200	130	200	28	200	80	21	125	200	200	
spit	1of1	2of2	2of3	4of5	5of5	2of4	1of1	1of1	2of2	1of1	1of1	1of1	1of1	2of8	1of1	
remains per 100 ml flot	1367	2129	1414	1487	1196	554	1123	1047	882.1	814	1030	647.6	548	440.5	512	

(+ = occasional; ++ = several; +++ = frequent; h = seeds still embedded in seed head fragment; p = legume pod fragments still attached to seed; cf. = unconfirmed identification)

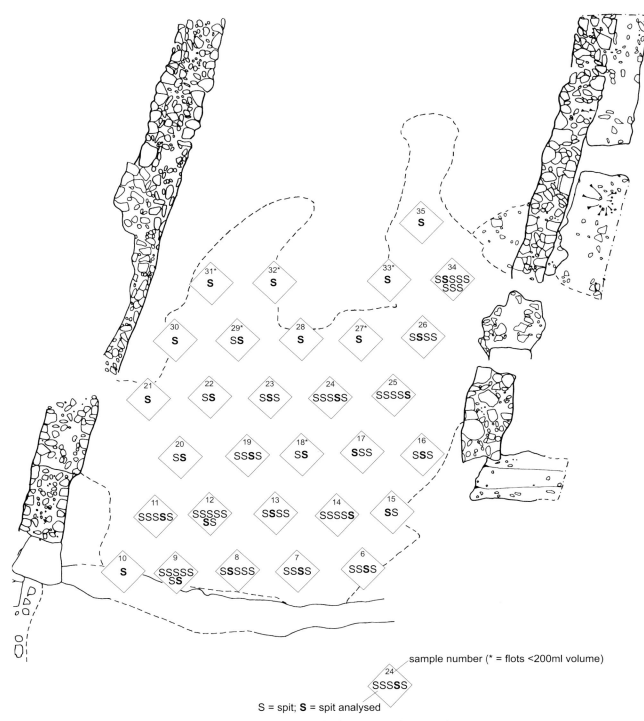

Fig. 114. Site 77 barn: location of the samples and the number of spits excavated. (E. Marlow-Mann)

Canoco Correspondence Analysis

In addition to analysing the data visually by plotting it on schematic diagrams, the data was subjected to Correspondence Analysis using Canoco. This work was carried out by Professor Marijke van der Veen (University of Leicester). Although the following interpretations of the data are primarily the responsibility of the author, she would like to thank Professor van der Veen for carrying out the analysis, for help in interpreting the results, and for very useful discussions concerning the barn assemblages. Professor van der Veen also provided the following description of Correspondence Analysis.

Correspondence Analysis is a type of multivariate statistics well suited to archaeobotanical data: it can cope with large numbers of taxa that do not appear in every sample, and it does not expect the data to be distributed normally (Gauch 1984; Ter Braak and Smilauer 2002). It arranges samples and species along two or more axes of variation, according to the co-occurrences of taxa in the samples. For ease of interpretation the plots are given separately for samples (Fig. 116) and species (Figs 117 and 118). The first axis is the horizontal one; this one accounts for most of the variation. The second, vertical one, accounts for the next amount of variation. Usually

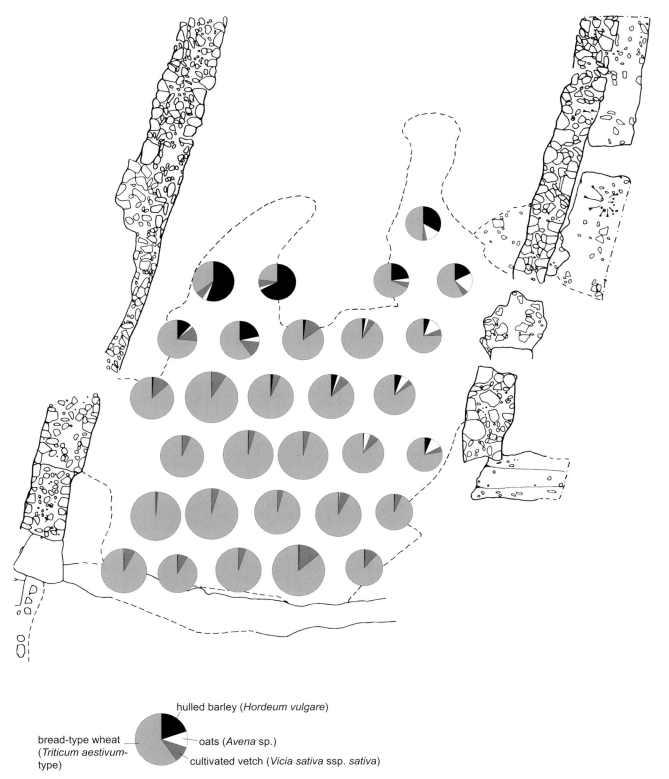

hulled barley (*Hordeum vulgare*)

bread-type wheat (*Triticum aestivum-*type)

oats (*Avena* sp.)

cultivated vetch (*Vicia sativa* ssp. *sativa*)

Fig. 115. Site 77 barn: the distribution of stored crop remains across layer 559. (E. Marlow-Mann)

only the first two axes are displayed, though more could be plotted. When looking for patterns in the data and similarities between groups of samples and/or species it is the direction away from the centre that matters, as well as the proximity of the samples/ species to each other. The areas of the plot are often referred to as the north-east, south-east, north-west and south-west quadrants.

Prior to running the Canoco analysis the data were prepared in the following way by Professor van der Veen:

non-numerical records such as legume pod fragments (scored for presence +) were removed
weed species occurring in less than 10% of the samples were removed

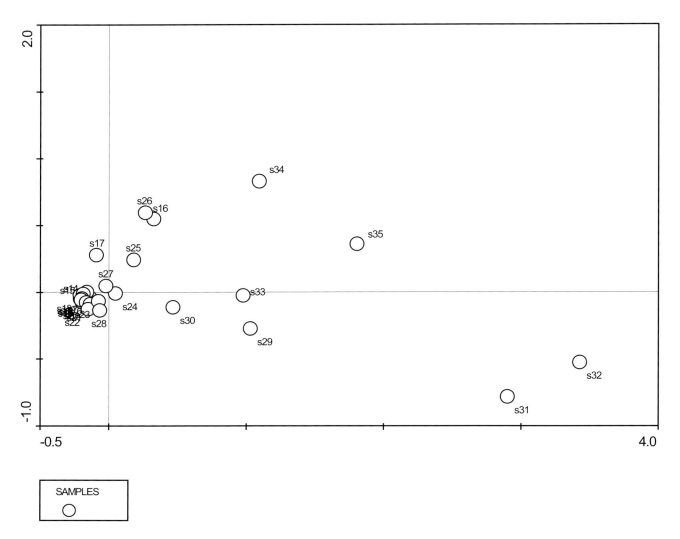

Fig. 116. Canoco sample plot.

taxa identified to both species level and to 'cf' level were merged e.g. the peas

rachis fragments of *Triticum* were combined as the data suggest that only one species was present

the indeterminate cereals were distributed amongst wheat and barley according to the relative proportion of positively identified grains (oats were not included as their more elongated shape meant that they had been recorded as *Avena* sp.)

Results and data analysis

Some notes on the state of preservation and identification of the crop plants

Because the charred deposit contained material burnt *in situ* in a thick (maximum depth 15cm), fairly undisturbed layer, a wide range of well-preserved cereal remains was recovered. The fact that the deposit had remained undisturbed was confirmed by the presence of rarely found charred items such as legume pods fragments still containing immature seeds (p in Table 64), weed seed heads with seeds still embedded (h in Table 64) and a few cereal grains still enclosed in chaff and attached to the

rachis, i.e. still 'in the ear' ('wheat grain in ear' in Table 64). Figure 114 shows the thickness of the deposit in terms of the number of vertical spits, providing some indication of how the charred deposit thickened to the south and east of the barn. Figure 119 shows the distribution of the notably well-preserved remains, i.e. weed seed heads, legume pod fragments and grains in the ear. It also gives cereal concentrations for each sample (standardised where flots of less than 200ml were analysed). Comparing these values with those in Figures 114 and 115, it can be seen that the highest concentrations of grain coincided with the predominantly bread-type wheat samples (wheat> 90%) and mostly with the thicker depth of charred material. Thus, it appears that a large deposit of wheat at the southern and central area of the barn was burnt, providing protection for the lower samples from damage and, therefore, excellent conditions of preservation. In the north-west corner of the sampled area a more thinly spread sample of barley was subjected to increased damage, possibly causing some loss of material. The barley/oat dredge (a mixed crop of barley and oats) was spread along the eastern wall of the barn. Lower cereal concentrations suggest that conditions of

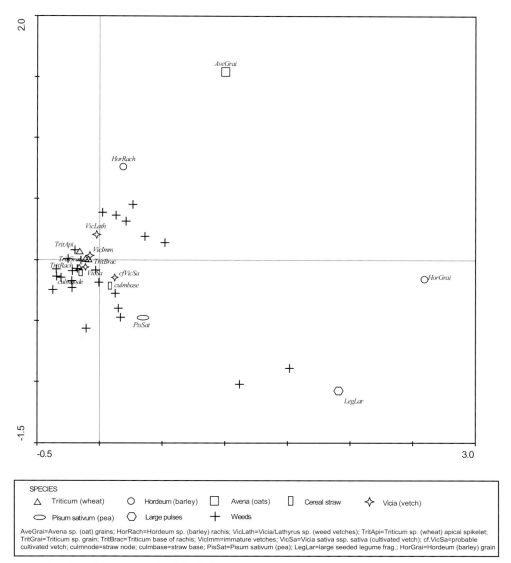

Fig. 117. Canoco species plot with crop remains labelled.

preservation were also poorer in this region, although the spit number information shows that a greater depth of deposit was preserved along the wall. Perhaps the charred deposit comprised more burnt thatch and building materials than stored crop along this side of the barn. Examination of the unprocessed soil samples showed that significant quantities of silt, stones and mortar from the walls were present in the outer samples, whilst a few of the centrally placed samples contained more fine ash and, in some cases (e.g. Sample 8), concretions containing grain still in the ear (discussed further below). It is clear that preservation conditions were more favourable in the central area of the deposit.

Canoco analysis results

When examined together, the samples (Fig. 116) and species (Figs 117 and 118) plots confirmed many of the impressions obtained from the visual spatial plots, and calculations of percentages and ratios.

The main cluster of samples occurred in the south-west quadrant, comprising the wheat-rich samples in the southern area of the barn floor. Most of the weed seeds and the wheat chaff (both rachis fragments and straw nodes) fragments also occurred in this tight cluster to the west of the vertical axis. Of particular note was the fact that the confirmed cultivated vetch seeds were located in the centre of this wheat-rich sample cluster and the probable vetch seeds were close by, on the edge of the group. This information was valuable in discussing the possible cultivation of vetch and wheat as a maslin (see discussion below).

Furthest removed from the central cluster were the two barley-rich samples (Samples 31 and 32) in the south-east quadrant, along with large legume fragments and two weed species (*Lolium temulentum, Silene vulgaris*). Also separated from the main group in an easterly direction were other samples containing higher proportions of barley, but with significant quantities of oats. The most characteristic of these probable dredge assemblages were from Samples 35 and 34, and these lay in the north-east quadrant together with three other samples located along the east wall of the barn. In addition to oats, the other

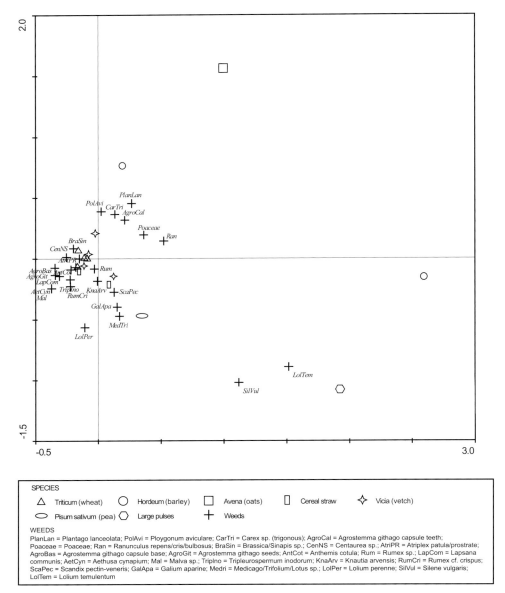

Fig. 118. Canoco species plot with weeds labelled.

SPECIES
△ Triticum (wheat) ◯ Hordeum (barley) ☐ Avena (oats) ▯ Cereal straw ✧ Vicia (vetch)
⬭ Pisum sativum (pea) ⬡ Large pulses + Weeds

WEEDS
PlanLan = Plantago lanceolata; PolAvi = Ploygonum aviculare; CarTri = Carex sp. (trigonous); AgroCal = Agrostemma githago capsule teeth; Poaceae = Poaceae; Ran = Ranunculus repens/cris/bulbosus; BraSin = Brassica/Sinapis sp.; CenNS = Centaurea sp.; AtriPR = Atriplex patula/prostrate; AgroBas = Agrostemma githago capsule base; AgroGit = Agrostemma githago seeds; AntCot = Anthemis cotula; Rum = Rumex sp.; LapCom = Lapsana communis; AetCyn = Aethusa cynapium; Mal = Malva sp.; TripIno = Tripleurospermum inodorum; KnaArv = Knautia arvensis; RumCri = Rumex cf. crispus; ScaPec = Scandix pectin-veneris; GalApa = Galium aparine; Medri = Medicago/Trifolium/Lotus sp.; LolPer = Lolium perenne; SilVul = Silene vulgaris; LolTem = Lolium temulentum

remains separated off in this direction were barley rachis fragments and a few weeds more characteristic of grassy habitats than arable fields (though they can be grown in a variety of disturbed places; e.g. *Plantago lanceolata, Ranunculus repens/acris/bulbosus,* Poaceae). Perhaps this area of the barn held feedstuffs, including dredge, hay and chaff. This is discussed further below.

The distribution of the weed taxa in the Canoco plots was a particularly useful part of the analysis, and this is discussed more fully below in the crop husbandry section.

Economic plants
The following identifications of economic plants were confirmed by the presence of chaff fragments (cereals) or hila (legumes):

Bread-type wheat *(Triticum aestivum-type)*
The majority of cereal grains were well-preserved, with no signs of sprouting through long-term storage in damp conditions and no obvious signs of insect damage.

Charring had not caused oozing or vacuolation, suggesting that the grain had been fully ripe with a low moisture content when stored, and that the combustion temperatures reached on the floor of the barn had not been too fierce. Where concretions of unprocessed material were examined (whole soil, not floated), remnants of the palea, lemma and glume were often still visible. These thin, papery chaff components are usually destroyed during charring and by flotation of the soil samples. Their presence in the unprocessed samples demonstrated that this element of the chaff had probably been mostly lost when the samples were excavated and floated. This observation was important in providing further evidence that the grain had been stored in an un-threshed state (see discussion below). Additional indications were the facts that some of the grains were still attached to the rachis.

The third line of evidence was that wheat chaff (rachis fragments) was present in relatively large quantities, with the ratio of grain to chaff fragments being roughly 5 to 1

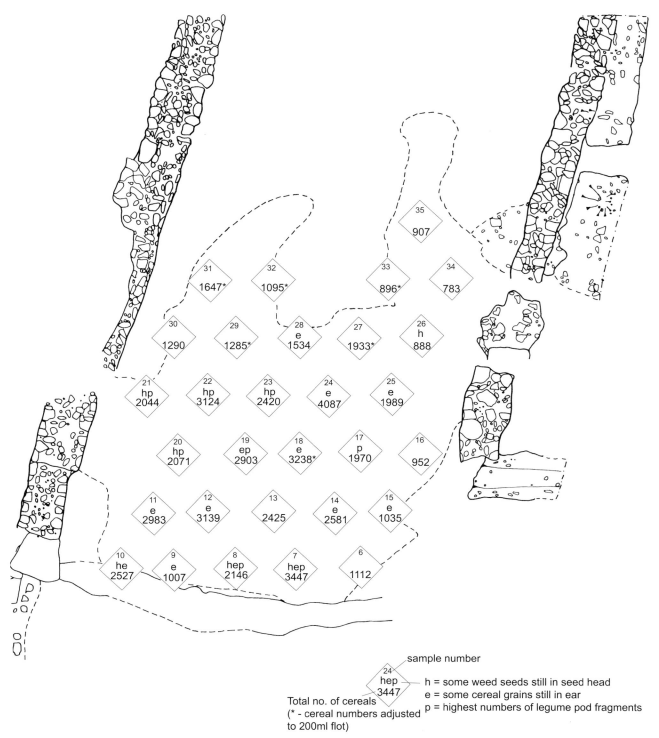

Fig. 119. Site 77 barn: grain density and preservation conditions. (E. Marlow-Mann)

(ranging from *c.* 3:1 to 8:1 in twelve wheat-dominant squares (>99% wheat)) (Fig. 120). The theoretical ratio of grain to chaff in an ear of wheat ranges from 2:1 to 6:1 grains to chaff fragments, as each spikelet at a rachis node can contain from 2 to 6 grains of wheat (Percival 1948). Although these figures have not been adjusted to take account of the unidentified cereal grains, accurate calculations cannot be made, as many small fragments of cereal grains and chaff in the flots could not be quantified. Besides, the underestimate of grains is probably balanced

out by the increased loss of rachis fragments during charring. Charring usually reduces the proportion of chaff, as rachis fragments are more delicate structures than grains (Boardman and Jones 1990). Taking these factors into consideration, the ratio of chaff appears to have been high enough to indicate that ears of wheat rather than threshed grains were present.

Finally, the very close association of the wheat rachis fragments and the wheat grains in the visual plots and in the Canoco plot (Figs 117 and 118) confirmed that the

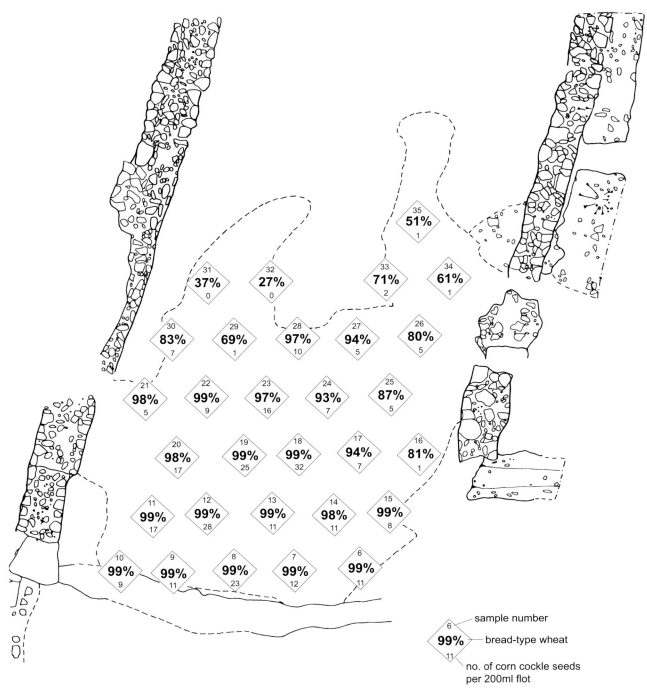

Fig. 120. Site 77 barn: bread-type wheat as a percentage of identifiable grain (%) and number of corn cockle seeds per 200ml flot (no.). (E. Marlow-Mann)

wheat had indeed been stored in the ear, most probably still in sheaves that had been brought in from the fields the previous summer. Percival (1948) suggests that in this area of the country the crop would probably have been harvested around mid-August, a suggestion that receives support from Henry Best's Farming Book, compiled just under a century later for a farm about 15km south-east of Wharram (Woodward 1984, 45-7; see below).

The grain morphology was generally of the rounded shape typical of bread wheat (Jacomet 1987) but was fairly varied, suggesting a genetically diverse crop. There was very little evidence to suggest that any other species

of wheat was being grown, for example rivet-type wheat (*Triticum turgidum;* see Moffett 1991). Although occasional rivet-like rachis fragments were observed in the samples (*c.* 0.5% of total rachis fragments), variations within ancient wheat crops and the fact that some of the identification criteria are not 100% reliable (Hillman, pers. comm.) mean that rivet wheat was probably not present. Small quantities of rivet-type wheat appear to have been grown at Wharram during the 13th and 14th centuries, since a few tetraploid rivet-type wheat rachis fragments were recovered from dumps of charred grain in the millpond at Site 71 (Jones 2005). The range of this

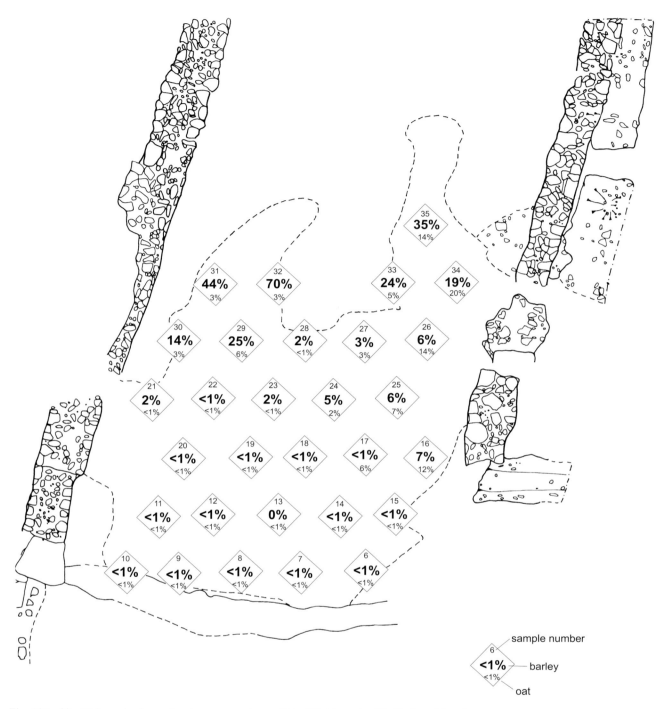

Fig. 121. Site 77 barn: barley and oat as a percentage of identifiable grain. (E. Marlow-Mann)

slightly tender species of wheat may have been greater with the milder climate of the earlier medieval period, when there was less danger of severe spring frosts and higher summer temperatures. By the 16th century the deterioration of the climate may have made it an unsuitable crop for a settlement as far north and as elevated (*c*. 150m above sea level) as Wharram.

Six-row hulled barley (*Hordeum vulgare* L. emend.)
Barley grains were present in all except one sample (Sample 13). Although six-row hulled barley was positively identified from the presence of paleas and

lemmas, and both straight and twisted grains, it is possible that some two-row hulled barley was present (straight grains only). Relatively few rachis fragments of barley were recovered from the samples, particularly the barley-rich samples, suggesting that this crop had been stored as processed grain. This suggestion is supported by the fact that the Canoco plot (Figs 117 and 118) separated the barley grains from barley chaff, particularly on the first axis of variation. The chaff that was present in the samples, therefore, did not show the same pattern of distribution as the grain, and it may have mainly been derived from the base coat of the thatched roof.

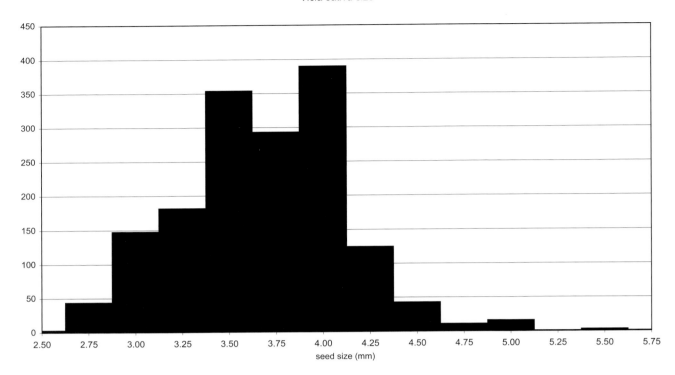

Fig. 122. Cultivated vetch (*Vicia sativa* ssp. sativa) seed sizes.

Barley does not produce a good thatching straw as it is too soft and absorbent, but a variety of waste material was often used as the base coat for thatch. John Letts (1999, 22) found barley remains in the base coat of three late medieval buildings in southern/central England. In the 1640s, and much closer to Wharram, Henry Best of Elmswell, near Driffield, reckoned that rye or wheat straw made the best thatch, but that barley was also acceptable if it lacked weeds and was not too short. He recommended that oat straw should be avoided (Woodward 1984, 145).

Cultivated and wild oats (*Avena sativa* L. and *Avena fatua* L.) Oat grains were present in all the samples, although often in fairly small quantities. Unfortunately the delicate floret bases and rachilla required to identify oats to species level rarely survive charring. The presence of a few well-preserved examples demonstrated that both wild and cultivated oats were present. The concentration of grains in the north-east, and, to a lesser extent, the north-west corners of the sampled area confirmed that cultivated oats were being grown as a crop, but perhaps only as dredge (see Figs 115 and 121). Occurrences of 3% or less in the samples probably represented wild weed oats and relict crops in fields where crop rotation was practised. This is discussed further below.

Cultivated vetch (*Vicia sativa* ssp. *sativa*)
This leguminous crop was positively identified in all but one sample (small volume Sample 32) from well-

preserved seeds possessing distinctive wedge-shaped hila and often a slightly square-shaped seed. Measurements of the identified seeds showed that the size range for the cultivated vetch seeds was wide (2.5mm to 5.75mm), but that 95% of the seeds fell within the 3-4.5mm range (Fig. 122). Unfortunately, most leguminous seeds are recovered without their identifying hila, since the seed coats are often damaged by charring. As weed seeds were not common in any of the samples, it was clear that the numerous medium-sized (3-4.5mm) unidentified vetch/tare seeds (*Vicia/Lathyrus* sp.) present in all samples were most likely to be from cultivated vetch rather than weed species. This was confirmed by the close relationship between all the vetch points in the Canoco plot, Figures 117 and 118. For these reasons, in Figure 115 the 3-4.5mm vetch seeds were added to the confirmed cultivated vetch records to present a clearer, more accurate impression of the proportions of each crop across the barn. Leguminous pod fragments still containing vetch seeds, which were sometimes small, flattened and immature, were recovered from most of the samples (87%). Tendril fragments were equally as common, suggesting that, like the wheat, vetch may also have been stored in the barn still on the straw. The distribution of vetch seeds and the possibility of cultivation as a maslin are discussed further below.

Peas (*Pisum sativum* L.)
The problem of poor preservation, i.e. loss of hila on charring, was also true for the large legumes present in

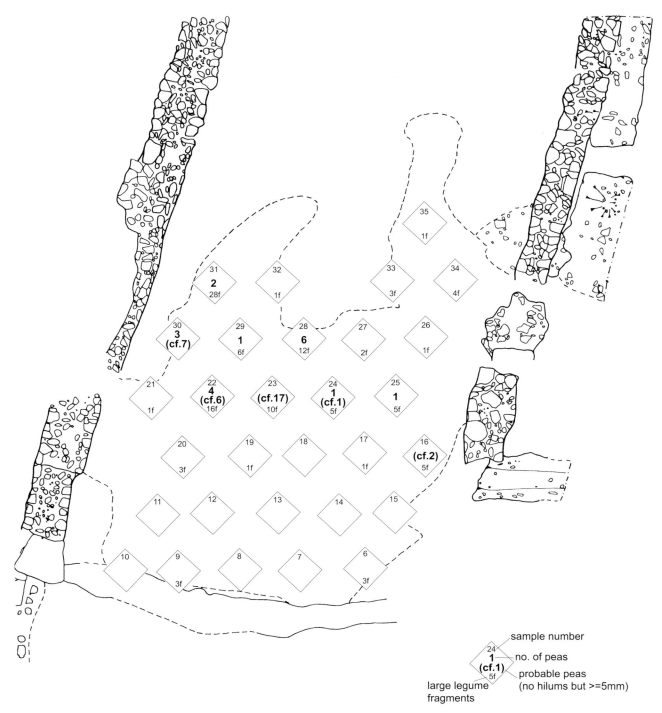

Fig. 123. Site 77 barn: number of peas, probable peas and large legume fragments. (E. Marlow-Mann)

the samples. This particularly causes identification problems for peas, as Celtic beans are more distinctive in their oblong shape when whole beans are present. No whole beans were recovered from the barn samples, although it is possible that some of the large legume fragments may have been from beans. Other Saxon and medieval samples from Wharram have only produced a single bean to date (Carruthers 2005), so beans do not appear to have been an important crop at Wharram Percy. In contrast, peas have been recovered in relatively large numbers from the Saxon and medieval samples. The presence of peas in the barn was confirmed in seven of the samples, due to the presence of small, rounded hilums on large round seeds (c. 5mm diameter or more). Some of the legume pod and tendril fragments may have been from the peas, although they were probably mostly from the more abundant vetches. Other large, round leguminous seeds were recorded as cf. pea if they were 5mm or larger in size. It should be noted that seed size is not a reliable method of distinguishing cultivated vetch seeds from peas, as a few of the positively identified *Vicia sativa* seeds possessing hilums were = or > 5mm (1%, 21 seeds) and peas can be less than 5mm in diameter. All the peas and cf. peas were recovered from the central area of the barn (Fig. 123). Although no definite associations with the barley concentration to the north-west were observed, the Canoco plots for barley, peas and large legume fragments were all in the same south-eastern quadrant (Canoco Figs 117 and 118). It is probable that the peas had been stored separately, close to the barley, although a barley and pea maslin could have been grown.

Discussion

The structure of the barn: the documentary and archaeological evidence

Chapter 1 of this volume has provided details of the 1555-6 court case involving two successive vicars of Wharram Percy, Marmaduke Atkinson and William Firby. The former had been the incumbent in 1553 when the fire had destroyed the vicarage and its barn. The precise date of this event is not known, but the records indicate that it occurred (during the night) at some point in late February or March in that year. Firby contended that Atkinson's replacement buildings were inadequate.

The pre-fire barn was described as a building of six posts or crucks. It had stood at the stable end of the vicarage house, and the house, stable and barn were all under one thatched roof. At the time of excavation the west wall of the barn was embedded into the hillside, but it may be that much of the overburden was due to land slippage in post-medieval times. Though the west wall as uncovered was continuous, without a gap to indicate a doorway, there was an area of looser rubble walling opposite the presumed main entrance in the east wall (see p. 70); this may indicate that the barn originally had opposed doorways that could be used to create sufficient draught for threshing. The west doorway would, however, have been blocked after the disuse of the building, when the west wall was incorporated into a boundary wall. Apart from the possible threshing floor position, the internal arrangements of the barn are unknown. The presence of a significant spread of nails towards the south end of the building may, however, indicate that there was an end loft.

Large fragments of charcoal were common in the samples, and in some cases the volume of charcoal equalled the volume of grain. There were no obvious patterns to the charcoal distribution, although samples around the southern and eastern walls of the barn generally produced larger quantities. Although the charcoal has not been analysed in detail by the author, oak heartwood (*Quercus* sp.; tyloses present, indicating heartwood) was by far the dominant taxon, with some ash (*Fraxinus excelsior*). The fragments of oak heartwood showing very little curve in the growth rings were likely to have been derived from the six oak posts and roofing timbers. Ash may have been used for smaller roof timbers and/or internal dividing panels.

The archaeobotanical evidence for thatch

Although well-preserved, *in-situ* charred plant remains were recovered from the samples, it has been difficult to determine with certainty whether or not some of the remains in the barn were derived from burnt thatch. Having been the uppermost, highly combustible layer exposed to the air, the thatch could have rapidly burnt away, leaving very little trace. Alternately, the opposite may be true, in that thatch is said to be permanently damp and so rarely catches fire (Letts 1999). Information retrieved by John Letts from thatchers in his survey of smoke-blackened thatch (1999, 32) suggested that, when a fire is started inside a house, although the timbers below the thatch may burn away and cause the roof to collapse, the thick upper layer of thatch may remain mostly unburnt:

'Hence only a portion of the thatch on the roof that is lost to fire is ever charred, but this material is quickly sealed by compost and colonising vegetation if the building is abandoned.'
(Letts 1999)

Letts suggests that, for this reason, burnt thatch is rarely found in archaeological deposits as charred remains, although base coats are more likely to be preserved, and thatch can be preserved by waterlogging.

Although straw or reed stems are usually completely destroyed by burning, the thickened stem joints or 'culm nodes' survive more frequently. An examination of the distribution of the straw nodes across the Wharram barn showed that their occurrence closely followed the pattern of distribution of the wheat grains. Further confirmation of this close relationship was found in the Canoco plot (Figs 117 and 118), as the wheat grains lay at the same point as the culm nodes along the horizontal axis, and the two were only separated a short distance by the second, vertical axis of variation. The evidence suggests, therefore, that rather than representing thatch, the straw nodes came from sheaves of wheat being stored in the barn.

Preservation was poorer at the northern end of the barn so it could be argued that the lack of straw nodes at the non-wheat end of the barn may have been due to differential preservation. Even where the preservation was reasonably good, in low-wheat squares, e.g. Sample 31, only a few straw nodes were present. This is further evidence supporting the suggestion that the barley and oats had been stored as threshed grain rather than in stooks.

A few small 'hand-picked' samples of charred 'thatch-like' material were examined, and in some cases these may have been burnt thatch. Straw fragments were seen to be aligned in one example (Sample 77/559/J), suggesting that either thatch or bundled straw was present. Bundled straw could equally as well have been from a sheaf of corn as from a fragment of thatch. In most cases the concreted lumps showed no structure or alignment, and these may represent general burnt waste, or possibly the base coat of the thatch. The thatch

question, therefore, remains unanswered. The author considers that the most likely explanation for the absence of clear evidence for thatch in this well-preserved deposit is the one given by Letts, i.e. that, if the fire had been started inside the barn, most of the damp thatch would have remained unburnt, falling onto the charred grain as the timbers burnt away. This would have provided a layer of protection to the burnt remains that gradually rotted away once the area was abandoned.

The stored crops

In the court case of 1555-6, one of the principal allegations made by Vicar Firby was that, after the fire, his predecessor should have replaced the barn with a new one, but had failed to do so. Atkinson responded that a new barn was unnecessary, because the two oxgangs of arable and two acres of meadow which formed the glebe in Wharram Percy township did not produce enough of a crop to warrant one. Each side called a number of witnesses as to the productive capacity of the glebe lands, and their written depositions provide considerable if contradictory detail. Firby's deponents broadly stated what two oxgangs *should* have produced – sixteen to twenty loads of corn and two to six loads of hay. Atkinson's witnesses stated what, they claimed, the land *actually* produced – three to six loads of corn and two of hay.

The cause of this disparity is clear from the various witness statements. Apart from two other oxgangs of land held by a chantry, the rest of Wharram Percy's open-field arable lands had been put down to permanent pasture over twenty years earlier, and this had impacted significantly on yields, presumably because the corn was growing in a sea of grassland which severely restricted opportunities for crop rotation to be practised. One of the deponents also implied that by 1555 the vicar's oxgangs, too, had been put down to grass. If so, this may have been a response to the barn's destruction.

It is possible, therefore, that the crops stored in the barn came from the two bovates of glebe land, but other potential sources need to be considered. Atkinson may, for instance, have bought crops in the sheaf from the farmers of neighbouring townships and stored them in his barn for household use; any such transactions are, of course, undocumented. For a few years after his admission to the vicarage, he had leased the Wharram Percy tithes from the crown, but his interest in them had evidently ceased long before the fire: in 1545 the crown had granted them on a 21-year lease to Thomas Kydall of York (*LP Henry VIII*, 20, *pt 1*, 682).

For a time Atkinson also had an interest in the chantry lands, which he had leased from the crown year on year (see p. 22). In 1552, however, the two bovates were put up for sale. The particulars were drawn up on 30th June 1552, but one of the clauses stated that the purchaser was to have the issues (i.e. the produce of the land) from the previous Easter (TNA PRO E315/68, f.439v). It seems unlikely therefore, that the two chantry bovates had contributed to the produce held in the barn early in 1553, even if they were still being cultivated.

Although some of the crop remains in the barn could have been left over from previous years, particularly small fragments of chaff and weed seeds, it is likely that storage areas would have been swept clean before the new harvest was brought in, so as to reduce spoilage from pests and diseases. The main crops being stored in the barn were as follows:

Wheat
The principal crop being stored in the barn at the time of the fire in 1553 was bread-type wheat (*Triticum aestivum*-type). Well-preserved wheat grains were recovered from all thirty samples, although it can be seen from Figures 115 and 120 that the main concentration occurred in the southern and central part of the sampled area. In seventeen of these southerly squares wheat comprised 97% to 99% of the identified grain. Some of the squares bordering the main concentration produced 80% or more wheat, and even in the areas where oats and barley were dominant, wheat still made up at least a quarter of the identifiable grain (Fig. 121).

The presence of frequent chaff fragments amongst the wheat grains demonstrated that this crop had been stored in the ear, probably still in the sheaves that had been harvested from the fields the previous summer. In describing the use of the 14th-century Great Barn at Bredon, Worcestershire, Dyer (1997, 27) suggests that the estate workers would have brought in cartloads of corn in the sheaf to be stacked in the barn. Wheat was primarily for use by the household, and threshing would take place gradually over the year when the weather permitted and when the labour force was available (Dyer, pers. comm.). The quantity of threshed and winnowed grain at Wharram was not sufficient to require a separate granary (in contrast to Bredon); it was probably stored in the upstairs rooms or loft spaces of the vicarage, as it still was in Wolds farmhouses of the early 18th century (Harrison and Hutton 1984, 238). Once free of the chaff, the naked grains of bread wheat are vulnerable to pests and diseases and are liable to sprout if kept in damp conditions. A traditional method was to store threshed grain in sacks or other containers in hammocks in the roof space of the house, so as to keep it dry and out of the reach of vermin. This type of storage would leave little archaeological trace.

Documentary evidence from harvest workers in southern and east England (Dyer 2000) demonstrated that, although barley was commonly used for workers' bread up to the 13th century, it was increasingly replaced by wheat during the 14th century. Higher status households would have consumed bread made primarily from wheat. It is likely, therefore, that the bread consumed at the vicarage would have been entirely made from wheat, since bread wheat produces a far lighter-textured loaf. Bread wheat, however, is more demanding of nutrients and needs to be kept free of weeds in order to obtain a reasonable yield. Being awnless, the ears are also more susceptible to pest damage than barley or oats. Crop rotation and/or manuring would be required if the land was continuously cropped. There is some evidence (see p.309 below) that adequate crop rotation and manuring was not being practised at Wharram and that yields suffered as a consequence.

Barley, oats and dredge
The archaeobotanical evidence from Wharram suggests that barley and oats were important crops from the Late Saxon period onwards, but that rye was never present in significant quantities (Carruthers 2005, 218). The barn samples contained what appears to have been threshed barley and oats, but only in the northern and eastern end of the sampled area (Figs 115 and 121). Pure barley, mixed with wheat spreading over from the southern end, was located in the north-west corner and a possible area of dredge was present against the east wall. The reason why these crops were stored as threshed grain is probably partly due to the fact that they both retain their husk when threshed, so are less vulnerable to pests and damp.

The prime use of barley and dredge was for brewing ale, with some being used for fodder. The vicar's household could well have drunk around 20-30 gallons of ale a week (Chris Dyer, pers. comm.), although no evidence for malting grain has yet been recovered from Wharram. Grain for brewing is likely to have been treated with care, and it may not have been stored for long periods, in order to achieve a high rate of uniform sprouting in the production of malt. If the barley and dredge were being stored for fodder, however, spoilage would have been less of a concern. The documentary evidence demonstrated that barley and dredge were grown in significant quantities at Bredon during the 14th century (Dyer 1997). Oats are a particularly useful crop on acidic soils in parts of the country with damp climates, such as south-east England, Wales and Scotland.

The free-draining, calcareous soils of the Yorkshire Wolds would have been well suited to the cultivation of barley, and it is a crop recorded as having been grown at Thixendale in the mid-16th century (Purvis 1949, 34-7), and in Wharram le Street towards the end of that century (Borthwick CP G.2577). Henry Best's Farming Book, 'a series of treatises and remembrances dealing with agricultural practice at Elmswell from the 1620s to the early 1640s' (Woodward 1984, xvii), is concerned with an estate near Driffield that contained carr land and clays, as well as wold land. It is clear from Best's advice and comments that he had been accustomed to grow barley on his wold land rather than on his clays (Woodward 1984, 56, 59).

Peas
Peas were present in the central area of the barn (Fig. 123) in fairly small numbers, perhaps indicating that by the spring of 1553 supplies of this crop were running fairly low. Dyer (1997) mentions peas as being used for pig fodder, particularly at times of the year when foods such as acorns were no longer available. At Wharram they may also have been used alongside dredge for sheep fodder (Chris Dyer, pers. comm.). As noted above, peas were grown during earlier periods of occupation at Wharram, but there was very little evidence for the cultivation of beans. They may have been grown as part of a crop rotation system, or as garden plants. Their association with barley in the Canoco plots suggests that peas could have been grown as a maslin. Dried peas were probably stored out of the pod in some type of container.

Cultivated vetch
The widespread and frequent occurrence of cultivated vetch remains in the barn samples was perhaps the most unexpected finding from this work, and possibly the most difficult to explain. Positively identified cultivated vetch seeds were recovered from all except the smallest sample (Sample 32), and vetch/tare seeds were present in numbers too large to indicate weed contamination (see discussion above). Ratios of cereal grains to vetch seeds (*Vicia sativa* ssp. *sativa* plus *Vicia/Lathyrus* sp.) varied erratically from 63:1 (Sample 11) to 10:1 (Sample 21). Since pod fragments and tendrils were also present in almost all samples, and vetch remains were fairly evenly distributed across the barn floor in a similar pattern to the wheat remains (Fig. 115), the most likely explanation is that unthreshed cultivated vetch was present amongst the sheaves of wheat. The Canoco species plot (Figs 117 and 118) confirms the close association between vetch and wheat.

Mixed cropping of vetch and wheat would seem to have been unlikely because bread wheat was generally sown in autumn but vetch was usually a spring-sown crop. Autumn sown varieties of vetch do exist today however (de Rougemont 1989) and a few varieties of bread wheat can be sown in spring. Percival (1948) notes that, prior to the 16th century, spring wheats were rare, however, he mentions documentary evidence from 1596 for 'March Wheat', a variety grown in the northern parts of Britain such as Kendal. In addition, the two existing varieties of spring-sown bread wheat that he describes, 'Spring White chaff bearded' and 'Welsh April Red Wheat', were both grown in the Welsh mountains. It is possible, therefore, that in the Yorkshire Wolds in periods of bad weather, spring-sown wheat and vetch maslins were worth growing, so as to avoid working the soil during the worst weather.

In addition, if the soil in the Wharram area had become as unproductive as the documentary sources suggest, it may have been worthwhile growing poorer yielding spring wheats with vetch in order to help restore fertility, reduce lodging (wheat plants lying flat) in a sparse crop, and provide some protection from pest damage. Since wheat was used for human consumption and vetch was only eaten by people during times of famine, a maslin of this nature would need to be separated after it was harvested. This may be possible after threshing using an appropriate sized sieve, although the author would need to try it experimentally before being convinced. The cultivation of vetches and wheat in a crop rotation would seem to be more sensible, but unless large numbers of vetch plants had grown up from seeds shed in the previous year, the ratio of vetch to wheat grains seems to be too high for this explanation to be likely.

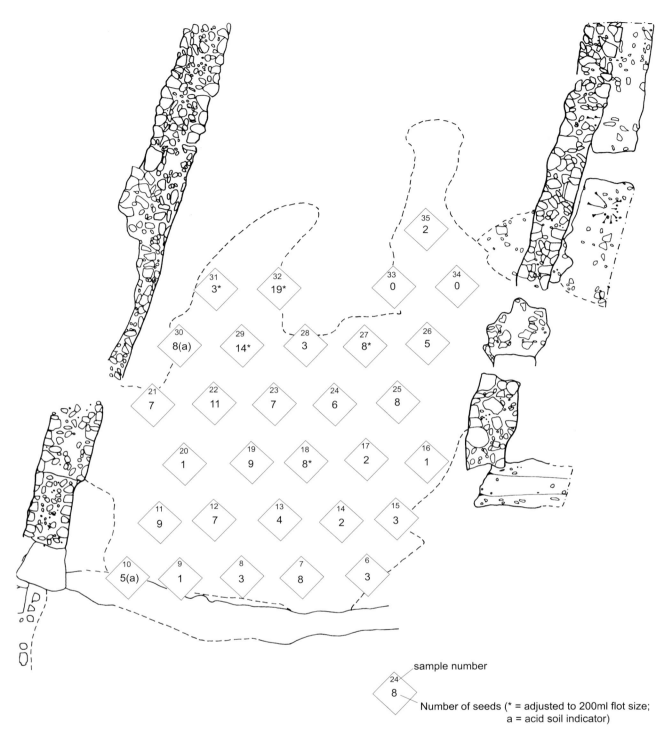

Fig. 124. Site 77 barn: weeds of cultivated meadows and pasture (includes: *Knautia arvensis, Prunella vulgaris, Medicago/Trifolium/Lotus sp., Rumex acetosella (a), Plantago lanceolata, Centaurea nigra/scabiosa, Poaceae, Lolium perenne/rigidum*). (E. Marlow-Mann)

An alternative explanation suggested by Professor van der Veen (pers. comm.) was that, where weather and pest damage had created gaps in the crop, vetch may have been sown as an infill crop in the spring. Although the crops may still have been harvested separately, some cross contamination would have been inevitable, particularly with a crop like cultivated vetch that forms tangled masses due to its twining tendrils.

Hay?

The law suit documents of 1555-6 state that the vicar's holding included two acres of grass, and hay is mentioned in many of the depositions (Chapter 1, above). It is uncertain whether hay was being stored in the barn, as this highly combustible material would have left very little trace. No slender, grass-sized culm nodes were recovered. Dyer (1997) found documentary references of hay being stored in the barn at Bredon, and it is likely that at least during some parts of the year the barn at Wharram was used for hay storage, whenever there was room. Some of the documents suggest a stable was also included in the building, so hay could also have been present as waste fodder.

A few of the weed taxa recovered from the samples were more characteristic of grassland habitats than arable fields, being perennials rather than annual early colonisers. Field scabious (*Knautia arvensis*), for example, is usually found in manured, slightly moist meadows. Its seeds were unusually common in the Wharram barn samples, along with occasional seeds of other grassland plants such as selfheal (*Prunella vulgaris*) and ribwort plantain (*Plantago lanceolata*). Charred remains from some of these taxa are occasionally found amongst cereal assemblages, suggesting perhaps the incorporation of plants growing around the margins of arable fields or the inclusion of waste hay. No clear distribution pattern was obtained in the barn samples (Fig. 124) to suggest whether, for example, the grassland herbs were more closely associated with one crop indicating rotations including fallow, although they were a little more frequent in the barley-rich samples. Because the seeds could have come from a variety of sources, including hay, arable field margins or the thatch base coat, no definite conclusions can be drawn.

Storage conditions

It is not possible to say whether the different crops were stored in separate compartments of the barn or whether the threshed cereals (barley, dredge and peas) were stored in containers such as baskets, sacks or wooden bins. When burnt, these types of container are unlikely to have left recognisable traces, unless preservation conditions were exceptional. The wheat sheaves (possibly together with entwined vetch plants) appear to have been stacked against the southern wall of the barn. It is notable, however, that even after about six to eight months of storage there was no definite evidence that any of the grain had sprouted due to damp conditions, or had been damaged by pests. Rodent droppings are sometimes preserved by charring, but none was found in these samples, nor were any rodent bones recovered. Storage conditions in the barn, therefore, appear to have been good.

Comparisons with crops recorded at Wharram in later centuries

An inventory of the farmhouse at Wharram Percy dated to 1699 (p. 4), listed £18 worth of corn in the barn and chamber and £12 of 'oats sown and ploughing the ground'. Estate valuation documents dated to 1806 concerning three farms at Wharram Percy provide useful insights into the nature of the local soils by the 19th century. Documents from two of the farms (Bella and Wharram Percy Farm) note that the tillage land was of a 'dead cold nature' and that it was only suitable for growing oats, and not other grains or turnips. At Wharram Grange Farm it was suggested that turnips and barley could be grown, but not wheat. An 1830 inventory of Wharram Percy Farm listed five wheat stacks and six oat stacks. Although some of the wheat listed in these documents could have been bought at market, the importance of oats as a crop in the area is evident. The degree to which this change over the centuries from growing wheat to the cultivation of less valuable crops such as oats and barley relates to climatic deterioration, to soil degradation or to the greater availability of wheat from more favourable soils, is unknown.

The quantity of grain being stored in the barn

Quantities of wheat, barley and oats present in the barn were calculated using the number of grains per 200ml flot and adjusting for total flot size, sample size per spit, and total number of spits. These figures are only a very rough approximation, as many of the variables had to be estimated or average figures used, e.g. the sizes of the un-analysed spits were probably variable and these figures were not known, so an average figure from the fully analysed spits was used (= 6.8 litres soil per spit). The numbers of grain were converted into volumes using figures from the fully analysed samples (*c.* 2600 grain per 100ml). Another figure that had to be estimated was the proportion of each cereal type in the indeterminate grain category. The indeterminate grains were divided amongst the barley and wheat according to the proportions of identified grains. Indeterminate grain numbers are likely to be a gross under-estimation, as fragments of grain smaller than half a grain were not counted. In addition to these under-estimations, some of the grain may have been completely destroyed by charring, or remained unburnt

Table 65. Quantity of grain being stored in the barn at Wharram Percy.

	estimated number of grains in deposit 577	estimated volume of crop in deposit 577	estimated quarters† of grain (not in sheaf)
wheat	115 million	4,440 litres	13.7 quarters
barley	4.7 million	182 litres	0.55 quarters
oats (possibly over-estimated as this includes cultivated and wild oats)	1.9 million	73 litres	0.22 quarters

[† as calculated in Dyer (1997)]

and rotted away. The final figures, therefore, provide only a very rough minimum figure for the quantities of crops originally stored in the barn (Table 65).

The Great Barn at Bredon had the capacity to hold 420 quarters of grain in the sheaf, but this was a large nine-bay barn of 132 by 44 feet (c.40 x 13m). The first year's records (1385-6) showed that it contained 44 quarters of wheat, 9 of rye, 75 of barley and dredge, 36 of peas and beans, and 25 of oats (=144 quarters). Although when the bishop was in residence 87 quarters were used to supply the household, in a later year when he was present less often (1395-6) only 13 quarters of mostly wheat were used for the household, with 12 quarters being used as fodder (Dyer 1997).

Bearing in mind that the quarters mentioned above for Bredon refer to grain in the ear, it can be seen that a substantial quantity of wheat was still present in the Wharram barn when it was burnt down, enough to supply a manor house, let alone a vicarage. Fodder grain, however, (barley, dredge and peas) was fairly sparse by February/April, probably because the economy was primarily focused around sheep by this time and it had been used up during the four to six winter months that had just passed. Fodder grain and hay would have been much in demand over winter in order to achieve good condition in the animals prior to lambing in the spring.

As indicated above, the witnesses provided by Vicar Firby in the court case of 1555-6 deposed that the two oxgangs glebe land should have produced sixteen to twenty loads of corn; whereas those who testified on behalf of Atkinson claimed that only three to six loads were actually achieved. Whichever is nearer the truth, the argument presupposes a common understanding of the quantity represented by 'a load'. It seems probable that the wains used to lead the sheaves from field to barn had broadly uniform capacities, making both accounting and the physical operation much more straightforward.

That said, the court records fail to tell us the quantity that was actually represented by a load. Fortunately, Henry Best's Farming Book supplies the figures that allow us to derive an approximate amount of threshed grain that could be generated from 'a load' of oats, or haver. He writes that a wain could carry 28 stooks of short and small haver, but only 20 or 22 stooks of large or 'loggery' haver (Woodward 1984, 54), again implying that a load represented a standard quantity. He then computes the capacity of the oat barn at Elmswell as follows:

'The furthest roomestead in the haver-barne next the East holdeth 34 loades; the middle roomestead or that which is next unto it holdeth xxvj; the hither roomestead 24 loades, viz. that which is next the threshing place. I have knowne allmost tenne score quarters of oates threshed out of these three roomesteads when they weare well mowed and well filled with good free oates that bledde well.'
(Woodward 1984, 54).

On this basis, 84 loads would generate 200 quarters or 1600 bushels, giving 2.4 quarters or 19 bushels per load,

though this seems to have been the most that might be expected in a good year rather than the average. Of course, these calculations relate to oats, and the figure for wheat is unlikely to be identical. Furthermore, Best's lands were undoubtedly more productive than those at Wharram even before the end of open-field farming, and so a more conservative estimate of 2 quarters per load might be more applicable for Wharram. It is a figure which looks about right in the context of the calculations given in another ecclesiastical cause, relating to the tithe of barley being grown in Thixendale. Two deponents estimated that, in the late 1540s, a load of barley rakings – the scattered corn raked up after the sheaves has been loaded onto the wain (Woodward 1984, 310) – would have yielded at least a quarter and a half of barley (Purvis 1949, 34-5).

If the Wharram lands produced about 2 quarters from a load, the 13.7 quarters of wheat estimated from the barn deposits represent about 7 loads, above the yield range indicated by Atkinson's deponents in 1555-6. If this was the produce of the glebe land (all or some of it may alternatively have been bought in from a neighbouring farm), and if it was used for domestic consumption, then it would suggest that the quantity generated at harvest time, six to nine months earlier, would have been much closer to the Firby estimates.

Crop husbandry at Wharram in the 16th century

Because of the unique nature of the barn deposit and the excellent state of preservation of the charred plant remains, it has been possible to look at crop-weed associations in more depth and recover some information about crop husbandry. Assuming that the barn's contents came from the locality, even if not from the vicar's two oxgangs, the documentary evidence (p. 304) and plant pathological information provided additional clues as to the state of arable agriculture in the Wharram area.

In ecological terms, all except one of the weeds growing with the crops were common weeds of disturbed and cultivated ground belonging to one of the three phytosociological classes: Chenopodietea (waste ground, garden and related arable weeds), Secalietea (weeds of cereal fields) or Artemisieta (persistent nitrophoilous ruderal weeds) (Ellenberg 1988).

In the first class (Fig. 125), waste ground and garden weeds such as orache (Atriplex patula/prostrata) and scentless mayweed (Tripleurospermum inodorum) were the most frequent taxa represented. Orache often grows in nutrient-enriched soils, and it is notable that all these taxa were located close to the wheat grains in the Canoco species plot (Figs 117 and 118). This group is often associated with manured garden plots, so some method of manuring the wheat fields was probably being practised, perhaps by folding sheep on the arable fields at night (Pretty 1990). Plants in this group indicative of other soil types include stinking chamomile (Anthemis cotula), a weed of heavy, damp clay soils, and corn spurrey (Spergula arvensis) and corn marigold (Chrysanthemum segetum), two arable weeds of acidic soils. Almost all the

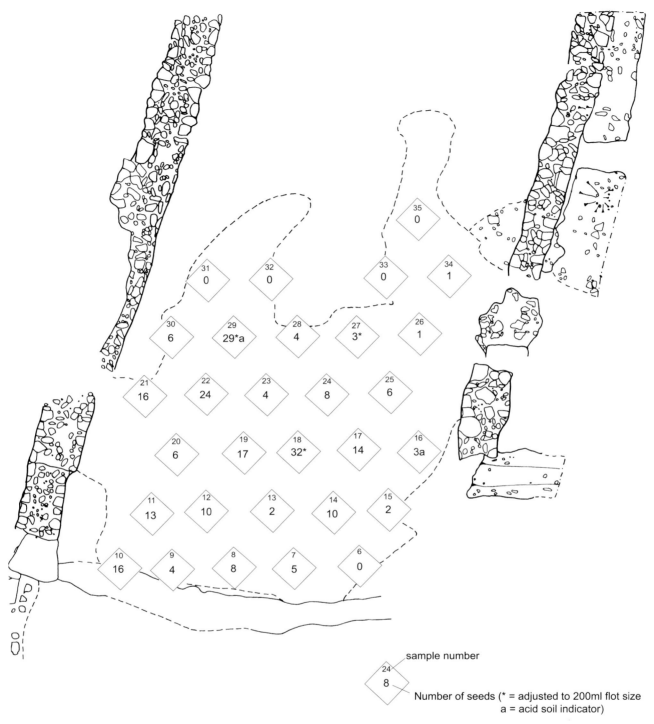

sample number

Number of seeds (* = adjusted to 200ml flot size
a = acid soil indicator)

Fig. 125. Site 77 barn: phytosociological class Chenopodietea: wasteground and related arable and garden weeds (includes *Atriplex patula/prostrata, Anthemis cotula, Tripleurospermum inodorum, Aethusa cynapium, Chrysanthemum segetum, Spergula arvensis* (a)). (E. Marlow-Mann)

stinking chamomile seeds came from the wheat-dominant samples. Since bread wheat prefers heavy, clay soils, it is clear that where such soils existed, wheat was the favoured crop. The acid soil indicators were few and far between so interpretations are very tentative, but two of the three seeds in this group came from samples containing reasonable quantities of oats. Of the three cereals, oats are best suited to acidic soils. The range of soils represented by these weeds suggests that a variety of different areas around the

vicarage were being cultivated, in addition to the well-drained, calcareous soils of the Wolds. This range in weed taxa could simply be due to the cultivation of damper, heavier pockets of soil around ditches, streams, troughs, gateways and trampled areas of the farm. Cereals may also have been brought in from further afield.

The Secalietalia is a class containing weeds that specifically grow amongst arable crops, such as corn cockle (*Agrostemma githago*), shepherd's needle

(*Scandix pecten-veneris*) and darnel (*Lolium temulentum*). These three taxa were all relatively common in most of the samples. Although no clear pattern emerges when all the taxa are examined together, single taxa plots (Fig. 120) and the Canoco plot (Figs 117 and 118) show that corn cockle was closely associated with the wheat crop, whilst darnel was more often a weed of barley fields. Both are introduced cereal weeds that became serious contaminants during the medieval period, particularly corn cockle which contains harmful alkaloids. Darnel can also contain poisons when infected by a common fungus, and these act on the nervous system and alimentary canal (Guerin 1899). Unfortunately there are no clear differences in these weeds' soil preferences to provide additional information about where the crops were being grown. It is interesting to note that the fact that weed-crop associations were observed in the Canoco plots suggests that the wheat and barley crops were kept quite separate, rather than grown on the same land in rotation.

The third phytosociological class, Artemsietea, are persistent nitrophilous weeds such as nipplewort (*Lapsana communis*) and cleavers (*Galium aparine*). These two taxa were more closely associated with wheat than the other cereals (Figs 117 and 118), once again suggesting the preferential manuring of wheat rather than the other two crops. It should be remembered, however, that the unthreshed sheaves of wheat are the most likely of the three cereals to have still contained a range of weed plants that had been gathered with the corn, particularly twining and climbing weeds such as cleavers. If the barley and dredge had been stored as processed grain, most of the weed seeds would have been removed during processing, apart from grain-sized seeds such as darnel. If destined to be used only for fodder, and not seed corn, the processing may not have been as thorough as would be the case with grain for human consumption, but the range of weeds and weed heads would still have been reduced. Figure 119 shows that all the weed seeds still in their seed heads were found in the wheat dominated squares (80% wheat or over). The species Canoco plot (Figs 117 and 118) demonstrated that very few weeds lay close to either the oats or barley, with most being centred around the wheat remains, lending weight to this suggestion.

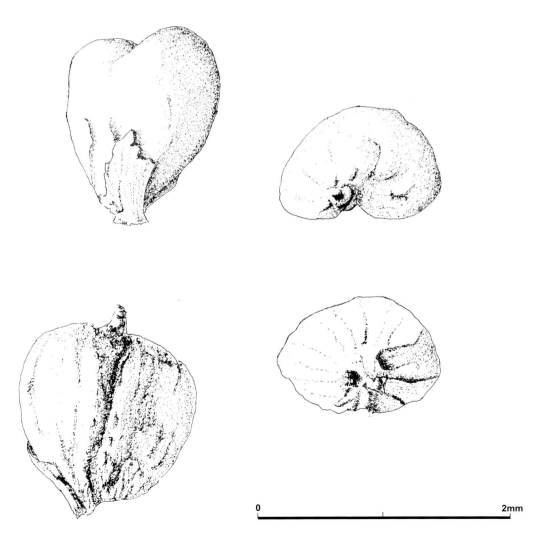

0 — 2mm

Fig. 126. Possible wheat-seed nematode galls or 'ear-cockles' (*Anguina tritici*). (K. Hunter)

311

Wheat-seed gall nematode, Anguina tritici

During the analysis frequent objects that were slightly smaller than wheat grains but of a similar shape were recovered from the samples (Fig. 126). It became apparent that the objects were distorted wheat grains, particularly when one of them was found still attached to a wheat rachis fragment. The distribution of the objects was also closely associated with that of wheat. The first suggestion that they might be wheat-seed nematode galls ('ear-cockles') came from Dr Allan Hall (University of York) to whom the author is very grateful. Dr Hall directed the author to web sites that provided photographs which very closely resembled the object, as far as could be seen from a photograph (e.g. www.invasive.org; http://plpnemweb.ucdavis.edu/nemaplex). A number of plant disease and gall experts were then sent examples of the gall in the hope that a positive identification could be made using reference material. The author is particularly indebted to John Southey (British Plant Gall Society) and Dr Ray Perry (Rothamsted Research) for providing their expert opinions, information and references.

Although some of the experts thought that the objects were quite likely to be charred *Anguina tritici* galls, the identification has not yet been confirmed. This is partly because of the difficulty in obtaining reference material, since this pest has been eliminated from British crops since 1956, and because the galls are charred. Whilst still trying to obtain reference material, the author is fairly certain (from photographs and drawings, e.g. Redfern and Shirley 2002) that Dr Hall's suggestion is correct and that these are nematode galls, rather than bunted grains or ergot sclerotia (already ruled out by a range of specialists).

Anguina tritici was a considerable problem in the past and still causes economic losses in some parts of the world, such as India and Romania. Infestations can be controlled by using crop rotations of one to two years in moist soil conditions, but in areas of drought the nematodes within the galls can remain viable in the soil for many years (nematodes have been revived from galls stored up to 28 years). Modern mechanical seed screening has led to the elimination of this pest from crops in Britain today, and in the past flotation in brine or water was used (Southey 1972). Although back in the 16th century there may not have been any understanding of the mechanism of infection by something as small as a nematode, the fact that the plants become grossly distorted and that the galls are brown or black in the ear should have allowed for some degree of disease control. Diseased plants could have been pulled up by hand and galls could have been hand picked from the harvested grain. Since the wheat was stored in the barn in the ear, some hand sorting of both galls and the harmful large black corn cockle (*Agrostemma githago*) weed seeds may have been undertaken once the sheaves had been threshed. The fact that 275 galls and 238 corn cockle (*Agrostemma githago*) seeds were recovered from the samples suggests that the crop had not been tended very diligently in the field.

Where crop husbandry practices were good, it might be expected that easily-spotted problems such as grossly distorted plants and bright pink corn cockle flowers would be removed as soon as possible.

Crop rotation

Because of the contradictory claims made by the deponents in the 1555-6 court case, there is considerable uncertainty with regard to precise yields obtained. The general impression, however, is that yields from the vicarage land were in decline. Infestation of the crop by wheat-seed gall nematode could have caused considerable reductions in yield. If crop rotation was not practised, the infestation would have built up over the years, perhaps causing the low yields described by several of the vicarage documents. The lack of crop rotation regimes would have led to pest, disease and weed build-up over time. It should be remembered that most fungal and bacterial cereal diseases, such as take-all and foot-rot, would not be observed in the archaeobotanical remains, but soil/plant debris-borne diseases such as these could have greatly reduced yields. It is interesting to note that experimental work has shown that cultivating leguminous plants on land affected by take-all prior to sowing wheat can help to reduce the disease, although presumably this would not have been known in the 16th century (Garrett and Mann 1948).

Since bread wheat is a very demanding crop in the levels of nutrients it requires, continuous cropping would soon have led to soil impoverishment, particularly on the light, calcareous soils of the Wolds. Although some of the arable weeds were indicative of manured ground, it may not have been applied at a high enough rate to maintain the soil fertility. The cultivation of vetches, either in rotation or as a maslin, would have helped to restore nutrient levels to some extent.

The question of whether crop rotation was being practised at Wharram vicarage is particularly interesting in view of the change to primarily sheep rearing in 1527, claims of low yields in the documents, the possible cultivation of a wheat/vetch maslin, and the recovery of wheat-seed nematodes galls. A statement from one witness could be significant in this respect. William Stanesby, vicar of Wharram-le-Street, stated that:

'if the vicar at Wharram Percy for the time being might be permitted to plough his arable ground through the Fields as other townships thereabouts doth his two oxgangs of Land were able to bear by his estimation one year with an other sixteen Loads of Corn'.
(Borthwick CP G.3537)

This suggests that, because the bulk of the former open fields had been put down to grass, the vicar was no-longer able to rotate his crops in the manner still practised in neighbouring townships that continued to support open-field systems. This was limiting yields from the two oxgangs, due to soil impoverishment and the build up of pests and diseases.

Table 66. The 'hand picked' plant remains from the North Glebe Terrace.

Context + AML no. in brackets	Site 74 311 (892451)	Site 54 context 1 (818712)	Site 77 s.2 321	Site 77 528/B (901847)	Site 77 405 SF406 (894554)	Site 77 566 SF772 (902203)	Site 77 523 (902201)	Site 77 405 SF408 (894555)	Site 77 405 (892777)
Period	UP	8.4	3.1	1-5	5.1	-	5.1	5.1	5.1
Context description	layer?	topsoil	layer	deposit	layer?	unstrat.	deposit	layer?	layer?
Location			Associated with burning in barn						
Plant remains	1 uncharred wheat spikelet (*Triticum* type)	1 uncharred plum stone (*Prunus domestica* ssp) *aestivum-domestica*	see Table 64	1 large uncharred hazelnut shell fragment (*Corylus avellana*)	1 large uncharred plum stone (*Prunus domestica* ssp *domestica*)	1 indeterm. vetch/tare (*Vicia/ Lathyrus* sp.)	1 frag. of large cf. plum stone	1 large robust cf. plum stone	1 large frag. charred hazelnut shell

Charred plant remains from other parts of the vicarage site

The only other sample of note from the vicarage site was Sample 2 from context 321, a Period 2 demolition layer from grid squares M/N in the north-east corner of the barn. This deposit is thought possibly to have been part of the charred grain context 559, although it was excavated at an earlier stage so the relationship was not confirmed (Ann Clark, pers. comm.).

Sample 2 produced large amounts of grain, with similar quantities of vetch seeds and no notable differences in weed taxa. Oats were particularly frequent (21% of the identified cereals) and barley was relatively common (6%), making the sample most resemble Samples 26 and 34 in layer 559 along the eastern wall of the barn. The cereal composition was 73% wheat and 27% dredge (or oats and barley), with cultivated vetch occurring at a ratio of 35:1 cereal grains to vetch seeds (see Table 64). In common with the context 559 samples, weed seeds were fairly sparse, although darnel and corn cockle were quite frequent.

The other hand-picked remains (Table 66) were mostly uncharred hazelnut shell fragments or plum stones (*Prunus domestica* ssp. *domestica*). It is uncertain whether these remains are contemporary with the vicarage or are more recent contaminants, since plum trees currently overhang the possible site of the barn and hazel is common in the area (A. Clark, pers. comm.). They are all robust, woody remains, so they could have survived in the soil for several centuries. If so, the evidence suggests that the vicarage owned at least one plum tree and that hazelnuts were either being collected from the hedgerows or grown in the garden for nuts. Documentary evidence concerning the vicar's house in 1716 mentions an orchard and garden, as does a terrier of 1853 which mentions an orchard planted with fruit trees (p. 25).

25 The Animal Remains
by J. Richardson

Introduction

Animal bones from Sites 21, 54, 73 and 77 have been examined and are referred to collectively here as those from the vicarage area. Bones identified from Sites 49, 51 and 74 are those from the farmstead area. These faunal assemblages date predominantly from the post-medieval period, although a minority of medieval material is also considered. Here the two areas are compared to each other by phase, deposits associated with the vicarage (Site 54) are compared to those of the farmhouse (Site 74), and the post-medieval animal bones are compared to the medieval and earlier bone assemblages from other parts of Wharram Percy. The latter may allow improvements in livestock as a result of the Agricultural Revolution to be identified (cf. Albarella and Davis 1996).

Methodology

In total, 21,111 bone fragments were recovered from the vicarage area and a further 6148 fragments from the farmstead area. Of these, 26% and 42% respectively were identified to species or a lower-order group. The difference in the proportions identified may be a reflection of the greater fragmentation of bones recovered from the vicarage area (see size index in Table 67), which resulted in fewer recordable diagnostic zones.

The methodologies used to record the bone assemblages from the vicarage and farmstead areas are the same as those detailed previously (Richardson 2004a, 257).

Table 67. Bone preservation and treatment by area and deposit type.

	Farmstead Area	Vicarage Area	Primary deposits	Secondary deposits
Size index	0.39	0.31	0.58	0.32
Condition index	1	1	1	1
Erosion index	0.99	0.99	1	0.99
% butchered	6.60%	3.70%	0.60%	5.00%
% gnawed	6.80%	4.90%	0.10%	6.10%
% burnt	0.20%	0.30%	-	0.30%
% fresh break	5.70%	8.70%	12.30%	7.30%
% loose teeth	23.80%	10.90%	-	21.50%

For the size, condition and erosion index, values closer to 1.0 indicate more complete or better preserved bones

Table 68. The articulated skeletons*.

Site 21	Context 97	Layer	Post-medieval	Near-complete cow skeleton
Site 54	Context 120	Wall rubble – Structure K	18th-century	Sheep's hock
Site 54	Context 150	Fill of rubbish pit 154	19th to later 20th-century	Sheep's hock
Site 54	Context 303	Fill of pit 289	18th-century	Near-complete cow skeleton
Site 54	Context 328	Fill of pit 321	17th-century	Near-complete calf skeleton
Site 54	Context 396	Wall footing – Structure H	16th to 17th-century+	Partial fowl skeleton
Site 54	Context 446	Fill of pit 447	17th-century	Near-complete piglet skeleton
Site 54	Context 598	Silting deposit	Medieval	Partial sheep hind limb
Site 77	Context 255	Hillwash	17th to late 18th-century	Partial dog skeleton

*The animal burial from pit 240, referred to on p.112 was not available for analysis.

Taphonomic bias

In order to assess the usefulness of the assemblages for the reconstruction of animal husbandry practices, bone recovery, formation process and bone condition/treatment have been assessed.

Bone recovery

On-site sieving was not carried out during the excavations on the North Glebe Terrace. This will have created a bias against the smaller bones of the smaller animals such as sheep and instead will have favoured the recovery of the larger bones of cattle and horse. Even smaller bodied animals such as rabbits, rats and the birds will have been biased against most severely. As a result, species proportions will have been compromised. Biases will also exist in terms of age data, as younger (hence smaller) bones will have been overlooked in greater proportions than the larger adult examples.

Formation processes

The presence of articulated skeletons and body parts (the articulation of three or more bones) of the domestic species have been used to identify the disposal of entire carcasses and the discard of low utility joints following primary carcass processing. These are listed in Table 68.

Two articulated parts, the sheep's hock from the wall rubble of Structure K and the cow skeleton from pit 289, displayed cut marks. The cow had been dismembered between the femur and tibia on both hind legs, presumably to facilitate disposal into the pit. None of the other partial skeletons was butchered. All the partial skeletons are likely to indicate the disposal of diseased animals or livestock that had died of unexplained causes and were deemed unfit for consumption. Certainly early church law prohibited the consumption of meat from animals that had died accidentally and that not been bled as part of the slaughtering process (Bieler 1975 cited in McCormick 2002, 30). The puppy incorporated into hillwash (the bones were disarticulated but clearly from the same animal) may have been a pet, but equally may have been culled as an unnecessary pest. Skeletons of rats, mice and hedgehogs are not included here as their intrusion into archaeological deposits is likely. The only other partial skeleton identified was a starling from an early 19th-century surface associated with the farmhouse (Site 74).

In contrast to these primary deposits, disarticulated bones (which account for the majority of the faunal assemblage) were much more heavily fragmented (see size index and % loose teeth in Table 67). Unlike the articulated bones which displayed neither eroded nor cracked or flaking surfaces (erosion and condition indices

Table 69. The proportion of butchered bones by site for all species, and knife and chop marks for cattle, sheep, pig and horse.

	Farmstead Area	Vicarage Area
Butchery marks %		
Cattle	13.8	5.8
Sheep	10.9	2.7
Pig	17.9	4.1
Horse	1.8	3.0
Deer spp.	50.0	-
Hare	3.8	1.8
Rabbit	1.3	3.3
Domestic fowl	8.0	1.7
Domestic goose	-	3.3
cf. Domestic duck	-	8.3
Large-size mammal	71.4	18.5
Medium-size mammal	31.8	5.1
Small-size mammal	54.8	14.0
Knife marks %		
Cattle	3.8	1.6
Sheep	5.6	1.1
Pig	5.3	1.3
Horse	-	0.8
Chop marks %		
Cattle	10.0	3.8
Sheep	5.4	1.1
Pig	12.6	2.8
Horse	1.8	2.1

Bones with both cut and chop marks are counted twice

in Table 67), some of the disarticulated bones had deteriorated since being discarded. The higher incidence of gnawed bones from secondary deposits also indicates that they were more likely to be exposed to dogs and rodents after disposal than those from primary deposits. These comparisons reveal that the articulated bones were buried rapidly, while the disarticulated bones were more frequently exposed to weathering, trampling and gnawing.

Pre-burial processes
While the butchering and burning of bones can result in bone loss, relatively few bones have been modified in this manner. Interestingly, however, nearly twice the proportion of bone was butchered from the farmstead area compared to the vicarage area (Table 67), although whether this resulted in disproportionate bone loss from the former is not quantifiable. The higher proportion of chopped cattle, horse and pig bones compared to bones which were cut is a reflection of their large carcass size when compared to smaller animals such as sheep (Table 69). Finally, butchery marks on the horse bones do not

necessarily indicate their consumption by people, particularly as eating horseflesh was prohibited (Rau 1968 cited in Grant 1988, 174). Instead horse carcasses would have been fully utilised for other purposes, such as bones for button-making, hair for mattresses, hides for leatherworking (Edwards 1987 cited in Dobney et al. 1996, 46) or for dog meat (Thomas and Locock 2000, 89).

Conclusions
As has already been identified from other Wharram Percy bone assemblages, pre-discard processes such as butchery, and post-discard processes such as weathering and gnawing have not significantly influenced bone destruction and/or biased the recovered bone assemblages. Although disarticulated bones were less well preserved than articulated parts, all bones were recovered in reasonable condition. In contrast, biases created by the lack of an on-site sieving strategy will have influenced the recovered assemblage. While the effect cannot be quantified, smaller bones will have been retrieved less efficiently than larger bones and this will have affected the smaller species and younger animals more severely.

Animal husbandry

Animal husbandry practices (breeding programmes, movement/trade of livestock, the exploitation of secondary products such as milk and fleeces, and ultimately slaughter patterns) have been investigated using species proportions, age, sex, metrical and pathological data. The range of animals consumed (species, age and body part) has also been used to assess the dietary preferences and status of those occupying the vicarage(s) and farmhouse(s).

Species proportions
The proportion of sheep, cattle, pigs and horse bones indicates that these animals would have outstripped the other species in terms of their economic importance (Table 70). In comparing the relative proportions of these animals from the vicarage (Site 54), tithe barn (Site 77), outbuildings (Site 51) and farmhouse (Site 74), it is clear that sheep (with sheep/goat) bones always predominated, while the proportion of cattle bones remained fairly constant (Fig. 127). The higher proportion of cattle bones from Site 54 is a reflection of the two near-complete cattle skeletons recovered from this area. Pig bones fluctuated from 9% in deposits associated with the outbuildings to just over 15% from the vicarage. Interestingly, the vicarage barn contained a much higher proportion of horse bones than the other areas and at nearly 30% of the domestic mammal total, this corresponds closely to the proportion of horse bones recovered from a 'butchery' deposit at Site 82K (Richardson 2004a, 261).

From the barn, however, butchery evidence was scarce (only four bones were marked) and no discrete horse-rich

Table 70. Fragment count by site.

Site	Farmstead Area			Vicarage Area			
	49	51	74	21	54	73	77
Cattle	13	58	89	29	898	21	95
Sheep	1	16	55		306	4	29
Goat					2		
Sheep/goat	11	152	231		1226	28	150
Pig	2	24	69		462	10	62
Horse	4	35	17		101	2	134
Dog		7	5		23	1	42
Canid spp.			1		1		
Cat	1	3	1		29		23
Fallow deer					1		
Roe deer							1
Deer spp.		1	1				
Badger					1		
Fox		1					
Hare		1	51		56		
Rabbit		86	217		179		2
Stoat					4		
Weasel							
Hedgehog						1	37
Mole			10		3		
Brown rat		133	951		551		1
Water vole		1			3		
Field vole							5
House mouse			32				
Amphibian spp.		6	7		7		9
Microfauna		18	29		180		9
Domestic fowl		10	16		155		22
Domestic fowl/pheasant			4		11		
Galliforme		4	1		4		
Domestic goose			11		58		2
Wild/domestic goose			5		16		4
cf. Domestic duck			3		10		2
cf. Mallard			1		1		1
Duck spp.		1	1		2		
Turkey					1		
Crane (Grus grus)					1		
Grey partridge			1				
Raven					2		
Crow/rook		3	2		26		2
cf. Jackdaw		1	2		19		1
cf. Song thrush/redwing			1				
cf. Blackbird		1	1				1
cf. Starling			8		8		
Grey or golden plover					2		
cf. Woodcock					1		
Rock dove			2		1		1
Columba sp.			3		1		3
cf. Barn owl		2					
Guillemot					1		
Passerine			2		7		
Bird spp.		1	19		35		3
Large-size mammal	1	6	28		92		16
Medium-size mammal		9	13		34		35
Small-size mammal		19	54		203		11
Total	33	599	1944	29	4724	67	673

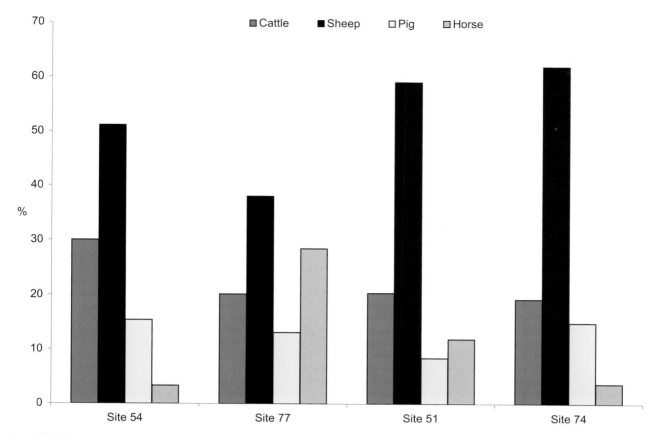

Fig. 127. The relative proportions of the main domestic animals by site. (J. Richardson)

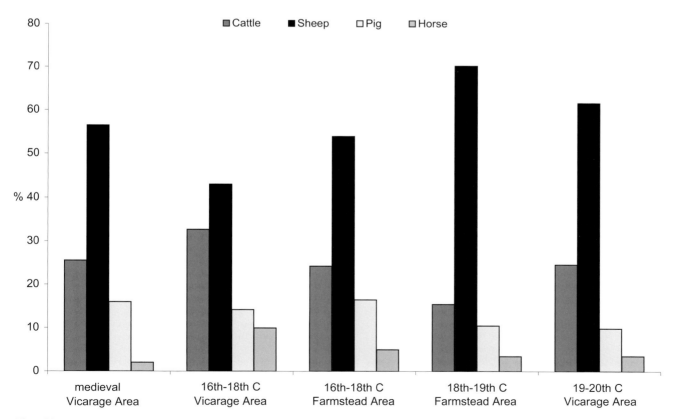

Fig. 128. The relative proportions of the main domestic animals by period. (J. Richardson)

Table 71. Fragment count by phase (excludes undated material).

	Farmstead Area					Vicarage Area		
	Iron Age/ Romano-British	Medieval	16th-18th-century	18th-19th-century	19th-20th-century	Medieval	16th-18th-century	19th-20th-century
Cattle	13	17	72	44	3	189	678	62
Sheep	1	4	34	26		91	143	33
Goat							2	
Sheep/goat	11	35	126	174	6	327	749	122
Pig	2	5	49	30	1	118	295	25
Horse	4	23	15	10		15	207	9
Dog		1	5	5		8	56	1
Canid spp.				1		1		
Cat	1		1	2		3	43	4
Fallow deer						1		
Roe deer							1	
Deer spp.			1	1				
Badger						1		
Fox				1				
Hare			19	32		1	28	27
Rabbit		1	129	90	1	2	69	110
Stoat								4
Hedgehog							37	1
Mole			9	1			3	
Brown rat		5	67	1008	4	3	173	375
Water vole				1		2		
Field vole							5	
House mouse				32				
Amphibian spp.		4	7			5	10	
Microfauna			22	23	1	1	68	120
Domestic fowl			10	6		51	76	14
Domestic fowl/pheasant			4			1	10	
Galliforme				3	1		4	
Domestic goose			1	10		14	20	1
Wild/domestic goose			2	3		3	14	2
cf. Domestic duck			3			1	5	5
cf. Mallard			1				2	
Duck spp.		1		1			2	
Turkey							1	
Grey partridge				1				
Raven							1	1
Crow/rook			1	4		1	26	1
cf. Jackdaw				3			20	
cf. Song thrush/redwing				1				
cf. Blackbird				1			1	
cf. Starling			1	7		3	1	4
Grey or golden plover						1		
cf. Woodcock							1	
Rock dove			2				2	
Columba sp.			2	1			4	
cf. Barn owl		2						
Guillemot						1		
Passerine			2				4	2
Bird spp.			17	2		4	15	8
Large-size mammal	1		17	12		16	76	4
Medium-size mammal		2	3	12		3	15	6
Small-size mammal		4	21	39		36	85	52
Total	33	104	643	1587	17	903	2952	993

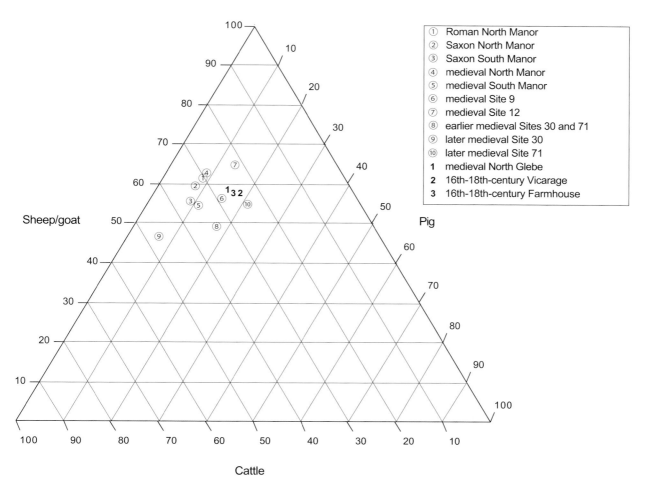

Legend

①	Roman North Manor
②	Saxon North Manor
③	Saxon South Manor
④	medieval North Manor
⑤	medieval South Manor
⑥	medieval Site 9
⑦	medieval Site 12
⑧	earlier medieval Sites 30 and 71
⑨	later medieval Site 30
⑩	later medieval Site 71
1	medieval North Glebe
2	16th-18th-century Vicarage
3	16th-18th-century Farmhouse

Fig. 129. The relative proportions of the three main 'meat' animals by site and period. (J. Richardson)

deposit was noted. Chicken and geese were farmed alongside the domestic mammals, albeit in small numbers, while dogs and cats may have had an economic and/or social role (Table 70).

Presenting the relative proportions of the main domestic animals by period reveals some fluctuations (Table 71; Fig. 128), but none so dramatic that clear changes were indicated in the mixed farming economy that had served the inhabitants of Wharram Percy since Roman times (Fig. 129). This economy was based on the knowledge that the thin, well-drained chalk soils of the Wolds favoured sheep rearing, but that cattle rearing was also valuable if a reliable water source was available. In addition, the fecund pig provided a readily renewable meat source, while horses were suitable as plough animals on the shallow, light soils of the area. When comparing deposits closely associated with the 16th to 18th-century vicarage and the 16th to 18th-century farmhouse, the proportion of domestic animals is uniform and as such reveals no evidence of disparity in diet (Table 72). The only notable difference is the much higher number of rabbit bones from the farmhouse.

From all the animal bone assemblages previously studied from Wharram Percy, domestic animals have always predominated, while wild mammals and birds have been scarce (e.g. Richardson 2005a, table 16). As

such, it is interesting that the vicarage and farmstead areas have revealed such high numbers of hare, rabbit and rat bones (Table 70). Hares were undoubtedly hunted, most likely with dogs, although traps may also have been used (Buczacki 2002, 482-3). Certainly they were consumed at Wharram Percy (Table 69), where they may have been considered a winter food (Buczacki 2002, 486). Only from Site 12 (Richardson 2005b, table 46) were rabbit bones retrieved in similar numbers to the North Glebe Terrace sites. Although rabbits, as burrowing creatures, may be intrusive in archaeological deposits, those from the North Glebe Terrace are believed to be legitimate as no articulated parts were noted and some of the bones were butchered (Table 69). Instead, it is likely that access to rabbits over the post-medieval period (see Table 71) had ceased to be the subject of status it had once been in the medieval period (O'Connor 2000, 169). The rats are also problematic as their intrusion into archaeological deposits cannot be dismissed categorically, but equally they may have established a commensal relationship with the people occupying the vicarage and farmhouse. As only the brown rat has been categorically identified here, it is likely that the large number of bones from post-medieval deposits reflects its introduction to Britain from the early 18th century and its rapid dispersal thereafter (cf. Clutton-Brock 1999, 189).

Table 72. Fragment counts from the 16th to 18th-century vicarage and farmhouse (excluding cattle skeletons).

	Farmhouse		Vicarage	
	Count	%	Count	%
Cattle	72	22.9	307	21.3
Sheep(/goat)	160	50.8	719	49.9
Pig	49	15.6	233	16.2
Horse	15	4.8	73	5.1
Dog	5	1.6	14	1.0
Cat	1	0.3	20	1.4
Domestic fowl	9	2.9	54	3.7
Domestic goose	1	0.3	18	1.2
cf. Domestic duck	3	1.0	3	0.2
Total of domestic animals	315		1441	
Deer spp.	1			
Hare	19		28	
Rabbit	129		67	
Mole	9		3	
Brown rat	67		172	
Amphibian spp.	7		1	
Microfauna	22		59	
Domestic fowl/pheasant	4		10	
Galliforme			4	
Wild/domestic goose	2		10	
cf. Mallard			1	
Duck spp.			2	
Turkey			1	
Raven			1	
Crow/rook	1		24	
cf. Jackdaw			19	
cf. Starling	1		1	
cf. Woodcock			1	
Rock dove	2		2	
Columba sp.			1	
Passerine	2		4	
Bird spp.	17		11	
Large-size mammal	17		60	
Medium-size mammal	10		3	
Small-size mammal	21		74	

Age, sex and pathological data for cattle, sheep, pigs and horses

Animal husbandry regimes, the targeting of secondary products such as milk and wool, and the production of meat, have been analysed by using age and sex data. Slaughter patterns based on fusion data have been assessed for cattle, sheep, pigs and horses (Tables 73-76), as well as the kill-off patterns based on dental eruption and wear data (Tables 77-80). These age data have been considered by phase and where possible by site.

Fusion data for cattle are not numerous (Table 73) and as a result are presented graphically by broad period only (Fig. 130). These data indicate that a slightly higher proportion of cattle were slaughtered for their meat in their third year during the medieval period when compared to the post-medieval period. During both periods, however, between 55% and 60% of animals were maintained to (osteological) maturity. Many of these older animals will have been kept as breeding stock, but also for their milk or traction capabilities. The presence of a breeding population

Table 73. Fusion data for cattle by period (zone > 0, F = fused, NF = not fused). Near-complete skeletons are excluded.

		7-18 months	24-36 months	36-48 months
Medieval	Fused	38	7	6
	Not fused	1	3	5
	% fused	97	70	55
16th to 18th-century	Fused	56	17	17
	Not fused	3	4	13
	% fused	95	81	57
18th to 19th-century	Fused	7	2	1
	Not fused	1	0	0
	% fused	88	100	100
19th to 20th-century	Fused	8	3	3
	Not fused	1	0	1
	% fused	89	100	75

7-18 months calculated from distal scapula, distal humerus, proximal radius, first phalanx, second phalanx
24-36 months calculated from distal metacarpal, distal tibia, distal metatarsal
36-48 months calculated from proximal humerus, proximal ulna, distal radius, proximal femur, distal femur, proximal tibia, calcaneus

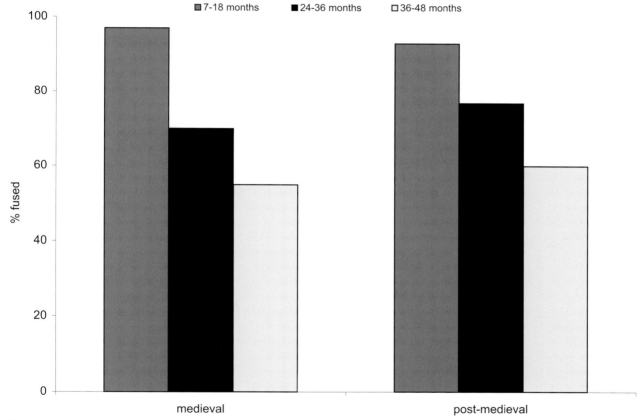

Fig. 130. Fusion data for cattle by period. (J. Richardson)

is supported by the identification of a few neonatal bones (0.5% of the medieval cattle assemblage and 2.2% from post-medieval deposits), as well as sex ratios of 0 males to 2 females from medieval deposits and 0 males to 7 females from post-medieval deposits. Although dental data were relatively scarce (Table 77), the high proportion of animals killed between 1 and 8 months may reflect calves that, once

they had established a reliable milk yield, were culled in order to free up milk for human consumption (Fig. 131). Slaughter of calves to this extent has not been identified previously from the medieval assemblages associated with the North Manor Area (Richardson 2004a, fig. 135), Pond and Dam (Richardson 2005a, fig. 67) and Sites 9 and 12 (Richardson 2005b, fig. 89).

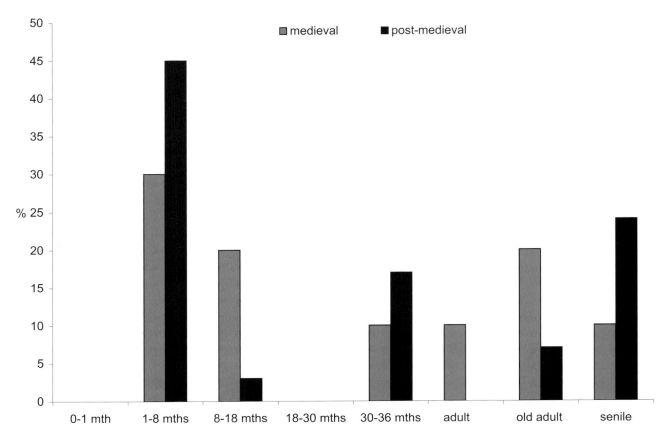

Fig. 131. Dental age data for cattle by period. (J. Richardson)

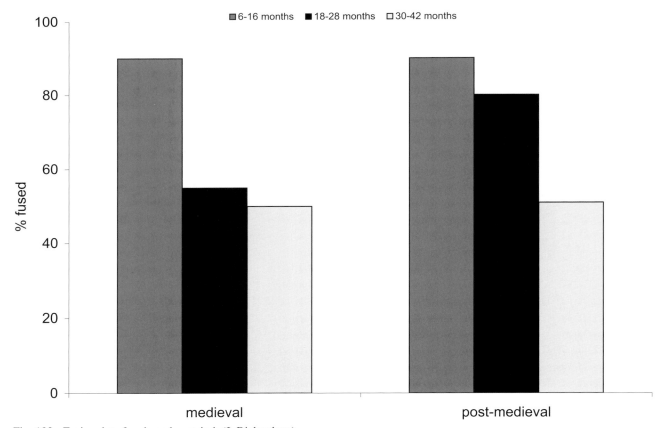

Fig. 132. Fusion data for sheep by period. (J. Richardson)

Table 74. Fusion data for sheep by period and site (zone > 0, F = fused, NF = not fused).

		6-16 months	18-28 months	30-42 months
Medieval	Fused	55	17	18
	Not fused	6	14	18
	% fused	90	55	50
16th to 18th-century	Fused	92	69	33
	Not fused	8	14	30
	% fused	92	83	52
18th to 19th-century	Fused	17	6	10
	Not fused	6	6	9
	% fused	74	50	53
19th to 20th-century	Fused	24	9	4
	Not fused	0	1	6
	% fused	100	90	40
16th to 18th-century vicarage	Fused	54	52	25
	Not fused	5	8	17
	% fused	92	87	60
16th to 18th-century farmhouse	Fused	15	13	3
	Not fused	3	3	8
	% fused	83	81	27

6-16 months calculated from distal scapula, distal humerus, proximal radius, first phalanx, second phalanx
18-28 months calculated from distal metacarpal, distal tibia, distal metatarsal
30-42 months calculated from proximal humerus, proximal ulna, distal radius, proximal femur, distal femur, proximal tibia, calcaneus

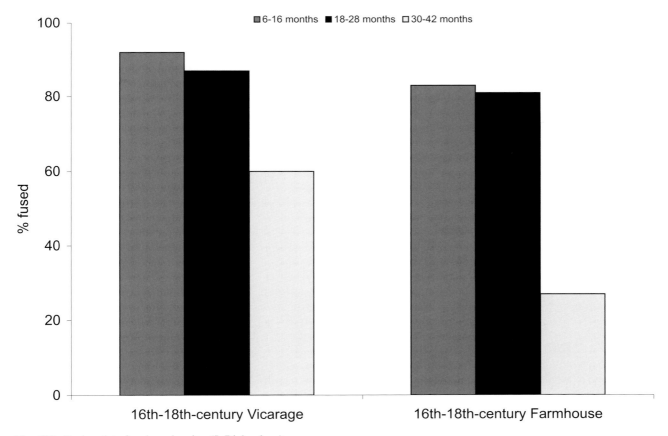

Fig. 133. Fusion data for sheep by site. (J. Richardson)

Interestingly, the dental eruption and wear data for cattle identified a discrepancy previously seen in the Sites 9 and 12 assemblages (Richardson 2005b, 234): the dental data indicate a higher proportion of juveniles slaughtered when compared to the fusion data. This inconsistency suggests that the mandibles and the limb bones each sampled a different population of individuals (O'Connor 2000, 96). This may have occurred if the dressed (i.e. decapitated) carcasses of young animals were sent to market leaving their heads to be deposited with the full range of body parts from older livestock that were routinely consumed by the medieval and post-medieval inhabitants of Wharram Percy. This hypothesis, however, can be countered by the fact that animals were typically sent to market on the hoof (Leatham 1794, 34). This avoided the difficulties of transporting heavy carcasses and the deterioration of meat following slaughter. The dearth of prime meat cattle between 18 and 30 months from both periods (Table 77, Fig. 131) may indicate that these animals were also traded off site, but this time on the hoof. Finally, the old and senile animals confirm the presence of breeding stock as suggested by the fusion data. The older cows will also have provided some milk, while traction cattle, apparently 'in yokes and for carriages' rather than for the plough (Leatham 1794, 35) were undoubtedly used despite the absence of possible work-related injuries.

The fusion data for sheep by period revealed similar slaughter patterns to those observed for cattle: again a higher proportion of sub-adult sheep were slaughtered during the medieval period when compared to the post-medieval period (Table 74, Fig. 132). These animals (aged somewhere between 16 and 30 months) were much too old to have been slaughtered in order to free up milk for human consumption, but were too young to have contributed any more than two fleeces at best. Instead they were killed for their meat. Subsequently, from both periods, around 50% of the flock was maintained to (osteological) maturity. Primarily, these older animals represent breeding populations with 0.7% of the medieval sheep assemblage and 7.1% of the post-medieval assemblage coming from neonatal animals, and sex ratios of 0 males to 2 females and 8 males to 16 females from medieval and post-medieval deposits respectively. In the absence of significant infant slaughter, neither the medieval nor the post-medieval flocks were run primarily for milk production, but fleeces would have been taken for local wool manufacture as well as for sale. Some inter-site variation is indicated, however, when the 16th to 18th-century vicarage is compared to the farmhouse (Table 74, Fig. 133). From the farmhouse less than 30% of the sheep were maintained to 30 to 42 months or beyond and this suggests that animals in their third year were more readily consumed by the inhabitants of the farmhouse than those occupying the vicarage.

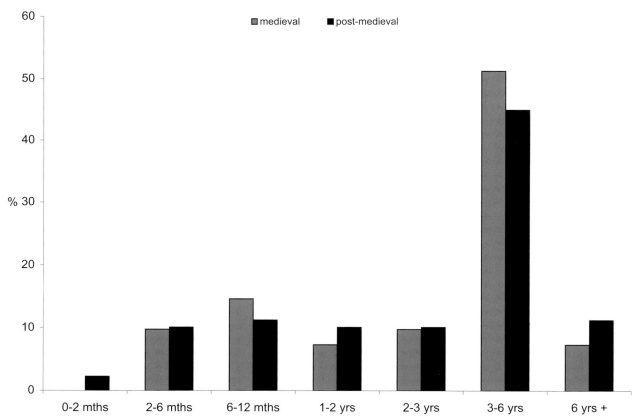

Fig. 134. Dental age data for sheep by period. (J. Richardson)

Table 75. Fusion data for pig by period (zone > 0, F = fused, NF = not fused).

		12 months	24-30 months	36-42 months
Medieval	Fused	7	1	0
	Not fused	0	13	2
	% fused	100	7	0
16th to 18th-century	Fused	19	5	0
	Not fused	3	14	9
	% fused	86	26	0
18th to 19th-century	Fused	1	1	0
	Not fused	1	0	1
	% fused	50	100	0
19th to 20th-century	Fused	3	2	
	Not fused	1	2	
	% fused	75	50	

12 months calculated from distal scapula, distal humerus, proximal radius, second phalanx"
24-30 months calculated from distal metacarpal, distal tibia, calcaneus, distal metatarsal, first phalanx
36-42 months calculated from proximal humerus, proximal ulna, distal radius, proximal femur, distal femur, proximal tibia

Table 76. Fusion data for horse by period (zone > 0, F = fused, NF = not fused).

		9-20 months	20-24 months	36-42 months
Medieval	Fused	7		2
	Not fused			
16th to 18th-century	Fused	32	10	17
	Not fused			3
18th to 19th-century	Fused	2		1
	Not fused			
19th to 20th-century	Fused		1	
	Not fused		2	

9-20 months calculated from distal humerus, proximal radius, distal metacarpal, distal metatarsal, first phalanx, second phalanx
20-24 months calculated from distal scapula, distal tibia
36-42 months calculated from proximal humerus, proximal ulna, distal radius, proximal femur, distal femur, proximal tibia, calcaneus

The dental data from sheep confirm that intensive milk production was unlikely given the absence and/or dearth of neonatal deaths (Table 78, Fig. 134), although the proportion of animals killed before six months of age was higher from the medieval and post-medieval North Glebe Terrace sites than from the medieval North Manor Area (Richardson 2004a, fig. 137), Pond and Dam (Richardson 2005a, fig. 70) and Sites 9 and 12 (Richardson 2005b, fig. 91). Apparently lamb consumed by those living in the North Glebe Terrace area was often from animals under six months old, while the inhabitants of the North Manor Area had ready access to lamb aged six to twelve months. Like all the previously studied medieval and later medieval sheep populations, though, the peak in slaughter from the North Glebe Terrace assemblages occurred between three and six years (Fig. 134). Some of these animals would have been young enough to provide high quality meat, while the oldest would have been killed when their breeding potential and/or fleece production had declined. An interesting pathology was noted on the elbow joint of some of the sheep: the ossification of ligaments following a strain or dislocation and commonly referred to as 'penning elbow'. As the name suggests, this trauma (leading to joint disease) can occur when animals are closely corralled (Baker and Brothwell 1980, 127). From medieval deposits 25% (one in four) of ulnas were

Table 77. Number of cattle jaws at various wear stages by period (after Halstead 1985).

	medieval	post-medieval
A: 0-1 mth		
B: 1-8 mths	3	13
C: 8-18 mths	2	1
D: 18-30 mths		
E: 30-36 mths	1	5
F: young adult	1	
G: adult		1
H: old adult	2	2
I: senile	1	7
Total	10	29

Table 78. Number of sheep jaws at various wear stages by period (after Payne 1973).

	medieval	post-medieval
A: 0-2 mths		2
B: 2-6 mths	4	9
C: 6-12 mths	6	10
D: 1-2 yrs	3	9
E: 2-3 yrs	4	9
F: 3-4 yrs	14	22
G: 4-6 yrs	7	18
H: 6-8 yrs	2	6
I: 8-10 yrs	1	4
Total	41	89

Table 79. Number of pig jaws at various wear stages by period.

	medieval	post-medieval
A: d4 unworn		1
B: d4 in wear, M1 unworn	1	2
C: M1 in wear, M2 unworn		1
D: M2 in wear, M3 unworn	1	2
E: M3 in early wear		3
F: M3 beyond wear stage c	1	1
Total	3	10

Table 80. Number of horse incisors (mandibular and maxillary) at various wear stages by period.

	medieval	post-medieval
A: decidous incisors present (< 2 yrs)	1	1
B: incisor erupted (2.5-4.5 years)		1
C: incisor first in wear (3-6 yrs)		
D: incisor with square enamel pattern (5-7 yrs)		2
E: infundibulum lost (7-9 yrs)		2
F: incisor with circular enamel pattern (8-10 yrs)	1	5
G: incisor with no enamel (14 yrs +)	3	16
Total	5	27

affected, compared to 6% (one in sixteen) from 16th to 18th-century deposits and 17% (one in six) from 18th to 19th-century deposits. Unfortunately the difference in the incidence of this pathology between periods may not be significant as the quantity of ulnas recovered was not particularly high.

The pig was kept as an animal ideally suited to turning food waste and arable by-products into meat. As such it made economic sense to kill them when they have gained the optimum amount of weight in relation to the quantity of food they had consumed. From the North Glebe Terrace, the fusion data indicated that this occurred between 12 and 30 months, by which time 93% of the medieval pigs and 67% of the post-medieval pigs had been culled (Table 75). Apparently no animals survived to (osteological) maturity, although the dental data indicate that a few animals over three years old were present (Table 79; the third molar erupts at three years according to Silver's (1969, table G) 18th-century data). Although the relatively high proportion of males does not represent the ideal breeding population (6 males to 8 females and 9 males to 13 females from medieval and post-medieval deposits respectively), local pig-rearing is indicated by the presence of neonatal bones: two from medieval deposits and 110 from post-medieval deposits, although 76 of the latter came from one piglet in its first few weeks. Only one pathological pig bone was identified, a lateral metapodial displaying a well-healed fracture from 16th to 18th-century deposits associated with the tithe barn.

In the absence of teeth that are indicative of donkeys or mules, the equid bones are 'horse', from pony-sized animals. The fusion data suggest adult animals predominated, although sub-adult animals were noted from 16th to 18th-century and 19th to 20th-century deposits (Table 76). The wear on incisors also reveals a few young animals, while the majority of horses appeared to exceed fourteen years (Table 80). Adult animals broken to the yoke or saddle would have been valuable plough and transport animals, and age and/or work-related traumas such as spavin and ring bone are indicated on both medieval and post-medieval bones. Curiously, one horse skull displayed bone destruction (porosity) as well as new bone growth immediately above the occipital condyles, although the aetiology of this probable infection is unknown. As has already been noted from other Wharram bone assemblages, the presence of young, unbroken animals suggests that horses were reared here, but in the absence of neonatal bones, this could not be confirmed.

Metrical data
Metrical data from the bones associated with the North Glebe Terrace sites were relatively scarce due to the high levels of fragmentation. Only some sheep and a few cattle bones provided sufficient data for an intra-site comparison, but unlike the previous analyses (Richardson 2005b, table 56) very few horse bones were measurable. Only one horse bone provided a wither height: a 16th to 18th-century radius indicative of a large pony of fourteen hands, one inch.

The greatest length of cattle metatarsals suggests that this animal tended to increase in height over time and this may be related to improvements in animal husbandry associated with the Agricultural Revolution of the 18th century onwards (Table 81). This pattern was

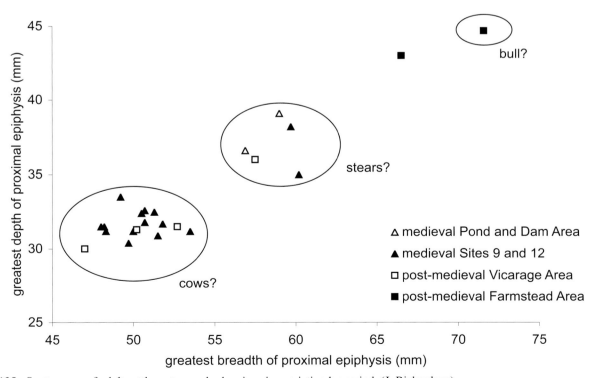

Fig. 135. Scattergram of adult cattle metacarpals showing size variation by period. (J. Richardson)

Table 81. Metrical data for cattle by site and period (in millimetres).

Site	Period	Species	Element	Measurement	Number	Minimum	Maximum	Mean	SD	Withers
SM	Medieval	Cattle	Metacarpal	GL	6	173.5	208.5	189.8	14.9	1063-1277
09+12	Medieval	Cattle	Metacarpal	GL	6	173.5	185.5	177.8	4.2	1063-1136
V	Post-medieval	Cattle	Metacarpal	GL	5	177.0	224.0	197.7	23.9	1084-1372
F	Post-medieval	Cattle	Metacarpal	GL	2	181.5	206.5	194.0	17.7	1112-1265
SM	Late Saxon	Cattle	Metacarpal	Bp	6	48.0	66.0	55.0	7.3	
PD	Medieval	Cattle	Metacarpal	Bp	2	56.9	57.5	57.2	0.4	
09+12	Medieval	Cattle	Metacarpal	Bp	17	48.0	60.2	51.7	3.5	
V	Post-medieval	Cattle	Metacarpal	Bp	6	46.3	66.5	54.0	8.1	
F	Post-medieval	Cattle	Metacarpal	Bp	2	59.0	71.6	65.3	8.9	
PD	Medieval	Cattle	Metacarpal	Dp	3	29.4	36.6	34.0	4.0	
09+12	Medieval	Cattle	Metacarpal	Dp	16	30.4	50.4	33.5	4.9	
V	Post-medieval	Cattle	Metacarpal	Dp	6	29.7	43.0	34.8	6.4	
F	Post-medieval	Cattle	Metacarpal	Dp	2	39.1	44.7	41.9	4.0	
SM	Saxon	Cattle	Metatarsal	GL	9	188.7	222.5	205.6	12.9	1028-1213
09+12	Medieval	Cattle	Metatarsal	GL	3	206.0	228.5	215.2	11.8	1123-1245
V	Post-medieval	Cattle	Metatarsal	GL	5	224.0	251.5	237.9	13.1	1221-1371

GL = greatest length, Bp = greatest breadth of proximal articulation, Dp = greatest depth of proximal articulation (after von den Driesch 1976)

SM = South Manor Area, NM = North Manor Area, PD = Pond and Dam Area, V = Vicarage Area, F = Farmstead Area

Table 82. Metrical data for sheep by site and period (in millimetres).

Site	Period	Species	Element	Measurement	Number	Minimum	Maximum	Mean	SD	Withers
SM	Middle Saxon	Sheep	Metacarpal	GL	13	105.2	126.1	116.9	5.8	514-617
SM	Late Saxon	Sheep	Metacarpal	GL	6	112.0	133.1	119.1	7.5	548-651
SM	Medieval	Sheep	Metacarpal	GL	5	100.2	114.1	108.1	6.5	490-558
NM	Medieval	Sheep	Metacarpal	GL	6	106.1	120.5	113.4	6.4	519-589
09+12	Medieval	Sheep	Metacarpal	GL	11	95.1	130.0	112.7	8.2	465-636
V	Medieval	Sheep	Metacarpal	GL	1	0.0	0.0	111.1		
V	Post-medieval	Sheep	Metacarpal	GL	10	114.4	137.0	122.5	8.1	559-669
SM	Middle Saxon	Sheep	Metacarpal	SD	14	12.8	15.9	13.8	0.9	
SM	Late Saxon	Sheep	Metacarpal	SD	6	11.7	16.0	13.2	1.5	
SM	Medieval	Sheep	Metacarpal	SD	5	12.1	12.8	12.4	0.3	
PD	Medieval	Sheep	Metacarpal	SD	1			13.0		
NM	Medieval	Sheep	Metacarpal	SD	6	11.1	12.4	11.7	0.5	
09+12	Medieval	Sheep	Metacarpal	SD	13	11.5	15.9	12.4	1.3	
V	Medieval	Sheep	Metacarpal	SD	1			13.7		
V	Post-medieval	Sheep	Metacarpal	SD	10	12.4	15.3	13.7	1.0	
NM	Iron Age/early Roman	Sheep	Metatarsal	GL	1			123.8		562
SM	Middle Saxon	Sheep	Metatarsal	GL	6	125.3	137.5	129.3	4.6	569-624
NM	Medieval	Sheep	Metatarsal	GL	4	100.5	131.9	122.0	12.3	456-599
12	Medieval	Sheep	Metatarsal	GL	8	114.0	140.4	128.3	10.0	558-637
V	Post-medieval	Sheep	Metatarsal	GL	3	122.3	140.0	131.7	8.9	555-636
SM	Middle Saxon	Sheep	Tibia	Bd	99	23.0	29.0	26.2	1.4	
SM	Late Saxon	Sheep	Tibia	Bd	42	22.9	29.8	25.8	1.6	
SM	Medieval	Sheep	Tibia	Bd	100	21.6	29.1	25.5	1.5	
NM	Medieval	Sheep	Tibia	Bd	11	20.3	27.2	25.3	2.0	
PD	Medieval	Sheep	Tibia	Bd	11	25.0	30.1	26.6	1.5	
09+12	Medieval	Sheep	Tibia	Bd	49	22.0	30.7	25.5	1.6	
V	Post-medieval	Sheep	Tibia	Bd	15	23.6	29.2	26.1	1.7	
F	Post-medieval	Sheep	Tibia	Bd	12	25.6	33.1	29.7	2.2	
NM	Medieval	Sheep	Tibia	Dd	9	16.4	21.5	19.8	1.6	
PD	Medieval	Sheep	Tibia	Dd	8	19.2	20.8	19.8	0.6	
09+12	Medieval	Sheep	Tibia	Dd	45	17.4	23.5	18.9	1.2	
V	Post-medieval	Sheep	Tibia	Dd	13	18.6	23.4	20.0	1.2	
F	Post-medieval	Sheep	Tibia	Dd	10	20.0	30.0	23.3	2.6	

GL = greatest length, SD = minimum shaft breadth, Bd = greatest breadth of distal articulation, Dd = greatest depth of distal articulation (after von den Driesch 1976)

SM = South Manor Area, NM = North Manor Area, PD = Pond and Dam Area, V = Vicarage Area, F = Farmstead Area

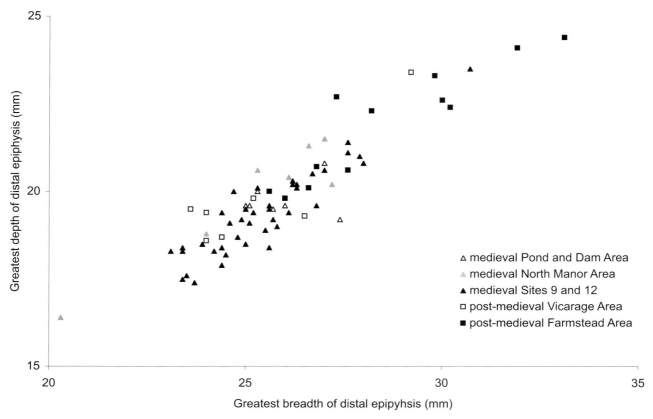

Fig. 136. Scattergram of adult sheep tibiae showing size variation by period. (J. Richardson)

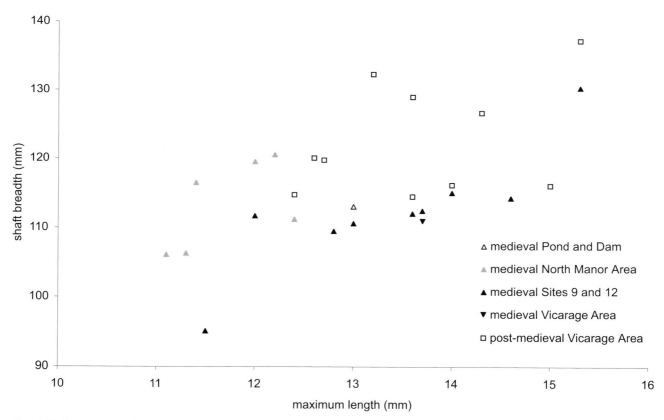

Fig. 137. Scattergram of adult sheep metacarpals by period. (J. Richardson)

corroborated by the metacarpals, although relatively few metapodials were measurable. Gender was mooted as an additional factor in size variation when the robusticity of the metacarpal was assessed, as this bone appeared to fall into one of three groups (Fig. 135). The variation in height indicated by the metapodials, therefore, may also be the product of gender rather than a reflection of husbandry advances over time.

Measurements taken of sheep tibiae indicate that this animal became increasingly robust when comparing post-medieval bones from the farmstead area to medieval examples, although evidence for a size increase from the post-medieval assemblage from the vicarage area was scant (Table 82). This variation in size is demonstrated when the breadth of the distal epiphysis of tibiae is plotted against its depth (Fig. 136), and it is clear that most of the more robust sheep were from the post-medieval farmstead area. Differing sex ratios are unlikely to account for this pattern: although the proportion of larger males from the post-medieval deposits of the North Glebe Terrace was relatively high (1 male: 2 females), Sites 9 and 12 had an even higher proportion of males (1 male: 1.4 females) but with no evidence for greater robusticity. In addition, the majority of bones identified as male from the post-medieval North Glebe Terrace sites came from deposits associated with the vicarage and not the farmstead. As a result, the higher proportion of robust animals from the farmstead area may reflect improvements in animal husbandry or the introduction of a new, larger breed. These data also suggest that the livestock being consumed by those occupying the vicarage area came from different flocks than those of the farmstead. Despite this variation in the post-medieval assemblages, larger animals in general appear to be associated with the later deposits as the plot of length against shaft breadth for sheep metacarpals shows a tendency for the post-medieval sheep (data available from the vicarage area only) to be amongst the taller and more robust individuals when compared to medieval animals (Fig. 137). This is reflected in the mean height (Table 82).

Carcass processing

Butchery marks made by knives, saws and/or cleavers were noted on a range of animals and with the exception of deer (saw marks to an antler) and possibly horse, many represent meat preparation and consumption (Table 69). These indicate that a meat diet rich in beef, lamb/mutton and pork was supplemented by meat from domestic fowl, goose and duck, as well as game in the form of rabbit and hare. In addition to meat, animal carcasses may also have been processed for their skins/feathers, horns and bones. Certainly, the use of horse skins and bones is possible, and saw marks to a metapodial from a medieval deposit are likely to indicate bone working as there is no usable meat around this part of the lower leg and the removal of the feet can be achieved more easily by cutting the relevant ligaments and tendons (Rixson 1989, 50). This bone also provides thick, straight and even pieces of

compact bone (Rixson 1989, 52), although no bone objects from the North Glebe Terrace sites were identified categorically as horse. Pig fibulae and a metacarpal, cattle tibiae and metapodials, and sheep/goat metapodials (Chapter 23), however, were fashioned into objects and this probably occurred on a local basis (pp 278 and 285).

The working of horncores was not identified categorically. Cattle horncores were rarely recovered, with all three coming from 16th to 18th-century deposits. One of these had chop marks around the horn's base, although whether this was to facilitate the removal of the skin or the horn sheath is not clear. Sheep horncores were more commonly noted, three from medieval deposits and twelve from 16th to 18th-century deposits, of which four had been chopped or sawn from the skull. Again, horn-working or skinning may be indicated, although no further cut marks indicative of skinning were noted on any metapodials or skulls from either sheep or cattle. The nasal bones of a rabbit, however, did reveal cut marks that are likely to have resulted from the skinning of the animal. Rabbit fur became increasingly popular for clothing from the 13th century (Bailey 1988, 1).

Typically, the majority of butchery marks relate to the reduction of carcasses during primary butchery (e.g. the removal of low-value parts such as the heads and feet) and secondary butchery (the division of the carcass into joints). Decapitation of sheep by severing the neck between the atlas and axis was indicated from both medieval and post-medieval deposits, while the beheading of post-medieval cattle was achieved by separating the atlas from the skull. Cut/chop marks to the mandibles of medieval sheep and post-medieval cattle and pigs may represent the removal of cheek meat (Rixson 1989, 56), while a cut to a hyoid of a post-medieval sheep indicates the removal of the tongue. Jointing the domestic mammals sometimes included the cleaving of carcasses into two halves once the animal was suspended by its hocks, although sagital chops through cattle, pig and sheep-sized vertebrae were only identified from 16th to 18th-century and later deposits. Subsequently, the halved carcasses were reduced to cuts of meat with dismembering marks to all the meat-rich joints, and meat removal was indicated in particular on the ribs. More rarely cut marks were noted on the smaller animals and birds; hare, rabbit, goose, chicken and duck (Table 69). Once cooked, the meat from these animals is easily torn from the bone without recourse to knives.

The relative proportions of body parts have also been used to assess carcass processing and these data have been analysed using a similar methodology to Pinter-Bellows (2000, 171) for the South Manor Area. To avoid over-emphasising minor deviations from the mean of 1, however, the standard deviation of the O/E ratio for each sample has been calculated and attention is given to elements for which the O/E ratio lies more than one standard deviation below or above the mean (after O'Connor 2000, 72). The distribution of elements for cattle, sheep and pig from both medieval and post-medieval deposits indicates that animals were slaughtered

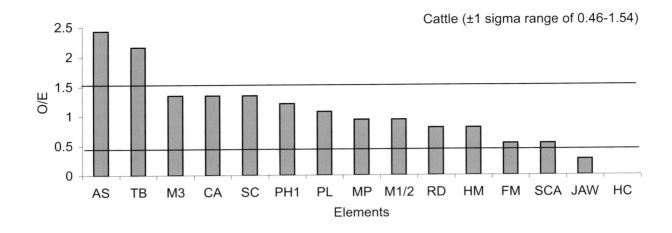

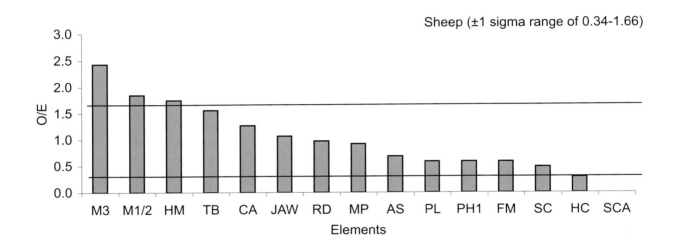

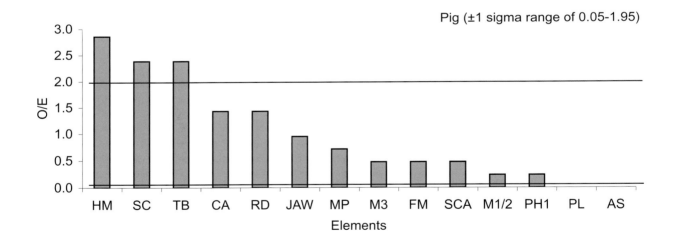

AS=astragalus, CA=calcaneus, FM=femur, HC=horncore, HM=humerus, M1/2=first/second molar, M3=third molar, MP=metapodials, PH1=first phalanx, PL=pelvis, RD=radius, SC=scapula, SCA=scaphoid, TB=tibia

Fig. 138. Distribution of skeletal elements: medieval. (J. Richardson)

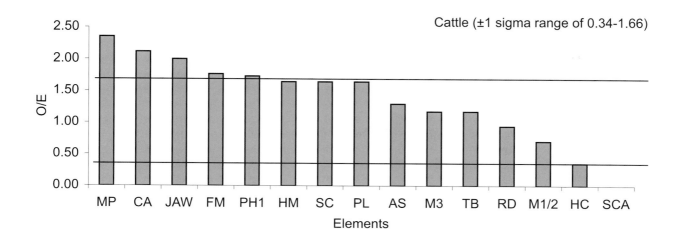

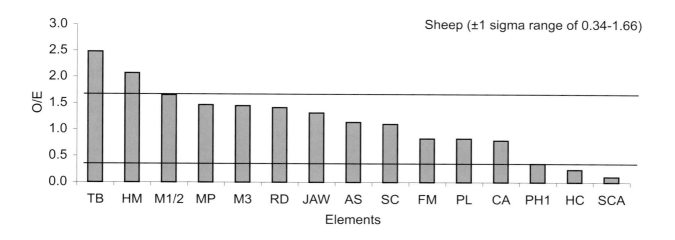

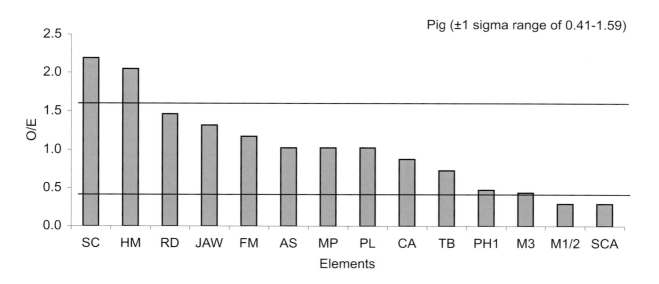

AS=astragalus, CA=calcaneus, FM=femur, HC=horncore, HM=humerus, M1/2=first/second molar, M3=third molar, MP=metapodials, PH1=first phalanx, PL=pelvis, RD=radius, SC=scapula, SCA=scaphoid, TB=tibia

Fig. 139. Distribution of skeletal elements: post-medieval. (J. Richardson)

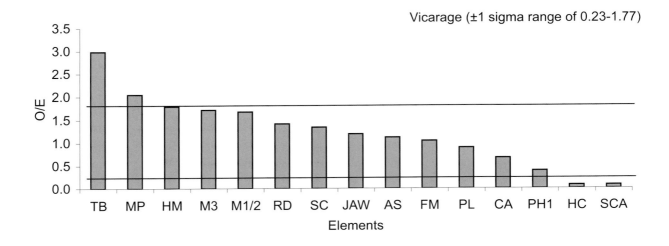

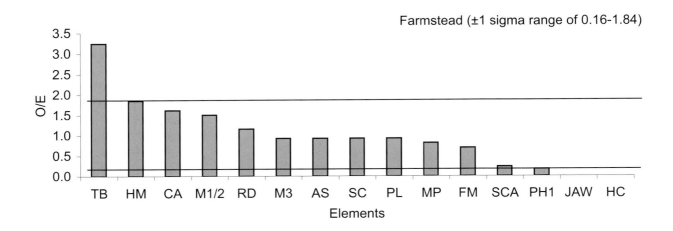

AS=astragalus, CA=calcaneus, FM=femur, HC=horncore, HM=humerus, M1/2=first/second molar, M3=third molar, MP=metapodials, PH1=first phalanx, PL=pelvis, RD=radius, SC=scapula, SCA=scaphoid, TB=tibia

Fig. 140. Distribution of skeletal elements: 16th to 18th-century sheep. (J. Richardson)

locally as the majority of body parts (e.g. heads, limb extremities and meat-rich joints) was present (Figs 138 and 139). Most of the missing elements represent the smaller bones that are often overlooked during hand excavation (e.g. scaphoid and astragalus), while a dearth/absence of horncores may indicate hornless varieties or alternatively the dispatch of this body part to a hornworker or with skins to the tanner. The absence of pig pelves from medieval deposits was unexpected as this bone is fairly large, robust and easily identified (Fig. 138). Perhaps this meat-rich haunch was traded beyond the village, although if this were the case, a similar dearth/absence of the accompanying femur may have been anticipated. Conversely, the other meat-rich joint, that of the shoulder (represented by the scapula and humerus), is over-represented for both the medieval and post-medieval pig. One final observation when comparing these data by period is that primary

butchery waste (such as metapodials, jaws and the first phalanx) is much more commonly recorded for cattle from post-medieval deposits when compared to the medieval material (cf. Figs 138 and 139). This suggests that the preliminary processing of cattle carcasses was carried out more frequently on the North Glebe Terrace during the later period.

Finally, the distribution of sheep bones has been compared from the 16th to 18th-century vicarage and farmstead (Fig. 140). This comparison reveals no significant difference between the two assemblages. From both, the meat-rich bones (scapula, humerus, pelvis and femur) all fall within the standard deviation of the mean of 1, and while primary butchery waste is more frequently observed from the vicarage (e.g. compare metapodials and jaws), the difference is not considered to be noteworthy.

Minor species

The minor species include birds and animals that were 'farmed' such as goat, goose, chicken, duck and turkey. These would have added variety to a meat diet dominated by beef, mutton and pork, as would the eggs from the poultry. Turkey is a relatively late import, the first documented record of turkey in England is from Cranmer's *Dietarie* of 1541 (Gurney 1921, 105), and it may still have been viewed as a high-status dish as late as the 18th century. The other domestic animals, cats and dogs, cohabited with their human masters but whether as beloved pets, working animals or poorly tolerated pests is unknown. The remaining bones represent game in the form of fallow deer, roe deer, hare, rabbit and partridge; animals that benefited from the presence of people and/or their buildings such as pigeon/dove, rat, house mouse and barn owl, and species representative of the wider environment such as badger, fox, stoat, jackdaw and starling (Table 71). Interestingly, a single guillemot bone, although unexpected, indicates contact with the east coast where guillemots still nest on cliffs during the spring and summer months. Historically, guillemots have been eaten, although their eggs, feathers and droppings were probably valued more highly (Buczacki 2002, 292). Finally, a single crane bone (unfortunately undated) is not exceptional as this bird was a fairly frequent visitor to Britain until the end of the 17th century (Buczacki 2002, 269). Roman deposits from West Heslerton (Richardson 2001) and medieval deposits from Beverley (Scott 1991, table 42) have also revealed the presence of cranes, while further afield examples are known from medieval Lincoln (O'Connor 1982, 44) and Barnard Castle (Jones *et al.* 1985, 26).

Discussion

The animal bones from the North Glebe Terrace sites have been used to consider husbandry practices over the medieval and post-medieval periods. With the molluscs (Chapter 26) and fish (Chapter 27), they have also been used to assess dietary intake and by comparing the data from the 16th to 18th-century vicarage and farmhouse, the diets of these particular households have been considered further. Finally, the faunal data have been compared to assemblages from other parts of medieval Wharram Percy.

In general, the animal bones from the North Glebe Terrace revealed a familiar farming practice that was well suited to the local environment and concentrated on multi-purpose sheep rearing for milk, wool, manure and meat. The Wolds were the preferred location for the breeding and fattening of sheep (Leatham 1794, 48) with the average Wold farm of the late 17th century carrying nearly three times as many sheep as its lowland counterpart (Harris 1961, 31). Sheep rearing was complemented by cattle (for milk, manure, traction, skins and meat) and to a lesser extent by pigs. Cattle herds were probably small-scale compared to the Vale of York and Holderness where water supplies were more reliable

(Harris 1961, 33-34). Horses completed the quartet of domestic livestock and given the presence of young individuals, this valuable animal was probably bred by the villagers to be used for traction and transport. Meanwhile, dietary variability was provided by poultry, goat, rabbit, hare, fallow deer and roe deer, shellfish (in particular oysters) and both marine and freshwater fish (although bones from the latter were very scarce) (Chapter 27). Rabbit warrens were also an important source of income for some Wold farmers (Harris 1961, 35), although the proportions of the identified bones and shells indicate that the domestic ungulates provided the majority of the calorific meat intake at Wharram Percy and that game and marine resources offered only rare alternatives.

Interestingly, documentary sources have indicated that open-field farming may have been in decline throughout the 15th century with the pastoral conversion completed by 1527 (pp 1-2). The likely result of this change would have been an increase in the size of the sheep flocks and probably in the fodder crops required for their over-wintering. Harris (1961, 31-2) has certainly identified an increase in flock sizes from the late 17th to mid-18th century for the Wolds in general. Such changes, however, do not appear to have been accompanied by any significant fluctuations in the proportions of the three main domestic animals from the North Glebe Terrace over time, or indeed from other parts of Wharram Percy (see Fig. 129).

Further differences in animal husbandry were anticipated, particularly given the changes in farming practices as a result of the Agricultural Revolution of the 18th century onwards. Osteologically, these would have been demonstrated most effectively by an increase in the size of livestock following improvements in breeding programmes for example. The metrical data for cattle indicated some increase in height and robusticity, but gender may have been a more significant factor in size variation (Fig. 135). Evidence for an increase in the size of sheep by the post-medieval period was clearer and this suggests that welfare practices had improved (for example the quality and quantity of feed) or that breeding programmes were selecting for larger livestock (Fig. 137). Certainly during the late 18th to early 19th centuries, the native slow-growing shortwool breed favoured by the Wold farmers was being replaced by Improved Leicesters (Bowie 1990, 118). Interestingly, an analysis of the metrical data from sheep tibiae revealed a significant difference in the robusticity of sheep from the post-medieval vicarage and farmstead areas (Fig. 136). It is possible that these data represent two distinct populations: perhaps the Vicar bought in meat from elsewhere, while the local farmer was successfully increasing the size of his animals beyond those of his neighbours.

To assess further the differences between the faunal assemblages of the two areas, the deposits associated specifically with the 16th to 18th-century vicarage and farmhouse were considered. Dietary differences were not extensive but pork and shellfish apparently made up a greater proportion of the diet of those occupying the vicarage, while rabbit was more commonly consumed by the farmhouse inhabitants. Comparing fusion data from the two properties, the slaughter patterns indicate that over 50% of the sheep consumed by those at the vicarage were osteologically mature, while under 30% of mutton eaten in the farmhouse came from animals 30 months plus (Table 74). Perhaps the farmer as a producer had greater access to prime lamb, while the vicar consumed animals that were somewhat older.

Finally, in comparing the North Glebe Terrace assemblages to those from other parts of medieval Wharram Percy differences in the slaughter patterns of cattle and sheep have been identified. From both the medieval and post-medieval deposits associated with the North Glebe Terrace sites, a higher proportion of cattle were killed between one and eight months than elsewhere in the village. Animals killed at around a month may have been slaughtered once their mothers' milk yield was established in order to free up the milk for butter and cheese making. Older calves at the end of this age range may have been slaughtered towards the end of the year as grazing became limited. The advantage of slaughtering livestock now was to preserve over-winter grazing/fodder for vital breeding stock, while also providing some meat for salting and drying to sustain the villagers over the lean months of the new year. Similarly, an early kill-off was also noted for sheep, with the proportion slaughtered before six months old higher from the North Glebe Terrace sites than elsewhere. It is tempting to assign some of these early deaths to an intensification of milk production, but more realistically they are likely to represent the slaughter of animals that were surplus to breeding requirements or poorer quality animals whose worth, following a second summer of grazing, was insufficient to take the trouble over-wintering them again.

Conclusions

The faunal assemblage from the North Glebe Terrace sites has confirmed the sheep-dominated husbandry of medieval and post-medieval Wharram Percy, but failed to identify any evidence for an increase in the importance/size of sheep flocks as indicated by contemporary documentary sources. Developments in husbandry, however, were proposed given the increase in the size of sheep (and possibly cattle also) by the post-medieval period. These changes, the introduction of new breeds and/or selective breeding programmes, were probably brought about as part of the Agricultural Revolution of the 18th century onwards. Despite the apparent stability and dominance of sheep-rearing at Wharram Percy, a comparison of the post-medieval data indicated that the meat supplied to the vicarage appeared to be drawn from a different flock than the one feeding those in the farmhouse. Social inequalities were also possible, with the residents of the farmhouse eating better-quality lamb and beef than those occupying the vicarage.

26 The Mollusca
by J. Richardson

In total, 87 marine shells (estimated by counting shell apices for gastropods and valve umbos for bivalves) were recovered from the North Glebe Terrace sites, with the majority retrieved from 16th to 18th-century deposits associated with the vicarage (Table 83). Oyster (*Ostrea edulis*) was the most commonly recovered species and given the presence of both lower and upper values, was probably introduced to the site unopened and ready for consumption. Scallops (*Pecten maximus*), cockles (*Cerastoderma edule*), mussels (*Mytilus edulis*) and periwinkles (*Littorina littorea*) may also have been consumed, but limpets (*Patella vulgata*) are considered rubbery and hence associated with times of hardship (Cerón-Carrasco 2005, 32). The Humber estuary is the most likely source for the esturine species such as oyster, cockles and mussel, while limpets (found on rocky shores), periwinkles (found on the lower shore) and scallops (found offshore) are likely to have been introduced from the coast.

Table 83. Mollusca from the North Glebe Terrace by site and period (excluding fragments)

	Oyster	Scallop	Cockle	Mussel	Limpet	Periwinkle
Vicarage: medieval	4		1			
Vicarage: 16th to 18th-century	28		18			
Vicarage: 19th to 20th-century	3	1	7			
Vicarage: undated	7			1		
Farmstead: 16th to 18th-century	4		1			1
Farmstead: 18th to 19th-century	1					1
Farmstead: 19th to 20th-century	6		2		1	
Total	53	1	29	1	1	2

27 The Fish Bone

by J. H. Barrett

Introduction

This report summarises a very small collection of fish bones recovered from the farmstead and vicarage sites at Wharram Percy. The material was collected by hand.

Fifteen specimens were examined from the farmhouse, only five of which were identified (Table 84). One of the latter was from the medieval phase. The remaining four were from the 18th to 19th-century phase. Four of the five identified specimens were from marine fish. The fifth, an eel bone, could represent either a saltwater or freshwater catch, but the latter is more likely.

Table 84. Farmhouse: number of identified specimens by phase.

Common name	Phase M	EPM	LPM	Total
Cod	1			1
Cod Family			1	1
Eel			1	1
Haddock			1	1
Ling			1	1
Unidentified	1	5	4	10
Total	2	5	8	15

M = medieval; EPM = 16th to 17th-century; LPM = 18th to 19th- century

A total of 172 specimens from the vicarage were examined, ranging in date from 'medieval' (43 specimens) to the 19th to 20th centuries (3 specimens). Most, however, were from the 16th to 18th centuries (118 specimens). Three were unphased. Only 48 specimens were identified to family, genus or species (Table 85).

As was the case for other collections from Wharram Percy (e.g. Barrett 2005), the bones are mostly from marine fish. The majority are members of the cod family (Gadidae) (cod (*Gadus morhua*), haddock (*Melanogrammus aeglefinus*), ling (*Molva molva*), pollack and saithe (*Pollachius*)), but flatfish (dab) and cartilaginous fish (thornback ray (*Raja Clavata*)) specimens are also present. Freshwater fish are represented by a single pike (*Esox lucius*) bone from the 16th to 17th centuries and a single carp family specimen from the 19th to 20th centuries. A single salmon or trout specimen from the medieval period could have been caught in saltwater or freshwater.

Methods

The assemblage was recorded following the York protocol (Harland *et al.* 2003). Twenty diagnostic

Table 85. Vicarage: number of identified specimens by phase.

Common name	M	EPM	Mod.	U	Total
Carp Family			1		1
Cod	6	17		1	24
Cod Family		5			5
Dab		1			1
Haddock		5		1	6
Ling	1	3			4
Ling?				1	1
Pike		1			1
Pollack		1			1
Saithe		1			1
Saithe/Pollack		1			1
Salmon and Trout Family	1				1
Thornback Ray			1		1
Unidentified	35	83	1	5	124
Total	43	118	3	8	172

M = medieval; EPM = 16th to 17th-century; Mod. = 19th to 20th- century; U = undated

Table 86. Vicarage: fish bone preservation characteristics by phase.

Phase	M	EPM	Mod.	U	Total
Percent completeness (diagnostic elements only)					
0-20%		5		1	6
21-40%	2	6			8
41-69%	1	6			7
61-80%	2	2			4
81-100%	1	2	1	1	5
Bone texture (diagnostic elements only)					
Good	4	16	1	1	22
Fair	1	4			5
Poor	1	1		1	3
Other modifications (all specimens)					
Carnivore gnawing	1	2			3

M = medieval; EPM = 16th-17th-century; Mod. = 19th-20th-century; U = undated

Table 87. Vicarage: element distribution for gadid fishes (see Barrett 1997 for definition of vertebra groups).

Element	M	EPM	Mod.	U	Total
Cod					
Abdominal Vertebra Group 2		1			1
Abdominal Vertebra Group 3	1				1
Articular	1	2			3
Caudal Vertebra Group 1		8		1	9
Ceratohyal	1	1			2
Dentary		1			1
Maxilla		1			1
Parasphenoid		1			1
Posttemporal		2			2
Quadrate	1				1
Scapula	1				1
Vomer	1				1
Cod Family					
Ceratohyal		1			1
Parasphenoid		1			1
Preopercular		1			1
Supracleithrum		2			2
Haddock					
Abdominal Vertebra Group 2		1			1
Abdominal Vertebra Group 3		1			1
Articular				1	1
Cleithrum		2			2
Preopercular		1			1
Ling					
Abdominal Vertebra Group 3	1	1			2
Supracleithrum		2			2
Ling?					
Parasphenoid				1	1
Pollack					
Abdominal Vertebra Group 3		1			1
Saithe					
Maxilla		1			1
Saithe/ Pollack					
Articular		1			1

M = medieval; EPM = 16th to 17th-century; Mod. = 19th to 20th-century; U = undated

Table 88. Vicarage, butchery marks (all identified specimens).

Element	Common name	Interpretation	EPM	U
Supracleithrum	Ling	decapitation	1	
Caudal Vertebra Group 1	Cod	removing anterior vertebrae	2	
Caudal Vertebra Group 1	Cod	filleting		1

EPM = 16th-17th-century; U = undated

elements are identified to the finest possible taxonomic group and recorded in detail – including, as appropriate, element, side, count, measurements, weight, modifications (e.g. burning and butchery), fragmentation, texture and estimates of fish size. 'Non-diagnostic' elements (quantification category 0) are only identified beyond class for special reasons. Examples include butchered specimens and bones of species otherwise missing from the assemblage. The assemblage has been quantified by number of identified specimens (NISP).

Preservation

The sample size from the farmhouse is too small to facilitate quantification of fish bone preservation, but in qualitative terms the material is comparable with other assemblages from Wharram Percy. The small size of the collection may thus not be due to preservation conditions (at least not alone).

Preservation of the fish bone from the vicarage was variable (Table 86). Many of the specimens were highly fragmented, but a few were over 80% complete. Moreover, the texture of the specimens was very solid, suggesting good preservation of the bone tissue despite sometimes high levels of fragmentation. Three specimens exhibited carnivore tooth impressions consistent with dog gnawing, implying that many fish bones will have been destroyed by farmyard scavenging.

Results

Farmhouse
The marine species present were cod, haddock and ling. The single eel (*Anguilla anguilla*) bone noted above probably represents a freshwater catch, although eels (a migratory species) can also be caught in the sea. None of the specimens exhibited cut marks, making it impossible to comment on butchery practices. Overall this assemblage can only be used to demonstrate the transport of marine fish from the coast.

Vicarage
As noted above, 172 specimens were examined, 48 of which were identifiable diagnostic elements (including one dermal denticle of a thornback ray) (Table 85).

Ten taxa are represented in the assemblage if one excludes broad groups such as cod family that are also represented by species level identifications. Seven of

Table 89. Vicarage, estimated total length.

Size	M	EPM	U	Total
Cod				
301-500mm		1		1
501-800mm	1	2		3
801-1000mm	1	2		3
>1000mm	3	3		6
Dab				
151-300mm		1		1
Haddock				
301-500mm		1		1
501-800mm		2	1	3
Ling				
801-1000mm		2		2
Saithe				
>1000mm		1		1
Saithe/Pollack				
>1000mm		1		1
Salmon and Trout Family				
801-1000mm	1			1

M = medieval; EPM = 16th to 17th-century; U = undated

these taxa are marine, two are freshwater and one is migratory between saltwater and freshwater. In rank order, the marine species are: cod (24 specimens), haddock (six specimens), ling (four or five specimens), pollack (one specimen), saithe (one specimen), dab (one specimen) and thornback ray (one specimen). The truly freshwater species were carp family (1 specimen) and pike (1 specimen). The single salmon or trout specimen could represent a fish caught in the sea or in freshwater. The paucity of freshwater fish overall may be partly due to poor recovery as many of the marine species are very large. Given sieving with fine mesh more cyprinids, for example, may well have been recovered.

The distribution of skeletal elements represented is not very informative due to the small sample size and the biases of hand collection. Nevertheless, it is clear that at least some of the cod family fish arrived whole, and thus possibly fresh, as bones from both heads and tails are represented (Table 87). Some cod may also have arrived as stockfish or a similar dried product, as two caudal vertebrae exhibit characteristic cut marks (Table 88). These are butchery marks on the side of the centrum in the transverse plane – created when the anterior vertebrae were removed as was often done prior to drying (e.g. Barrett 1997). Both vertebrae cut in this way are from the 16th to 18th centuries. Two further cut marks, one on a ling supracleithrum and one on a cod caudal vertebra, are indicative of decapitation and filleting respectively. These could indicate the manufacture of a dried product *or* butchery of fresh fish and are thus less informative.

Many of the bones are from very large fish, some in excess of 1m in total length (Table 89). This is not surprising given the recovery methods employed. The presence of some specimens from individuals of less than 500mm total length implies that both small and large fish may originally have been consumed. The estimates provided in Table 89 are based on comparison with reference specimens of known size. Too few measurements could be taken to justify quantitative analysis.

Discussion

The observations in this report apply principally to the 16th to 18th centuries, as virtually all the material derives from that period. Like previous results from Wharram Percy, this small assemblage indicates that a diverse range of marine fishes was transported from the coast. Some arrived as whole (possibly fresh) fish, others probably as dried stockfish (or a similar product). Freshwater species were also exploited, and may be greatly under-represented due to recovery by hand collecting. Little more can be said due to the modest sample size.

Part Seven
Discussion

28 The Post-medieval Settlement and its Buildings
by S. Wrathmell

The depopulation of the medieval settlement

In the first of this series of publications, Maurice Beresford summarised his thoughts on the chronology of depopulation and the decline of open-field agriculture at Wharram Percy:

'The system of open field farming evidenced in 1368 was in use in 1440, and at least sixteen houses were still occupied in 1435 and 1458, when the fields were yielding corn for the manorial mill, but there were tax reliefs from 1433 and some poor quality woodland had returned by 1435. In 1440 the vicarage income was reduced from the sum agreed in 1327 by more than a half. This shrinking community was reduced further, probably as a result of the general substitution of grass for arable characteristic of that period. If so, most of the depopulation occurred before 1488, since only four houses were pulled down between 1488 and 1517'
(*Wharram I*, 16).

He envisaged a community in economic as well as demographic decline during the 15th century, though one piece of evidence cited in support of this – the reduction in the vicar's income – was, as the archbishop's letters make clear, related to the financial problems of Haltemprice priory, rather than to the impoverishment of the village community. The economic condition of Wharram's late medieval farming families will be discussed further in *Wharram XIII*.

On the basis of the recorded tenements, and of the tofts and crofts represented by earthworks, the mid-15th-century population was perhaps only half that of the 13th-century community, but it would be wrong to assume that the four tenements destroyed between 1488 and 1517 represented the final depopulation of the village: Robert Pickering's testimony that the township was laid to grass in 1527 suggests that a significant number of open-field holdings, in addition to the vicarage and chantry bovates, continued to be cultivated until that time. The pulling down of four houses between 1488 and 1517 marked a stage in the reduction of the community, not the final act of depopulation which came a decade or more later.

It seems very probable that, when the final depopulation came, it was instigated by a wealthy grazier, John Thorpe of Appleton in the Vale of Pickering. There is no reason to suppose that the tenants evicted at that time were simply scraping a living, or unable to pay the rent that the Hiltons demanded. It is just as likely that Thorpe had identified a valuable asset to add to his enterprise – good Wolds sheep pasture close to the Vale and with a reliable supply of water – and that he was willing to pay a big enough rent to persuade the Hiltons to put the whole township down to grass.

Whoever lived at Wharram in the middle decades of the 16th century – and it seems there were still a few resident smallholders and labourers from time to time – it is probable that there was no cultivation in the township at this period, other than perhaps in a few garden plots, and no resident farmer. By the early 1570s, however, a new farm had been established, its lands occupying the whole of the township, and its buildings including a substantial farmhouse described in the early 17th century as the 'chief house of the manor'. As yet, we cannot say where that house was located, or whether it was a new building or one of the old village houses that had continued to be occupied. The status of at least one resident family, the Richardsons, might imply a house of some substance and sophistication. The earlier of the two excavated farmhouses in Site 74, on the north side of the churchyard, appears to have been built no earlier than the late 17th century and so cannot have been the home of the Richardsons or their predecessors.

The farmhouse and its outbuildings (Fig. 141)

The archaeological remains of these two successive farmhouses accorded well with the documentary descriptions of the buildings in 1699, 1806 and 1830. There were, however, some other aspects of what seemed at the time to be a straightforward and highly productive excavation that appear less so in the light of the finds analyses. By separating out contexts that were thought to relate to construction phases from those that represented periods of occupation (both within the house and outside it in the case of Period 3) it was hoped that greater definition could be achieved for the activities that took place during the use of those buildings. Regrettably, this ambition was thwarted by the degree of contamination from subsequent activity on the site, especially after the demolition of the final house.

The other disappointment in relation to Site 74 was, as noted above, the failure to identify Period 1 remains that might belong to the chief house recorded in the late 16th and early 17th centuries. The pottery and clay pipe reports suggest that this earlier building lay elsewhere – whether in the valley or on the plateau we cannot say – but it is worth introducing a note of caution over this

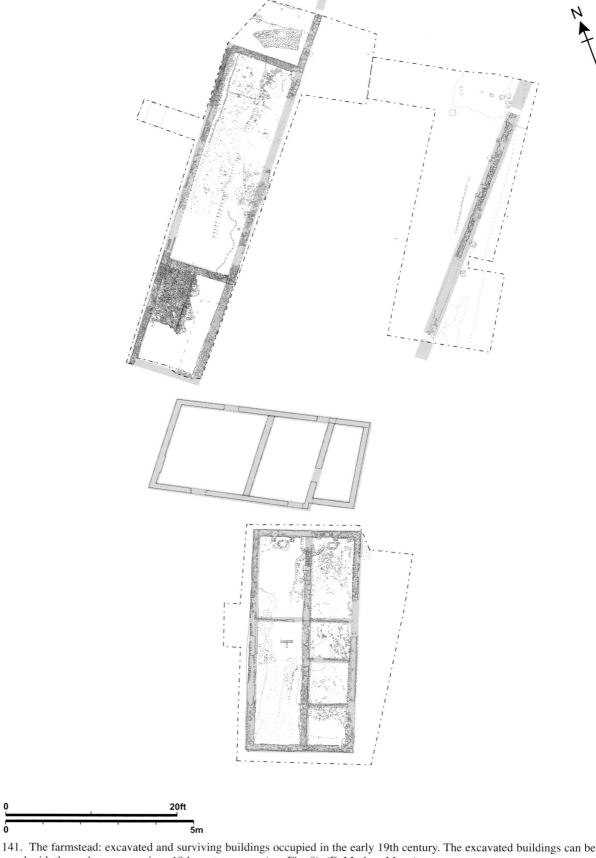

0   20ft

0   5m

Fig. 141. The farmstead: excavated and surviving buildings occupied in the early 19th century. The excavated buildings can be compared with those shown on various 19th-century maps (see Fig. 8). (E. Marlow-Mann)

conclusion. If we look at the pottery assemblages from the neighbouring vicarage sites there is only a small component of identifiably 16th-century pottery (pp 176-7, above), despite the wealth of information regarding resident vicars in that period. It is just possible that the ceramic and other assemblages have been shaped more by their social and economic context rather than by the simple presence or absence of activity at particular periods in particular parts of the village area.

Finally, it is still uncertain whether the Hearth Tax return of 1674 described the Period 2 house that was uncovered in Site 74. Though the pottery report implies that the return may be too early for the excavated house, it is worth noting that the record of three hearths would fit admirably this earliest excavated house if the artefact dating could be stretched to accommodate such an identification. The plan form and structural aspects of this house, and those of its much more spacious successor, are discussed by David Neave in the next section of this chapter, in the context of vernacular building traditions on the Wolds.

Turning to the outbuildings to the north, the earliest remains in Site 51 were clearly medieval, and it would be reasonable enough to assume that the peasant tofts and crofts visible as earthworks to the north of the site had simply once run through it, towards the church. This may, indeed, be the best model for medieval settlement in the valley north of the vicarage, although the discovery of what appears to have been a rock-cut undercroft – and one with a coin of Henry I on its floor – may suggest a different settlement history for this part of the village. It is a suggestion that may be supported by the recovery (admittedly from unstratified contexts) of two pottery forms that are rare at Wharram: a possible Stamford Ware bottle, and a Scarborough ware lamp. It should perhaps be noted in this context that the Wharram rectory, as a physical entity, makes its sole appearance in 1368 when it was said to lie next to a waste toft. The rectory buildings might well have been sited not far from the church.

The remains of the post-medieval farm buildings, or some of them, are presumably to be related to the documented improvements of the 1770s, but given their poor survival overall, the question is whether what survived to be excavated is what was recorded in the building accounts. It is easy to assume that Monkman's barn is to be identified as the West Range, simply because it looks like a barn and it survived, but we cannot rule out the possibility that the documented buildings have been lost, and the excavated buildings are undocumented in the late 18th-century building accounts.

That said, the case for this identification receives some support from the West Range's dimensions. Its internal width is 18 feet, in accordance with the analysis of the Monkman's barn documents in Chapter 1. Furthermore, the floor slots which presumably accommodated joists for a boarded floor occupy an area of 15 feet by 18 feet, as against the recorded measurements which give 14 feet 9 inches by 17 feet 10 inches. It has been suggested in Chapter 1 that the boarded floor represented just the part

of the barn that was used for threshing. The excavated remains included a doorway (later blocked) in the west wall of the room with the floor slots; the east wall, and any doorway it might have contained to provide a through draught for threshing, had been entirely lost through erosion. Though the remaining documented measurements are far less easy to fit into the excavated building, it is possible that other rooms were stables and (perhaps at first floor) a granary. The southern end of the range, with its cobbled floor and edged brick drains, certainly seems to have been a stable in its final structural period (cf. Hayfield 1998, 120).

In the valuation of 1806, which gives a more comprehensive description of the farmstead than the building accounts, the 'new' barn at Wharram Percy Farm was no doubt Monkman's barn of the 1770s, just as the 'new' dwelling house at Wharram Grange was the one that had been built in the same decade. Monkman's barn was again associated with stables and granary, presumably all these functions contained in one range, the West Range. The small wagon shed and cow house may have been located in the South Range of outbuildings, now the cottages: the wall sockets for timbers in the west wall of Room 2 (Fig. 26) may have supported a feeding trough, and the rounded inner corners of the entrances suggest that animals were intended to pass through them (cf. Hayfield 1998, 116).

The detached stone and thatch wagon shed of 1806 may have been represented by the ephemeral remains of the East Range, the thatch later being replaced by tiles. Colin Hayfield has noted that at Vessey Pasture, to the south-west of Wharram, the wagon sheds, 'as was usual, opened out not into the foldyard but out onto the fields' (Hayfield 1998, 120). At Wharram Percy this would not have been possible (except in the North Range) because of the topography, and such constraints would probably have contributed to the decision to abandon this farmstead in favour of the present one, sited on the Wold plateau.

A wider context for the kind of structural developments seen at Wharram Percy has been supplied by Paul Barnwell and Colum Giles in their survey of English farmsteads in the period 1750-1914, and it is worth quoting from their general conclusions:

'The farmsteads recorded can be divided into two broad categories: those which were planned as a whole, including "model" farmsteads, and those which reached their mature form through a process of evolution. The former, whether built primarily as showpieces or as efficient working farms, are readily set in a context derived from the contemporary literature... What is much more difficult is to make sense of the vast majority of farmsteads – often of little strictly architectural merit – which reached their mature form through a process of evolution, which in many cases may have begun before the period at which the earliest extant structures were erected'
(Barnwell and Giles 1997, 146).

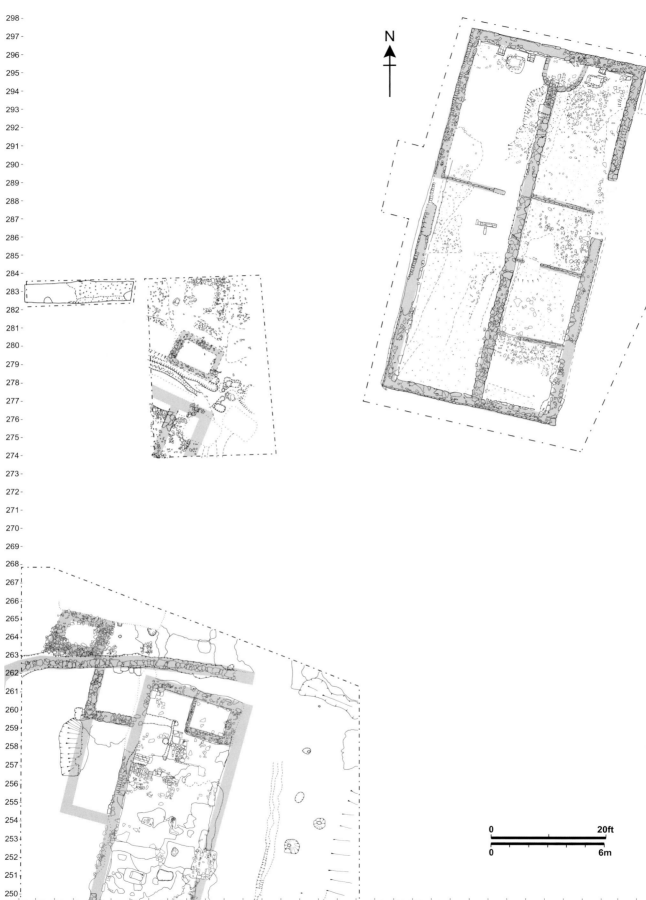

Fig. 142 Remains of outbuildings on Site 73, between the farmhouse and vicarage (E. Marlow-Mann)

344

As they emphasise, it is these 'ordinary', evolving farmsteads that provide evidence for the wider impact of new ideas (Barnwell and Giles 1997, 156), though the assessment of impact at the level of the individual farmstead needs to take into account the constraints of topography and existing buildings in a context where capital was insufficient to provide an opportunity for wholesale replacement. In the case of Wharram, it is likely that the constraints imposed by the farmstead's location deterred more than modest, piecemeal investment, and were such that, when major investment was considered appropriate, it was directed to a more convenient site elsewhere in the township. That site was High House, one of the many early 19th-century Wolds 'high barns' that already included some domestic accommodation (see Beresford and Hurst 1990, 119-21; Hayfield 1991, 41).

Fragments of another outbuilding, or group of outbuildings, were excavated in Site 73, south-west of the early 19th-century farmhouse and north of the contemporary vicarage (Fig. 142). Virtually nothing can be said about them, except that they seem to have followed broadly similar orientations to the farmhouse and vicarage. A small building is shown in this location on the 1836 map and, sited just north of the northern glebe boundary, it has been tentatively identified as the farmer's stable (Ch. 3 and Fig. 8).

The vicarage buildings

The discussion of the post-medieval farmhouse has provided, in the main, a coherent and intelligible history supported by, and refined through the various strands of information and analysis – documentary, stratigraphic, artefactual. The same cannot be said for the late medieval and early post-medieval vicarage buildings. Readers will have noted that the extensive documentary evidence and the excavation data for these buildings have been treated quite separately in Parts One and Two of this volume, and may assume that this approach has been adopted in order to invest the analysis of the archaeological remains with a spurious air of objectivity. This is not the case. The reason is that, for the vicarage sites, it has proved enormously difficult to tie the two forms of evidence together, and it is quite possible to assemble alternative interpretations that are equally as valid as each other. The reasons for this will be considered in the concluding section of this chapter.

The two main excavations which explored the vicarage area were those of Site 54 and, on its west side, Site 77. Parts of Site 54 were excavated completely at least as far back as Romano-British levels, and it was here that the earliest, pre-vicarage features were recorded, as Structures A, B and C. These are all likely to date to well before the later Middle Ages, and will be considered further in *Wharram XIII* in the context of Romano-British and Anglo-Saxon activity in the valley. Site 77 was, however, excavated only as far as the late medieval levels; and though the presence of earlier structures was

detected beneath these levels, nothing useful can be said about them. The main late medieval vicarage buildings were found in Site 77 and to the south, in Site 26, though it is also likely that further remains await investigation in the unexcavated ground west of Site 26. During the 16th, 17th and 18th centuries, however, the successors to the late medieval vicarage buildings seem gradually to have shifted eastwards, into the area investigated as Site 54.

On Site 77, the earliest coherent excavated structure was the barn occupying its north end (Fig. 143). It was clearly not the earliest building erected there: a trial trench cut through its floor revealed levelling layers and surfaces below, and an experimental GPR survey appeared to indicate a wall on a different orientation. There is, however, no reason to doubt that the excavated structure was the barn recorded as being destroyed by fire in 1553, or that it had stood there since at least the new ordination of the vicarage in 1440.

The barn's contents at the time of its destruction have been fully discussed in Chapter 24, but its form and size deserve further consideration. In 1555 it was said to have measured the equivalent of about 6.4m in width and about 7.3m in length. The first of these dimensions has been confirmed by excavation, but the second has not: it is significantly shorter than the excavated length (11m), and there is an unknown further extent of barn surviving beyond the northern edge of excavation.

It may be that the vicars who surveyed the remains in 1555 observed only part of the structure, the rest perhaps already obscured by accumulating hill-wash. But we should consider two alternative possibilities. The first is that the barn had by this time been substantially reduced from its original length. There were no structural remains to attest such a shortening, but the distribution of charred crops and timber – confined to the southern 8m of the building – might be cited in support of this suggestion. The second relates to the statement of one of the deponents, Thomas Marshall, that the pre-fire buildings included a stable, and that the stable stood between the house and barn. If the stable had been built within the barn – presumably in its south end – its area may not have been included in the quoted dimensions of the barn.

The 1555 statements in relation to the number of posts or crucks in the building – six – may support any of these suggestions, and are themselves open to several possible interpretations. In the first place, the building may have had three trusses, formed by three pairs of crucks creating two full bays, with a truss in each gable end wall. On the basis of truss spacings in the late medieval farmhouse on Area 6 (Building 1), this barn would have been about 8m long (see *Wharram VI*, fig. 15).

Alternatively, two of the crucks may have been 'end forks', giving a configuration of one full bay formed by two trusses and two end bays supported by a pair of end forks (see *Wharram VI*, fig. 3). This again would give a barn about 8m long. Only if the three pairs of crucks formed two bays with unrecorded end bays beyond them could the 1553 barn match the excavated length of barn walling and flooring. Even more confusingly, as noted in

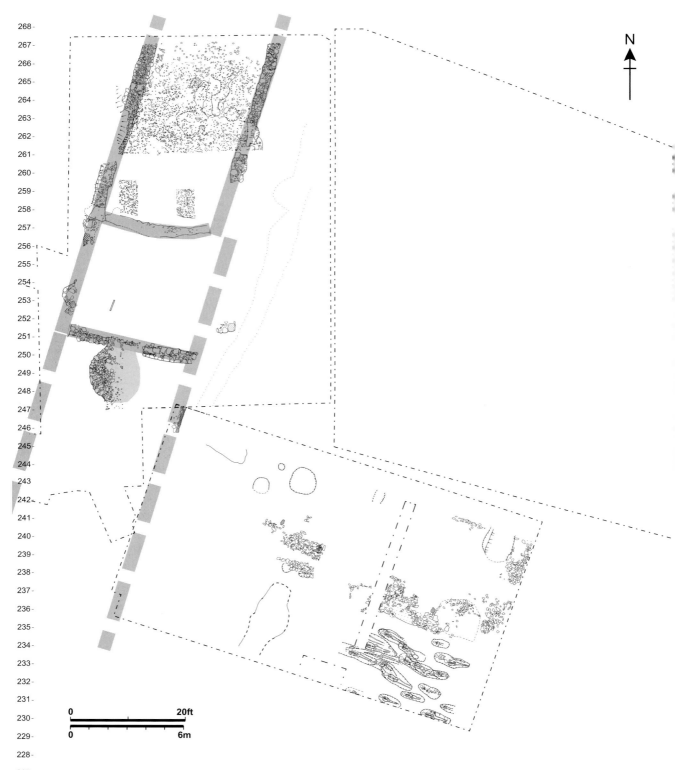

Fig. 143. Pre-fire vicarage: alternative A. (E. Marlow-Mann).

Chapter 2, one of the 1555 witnesses, Hugh Collome, said that the barn had been of three 'rooms'. If these three rooms were bays, they should have been framed by four, not three pairs of cruck blades.

The southern end of the barn's east wall, and the whole of its south end wall, had been robbed out. Nevertheless, the course of the end wall is clear, and is confirmed by the corresponding sharp edge to the burnt deposits on the barn floor. The slightly convex shape of the south-end robber trench may signify the use of an endfork to support a hipped roof, at least until Atkinson's additional building was erected in the gap between the barn and the house. The large quantity of burnt nails from the deposits in the barn, some bearing evidence of having been driven through planking, may indicate that the southern end of the building had a loft – a suggestion that might be seen to support the idea of a stable in this location.

The datable finds from the barn floor were few, but included, as probably the latest chronologically, seven sherds of a 15th-century Humber ware jug (see p. 138, Table 10). There was no pottery of characteristically 16th-century date. It can of course be argued that pottery employed in a barn might be unrepresentative of what was contemporaneously used in the household. Nevertheless, it has to be said that without such a clear mid-16th-century record for the destruction of the barn, there would have been no reason to date its use beyond the late 15th century.

South of the barn, the archaeological remains of the documented buildings are much more elusive (Fig. 143). This was, according to the 1555 witness statements, an area of void ground, measuring 15 by 12 yards, until about 1545 when it was filled with parlours, chambers and chimneys. The last of these are described by one witness as two chimneys, by another as a double chimney, perhaps indicative of back-to-back hearths. An east-west stretch of walling parallel to and about 6m south of the south end of the barn may be a remnant of these structures, along with a semi-circular stone based structure extending further south. If the base was originally circular it would have been over 3m in diameter, perhaps accommodating a very large oven – or even marking the base of a small spiral staircase giving access to the chambers above. The hearth recorded in section at a lower level to the north of these remains might be associated with them: the failure to carry through excavation of Site 77 beyond the upper levels means that its stratigraphic associations are ambiguous.

Fragments of walling continuing the line of the barn's west wall included another semi-circular structure, possibly a projecting oven or chimney base. On the line of the barn's east side was a short stretch of walling largely cut away by the conduit trench, perhaps continued further south by wall 83 in Site 26, allocated there to Period 4, Phase 1 (*Wharram XI*, 41, fig. 36). If these remains are correctly associated with each other, they suggest that the parlours and chambers erected in the former void ground replicated the width and axial alignment of the barn. Furthermore, if this alignment was continued by the pre-fire vicarage house – as has been

inferred purely from a reading of the 1555 witness statements – then the site of the house must lie in unexcavated ground, just beyond the western end of Site 26 and just beyond the southern end of Site 77 (Fig. 143). Site 99, the extension southwards from Site 77, was opened up to record the full extent of wall 182 as far as the conduit trench, but not excavated more deeply.

There is, however, an alternative interpretation that might better accord with the excavated structural remains (Fig. 144), not only on Site 77 but also on Site 26 (reported in *Wharram XI*). Wall 182, mentioned above, seems at least in its later life to have been the vicarage's enclosure wall, on the west side following the alignment of – and incorporating – the west wall of the defunct barn. It probably continued south on that alignment to the point where it met the east-west wall 711; thence it changed course, from south south-west to south south-east, possibly reflecting the alignment of a trackway and steps that came, at this point, down the steep slope from the plateau. In Site 99 wall 182 turned yet again, just west of the gap created by the later conduit trench, and continued south-eastwards through Site 26 as wall 74 and 20, the two context numbers given to the separate stretches of walling on each side of a gateway linking vicarage to churchyard (*Wharram XI*, 46, fig. 39).

Wall 182 unquestionably functioned as a continuation of the boundary formed by walls 74/20 in Site 26, even though the character of the walling at the angle just west of the conduit might indicate that this was a realignment from an earlier course (see Plate 16). What cannot be determined closely is the date at which this boundary was created. In the full report on Site 26 it was assigned to Period 5, which was dated broadly to the late medieval period (from the mid-14th to the early 16th centuries: *Wharram XI*, 45-9). Similarly, in Site 77 there was no characteristically post-medieval pottery assigned to this phase. On this basis, the wall would seem to pre-date the vicarage fire.

On the other hand, the Site 26 report also notes the presence, in Period 4, Phase 6, of an unidentified jug which 'might be dated as late as the 16th century', and two post-holes assigned to the same phase had evidence of burning in their fills (*Wharram XI*, 45). Furthermore the fill of a cut feature 318 assigned to Period 5, Phase 1 (the phase that saw the construction of wall 74/20), contained carbonised grain (*Wharram XI*, 49). Though the records do not show whether the jug was sealed by the wall, it was in chalk rubble believed to have accumulated before the wall's construction (*Wharram XI*, 45). Along with the burning and the carbonised grain, it might therefore be cited in support of wall 182 being of post-fire construction. Similarly, on Site 77 the absence of characteristically post-medieval pottery in any of Periods 1-3 or indeed, save for one sherd, in Period 4, means that we cannot rely on the presence or absence of such wares to indicate pre-fire or post-fire activity.

The only other evidence that might be brought to bear on this problem is the reuse of building materials; for if a quantity of distinctive stonework was released at a

Fig. 144. Pre-fire vicarage: alternative B. (E. Marlow-Mann)

specific point by the demolition of a building, this event would provide a *terminus post quem* for the erection of any structures which reused the stonework. The relevant material recovered from the excavations can be divided into two groups: dressed architectural stonework derived from the church for secondary use in the vicarage, and sandstone roofing slabs which might have had their first use either on the vicarage buildings or on the church.

In the full report on Site 26 it was suggested that the architectural stonework reused in the gateway between walls 74 and 20 had come from the north aisle of the church, the demolition of which was ascribed to the late 15th or early 16th century (*Wharram XI*, 49). It has also been suggested that the east end of that aisle contained a chantry chapel which was demolished *c*.1550, after the suppression of chantries (*Wharram III*, 84-5). Though the chapel may have been built in the 14th century to house the Scrope chantry (see Chapter 2), it could later have been used for the Towthorpe chantry – the only one recorded in the 16th century. Whatever its precise location in the church, the Towthorpe chantry's suppression in 1547 might have occurred in time to release architectural stonework for Vicar Atkinson's additions to the pre-fire vicarage; and if not, for his post-fire reconstruction of the vicarage.

The sandstone roofing slabs may also have come from a dismantled aisle of the church, though they might equally have originated in the vicarage itself. The deponents of 1555 say little about the types of roofing material on the vicarage buildings. One of them, Robert Ryvar, 'did thatch him self' one of the outshots attached to Atkinson's parlours and chambers, and Robert Pickering claimed to have spent six weeks 'theakinge' the post-fire vicarage, and said that after him there were other 'theakers and wallers'. Two of the Askham Bryan deponents commented on the walls and 'thack' of the post-fire building. Despite these references, however, we cannot be absolutely certain that the vicarage buildings were at any stage covered in thatch as opposed to stone slates: 'thack' might be simply translated as 'roof covering' rather than as, specifically, 'thatch'. In West Yorkshire's medieval records, stone slates are often called 'thackstones', and the occupational name 'le thecker' may refer to people who roofed in stone or shingles, as well as those who covered buildings in thatch (Faull and Moorhouse 1981, 810).

It would have been helpful if the excavation record could have been used to clarify the materials used to cover the roofs of the vicarage buildings, but that record is very ambiguous. No less than 650 fragments of Brandsby Roadstone roofing slabs were recovered from the area of the barn, but only a limited number in or immediately above the remains of the barn itself – too few to suggest the collapse of a fully stone-slated roof. There were numerous fragments of roofing slabs in the debris that lay along the inner face of the barn's west wall, and others along the outer face of its east wall. Some of the pieces showed signs of heat reddening (p.204).

This distribution may point to a hybrid roof covering, with courses of sandstone slabs on each side of the building forming the lower edges of the roof, to give added protection to the walltops. Above them, the roof would have been thatched. It had been hoped that the recovery of thatch samples from the burnt deposits in the barn might have provided further clarification, but as the report makes clear (Chapter 24), the absence of thatching material in the debris might be explained through taphonomic processes, rather than simply as an absence of thatching.

Much larger quantities of sandstone roofing slabs were recovered from the demolition layers associated with the post-fire building of Period 4, suggesting that this was, indeed, covered in stone rather than thatch. Further fragments were found on Site 26: they constituted the largest part of a dump of rubble recorded as context 288 in Period 5, Phase 1, the same phase that saw the erection of enclosure wall 74/20 (*Wharram XI*, 49), and one piece also came from that wall. On Site 77, fragments of sandstone roofing slab were used to level up the foundation of wall 182, including the only near complete slab. If this roofing material was derived from the fire-damaged vicarage, or from the north aisle and chantry chapel of the church, then enclosure wall 182/74/20 is also likely to have post-dated the fire. Unfortunately, we cannot substantiate either of these hypotheses.

To sum up, in terms of the location of vicarage buildings in the first half of the 16th century, the possibilities are as follows. If wall 182/74/20 was a post-fire construction, the pre-fire vicarage house may lie south of Site 77 (Fig. 143: alternative A), following the alignment of the barn, as was inferred in Chapter 2 on the basis of the 1555 depositions. On the other hand, if wall 182/74/20 was a pre-fire structure in origin, it indicates that the contemporary vicar's house was not on an axial alignment with the barn, but must have run west to east, or at least north-west to south-east, to be accommodated within the space it enclosed (Fig. 144: alternative B). Indeed, given that the west wall of the barn was incorporated into the enclosure wall, the wall of the dwelling may have been similarly reused. The excavation of Site 26 uncovered the other fragmentary structural remains in this area, but these were dated to the mid-14th century (*Wharram XI*, 62-3): they might belong to an earlier vicarage or outbuilding. The only walling in Site 26 attributed to the same period as the enclosure wall are two stretches of a north-south wall 88 (*Wharram XI*, 49).

Whatever the precise location and orientation of the vicarage buildings, the depositions of 1555 broadly suggest that the sites of the pre-fire barn and house lay north and south of the post-fire house. The Site 77, Period 3 remains can therefore be identified with a measure of confidence as part of Atkinson's post-fire vicarage (Fig. 145). Furthermore, the ovoid hearth and ?oven base that appear to project from the west end of the building suggest that this part represents internal kitchens, perhaps with an attached fuel store.

N

Gravel path

Fig. 145. Late 16th-century vicarage. (E. Marlow-Mann)

The pairing of an ovoid hearth and oven can be found in another excavated Wolds house occupied in the 16th to 17th centuries, in the deserted village of Cowlam (Hayfield 1988, 46-7, 88). The Cowlam house (Building C), however, had a 'hearth-passage' plan (see Neave, below), whereas the Wharram vicarage, whatever its plan form, does not seem to have been of this type. Ovoid ovens continued to be incorporated into Wolds farmhouses into the late 18th and early 19th centuries on the evidence of the contemporary plans redrawn here (see Figs 151 and 152 below), including one that was envisaged as projecting from the external wall face.

Vicar Atkinson was said by Robert Ryvar to have erected two buildings after the fire: the new 'hall house', and 'a kitchen', the latter built where there had been no buildings at the time of the fire. The 'kitchen' was presumably not, therefore, the building containing the hearth and oven described above: as the Period 3 structural remains are on the site of the earlier building, they presumably mark the west end of the hall house rather than a detached 'kitchen'. They are unlikely to belong to a rear wing of that house, as the measurements that are given indicate a simple rectangular structure 25 yards long and 6 yards wide, rather than a T-shaped building.

Given the recorded length of the post-fire house, it will, if aligned west to east, have extended across the western half of Site 54, as far as the west side of the last vicarage house (Fig. 145). Though the apparent alignment of the Site 77, Period 3 building is somewhat at variance with virtually all the structural features on Site 54, this is no doubt partly because much of the alignment is indicated by robber trenches rather than walls: some (though probably not all) of the elements of Structures E, F and G might conceivably be part of this building. These structures on Site 54 have been assigned to Periods 3.3 to 4.3. Apart from evidently intrusive sherds, the pottery from these periods included little that could be dated to the 16th century or later, although a couple of pieces of Ryedale ware, probably 17th-century, came from Periods 4.2-4.3. On the other hand, as we have seen, Period 3 in Site 77, the immediate post-fire period, contained no post-medieval pottery at all.

Few other comments can be made about these Site 54 structures. The walling of Structure E in Period 3.3 might be a continuation of the south side of the post-fire vicarage. The slots marking Structure G in Period 4.3 could well have housed joists for a raised, boarded floor similar to that in the farmstead barn (Site 51). If the context here is domestic rather than agricultural, it could be another floor of deal boards: Henry Best indicates that the import of such floorboards through Hull was already well established by the middle of the 16th century (Woodward 1984, 131-3). Finally, it was presumably this building that the path from the gateway in the Site 26 enclosure wall was intended to serve (*Wharram XI*, 48-9).

The next three buildings in the sequence on Site 54 are Structures H, J and K (Figs 146 and 147), and it will be useful to begin by considering (in reverse order) their

chronological indicators in relation to the conduit channel that cut through Sites 26, 77 and 54 to carry water to the area occupied by the farmhouse. The construction of the conduit has previously been assigned to the late 18th century (e.g. *Wharram XI*, 64), on the assumption that it was part of the improvements made at the time of the township's enclosure. The identification of records indicating that the 1770s improvements included the digging of a well serves to challenge that assumption. In Site 77, the pottery from the fill of the conduit trench provides a *terminus post quem* for its backfilling in the early 18th century, and that may, indeed, be the period of its construction, rather than later in the century. Though late 18th to early 19th-century pottery was recovered from the upper parts of the backfill in Site 54, this may simply be the later levelling up of the hollow created by the settlement of the fill.

Given the apparent destination of the conduit (its outflow has not yet been located), the course it takes through the vicarage grounds can be explained only by its need to avoid extant buildings. It should therefore enable us to determine which buildings were in existence in the early 18th century, which had already been demolished (the conduit trench cutting through their foundations), and which had yet to be built (the fill of the conduit trench underlying their foundations).

It will by now come as no surprise to readers of this volume that the evidence is not as straightforward as might have been hoped. The course of the trench appeared designed to avoid Structure K, the last building in the sequence and one that can be equated to the first detailed written description of the vicar's house, in the Glebe Terrier of 1764 (Chapter 2). The trench also appeared to avoid Structure J, the 'cellar' on the west side of Structure K. The report on post-medieval pottery from Structure J (Chapter 13) questions whether any of that material should be regarded as providing a *terminus post quem* for its construction, but proposes one in the early to mid-18th century for its disuse and backfilling. This is supported by the glassware (mainly early 18th-century) and the clay tobacco pipes. Furthermore, the cow burial (289, context 303) cut into the backfill may well date from the cattle plague of 1747-56 (D. Neave, pers. comm.; see Neave, 2002, 22-8). Given the likely proximity of the 'cellar' to the contemporary vicarage (see below), its backfilling was probably a single and immediate event rather than a gradual process that took place over decades. Therefore its demolition and disuse may have come a few decades after the construction of the conduit.

Structure J will not have existed as an isolated building. Very few cellars are recorded in northern Wolds houses of the period 1660-1730, but the expectation is that it would have been attached to a house, and not a free-standing structure (D. Neave, pers. comm.). The question remains, whether it was attached to a house on its east side (represented by an earlier version of Structure K), set in a rear outshot, or whether it had been created within the north-east corner of the more ephemeral Structure H, a

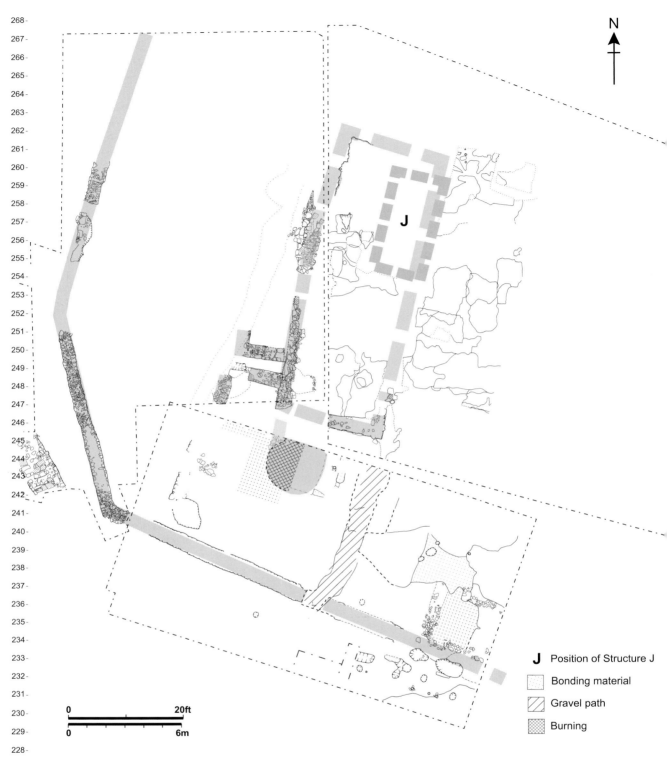

N

J Position of Structure J

▢ Bonding material

▨ Gravel path

▨ Burning

0   20ft

0   6m

Fig. 146. 17th-century vicarage. (E. Marlow-Mann)

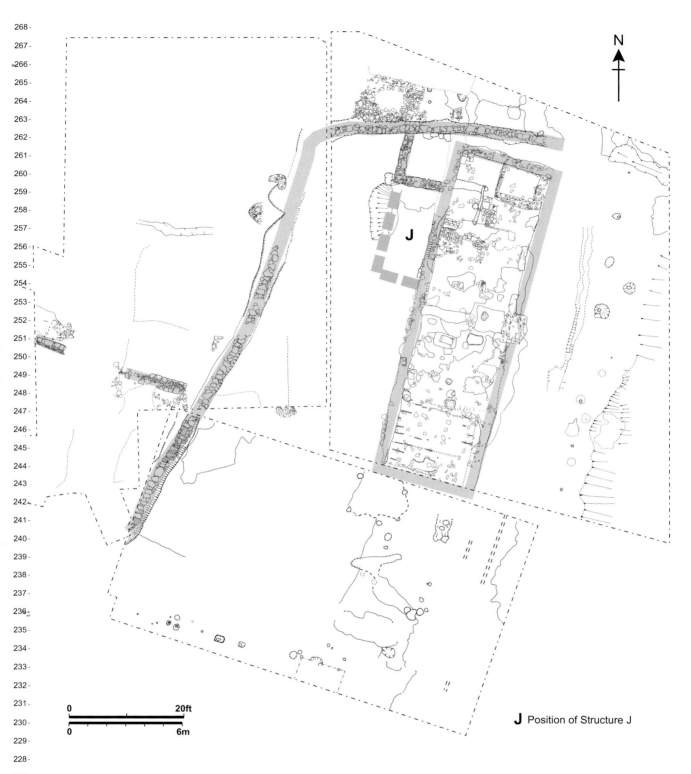

N

J Position of Structure J

J

Fig. 147. 18th-century vicarage and conduit. (E. Marlow-Mann)

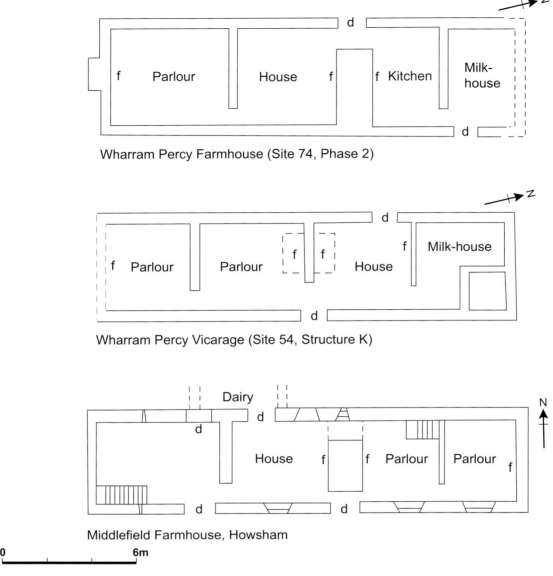

Fig. 148. Simplified diagrams comparing the building layout of Wharram Percy farmhouse and vicarage with Middlefield Farmhouse, Howsham. (E. Marlow-Mann)

building on the same alignment as Structure K, and of broadly similar dimensions, immediately to its west (Fig, 146). If the 'cellar' actually served as a partly subterranean dairy, then it may, like the dairy of North Grimston vicarage, have been located in an addition to the rear of the vicarage, with the house on its east side. Neave has also drawn our attention to a later dairy at Middlefield Farm, Howsham (Fig. 148), which is in an outshot, and sunken, though it cannot be called a cellar.

The succession of archaeological contexts described in Chapter 10 places the excavated west wall of Structure K after the demolition of Structure J, and before the digging of the conduit trench. There are, however, reasons for questioning what the stratigraphy appears to be telling us. Structure K is unquestionably the building recorded in the 1764 Glebe Terrier, but the pottery associated with it has provided somewhat later dating: its west wall included early 19th-century pottery sherds; its east wall appears to

have a *terminus post quem* of the late 18th century, and hearth 117 in Room 2 seems to date no earlier than the 19th century; whereas the make-up for the lobby-entry flooring, 125, has a *terminus post quem* provided by '17th-century' Ryedale Ware.

We know from documentary sources that the building was in disrepair in the early 19th century, and was converted to a cottage in the final phase of its occupation. The excavated remains may well date rebuilding activity rather than initial construction, allowing the structure a significantly earlier origin than appears in the archaeological record. In such a reading it may have been created in the early 18th century, with an attached sunken-floored dairy (Structure J) and an adjacent coal store (Structure L), both housed in a rear outshot. By the time of the 1764 Glebe Terrier both had been removed, and the pantry was now housed within the footprint of the main building, at its north-east corner.

The predecessor of Structure K was Structure H. It has a *terminus post quem* for its erection, provided by 17th-century Ryedale Ware in context 452. This layer sealed the remnants of Structures F and G, and was built over by the Structure H wall footing 254. The conduit trench seems not only to avoid Structures J and K; it also skirts, much more tightly, the western wall (358) and the assumed north-west corner of Structure H. Had this building not been standing when the conduit was installed, it might be expected that the trench would have been cut on an alignment to take it much closer to the north-west corners of Structures J and K. The occupation of Structure H may, therefore, be dated broadly to the later 17th and early 18th centuries. It can tentatively be identified as vicar Luck's two-hearth house of 1674.

There is, however, some contradictory evidence that indicates Structure H – or at least parts of it – had been demolished by the time the conduit trench was dug. In Site 77, the wall footings 506 and 358 seem to mark the west wall of Structure H. It was abutted by walls 569, 281 (with return 282) and 280 (with return 579), apparently forming successive outshots. These outshots seem, however, to have been cut by the conduit trench, and had therefore gone out of use by the time the conduit was inserted. More significantly, the later layer 144 in Site 77, assigned to Period 5.1 and seemingly also cut by the conduit trench, was recorded as partly overlying the footings of the west wall of Structure H. The apparent relationship between the conduit and the western side and northern end of Structure H is presumably, therefore, more apparent than real.

There seems at present no way of resolving these contradictions. All that can be said is that, in the broadest terms of structural development, the pre-1553 buildings lay in the western and southern parts of the vicarage plot, in Sites 26 and 77, and possibly south of them (Fig. 143-4); that the immediate post-1553 house lay roughly east to west, extending from Site 77 into Site 54 (Fig. 145); that this was replaced sometime in the 17th century by Structure H on a north-south axis (Fig. 146), and that Structure H was replaced, perhaps in the early 18th

century, by Structure K (Fig. 147). Structure K had a dairy in a rear outshot that was demolished in the mid-18th century, soon after the water conduit trench had been cut through the vicarage plot. It then continued in use, though with various modifications and rebuildings, occasioned by its use as a cottage and its documented state of disrepair, until it was finally demolished in the 1830s.

29 The Late 17th to Early 19th-century Farmhouse and Vicarage House, and the Vernacular Building Tradition of the Northern Wolds
by D. Neave

The evidence for the plan and construction of the principal post-medieval buildings at Wharram Percy is limited by the lack of any substantial walling and by the extent of the robbed foundations. As with the reinterpretation of the medieval longhouses by Stuart Wrathmell (*Wharram VI*) much can be learnt from contemporary documents and surviving buildings to suggest what would have been the likely layout and construction of the post-medieval houses.

This is particularly relevant to the vicarage (Site 54, Structure K) and the earlier farmhouse (Site 74, Period 2) which, as excavated, were similar in size and layout, and typical of the larger village houses on the northern Wolds in the late 17th and early 18th centuries.

The vicarage and earlier farmhouse

House size
The vicarage and the farmhouse were one room deep with four rooms in a line on the ground floor, and documentary sources show that at one stage they each had four first-floor rooms. Externally the vicarage was about 18.5m long and 5.5m wide and the farmhouse, of which the north wall was not located, was at least 17.5m long and

Table 90. Buckrose Wapentake: Parsonage House Measurements (Borthwick, TER.K)

Place	Date	Ground-floor Rooms	Measurement of building given in yards	Measurement of building in metres
Acklam	1716	3	20 x 6	18.3 x 5.5
Bugthorpe	1726	3	18 x 5	16.5 x 4.5
Burythorpe	1716		14 x 7	12.8 x 6.4
Helperthorpe	1764	3	13.5 x 3.5	12.3 x 3.2
Kirby Grindalythe	1743	3	16 x 5	14.6 x 4.5
Langton	1764	3	15 yds long	13.7 m long
North Grimston	1764	3	17 x 5	15.5 x 4.5
Westow	1764	4	20 x 6	18.3 x 5.5
Wharram Percy	1764	4	19 x 4.5	17.4 x 4.1
Yedingham	1764	3	15 x 6.5	13.7 x 5.9

5.5m wide. These measurements are comparable to those of a number of parsonage houses in Buckrose Wapentake (Table 90) as recorded in early to mid-18th-century glebe terriers. (Borthwick, TER.K)

These are likely to have been rough calculations made by the clergyman drawing up the terrier and, as is probable with the Wharram Percy figures, may sometimes be based on internal rather than external measurements. The average size of the parsonage houses was 15.3m by 4.9m.

There is no doubt that the vicarage at Wharram Percy as described in the glebe terrier of 1764 is the building that was excavated, but it is uncertain when it was built.

The hearth tax returns indicate that the two Wharram Percy properties were more substantial than the majority of local village houses. The 1672 hearth tax returns list 1,419 households in 44 townships in Buckrose wapentake, of which 1,231 (87 per cent) had only one hearth, 108 (7.5 per cent) had two hearths, and 33 (2.5 per cent) had three hearths (Purdy 1991, 52-3; Neave and Neave 2006, 127). Buckrose had the highest percentage of one-hearthed houses amongst the wapentake divisions of the East Riding (Purdy 1991, 52-3; Neave and Neave 2006, 127). Within Buckrose, the joint parish of Wharram Percy and Wharram le Street, not separately entered in the 1672 returns, was, with the exception of Yedingham, the best-hearthed parish. There were 54 households listed in the two Wharrams, of which 40 had one hearth, 8 had two hearths, 5 had three hearths and 1 had seven hearths. (Purdy 1991, 53; TNA PRO E179/205/514.)

The number of hearths is only a rough guide to the size of a house; a one-hearthed house could consist of a single room or have two or more rooms on a floor. Probate inventories that list individual rooms and their contents provide a more reliable indication of house size and status.

Number and use of rooms

Of the houses recorded in 100 inventories from the northern Wolds for the period 1660-1730, 69 had no more than four rooms (see Table 91; Borthwick, Wills: York; Dean and Chapter; Fridaythorpe Prebend; Langtoft Prebend; Wetwang Prebend). Forty-eight had two rooms on the ground floor, 24 had three rooms and 15 had four rooms. Almost three-quarters of the houses had a room or rooms on the first floor, but only one also had garrets.

The main room used during the day and for cooking and eating was termed the 'house' in 56 per cent of the inventories and 'forehouse' in 25 per cent. Other names used for this room were 'hall', 'hall house', 'fore room' and 'firehouse'. All but six of the houses had parlours, and of these 85 per cent were used for sleeping. Nineteen of the houses had a milk house or dairy and fifteen had a kitchen. Only nine of the houses had both a kitchen and a milk house or dairy. Other service rooms included a buttery in nine houses and a cellar in four. The probable use of the first-floor chambers is indicated by the contents in 62 inventories. In sixteen cases they were used for storage of crops and other goods, in 22 cases only beds are recorded, and in 24 there are both beds and goods.

The Wharram Percy farmhouse as recorded in the inventory of William Botterell drawn up in March 1699 had four rooms on the ground floor, a parlour, a fore room, a kitchen, and a milkhouse, and three rooms on the first floor, a fore chamber and a kitchen chamber with beds and a parlour chamber containing wool and other goods. (see p. 4, above; Beresford and Hurst 1990, 111). In 1806 the farmhouse had two parlours, a kitchen and a dairy on the ground floor with four lodging rooms above. (see p.13.)

The vicarage at Wharram Percy was described in the 1764 glebe terrier as having 'three rooms below stairs with a pantry' and 'above stairs four chambers'. (Borthwick, TER.K, Wharram Percy). It was one of the better-roomed of the nineteen parsonages where rooms are given in Buckrose Wapentake glebe terriers (Table 92). The vicarage at North Grimston was the only other with eight rooms. Here there were three ground-floor rooms with a dairy and four chambers above. The layout of the two vicarages differed; at North Grimston the dairy was evidently an addition at the back of the house whilst at Wharram Percy the pantry was 'in one straight building' with the rest of the ground-floor rooms as revealed in the excavation.

Plan type

There were two main plan types for housing on the Yorkshire Wolds in the late 17th century: *hearth-passage* and *lobby-entry*. The houses of each plan type would have had a linear form with two, three or more main rooms laid out, as at Wharram Percy vicarage, in one straight line. The main difference between the plan types related to the position of external doorways and hearths.

The *hearth-passage* plan was derived from the longhouse plan. The medieval houses excavated at Wharram Percy were longhouses where under one roof, initially with no internal partitions, there was a living area

Table 91. Northern Wolds Probate Inventories 1660-1730 – Number of rooms

Number of rooms	0	1	2	3	4	5	6	7	8	9 +	Total
Total rooms in house		3	23	26	17	8	9	8	2	4	100
Ground-floor rooms*		5	48	24	15	3	4		1		100
First-floor rooms	27	42	21	8	2						100
Service rooms	67	14	10	4	5						100

*includes service rooms

Table 92. Buckrose Wapentake. Early to mid-18th-century Glebe Terriers – Number of rooms in parsonage houses (Borthwick, TER.K)

Number of rooms	0	1	2	3	4	5	6	7	8	11-12	Total houses
Total rooms in house			2	3	5		2	1	2	4	19
Ground-floor rooms*			6	5	5		2	1			19
First-floor rooms	6		4	4	2	3					19
Service rooms	9	7		3							19

*includes service rooms

with central hearth for the humans then a cross-passage with opposing external doorways providing a common entrance and on the low-side of the passage a byre for cattle. (Beresford and Hurst 1990, 39-40; *Wharram VI*, 11-12). The passageway would in time be screened off from the living area, and the hearth placed against the screen and perhaps given a timber-framed hood and later a stone or brick chimney-stack inserted. Then the cattle would be removed and the low-side room would become a store or service room. An account of a longhouse in transition to the hearth passage plan is provided by the much-quoted late 19th-century descriptions of the cruck houses at Fimber (*Wharram VI*, 10-11).

The usual hearth-passage house, built as such, was a three-cell building of one or two storeys with a through passage. On one side would be the house, the main living room, with a hearth backing onto the passage, and a parlour, possibly unheated. The room on the other side of the passage may be a second parlour, or more likely a service room. In the East Riding hearth-passage houses, probably of the late 16th or early 17th century, are to be found at Octon and South Dalton, and another was excavated at Cowlam, all on or close to the Wolds (Pevsner and Neave 1995, 81-2; Hayfield 1988, 45-8, 88-9, 106-7). There are later examples at Hunmanby and Filey, both dated in the 1690s (Pevsner and Neave 1995, 81).

No evidence was found for a through passage in the excavation of the farmhouse and vicarage at Wharram Percy, and therefore it is assumed that they were not of a longhouse or hearth passage plan. None of the identified external doorways was matched by another on the opposite wall, although the traces of any such opening could have been removed when sections of walling were totally robbed. The main entrance to the farmhouse has been identified in the centre of the west wall and that of the vicarage in the centre of the east wall. In both cases there was a hearth, or pair of hearths opposite the entrance (Fig. 148). This suggests the *lobby-entry* plan, the commonest plan-form in surviving East Riding houses from the mid-17th to early 18th centuries.(Pevsner and Neave 1995, 81-2).

The simplest form of a lobby-entry house consists of a two-cell building with a central entrance door which opens into a small enclosed lobby. Directly in front is a wide chimney-stack and to the left and right are doorways, one leading to the main living-eating room, the other to the parlour. Many of the surviving houses are three-cell with a second parlour to one end, but the farmhouse and vicarage at Wharram Percy were seemingly four-cell having the addition of a service room. Directly comparable in size and plan to the Wharram Percy houses is the surviving Middlefield Farmhouse at Howsham, some 7 miles to the south-west on the edge of the Wolds (Fig. 148). Built of iron-rich sandstone, Middlefield Farmhouse dates from around 1700 (YVBSG 612, 1979; D. Neave, sketch survey, 1971; Harrison and Hutton 1984, 150). The entrance door in the centre of the south wall opens onto a chimneystack with two parlours off to the right, and the house or hall and a service room or store to the left. There is a secondary entrance to the last, opposite which is a blocked door indicating a former through passage, derived from the longhouse plan. The dairy at the rear is a later addition. Access to the first floor is provided by a staircase in the north-east corner of the first parlour.

Building materials and construction
The houses of the northern Wolds in the late 17th and early 18th centuries would have been constructed of stone and/or timber, and thatch. The older surviving buildings in the area are stone walled. Those in the eastern half are largely of chalk, but in the western half the buildings are of the more durable stones from the Jurassic belt. These include North Grimston cement stone, Malton oolite and coral rag, Whitwell oolite, Birdsall calcareous grit and dogger, a brown iron-rich sandstone (Myerscough 2005; Neave and Ellis 1996, 56-7). Buildings at Wharram-le-Street are of a mixture of Malton oolite, North Grimston cement stone, chalk and Birdsall calcareous grit. The last, the best quality building stone, was used for quoins and as a facing stone (Myerscough, 2001).

The excavated foundations of the farmhouse and vicarage at Wharram Percy are of a mixture of stones from the Jurassic belt and chalk. The extent to which these buildings were stone walled is unknown, but there is evidence that both were, at least in part, timber-framed. The change in alignment of the east wall of the farmhouse (see above – Site 74, Periods 2-3, Discussion) has been taken to suggest that it was cruck built like the late medieval buildings on the plateau (*Wharram VI*). The evidence for the vicarage being timber-framed is however documentary rather than from the excavation. Of the eighteen parsonages in Buckrose Wapentake for which building materials are given in 1764, ten were of stone, one of stone and timber, one of stone and brick, three of brick, one of mud and in two cases only timber was mentioned. The last are the vicarages at North Grimston and Wharram Percy. Of the house at North Grimston the glebe terrier records that 'most of it' was built with oak timber in 1739, suggesting that it was timber-framed (Borthwick, TER.K, North Grimston). The statement in the Wharram Percy terrier that 'the timber of the house consists of ash wood and deal poles', is more ambiguous, but the fact that it was mentioned, unlike in the majority of local glebe terriers, suggests that it was structural and visible (Borthwick, TER.K, Wharram Percy).

Ash was evidently more plentiful on the Wolds and was the more commonly used timber for building. Eighty-seven per cent of the 1581 trees sold from Settrington woods in the later 1590s to 158 people from 37 townships in and around the northern Wolds were ash, and only 213 of the trees were oak (King and Harris 1962, 87-95). Seven inhabitants of Wharram, seemingly Wharram-le-Street, purchased 46 of the trees. Some of the trees would have been bought for repairs or other uses, such as wagon making, but some would have been for house building (King and Harris 1962, 89, 92). The greater part of the houses at Warter, on the Wolds north of Pocklington, were timber built and in 1742 it was said that as 'a great many of them [have] been built with ash wood they are continually coming to decay' (Neave 1990, 248-9).

The 'deal poles' in Wharram Percy vicarage were imported softwood. A deal is a plank of fir-wood, and imported deals were being used on the edge of the Wolds within ten miles of Wharram by the early 1640s (Woodward 1984, 116-7, 131-3). One of the rooms at the vicarage, presumably the parlour, was floored in deal in 1764, in common with the parlours at half-a-dozen other Buckrose parsonages (Borthwick, TER.K).

Although there is evidence for some post and truss timber-framing on the Yorkshire Wolds including a remnant at the Manor Farm at Huggate, six miles south of Wharram, the farmhouse and vicarage are most likely to have been cruck-framed (Neave and Ellis 1996; Pevsner and Neave 1995). The use of crucks on the northern Wolds has been fully explored by Wrathmell in *Wharram VI*. In addition to documentary and printed references, including the detailed accounts of crucks at Settrington and Fimber, and the evidence from excavations at Cowlam and Wharram Percy, there is a handful of surviving examples of which the most significant is the former farmhouse at Glebe Farm, Octon, 11 miles east of Wharram. (*Wharram VI*; Pevsner and Neave 1995, 79). The chalk and brick walled three-bay building retains two pairs of crucks which are thought to be of ash, as may have been the case at Wharram Percy vicarage (recorded by YVBSG 2005-6, information from David Cook). The vicar of North Grimston had three pairs of ash 'forks', or crucks, in his garth in 1617 (Alcock and Blair 1986, 37).

Thatch was the principal roofing material throughout Buckrose, and indeed the whole East Riding, in the mid-18th century (Neave 1993, 43-9). Fourteen of the twenty Buckrose parsonages where the roof material was specified in 1764 were thatched, and two part-thatched. The vicarage at Wharram Percy was thatched and remained so until it was demolished in the 1830s (Borthwick, TER.K, Wharram Percy 1853). Wharram Percy farmhouse, like Wharram Grange, would have been thatched up until the late 1770s, when it was probably tiled as recorded in 1806 (see p.13). At that date the only building on the farm still with a thatched roof was the wagon shed (see Chapter 1).

The early 19th-century farmhouse

The farmhouse was evidently rebuilt soon after 1806 and on a grander scale (see Chapter 1). The plan revealed by excavation was double pile with two substantial rooms, and one small central room in the front section, and one large room and three smaller rooms in the slightly narrower rear section (Site 74, Period 4; Fig 149). Double-pile plans are typical of late 18th and early 19th-century East Riding farmhouses but the Wharram Percy building was unusual in its length and overall dimensions. Post-enclosure farmhouses are more likely to have had a shorter main front and to be L-shaped or approximately square.

No exact comparison has been found for the early 19th-century farmhouse, but a number of original plans for late 18th to early 19th-century farmhouses on the nearby Sledmere estate show similar layouts (plans at Sledmere House and the Estate Yard, Sledmere, 2002). An undated plan for an unidentified farmhouse (Fig. 150) is nearest in size and layout to the Wharram Percy farmhouse, but it also has service rooms in wings to the rear. There are two large rooms and entrance hall in the front section and four rooms in the rear section which, as at Wharram Percy, is narrower. The farmhouses to be built at Tibthorpe and Thixendale (Figs 151 and 152) have similar plans but on a smaller scale.

These plans add to the interpretation possible from the bankruptcy inventory of 1830 (see Chapter 1 and Discussion after Site 74 Period 5). Referring to the rooms as numbered in the excavation report, Room 1 was almost certainly the main kitchen/living room with a fireplace on the north wall and an oven in the north-east corner. Room 2, only 1.5 m wide would have been an entrance hall, and Room 6 the sitting room for the farmer's family. It is very likely that there would have been a fireplace on the south wall of Room 6 but no evidence of this was found in the excavation. The commonest form of farmhouse plan in the East Riding at this time had chimney stacks at the gable ends (Pevsner and Neave 1995, 85-6).

Of the rooms in the rear section, Room 3 would have been the back kitchen with fireplace on the northern wall and a large oven in the north-west corner. This room would be the cooking, eating and living room for the hired men and women who lived on the farm, of which

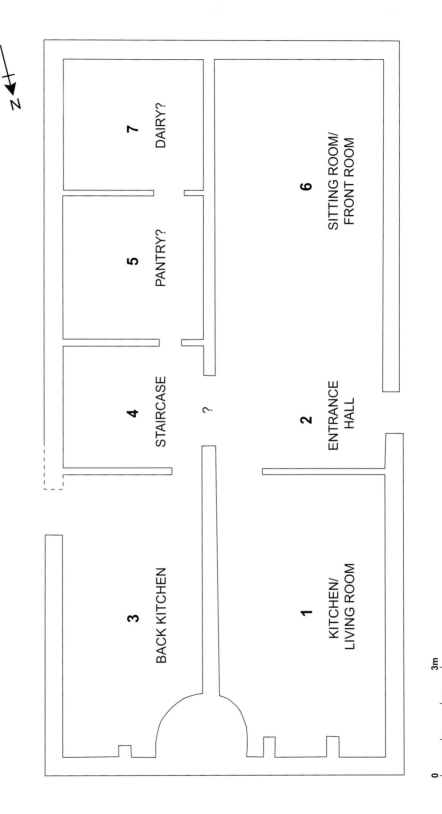

Fig. 149. Simplified plan of later farmhouse (Site 74: Period 4). (E. Marlow-Mann)

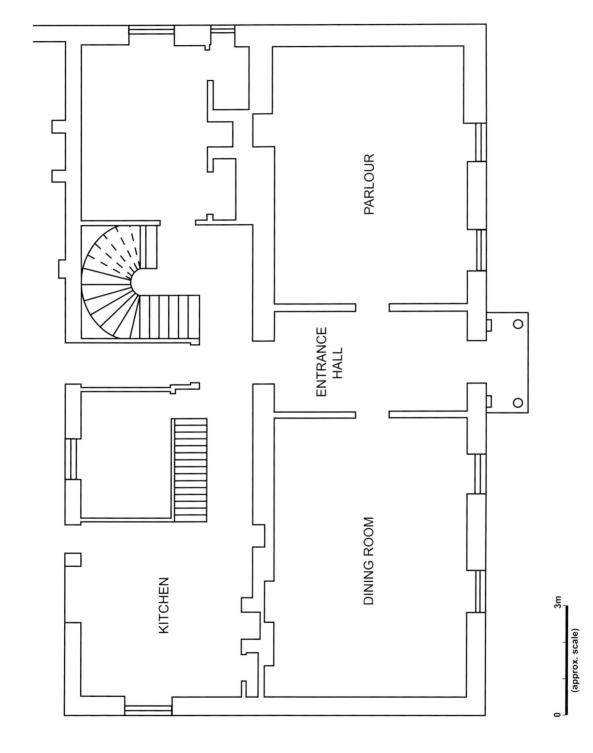

Fig. 150. Plan for a farmhouse on the Sledmere estate, early 19th-century (redrawn from scanned photograph of plan) (E. Marlow-Mann)

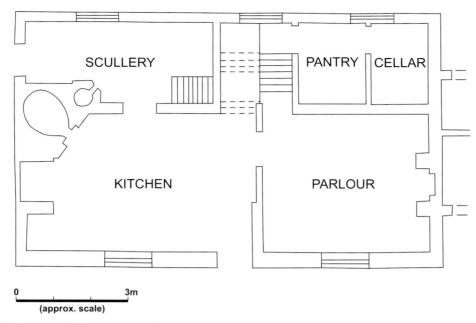

Fig. 151. Plan of farmhouse at Tibthorpe 1799 (redrawn from photograph of plan) (E. Marlow-Mann)

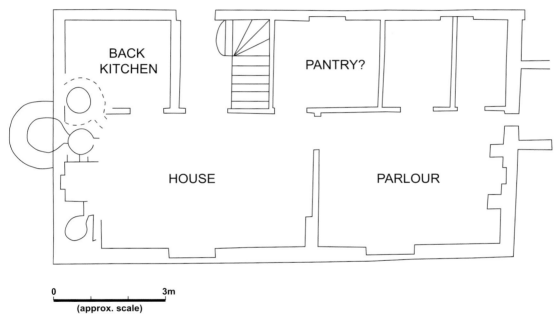

Fig. 152. Plan of farmhouse at Thixendale (redrawn from photograph of plan - the positions of some of the ovens represent alterations to the drawings) (E. Marlow-Mann)

there were seven men and two women in 1841 (see Chapter 1; Hayfield 1994, 7-28). It is probable that there was a servants' staircase in this room as in Figure 151, or leading off the room as in Figure 150. The back kitchen would have had a separate external entrance. Room 4 was most likely to have been the location of the main staircase leading from the entrance hall and with rear access in the east wall, to and from the farmyard (see Figs 150-152). Rooms 5 and 7 were probably the pantry and dairy.

The inventory indicates that there were four rooms on the first floor: two front chambers and behind a back bedroom and a female servants' bedroom. The hired men slept in the garret above.

The materials used for the construction of the Wharram Percy farm, its unusual proportions, and its demolition after less than 50 years suggest that it was neither particularly well built nor was it a 'model' farm built to impress both tenant and fellow landowner, as others on the Birdsall and Sledmere estates. The walls were of chalk and sandstone, with the main façade, that is the western wall, and the southern wall faced in brick, and the eastern and the northern walls faced with reused sandstone blocks. Many late Georgian buildings on the Wolds have inner chalk walls faced in brick, but it is usual to have the brick skin on all the external walls (cf. Life Hill Farm, Sledmere; Hayfield and Wagner 1998, 10; Larkham 1992, 119-28).

30 The Finds Assemblages from the North Glebe Terrace Sites

by E.A. Clark

Medieval and earlier activity

A background of material from earlier periods is normal in most parts of the village, and a small amount of Roman material was recovered from the North Glebe Terrace sites. More interestingly, among the medieval pottery relating to the Period 1 building in the north-west corner of Site 51, and from other Period 1 contexts in and around the courtyard buildings, were forms and decoration either not common or not previously present among the large amounts of medieval pottery found elsewhere in the village. Also from this area but found in later contexts are, along with other medieval pottery and iron objects of probable medieval date, a very fine padlock key (again a new type at Wharram; Chapter 22, No. 101), a bone mount and a bone 'whizzer' (Chapter 23, Nos 6 and 4), a 12th-century coin (Chapter 20, No. 9), and four fragments of glass from one or more vessels of uncertain type (Archive 469 and 477). In contrast there was virtually no medieval material other than pottery in the area immediately south of the cottages.

Medieval activity in the area of the vicarage and its barn is represented largely by pottery, again including some types rarely found elsewhere at Wharram. Only a few other objects from the vicarage can be dated earlier than the 16th century. Among them are another 12th-century coin (Chapter 20, No. 10), fragments of two glass jugs (Chapter 19, Nos 47 and 48), two bone mounts and a stylus (Chapter, 23, Nos 7-9). These objects may suggest establishments with a higher standard of living than that achieved in other homesteads in the medieval village: they will be reviewed as part of the whole medieval assemblage in *Wharram XIII*.

The material culture of Wharram's post-medieval households

The finds have not been helpful in identifying the use of rooms, or even of buildings: many of the identifiable objects were recovered from demolition rubble or from unstratified deposits, and others from dumps which are likely to have originated in other parts of the site; only a few were found in what might be interpreted as their place of use. For example, a weedhook and a sickle blade (Iron Archive 1034 and 1031), an iron weight (Archive 286), two horseshoe fragments and an iron buckle that might have been used in harness (Iron Archive 1085 and 1086; Archive 155) are the only objects that were probably related to the use of the Period 2 buildings in the West Range of Site 51. Finds from the rooms of the houses were even less helpful, although a few pins from beneath the 'deal floor' of the vicarage may indicate that sewing took place in this room. The Period 1 context, 341, beneath the floor of the 17th-century farmhouse, had on its surface a mixed group of objects of domestic origin, and it has been

suggested that they too may have fallen through the floor boards. Some of them, such as the pins (Non-ferrous Archive 426-508), might indeed have been deposited in this way, but others seem rather large for this to be an entirely satisfactory explanation for their presence.

On the other hand, given that it is unlikely that rubbish would have been removed from the village before the 20th century, or that goods were brought to Wharram other than for the purpose of being used there, it can be assumed that the assemblage taken as a whole represents the surviving, largely inorganic component of the goods and chattels used by the inhabitants of a farmhouse and a vicarage in a Wolds hamlet. Although the total number of any group of objects is small, some interesting differences are worthy of comment.

Agriculture and related activities

Some of the structural objects can be related to the farm buildings, although it is rarely possible to pin them down to specific periods. Many nails, a couple of large iron studs, an iron ring and a hasp (Archive 195, 196 and 616; Chapter 22, No. 103) were found in the barn that was destroyed in 1553. Another hasp and five more studs (Chapter 22, No. 102; Iron Archive 960-63 and 967) also came from the barn area, but from later phases where the finds also included such items as a lace end, a strap ornament, window cames and a pair of tongs, all suggesting a more domestic origin and presumably derived from the vicars' house. The nails from the barn have been discussed in detail in Chapter 22, and the rich organic layer made up from the burnt remains of the crops stored there has been discussed in Chapter 24.

Apart from some tools and a few items relating to animals – objects that are found throughout Wharram – there was nothing to identify the use of the courtyard buildings north of the farmhouse. A wider variety of objects used in the care and management of animals was found around the vicarage site, and despite not being related to specific areas or buildings all these objects add some detail to farming activity in the village.

It is interesting to note that, though the actual quantities are small, 76% of the ox shoes and 87% of the shears blades (Iron Archive 1138-54, 1044 and 1053-59) recovered from both areas are from the barn and other buildings around the vicarage. Although the earliest context for the ox shoes is 17th-century, they may reflect the time in the late 16th century when the vicarage was leased to farmers. As a reminder that absence from an archaeological assemblage is not proof of a real absence, it should be noted that eight oxen and eight young beasts are listed, together with eight horses old and young, in the farm inventory of 1699; by the time of the 1830 inventory only horses are listed. Other agricultural tools and the many horseshoes are more equitably spread between the two areas. Some of the fragments of chain (Archive 439-451) and other iron objects may have come from items of harness for farm wagons and machines such as the wain, ploughs and harrows mentioned in the 1699 inventory. At nearby Cowlam, in 1579, William Milner was using cattle to pull his wain and horses on his ploughs (Hayfield

1988). The inventories are also a reminder of the many agricultural tools made entirely from organic material such as wood and leather, which have left no trace. A rapid survey of Henry Best's farming book (Woodward 1984, 3-155) suggests he was using and purchasing very few objects made of metal.

The activities of shooting and fishing have always been sparsely represented among the finds from Wharram, and this period is no exception. A single fish hook (Iron Archive 1050) came from the vicarage. The arrowheads representing the bows and arrows of the medieval period are now replaced by ammunition for guns, such as the stone shot (Stone Archive 73-83) found in the farmhouse on the surface of context 341 and elsewhere, as well as many later cartridge heads. The remains of eleven traps (Iron Archive 1035-43, 1051 and 1052), some virtually complete, found mainly in and around the farm buildings, are probably from the time when the cottages were occupied by the estate gamekeeper. Rabbit bones with cut marks (Chapter 25) suggest that these were among the animals being trapped.

The North Glebe Terrace sites have also produced objects which may be derived from metalworking. Slag is found throughout the village and, although there is presently no structural evidence for a post-medieval smithy, it would not be surprising for a farming community of this kind to have had the facilities to carry out its own metalwork repairs. This is perhaps suggested by the presence of three partly-forged bars and a length of strap (in contexts from the late 17th century onwards; Iron Archive 402, 416, 421 and 864, although metallurgical analysis would be needed to confirm that they do not originate from the Anglo-Saxon smithy on the chalk plateau to the north-west). Scraps of molten lead and copper may be the result of heavy burning, but the presence of a lead bar inscribed with an M (Chapter 21, No. 123) suggests some more purposeful working.

Residential buildings

The presence of leaded windows in the vicarage is indicated by numerous lead cames (Non-ferrous Archive 786-866), some showing their original diamond shape, together with other window furniture such as the iron stay and bar (Chapter 22, Nos 69-74 and 81), and lead ties (Chapter 21, Nos 111 and 112) from 17th-century and later contexts on Site 54. These objects, and the door handle, latch fasteners and the decorative wall hooks (Chapter 22, Nos 85-87 and 75-80), reflect the high standard of ironwork found at other houses of these periods (see Hall 2005). Door handle No. 83 (Chapter 22) is the only decorative object to survive from the farmhouse, where window cames (Chapter 21, No. 110; Non-ferrous Archive 748-85) also occur in 17th-century and later contexts.

Most other objects related to the residential buildings occurred in similar proportions across both sites. An exception was the spikes (Iron Archive 634-56) and it is not obvious why 70% of these were recovered from the vicarage sites. Nor is it clear why no keys or lock parts were found in any contexts earlier than the 19th century on the farm sites, in contrast to the vicarage sites where seven keys, a box padlock and a possible lock part (Chapter 22, Nos 105-111; Iron Archive 583; Chapter 22, No. 104 and Iron Archive 578) were all recovered from 17th and 18th-century contexts. The vicars may have had more need for locks and security than the farmers, perhaps because of the greater value of their possessions, though also, perhaps, because of their frequent absences in other parts of the parish and beyond.

A tanged candlestick (Chapter 22, No. 56) found in an 18th-century context in the vicarage barn could be from an earlier period, but the other items relating to lighting, including a possible candlesnuffer, are likely to be 19th or 20th-century in date (Chapter 22, No. 55), and to derive from the cottages. Hearths and fire grates, and the bars from them, were found in both the vicarage and farmhouse (Iron Archive 310-26, 328-43 and 345-48); the grate from Room 2 in the 18th-century vicarage retained most of its bars and plates. Widespread fragments of coal, cinder and other burnt material were presumably the residue of fuel used in these hearths; burnt mudstones, from coal-bearing sequences in north-east Yorkshire, suggested that some of the fuel was local and of poor quality. Again, this material was associated with both dwellings.

A small delicate shovel and parts of two pairs of tongs (Chapter 22, Nos 57-59) are examples of hearth equipment; those found archaeologically are all from around the vicarage, but a fire iron and fender are among John Cattle's belongings in the 'Front Room' of the 1830 farmhouse, according to the inventory of that year. A bar found in the farmhouse kitchen has unusual diagonal cuts down its length which are identical to those on two spikes found around the vicarage (Iron Archive 410, 647 and 652). These, together with another purposefully-shaped metal object found in a hearth (Iron Archive 344), might be part of hanging devices over the hearths, but further research is needed to confirm this.

Only two decorative iron hinges survive from the vicarage, a butterfly-hinge and an H-hinge (Chapter 22, Nos 99 and 100); another butterfly hinge (Chapter 22, No. 93) found on Site 51 is perhaps from a door reused in the farmstead. A large copper-alloy hinge from Site 54 (Non-ferrous Archive 707) has an integral lock plate and is probably from a chest. A number of rings, similar to those identified in Lincoln as curtain rings (Mann 2008), upholstery tacks and a few handles (Chapter 21, No. 113; Non-ferrous Archive 725, 730A-E and 732-36) are reminders of the furniture, hangings, bedding and linen mentioned in the inventories, all likely to have been removed prior to demolition.

This assemblage also highlights the continuous reuse of stone within the village. This will be discussed in more detail in *Wharram XIII*, but some points are worth noticing here. A glance at the stone objects recovered from the vicarage might suggest that stone querns and mortars remained in use into the post-medieval period. A closer look, however, reveals that some were reused in walls, one having mortar still adhering to the surface. Part of a window, possibly from a secular building, was reused as a hearth on Site 77, where other walls contained stone reused from a substantial medieval building, either the church or a secular building. Pieces of reused dressed stone were found in a Period 1 wall of the North Range of the courtyard. This raises the question of how these stones came to be available for reuse: was there a village policy to collect stone, and were piles of stone, awaiting reuse, simply part of the village scene?

It should be noted here that the word 'flagstone' as used in the excavation texts does not refer to a specific type of stone. The only stones definitely used for flooring among the finds assemblage are of limestone. They are well-made with neatly dressed edges (Chapter 15, No. 39 from the vicarage is about 200mm x 180mm, and 90mm thick), and were recovered from both vicarage and farmstead areas. Two other stones (Archive 1559 and 1560), one a sandstone with an artificially-smooth surface, possibly Brandsby Roadstone, and one of limestone which is so calcareous as to suggest it might also be Brandsby Roadstone, are thick enough to have been used for flooring rather than roofing. Brandsby Roadstone occurs on most excavated sites throughout the village and from most periods, and sufficient fragments of semi-complete tiles, or tiles with holes for suspension, have been found to be certain that roofing was its main purpose. As with the large quantities found in Site 77, however, it was often removed and reused, making it difficult to be sure from which buildings it originated.

Domestic life

Much of the work within both of the households would have revolved around the provision of food and drink for the families and workers, and this is reflected in the large number of objects connected to this aspect of domestic life. Surviving items are made of a wide range of material, but, as with the agricultural objects, it is necessary to remember the many items that would have been made from organic substances, including wooden vessels, woven baskets and leather bottles, and which are therefore missing from the record. For example, in 1699 William Botterell had a salting tub, a churn, and bowls with other wooden vessels worth £1.15s in his milk house.

There are immediately obvious differences in the content of the post-medieval assemblage when compared with those from earlier periods. Glass vessels, rare in the medieval period, are more common, though the bulk of the fragments are from wine bottles. Pewter objects appear among the metalwork; and a greater number of bone handles seem to have survived. As far as the post-medieval pottery is concerned, budgetary constraints have limited the amount of detailed analysis that could be undertaken. Nevertheless, this work has indicated that the greater variety of forms and pottery types that can be seen in the vicarage in the medieval period (in contrast to other sites in the village), appears to continue into post-medieval times.

McCarthy and Brooks (1988, 102-04) have discussed the varied uses to which medieval ceramic vessels might

be put, and the same applies to these later periods and vessels of all materials: see, for example, the wine bottle with a green powdery residue that is unlikely to be wine (Chapter 19, No. 167). As far as storage containers are concerned, a copper-alloy tap from a barrel (Chapter 21, No. 87), found in the farmhouse, and the pottery cisterns and jugs, as well as the large numbers of glass wine bottles and phials, all indicate the need to store liquids for drinking and cooking.

A wide variety of drinking vessels was recognised. The glass goblets and beakers of the late 16th and 17th centuries, only found at the vicarage, were replaced by wine glasses and tumblers, now from both households but in smaller quantities in the farmhouse. Ceramic drinking vessels range from a Cistercian-ware three-handled cup (Chapter 13, No. 67) and a variety of imported stone wares and other ceramic types, to the fine quality tea bowls and cups of the 18th and 19th centuries. Fragments from the pots for serving both the new drinks of tea and coffee were recovered, as were plates and bowls in some of the finer wares. One tiny piece of Chinese porcelain, and a glass stand (Chapter 13, No. 75) and jelly glass (Chapter 19, No. 78) both 18th-century in date, all hint at the level of fashion that might reach even a small Wolds village. One decorated fragment probably from a pewter plate (Chapter 21, No. 86), found near the farmhouse, is a tangible reminder of the eleven pewter dishes, six plates and two pewter tankards that William Botterell had in the 'fore room' of his house.

The most numerous glass vessels are the wine bottles which make up a large proportion of the vessels in both households, with nearly 2,000 fragments from in and around the vicarage and less than half that number from the farmstead. The vast majority in both areas are from 17th and 18th-century bottles, although the greater proportion of 19th and 20th-century bottles from the farm area suggests that wine was not unknown when the cottages were inhabited. It is not clear whether the 18th-century fragments (18% of them) appearing in 16th and 17th-century contexts are due to disturbance, or to some other factor. Other glass vessels, though present from the medieval period onwards, dominate the 19th and 20th-century contexts, especially around the cottages.

In contrast to the earlier medieval assemblages, spoons and forks are now found among the numerous knives. Pewter spoons of types datable from the late medieval period to the 18th century (Chapter 21, Nos 72-78) were recovered from the vicarage, with those of other metal, including two of silver (Chapter 21, Nos 79 and 80), appearing from the 18th century onwards. In contrast, the earliest spoon to be found in the farmhouse is the small 18th-century bone spoon (Chapter 23, No. 15), perhaps a cheap form of a type known in silver, whilst those of other metals are all likely to be of 19th-century and later date.

Although knives are a frequent find, most of them only retaining the tang for the now-missing organic handle; other cooking implements are entirely absent from the assemblage. Although ceramic cooking pots dominate the medieval assemblages at Wharram, fragments of copper-alloy pots are also present. This pattern seems to remain the same in the early post-medieval period, with the Ryedale and other coarse ware cooking vessels, including dripping pans, pipkins and chaffing dishes, being supplemented by metal – although the evidence for metal vessels is sparse. It is generally accepted that copper-alloy vessels gave way to cast-iron ones between 1700 and 1850 (Butler, Green and Payne 2009, 1), but the small fragments of copper-alloy vessels (Chapter 21, Nos 89-91) are similar to those in the medieval assemblage, and most of the iron fragments likely to originate from vessels are from very late or unstratified contexts. The only substantial fragment is part of an iron cauldron (Chapter 22, No. 48) from a 16th to 17th-century context in the vicarage. The lack of evidence is likely to be a result of recycling and/or removal rather than true absence, and indeed brass vessels are among the goods listed in William Botterell's kitchen in 1699.

As there are no organic remains from these sites, only small metal and bone objects used functionally and/or decoratively give a glimpse of fashion and of the garments referred to as 'apparel' in the 1699 inventory. The presence of items of cloth needing to be washed and ironed can be inferred from the presence of a heating plate from a box iron of a type used in the area in the early 20th century (Megginson 1987, 50), and also from the reference to a mangle in the 1830 inventory.

Clothing

Objects representing clothing include some eighteen lace ends (Archive 224-52), a traditional method of fastening clothes carried forward from the medieval period. Although total numbers of these small objects are low (and it has to be acknowledged that they are easily missed in excavation), it is notable that fourteen (78%) occur in 16th and 17th-century contexts in the vicarage, but only four in the farmhouse. Buttons, which occur from 17th-century contexts in the farmhouse, do not appear in the vicarage until 18th-century contexts, a difference which might equally be the result of function or fashion. Hooked fasteners of varying dates have been found in the village; the 17th-century example (Chapter 22, No. 20) found in the barn is very similar to another from a household up on the chalk plateau.

By the 17th century, buckles might be used on almost any part of the body from hats to shoes, and examples of buckles for use on shoes, knee breeches and spurs have all been identified in this assemblage. Only a few of those found in the North Glebe Terrace sites are closely datable, and many of the larger ones, especially those of iron, are likely to have been used on harness and for other agricultural and non-dress purposes. The more decorative ones, such as Numbers 3 and 17 in copper alloy (Chapter 21), an iron buckle with pitchfork tongue (Chapter 22, No. 6), and the small copper-alloy knee buckle (Chapter 21, No.13), can confidently be identified as dress accessories. Also recovered were parts of pots that had contained boot blacking (Chapter 13, Nos 29 and 64).

Together with the ointment pots (Chapter 13, Nos 42, 129 and 164), they also demonstrate the wide variety of goods becoming available at local market centres.

Iron plates to protect the toes and heels of shoes and boots are frequent finds (Iron Archive 117-50), the earliest occurring in an 18th-century context in the barn. Pattens to raise the wearer above the mud were made in both wood and iron; the four iron examples (Chapter 22, Nos 1-4), three from the farm buildings, are all from 19th-century and later contexts, but this type of iron patten is known to have been worn by all classes of society from the 17th century onwards.

One bone comb of 18th-century or later date was recovered from each of the households (Chapter 23, Nos 13 and 14); they, together with the 18th-century clay wig curler (Chapter 17, No. 8) from the vicarage, are reminders of hair styling. A small group of bone objects and one in horn (Chapter 23, syringe No. 51; stick handle No. 52; finial No. 56 and horn plates No. 57) are surviving examples of the many other types of object used by Wharram's inhabitants.

The need for dressmaking and sewing skills in any household, effectively supplementing the work of haberdashers, milliners and dressmakers among the shop-owners in nearby Malton, is reflected in another small group of objects. Numerous pins and a few needles occur across both areas, whilst thimbles and scissors (Chapter 21, Nos 105; Non-ferrous Archive 282-679; Chapter 22, Nos 50-54 and Chapter 21, 98-103; Non-ferrous Archive 273-81 and Iron Archive 288-309) in a variety of shapes and sizes occur from the 17th century.

Evidence for literacy and enquiry

Evidence for literacy, in the form of decorative clasps, hinges and mount from books (for example Chapter 21, Nos 44-46 and 54-56) and writing implements of both lead (Chapter 21, Nos 48, 57 and 58; although these are likely to be medieval in origin) and slate (Chapter 15, Nos 7 and 9; Stone Archive 86-100), occurs from at least the 17th century in the vicarage, and from the 18th century in the farmhouse (where John Cattle's secretary (or desk) and bookcase containing a number of books, are among his goods listed in 1830). The presence of fragments of school-type slates (Chapter 15, Nos 6 and 7; Stone Archive 85) might be associated with the school mentioned by one of the witnesses to the legal case about the 1553 fire in the vicarage barn. The school had undoubtedly ceased to exist by the time of the final abandonment of the village in the late 1520s, and the contexts of two of the three fragments (one in the vicarage barn and another among the courtyard buildings of the farmstead), make an agricultural use more likely.

Geoff Gaunt has commented on the unusually high number of fossils and the presence of some non-local pieces of ironstones found in and around the vicarage. Fossils occur naturally in the chalk and have been among the retained items on most sites. Among the sites excavated on the North Glebe Terrace, 70% of the fossils came from Site 54, with another 19% from Site 77, with the majority of those coming from 17th and 18th-century contexts. One explanation might be a vicar with an enquiring mind, the same type of person as those in Malton who were collecting the objects of antiquarian and geological interest that would eventually form the early museum collections there.

Other objects might lend weight to that suggestion. Two pairs of possible dividers, found in the vicarage buildings, an iron one (Chapter 22, No. 22) in the 17th-century demolition material of Structure H2, the other, copper-alloy one (Chapter 21, No. 49) in a pit fill associated with Structure L, imply an owner able to make numerical calculations. Nuremberg jetons (Chapter 20, Nos 32-35), found on both these sites as well as in other parts of the village, were frequently used for calculating. The need for timekeeping is reflected in the possibly 17th-century sundial and the later watch and clock parts (Chapter 21, No. 109; Non-ferrrous Archive 741-46), including a small iron clock key (Chapter 22, No. 112). John Cattle's barometer was an obviously useful object for a farmer.

Jews' harps in both iron (Chapter 22, Nos 23-26) and copper alloy (Chapter 21, No. 60) were found in 18th-century and later contexts; apart from a fragment of a medieval bone flute (Chapter 23, No. 12) and 20th-century harmonium and mouth organ parts (Chapter 21, No. 61; Non-ferrous Archive 255-59), these are the only musical instruments from either site. Apart from drinking, the only other activity that might be associated with leisure moments is smoking, evidenced by the frequent finds of clay pipe fragments (see Chapter 18).

Coins, rare losses from the medieval period, are more numerous in these later centuries. The trade tokens from Malton and elsewhere (Chapter 20, Nos 50-52), together with objects such as the fragments of marked pots from Malton and Pickering firms (Chapter 13, Nos 176 and 184) are interesting glimpses of the links that post-medieval Wharram had with its surrounding market centres. The greater variety of goods already referred to above suggests that even a Wolds village was caught up into the growing consumerism of the 17th and 18th centuries. Malton was only one of the busy market towns in the area (Rushton 2003, 239 and 308-10). Henry Best is very specific about where to buy and sell certain goods: Malton was where he bought wooden agricultural implements such as hay rakes; Beverley market was a good place to sell oats when conditions in the Humber estuary allowed Lincolnshire men to cross over to Hull (Woodward 1984, 36, 105-108). He was concerned mainly with the equipment he needed to run his farm, and the sale of its produce, but he also mentions household goods such as the butter he preferred to buy at Beverley, and various types of cloth. The same markets would have been available to the Wharram households.

Conclusion

The finds have not been helpful in identifying rooms and their uses within the various vicarage and farmstead buildings, largely because both homesteads were thoroughly demolished and removable objects were taken away; the objects that remained were found mainly in demolition layers. They have, however, given more than a glimpse of life in the two households. Despite the broad similarities in their 17th and 18th-century assemblages, some interesting differences can be seen, with those living in the vicarage aspiring to a greater variety and quality of goods in all parts of the house, from the kitchen to the parlour. The question as to how far the surviving assemblage from two households in a small village in the Wolds reflects daily life of the period as it known from other sources remains for others to address.

31 Conclusions: the Lessons Learned
by S. Wrathmell

As has been made clear in an earlier section of this chapter, one of the great disappointments during the preparation of this volume has been the writers' inability to create a more coherent story of the structural development of the farmstead and vicarage on the basis of documentary descriptions and excavated remains. This is particularly true for the vicarage, for which there are, paradoxically, extensive and detailed written descriptions. The reasons for this are partly historical, partly technical and partly conceptual.

After the last remaining medieval farmsteads on the plateau were abandoned in the early 16th century, their sites were left largely undisturbed, as the chalk rubble foundations were not worth recycling or clearing. In the early years after the township had been put down to grass in 1527 there was probably little cultivation at all; and when the infield was developed, the village site contained too much stonework to be worth ploughing. Even the era of Improvement evidently left the former tofts and croft largely untouched, and so they remained until the archaeological excavations began.

The history of the homesteads in the valley, immediately north of the church, was entirely different. Occupation and disturbance continued until 1990, albeit intermittently after 1976, when the last of the cottages ceased to be occupied on a permanent basis. The sites of the farmhouse and farm buildings continued to be gardened in the 20th century, sometimes with the aid of a tractor and plough, and in the early years of the excavation programme rubbish pits were dug in this area, along with exploratory trenches that were not fully recorded. This no doubt accounts for the scattering of late pottery and clay pipes in contexts that were thought, at the time of excavation, to represent much earlier activity. It also accounts, no doubt, for our misreading of the deposits at the north end of Site 74, close to the cottages, which were thought to represent 16th-century and earlier occupation, but have been shown by the finds analyses to contain evidence of much more recent activity.

The vicarage site, similarly, has produced 19th-century pottery from contexts that were thought much earlier, and probably were, though with later, undetected disturbance.

The foundations of successive vicarages were largely robbed out, and their sites cut away by terracing, as their occupants attempted to prevent the western part of the vicars' plot being overwhelmed by hill-wash soil. The largely undisturbed deposit of burnt crops on the floor of the 16th-century barn, underlying deep layers of hill-wash, suggests that soil erosion became a serious problem in the years after the depopulation of the last remaining tenant farms, perhaps as a consequence of increasing and unregulated activity by rabbits (which are far more numerous in the post-medieval faunal record than in the medieval one). In the end, the vicars responded by relocating their houses further to the east.

Some of the problems of interpreting these sites are, however, the result of strategic and technical decisions made in the course of the archaeological investigations. The 1983 *Mid-term Guardianship Report*, prepared for the then Department of the Environment, outlined the strategy of displaying to the public the sites of the 18th-century farmstead and vicarage, and recognised that this would involve 'leaving the earlier remains sealed underneath as a sample of the terrace for future generations to study' (see Hurst 1984, 108). In terms of displaying the site, this was a sensible strategy, as the post-medieval sites stood a better chance of being understood by the non-expert and, located within the fenced part of the guardianship area, were less liable to be damaged by cattle.

In terms of understanding and dating what had been found, however, its impact was less welcome. On Site 51 medieval structural remains could be uncovered in places where later buildings had been eroded away by gardening, but not where well-preserved 18th-century structures survived. On Site 54 the 18th-century vicarage was removed, but the road was retained, and the northern part of the site was not explored below the Period 5 remains because of the depth of deposits. In contrast, the area immediately west of the latest vicarage house was excavated down to pre-medieval levels. Such variations in depth of excavation have hampered our understanding not only of the underlying 'prehistoric, Roman and Saxon remains' envisaged in the *Mid-term Guardianship Report*, but, in the event, of 15th, 16th and 17th-century activity as well.

It should also be acknowledged that the resources available for excavating the post-medieval sites were insufficient for complex, open-area excavations. In the early years of the Research Project only one major site was opened at a time; the post-medieval sites had, however, to compete for labour and technical expertise with other major excavations on the plateau. The traditional absence of strong central control over methods of excavation and techniques of recording meant that the two parts of the vicarage area, Sites 54 and 77, were investigated and documented in very different ways, and this, together with the location of the conduit trench and the problems that always occur at the interface of two sites under separate supervision, compounded the difficulties of interpretation.

The final, and in some ways least-expected issue affecting our understanding of these sites has been conceptual: our inability to read in the archaeological record the story that we thought the documents were telling us. The most obvious example of this was the date at which the latest farmhouse was erected. During the early years of his post-medieval historical research, Beresford located the expenditure accounts of Sir Charles Buck, and these demonstrated that Wharram Percy township experienced wholesale Improvement in the 1770s. The documented work included not only the creation and fencing of new fields, but also the erection of new houses at Bella and Wharram Grange and the reconstruction of farm buildings at Wharram Percy. Thousands of bricks were brought to Wharram, and it is entirely understandable that, though specifically unrecorded in any of the surviving papers, the rebuilding of Wharram Percy farmhouse was assumed to have taken place at the same time.

The valuation of 1806 was discovered many years later in the Birdsall estate office; and though this clearly records a house that was *not* the final, brick-faced farmhouse, the concept of rebuilding in the 1770s was so embedded in the minds of all of us working on Wharram that its significance remained undetected: the date of rebuilding had ceased to be in question. It was not until Didsbury's insistence that the post-medieval pottery demanded a date after 1800, and Davey's confirmation that the clay tobacco pipes were in agreement, that the issue was reopened.

At this point in the research on Wharram, we can at least say that the documentary evidence for the development of the farmhouse and outbuildings appears to accord with (or, perhaps, does not conflict with) the archaeological record. The same cannot be said for the far better documented 16th-century vicarage. No documentation is neutral; and without an understanding of its purpose and context it is difficult to appreciate what it is telling us, and more particularly what it is not telling us. The articles recited in the dilapidations cause of 1555-6 provide a context for the information contained in the depositions; and whilst the depositions were made in support of one party or the other, we have plenty from both sides and so it should have been easy to identify common ground and therefore the more reliable parts of the testimonies.

Yet one of the key issues – the location of the pre-fire vicarage house – is entirely unresolved, as the excavation failed to confirm what appeared to be a clear indication in the documentation. Furthermore, even though the documents record the burning of a vicarage barn, and though the excavation revealed a burnt barn in the vicarage, the historical and archaeological data for the length of the building are seemingly irreconcilable. We are unable to conceive of a line of argument that would satisfy both the documentary and the archaeological evidence either for the location of the pre-fire house or for the length of the barn – although there must be one, and other researchers will, no doubt, identify it at some point in the future.

For other aspects of life in the post-medieval settlement at Wharram, the problem is less an issue of conflicting evidence, more a question of being faced with alternative inferences that appear to have equal validity on the basis of current information. A case in point is the ceramic evidence for activity in the 16th century. As noted earlier in this chapter, had there been no documentary evidence for the vicarage barn's destruction, its archaeological event would almost certainly have been dated, on the basis of pottery, to the second half of the 15th century, rather than to the mid-16th century. Moreover, there are no distinctly post-medieval pottery types and forms associated with any of the immediate pre-fire and post-fire phases of occupation.

Given that the vicars are supposed to have resided at Wharram in this period, the paucity of early post-medieval tablewares – for example Cistercian Ware – is likely to be a matter of choice rather than necessity: the vicars had pewter on the table rather than ceramics. Yet in Chapter 13 it has been suggested that a similar absence of 16th-century pottery on the site of the later farmstead signifies an absence of 16th-century occupation. Is one answer more reliably grounded than the alternative on either of these sites? In this case there are two other strands of evidence that support the proposition with regard to the farmhouse. The first is an absence of whittle-tang knives from the site (in contrast to the vicarage). The second is the relatively small proportion of 'transitional' pottery in the Site 74 assemblage (just under 16%) as against the vicarage sites (over 41%). In many other cases, however, we are left with equally plausible alternatives.

Post-medieval settlement at Wharram falls into two parts, lay and clerical, and it had been hoped that the finds assemblages from these distinct areas would provide instructive similarities and contrasts. Once again, our expectations were rather too high, though not completely unrealised. The pre-Dissolution vicars seem to have had more ready access to imported ceramics, and to glass jugs, than had Wharram's other residents, presumably because of the Haltemprice connection. Yet Haltemprice's financial difficulties had reduced significantly the value of the living, and this reduction was not reversed at the Dissolution. Thereafter, the general impression is that expenditure on maintaining the physical infrastructure of the vicarage was kept to a minimum: there are hints that Atkinson used building material recycled from the church, and there seems to have been much recycling of brickwork in later centuries. On the other hand, the 'cellar', Structure J, must represent a significant investment in a kind of facility that is only rarely recorded in the region.

The farmers of the 17th and 18th centuries lived in a house that seems, from its plan form, to have been very similar to the vicarage Structure K. Nevertheless, the documentation that has been found suggests that the Richardson and Botterell families had money: they simply chose not to spend it (certainly in the Botterells' case) on the houses they occupied. They were tenant farmers, and subscribed to the view of tenant farmers everywhere, that there is not much point in spending money on a property you do not own (a sentiment that can be applied equally, of course, to vicars). So the Botterells spent their money on personal possessions and commodities such as wine (as evident from the large number of late 17th to early 18th-century wine bottles from Site 74) rather than on improving their dwelling. Improvements in housing and farm buildings depended almost entirely on the investment decisions made by the landowner, a tradition that at Wharram probably originated in the late Anglo-Saxon period, and continues even today.

Appendices

Appendix 1: The Clay Tobacco Pipe Recording System employed for the Wharram Percy Assemblage
by P. Davey and S. White

Introduction

The Wharram Percy clay tobacco pipe finds have been entered onto an Excel spreadsheet, which has been designed to allow all the pipe fragments to be recorded in a standard manner. Each of the columns of the spreadsheet represents a different variable that has been selected as being of possible significance in the interpretation of excavated groups. Each of the rows contains details of an individual fragment(s) from a specific archaeological context.

In order that the Wharram material can be compared closely with other excavated groups, the variables included are essentially those defined in the recording system devised by Davey and Higgins and last revised in 1994. It has subsequently been used to document many excavated assemblages. A copy is held in the Site Archive and will be made available through the Archaeology Data Service along with lists and databases relating to the Wharram finds assemblages.

The Excel Clay Tobacco Pipe Record

The pipe fragments are recorded in site and context order. Each line is used to record an individual fragment or a group of fragments if their attributes are all the same. For each different context the bowls, stems, mouthpieces and heel/spur junctions are listed, in that order, with marked or decorated pieces coming before the plain examples within each category. The symbols /, 0 or - are used to mean 'yes', 'no' or 'can't tell' respectively. The following classes of information are then recorded:

Identification
Site number The first column (ST) on the left records the site number.

Context number The second column (Cxt) records the context number.

Laboratory number The third column includes the Lab No, where one has been allotted. This column is not included in the tables in this volume.

Small find number The fourth column records the SF number where one has been given.

B S M H/S
The number of bowl (B), stem (S), mouthpiece (M) and heel stem junction (H/S) fragments recovered from each context is entered in these three columns. As entries on the right hand side of the sheet must relate to all the fragments entered in these first columns, a number of different lines are usually required to build up a complete record of each context group.

The numbers of fragments entered are the numbers as excavated. Two or more joining pieces which have clearly been damaged during recovery or handling are counted as one piece. Reconstructed fragments, which were damaged before deposition, are counted individually, being listed in their appropriate columns but on the same line. A note of any such joins or of other cross context joins is placed in the final column.

If an unbroken pipe is recovered, it is counted under the bowl column and an arrow (->) drawn across the stem and mouthpiece columns. The fact that the pipe is complete is noted in the 'comments' column where details of the stem length, mouthpiece form and finish can be given. In this way details of the pipe can still be found on the form without distorting the count of fragments recorded in the columns.

Bowls (B) A bowl fragment is defined as any fragment with part of the base of the heel or spur surviving with enough of the bowl to show its thickness (i.e., with any part of the internal bowl cavity surviving). The length of any surviving stem is irrelevant and is not counted separately in the stem column. This does not apply to reassembled fragments of stem, which have been joined to a bowl fragment. These are counted under the stem column on the same line.

Stems (S) A stem is any fragment with neither bowl, mouthpiece nor heel or spur surviving.

Mouthpieces (M) A mouthpiece is any piece with some or all the mouthpiece surviving.

64
This records the stem bore(s) of the fragments listed on each line in 64ths of an inch, '7', for example, representing a fragment with a bore of 7/64". For the Wharram Percy assemblage the butt ends of imperial drill bits have been used to measure the stem bores. Where the diameter of the bore at either end of a fragment varies, only the smaller measurement is recorded. For mouthpieces only the broken end is measured.

DATE
The date range for the piece(s) recorded. This is an estimate of the likely period during which the pieces were made.

BUR

Records burnishing on the fragments(s). This can either be a yes tick (/) where burnishing is present or it can be further graded as fine (F), good (G), average (A) or poor (P). A fine (F) burnish is when the polishing lines are so closely spaced and even that there are no gaps between and a fine very glossy surface is created. A good (G) burnish is well applied with close, even strokes. An average (A) burnish will have gaps of roughly equal width to the burnish lines and may be light and uneven. A poor (P) burnish is very scrappy and irregularly applied. Burnishing on the stem is usually less well applied than that on the bowl and can often only be noted as being present rather than being graded. Great care must be taken on the identification of burnishing, especially where naturally glossy fabrics are used. Burnished pipes exhibit the slight facets caused by polishing and, usually, an alternating surface of glossy and matt strips.

BOWL

Three columns deal with various attributes of the bowl. These are:

X Internal bowl crosses. The most common marks found on the internal base of a bowl are crosses. When viewed with the stem pointing down these can either appear as '+' or 'x'. These symbols are used to indicate which type is present. If some other symbol or letter is found * is entered and the mark is described in the comments section.

M4 Milling. The amount of milling around the rim is estimated to the nearest quarter of a complete circumference so, for example, a half milled pipe is entered as 2. If no milling is present a 0 is entered, if milling is present but the rim damaged a / is entered, if no rim survives X - is entered.

RIM Rim finish. The way in which the rim has been treated is coded:

C   Cut: the rim is formed by just a single horizontal knife cut.
B   Bottered: the rim has been smoothed with a bottering tool giving a rounded profile.
I   Internal knife cut: a knife has been used to cut clay from the inside of the bowl to make a thinner, finer rim.
W   Wiped: the rim has been wiped or smoothed (as opposed to being bottered).

These codes may be used together. Thus CW is a rim that has been cut and wiped or IB is a rim that had been internally knife cut and bottered. These last two techniques are often very difficult to distinguish where they occur together and any results should be regarded cautiously looking for general trends rather than exact figures. As a general rule bottering produces a smooth, rounded and 'wiped' appearance near the rim as opposed to knife trimming which produces less even and deeper marks within the bowl with a fresher 'scraped' appearance to the surface.

TIP

These two columns describe the tip or mouthpiece of the pipe. They record the type of mouthpiece (TT) and finish (TF) applied to it.

The types of mouthpiece (TT) are coded as follows:

C   Cut; the mouthpiece is formed by a simple cut end to the stem and no other moulded shape is present.
R   Rounded: the mouthpiece is formed in the mould as a simple rounded end.
N   Nipple: a circular sectioned stem, which terminates with a moulded nipple.
D   Diamond shaped: the stem ends with a diamond shaped cross section but without a nipple.
DN Diamond nipple: where the stem takes on lozenge or sharply oval section in shape directly before the nipple.
FO Flattened Oval: the stem takes on a flat, oval, section at the tip, without a nipple.

The types of finish (TF) are coded as follows:

0   No visible finish
RW   Red Wax
GW   Green Wax
GG   Green Glazed; often thin and light in colour
YG   Yellow Glaze
CG   Clear Glaze Other; specify under 'comments'

MARK

The next six columns deal with any maker's mark. A sketch or transcription of the mark is written under other.

NCAT The National Catalogue number of any stamped mark. This is intended to relate specifically to the National Stamp Catalogue, which is being compiled at the University of Liverpool.

CN The first name or initial as it appears on the pipe.

SN The second name (surname) or second initial, as it appears on the pipe.

Other A sketch, transcription or additional description of the mark is given here.

P The position of the mark on the pipe is recorded. The codes are:

H   On the base of the heel.
SP   On the base of the spur.
BB   Beneath the bowl where a pipe has neither heel nor spur.
SH   On the sides of the heel.
SS   On the sides of the spur.

BF On the bowl facing the smoker.
BL On the bowl, on the left hand side as smoked.
BR On the bowl, on the right hand side as smoked.
BA On the bowl facing away from the smoker.
BS On the bowl sides.
SX On the top of the stem, reading across it.
SL On the stem, reading along it.
SM Multiple individual stamps right around the stem, as a band or pattern.
RS Roll stamped stem, a continuous band or zone around the stem. This may be plain or decorated but does not include milled decoration.
SP Spiral stem stamp (one line mark applied on a spiral).
ST Stem twist, a specific form of roll stamp forming a spiral of shallow grooves around the stem.

T The type of mark is recorded:

I The primary pattern or motif is incuse.
R The primary pattern or motif is in relief.
A Applied mark formed of some medium other than clay such as a rubber stamp, transfer print or hand written mark.

M The method by which the mark was formed:

M   Moulded mark
S   Stamped mark
I   Ink stamp (rubber stamp)
TP Transfer printed mark
HW Hand written mark
*   Other, specify the exact type under comments

DEC/MODIFICATION
Any decorative treatment of the pipe, or any modification of it, such as whittling on stems, is described or sketched.

DR
Drawing. Three sets of codes have been used to refer to individual drawings:

PJD Drawings made by Peter Davey in his preliminary study of the pipes carried out between 1983 and 1987. These drawings which were made as record sketches and not intended for publication are given letter codes A to Z, AA-AZ etc.

SDW This series of numbers relates to drawings made by Susie White, between 1996 and 2004, during fieldwork for her PhD on Yorkshire clay tobacco pipes. Some of the drawings were published in her thesis and can be found in BAR, British Series 374, 2004.

DN The number given to each pipe fragment, a drawing of which is to be published. A version of this number will be added to the database following publication.

COMMENTS
Any comments or notes on the pipe(s) recorded. These range from notes about the degree of preservation of individual pieces, the presence of spots of glaze or residues and notes about joining pieces. A particular note is made to expand any column where * or an arrow has been entered and to note features such as cross context joins.

Appendix 2: A Note on the Burnt Clay

Fragments of burnt clay were recovered from both the farmhouse (Sites 49, 51, 73 and 74) and the vicarage buildings (Sites 54 and 77), and across most periods. They appear in small quantities and the majority are likely to be residual. Both the main types of burnt clay recovered across the village, one with a soapy texture, the other harder and sandier, were among this assemblage. Only a few showed the impressions of wattles, but those doing so included a small group from Site 54, context 298, in Period 6.3, with a very different brown, light dusty texture.

Appendix 3: A Note on Objects of Wood, Shell, Leather and Other Materials

More than a hundred fragments of wood were recovered, a much larger number than from other sites within the village. Some are relatively modern, the remains of stakes and fence posts for example. Most are off-cuts with no form, but three are shaped. Archive 69 may be the remains of a handle plate; Archive 70 may be part of a button or a bead; and Archive 71 is a flat button identical to others in bone. Four mother of pearl buttons all came from around the Farmhouse, two (Archive 111 and 114) from occupation phases.

Only four small fragments of leather were found, all around the cottages and likely to be modern.

Appendix 4: A Note on the Mortar and Plaster

Fragments of mortar and/or plaster were recovered from both groups of buildings. Mortar, including samples, was recovered, but no further work has been done.

Fragments of plaster occurred both around the vicarage and the farmhouse, some showing colour which may be the residue of decorative designs. Material from the early 19th-century Farmhouse (Periods 4 and 5) has red and blue colour, whilst some indications of colour and black lines can be seen on plaster from phases associated with the 17th-century vicarage.

Appendix 5: A Note on the Charcoal

It is normal to find fragments of charcoal and/or burnt wood in any excavation at Wharram and those discussed in this volume were no exception. There was however an unusual amount of material from Site 77, particularly in the layers connected with the fire. Some was identifiable as charred planks, whilst others had a more rounded profile and may have originated as wattles.

Appendix 6: A Note on the Coal, Cinder and Burnt Material

Coal was, as is usual at Wharram, found on almost every site, although collection is unlikely to have been total. The presence of a possible coal store at the Vicarage (Site 54), as well as hearths both there and in the Farmhouse, suggest that coal was burnt by both households. In the Farmhouse (Site 74) some 60% comes from 19th-century phases, whilst on Site 54 85% is from contexts dating from the 17th-century onwards.

Fragments of burnt material (described as burnt shale), found within both buildings and from contexts with a similar date range, have been identified by G.D. Gaunt who comments:

'Nearly half of this material is carbonaceous and some, notably from Site 54, contain thin (generally <1.5mm thick) layers of poor quality coal. These characteristics, and the fact that most of them have been burnt, some severely, strongly suggest a source in one of the coal-bearing non-marine sequences such as the Saltwick Formation or the Sycarham or Gristhorpe Member of the Cloughton Formation, all the Middle Jurassic of north-eastern Yorkshire.'

These areas may therefore have been the source of cheap coal.

Appendix 7: The Metalworking Residues

The small quantity of slag recovered across most of the sites, mainly consists of smithing slag, but includes hearth bottoms, fuel ash slag, hearth lining, and a possible fragment of hammer scale (see p. 363 for a discussion of possible source). Small amounts of copper-alloy slag and/or dribbles may relate to the copper-alloy working known to have taken place within the village, although the bell pit within the church is another possible source. An unusual item, and one of interest is the lead bar, No. 123 (Chapter 21), suggesting that lead was being worked near by, but at what period is not known.

Appendix 8: Concordance of the Contexts containing Pottery, Small Finds, Metallurgical and Environmental Remains, and of all Contexts mentioned in this volume, by Site, Phase and Context

The concordance lists all pottery by sherd count and weight; catalogue numbers of illustrated sherds are given in brackets. The published or Archive catalogue numbers are given for small finds of stone (including memorials), clay, illustrated clay pipe, metal, wood, bone or ivory, leather, and for published glass objects and vessel glass. The remaining vessel glass is listed by number of fragments (bracketed), as are brick, nails (Site 54/516 and Site 77 only), clay tile, unillustrated clay pipe fragments, burnt clay and published animal bone; animal bone in other contexts is not recorded here. Metallurgical waste, cinder, coal and charcoal are listed by weight and, finally, mortar, plaster, burnt shale, fish bone (see archive for complete catalogue) and molluscs by presence. The 'phases' listed in the concordance are equivalent to the 'periods' referred to in the earlier chapters. They have been converted to periods after being given date ranges. It has not been possible to create overall periods covering all the sites reported in this volume: there is no necessary chronological equivalence of the periods of one site with those of any other.

Abbreviations

Pottery:
Pre.: Prehistoric pottery
Rom.: Iron Age and Roman pottery
Med.: Saxon and medieval pottery
PM: post-medieval pottery

Small Finds:
Bone: bone or ivory artefact
Brick: brick fragments
Clay: clay artefact
Coin Rom.: Roman coin
Coin med.: medieval coin
Coin pm: post-medieval coin
Copper: non-ferrous metal object
Cp: clay pipe
Glass: glass object
Iron: iron artefact
Lst.: limestone
Mem.: stones related to burial and memorial
Nail: nail including fragments (the second no. is nails from animal shoes)

Quern: quernstone
Roof.: roofing stone (including slate)
Sst.: sandstone
Stone: stone artefact other than quern, including stone possibly used for flooring
Tile: clay tile
Vess.: vessel glass
Wood: objects of wood, shell, leather and other materials

Environmental and Technological Remains:
An.: animal remains
BS: burnt shale
Burnt: burnt clay fragments
Char.: charcoal
Cin.: cinder
Coal: coal
Fish: fish bone
Moll.: molluscs
Mortar: mortar
Plas.: plaster
Slag: metallurgical waste

Phase	Context	Description	Fig. Nos	Artefacts and environmental remains

Farmhouse sites

Site 11

Phase	Context	Description	Fig. Nos	Artefacts and environmental remains
-	1	No context information		Copper A680
-	2	No context information		
-	3	No context information		Med. 3:41; PM 17:373 (58); Brick (1); Vess. (1)
-	4	No context information		Roof. A747; Tile (2)
-	5	No context information		Med. 22:203; Brick (5); Vess. (2); Plas.
-	6	No context information		PM 24:112; Glass A198; Tile (5)
-	7	No context information		
-	8	No context information		
-	9	No context information		
-	10	No context information		
-	Cesspit	No context information		PM 1:7

Site 15

Phase	Context	Description	Fig. Nos	Artefacts and environmental remains
-	1	Hole for electricity pole 1		
-	2	Hole for electricity pole 2		Bone 31
-	3	Hole for electricity pole 3		
-	4	Hole for electricity pole 4		PM 4:539 (62); Cp (3); Iron 116
-	5	Hole for electricity pole 5		
-	6	Trench for electricity poles		PM 60:2151 (59-61); Cp (1); Iron 83, A430, A659, A946; Roof A1486; Vess (4)
-	7	Trench for electricity poles		PM 50:2337; Cp (3); Iron A740, A1028
-	8	Trench for electricity poles		Copper A699; Cp (3); Iron 1
-	9	Trench for electricity poles		
-	10	Trench for electricity poles		PM 3:148; Iron A117, A356
-	11	Trench for electricity poles		
-	12	Trench for electricity poles		
-	13	Trench for electricity poles		
-	14	Trench for electricity poles		
-	15	Trench for electricity poles		
-	16	Trench for electricity poles		
-	17	Trench for electricity poles		

Site 49

Phase	Context	Description	Fig. Nos	Artefacts and environmental remains
3	1	Topsoil	32	PM 53:1300; Copper A132, A713; Cp 43, 48, 51 (16); Iron A193, A532, A565, A1138, A1168; Tile (4); Vess. (2); Wood A124; BS; Coal 60g; Mortar; Plas.
3	2	Overburden	32	PM 495:2815; Bone 61; Brick (24); Copper 69, A134, A255, A273, A700, A741, A919, A946; Cp 38, 49 (16); Glass A172; Iron 55, A118-120, A228-230, A292, A315, A316, A492, A540, A568, A584, A588, A741-744, A970, A979, A1155, A1397-1399; Roof. A1485, A1517; Tile (46); Vess. (100); Wood A1-3; BS; Cin. 40g; Coal 24g; Slag 93g; Plas.
2	3	Road repair	32	PM 1:15; Tile (3); BS; Cin. 56g; Coal 30g; Mortar
2	4	Road repair	32	Vess. (6); Cin. 4g; Coal 2g
2	5=20	Road repair	32	PM 16:179; Copper A748; Iron A458; Lst A722; Tile (1); Vess. (3); Char. 1g; Cin. 3g; Coal 7g
3	6	Redeposited deposit		Brick (1); Cp (4); Sst. A198; Tile (4); Wood A4
3	7	Redeposited deposit	32	PM 3:10; Copper 41; Tile (1); Vess. (6); Wood A5, A111
2	8	Brick wall		
3	9	Mortar deposit	32	
3	10	Chalk pad	32	Med. 2:10; PM 2:54; Clay 1; Iron A164; Stone 2; Vess. (1)
3	11	Sand deposit	32	PM 89:433; Brick (18); Cp (3); Iron A459, A460, A518, A546, A1400; Tile (26); Vess. (6); Wood A6; Cin. 1g; Mortar; Plas.
2	12	Rubble wall core		
3	13	Tent pegs		
3	14	Post-pipe		
3	15	Post-hole (cut & fill)		Iron A121, A240; Tile (2)
-	16	Chalk post packing		
2	17	?Brick structure	33	
2	18	Plaster & brick pad	33	Plas.
2	19	Destruction debris		
2	20=5	Road repair		
2	21=26	Humic deposit		Med. 2:29; PM 4:55; Brick (5); Copper 86, A133, A256, A708, A992, A1037; Cp (5); Glass A216; Iron 23, A431, A461, A541, A589, A1169; Roof. A1518; Tile (20); Vess. (40); Wood A7, A116; Cin. ≤1g; Coal 5g

Phase	Context	Description	Fig. Nos	Artefacts and environmental remains
1	22	Pebble surface	32	Vess. (1)
2	23	Gravel surface	32, 33	PM 5:14; Glass A213; Tile (1); Vess. (1); Wood A8
2	24	Flint surface	32, 33	
2	25	Foundation wall		
2	26=21	Humic deposit	32	Med. 5:118; PM 85:813; Brick (30); Coin pm 50, 51; Copper 109, 121, A282, A283, A749; Cp 20 (4); Glass A171; Iron A673, A1075, A1170, A1244; Roof. A774, A775; Stone A41; Sst. A199; Tile (12); Vess. (8); BS; Coal 11g
2	27	Pebble deposit		
-	28	Misc. pot		Tile (1)
2	29	Post-hole (cut and fill)		Rom. 2:54; Lst. A727; Stone 22
2	30	Black ditch fill		Rom. 48:1445 (1-3); Stone A42; Burnt (2); Char. 4g
1	31	Road repair	32	Rom. 1:10; Med. 21:76; PM 11:87; Brick (15); Copper 1, A947; Iron A1076; Roof. A776; Tile (6); An. (29); BS; Cin. 25g; Coal 30g
2	32	Humic deposit		PM 13:131; Iron A547, A1401; Stone A43
2	33	Destruction debris		
2	34	Cobble surface	33	
1	35	Road repair		
2	36	Destruction debris	33	
2	37	Bonding bricks		
1	38	Yard surface		
1	39	Yard surface		
3	40	Turf		
3	41	Modern overburden		
3	42	1958 excavation trench		
2	43	Sandstone wall		
1	44 (Site 74 351?)	Foundation wall?		
2	45	Red brick wall		
2	46	Rubble wall core		
2	47	Mortar bonding		
2	48	Rubble wall core		
2	49	Chalk wall		
3	50	C20th refuse		
2	51	Post-hole (cut and fill)		
2	52	Post-hole (cut and fill)		Rom. 1:16
2	53	Post-hole (cut and fill)		
2	54	Post-hole (cut and fill)		
2	55	Post-hole (cut and fill)		
2	56	Post-hole (cut and fill)		
2	57	Post-hole (cut and fill)		
2	58	Post-hole (cut and fill)		
2	59	Post-hole (cut and fill)		
2	60	Stake-hole (cut and fill)		
2	61	Stake-hole (cut and fill)		
2	62	Stake-hole (cut and fill)		
2	63	Stake-hole (cut and fill)		
-	64	Eavesdrip gully?		
2	65	Ditch		
2	66	Post-hole (cut and fill)		
2	67	Post-hole (cut and fill)		
2	68	Shallow depression - ?natural		
-	69	Natural chalk		
2	70	Natural gully		
3	71	Brick pathway		
3	72	Construction/destruction debris		Iron A533
3	73	Stone wall course		
3	74	Stone wall course		
2	75	Chalk pathway	33	PM 9:17; Clay A13; Copper 123; Sst. A571; Vess. (3)
3	76	Pit cut and fill		Med. 1:6; PM 9:31; Cp (1); Iron A1082; Tile (2); Vess. (2); Wood A9, A117
3	77	Post-hole (cut and fill)		
-	78	Rock deposit		PM 49:291; Brick (3); Copper 61, A135; Cp 50 (1); Iron 43, A186, A231, A358, A519, A1402, Sst. A572; Stone A44, A86; Tile (1)
3	79	Black soil		PM 57:650; Copper A136, A701; Iron A310, A1245; Vess. (4)
3	80	Post-hole		
3	81	Post-hole packing		Rom. 1:8 (4); Tile (1); Coal ≤1g
3	82	Post-hole packing		
3	83	Pit cut		Iron A1032, A1403; Vess. (2)
3	84	Pit fill		PM 26:128; Tile (6)
2	85	Squarish depression		

374

Phase	Context	Description	Fig. Nos	Artefacts and environmental remains
-	86	Shallow depression cut		
3	87	Pre-1972 turf level		
3	88	Post-hole cut		
3	89	Decayed post		
3	90	Truncated depression		
3	91	Pit		
3	92	Pit fill		PM 1:10 (63 pt)
-	93	Pit fill		
3	94	Pit cut		
2	95	Levelling path deposit		PM 6:23; Vess. (6); Wood A10
3	96	Pit base layer		
3	97	C20th rubbish pit		
3	98	Post-hole and post packing		
3	99	Post-hole fill		
3	100	Mortar dump		
3	101	Post-packing		
2	102	Road levelling deposit		Med. 1:107; PM 2:3; Brick (2); Tile (1); Vess. (2); Cin. 5g
-	103	Trench fill unexcavated		
-	104	Construction trench?		
-	105	Trench/drain/ditch unexcavated		
-	106	Trench/drain/ditch fill unexcavated		
3	107	Post-hole (cut and fill)		Cin. 2g; Coal 4g
3	108	Stake-hole		
3	109	Stake-hole		
3	110	Stake-hole		
-	111	Irregular depression		PM 1:2
3	112	Pit		
3	113	Pit fill		PM 1:1
3	114	Post-hole fill		
3	115	Post-hole cut		
3	116	Post-hole cut		
3	117	Post-hole fill		PM 1:2; Tile (2); Cin. 6g; Coal 27g
3	118	Post-hole cut		
3	119	Post-hole fill		PM 2:3; Brick (1); Tile (2); Cin. ≤1g; Coal 1g
	120-342	Unused context		
-	343	No context information		Sst. A200-204
	344-499	Unused context		
3	500 (Site 73/1)	Topsoil		Med. 1:1; PM 40:612; Brick (6); Copper 43, 66; Cp (1); Iron A151, A154, A293, A311, A312, A350, A619, A674; Quern A114; Roof. A1519; Stone A45; Tile (12); Vess. (11); Cin. 1g; Coal 21g; Slag 11g
3	501=523 (Site 73/2)	Chalk rubble		Rom. 1:3; PM 11:62; Bone 32; Brick (3); Copper A264, Iron 7, 28 A1077; Lst. A734; Roof. A777-780; Sst. A205; Tile (7); Vess. (1); Cin. 4g; Coal ≤1g
3	502	Rubbish pit		Rom. 2:5; Med. 1:4; PM 22:888; Brick (1); Iron A1246; Vess. (1)
3	503	Rubbish pit fill		PM 250:11503; Copper A709; Vess. (1)
3	504	Shallow depression (cut)		
2	505	Clay deposit		
2	506	Loam deposit	32	Rom. 1:9
1	507	Hillwash?	32	Rom. 2:28; An. (2)
1	508	Buried soil layer	32	Rom. 5:22; An. (2); Slag 4g
3	509	Undefined feature cut		
1	510	Natural bedrock	32	
1	511	Pea grit layer	32	
2	512	Undefined feature cut		
3	513 (Site 73/13)	Rubbish pit cut	33	
3	514 (Site 73/14)	Rubbish pit fill		Med. 1:3; PM 23:646; Vess. (4); Iron 2, A1171; Plas.
3	515	Cess pit layer		
3	516	Cess pit layer		
3	517	Depression fill		
	518	Unused context		
3	519	Clay loam deposit		
2	520	Loam deposit/fill of ?natural hollow		
2	521	Ditch		
2	522	Ditch fill		Med. 3:13
2	523=501 (Site 73/2)	Chalk layer		Med. 5:32; PM 3:10; Vess. (1)
2	524 (Site 73/11)	Cobble surface		

Phase	Context	Description	Fig. Nos	Artefacts and environmental remains
2	525	Cut of pit		
2	526	Pit fill		
2	527	Loam deposit	32	
1	528	Hillwash	32	
2	529	Post-medieval depression	33	
2	530	Ditch fill		
2	531	Ditch cut		
2	532	Ditch fill		
2	533	Depression		
2	534	Ditch fill		
2	535	Cobbled yard layer		
2	536	Clay layer		
2	537	Clay layer		
1	538	Natural		
1	539	Natural		
3	540	Stake-hole cut	33	
3	541	Stake-hole fill		
3	542	Stake-hole cut	33	
3	543	Stake-hole fill		
3	544	Stake-hole cut	33	
3	545	Stake hole fill		

Site 49/51

-	1			PM 62:1371

Site 51
West Range

Phase	Context	Description	Fig. Nos	Artefacts and environmental remains
2.4	466	Road surfacing/make-up	18, 22	Med. 1:8; Coin pm 41; Iron A604, A1062, A1183
2.4	467	Topsoil	22	Med. 18:93; PM 32:147; Brick (10); Copper A140; Cp (4); Glass A178, A201, A218; Iron A252, A262, A265-267, A281, A353, A464, A605, A688, A948, A996, A1039, A1184, A1186, A1266, A1429; Lst. A737; Quern A116; Roof. A789; Tile (101); Vess. (12); Wood A35, A36; BS; Char. 13g; Cin. 32g; Coal 18g; Mortar; Plas.; Slag 60g
Mod.	468	Trench backfill		PM 2:9; Copper A994; Iron 92, A689, A1185, A1187; Roof. A790; Tile (1); Char. 9g; Coal 1g
2.4	469	Buried soil layer	18, 21	Med. 45:344; PM 158:1329 (51); Bone 34, 63; Brick (11); Copper A743, A747, A892, A893, A929, A995; Cp (2); Glass A179, A202, A203; Iron A187, A253, A254, A263, A296, A322, A323, A359, A361, A362, A448, A465, A466, A539, A542, A569, A606-608, A712, A757, A949, A1160, A1188-1191, A1267, A1430, A1431; Lst. A605; Roof. A791, A792, A1491, A1526, A1527; Sst. 576; Stone 1, 7, 16; Tile (42); Vess. (51); Wood A126; BS; Char. 2g; Cin. 12g; Coal 1g; Plas.; Slag 2g
2.3	470	Make-up layer	18, 20, 21	Med. 8:109; PM 3:10; Brick (4); Iron 93, A285; Lst. A606-609; Sst. A216; Tile (90); Vess. (2); Wood A37; An. (6); Cin. 1g; Mortar; Plas.
2.2	471	Make-up layer	18, 20	Med. 352:3156; PM 1:3; Brick (2); Copper 2; Iron A609; Roof. A793-795; Stone A46, A47; Tile (20); Vess. (1); Wood A38; An. (46); BS; Burnt (3); Cin. 20g; Coal 2g; Fish; Mortar; Slag 337g
1	472=46 =555	Chalk floor surface	17, 18	
2.1	473=514= 518=519= 525=567= 571	Wall		
-	474	Core and inner face of wall		
2.1	475	Wall filling		An. (26)
2.1	476=740	Wall		
2.1	477=45?	Mortar surface	18	
2.1	478	Gully	17, 18	
2.1	479	Gully fill		Brick (4)
-	480	Post-pit		
-	481	Post-pit fill		
-	482	Post/stake-hole		
-	483	Post/stake-hole		
-	484	Associated feature of 480		
-	485	Associated feature of 480		
2.1	486	Post-hole		
2.1	487	Post-hole fill		An. (1)
-	488	Post-hole		

Phase	Context	Description	Fig. Nos	Artefacts and environmental remains
-	489	Post-hole fill		
-	490	Post-hole		
-	491	Post-hole fill		
-	492	Post-hole		
-	493	Post-hole fill		
-	494=36= 496	Post-hole		
Mod.	495	Trench backfill		
-	496=36= 494	Post-hole		Wood A39
-	497	Post-hole fill		
-	498	Post-hole		
-	499	Post-hole fill		
2.1	500=574= 601=603	Foundation trench	18	Med. 1:5; Tile (2); An. (6)
2.1	501	Foundation trench fill	18	Rom. 1:20; Med. 27:265 (44); Tile (2); An. (7)
2.3	502	Road surface	18, 21	An. (1)
-	502/538	No context information		Iron A591
2.1	503	Cobble surface	17, 18	Iron A155
2.4	504	Trench fill	18	
2.1	505	Chalk footings	18	
2.2	506	Mortar layer	19	
-	507	Post-hole		
-	508	Post-hole fill		Rom. 1:2; Med. 37:281 (4); Brick (1); Iron A255, A391, A628; Stone 13; Tile (10); Wood A40; Char. <1g; Cin. 1g
2.1	514=473 =518=519 525=567 =571	Wall		
-	515	Foundation trench fill		
-	516	Cut		Vess. (48)
-	517	Fill (? relating to 478)		
2.1	518=473 =514=519 =525=567 =571	Wall	17, 18, 20, 21	
2.1	519=473 =514=518 =525=567 =571	Brick wall skin	17, 18, 21	Brick (1)
2.4	520	C20 pit cut	21	
-	521	Demolition debris		Brick (10); Tile (58); Vess. (2)
-	522	Demolition debris		
-	523	Chalk deposit		
-	524	Pit cut		
2.2	526	Wall	19, 20, 21, 22	
-	527	Wall foundation		
2.4	528	Loam deposit	18, 21	PM 5:18; Brick (3); Iron A467, A758; Tile (5)
2.4	529	Hillwash	21	
2.1	532	Pebble surface	21	
-	533	? C20 feature		
2.1	534	Drainage ditch	17, 18, 19	Med. 1:1
2.4	535	Drainage ditch fill	18	PM 2:4; Brick (1)
-	536	Rut/gully		
-	537	Gully fill		
2.1	538	Pebble surface	18, 19	Tile (4)
-	541	Pit cut		
2.4	542	Topsoil	18	Iron A762; An. (1)
-	543	Road debris		Brick (2)
2.4	544	Clay loam/cart rut	18, 21	PM 5:76; Tile (4); Vess. (20)
2.1	545	Cobble surface bedding		
1	546	Clay loam & chalk deposit	18	Brick (1)
2.4	549	Hillwash		
-	550	Clay & chalk deposit		
-	551	Pit fill		
-	552	Natural bedrock	17	
-	553	Number for box section		Med. 5:22; Tile (1); Coal 1g; Slag 2g
-	554	C20 pit and fill		
-	556	Part of 540		Tile (3)
-	557	Loam & chalk deposit		Med. 6:31; PM 1:29; Coal 2g; Slag 58g

Phase	Context	Description	Fig. Nos	Artefacts and environmental remains
2.4	558	Demolition debris	18, 21	PM 48:283; Cp (1); Lst. A610; Tile (10); Vess. (2); Cin. 9g
2.3	559	Floor surface	18, 21, 21	
2.3	560	Seating for upright timber	21	
2.1	561	Post-pipe fill	19, 21	Iron A690, A763; Wood A41
2.1	562	Post-pipe fill	17, 18, 19, 21	Wood A42
2.2	563	Floor level	18, 19, 20	Med. 25:78; Brick (1); Tile (14); An. (4); BS; Char. 6g; Cin. 1g; Coal 7g
2.2	564	Post-hole		Iron A162; Vess. (11)
2.1	565	Chalk surface	18, 19	PM 1:1; Iron A286; Tile (6); Vess. (1); An. (21)
2.1	566	Fill of wall trench	19	Med. 1:6; Brick (4); Mortar
2.1	567=473 =514=518 =519=525 =571	Wall		
2.3	568	Surface	21, 22	
2.4	569	Layer		PM 7:233; Cp (2); Iron A1193; Tile (2); Vess. (13); Coal 1g; Plas.
2.3	570	Cart rut		
2.1	571=473 =514=518 =519=525 =567	Wall		
2.3	572	Cobbled surface		
2.2	573	Anchorage for wall partition	19	
2.1	574=500 =601=603	Foundation trench		
2.2	575	Rubble dump	20	
2.3	578	Wall tumble	22	
-	579	No context information		Vess. (2); Wood A43
	580-81	Unused context		
2.1	582	No context information		
	583	Unused context		
2.1	584=594	Foundation trench fill		Med. 1:58
2.2	585	Flint cobble path	19, 21	Tile (4); An. (1)
2.3	586	Gully fill		Med. 1:10; Iron 6; Tile (1); Vess. (1); An. (1)
2.1	588=830	Pebble surface		
2.1	589	Sandstone flagging	17	Med. 1:3; Iron A902, A1085; Tile (15); An. (20); Cin. ≤1g
2.1	590	Post-hole fill		
2.1	591	Post-hole		
2.1	592=663	Worn surface		
2.2	593	Gully fill		Copper A956; Cp (1); Iron A1031; Tile (10); Vess. (1); An. (4); Cin. 2g; Coal 2g
2.1	594=584	Foundation trench fill		Iron A392, A950, A1078; Vess. (2)
2.1	595=835	Foundation trench	17, 18	
2.2	596	Pit fill	18	Brick (4); Iron A764; An. (2); Cin. 3g; Coal 3g
2.2	597	Pit		
	598	Unused context		
	599	Unused context		
2.1	600	Gully fill		Vess. (1)
2.1	601=500 =574=603	Foundation trench		
2.1	602	Gully fill		Copper A141; Tile (1); An. (71); Cin. 6g; Mortar
2.1	603=500 =574=601	Foundation trench		
2.1/2.2	604	Post-pipe		
2.1/2.2	605	Support for wall partition	19	
2.1	606	Loam and stone deposit	17, 18	PM 1:1; Iron A235; An. (2)
-	607	No context information		
	608	Unused context		
2.1	609	Gully fill	18	Med. 11:68; PM 1:58; Brick (8); Stone A91; An. (4); Cin. 9g; Fish; Mortar
2.1/2.2	610	Post-pipe fill		
2.1/2.2	611	Post-pipe	19	Tile (2); An. (1)
2.1/2.2	612	Post-pit packing		Tile (3); An. (1)
2.1/2.2	613	Post-pit	19	
2.1/2.2	614	Post-pipe fill		Brick (4); Mortar
2.1/2.2	615	Post-pipe void fill	19	
2.2	616	? Post-hole fill		Brick (1); Tile (12)
2.2	617	? Post-hole		
2.2	618	Post-pipe fill		Wood A44
2.2	619	Post-pipe void	19	
2.1	620	Post-pipe fill		
2.1/2.2	621	Post-pipe void		

Phase	Context	Description	Fig. Nos	Artefacts and environmental remains
2.1	622	Floor repair	18, 19	Med. 1:2; An. (3)
-	623	Post-hole fill		
-	624	Post/stake/rat-hole		
2.2	625	Post-pipe fill		
2.2	626	Post in partition wall	19	
2.2	627	? Turf layer		
2.1	628	Post-pipe fill		
2.1/2.2	629	Post-pipe void	19	
2.1	630	Post-pipe void fill		
2.1/2.2	631	Post-pipe void	19	
2.1/2.2	632	Post-pipe void	19	Brick (1)
2.1/2.2	633	Post-pipe void fill		
2.2	634	Wall partition	19	Rom. 1:24
2.1/2.2	635	Post-pipe void fill		
2.1/2.2	636	Post-pipe void	19	
2.1	637	Stake-hole fill		
2.1	638	? Stake-hole		
2.1/2.2	639	Stake-hole fill		
2.1/2.2	640	Stake-hole	19	
2.1	641	Post-pipe fill		
2.1	642	Post-pipe void		
	643	Unused context		
-	644	No context information		Med. 19:242; Quern 28; Roof. A798; Tile (1)
	645-647	Unused context		
2.1	648	Post-hole/post-pipe fill		Iron A1194
2.1	649	Post-pipe void		
	650-7	Unused context		
-	658	?Pit/post-hole		
	659	Unused context		
-	660	Surface		
-	661	Interface		Iron A765, A1195
2.1	662	Post-packing fill		
2.1	663=592	Chalk & pea-grit surface		Copper A284; Iron A1086
Nat.	664	Bedrock/natural		
-	665	No context information		PM 1:2
	666	Unused context		
-	667	No context information		Wood A45
-	668	?Pit/post-hole		
	669-74	Unused context		
-	675	?Pit/post-hole		
	676-9	Unused context		
2.1	680=703	Post-pipe packing		
-	681	Post-hole		
-	682	Fill		Brick (1)
-	683	No context information		Med. 5:42
2.1	684	Wall		
2.1	685	Post-pipe void		
2.1	686	Post-pipe void		
2.1	687	Post-packing		
2.1	688	Post-pit		
-	689	Natural bedrock		
2.1	690=723	Gully	17, 18	
2.1	691	Gully fill		Copper A894; Quern A117; Roof. A799; Stone A48; Tile (8); Coal ≤1g; Mortar
2.1	692=727	Gully	17, 18	
2.2	693	Chalk pebble floor	19	Iron A1034
2.1	694	Post-pit fill		
2.1	695	Post-hole packing		Brick (3); An. (7); Burnt (4)
2.1	696	Post-pit	17	
2.1	697	Gully fill		
2.1	698=725	Gully	17, 18	
2.1	699	Gully fill		Tile (3); An. (1); Cin. 19g
2.1	700	Gully	17, 18	
2.1	701	Gully fill		Med. 1:2
2.1	702	Gully	17, 18	
2.1	703=680	Post-packing		
2.1	704	Post-pit		
-	705	Post-pipe void fill		
-	706	Post-pipe void		
2.1	707=728	Post-pit (708) fill		
2.1	708	Post-pit		

Phase	Context	Description	Fig. Nos	Artefacts and environmental remains
2.1	709	Post-pit	17	
2.1	710	Post-pit fill		
2.1	711	Post-pit	17	
2.1	712	Post-pit fill		
2.1	713	Post-pit	17	
2.1	714	Post-pit fill		
2.1	715	Post-pit		
2.1	716	Post-packing		
2.1	717	Post-pit		
2.1	718	Post-pipe fill		
2.1	719	Post-pipe void	17, 18	
2.1	720	Post-pit packing	18	
2.1	721	Post-pit	17	
2.1	722	Post-hole fill		
2.1	723=690	Post-pit		
2.1	724	Post-hole fill		
2.1	725=698	Post hole		
2.1	726	Post-hole fill		
2.1	727=692	Post-hole		
2.1	728=707	Post-hole in larger post-hole		
-	729	Post-hole fill		
2.1	730	Post-pipe fill		
2.1	731	Post-pipe void	17, 18	
	732	Unused context		
-	733	Chalk & sandstone rubble		Sst. A220
-	734	No context information		Tile (1)
-	735	Pit/post-hole		
	736	Unused context		
-	737	No context information		Med. 1:23
	738	Unused context		
2.1	739	Gully fill		Med. 1:10
2.1	740=476	Gully	17, 18	
	741	Unused context		
	742	Unused context		
-	743	Pit/post-hole		
	744	Unused context		
-	745	No context information		Brick (1); Roof. A800; Tile (4)
-	746	Pit/post-hole		
-	747	No context information		Med. 1:5; Sst. A221
-	748	Pit/post-hole		
-	749	No context information		Med. 2:9
-	750	No context information		Rom. 1:41; Med. 3:13
-	751	No context information		Vess. (1)
-	752	Pit/post-hole		
	753-754	Unused context		
-	755	No context information		Med. 7:29; Copper A957; Sst. A222; Burnt (1)
-	756	No context information		Sst. A223
	757-758	Unused context		
-	759	Pit/post-hole		
	760-2	Unused context		
-	763	Pit/post-hole		
-	764	No context information		Med. 1:11
	765	Unused context		
-	766	Pit/post-hole		
-	767	No context information		Med. 4:26; Roof. A801, A802
	768	Unused context		
-	769	Pit/post-hole		
-	770	No context information		Med. 1:1; Tile (1)
-	771	Pit/post-hole		
-	772	No context information		Med. 14:141; PM 1:1; Copper A996
	773-74	Unused context		
-	775	Pit/post-hole		
	776	Unused context		
-	777	Pit/post-hole		
-	778	Pit/post-hole		Med. 8:51; Brick (1)
	779-780	Unused context		
-	781	No context information		Med. 1:7; Iron A189
-	782	No context information		Lst. A611; Roof. A803; Sst. A224-226
-	783	No context information		PM 2:102; Coal 2g
-	784	No context information		Med. 2:3; Sst. A227
	785	Unused context		

Phase	Context	Description	Fig. Nos	Artefacts and environmental remains
-	786	No context information		Lst. A612, A613; Roof. A804-806
-	787	No context information		Med. 1:24; Coal 42g
	788	Unused context		
-	789	No context information		Med. 1:9
	790-793	Unused context		
-	794	No context information		Coal 1g
	795-799	Unused context		
2.3	800	Floor make-up	18, 19	Med. 4:13; Brick (1); Vess. (2); Cin. 20g; Coal -g
-	801	Interface layer		Iron A497, A1063, A1158
2.1	802	Gully fill		
2.1	803	Gully	17, 18	
-	804	? Topsoil		Med. 25:116; Wood A119; Cin. 7g
-	805	Demolition debris		
-	806	Blocked/raised doorway		
-	807	Drain/?central soak-away		
-	808	Limestone cobbles		
-	809	Wall		
-	810	Fill of 811		
-	811	Cut of feature		
2.1	812	Post-hole		
2.1	813	Post-hole fill		
-	814	Undefined depression		
-	815	Fill of 814		
	816	Unused context		
-	817	Post-pipe fill		
	818	Unused context		
-	819	Sandy fill		Lst. A614-625; Tile (10)
2.1	820	Post-hole		
2.1	821	Post-hole fill		
2.1	822	Post-hole		
2.1	823	Post-hole fill		
2.1	824	Post/stake-hole		
2.1	825	Post/stake-hole fill		
2.1	826	Post-hole		
2.1	827	Post-hole fill		
2.1	828	Post-hole		
2.1	829	Post-hole fill		
2.1	830=588	Flint surface	17, 19, 20	
2.1	831	Drainage gully	17, 19, 20	
2.2	832	Foundation trench		
2.3	833	Pit fill		
2.2	834	Pit		
2.1	835=595	Foundation trench		
2.1	836	Post/stake-hole	18, 19	
2.1	837	Post/stake-hole fill		
2.1	838	Post-hole		
2.1	839	Post-hole fill		
2.1	840	Post-hole		
2.1	841	Post-hole fill		
2.1	842	Post-hole		
2.1	843	Post-hole fill		
2.1	844	Post-hole		
2.1	845	Post-hole fill		
2.1	846	Post-hole		
2.1	847	Post-hole fill		
2.1	848	Post/stake-hole		
2.1	849	Post/stake-hole fill		
2.1	850	Post/stake-hole		
2.1	851	Post/stake-hole fill		
2.1	852	Post/stake-hole		
2.1	853	Post/stake-hole fill		
2.1	854	Post-hole		
2.1	855	Post-hole fill		
-	856	Post-hole		
-	857	Post-hole fill		
	858-867	Unused context		
-	868	No context information		Med. 1:3
	869-870	Unused context		
-	871	No context information		Sst. A228-235
	872-875	Unused context		
-	876	No context information		Brick (2); Roof. A807

Phase	Context	Description	Fig. Nos	Artefacts and environmental remains
	877-878	Unused context		
-	879	No context information		Med. 8:56; Lst. A723; Sst. A236
2.2	880	Post-hole	19	
2.2	881	Post-hole fill		
-	882	No context information		Med. 3:12; Coal 1g
	883-886	Unused context		
-	887	Clay dump		Med. 1:36
-	888	Post-hole		
-	889	Post-hole fill		
-	890	Post-pipe		
-	891	Post-pipe fill		
2.1	892	Post-pipe	17	
2.1	893	Post-pipe fill		
Mod.	894	Stake-hole		
Mod.	895	Stake-hole fill		
Mod.	896	Stake-hole		
Mod.	897	Stake-hole fill		
2.1	898	Post-pipe		
2.1	899	Post-pipe fill		
Mod.	900	Stake-hole		
Mod.	901	Stake-hole fill		
Mod.	902	Post-pipe		
Mod.	903	Post-pipe fill		
2.1	904	Stake-hole		
2.1	905	Stake-hole fill		Med. 1:6
2.1	906	Stake-hole	17	
2.1	907	Stake-hole fill		
2.1	908	Stake-hole	17	
2.1	909	Stake-hole fill		
2.1	910	Stake-hole	17	
2.1	911	Stake-hole fill		
-	912	Chalk slot depression		
-	913	Brown soil deposit		
2.1	914	Post-pipe	17	
2.1	915	Post-pipe fill		Tile (4); An. (1)
2.1	916	Post-pipe	17	
-	917	Post-pipe fill		
2.1	918	Post-pipe	17	
-	919	Post-pipe fill		
2.1	920	Post-hole	17	
2.1	921	Post-hole fill		Tile (2)
2.1	922	Post-hole	17	
2.1	923	Post-hole fill		Med. 1:6; PM 3:4; Iron A766
2.1	924	Post-hole	17	
2.1	925	Post-hole fill		
2.1	926	Post-hole	17	
2.1	927	Post-hole fill		
-	928	Stake-hole		
-	929	Stake-hole fill		
2.1	930	Stake-hole	17	
2.1	931	Stake-hole fill		
2.1	932	Foundation trench		
2.1	933	Foundation trench fill		Med. 8:43; Copper A285
2.1	934	Post-hole	17	
2.1	935	Post-hole fill		PM 6:8; Tile (6)
-	936	Post-pipe		
-	937	Post-pipe fill		
-	938	Post-pipe		
-	939	Post-pipe fill		
2.1	940	Post-pipe	17	
2.1	941	Post-pipe fill		Tile (1)
2.1	942	Post-hole	17	
2.1	943	Post-hole fill		
-	944	Mortar deposit		Wood A46
2.1	945	Stake-hole	17	
2.1	946	Stake-hole fill		
2.1	947	Stake-hole	17	
2.1	948	Stake hole-fill		
2.1	949	Stake-hole		
2.1	950	Stake-hole fill		
-	951	Chalk deposit		

Phase	Context	Description	Fig. Nos	Artefacts and environmental remains
	952-953	Unused context		
-	954	No context information		Char. ≤1g
-	955	No context information		Med. 1:2
-	956	No context information		Roof. A808
	957-958	Unused context		
-	959	No context information		Sst. A237
	960-963	Unused context		
-	964	No context information		Med. 1:2; Iron A660; Slag 6g
	965-975	Unused context		
2.1	976	Stake-hole		Rom. 2:15; An. (1)
2.1	977	Stake-hole fill		
2.1	978	Stake-hole	17	
2.1	979	Stake-hole fill		
2.1	980	Stake-hole	17	
2.1	981	Stake-hole fill		
2.1	982	Stake-hole	17	
2.1	983	Stake-hole fill		
2.1	984	Clay & chalk pebble surface	17	Med. 2:21; PM 1:1; Roof. A1492; An. (3)
2.1	985	Chalk surface	17	
1	986	Clay & chalk deposit		Rom. 1:3; Med. 30:277 (64); An. (9); Slag 6g
2.2	987	Wall foundation trench		
-	988	Foundation trench fill		Brick (2); Quern A118; Tile (1)
-	989	Post-pit		
-	990	Post-pipe packing fill		Brick (8); Iron A997
-	991	Loam and brick deposit		Sst. A238; Coal 14g
	992-999	Unused context		
-	1000	No context information		PM 60:888; Copper A710; Tile (1); Vess. (2)
-	1001	No context information		PM 2:12; Plas.
	1002-1021	Unused context		
-	1022	Rubble fill		Med. 1:2
-	1023	Burnt area		
-	1024	Chalk pebble surface		
1	1025	Post-pit	16	
-	1026	Post-pit packing		
-	1027	Post-hole		
-	1028	Post-hole fill		
2.4	1029	Post-hole		
Mod.	1030	Post-hole fill		
1	1031	Make up layer		Rom. 1:5; Med. 13:114; Stone 15; Tile (1); An. (5); Coal 8g
1	1032	Chalk rubble deposit		
2.1	1033	Foundation trench	16	
2.1	1034	Foundation trench fill		Med. 12:77; Brick (5); Coin med. 9; Tile (12); An. (2); Cin. 8g; Slag 124g
1	1035	Feature cut		
1	1036	Rubble deposit		Med. 48:597 (2, 6, 18); Iron 27; Lst. A626, A627; Quern A119; Sst. A239; An. (19); Char. ≤1g; Slag 9g
1	1037	Gully	16, 20	
1	1038	Linear feature fill	18	Rom. 1:7; Bone 6; Roof. A1493; Char. 1g
1	1039	Clay & chalk pebble deposit	18	
1	1040	Wall tumble/rubble	16	Med. 25:117; Iron 84, 101, 115; Quern A120; Roof. A1494; Stone A49; An. (19); BS; Coal 1g
2.2	1041	Foundation trench		
2.2	1042	Foundation trench fill		Med. 1:14
1	1043	Wall	16	
1	1044	Burnt surface layer	16	Med. 8:58; Roof. A809; An. (3)
2.2	1045	Foundation trench		
2.2	1046	Foundation trench fill		
2.2	1047	Foundation trench		
2.2	1048	Foundation trench fill		Lst. A628; Tile (2)
2.2	1049=246	Foundation trench		
2.2	1050	Foundation trench fill		
1	1051	Linear feature		
1	1052	Linear feature fill		Med. 1:28 (8)
1	1053	Make up layer		
1	1054	? Chalk surface	16, 20	Med. 3:5; An. (2); Cin. ≤1g; Fish
1	1055	Gully	16	
1	1056	Linear feature fill		Med. 3:9; An. (2); Fish
1	1057	Wall/robber trench	16	
1	1058	Pea-grit deposit		Bone 4; An. (4)
1	1059	Linear feature	16	
1	1060	Linear feature fill	16	PM 1:87; An. (1)

Phase	Context	Description	Fig. Nos	Artefacts and environmental remains
1	1061	Chalk rubble fill		Rom. 1:21; Med. 1:6; Iron A1196; Quern A121; Sst. A240; An. (6); Slag 41g
2.1	1062	Robber trench fill	16	Med. 7:39; Iron A1197; Lst. A629; Sst. A241, A242; An. (1); Char. ≤1g
1	1063	Clay & pebble deposit		
1	1064	Unexcavated feature	16, 20	
1	1065	Unexcavated feature fill		
Nat.	1066	Terraced/levelled chalk natural	16	
1	1067	Pad-stone	16	
-	1068	No context information		
u/s	9000	Unstratified		PM -:- (50); Brick (1); Iron A1273; Vess. (8)

North Range

Phase	Context	Description	Fig. Nos	Artefacts and environmental remains
-	509	Pit cut		
-	510	Pit fill		
2.4	511	Brick path	19	
2.4	512	Chalk edging		
2.1	513	Clay loam deposit	22	Med. 6:70; Brick (3); Iron A1268; Stone 6; Tile (5); An. (5)
2.1	525=473 =514=518 =519=567 =571	Wall foundation (renumbering of 514)		
1	530	Paving/wall		Sst. A217, A218
1	531	Hearth		
2.2	539	? Rubble layer	22	Med. 16:53; PM 45:349; Brick (2); Cp (1); Iron A156, A188, A256, A354, A449, A450, A635, A709, A759-761, A1269, A1432; Sst. A219; Tile (13); Vess. (2); An. (7); Coal 34g; Fish; Slag 53g
2.1	540	Pebble surface	23	Med. 2:11; Coin pm 32; Tile (21); An. (4)
1	547	Deposit	23	Med. 1:2; Iron A520, A982, A1270, A1271
2.1	548	Silty loam deposit		Med. 57:377; Copper A1038; Iron 9, 26, A545, A1139, A1192, A1272; Roof. A796, A797; An. (20); Char. 1g; Cin. 6g; Coal 3g
1	555=472 =46	Pebble surface	23	
2.1	576	Wall	22, 23	
2.1	577	Robber trench (cut & fill)	22	
2.2	587	Wall core		Med. 1:2; Brick (1); Tile (5); An. (1)

East Range

Phase	Context	Description	Fig. Nos	Artefacts and environmental remains
Mod.	1=100	C20 landscaping material		Med. 63:471; PM 424:2096 (64); Brick (1); Clay A14; Coin pm 9; Copper 32, 67, A257; Cp 42 (7); Glass A217; Iron A313, A369, A387, A505, A745, A746, A1247-1249, A1404, A1405; Roof. A1487; Tile (28); Vess. (10); Cin. 22g Coal 19g
Mod.	2	Rubble deposit		Med. 39:204; PM 2:69; Bone 33; Brick (2); Cp 40 (1); Iron 5, A620; Lst. A728; Tile (5); Vess. (6); Wood A125; Cin. 6g; Coal 2g
-	3	Post-hole		
-	4	Post-hole fill		Coin pm 44
-	5	Post-hole		Roof. A1488
-	6	Post-hole fill		Coin pm 19
-	7	Post-hole		Wood A11
-	8	Post-hole fill		Med. 1:1; PM 8:151; Tile (1); Vess. (23); Mortar; Plas.
-	8/9			PM 1:2
-	9	Cobbled surface		
-	10	Chalk deposit		
-	11	Mortar surface		
- (ER)	12	Post-hole		
-	13	Post-packing		
-	14	Post-hole fill		
2 (ER)	15=141	Wall foundation		
-	16=35?	Wall		
-	17	Wall core		
-	18	Chalk deposit		
-	19	Road surface		
-	20	Edging stones		PM 1:19
-	21	Rubble deposit		
-	22	Brick path		
-	23	Natural/weathered surface		Coin Rom. 19
-	24	Wall core make-up		
-	25	Cobble surface		

Phase	Context	Description	Fig. Nos	Artefacts and environmental remains
-	26	? Interior wall face/worn threshold		
2.4	27	Subsoil		Brick (3); Iron A122, A980, A1172, A1406; Tile (4); Char. 3g
2.3	28	Destruction debris/make-up		Brick (6); Char. 26g
-	29=31?	Post-hole		
-	30	Post-hole fill		
-	31=29?	Post-hole		
-	32	Post-hole fill		
2 (ER)	33	Wall/worn path		
2 (ER)	34	Cobble surface		Med. 3:13; PM 25:180; Tile (5); Vess. (1); An. (1); Cin. 1g
-	35=16?	Wall		Med. 7:111; Brick (8); Tile (1)
-	36=494 =496	? Double post-hole		
-	37	Post-hole fill		PM 23:41
-	38	Wall		
-	39	Wall extension		
Mod.	40	C20 pit		Med. 1:4; PM 11:74; Brick (1); Iron A241, A317, A678, A1035, A1407; Roof. A1520; Vess. (8); Wood A12; Cin. 2g
Mod.	41	C20 pit fill		
-	42=44?	Chalk surface		
-	43	Clay/chalk deposit		
-	44=42?	Chalk surface		
2.1	45=477?	Mortar surface		PM 7:7; Brick (4)
1	46=472 =555	Surface		
-	47	Rubble		Med. 16:200 (14)
-	48	Faced chalk stone		
Mod.	49	C20 pit		
-	50	Flint & brick surface		
Mod.	51	Feature		
-	52	Chalk & mortar deposit		
-	53	Chalk pebble deposit		
-	54	Burnt area		
-	55	Shallow pit		
-	56	Pit fill		
-	57	Rubble layer/make-up		
-	58	Cobbles/make-up layer		
-	59	Gravel/make-up layer		
-	60	Post-hole fill		
-	61	Post-hole		PM 1:10
-	62	Post-hole packing		
-	63	Gravel/make-up layer		
-	64	Double post-hole		
-	65	Post-hole fill		
-	66	Chalk pebbles/make-up layer		
-	67	? Robber trench cut		
-	68	Robber trench fill		
	69	Unused context		
	70	Unused context		
-	71	? Edge		
Mod.	72	Garden soil layer		Med. 1:3; PM 29:1025 (47); Clay A15; Copper A884, A920, A948, A978, A979; Cp (2); Iron A242, A318-320, A363, A364, A676, A747, A1036, A1045, A1173-1175, A1250-1252, A1408-1412; Tile (2); Vess. (20)
-	73	Wall		PM 7:33; Tile (1); Coal 11g
Mod.	74	Garden soil layer		PM 7:550; Bone 62; Copper A921; Glass A173; Iron A351, A367, A566, A748, A891, A892, A1253; Sst. A206; Tile (9); Vess. (1); Cin. ≤1g; Mortar
-	75	Disturbed natural		
-	76	Building foundation		
-	77	Wall footing		
-	78	Demolition/construction debris		
	79	No context information		Coal 26g
	80-99	Unused context		
Mod.	100=1	C20 landscaping material		Med. 35:333; PM 267:2434 (48, 49); Brick (67); Cp 41, 44 (5); Copper 36, A128, A137, A258, A260, A885-888, A993, A1031; Glass A174-176, A190-192; Iron 8, 16, A123-126, A142, A232, A243-245, A260, A261, A264, A280, A294, A388, A389, A439-A443, A488, A489, A493, A506, A600-602, A621-623, A657, A677-681, A749-751, A893-895, A989, A990, A1156, A1157, A1176-1178, A1413-1418; Roof. A781, A1521-1523; Sst. A573; Stone A87-89; Tile (46); Vess. (236); Wood A13, A14, A118, A122, A127; BS; Burnt (2); Char. 19g; Cin. 51g; Coal 135g; Mortar

Phase	Context	Description	Fig. Nos	Artefacts and environmental remains
-	101=112?	Make-up layer		
Mod.	102	Post-hole		
Mod.	103=105	C20 pit		
Mod.	104=106	C20 pit fill		Med. 11:112; PM 136:2919; Cp (1); Iron A233, A624; Tile (5); Vess. (35)
Mod.	105=103	C20 pit		
Mod.	106=104	C20 pit fill		
Mod.	107	Cess pit		
Mod.	108	Cess pit fill		
Mod.	109	C20 post		
Mod.	110	C20 post		
Mod.	111	Group context number		
-	112=101?	? Vault of deep plough		Iron A1419
Mod.	113	Post-hole		
Mod.	114	Garden path		
	115	Pit		
	116	Pit fill		
Mod.	117	C20 post-hole		
-	118	Post-hole fill		
-	119	Post		
Mod.	120	C20 post-hole		
-	121	Feature		
-	122	Fill		
- (ER)	123	Post- hole fill		
- (ER)	124	Post-hole		
- (ER)	125	Post- hole fill		
- (ER)	126	Post-hole		
- (ER)	127	Post- hole fill		
- (ER)	128	Post-hole		
- (ER)	129	Post- hole fill		
- (ER)	130	Post-hole		
- (ER)	131	Post- hole fill		
- (ER)	132	Post-hole		
- (ER)	133	Post-hole packing		
- (ER)	134	Post-hole		
- (ER)	135	Post- hole fill		
- (ER)	136	Post-hole		
- (ER)	137	Post- hole fill		
- (ER)	138	Post-hole		
- (ER)	139	Post- hole fill		
- (ER)	140	Post-hole		
2 ((ER))	141=15	Wall	24	Iron A161, A444; Vess. (1)
- (ER)	142	Post-hole		
- (ER)	143	Post- hole fill		
- Mod.	144	C20 cat burial		
- Mod.	145	Post- hole fill		PM 2:8
- (ER)	146	Post-hole		
- (ER)	147=149	Post-hole fill		
- (ER)	148	Post mould		
- (ER)	149=147	Post-hole fill		
- (ER)	150	Post-hole	24	
- (ER)	151	Post-hole fill		
2 (ER)	152	Flint surface	24	Brick (2); Iron A1420; Tile (10); Wood A15; An. (13); Cin. 11g
2 (ER)	152/153			An. (2); Cin. 8g
2 (ER)	153	Surface	24	Med. 2:57; Tile (2); An. (2)
- (ER)	154	Robber trench fill		Med. 2:29; PM 1:2; Tile (5); Mortar; Plas.
- (ER)	155	? Pit		
- (ER)	156	? Pit fill		
Mod.	157	Post-hole		
Mod.	158	Post-hole fill		
- (ER)	159	Post-hole		Brick (2); Tile (10); Wood A16
- (ER)	160	Post-hole fill		
- (ER)	161	Post-hole		
- (ER)	162	Post hole mould		
- (ER)	163	Post-hole fill		
2 (ER)	164	? Floor	24	
- (ER)	165	Post-hole		
- (ER)	166	Post-hole fill		
- (ER)	167	Post-hole		
-	168	? Fill		
- (ER)	169	Post-hole		
- (ER)	170	Post-hole		

Phase	Context	Description	Fig. Nos	Artefacts and environmental remains
- (ER)	171	Post-hole fill		
- (ER)	172=182	Post-hole fill		
- (ER)	173	Post-hole		
- (ER)	174	Post-hole fill		
- (ER)	175	Robber trench		
- (ER)	176	Post-hole		
- (ER)	177	Post-hole fill		
- (ER)	178	? Scoop/post-hole		
- (ER)	179	Post-hole fill		
Mod.	180	? Cat burial		
Mod.	181	C20 cat burial		
- (ER)	182=172	Pit fill		
- (ER)	183	Post mould	24	
-	184	Post mould fill		
-	185	Post-hole		
-	186	Post packing		Med. 1:6; Cin. 3g
- (ER)	187	Post-hole		
-	188	Post-hole		
	189	Unused context		
- (ER)	190	Post-hole		
- (ER)	191	Post-hole fill		
-	192	Stake-hole		
-	193	Stake-hole		
- (ER)	194	Post-hole		
- (ER)	195	Post-hole fill		
- (ER)	196	Levelling material		
- (ER)	197	Chalk pebble deposit		
- (ER)	198	Chalk surface		
- (ER)	199	? Pad stone/step		
- (ER)	200	Group context		Copper A271
Mod.	201	C20 turf layer		PM 6:72; Copper 47, 65, 92, A272, A949; Cp (1); Iron 128, A127, A1421; Roof. A782; Tile (6)
Mod.	202=210	Garden soil layer		Med. 2:70; PM 207:852; Brick (9); Copper A261, A742, A867, A889, A922, A950; Cp 47 (7); Glass A199, A214; Iron A129, A130, A131, A143, A295, A321, A357, A494, A507, A534, A682-684, A752, A991, A1037, A1083, A1179, A1180, A1254, A1422; Lst. A729; Roof. A783, A784, A1489, A1490, A1524; Tile (16); Vess. (174); Wood A17; Cin. 6g; Coal 9g; Plas.
Mod.	203	Cat skeleton		
Mod.	204	Cat skeleton		Med. 1:3; PM 5:27; Copper A923; Cp (1); Vess. (2)
Mod.	205	Cat skeletons		
Mod.	206	Cat skeleton		
Mod.	207	Cat skeleton		
- (Ctyard)	208	Demolition debris		Med. 1:8; PM 1:8; Copper A924; Cin. 4g
Mod.	209	C20 rubbish deposit		Med. 2:20; PM 115:624; Brick (3); Copper A714, A715, A925, A951; Cp (2); Iron 44, A144, A432, A445, A590, A625, A626, A658, A685, A896, A1038, A1181, A1423; Vess. (51); Wood A18; Char. 2g; Coal 3g
Mod.	210=202	C20 garden soil layer		
- (Ctyard)	211	Soil accumulation		Med. 6:25; PM 54:267; Brick (13); Copper A683, A926; Cp (5); Glass A200; Iron A246, A446, A603, A686; Lst. A593, A730; Roof. A1525; Stone 12, A181; Vess. (9); Char. 2g; Cin. 10g; Coal 4g; Plas.
Mod.	212	Cat skeleton		Cin. 2g
Mod.	213	Cat skeleton		
-	214	Site clean-up material		
2.3	215	Demolition debris		Brick (7); Vess. (1); An. (6)
Mod.	216	Cat skeleton		
Mod.	217	Cat skeleton		
Mod.	218	Demolition debris		PM 4:7; Copper A927; Iron A1255; Vess. (1)
2.4	219=220	Stony loam deposit		PM 2:2; Iron A1256; Vess. (5); Wood A19
2.4	220=219	Stony loam deposit		
1	221=225	Rubble layer		
2.4	222	Wall demolition layer		
2.4	223	Demolition deposit		PM 6:11; Brick (6); Copper A928; Lst. A735
-	224	Chalky loam deposit		Med. 3:13; Sst. A207; Mortar
1	225=221	Rubble layer		Med. 2:35; PM 2:4; Tile (1); Vess. (12); An. (2)
-	226	Demolition debris		Med. 2:4; Lst. A594
-	227	Wall/wall tumble		Brick (2); Iron A1257
2.1	228	Chalky loam deposit		Med. 3:9; PM 2:3; Wood A20; An. (7); Cin. 2g
2.1	229	Chalky loam deposit		Med. 6:20; Lst. A595, A736; Sst. A208; An. (8)
- Mod.	230	Cat skeleton		
- Mod.	231	Cat skeleton		

Phase	Context	Description	Fig. Nos	Artefacts and environmental remains
2.2	232	Wall		
1	233=243	Rough surfacing deposit		Med. 13:97; PM 3:32; Brick (11); Iron A947; Lst. A596-601; Roof. A785, A786; Sst. A209; Tile (27); Vess. (2); An. (30); Coal 2g
1	234	? Solution hole		
-	235	Fill of 234		Med. 1:5
1	236	? Post-hole		
1	237	Post-hole fill		Med. 1:4; Brick (8); Iron A753, A897; Tile (16); An. (2); Coal 9g
Mod.	238	Cat skeletons		
Mod.	239	Cat skeleton		
1	240	Unexcavated yard surface/ levelling material		
-	241	Wall make-up		
-	242	Wall make-up		
1	243=233	Rough surfacing deposit		Lst. A602, A603; Sst. A210-213; Tile (47)
1	244	Post-hole		
1	245	Post-hole fill		
2.2	246=1049	Foundation trench		
	247	Unused context		
-	248	Fence posts		
- (ER)	249	C20 fence post		
- (ER)	250	Fence post		
- (ER)	251	C20 fence post		
- (ER)	252	Gate post		
- (ER)	253	Gate post		
- (ER)	254	Fence post		
- (ER)	255	Fence post		
- ER)	256	Fence post		
- (ER)	257	Fence post		
- (ER)	258	Fence post		
- (ER)	259	Fence post		
- (ER)	260	Fence post		
- (ER)	261	Fence post		Med. 3:9; PM 4:22; Brick (3); Tile (1); Cin. 2g
- (ER)	262	Fence post		Vess. (109)
3 (ER)	263	Bank		Med. 2:11; PM 31:385; Brick (3); Copper 6, A716; Iron A462, A543, A1029, A1258; Roof. A787, A788; Tile (2); An. (17); Mortar
3 (ER)	264	Demolition debris/make-up		Med. 8:79; PM 120:2718 (43-45, 46 pt); Brick (10); Clay (5); Copper 5, A129, A138, A711, A952; Cp (1); Glass A177, A193; Iron 14, A247, A248, A365, A447, A491, A544, A687, A981, A1061, A1259, A1260; Tile (14); Vess. (12); An. (87); Burnt (1); Cin. 3g; Coal 5g; Plas.
- (ER)	265	Water pipe	22, 24	Copper A953; Vess. (64)
- (ER)	266	Water pipe trench fill		
2 (ER)	267	Construction debris	24	
-	268	Post-hole		
-	269	Post-hole fill		
-	270	Post-hole		
-	271	Post-hole fill		
-	272	Post-hole		
-	273	Post-hole fill		Iron A463
- (ER)	274	Post-hole		
- (ER)	275	Post-hole fill		Copper A139
2 (ER)	276	Post-hole		
2 (ER)	277	Post-hole fill		Brick (1); Wood A21
- (ER)	278	Post-hole		
- (ER)	279	Post-hole fill		PM 1:2; Cin. 5g; Coal 6g
2 (ER)	280	Post-hole	24	
2 (ER)	281	Post-hole fill		Med. 2:4; Brick (27); Iron A1261, A1262; Lst. A604; Wood A22; Coal 10g; Plas.
- (ER)	282	? Levelling/make-up layer		
- (ER)	283	Post mould		
- (ER)	284	Post-hole fill		
- (ER)	285	Post-hole		
- (ER)	286	Post-hole fill		
- (ER)	287	Post-hole		
- (ER)	288	Post-hole fill		
- (ER)	289	Post-hole		
- (ER)	290	Post-hole fill		
- (ER)	291	Post-hole		
- (ER)	292	Post-hole fill		
2 (ER)	293	Post-hole		
2 (ER)	294	Post-hole fill		
2 (ER)	295	Post-hole		

Phase	Context	Description	Fig. Nos	Artefacts and environmental remains
2 (ER)	296	Post-hole fill		
- ER	297	Post-hole		
- ER	298	Post-hole packing		
- ER	299	Post-hole		
- ER	300=302 =305	Post-hole packing		
- ER	301	Post-hole		
- ER	302=300 =305	Post-hole packing		
2 (ER)	303	Post-hole	24	Med. 1:5; An. (1)
2 (ER)	303/312			Iron A352, A1424-1426; Wood A23; Cin. 18g; Coal 4g; Mortar
2 (ER)	304	Post-hole fill		
- ER	305=300 =302	Post packing		Brick (15); Cin. 2g; Coal 5g
2 (ER)	306	Post-hole/scoop	24	
2 (ER)	307	Post-hole fill		Brick (3)
- (ER)	308	Stake-hole		
- (ER)	309	Post-hole fill		
- (ER)	310	Post-hole		Brick (11); Quern A115; Tile (3); Char. 3g
- (ER)	311	Post-hole fill		
2 (ER)	312	Post-hole		
2 (ER)	313	Post-hole fill		
2 (ER)	314	Post-hole/scoop		
2 (ER)	315	Post-hole fill		Brick (2); Wood A24
2 (ER)	316	Post-hole mould		
2 (ER)	317	Post-hole fill		
- (ER)	318	? Levelling/make-up layer		PM 1:1
2 (ER)	319	Post-hole	24	Brick (10); An. (1)
2 (ER)	320	Post-hole fill		
- (ER)	321	Post/stake-hole		
- (ER)	322	Post-hole fill		
2 (ER)	323	Floor level	24	Rom. 1:4; Med. 11:79; PM 21:83; Brick (15); Iron A754, A898, A1427; Tile (12); Vess. (3); Wood A25; An. (30); BS; Char. 2g; Cin. 21g; Slag 73g
-	323/324	No context information		Iron A755
- (ER)	324	? Occupation surface/yard		Med. 7:40; PM 2:2; Copper A262; Iron A234, A1263; Tile (22); Wood A26; Cin. 13g; Coal 3g; Slag 11g
- (ER)	325	Post-hole		
- (ER)	326	Post-hole fill		Brick (12); Wood A27; Cin. ≤1g
- (ER)	327	Post/stake-hole		
- (ER)	328	Post-hole fill		
- (ER)	329	Post/stake-hole		
- (ER)	330	Post-hole fill		
-	331	? Destruction layer		
- (ER)	332	Post/stake-hole		
- (ER)	333	Post-hole fill		Cin. 9g
2 (ER)	334	Post-hole		
2 (ER)	335	Post-hole fill		Med. 1:3; Wood A28; An. (1)
2 (ER)	336	Post-hole	24	
2 (ER)	337	Post-hole fill		Brick (18); Wood A29; An. (2)
- (ER)	338	Post-hole		
- (ER)	339	Post-hole fill		Med. 1:4
Mod.	340	Cat skeleton		
- (ER)	341	Post/stake-hole		
Mod.	342	Post/stake-hole fill		Brick (3); Cin. 10g
Mod.	343	Cat skeleton		
-	344	Animal skeleton		Iron A250
- (Ctyard)	345	Post/stake-hole		Iron A1182; Char. 35g
- (Ctyard)	346	Post/stake-hole fill		
- (ER)	347	Post-hole	24	
- (ER)	348	Post-hole fill		Med. 3:25; PM 1:2; Brick (1); Iron A899; Vess. (23); Char. 2g; Cin. 8g
2 (ER)	349	? Plough line		
2 (ER)	350	Post-hole		
2 (ER)	351	Post-hole fill		Cin. 6g
- (ER)	352	Post-hole mould		
- (ER)	353	Post-mould fill		
- (ER)	354	Post-hole		Med. 1:10
- (ER)	355	Post-hole fill		Med. 4:6; Iron A1084; Coal 4g
- (ER)	356	Group context		
- (ER)	357	Post-hole	24	
- (ER)	358	Post-hole fill		Brick (1)
- (ER)	359	Fence line		

Phase	Context	Description	Fig. Nos	Artefacts and environmental remains
- (ER)	360	Post-hole	24	
- (ER)	361	Post-hole fill		
- (ER)	362	Post/stake-hole		
- (ER)	363	Double post-hole		Brick (5)
- (ER)	364	Post-hole fill		
- (ER)	365	Post-hole		
- (ER)	366	Post-hole fill		
2 (ER)	367	Pit	24	Brick (1); Char. 3g
2 (ER)	368	Pit fill		Med. 7:39; PM 1:3; Brick (1); Copper A890; Tile (3); Wood A30; An. (2); Cin. 2g; Mortar
-	369	? Linear slot		
2 (ER)	370	Post-hole		
2 (ER)	371	Post-hole fill		
2 (ER)	372	? Surface	24	
- (ER)	373	? Pit/well		Copper A891
- (ER)	374	Pit/well fill		Med. 1:18; PM 2: 27; Brick (5); Iron A992, A993; Sst. A574; Tile (2); Vess. (3); Wood A31; Cin. 12g; Coal 10g
- (ER)	375	? Surface		
- (ER)	376	Flint collar		
2 ((ER))	377	? Surface		Rom. 1:16; Med. 24:170 (71); Bone 17; Clay 2; Iron A360, A390, A708, A1264; Tile (4); Vess. (1); An. (10); Char. ≤1g;
- (ER)	378	? Edge		
- (ER)	379	? Roof/partition support	24	
- (ER)	380	Post-hole		
2 (ER)	381	Surface spread		
- (ER)	382	? Make-up layer		PM 1:7
2 (ER)	383	Shallow scoop		Med. 1:5; Iron A251
2 (ER)	384	Shallow scoop fill		Med. 3:6; An. (1)
-	385	Demolition debris/make-up		Med. 3:48; PM 2:28; Sst. A214, A575
	386	Unused context		
	387	No context information		Med. 5:19
-	388	? Make-up layer		
- (ER)	389	Post-hole		
- (ER)	390	Post-hole fill		Wood A32
- (ER)	391	Post-hole		
--(ER)	392	Post-hole fill		Med. 3:22; Char. 3g; Cin. 6g; Mortar
2 (ER)	393	Post-hole	24	
2 (ER)	394	Post-hole fill		An. (2); Cin. 2g
- (ER)	395	Post-hole		
- (ER)	396	Post-hole fill		
- (ER)	397	Post-hole		
- (ER)	398	Post-hole fill		
- (ER)	399	Roof/stall support	24	
- (ER)	400	Post-hole fill		
2 (ER)	401=409	Level surface		
-	402	? Layer		
- (ER)	403	Post-hole		
- (ER)	404	Post-hole fill		
- (ER)	405	Pit cut/? Beam slot		
- (ER)	406	Fill of 405		Med. 1:5; Iron 19; Char. 7g; Slag 18g
2 (ER)	407	Foundation trench	22	Med. 3:11; PM 17:99; Tile (9); Vess. (1); An. (1); Cin. 46g; Coal 1g
2 (ER)	408	Wall foundation course	22	
2 (ER)	409=401	Foundation trench fill	22	PM 1:2; Brick (11); Iron 33; Tile (35); An. (3); Cin. 22g
1 (ER)	410	Floor make-up		Med. 2:22; Brick (6); Tile (17); An. (1)
1 (ER)	411	Backfill to support wall/ ? floor levelling		Med. 20:174; Clay 6; Tile (2); Vess. (1); An. (11); Char. 1g; Cin. 2g; Coal 13g; Mortar
- (Ctyard)	412	Post-hole		
- (Ctyard)	413	Post-hole fill		Med. 3:11
- (Ctyard)	414	Post-hole		
- (Ctyard)	415	Post-hole fill		Med. 1:3; Char. ≤1g; Tile (22)
-	416	Post-hole		
-	417	Post-hole fill		
- (Ctyard)	418	Post-hole		
- (Ctyard)	419	Post-hole fill		
1 (ER)	420	? Layer		Med. 9:52; PM 1:1; An. (4); Char. 5g; Cin. 5g; Slag 17g
- (Ctyard)	421	Post-hole		
- (Ctyard)	422	Post-hole		Tile (1)
- (Ctyard)	423	Post-hole fill		
- (Ctyard)	424	Post-hole		
-	425	Post-hole fill		Med. 3:11; PM 2:3; Tile (2)
-	426	Post-hole packing		Med. 7:28; Brick (3); Vess. (1); BS

Phase	Context	Description	Fig. Nos	Artefacts and environmental remains
-	427	Loam rubble		
2 (ER)	428	Loam rubble		
2 (ER)	429	Loam rubble		
-	430	Post-hole		
-	431	Post-hole fill		Med. 1:2; Iron A971; Vess. (2)
-	432	Post-hole		
-	433	Post-hole fill		
2 (ER)	434	Post packing		
2 (ER)	435	? Post-hole mould		Burnt (1)
Mod.	436	Animal burrow		
Mod.	437	Animal burrow		
2 (ER)	438	Chalky loam		PM 1:4; Iron 24; Tile (19)
2 (ER)	439	Make-up levelling layer		
2 (ER)	440	Floor make-up		
-	441	Wall make-up layer		
Mod.	442	Root-damage tree throw		
Mod.	443	Tree throw fill		
-	444	Loam with compacted pebbles		Med. 8:33; Sst. A215; Vess. (1); Char. ≤1g
-	445	Post-hole		
-	446	Post-hole fill		Med. 3:10; Brick (5)
-	447	Post-hole		
-	448	Post-hole fill		Brick (1)
-	449	Trench		
-	450	Trench fill		PM 1:4; Brick (2); Copper A954; Wood A33; Cin. 6g
Mod.	451	Animal burrow		
2 (ER)	452	Clayey loam		
-	453	Trench fill		Med. 4:55; PM 3:12; Brick (13); Copper A955; Glass A194; Iron A756, A900, A901, A994, A995, A1265, A1428; Stone A90; Tile (38); BS; Burnt (1); Cin. 83g; Slag 54g
-	454	Trench fill		Brick (1); Iron A627
Mod.	455	C20 pipe		
-	456	Post-hole		
-	457	Post-hole fill		
-(ER)	458	Late med. backfill		
-	459	Mortar layer		
-	460	Post-hole		
-	461	Post-hole fill		Med. 1:19
-	462	Post-hole		
-	463	Post-hole fill		Brick (1); Wood A34; Cin. 24g
-	464	Post-hole packing		
-	465	Post-hole fill		

Back and front of cottages

Cottage	9000	Topsoil		PM 435:4475
General	9000	Unstratified		PM 84:1009 (54-57)

Site 55

	1	Path in north-west corner of Glebe		Copper A142
-	1	Path in north-west corner of Glebe		Copper A142
-	2	On track near cottages		Slag 9g
-	4	Garden in front of cottages		Quern A134
-	5	Unstratified find		Bone 21
-	9	Found loose in box		Copper A682
-	15	In rubble in front of cottages		Iron A370
-	17	In bank along track, w of cottages		Iron A767
-	18	Demolition debris from farmhouse		Copper A930
-	19	Found in cottages		Iron A1064
-	20	Found in cottages		Iron A1065
-	21	Found in cottages		Iron A1066
-	22	Found in cottages		Iron A1067
-	23	Found in cottages		Iron A1068
-	26	From dump between cottages and Vicarage		Stone 25
-	28	From dump between cottages and Vicarage		Vess. (1)
-	31	Material from farmhouse		Bone 16
-	32	Found in cottages		Iron A132
-	33	Garden in front of cottages		Iron A570
-	34	Bank on west of track by cottages		Iron A903
-	35	Unstratified find		Iron A364

Phase	Context	Description	Fig. Nos	Artefacts and environmental remains
-	40	Site 74 unstratified		Iron A1069
-	42	Site 74 stone heap		Stone A105
-	43	Found in cottages		Iron A1070
-	45	Found in cottages		Iron A1071
-	46	By water trough north of Site 51		Copper 88

Site 73

Phase	Context	Description	Fig. Nos	Artefacts and environmental remains
3	1 (Site 49/ 500)	Topsoil		Med. 4:137 (7, 27); PM 352:6113; Bone 35; Brick (1); Copper 44, 93, 114, A130, A143; A698, A895-896, A958; Cp (21); Glass A204, A205; Iron A133, A134, A153, A282, A426, A451, A468, A490, A571, A691, A973, A1030, A1044, A1072, A1198-1200; Roof. A1505, A1506; Tile (13); Vess. (124)
2	2 (Site 49/ 501) = (Site 49/523)	Chalk rubble deposit		PM 3:32; Iron A194
2	3	Decayed chalk surface		
2	4	Wall		
2	5	? Natural hollow fill		Iron A904, A905; Coal 4g
3	6	Modern pit	35, 36	Med. 1:24
3	7	Pit fill		
2	8	Cobble surface	35	Med. 1:6; Iron A1274-1276, A1433
2	9	West wall	35	
3	10	C20 pit	35	
2	11 (Site 49/524)	Road surface		
3	12	C20 pit	35	
3	13 (Site 49/513)	C20 pit	35	
3	14 (Site 49/514)	Fill of pit 13		Med. 1:31; PM 7:72; Tile (2); Vess. (1); Wood A47
3	15	Fill of pit 10		Med. 2:11; PM 42:1070; Cp (1); Copper 7; Tile (1); Vess. (4)
3	16	Fill of pit 12		Med. 1:3; PM 2:23; Cp (1); Roof. A1507; Tile (10); Vess. (1); Coal 6g
3	17	C20 pit	35, 36	
3	18	Fill of pit 17		PM 58:2033; Vess. (1)
3	19	? Tree-hole/pit		
3	20	Fill of 19		PM 2:6; Copper A259; Vess. (3)
3	21	Pit fill		
2	22	? Burnt sill-beam slot		
2	23	Mortar layer		
2	24	Layer		
-	25	? Midden fill		
2	26	? Drain cover/floor		PM 4:63
2	27	Rubble surface		
2	28	Rubble deposit		
2	29	Levelling surface		
2	30	Layer		
2	31	Pit fill		
1	32	Natural		
2	33	Pit fill		
2	34	Pit fill		
2	35	Layer	35	
2	36	Pit		
2	37	Pit		
2	38	Layer		
2	39	Layer		
2	40	Post-pipe fill		
2	41	Post-pipe fill		
1	42	Chalk layer		
2	43	Post-pipe		
2	44	Pit		
2	45	Layer		
2	46	Demolition debris		Med. 5:29; Burnt (1)
2	47	Wall footing	35	
2	48	Rubble deposit	35	
2	49	Wall	35	
3	50	Unstratified material		Med. 2:22; PM 19:232; Brick (1); Iron A195, A196, A951, A998; Tile (4); Vess. (6); Coal 2g
2	51	Surface layer	35	Med. 11:73; PM 2:11; Iron A190, A197, A768, A1140, A1434; Roof. A926-928; Sst. A358-360; An. (10); Char. 3g; Coal 5g

Phase	Context	Description	Fig. Nos	Artefacts and environmental remains
2	52	Wall	35	Char. ≤1g
2	53	Pillar base	35	Rom. 1:5
2	54	Chalk rubble deposit		Tile (2)
2	55	Yard surface	35	PM 13:19; Copper A224; Cp (1); An. (1)
3	56	C20 post-hole		
3	57	C20 post-hole		PM 1:5
3	58	Post-hole fill		Tile (1)
3	59	Post-hole fill		PM 1:22
2	60	? Pit fill	35	An. (1); Char. 2g
2	61	Hillwash		
2	62	? Natural		
2	63	Surface layer	35	Rom. 2:7; Copper A959; An. (2)
2	64	Cobble surface		
2	65	Chalk surface		Med. 6:73; Lst. A659; An. (1)
2	66	Stake-hole		
2	67	Stake-hole fill		
-	68	Post-hole		
-	69	Post-hole fill		Tile (1)
2	70	? Surface layer		
2	71	Ditch	36	Med. 1:2; An. (4)
2	72	Ditch	35, 36	Med. 7:54; PM 1:2; Tile (4); An. (1)
2	73	Pit fill	35	Tile (2); Burnt (1)
2	74	Stake-hole		
-	75	Post-hole		
-	76	Post-hole fill		PM 2:43; Wood A48
-	77	Stake-hole		
-	78	Shallow pit		
-	79	Pit fill		PM 3:6
2	80	? Layer	35	
2	81	Post-pipe		
2	82	Remains of post	35	Wood A49; An. (1)
2	83	Fill of 82		
-	84	Post-hole		
-	85	Post-hole fill		
2	86	Post-hole		
2	87	Post-hole fill		
2	88	Build-up layer	35	Roof. A929; An. (5); BS; Cin. 1g
2	89	? Fill of ditch		PM 1:18; Iron A198; Tile (6)
2	90	Chalk surface	35	
2	91	? Layer		
2	92	? Wall	35	
2	93	? Post packing		
-	94	Stake-hole		
2	95	? Layer		
-	96	? Layer/surface		
2	97	? Surface/layer		Plas.
2	98	? Layer/surface	35	PM 1:8
2	99	? Post packing	35	PM 2:6; Iron A906
3	100	Overburden/topsoil		PM 10:163; Med. 11:120; Copper A750; Iron A769-771, A907, A974, A1435, A1436; Stone A65; Vess. (9)
-	100/150	No context information	36	PM 1:3; Tile (1); Coal 18g
2	101	Garden soil	36	Med. 20:102; PM 1:3; Brick (4); Quern A135; Roof. A930; Tile (3); Vess. (1); An. (10); Cin. 12g; Fish
3	102	C20 surface		Med. 6:34; Brick (1); Copper A751, A752; Iron A1437; Tile (2); Vess. (4)
2	103	Hillwash	36	Med. 19:217; PM 1:10; Copper 122; Mem. A177; Quern A136; Sst. A361; Tile (1); An. (10)
2	104	Hillwash	36	PM 3:19; An. (12)
2	105	Pit		Iron A772
2	106	Pit fill		PM 3:42; Brick (3); Lst. A731; Quern A137; Roof. A932; Sst. A362; An. (2); Cin. 6g; Coal 1g
2	107	Pit	36	
2	108	Pit fill	36	Med. 1:2; An. (1)
2	109	Pit		
2	110	Pit fill		Med. 1:2; Iron A1079; An. (1)
1	111	? Natural	36	
1	112	Natural	36	Iron A1438
2	113	Post-hole packing		Sst. A363; An. (1); Coal 1g
2	114	? Gully/Ditch		Med. 1:5
2	115	? Layer	35	
2	116	Stake-hole		
2	117	? Post-hole		

Phase	Context	Description	Fig. Nos	Artefacts and environmental remains
2	118	? Floor surface		Med. 2:14; PM 1:162; Roof. A934-936; An. (1)
2	119	? Layer		
2	120	? Layer/post-pit		Med. 2:15
2	121	? Layer/surface	35	An. (2)
-	122	? Stake-hole		
-	123	Rubble deposit		
2	124	Pit fill		
2	125	Pit	35	PM 3:9
2	126	Pit	35	
2	127	Post-hole	35	
2	128	Post-hole	35	An. (1)
2	129	Post-hole	35	
2	130	Pit	35	
2	131	Surface	35	Med. 3:8
2	132	Pit		
2	133	Pit fill		
2	134	Pit	35	
2	135	Pit fill		
3	136	Build-up material		Rom. 3:21; PM 1:1; Quern A138; Wood A50; Coal 3g
2	137	Depression		
2	138	Post-hole		
2	139	Post-hole		
2	140	Post-hole		
2	141	Post-hole fill		
2	142	Sandy deposit		
2	143	Pit		
2	144	Pit fill		
2	145	Post-pipe		
-	146	Post-hole/pit		
-	500	No context information		Wood A51

Site 74

Phase	Context	Description	Fig. Nos	Artefacts and environmental remains
6	1	Garden levelling deposit		Vess. (1)
	2 - 33	Unused context		
-	34	No context information		Brick (1)
	35-92	Unused context		
	93	No context information		Burnt (1)
	94-97	Unused context		
-	98	No context information		Brick (4)
	99	Unused context		
4	100	Wall/demolition debris	14	PM 4:27; Brick (8); Copper A931; Cp (1); Tile (3); Vess. (6); An. (4); Coal 2g; Mortar
6	101	Demolition debris		PM 143:1305 (26, 27); Copper A897; Cp (8); Iron A393, A433, A692, A773-775, A908, A1277; Roof. A1508, A1535, A1536; Sst. A364; Tile (3); Vess. (7); Wood A128; BS; Mortar
4	102	Floor surface	14	PM 89:744 (23); Bone 41; Brick (23); Copper 35, A144, A286, A287, A997; Cp (10); Iron 32, A434, A636, A693, A1159, A1201, A1278-1281; Tile (384); Vess. 6, 22, (6); An. (41); Coal 2g; Plas.; Slag 3g
6	103	Floor surface/modern dump		PM 3:9; Cp (1); Iron 61; Tile (1); Vess. 13
4	104	Wall	14	PM 3:3; An. (1); Mortar
4	105A	Brick partition wall	14	Cp (2)
6	105B	Demolition rubble		PM 7:130; Bone 11; Tile (3); Vess. (2)
3	106	Layer	12, 14	Med. 9:72; PM 355:5561 (10-17); Bone 1, 19, 36; Brick (20); Copper 42, 115, A145-147, A225, A288, A289, A753-758, A932, A960; Cp 2, 5, 12, 27 (30); Iron 15, 60, A157, A199, A200, A201, A236, A288, A394, A548, A776, A777, A952, A1202, A1282-1284; Stone A75; Tile (191); Vess. 15, 18, 26 (57); Wood A129; An. (101); BS; Char. 1g; Cin. 10g; Coal 78g; Fish
6	107	Modern dump		Iron A661
6	108	Layer/wall		PM 12:20; Brick (1); Copper A148, A290, A759; Cp (1); Iron A469; Tile (69); Coal 1g; Plas.
6	109A	Post-1958 pathway		
6	109B	Layer		PM 17:92; Bone 60; Brick (4); Iron 29, A395, A396, A508, A1040-1042, A1203, A1285, A1286; Roof. A1537; Tile (12); Vess. (1); Wood A52-56; Char. ≤1g; Cin. 7g; Coal 5g
6	110	Rubbish pit		PM 3:13; Iron A397, A535, A778
6	111	Rubble tip		PM 11:37; Cp (1); Iron A202, A398, A536, A694, A1287; Vess. (3); Cin. 12g
6	112	? floor surface		PM 31:326 (28); Brick (91); Clay 7; Copper A149; Cp (3); Iron A203, A283, A521, A909, A910; Lst. A660-662; Mem. A178; Sst. A584; Tile (136); Vess. (3); BS; Burnt (1); Char. 19g; Cin. 22g

Phase	Context	Description	Fig. Nos	Artefacts and environmental remains
4	113=?115	Floor packing		
6	114	Modern path		Iron A289
4	115=?113	Floor layer		PM 2:17; Cp (1); Vess. 4; An. (5); Mortar
6	116	Modern drain		Copper A980; Iron A972
6	117	Infill of wall		PM 16:78; Copper A744; Cp (4); Iron A509, A779; Vess. (1); Cin. 4g
6	118	Garden soil		PM 29:218; Glass A195, A196; Iron A573; Vess. (2)
6	119	Garden soil		PM 1:14; Copper 31; Iron A470
4	120	Mortar floor surface		PM 1:1
6	121	Pit		
6	122	Ashy deposit		
6	123	Chalk surface		PM 45:314; Copper 21, A868; Cp (2); Iron A237, A399, A498, A592, A780, A781, A911, A975, A999, A1288-1290, A1439; Lst. A663; Tile (2); Vess. (17); Cin. 1g; Slag 15g
6	124	Post-hole		
6	125	Rubble dump (including rodent skeleton)		Med. 1:22; PM 242:1887 (29); Bone 13; Brick (5); Copper A898, A981, A998; Cp 33, 37 (30); Iron 3, A238, A324, A471, A495, A496, A537, A662, A695, A782-791, A912, A912A, A983, A984, A1291-1295, A1440-1442; Tile (73); Vess. (17)
6	126	Floor surface		PM 242:1832 (30 pt); Coal 4g; Mortar
6	127	Mortar floor		PM 2:5; Bone 64; Iron A696, A100, A1444; Coal 1g
4	128	Internal wall		Mortar
-	129	No context information		
4	130	Wall	14	PM 1:1; Cp 15 (1); An. (3); Mortar
6	131	Floor packing		PM 3:22
6	132	Floor packing		PM 1:2; Vess. (67)
6	133	Rubble deposit		
6	134	Floor packing		Rom. 1:20; PM 28:231; Cp (5); Vess. (1); Wood A112; Coal 9g; Mortar
6	135	Pit		PM 48:403; Brick (2); Copper A150, A267, A268, A684; Cp (7); Iron A400, A574, A637, A792, A793, A1204, A1296, A1297; Lst. A740; Tile (69); Vess. 44, (89); Wood A57, A58, A123, A130; Char. 1g; Cin. 61g; Coal 8g; Plas.
6	136	Pit		PM 9:18; Iron A1001, A1002; Roof. A1538; Tile (1); Char. 17g; Coal 4g
6	137	Pit fill		PM 1:9
-	138	No context information		PM 4:37; Cp (2)
6	139	Gravel floor		PM 2:26; Iron A610; Tile (3); Cin. 15g
4	140	Demolition debris		PM 11:66; Coin pm 49; Iron A435; Roof. A1509; Tile (11); Vess. (145); An. (10); Cin. 7g
4	141	Internal wall	14	Mortar
4	142	Internal wall	14	Vess. (1); Mortar
6	143	Mortar floor surface		
6	144	Mortar floor surface		PM 1:2
6	145	Mortar floor surface		Vess. (27)
6	146	Floor surface		PM 10:1087; Bone 65; Brick (2); Cp (3); Iron A314, A1298, A1445; Sst. A365; Vess. (7)
6	147	? yard surface		PM 6:27; Glass A206; Vess. (1)
6	148	Demolition debris		
6	149	Demolition debris		PM 1:10; Iron A710; Tile (5)
-	150	No context information		PM 7:83 (30 pt, 31); Cp (5)
6	151	Demolition debris		PM 31:111; Iron A158, A711, A794; Vess. (3)
6	152	Pit fill		PM 11:33; Cp (2); Iron A239, A257; Vess. (14)
6	153	Rubbish pit		PM 8:49; Brick (1); Copper 49; Cp 34 (10); Glass A207; Iron A499, A638, A697, A795, A796, A1073, A1088, A1205
4	154	Wall	14	PM 3:3; Copper A999; Cp (1); Tile (6); Vess. 10; An. (3); Plas.
-	155	No context information		
6	156	Demolition debris		PM 28:215; Vess. 23; Wood A59; Coal 5g
6	157	Compacted surface		PM 2:7
6	158	Demolition debris		PM 3:133; Coin pm 48; Vess. 28, 46
6	159	Pit fill		PM 2:7; Iron A401; Wood A60
6	160	Pit fill		Tile (3); Vess. (2)
6	161	Pit fill		PM 2:2; Vess. (1); Cin. 10g
6	162	Pit fill		
6	163	Pit fill		PM 4:9; Cp (1); Iron A664; Tile (1); Vess. (1); Cin. 8g; Coal 13g
4	164	Floor surface		Roof. A937
3	165	Surface	12	Med. 1:29; PM 128:3132 (13 pt, 18-19, 20 pt); Brick (1); Copper A291, A685, A760; Cp (5); Iron A402, A403; Tile (18); Vess. 11, 17, 20, 21, 27, 29-32, 34, 41, 42, (277); An. (37); BS; Cin. ≤1g; Coal 4g
4	166	Garden soil		Copper A1000; Iron A258; Vess. (4)
4	167	Clay deposit		PM 1:10; Tile (2)
6	168	Mortar surface		
4	169	Layer?		Cp (1)
6	170	Pit fill		

Phase	Context	Description	Fig. Nos	Artefacts and environmental remains
4	171	Surface		
6	172	Chalk deposit		
6	173	Burnt deposit		PM 5:33; Wood A61
6	174	Blocked surface		
2?	175	Chalk & mortar bank		
4	176	Clay deposit		
6	177	Floor make-up		
6	178	Dog burial		
-	179	No context information		Iron A797
6	180	Lime/chalk floor surface		PM 1:1; Brick (1); Cp 29 (7); Iron A1206; Stone A97, A98; Tile (2);
5	181	Pit fill	14	Wood A62; BS; Char. ≤1g; Cin. 134g; Coal 5g
6	182	Layer over ash pit		PM 9:144 (32); Iron A593, A698; Tile (1)
6	183	Burnt area		PM 46:224; Tile (1); BS; Char. ≤1g; Cin. 4g; Coal 13g
6	184	Pit fill		PM 5:3; Bone 52; Tile (2); Wood A63; Cin. 1g; Coal 2g
6	185	Post-hole		
-	186	No context information		PM 13:29; Brick (1); Cp (1)
2	187=220	Cobbled flint surface		
6?	188	Pit/post-hole		PM 2:2
6?	189	Post-hole/pit fill		PM 2:5; Copper A151; Cp (1); Coal 1g
6	190A	Post-hole		
6	190B	Layer		Coal 20g
6	191	Post-hole fill		PM 4:4; Cin. 1g
6	192	? Feature		
6	193	Feature fill		PM 15:23; Brick (8); Tile (5); Wood. A113; Cin. 1g; Coal 5g
6?	194	Pit		
6?	195	Pit fill		Iron A191
4	196	? Ash pit		
6	197	Robber trench	14	
6	198	Robber trench fill	14	PM 14:21; Coin pm 21; Tile (2); Vess. (2); Cin. 15g; Plas.
4	199	Make-up surface	14	PM 14:103; Brick (12); Iron A798; Lst. A664; Roof. A1539; Sst. A366; Tile (75); An. (28); Cin. 7g; Coal 69g; Plas.
6	200	Make-up surface		
6	201	Mortar floor surface		
4	202	Make-up surface		
6?	203	Rubble layer		PM 2:4; Brick (8); Lst. A665, A666; Tile (89); Vess. (3); Wood A64; Cin. 62g; Coal 24g
4	204A	Brick fireplace	14	
6	204B	Make-up for floor		Coal 1g
4	205A	Brick fireplace	14	
6	205B	Surface		PM 1:6; Brick (1); Copper A152; Cp (2); Iron 25, A799-801; Tile (8); Vess. (2); Wood A65; BS; Cin. 49g; Coal 77g; Plas.; Slag 3g
4	206	Gravely-mortar spread		
6	207	Mortar surface		Iron A802
6	208	? Compacted rubble spread		PM 11:114; Copper 104; Vess. (2); Coal ≤1g; Plas.
6	209	Rubble spread		PM 5:12; Cp (2); Vess. (3); Coal 4g; Mortar
6	210	Rubble spread		Med. 1:3; PM 6:181; Copper A153, A292; Iron 94, A1299, A1300, A1446; Lst. A667-674; Sst. A367, A368; Stone 14; Tile (25); BS; Cin. 15g; Coal 1g; Mortar; Plas.
5	211	? Floor packing material		PM 22:487 (24); Brick (7); Copper A154, A293; Iron A803; Sst. A369, A370; Tile (25); Vess. (6); An. (89); Cin. 10g; Mortar; Plas.
6	212	Post-hole		
6	213	Post-hole fill		
6	214	Post-hole		
6	215	Post-hole fill		
6	216	Post-hole		
6	217	Post-hole fill		PM 2:8; Tile (5); Plas.
6	218	Post-hole fill		
2	219	Yard surface	12	PM 22:119; Bone 10; Copper 3, 27, A294; Cp (5); Iron A404, A405, A913, A1089, A1301; Tile (3); Vess. (7); An. (2); Cin. ≤1g
2	220=187	Cobbled pathway	12	
2	221	? Wall	12	An. (2)
2?	222	Surface layer		
4	223	Ash pit	14	PM 2:3; Tile (2); An. (2)
5	224	Ash pit fill		PM 3:79; Cp (4); Vess. (1); Wood A66; An. (2); Cin. 4g; Coal 114g; Plas.
5	225	Ash pit fill		
6	226	Demolition debris		PM 7:120; Brick (1); Iron A1447; Tile (1)
4	227	Wall	14	
4	228	? Oven base	14	
4	229	? Oven base	14	PM 4:103

Phase	Context	Description	Fig. Nos	Artefacts and environmental remains
3	230	? Hillwash		PM 157:1211; Copper A295, A296, A761, A1001; Cp (1); Iron 50, A699, A804-806, A1302-1304; Tile (2); Vess. (4); Wood A114; An. (9); BS
4	231	Foundation trench		Med. 1:23
4	232	? Floor layer	14	PM 4:10; Iron A1305; Tile (46); Vess. (1); An. (1); Fish; Mortar
4	233	Foundation trench		
4	234	Foundation trench fill		Copper A155
6	235	Demolition debris		
4	236	Mortar/wall plaster layer		Vess. (1)
4	237	Pea-grit deposit	14	PM 13:641; Copper A297, A298; Cp (2); Iron A807; Lst. A675-683, A741; Roof. A1540; Sst. A371-373, A585, A586; Stone A185; Tile (15); Vess. (1); An. (23); Plas.
3	238	Silty clay bank	14	PM 22:432; Cp (3); Iron A1306; Vess. (1); An. (5); Char. ≤1g
6	239	Robber trench		
4	240	Robber trench fill		
4	241	Floor make-up	14	
4	242	? Make-up for floor	14	PM 2:56; Iron A808, A809; An. (22)
4	243	Demolition material/make-up		Tile (1); An. (22)
4	244	Mortar rich surface/floor	14	PM 7:24; Brick (1); Copper 28, A299; Cp (1); Lst. A684; Tile (11); Vess. (1); An. (67); Coal 5g; Plas.
4	245	Rubble dump	14	Med. 2:13; PM 2:3; Copper A300; Cp (1); Iron A953; Tile (2); Vess. 35, 36; An. (30); Plas.
4	246	Mortar layer	14	Iron A1307
4	247	Foundation trench	14	
4	248	Foundation trench fill	14	
4	249	? Hardcore dumping		An. (103)
6	250	Post-hole		PM 1:22; Iron A810; Vess. (3)
6	251	Post-hole fill		Brick (1)
4?	252	Layer		Vess. (3)
3	253	Layer		Copper A156-158, A301, A762, A763, A982; Iron A406, A700, A811, A1308; Cin. 25g
2	254	Surface	12	
3	255	? Demolition burning event		Med. 1:2; PM 29:156 (21, 22); Brick (1); Coin pm 20; Cp (1); Tile (44); An. (6); Cin. 11g
6	256	Feature		
6	257	Feature fill		PM 2:22; Tile (2)
6	258	Soft mortar deposit		PM 2:41; Vess. 19
4	259	Foundation trench fill		PM 2:7; Iron A1448; Plas.
-	260	No context information		
2	261	Wall face		
4	262	Robber trench		PM 4:65 (33); An. (1)
3	263	Robber trench fill		PM 2:75; An. (10); Fish
3	264	Floor make-up		PM 23:117; Bone 37; Brick (6); Copper A302-315; Cp (4); Tile (12); Vess. (4); An. (57); BS; Cin. 1g; Mortar
3?	265	Floor		
-	266	No context information		PM 1:4; Cp (1)
-	266/267	No context information		PM 1:7
4	267	Demolition debris/floor make-up	14	Med. 2:138; PM 29:288; Bone 50; Brick (7); Cp (1); Roof. A1510; Sst. A374, A375; Tile (12); Vess. (7); An. (27); Coal 58g
4	268	Floor surface	14	Vess. (1); An. (1)
4	269	Robber trench fill	14	PM 3:6; Copper A316; Cp (1); Iron A1080; Tile (13); Vess. (2); An. (2); Mortar; Plas.
4	270	Wall plaster debris		PM 1:3; Copper 39, A159, A1002; An. (2); Plas.
2	271	Surface		PM 1:2; Cp (1); An. (2)
6	272	Wall core		Med. 6:63; PM 33:486 (34-37); Brick (10); Copper 48, A317, A717; Cp (4); Iron A1207, A1208, A1309-1312; Lst. A741; Stone A76; Tile (19); Vess. 5, 40; Cin. 1g; Coal 15g; Plas.
6	273	C20th excavation trench		Plas.
6	274	C20th rubbish gully fill		
6	275	C20th feature fill		Med. 7:58; PM 48:227 (38, 39); Copper 29, A160, A226, A318-322, A764; Cp 13 (5); Iron A1209, A1313, A1314; Roof. A1511; Tile (15); Vess. 12 (23); BS; Cin. 19g; Coal 39g
6	276	? Layer		Med. 16:69; PM 42:347; Brick (3); Iron A701, A914, A1449; Tile (39); Vess 2 (5); Cin. 9g; Coal 9g
3	277	? Layer	12	Rom. 2:11; Med. 21:258; PM 51:971; Bone 40; Copper A933; Cp (3); Sst. A376, A377; Tile (11); Vess. (27); An. (32)
2	278	Hard surface		Med. 2:5; PM 8:128; Brick (1); Copper A263; Iron A812; Roof. A1541; Sst. A378, A379; Tile (2); Vess. (6); An. (2); BS; Coal 1g
3	279	? Demolition debris		An. (3)
-	280	No context information		PM 4:12; Brick (6); Sst. A380; Tile (6); BS
6	281	Garden structure platform		Med. 4:38; PM 10:37; Brick (1); Iron A407; Tile (12)
4	282	Demolition layer		PM 2:5; Iron A713, A1315; An. (14); Mortar

Phase	Context	Description	Fig. Nos	Artefacts and environmental remains
4	283	Construction trench	14	
4	284	Foundation trench fill	14	Med. 1:2; PM 22:155; Brick (2); Cp 6 (4); Vess. 39, 45; An. (3); Coal 34g
4	285	Foundation trench		
4	286	Foundation trench fill		PM 15:114; Copper A765; Cp 8 (1); Iron A159, A702, A1141; Tile (10); Vess. (3); An. (3); Char. 2g; Cin. 3g; Coal 4g
3	287	Soil deposit		Med. 4:20; PM 16:189 (8); Copper A766; Cp 4, 7 (2); Iron A408; Tile (4); Vess. 33; BS
4	288	Layer beneath make-up material		Iron A813; An. (1)
4	289	Foundation trench fill	14	An. (1); Plas.
4	290	Foundation trench	14	
3	291	? Layer		
2	292	? Internal wall	12	
4	293	? Layer		
2	294	? Floor layer	12	Copper 87
4	295	? Floor layer		
2	296	Floor	12	
4	297A	Foundation trench fill		Copper 60
4	297B	Foundation trench		
4	297C	Foundation trench fill		
4	298	Demolition debris		
3	299	Building/garden levelling material		PM 58:461; Copper 110, A323-327, A767-776, A934, A1003; Cp 3 (6); Iron A290; Tile (61); Vess. 9, 24 (5); An. (23); Char. ≤1g; Cin. 5g; Coal 10g
2	300	Robber trench fill	12	PM 24:419 (6, 7); Coin med. 32; Copper A383-331, A777-780; Cp (1); Tile (11); Vess. (3); An. (3)
3	301	? Layer		PM 3:4; An. (2)
6	302	Post-hole		
6	303	Post-hole fill		
2	304	Dividing wall		An. (1)
6	305	Rubble layer		PM 2:17; Iron A1316; Sst. A381; Tile (1); Coal 9g
4	306	Gully fill		PM 3:65
4	307	Linear gully	12	
6	308	Post-hole		
6	309	Post-hole fill		PM 1:17; Brick (3); Tile (3); Vess. (1)
5?	310	Layer	14	Med. 23:237; PM 21:426; Cp (3); Iron A1317; Tile (147); Vess (1); An. (7); Cin. 6g
-	311	? Layer		PM 2:30; Iron A814; Vess. (3)
4	312	Demolition layer		PM 10:165; Copper 8, A161; Iron A815, A1210; Vess. (1); An. (15); Burnt (9)
6	313	Mortar floor base/make-up rubble layer		Med. 2:35; PM 30:247; Brick (22); Coin pm 3; Cp (3); Iron A816, A1318; Tile (56); Vess. (11); Burnt (2); Cin. 16g; Coal 133g
4	314	Layer beneath floor	14	PM 139:1032 (40); Coin pm 12, 27, 43; Copper 4, 46, A131, A162-168, A227, A274, A332-409, A880-882, A899, A900, A1004; Cp (14); Glass A180; Iron 30, A297, A472, A510, A817, A818, A1003, A1090, A1319; Lst. A685; Stone A77; Tile (6); Vess. 1 (11); An. (342); Burnt (2); Char. ≤1g; Coal 8g; Fish; Plas.
6	315	? Cess pit/robber trench		PM 6:20; Bone 38; Cp (1); Tile (1); Coal ≤1g
6	316	Cess pit/robber trench fill		PM 15:71; Bone 39, 58; Brick (2); Copper A410; Cp (3); Iron A409, A1091; Tile (7); Char. 1g; Cin. 20g; Coal 85g
6	317	Robber trench		
6	318	Robber trench fill		
2	319	? Ash pit	12	Copper 98; Mortar
3	320	Ash pit fill		PM 1:1
2	321	? Cobble pathway	12	PM 25:95; Copper A411; Cp 19 (2); Sst. A382; Tile (1); Vess. (7); An. (37); Cin. 8g; Coal 75g
6	322	Linear robber trench		
2	323	Bedding sand layer	12	PM 12:89 (3, 4); Copper A412, A413; Cp (1); An. (1)
5?	324	Ash layer		
4?	325	Water drain		
6	326	Ashy fill of conduit		PM 3:4; Tile (2); Cin. 14g; Coal ≤1g
4?	327	Construction trench for conduit		
2	328	Floor base layer	12	Copper A414
4	329	Foundation trench	14	
4	330	Foundation trench fill	14	Copper A686
-	331	? Layer		
6	332	C20th cess pit fill		Iron A259; Tile (1); Vess. (1)
6	333	Post-hole fill		
4	334	Construction trench		PM 1:7 (25); Bone 51; Copper A415, A416, A869; Cp (1); Vess. 3; An. (4)
4	335	Foundation trench fill		PM 2:5; An. (1)

Phase	Context	Description	Fig. Nos	Artefacts and environmental remains
4	336	Foundation trench	14	Vess. (1); An. (8); Coal 3g
4	337	Construction trench		Med.2:12; PM 8:210 (41); Cp (2); Iron A204; Tile (8); Vess. (1); An. (2); Char. ≤1g; Coal 6g; Mortar
4?	338	Construction trench spoil		PM 1:3; Copper A417-419; Iron A585; Vess. (2); An. (341)
4	339	Pea-grit bedding layer		Med. 2:35; PM 7:70; Brick (2); Copper A420-423; Cp (1); Tile (3); Vess. (6); Wood A67; An. (43); Char. ≤1g; Cin. 3g; Plas.
4	340	Layer underneath 339	14	PM 1:14; Bone 18; Copper A424, A425; Vess. (1); An. (3)
1	341	Sub-floor base /?natural	11	Med. 8:16; PM 69:361 (1, 2); Bone 15, 20; Brick (1); Copper 26, 30, 70, 99, A169-172, A228, A229, A426-508, A687, A718-721, A737, A738, A870-877, A883; Cp 46 (8); Glass A181; Iron A291, A819, A915, A1320, A1321; Stone A78-83; Tile (14); Vess. (6); Wood A68; An. (253); Cin. 4g; Coal 6g; Fish; Plas.
2	342	? Partition layer	12	PM 4:61 (5); Copper A509, A510; Iron A410; Tile (16); An. (2)
2	343	? Floor layer		
2	344	Construction debris	12	PM 3:85; Brick (5); Copper A173, A174, A511, A512; Glass A182; Sst. A383; Tile (10); Vess. (1); An. (3)
2	345	Layer below 344		PM 12:61; Copper A781, A782; Cp (1); Iron A1322; Tile (5); Vess. (18); An. (26); BS; Cin. 5g; Fish
1	346	? Layer beneath floor		Tile (1); An. (2)
4	347	Construction trench fill	14	PM 2:2; Copper A513; Iron A703, A1323; Vess. (1); An. (1)
4	348	Robbed/demolition material		
4?	349	Hearth/feature related to conduit		PM 5:15; Coin pm 29, 45; Copper 71; Cp 9 (1); Tile (5); An. (7)
6	350	Post-hole		
2	351	Wall	12	
2	352	Circular mortar feature fill	12	
6	353	Robber trench fill		Copper A514
2	354	Construction fill for ash pit	12	Med. 1:4; Lst. A686
2	355	Pit	12	
2	356	Beam slots	12	
2	357	Layer under flagstone floor	12	
6	358	? Fill of 315		
2?	359	? Mortar surface		
1	360	Burnt area	11	PM 3:27; Copper 116; Vess. 7; An. (2)
1	361	Wall		Copper A515; Cp (3)
3?	362	Burnt area		Med. 1:6; PM 22:214 (9); Brick (1); Copper A230, A783, A1005; Iron A185, A639, A1324; Sst. A587; Tile (44); Vess. 8 (15); An. (29); Char. 1g; Cin. 2g; Coal 8g
2	363	Floor make-up	12	Med. 1:14; PM 1:10; Copper A516; An. (2)
3?	364	Black deposit		Iron A1325
2	365	Rubble dump	12	Copper A1006; Vess. (2)
1	366	Wall	11	An. (1)
1	367	Yard surface	11	
2	368	Chalk block deposit	12	
2	369	Surface	12	
1	370	Chalk pebble surface	11	
1	371	Chalk block structure		
1	372	Chalk block structure fill		
1	373	Demolition layer	11	Copper A784
3?	374	? Layer		PM 9:112
2	375	Threshold	12	
3?	376	? Layer		Med. 3:46; PM 3:83; An. (4)
6	377	Post-hole fill		Tile (1)
-	422	No context information		Brick (1)
-	469	No context information		Iron A500
-	598	No context information		Char. ≤1g
-	740	No context information		Brick (5); Tile (93)
u/s	9000	Unstratified		PM 1094:5650 (30 pt, 42); Bone 53, 59; Brick (4); Coin pm 18, 26, 40; Copper 33, 34, 40, 62-64, 68, 106, A175-181, A269, A275, A567, A681, A705, A706, A712, A722-724, A739, A785, A901-904, A935-941, A961, A1007, A1008, A1032; Cp 26, 39, 52 (91); Glass A183-186, A197, A208-211; Iron 31, A135-141, A160, A163, A165, A192, A205, A284, A298, A325, A326, A355, A366, A368, A371, A411-415, A473, A511, A522, A538, A575, A629-632, A640, A704-707, A820-828, A916-920, A954, A985, A1004-1007, A1043, A1074, A1081, A1092, A1211-1218, A1326-1333, A1450-1457; Lst. A725; Roof. A1512, A1542-1547; Sst. A588; Stone A84, A99, A100, A102, A103; Vess. 14, 16, 25, 37, 38, 43 (67); Wood A69-73, A131-136; BS; Char. ≤1g; Cin. 39g; Coal 199g; Mortar; Plas.

Phase	Context	Description	Fig. Nos	Artefacts and environmental remains

Site 79

Phase	Context	Description	Fig. Nos	Artefacts and environmental remains
-	1	No context information		Med. 4:156; Vess. (3)
	2-9	Unused Context		
-	10	Topsoil		Med. 2:26; Iron A1033; Tile (2)
-	11	Topsoil		
-	12	Make-up layer		
-	13	Make-up layer		
-	14	Yard surface		
-	15	Make-up layer		Med. 1:27
-	16	Chalk deposit		Med. 2:15
-	17	Chalk deposit		
-	18	Chalk deposit		Med. 1:4
-	19	Chalk deposit		Med. 2:20
-	20	Quarry pit fill		
-	21	Chalk deposit		Med. 2:18
-	22	Revetment wall/structure		

Site 97

Phase	Context	Description	Fig. Nos	Artefacts and environmental remains
-	10	No context information		PM 9:282; Bone 42; Copper 45; Iron A586

Vicarage Sites

Site 20

Phase	Context	Description	Fig. Nos	Artefacts and environmental remains
-	24	No context information		PM 1:12
-	36	No context information		PM 2:20; Iron A1142; Quern A107, A108; Sst. A187
-	39	No context information		Sst. A188; Char. 3g; Coal 15g
-	49	No context information		PM 2:8; Iron A276, A1161; Roof. A748-756; Sst. A189; Stone A180; Coal 1g
-	54	No context information		Roof. A757, A758
-	57	No context information		Roof. A759; Slag 192g
-	58	No context information		Quern A109; Roof. A760, A761, A762-764; Sst. A190; Char. 3g
-	u/s	No context information		PM 3:13; Copper A1033; Iron A1458; Lst. A590, A591

Site 21

Phase	Context	Description	Fig. Nos	Artefacts and environmental remains
-	28	No context information		Lst. A592; Quern A110, A111; Roof. A765-768; Sst. A191-195
-	62			Rom. 1:1
-	97	No context information		An. (29); Char. 4g
-	9000	Unstratified		PM 1:2; Quern A112
-	-	No context information		PM 3:6; Copper A905; Iron A206, A268, A1053, A1101, A1116; Roof. A769-773; Sst. A196, A197

Site 54

Phase	Context	Description	Fig. Nos	Artefacts and environmental remains
8.4	1	Topsoil		Rom. 2:31; Med. 79:1094; PM 971:12867 (46 pt, 121 pt, 126 pt, 166 pt, 167 pt, 174-178); Bone 22, 43, 44, 47, 49, 55; Brick (33); Coin pm 32, 42; Copper 17, 19, 22, 24, 83, 120, 124, A182, A183, A270, A276, A277, A702, A707, A725-728, A745, A786-788, A906-908, A942, A962-967; Cp 32, 35 (47); Iron 4, 40, 42, 47, 57, 69, 75, 76, 82, 85, 95, 100, A145, A171, A172, A269, A270, A277, A306, A327, A334-337, A373, A374, A377-379, A381, A382, A416-418, A436, A452, A474-477, A501, A512, A523, A524, A549, A550, A554, A556, A557, A576, A577, A587, A594-598, A611, A612, A633, A641-463, A665, A671, A714-716, A730, A731, A736, A829-843, A921-923, A976, A977, A986, A987, A1008-1011, A1046-1048, A1054, A1093-1097, A1101-1104, A1166, A1219-1228, A1334-1336, A1456; Lst. A738; Quern A122; Roof. A810-824, A1495, A1496, A1528-1530; Sst. A243, A244, A577; Stone A92; Tile (247); Vess. 54, 71, 75, 76, 80, 85, 86, 101, 115-121, 161 (258); Wood A74, A75, A115, A120; BS; Char. 5g; Cin. 9g; Coal 278g
8.4	2	Demolition debris		Med. 1:3; PM 41:460 (179); Copper A184, A729; Cp (2); Iron A1055, A1056, A1337; Vess. (2)
8.4	3	Demolition debris	65	Med. 2:28; PM 78:878; Copper A930A, A909; Cp (1); Roof. A1497; Tile (44); Vess. (6); Coal 33g
8.4	4	Demolition debris		Med. 5:25; PM 103:546; Brick (5); Copper 100, A746; Coin pm 22; Cp (4); Glass 168, 170; Tile (18); Vess. 78, 122 (4); Cin. 9g; Plas.

Phase	Context	Description	Fig. Nos	Artefacts and environmental remains
8.1	5=5A	Demolition debris		Rom. 2:29 (5); Med. 32:746 (53 pt, 68); PM 839:16521 (121 pt, 122 pt, 142 pt, 151-153, 154 pt, 155-156); Bone 45-46, 48, 56-57; Brick (13); Coin pm 33, 52; Copper 18, 38, 50, 79-81, 94, 95, A185-195, A278, A517-519, A688-692, A730B-E, A789-791, A1039, A1040; Cp 25 (23); Iron 70, 71, 77, 86, 87, A146, A182, A217, A271, A338-340, A437, A453, A478-780, A502, A525, A526, A551, A555, A558, A561, A580, A581, A644-650, A666, A717, A732, A737, A844-849, A924, A925, A955, A1051, A1338, A1460, A1461; Roof. A1498, A1499, A1531-1533; Sst. A245-247; Stone 9, A85, A93-95; Tile (73); Vess. 87-89, 102-104, 123-125, 162-166 (152); Wood A76; Burnt (1); Char. 2g; Cin. 19g; Coal 176g; Mortar; Plas.; Slag 35g
8.1	6	Topsoil interface		
8.2	7	Surface deposit		Med. 1:6; PM 170:2453 (170-172); Brick (4); Copper A196, A792; Cp (3); Iron 58, 72, 99, A173, A218, A341, A342, A376, A383, A419, A427, A454, A481, A668, A718, A978, A1229; Lst. A630-632; Mem. A174; Sst. A248-251; Tile (28); Vess. (10); Coal 39g; Mortar
8.4	8	Topsoil & rubble		Rom. 1:22; PM 257:2498; Brick (1); Copper A520, A521, A703, A793, A794, A910; Cp (6); Iron 78, 79, A307, A651, A1098, A1162; Lst. A633-636; Mem. 33 (pt); Quern A123, A124; Roof. A825-828; Sst. A253, A254, A578-580; Stone A1559; Tile (4); Vess. 126 (50); Burnt (1); Coal 10g
-	8A	No context information		Copper A279
7.8	9	Pit fill	65, 67	Med. 1:22; PM 88:1788 (145-148); Coin pm 6, 25; Cp 36 (1); Iron 73, A455; Sst. A581; Tile (3); Vess. 90 (8); An. (25); Coal 16g
7.8	10=16	Cobbled surface	67	
8.2	11	Silt deposit	65	Med. 3:15; PM 4:29 (160); Copper 108, A197; Cp (2); Iron 80, A168, A328, A456, A850, A1099; Sst. A255; Tile (1); Vess. (2)
7.8	12=27	Drain fill/sandstone capping	67	Med. 1:3; PM 28:237 (150); Bone 9; Copper A198, A795; Iron A553; Lst. A637; Tile (1); Vess. (4); An. (9)
8.2	13	Topsoil deposit		Med. 17:479 (24, 57); PM 10:75; Stone 20; Vess. (11)
8.2	13/14	No context information		PM 45:441; Vess. 91; Coal 44g
8.2	14	Rubble deposit	65	Med. 1:52; PM 7:128 (173); Coin pm 55; Cp (1); Stone 4; Tile (6)
7.8	15	Cobbled surface repair	67	
7.8	16=10	Cobbled surface	65, 67	Med. 1:92; PM 6:17; Iron A956
8.1	17	Topsoil deposit	65	Med. 3:78; PM 55:982; Brick (1); Cp 1 (3); Iron 45, A166, A167; Tile (6); Vess. 92 (7); Cin. 3g; Coal 20g; Mortar; Plas.
7.7	18	Construction trench	65, 66	
7.7	19	Wall	66	Mortar
7.7	20	Wall	66	Mortar
7.7	21	Cobbled surface		PM 27:136; Med. 20:332; Brick (53); Copper 117; Iron 37, A117; Roof. A830; Tile (1); Vess. (9); An. (10)
7.7/7.8	21/34	No context information		PM 9:33; Iron A1339; Tile (2); An. (5); Coal 3g
7.7/7.2	21/72	No context information		PM 22:339; Lst. A638; Roof. A831; Tile (8); An. (10); Char. 1g; Cin. 6g; Coal 3g
-	21/74	No context information		Iron A420
7.5	22=?183= ?214=?261	Wall footing	64	Med. 1:6; PM 5:127; Iron A513; Vess. 127 (4); An. (10); Coal 22g
6.1	23	?Hillwash	51, 60	Med. 5:93; PM 4:19; Vess. 127 (5); Coal 1g
-	23A	No context information		PM 2:58
-	23/18	No context information		PM 1/26
8.2	24	Topsoil dump		
7.7	25	Construction trench fill		
7.8	26	Rubbish pit	67	
7.8	27=12	Surface dump/?fill	67	
8.1	28=5=5A =?76	Demolition debris		Brick (1)
8.3	29	Post-hole fill		Med. 1:3; PM 13:296; Brick (1); Cp (1); Iron A457, A618, A669; Sst. A256; Tile (2); Vess. 93; Cin.. 3g
8.3	30=?49	Construction trench		
8.1	31	Demolition debris/hillwash	51	PM 60:948 (142 pt, 157); Brick (2); Copper A199; Cp (1); Iron A384, A482, A613, A851, A852, A1340-1343; Tile (14); Vess. 82 pt (4); An. (41); Coal 4g; Mortar
-	31/97	No context information	51	PM 42:808; Copper A796; Cp (1); Iron 35, A733, A719, A853; Vess. 82; An. (4)
8.4	32	Rubbish pit	65	
8.4	33	Rubbish pit fill		Med. 1:99 (56); PM 2:108; Vess. (1)
7.6	34	Surface dump/demolition debris		PM 14:60; Vess. (4); An. (1); Coal 19g
8.3	35	Construction debris		
8.3	36	Construction debris		PM 2:14
8.3	37	Construction debris		PM 2:21; Tile (1)
8.3	38	Stake-hole		

Phase	Context	Description	Fig. Nos	Artefacts and environmental remains
8.3	39	Post-hole		
8.3	40	Post-pipe		
8.3	41	Post-pipe		
8.3	42	Stake-hole		
8.3	43	Post-pit fill		
8.3	44	Post-hole		
8.3	45	Post-pit fill		PM 3:23; Brick (2); Vess. (1)
8.3	46	Post-hole fill		PM 1:26
8.3	47	Post-hole fill		Tile (1)
8.3	48	Post-hole		Vess. 94
8.3	49=?30	Construction trench		
7.8	50	Loam, ash & coal dump	67	Tile (11)
8.3	51	Stake-hole		
7.8	52	Post-hole	67	
7.8	53	Post-hole fill		An. (1); Cin. 3g; Mortar
7.8	54	Post-hole	67	
7.8	55	Post-hole fill		
7.8	56	Post-hole	67	
7.8	57	Post-hole fill		Med. 1:2; PM 22:44; Tile (1); Vess. 81; An. (3)
7.8	58	Post-hole		
7.8	59	Post-hole fill		Med. 2:22 (67); PM 3:5; Copper A731; Cp (1); Roof. A1500; Vess. (2); An. (3); Coal 9g
-	60	Stake-hole void		
-	61	Stake-hole void		
7.8	62	Post-pipe	67	PM 1:1
7.8	63	?Post-hole	67	
7.8	64	Post-hole fill		
7.8	65	Stake-hole void	67	Coal 1g
7.8	66	Post-pipe		
7.1	67	Make-up deposit		An. (7)
5.2	68	Surface deposit		
7.1	69	Wall footings		
7.8	70	? Road surface	67	
7.1	71=121	Threshold deposit	63	
7.7	72	Surface dump/deposit		PM 2:15
7.1	73	Surface deposit	63, 65	
7.2	74	Surface deposit		Copper A732
7.4	75	Soak-away deposit	64	Med. 12:444; PM 32:387 (124, 125-126 pt); Brick (4); Copper A522, A797, A798; Cp (1); Mem. 34; Iron A299, A1012; Lst. A639, A640, A739; Roof. A832, A833; Sst. A257-266; Stone A182, A1560; Tile (2); Vess. 66 (pt), 68 (7); An. (3); Burnt (11); Char. 3g; Cin. 3g; Coal 3g; Fish; Plas.
8.1	76=?5=?5A=?28	Demolition debris		
8.2	77	Loam & rubble deposit		PM 14:337; Iron A854; Lst. A641; Vess. (6)
5.3	78	Wall	59	Sst. A267
8.1	79	Loam & chalk deposit		Sst. A582
7.8	80	Stake-hole void	67	
7.8	81	Stake-hole void		An. (1)
8.2	82	Rubbish pit fill		PM 43:582 (142 pt, 168, 169); Iron A300, A503, A652; Tile (2); Vess. 128 (2); Wood A77; Coal 1g; Plas.
7.8	83	Charcoal & burnt loam deposit	65, 67	Wood A78; An. (1)
8.2	84	Conduit fill	65	
8.1	85	Clay & chalk deposit		PM 2:14; Roof. A834; Sst. A268; Med. 7:112
7.7	86	Demolition debris		PM 8:17; Lst. A642; Tile (9); Vess. (6); An. (13)
7.7	87	Clay & chalk deposit		PM 3:90 (143); Iron A855; Vess. 129 (11); An. (12); Coal 2g
7.4	88	Surface deposit	64	Med. 1:16; PM 2:12; Vess. (2); Coal 53g
7.8	89	Post-hole	67	
7.8	90	Post hole fill		Tile (1)
7.7	91=97	Silt deposit	66	
8.1	92	Robber trench		PM 1:2
8.1	93	Robber trench fill		Pre. 1:8; Med. 1:17; PM 41:745 (131 pt, 142 pt); Copper A799, A800; Cp (2); Iron A343, A527, A734, A856, A1344; Sst. A269; Tile (5); Vess. 105 (17); Coal 55g; Mortar; Plas.
-	93/98/123	No context information		PM 28:476
8.2	94	Rubbish pit/animal burial		
8.2	95	Rubbish pit fill/animal burial		PM 46:501 (120 pt, 142 pt); Coin pm 37; Copper A801; Iron A1013; Roof A1501; Vess. 130 (39); Coal 23g; Plas.
7.8	96	Drainage gully fill		Med. 2:7; PM 70:361 (149); Copper A802; Cp 31 (2); Iron 18, A720, A1230; Vess. 95; An. (11)

Phase	Context	Description	Fig. Nos	Artefacts and environmental remains
7.7	97=91	Hillwash deposit	66	Med. 6:37; PM 45:645 (126 pt, 144); Brick (2); Copper 55, A200, A1009; Cp (1); Tile (10); Vess. 82 pt (16); An. (63); Coal 48g
7.7	98	Surface deposit		Med. 8:283; PM 19:246 (131 pt); Bone 23; Brick (1); Copper A523, A803; Iron A1345; Sst. A270, A271; Tile (2); Vess. (7); An. (96)
7.7	99	Surface deposit	51	Med. 2:63; PM 16:237; Sst. A272; Tile (4); Vess. 167; An. (2)
7.1	100	Make-up deposit		Med. 9:21; PM 4:37; Brick (1); Copper A231; Coin pm 14; Tile (4); An. (21)
7.1	101=118	Wall footings		Med. 1:15; PM 2:18 (120 pt); Quern 30; Tile (1); An. (1)
8.1	102	Robber trench		Med. 2:12
7.1	103	Surface deposit	63	
7.8	104	Silt deposit	67	Med. 5:26; PM 3:6; Copper A524
7.1	105	Wall footings		
7.7	106	Silt deposit		PM 1:29
7.2	107	Post setting		
8.1	108	Demolition debris		
7.2	109	Hearth	64	Brick (1); Mortar
7.8	110	Surface deposit	67	Med. 5:51; PM 1:10; Brick (2); Iron A552; Tile 92); Vess. (1); Char. ≤1g; Cin. 3g
8.1	111	Demolition debris		Med. 3:24; PM 80:282 (154 pt, 158); Bone 70; Coin pm 10, 23; Copper 13, 37, 78, 113, A201-214, A280, A525-535, A733-736, A1010, A1041; Cp (15); Glass A212; Iron 46, 51, 110, A614, A721, A926, A927, A1231; Stone A69-72; Tile (8); Vess. 106 (43); Wood A79, A80; An. (681); Char. ≤1g; Cin. 130g; Coal 75g; Fish; Mortar
7.1	112	Partition base	63	Med. 1:3; PM 1:3; Roof. A835; An. (3)
8.1	113	Demolition debris		Rom. 1:2; Med. 22:270; PM 64:194 (159, 166 pt); Bone 14, 66; Coin pm 34-36; Copper 56, 107, A215, A216, A536-563, A804, A1043; Cp (5); Iron A213, A857, A928, A1014; Lst. A643; Roof. A836-842; Tile (41); Vess. 74, 96, 107 (12); An. (1); BS; Cin. 9g; Coal 86g; Fish; Mortar
7.2	114	Floor deposit	63, 64	Lst. 39
8.1	115=185	Demolition debris		
7.2	116	Hearth setting		
7.2	117	Hearth	64, 67	Med. 7:18; PM 27:614 (121 pt); Bone 67; Copper A564; Cp (4); Iron A329-333, A344-348, A483, A1232, A1233, A1346, A1347; Roof. A1502, A1534; Tile (2); An. (10); Cin. 6g; Coal 1g; Mortar
7.1	118=101	Wall footing	63, 64	Med. 5:18; PM 7:84; Copper A805; Tile (1); An. (133)
7.2	119	Wall footing	64	
7.2	120=159	Wall bonding	64	Med. 1:9; Tile (2); An. (5); Coal 4g
7.1	121=71	Threshold kerb	63	Med. 1:6; PM 2:2; Brick (3); Cp (2); Coal ≤1g
7.4	122	Wall	64	
7.4	123	Construction debris		Med. 3:7; PM 14:153 (130, 131 pt, 132); Copper A806-809; Cp (1); Tile (1); Vess. 131 (13); An. (9); Coal 32g
7.5	124	Surface accumulation		Med. 11:170; PM 243:1822 (125 pt, 139 pt, 141 pt); Bone 24, 30; Brick (9); Copper A232, A565, A566, A810, A811, A911, A968, A1042; Cp (5); Iron A207, A421, A514, A1143, A1144; Roof. A843, A844; Sst. A273, A274; Tile (9); Vess. 50, 132, 133; An. (47); BS; Burnt (1); Cin. 1g; Coal 34g
7.1	125	Make-up deposit	63	Med. 19:80; PM 7:160 (126 pt); Brick (5); Copper A567-570; Iron A167, A1118; Roof. A845; Tile (37); An. (10); Burnt (3); Cin. 2g; Coal 19g
7.1	126	Threshold deposit/step	63	Brick (2); Vess. 67; An. (1)
7.1	127=195	Make-up deposit/bedding for flag stones		Copper 102
7.1	128	Ash pit	63	
7.1	129	Hearth deposit	63	Brick (2); Tile (3); Burnt (1)
7.2	130	Surface deposit/flooring	64	Brick (1)
7.2	131	Surface deposit		PM 2:51 (122 pt); Lst. A644
7.2	132	Structure slot	64	
7.2	133	Make-up deposit	64, 67	Med. 3:10; PM 2:88; Copper A969; Tile (2); Vess. (2); An. (7); Coal 62g; Fish; Plas.
7.2	134	Wall footing	64, 67	PM 7:168; Iron A858; Sst. A275; Vess. (1); An. (10); Cin. 23g; Coal 2g; Plas.
7.2	135	Wall	64, 67	Med. 2:9
7.1	136	Wall	63, 64	Tile (2); Vess. 97; An. (1); Coal 8g; Mortar
7.1	137	Hearth deposit	63	PM 1:39; Brick (8); Copper A571; Roof. A846
5.2	138	Cobbled surface	58, 59	Med. 7:92; PM 4:12; Copper A812; Iron A859, A1105; Vess. (17); An. (3); BS
8.1	139	Pit/scoop fill		PM 2:30; Sst. A276; An. (3); Coal 4g
8.1	140	Pit/scoop		
8.1	141	Surface deposit	51	Med. 2:28; PM 94:977 (167 pt); Copper A572-574, A813-815; Cp (7); Iron A1167; Vess. 108, 134, 135 (27); An. (39); Coal 23g
8.1	142	Demolition debris		

Phase	Context	Description	Fig. Nos	Artefacts and environmental remains
8.1	143	Demolition debris		PM 2:4; An. (2); Coal 10g; Mortar
7.1	144	? Wall footing		
7.1	145	Hearth		Char. ≤1g; Mortar
7.1	146	Hearth fill	63	BS; Coal 3g; Mortar
7.1	147	Depression		
7.1	148	Hearth fill	63	BS
8.1	149	Demolition debris		PM 7:19; Copper A217, A233; Iron A1462; An. (5); Coal 36g
8.1	150	Rubbish pit fill		Med. 2:14; PM 210:1718 (161-165, 167 pt); Copper A575, A816; Cp (3); Iron A385; Vess. 63, 113, 136-138 (46)
7.1	151	Hearth	63	Wood A81; An. (86)
7.1	152	Hearth	63	
7.1	153	Hearth fill	63	An. (105); Cin. 14g
8.1	154	Rubbish pit		Med. 1:8
8.1	155	Demolition debris		PM 10:81; Copper A817; Iron A562, A860; Roof. A847; Tile (2)
7.1	156	Post-pit	63	
7.1	157	Post-pit fill		PM 12:37; Cp (1); Vess. 51, 53, 57 (2); An. (1); BS; Slag 2g
7.7	158	Rubbish pit fill		Rom. 2:8; Med. 1:1; PM 14:95; Iron 113; Sst. A277; Tile (10); Vess. 139 (28); An. (5); BS; Burnt (1); Char. 3g; Coal 20g
7.1	159=120	Wall footing	63	Med. 1:2; An. (1)
7.2	160	Wall footing		
7.2	161	Wall footing		
8.1	162	Demolition debris		Med. 1:4; PM 26:67 (166 pt); Bone 69; Brick (1); Coin pm 54; Copper 51, A218-220, A281, A576-585, A818; Cp (4); Iron A303, A563, A861; Vess. 77 (2); BS; Cin. 4g; Coal 21g
8.1	163	Post-hole		An. (27)
8.1	164	Post-hole fill		PM 14:439 (117 pt); Iron A653, A722; An. (3)
7.7	165	Rubbish pit		
7.5	166	Floor bedding	64	Vess. (3)
7.6	167	Surface/path		Med. 6:34; PM 11:98 (142 pt); Vess. (4); Wood A82; An. (10)
7.5	168	Surface/yard	64	PM 23:283; Brick (1); Cp (1); Tile (1); Vess. (16)
7.5	169	Fill of 284/wall footing		Med. 1:13; Copper 53; Roof. A848; An. (1); Plas.
7.6	170	Conduit trench fill		Med. 9:82; PM 21:325; Copper A819; Iron 17, A929, A1106; Tile (4); Vess. 140 (28); Wood A83; An. (12); Mortar
7.2	171	Floor bedding	64,	Med. 1:4; PM 2:3; Tile (1); An. (7); Cin. 1g; Coal 58g; Plas.
8.1	172	Demolition debris		
7.5	173	Surface		PM 16:291; Copper A586, A820, A821; Vess. (14); An. (4); Coal 7g
7.5	174	Surface		PM 2:17
7.6	175	? Stake-hole		Vess. 58
7.6	176	Stake-hole fill		
7.6	177	Stony deposit		Stone A73
7.1	178	Rubble deposit/post packing		
7.1	179	Post-hole		
7.1	180	Post-hole fill		PM 2:24; Copper A822
7.1	181	Post-hole	63	
7.1	182	Post-hole fill	63	PM 4:48; Coin pm 38; Copper 111, A221, A222, A587, A588; Cp (1); Iron A304; An. (5)
7.5	183=?22=		64	
	214=?261	Wall footing	64	PM 3:124; Stone A51
7.6	184	Conduit fill	51	Med. 19:132; PM 37:565; Brick (1); Iron A287; Tile (3); Vess. 64, 141, (4); An. (26); Cin. 18g; Coal 84g; Fish
8.1	185=115	Demolition debris		PM 4:29; An. (1); Cin. 4g; Coal 22g
7.6	186	Demolition debris		PM 7:34; Vess. (8); An. (1); Cin. 4g; Coal 60g
7.1	187	Post-hole	63	
7.1	188	Post-hole fill		Copper A589; Tile (1); Coal 15g
7.5	189	Stake-hole		
7.5	190	Stake-hole fill		
7.7	191	Surface		PM 11:203; Coin pm 28; Vess. (2); An. (19); Coal 41g
7.5	192	Floor bedding	64	PM 22:443; Cp (2); Iron A174, A386, A578; An. (41); Cin. 1g; Coal 4g
7.5	193	Stake-hole		
7.5	194	Stake-hole fill		
7.1	195=127	Floor bedding		PM 1:67
7.7	196	Loam, flint & sandstone deposit		PM 4:136
7.7	197	Demolition debris	66	PM 1:3; An. (2)
7.1	198	Joist supports	63	Brick (2); Sst. A278
7.1	199	Wall footing	63	Med. 1:8; PM 1:9
7.1	200	Floor bedding	63	Med. 2:18; PM 2:2 (118 pt); Bone 26; Copper A590, A693, A1044; Iron A1015; Tile (9); An. (3)
7.5	201	Surface		PM 36:328; Copper A823; Vess. (3); An. (2)
7.5	202	Hillwash	64	Rom. 1:21; Med. 59:548; PM 2715:12300 (108-114 pt, 116 pt, 123, 126 pt, 128 pt, 133-138, 139 pt, 140, 141 pt); Brick (1); Coin pm 7; Copper 14, 72, 91, 96, A234, A591-594, A824, A983, A984; Cp 14, 24

Phase	Context	Description	Fig. Nos	Artefacts and environmental remains
				(14); Glass A187; Iron 36, 38, 88, A175, A219, A515, A862-865, A930-933, A1145, A1234, A1348-1352; Lst. A645, A724; Mem. A168; Roof. A849; Sst. A279-283; Stone 17; Tile (12); Vess. 62, 84, 109-112, 142-144 (104); An. (157); BS; Burnt (1); Cin. 193g; Coal 188g; Fish; Mortar; Slag 136g
-	202/247	No context information		PM 14:121
7.1	203	Fill of rubbish pit 207		Rom. 1:2; Med. 4:16 (3); PM 1:43; Tile (1); Vess. (3); An. (6); Coal 29g; Plas.
5.2	204	Hearth/dump	59	
7.1	205	Wall footing	63	Med. 1:3; PM 3:7; Iron 74; An. (2); Char. ≤1g; Coal 39g
7.1	206=?244	Stone slab, coal, brick and burnt dump		
7.1	207	? Fill/?cut		
5.2	208	Compact clay deposit	58, 59	Rom. 18:194 (6)
5.2	209	Clay surface	50	Med. 3:6; PM 5:52; Coin med. 10; Tile (1); Vess. (2); An. (6)
7.1	210=?224	Wall footing	63	Med. 1:29; PM 5:239; Tile (10)
7.1	211	Make-up for threshold		PM 7:25; Iron A169; Mem. 33 (pt); An. (1); Coal 4g
7.2	212	Make up deposit		Med. 22:106; PM 5:52; Copper A595; Iron A208; Vess. (1); An. (8); BS; Coal 42g; Plas.
7.2	213=258	Wall	64, 67	Roof. A850; Sst. A284, A285; An. (1); Coal 9g
7.5	214=?22= ?183=?261	Wall footings		
5.2	215=?216	Cobbled surface	58, 59	Med. 1:132; Brick (1); Tile (4)
5.2	216=?215	Cobbled surface	58, 59	Med. 5:57; PM 1:85; Brick (1); Roof. A851; Sst. A286-288; Tile (32); An. (2); Fish
5.2	217	Surface	58, 59	
5.2	218	Surface	58, 59	
5.2	219	Surface	58, 59	
5.2	220	Cobbled surface	58, 59	Med. 2:163; Tile (3); Wood A84; An. (1)
5.2	221	Surface	58, 59, 65	PM 1:1; An. (1); Cin. 3g
5.2	222	Cobbled surface	58, 59	Med. 1:2
5.2	223	Surface	58, 59	
7.1	224=?210	Wall footing	63	Tile (3)
5.2	225	Surface	58, 59	
7.4	226	Surface		Med. 4:27; PM 19:222; Bone 68; Clay 8; Copper A596; Cp (1); Lst. A646; Tile (2); Vess. 60 (pt) (24); Fish
7.4	227	Robber trench fill	65	Copper A253; Sst. A289; Tile (17); An. (5); Burnt (7)
6.2	228	Construction cut	65	
7.4	229	Demolition debris		
7.4	230	Burnt clay & cobble deposit		PM 7:27; Vess. (3); Cin. 3g
7.4	231	Surface		PM 61:277; Brick (5); Iron A170; Vess. 145 (112); Burnt (1); Cin. 52g; Coal 21g
6.2	232	Construction cut fill		
7.6	233	Demolition debris		Copper 15; Vess. (2)
7.1	234	Wall footing	63, 64, 67	PM 3:10; Copper A825; Roof. A852; Sst. A290; BS; Coal 7g; Mortar
7.6	235	Construction trench	51, 64, 65	
7.1	236	Slot	63	
7.1	237	Clay & chalk deposit		Med. 1:1; PM 2:3; Copper A597; Tile (4); An. (3)
7.1	238	Stone slab surface		
7.1	239	Post-hole	63	
7.4	240	Pit for animal burial	64	Med. 1:20; An. (1)
6.3	241	Demolition debris		Med. 5:77; PM 35:907 (119 pt); Copper A1045; Cp (1); Iron A220, A1235; Tile (1); Vess. (4); Wood A85; An. (70); Cin. 3g; Coal 150g; Fish; Slag 2g
-	242	Pit		
6.3	243	Demolition debris		Med. 6:39; PM 1:49; Bone 25; Copper A826; Tile (2); An. (1); Cin. 1g
7.1	244=?206	Pad-stone		Rom. 1:31 (7); PM 1:62;
6.3	245	Demolition debris		Pre. 1:2; Med. 4:99; PM 21:237; Brick (1); Copper A598, A912, A1034; Cp (2); Roof. A853; Tile (1); Vess. 79
7.1	246	Post-hole fill		
7.4	247	Pit fill with animal burial		Med. 5:28; PM 81:518 (113 pt, 114 pt, 127, 128 pt); Bone 27; Copper 59; Cp (2); Iron A176, A221, A272, A865; Vess. (6); An. (10)
7.6	248	Repair deposit		Iron A1353
6.3	249	Demolition debris		PM 4:67; Brick (1); Copper A1011; Stone 32
7.5	250	Construction material		PM 1:2; Brick (1); Cp (1)
7.4	251	Skeleton (animal)	50, 64	
7.1	252	Wall footing	63	Med. 1:61; PM 7:66; Brick (2); Copper A970; Cp (1); Roof. A1503; An. (5)
5.3	253	Wall footing/ bonding		
5.2	254	Wall	50, 58, 59	Med. 1:2; Lst. A647, A648; Mem. 37; Sst. A291; Stone 24; Tile (4); Vess. 47; An. (10); Fish; Mortar; Slag 1g

Phase	Context	Description	Fig. Nos	Artefacts and environmental remains
7.1	255	Wall footing	63	Med. 1:1; Brick (2); Tile (3); Wood A86; An. (2); Coal ≤1g
5.3	256	Wall footing/bonding		Wood A87; An. (1); Burnt (2); Char. 2g
7.1	257	Post burnt *in situ*		Burnt (2); Char. 4g; Plas.
7.1	258=213	Wall	63	Rom. 1:7
5.2	259=?361	Surface	58, 59	PM 2:87
6.3	260	Demolition debris		Med. 1:3; PM 15:380; Copper A827, A828; Iron 22, 98; Stone A52; Tile (1); An. (2); BS; Char. ≤1g; Fish
	260?			PM 1:88
7.5	261=?22=?183=?214	Wall foundation		
8.1	262	Post-hole		
8.1	263	Post-hole fill		Burnt (1); Char. 3g
6.3	264	Demolition debris		Med. 2:26; PM 24:554; Brick (2); Iron A615, A667, A723, A866, A867; Roof. A854, A855; Tile (1); Vess. 83; An. (7); Coal 45g; Fish
7.1	265	Wall footing	63	PM 2:15
6.3	266	Demolition debris		Med. 8:74; PM 48:2198 (118 pt, 119 pt); Copper A235, A971; An. (6); Fish
-	266/242	No context information		PM 5:17
5.2	267	Dump from hearth	58, 59	
7.5	268	Post-hole fill		PM 2:6; Cin. 13g
7.4	269	Surface		Med. 4:72; PM 33:609; Brick (3); Iron 10, A484; Tile (4); Vess. 56 (21); Coal 52g; Fish
7.3	270	Post-hole fill/post-pad		PM 2:16; Brick (10); Iron A209; Sst. A292; Vess. (2); An. (2); Coal 36g
5.2	271	Dump of burnt material	58, 59	Rom. 1:7; Med. 8:99; PM 6:54; Copper A599; Tile (18); An. (7); Cin. 2g; Coal 7g
7.4	272	Surface		Med. 3:12; PM 3:18; Copper A600; Iron A1163, A1354; Vess. (1)
7.1	273	Wall bonding	63	Med. 1:2; Sst. A293
7.1	274	Wall footing/bonding		
7.6	275	Conduit stone channel	51, 64	
7.3	276	Post-pipe		
7.3	277	Post-hole		Brick (1)
7.3	278	Post-hole fill		
7.3	279	Post-hole		
6.3	280=410	Surface	51	Vess. (1)
7.3	281	Post-hole fill		PM 2:31; Cin. 2g
7.5	282	Post-hole		
7.5	283	Hearth		
7.4	284	Post-pad		
7.3	285	Post-pad		
7.4	286	Post hole fill		PM 1:13 (129)
7.4	287	Post-hole		
7.4	288	Pit fill with animal burial		PM 128:1528 (119 pt); Copper A236, A601, A829, A830; Cp (2); Iron A1016, A1355; Tile (1); Vess. 98 (4); An. (27); Cin. 6g; Coal 31g
7.4	289	Pit with animal burial	64	
7.4	290	Wall	64	PM 1:1; An. (1); Coal ≤1g
7.4	291	Wall footing	64	PM 1:6
6.1	292	Surface		PM 2:7; Iron 105
7.1	293	Wall footing		
7.1	294	Wall footing		Copper A831
6.3	295	Demolition debris		
6.3	296	Post-hole		
6.3	297	Post-hole fill		Iron A735
6.3	298	Demolition debris		Cp (1); Burnt (16)
5.2	299	Surface/finds only	59	Rom. 1:7; PM 1:18
u/s	300	u/s 1983		Rom. 1:36 (8); Mem. 3:22; PM 26:898; Copper 103; Iron A1356; Mem. A169; Tile (2); Coal 1g; Plas.
7.4	301	Gully	63, 64	
7.2	302	Plaster face deposit	64, 67	
7.4	303	Skeleton (animal)	64	An. (162); Fish
7.1	304	Construction trench		
7.1	305	Wall	63	Med. 1:1; Stone A53; An. (1)
7.1	306	Surface		
7.3	307	Hillwash		
7.3	308	Surface		Med. 4:27; PM 14:132 (123 pt); Copper 101; Cp (1); Iron A1357; Tile (1); Mortar
7.3	309	Post-hole fill		
6.1	310	Clay & rubble dump		Rom. 1:4; Brick (28); Copper 11; Sst. A294; Tile (2); Vess. (2); An. (2); Coal 99g
7.3	311	Animal disturbance		Copper A602; Char. ≤1g
7.3	312	Surface		PM 2:10; Copper A740; Char. 1g; Coal 6g
6.1	313	Surface	60	Copper A603, A604

Phase	Context	Description	Fig. Nos	Artefacts and environmental remains
7.3	314	Surface		Med. 2:4; PM 4:31; Brick (2); Copper A605, A1046; Iron A214; Vess. (10); Cin. 5g; Coal 11g
7.4	315	Surface		PM 6:12; Brick (2); Tile (1); Vess. (20); Burnt (5); Cin. 1g; Coal 17g
7.4	316	Pit fill/dump		PM 3:18; Tile (1); Vess. 146, 153, 154 (154); Char. 2g; Cin. 1g; Coal 5g
6.1	317	Surface	60	
7.4	318	Rubbish pit		Quern A125; Tile (3); Burnt (1)
7.4	319	Rubbish pit fill		
6.3	320	Surface		Med. 14:240; PM 3:30; Iron 20; Roof. A856-861; Tile (62); An. (13)
6.3	321	Pit for animal burial		
5.3	322	Hillwash	50, 51	Med. 22:165; PM 5:9; Tile (4); An. (11)
6.1	323	Make-up deposit	60	Med. 1:2; PM 21:477; Brick (2); Copper A606-608, A832-834; Cp (1); Iron 41, 106, A422, A724, A1049, A1358; Tile (1); Vess. 147 (16); An. (8); Coal 27g
-	323/350	No context information		PM 1:2
5.2	324	Post-hole	58, 59	
5.2	325	Post-hole fill		
6.3	326	Pit fill with animal burial		PM 1:14; An. (6); Burnt (1)
5.2	327	Surface	58, 59	
6.3	328	Skeleton (animal)		An. (123)
5.2	329	Stake-hole	58, 59	
5.2	330	Stake-hole	58, 59	
7.1	331	Construction trench		
7.1	332	Construction trench fill		
7.1	333	Construction trench		
5.3	334	Wall footing/deposit		Med. 2:12; An. (1); Burnt (3); Char. 4g; Cin. 1g
7.1	335	Surface		PM 1:1; An. (3); Coal 15g; Fish
7.2	336	Plaster face deposit		Plas.
7.3	337	Post-hole		
7.4	338	Dump deposit		Rom. 1:4
6.1	339	Surface	60	
6.2	340	Wall	60, 61	Sst. A295
6.3	341	Demolition debris	51	Med. 3:24; PM 1:1; Copper A609, A835, A836; Iron A1017; An. (3)
	341?			PM 1:4
5.3	342	Clay & chalk deposit	50, 51	Med. 21:119; PM 5:70; Iron A1107, A1119, A1120, A1359, A1360; Tile (1); An. (107); Fish
6.1	343	Surface		PM 2:8; Lst. A649; Sst. A296-308; Burnt (3); Cin. 4g; Coal ≤1g; Plas.
6.1	344	Post-hole		
6.1	345	Post-hole fill		
6.1	346	Post-hole		
6.1	347	Post-hole fill		
7.1	348	Post-hole fill		
7.1	349	Post-hole	63	
7.4	350	Surface	50	Med. 4:29; PM 38:536 (115 pt); Roof. A862; Sst. A309; Vess. (5); An. (5); Burnt (2); Cin. 11g; Coal ≤1g; Fish
7.4	351	Surface	64	Med. 6:43; PM 8:53; Vess. 99 (4)
7.1	352	Slot	63	Med. 1:3
6.3	353	Clay & stone deposit		Plas.
6.1	354	Post-hole fill		Char. 1g
7.5	355	Make-up deposit	63	PM 13:52; Copper A837; An. (1); Coal 12g
7.1	356	Construction trench		
7.3	357	Robber trench fill		Med. 3:32 (58); PM 152:2394; Copper A610, A878, A971; Iron 12, 13, A868, A1361, A1362; Mem. 35, A170; Roof. A863; Sst. A310, A311; Tile (1); Vess. (9); An. (54); BS; Char. ≤1g; Coal 3g; Fish; Slag 54g
7.1	358	Post-hole		Brick (1)
7.1	359	Post-hole	63	
6.3	360	Demolition debris	51	Med. 1:42; Copper A611; Iron A869, A934, A1363; Tile (2); Burnt (2)
5.2	361=?259	No context information	361	PM 1:1; Copper A913; Iron A1146; Tile (1)
6.1	362	Timber post		Wood A88
6.1	363	Post-hole		
7.3	364	Post-hole fill		Med. 1:2; PM 1:2; Vess. (3); An. (1); Coal 4g
7.3	365	Post-hole		
6.1	366	Post-hole		
6.3	367	Demolition debris	51	Rom. 1:2; Med. 8:43; PM 4:30; Copper A237; Roof. A1504; Sst. A312; Stone A183; Tile (1); An. (4); Burnt (6); Coal 2g; Plas.
6.3	368	Clay loam deposit		
6.3	369	Demolition debris	51	Med. 29:355; PM 44:704; Bone 28; Coin med. 33; Copper A238-240, A838-841; Iron A423, A870, A871, A935, A1236; Roof. A864; Tile (3); Wood A89; An. (11); Burnt (1); Coal 3g
-	369/393	No context information		Iron 114; Sst. A313
7.3	370	Robber trench		
5.3	371	Wall footing		Med. 1:2 (31 pt); PM 1:4; Roof. A865; Sst. A314; Tile (5)

Phase	Context	Description	Fig. Nos	Artefacts and environmental remains
6.1	372	Silt deposit		PM 1:2; An. (1); Cin. 9g; Coal 16g
6.1	373	Silt deposit		
6.1	374	Surface	60	Coin pm 46; Iron A957
6.1	375	Surface	60	Copper A612
6.1	376	Make-up deposit		Tile (1); An. (1)
6.1	377	Rubble filled feature	60	Med. 3:3; Cin. 2g; Coal ≤1g
6.1	378	Post-hole fill	60	
6.1	379	Hillwash		
6.1	380	Make up deposit		Tile (1)
6.1	381	Surface	60	Brick (1)
7.3	382	Make-up deposit		
6.1	383	Sandy mortar deposit	60	
7.4	384	Animal disturbance		
4.1	385	Surface	56	An. (2)
4.1	386	Surface	56	PM 1:13; Tile (2); An. (5)
6.1	387	Post-hole		
6.1	388	Post-pad		
6.1	389	Make-up deposit	60,	Med. 6:33; PM 49:822; Bone 7, 8; Brick (46); Copper A613-620; Iron A177, A1364-1366; Quern A126; Sst. A315-318; Tile (1); Vess. (7); An. (14); Char. 20g; Fish
6.3	390	Structure J backfill		Med. 71:294; PM 156:288; Brick (2); Copper A621, A842; Tile (3); Vess. 100; An. (17); Coal 19g; Fish; Mortar; Slag 9g
6.3	391	Structure J backfill		Med. 6:17; PM 1:1; Brick (9); Tile (1); An. (2); Coal 20g; Plas.
u/s	392	u/s 1984		Rom. 1:15; Med. 6:160; PM 5:83; Brick (2); Copper A622; Roof. A866; Sst. A319, A320; Tile (7); Vess. (2); Char. ≤1g; Coal 6g
5.3	393	Surface		Med. 1:26; PM 2:6; Copper 75, A241, A623; Roof. A867; An. (3)
5.3	394	Wall footing	51, 59	Med. 2:13; Copper 73, 76; Sst. A321; Iron A1367; An. (1)
5.3	395	Wall footing	51, 59	PM 3:364 (76, 77); Copper A1035; Iron 48; An. (1)
5.3	396	Wall footing	51, 59	Med. 8:28; PM 6:22; Copper A843; Iron A872; Roof. A869; An. (15); Cin. 12g; Coal 139g; Fish
5.3	397	Wall footing	59	
6.1	398	Make-up deposit		Roof. A868
5.2	399	Surface		Med. 31:225; PM 6:121; Roof. A870-872; Stone A54; Tile (38); An. (73); Char. 1g; Cin. ≤1g; Fish; Slag 7g
-	399/215	No context information	50	PM 1:5
5.2	400	Stake-hole	50	PM 4:5; An. (2)
3.3	401	Wall	55	Sst. A322, A323
5.2	402	Post-hole		
5.2	403	Post-hole fill		An. (41)
5.2	404	Scoop fill		Bone 2; An. (1)
5.2	405	Scoop		
5.2	406	Post-hole fill		Med. 1:6
5.2	407	Post-hole		
7.4	408	Silt & chalk deposit	51	Med. 14:136; PM 10:111
6.1	409	Surface	51, 60	Med. 22:218; PM 3:77; Roof. A873; Tile (4); An. (5); BS; Char. 1g; Cin. 4g; Plas.
6.3	410=280	Surface	51	Med. 1:5; PM 1:6; Iron A1147
5.3	411	Make-up deposit		Tile (1); An. (3)
6.3	412	Demolition debris		Med. 1:3; PM 1:2; Copper 16, A242, A844; Tile (1); An. (7); Burnt (1); Fish
5.2	413	Surface	58	Med. 4:9; PM 3:42; Copper A254; Iron A1121, A1368; Roof. A874; Tile (1); Wood A90; An. (34); Fish
5.3	414	Surface		PM 1:13; An. (1); Burnt (1); Mortar
5.3	415	Surface		PM 1:1; Copper A243; Iron 11, A485; An. (1); Burnt (1); Char. 3g
3.3	416	Surface		Med. 2:5; Copper A1047; Tile (1); Wood A91; An. (99); Fish; Mortar
5.2	417	Surface		
5.2	418	Demolition debris	59	
5.2	419	Construction debris	50, 58, 59	Med. 1:2; Quern A127; An. (13)
3.3	420	Burnt area	55	
6.3	421	Clay & chalk deposit		
7.4	422	Rubbish pit fill		Med. 1:1; PM 2:18; Brick (1); Cp (1); Lst. A650; Sst. A324; Coal 4g
7.4	423	Rubbish pit		
6.3	424	Surface		Med. 3:10; PM 3:8; Iron A1018; An. (1); Burnt (1); Coal ≤1g
6.1	425	Silt & chalk dump		
5.3	426	Post-hole		
5.3	427	Post-hole fill		An. (4)
5.2	428	Post-hole	58, 59	
5.2	429	Post-hole fill		
5.2	430	Threshold deposit	58, 59	Sst. A325; An. (1)
6.1	431	Surface	60	Med. 12:123; PM 10:118 (78); Copper 54, A624, A625; Iron A1019; Roof. A875, A876; Tile (14); Vess. 59; An. (18); Burnt (1); Cin. 5g; Fish

Phase	Context	Description	Fig. Nos	Artefacts and environmental remains
6.1	432	Clay deposit		
6.1	433	Clay & chalk deposit		Med. 4:11; PM 3:62; An. (1)
6.1	434	Clay & chalk deposit		
7.1	435	Construction trench		
4.1	436	Make-up deposit	56	Med. 1:1
6.3	437	Rubbish pit fill		Med. 1:2; PM 29:304; An. (1)
6.3	438	Rubbish pit		
3.3	439	Post-hole fill		
3.3	440	Post-hole	55	
5.2	441	Surface		
5.3	442	Surface	51, 59	
5.2	443	Surface	51, 58	Med. 2:9; PM 1:29; Brick (1); Clay 10; Copper A1012; An. (4); Fish
6.1	444	Silt & sandstone deposit		Med. 1:14; Stone A74; Tile (2); An. (2); Char. 40g
6.3	445	Pit fill with animal burial		PM 3:5; Brick (1); An. (3)
6.3	446	Skeleton (animal)		An. (98)
6.3	447	Pit for animal burial		
5.2	448	Hearth	58	PM 1:4; Iron 89, A1148; An. (18); Fish; Slag 5g
5.2	449	Surface		
5.3	450	Surface	50, 51	PM 1:1
5.3	451	Surface		Med. 2:10; PM 5:8; Roof. A877; Vess. (1); An. (4); Fish
5.2	452	Make-up deposit	51	Med. 4:26; PM 11:110; Brick (1); Copper 74; Iron 64; Tile (11); An. (23); Char. ≤1g; Coal 15g
5.3	453	Surface		Iron A1108; Cin. 55g
6.3	454	Demolition debris		PM 25:174 (116 pt); Brick (1); Tile (3); Vess. 66 (pt) (1); An. (1); Burnt (3); Cin. 14g; Coal 68g
6.3	455	Structure J backfill		Med. 5:32; PM 1:148; Brick (1); Tile (1); An. (1); Cin.; Coal ≤1g
6.3	456	Structure J backfill		Med. 1:1; PM 2:13; Cp (1); Stone A104; An. (1)
3.3	457	Stake-hole	55	
3.3	458	Deposit		Med. 14:151 (12 pt); Copper A973; Iron A564; An. (31)
3.3	459	Surface/repair	55	Med. 1:6
3.3	460	Stake-hole	55	
6.3	461	Structure J backfill		Med. 2:43; PM 3:18; Brick (1); Copper A626, A627; Iron 107, A461; An. (5)
6.3	462	Structure J backfill		Med. 13:39; PM 35:375 (63 pt, 117 pt); Brick (2); Copper A244, A845, A1048; Cp (2); Iron 81, A369; Mem. A171; Stone A55, A56; Vess. (1); An. (12); Cin. 4g; Coal 3g
3.3	463	Post-hole	55	
3.3	464	Post-hole fill		Tile (3); An. (1); Char. ≤1g
3.3	465	Post-pit	55	
3.3	466	Post-hole fill/hearth deposit		Med. 4:22; An. (1)
3.3	467	Post-pipe	55	Wood A92
3.3	468	Post-hole fill		Med. 2:14; Iron A873; An. (8)
3.3	469	Post-hole	55	
3.3	470	Post-hole fill		
6.3	471	Structure J backfill		Med. 4:38 (61); PM 36:771; Brick (5); Clay 9; Copper A628-630, A846; Glass A219; Lst. A651; Sst. A326-329; Tile (2); Vess. 72 (2); An. (5); Cin. 6g; Coal 11g
3.3	472	Hearth		Med. 2:33; Roof. A878; Cin. 9g
3.3	473	Post-hole		
3.3	474	Post-hole fill		Roof. A879
3.3	475	Post-hole	55	
3.3	476	Post-hole fill		
3.3	477	Post-hole	55	
3.3	478=482	Post-pit fill		Med. 1:6; An. (2)
3.3	479	Levelling deposit	55	
3.3	480	Surface	55	Rom. 1:4; Med. 8:19; An. (20); Char. ≤1g; Slag 123g
6.3	481=520	Structure J backfill		Med. 2:6; PM 21:111; Brick (19); Sst. A330; Vess. (4); Wood A93, A94; An. (4); Cin. 20g; Coal 125g; Fish
3.3	482=478	Post-pit fill		An. (6)
3.3	483	Stake-holes/post-pit	55	
5.2	484	? Pit fill		Rom. 1:5; Med. 1:2; Coal 6g
5.2	485	? Pit	57	
4.3	486	Post-hole/slot fill		Char. 3g; Coal 51g
4.3	487	Post-hole/slot		
5.2	488	Make-up deposit	57	Coal 35g
5.2	489	Clay loam deposit	57, 58	PM 1:3
3.3	490	Burnt area	55	
3.3	491	Surface repair deposit		Med. 1:2; Tile (3); An. (1)
5.2	492	Surface		An. (1)
3.3	493	Post-hole	55	

Phase	Context	Description	Fig. Nos	Artefacts and environmental remains
3.3	494	Post-hole fill		Tile (3)
3.3	495	Post-hole fill		An. (2)
6.3	496	Rubbish pit fill		Copper A631-633
6.3	497	Rubbish pit		
5.2	498	Surface		
4.3	499	Slot fill		An. (1); Char. 11g
4.3	500	Slot fill	50	An. (3); Burnt (1); Char. 5g
4.3	501	Slot fill		Burnt (2)
4.3	502	Loam deposit	57	
5.2	503	Surface		
4.3	504	Slot fill		Coal 10g
4.3	505	Slot fill		
4.3	506	Decayed timber deposit	57	
4.3	507	Slot	57	An. (1)
4.3	508	Slot	57	
4.3	509	Slot	57	
3.3	510	Post-hole	55	
5.2	511	Stake-hole		Brick (2)
5.2	512	Stake-hole		
5.2	513	Stake-hole		
5.2	514	Stake-hole		PM 4:40 (75 pt)
3.3	515	Scoop	55	
6.3	516	Structure J backfill		Med. 31:375 (51); PM 1053:17288 (75 pt, 79-107, 108-117 pt); Bone 29; Brick (165); Clay 11, 12; Coin med. 34; Copper 57, 77, 97, 105, A245, A246, A634-650, A847-852, A879, A974, A1054, A1055; Cp 22, 23 (7); Iron 52-54, 96, A178, A222, A301, A302, A438, A486, A487, A725, A874-876, A936, A937, A958, A1020-1022, A1122, A1149, A1150, A1370-1380; Mem. A172; Nail 64:1; Quern A128; Roof. A880-888; Sst. A331-346; Stone A57; Tile (26); Vess. 49, 55, 66, 70, 114, 148-152, 158-160 (123); Wood A121; An. (134); BS; Burnt (9); Cin. 67g; Coal 354g; Fish; Mortar; Plas.
5.2	517	Clay & chalk deposit	58	PM 2:12
6.2	518	Construction cut	60	
6.3	519	Clay & chalk deposit		PM 2:46; Tile (4); Vess. 69; An. (1); Char. ≤1g; Cin. 1g; Coal 19g
6.3	520=?481	Structure J backfill		Med. 5:14; PM 108:1311; Brick (9); Copper A651-662, A975, A1050, A1052; Iron A1050, A1164, A1381, A1382; Tile (2); Vess. 60 (pt) (2); An. (20); BS; Burnt (2); Cin. 33g; Coal 123g; Fish
5.2	521	Clay & coal deposits	58	Med. 1:10; PM 3:16; An. (1); Coal 29g
3.3	522	Fill of scoop 515		Med. 16:81; Stone A58; An. (12)
3.3	523	Scoop		
3.3	524	Fill of scoop 523		Med. 41:198; Glass A215; Roof. A889, A890; Sst. A347; Tile (5); Vess. (3); An. (22); Char. 2g; Fish; Slag 78g
3.3	525	Scoop fill		An. (2)
3.3	526	Scoop		
3.3	527	Fill of scoop 526		Rom. 1:5; Med. 3:37; Roof. A891; Tile (1); An. (7); Fish
4.1	528	Surface	51, 56	Med. 1:6; PM 2:25
4.1	529	Wall footing	51, 56	Tile (3)
4.1	530	Wall footing	56	Tile (1)
4.3	531	Slot	57	
4.3	532	Slot	57	
4.3	533=1049	Clay & pebble deposit	51	
5.2	534	Surface	51	Roof. A892; An. (2); Coal 2g
4.3	535	Post-hole fill		
4.3	536	Post-hole	57	
4.3	537	Slot fill		Tile (2); An. (2)
4.3	538	Slot fill		Coal 51g
4.3	539	Slot fill		Char. 1g; Coal 19g
-	540	No description		
3.3	541	Scoop fill		
3.3	542	Scoop		Med. 5:16; An. (2); Fish
3.3	543	Post-hole void		
3.3	544	Post-hole void		
3.3	545	? Rubble dump	55	
u/s	546	u/s 1985		Med. 11:100 (25); PM 16:359; Brick (5); Iron A1109; Tile (3); Coal 11g; Plas.
-	547	Finds only 650/643 etc.		Brick (1)
3.3	548	Clay dump		
3.3	549	Fill of 522		Med. 1:2; Roof. A893; An. (1); Slag -g
3.3	550	Post-hole fill	50	An. (2); Fish
3.3	551	Post-hole		
3.3	552	Scoop		

Phase	Context	Description	Fig. Nos	Artefacts and environmental remains
3.3	553	Post-hole fill		An. (1)
3.3	554	Post-hole		
-	555	Redeposited fill 1984		Med. 1:3; PM 1:2
-	556	?		
3.3	557	Surface	50, 55	Rom. 1:3; Med. 91:705 (31 pt); PM 1:22; Copper A1014, A1053; Quern A129, A130; Roof. A894; Tile (20); Wood A95; An. (44); Burnt (2); Char. 1g; Cin. 3g; Coal 2g; Fish; Slag 68g
3.3	558	Surface	55	Med. 2:6; An. (2)
3.3	559	Fill of 552		Med. 7:14; An. (4)
3.2	560	Surface		Med. 11:48; Sst. A348, A349; Tile (1); An. (11)
4.3	561	Post-hole fill		
5.2	562	Surface	51, 57	
4.3	563	Burnt area		
5.2	564	Stake-hole	57	Char. ≤1g
5.2	565	Surface		
6.3	566	Dump		
4.3	567	Slot	57	
4.3	568	Slot	57	
4.3	569	Slot	57	
5.2	570	Surface	51	Med. 4:9; Roof. A895; An. (5); Coal 36g
4.3	571	Dump/pad-stone	57	An. (6)
4.3	572	Scoop fill		
3.3	573	Post-hole fill		
3.1	574	Burnt area	54	Med. 12:83; An. (1); Char. ≤1g
3.2	575	Clay & chalk deposit	50	Med. 2:15; An. (5)
3.1	576	Rubbish pit fill		Med. 11:40; Glass 169; An. (13)
3.1	577	Rubbish pit fill		Med. 1:3; An. (9); Fish
3.2	578	Make-up deposit		Rom. 1:2; Med. 27:161; Iron A654; Lst. A652; Quern A130; Stone A59; An. (19); Slag 7g
3.1	579	Pit	54	Med. 2:15
4.1	580	Chalk dump		Coal 9g
4.1	581	Post-hole fill		
4.1	582	Post-hole fill		
4.3	583	Post-hole	57	
4.1	584	Post-pipe	56	
4.1	585	Post-hole	56	
4.1	586	Post-hole fill	51, 54,	
4.1	587	Burnt area	51, 56	
4.1	588	Post-hole fill	51	Copper 89, A247, A663; Iron A877, A938; Tile (1); An. (1); Coal 2g; Fish
4.3	589	Pit	57	Med. 18:96; PM 6:280; Brick (5); An. (11)
5.3	590	Wall footing	51, 59	
6.3	591	Clay & chalk deposit		PM 1:11; Burnt (1)
4.3	592	Post packing	57	Sst. A350
2.4	593	Post-pit	53	
2.4	594	Post-pit fill	65	Rom. 1:3; Med. 2:13 (1); An. (8); Fish
2.4	595	Post setting		
2.4	596	Post-hole fill		
3.1	597	Clay & chalk deposit	54	An. (4)
3.1	598	Surface/hillwash	50, 54, 65	Rom. 2:20; Med. 95:203; Brick (1); Copper A1013, A1049; Roof A896; Stone 10, 19; Tile (3); An. (194); Burnt (1); Fish
3.1	599	Wall footing	54	Med. 24:134
4.3	600	Clay & chalk deposit	50	Med. 2:38; Copper 25; Tile (2); An. (16); Slag 10g
4.1	601	Burnt area	56	
4.1	602	Post-pit	51, 56	
4.1	603	Clay & chalk deposit	56	Med. 3:44; Iron 34, A223; Lst. A853; Quern A132; Roof. A897; An. (15); Fish
2.2	604	Post-hole		
2.2	605	Post-hole fill		An. (6)
2.2	606	Stake-hole		
4.1	607	Burnt area		
4.1	608	Burnt area	56	
2.4	609	Post-hole fill		
4.1	610	Clay & chalk deposit		
2.4	611	Post-hole		
6.3	612	Structure J backfill		Med. 2:22; PM 64:952; Brick (8); Copper A664; Roof. A898, A899; Sst. A351; Stone A60; Tile (2); Vess. 65, 73, 155-157; (128); An. (8); Coal 27g; Plas.
6.3	613	Surface		
6.3	614	Lens		Copper A665; Vess. (3)
3.3	615	Sandstone dump	55	

Phase	Context	Description	Fig. Nos	Artefacts and environmental remains
4.3	616	Make-up deposit	51, 57	Rom. 1:33; Med. 8:77; Brick (1); Copper A1015; Tile (8); An. (8); Coal 17g
2.4	617	Post-hole		
2.4	618	Post-hole fill		
2.4	619	Post-hole		
2.4	620	Post-hole fill		
	621	Unused context		
6.2	622	Wall	60, 62	Tile (2)
6.2	623	Wall	60, 61	
6.2	624	Wall	60, 61	
6.2	625	Make-up deposit	60	Med. 1:3; PM 6:70; Brick (1); Copper A853; Cp (1); Iron A959; Vess. (20); An. (1); Cin. 2g
4.1	626	Wall footing	56	
6.2	627	Drain	60	
2.3	628	Gully fill		Rom. 1:4; Med. 2:4; Quern A133; An. (23); Char. 1g
2.3	629	Gully	50, 53	
3.3	630	Post setting		Roof. A900; Stone A61
3.3	631	Surface	51, 55	An. (4)
3.3	632	Post-hole fill		
3.3	633	Post-hole	55	
3.3	634	Post setting	55	
3.3	635	Depression	55	
2.1	636	Surface	49, 50, 51	An. (2)
2.2	637	Surface	52	Rom. 2:36; Med. 1:6; Copper A248; Glass A188; Tile (1); An. (64); Char. ≤1g
2.3	638	Surface	50, 53	Rom. 2:18; Med. 4:16; Copper A985; Stone A62, A63; An. (31); Mortar
2.3	639	Post-hole fill		
2.3	640	Post-hole	50, 53	
3.3	641	Post-hole fill		Roof. A901-903; Sst. A352; Tile (2); Vess. 48; An. (2)
4.1	642	Surface	56	Tile (2)
2.3	643	Rubbish pit fill		Med. 54:450 (12 pt); An. (17); Burnt (1); Fish
2.3	644	Rubbish pit	53	An. (1); Burnt (2)
2.3	645	Scoop fill		Med. 1:6
2.3	646	Scoop	53	
2.3	647	Scoop fill		An. (1)
2.3	648	Scoop	53	
3.1	649	Silty loam deposit	54	Rom. 1:2; Med. 1:6; Copper A914; An. (31)
3.1	650	Levelling/make-up surface	50, 54	Med. 1:6; PM 1:1; Iron A670; An. (99); Fish; Slag 270g
3.1	651	Surface	50, 54	Med. 1:2; An. (1)
2.2	652	Scoop fill		Med. 1:22; An. (1)
2.2	653	Scoop		
2.2	654	Post-hole fill		An. (6)
2.2	655	Post-hole		
3.3	656	Post-hole fill		
2.2	657	Post-hole fill		Copper A249; An. (14)
2.2	658	Post-hole	52	
2.2	659	Post-pipe	52	
4.1	660	Wall footing	56	Wood A96
4.1	661	Loam & chalk deposit	56	
3.3	662	Post-hole	55	
2.3	663	Post-hole fill		Glass A189; Iron A1123, A1124; Roof. A904; An. (4); Burnt (1)
2.3	664	Post-hole	53	
3.1	665	Post-hole fill		An. (2)
3.1	666	Post-hole	50, 54	Med. 1:2; An. (1)
3.3	667	Stake-hole fill		
3.3	668	Stake-hole	55	
2.3	669	Post-hole fill		
2.3	670	Post-hole	53	Med. 1:12
2.3	671	Post-hole fill		
2.3	672	Post-hole	53	
2.2	673	Post-hole fill		
2.2	674	Post-hole	52	An. (1)
2.2	675	Post-hole fill		
2.2	676	Post-hole	52	Rom. 2:33; An. (5)
2.4	677	Surface	51, 53	
1	678	Stake-hole (cut and fill)		
4.3	679	Gully fill		An. (9); Char. 1g
1	680	Stake-hole (cut and fill)		
1	681	Post-hole fill		
4.1	682	Gully fill		An. (32)
2.2	683	Post-hole fill		Sst. A353; An. (7); Slag 3g

Phase	Context	Description	Fig. Nos	Artefacts and environmental remains
2.2	684	Post-hole	52	
4.3?	685	Surface	57	An. (2)
4.3?	686	Surface	57	
3.3	687	Post-hole	55	
2.4	688	Pit/post-hole fill		
2.4	689	Pit/post-hole fill		Med. 2:146; An. (2)
2.4	690	Pit/post-hole fill		
4.3	691	Gully	57	
2.2	692	Post-hole fill		
2.2	693	Post-hole		An. (14)
2.1	694	Post-hole fill		
2.1	695	Post-hole		
2.3	696	Post-hole fill		Med. 1:3; Wood A97; An. (6)
2.3	696/700	No context information		An. (14); Char. 2g
2.3	697	Post-hole	53	
2.1	698	Stake-hole		
2.1	699	Stake-hole		
2.3	700	Post-hole fill	50	An. (11)
2.3	701	Post-hole		
2.4	702	Post-hole fill		Tile (3)
1	703	Post-hole	48	
2.1	704	Stake-hole (cut and fill)		
2.3	705	Post-pit fill		Copper 23; An. (25)
2.2	706	Post-hole fill		Rom. 1:2; Iron 49; An. (12); Char. ≤1g
2.2	707	Post-hole		
2.2	708	Scoop fill		
2.2	709	Scoop		
2.4	710	Stake-hole		
2.4	711	Stake-hole		
4.3?	712	Post-hole	57	
4.3?	713	Post-hole fill		
4.3?	714	Post-hole fill		An. (1); Burnt (1)
4.3?	715	Post-hole	57	
4.3?	716	Post pad fill		
3.3	717	Stake-hole	55	
2.4	718	Clay & chalk deposit	53	
2.4	719	Post-hole fill	53	
2.4	720	Post-hole	53	
4.1	721	? Pad-stone	56	
2.4	722	Post-hole fill		
2.4	723	Post-hole		
2.4	724	Stake-hole		
2.1	725	External surface	49	Rom. 1:3; Tile (1); An. (10); Burnt (1); Char. ≤1g
4.1	726	Wall footing	51, 56	Copper A1057; Mortar
2.3	727	Scoop	53	
2.3	728	? Levelling deposit		An. (35); Char. ≤1g
2.3	729	Post-hole fill		An. (3)
2.3	730	Post-hole	53	An. (1)
2.3	731	Post-pipe		
2.3	732	Post-pipe		
4.3?	733	Post-hole fill		An. (1)
4.3?	734	Post-hole	56	
4.1	735	Post-hole fill		
4.1	736	Post-hole fill		
2.2	737	Post-hole fill		
2.3	738	Post-hole fill		Med. 1:6; An. (5)
2.3	739	Post-hole	53	
2.3	740	Post-pit	53	
4.1	741	Gully	56	
2.4	742	Post-hole	53	
4.1	743	Post-hole	56	An. (1)
4.1	744	Post-hole	56	
4.3	745	Post-hole fill		Med. 1:2; An. (4)
2.2	746	Post-hole	52	An. (3)
2.3	747	Post-pipe		
2.3	748	Post-pipe		
4.3?	749	Post-hole fill		
4.3?	750	Post-hole	50, 56	
4.3?	751	Pit fill		An. (2)
4.3?	752	Pit		
4.3?	753	Post-hole fill		

Phase	Context	Description	Fig. Nos	Artefacts and environmental remains
4.3?	754	Post-hole	56	
3.4?	755	Topsoil & demolition debris	51	Med. 31:233; PM 1:2; Roof. A905; Tile (22); An. (12); BS; Char. 2g; Coal 55g; Fish
6.1	756	Make-up deposit		Med. 3:63; An. (1)
6.1	757	Silt & rubble deposit		Med. 13:117; PM 13:247; Copper A666, A667; Iron A1237; An. (4); BS; Coal 2g
4.1	758	Hillwash	56	An. (1)
4.3	759	Post-hole	57	
4.2	760	Terracing cut	51, 57	Med. 1:59; PM 1:6; Brick (3); BS
4.3?	761	Fill of hearth 960	56, 57	Med. 1:3; Copper A668; Roof. A906; Tile (1); An. (2); Burnt (bag); Cin. 4g
2.3	762	Silty clay deposit	53	An. (20)
2.2	763	Stake-hole		
2.2	764	Scoop fill		
2.2	765	Scoop	50	
3.3	766	Stake-hole	55	
1?	767	Post-hole fill		
6.1	768	Post-hole fill		PM 1:1; Iron A939; Coal 6g
6.1	769	Post-hole		
4.1	770	Hillwash	56	Med. 2:10; Stone 11, A184; An. (75); Char. 3g; Cin. 22g
2.2	771	Post-hole fill		An. (1)
2.2	772	Post-hole		
2.3	773	Post-pit fill		An. (10); Cin. 1g
2.1	774	Post-hole fill		
2.1	775	Post-hole	49	
2.1	776	Post-hole fill		An. (3)
2.1	777	Post-hole	49	
2.1	778	Post-hole fill		Rom. 1:5; An. (6)
2.1	779	Post-hole fill		
2.1	780	Post-hole	49	
4.1	781	Clay surface	56	Coal 17g
2.1	782	Post-hole fill		An. (3)
2.1	783	Post-hole fill		An. (4); Slag 9g
2.1	784	Post-hole	49	Stone A96
2.1	785	Post-hole	49	
2.1	786	Post-hole	49	
2.1	787	Post-hole fill		
2.1	788	Post-hole	49	
2.1	789	Post-hole fill		
6.1	790	Clay silt & chalk deposit		
6.1	791	Pit fill		Med. 2:15; Iron A210; Stone A64; An. (2)
6.1	792	Pit		
6.1	793	Deposit		
u/s	794	u/s 1986		Med. 14:189; PM 21:572; Copper A669, A1056; Iron A179, A180, A582, A1110; Sst. A354; Tile (2); Vess. 52 (3)
2.4	795	Post-hole fill		An. (4); Char. 12g
2.4	796	Post-hole		
2.1	797	Silt deposit		
2.1	798	Stake-hole cut & fill	49	Med. 4:68; An. (5)
2.1	799	Post-hole fill		An. (6); Char. ≤1g
2.1	800	Post-hole	50	
2.1	801	Scoop fill		
2.1	802	Scoop		
2.1	803	Post-hole fill		
2.1	804	Post-hole	49	
2.1	805	Post-hole fill		An. (3)
2.1	806	Post-hole	49	
2.1	807	Post-hole fill		An. (3)
2.1	808	Post-hole	49	
2.1	809	Post-hole fill		An. (2); Char. ≤1g
5.4	810	Pit fill	59, 65	Med. 1:1; Brick (5); Copper A1016; Roof. A907-918; Sst. A355; Tile (3); BS; Char. ≤1g; Cin. 1g
4.3?	811	Post-hole fill		Coal 9g
4.3?	812	Post-hole	57	
1?	813	Post-hole fill	65	
1?	814	Post-hole	65	
6.1	815	Hillwash		PM 5:63; Roof. A919; Tile (2); BS; Char. 5g; Coal 2g
2.1	816	Post-hole	49	
2.1	817	Stake-hole (cut and fill)	49	Char. ≤1g
4.3?	818	Post-hole fill	65	
4.3?	819	Post-hole fill		

Phase	Context	Description	Fig. Nos	Artefacts and environmental remains
4.3?	820	Post-hole	57	
2.1	821	Post-hole fill		
2.1	822	Post-hole	49	
2.1	823	Post-hole fill		
2.1	824	Post-hole	65	An. (3)
2.1	825	Post-pipe	49	An. (2); Char. ≤1g; Coal ≤1g
1.1	826	Stake-hole (cut and fill)		
1	827	Stake-hole (cut and fill)		
1	828	Post-hole fill		
1	829	Post-hole	51	
1.1	830	Natural Chalk		
5.4	831	Post-hole fill		
5.4	832	Post-hole		
5.4	833	Stake-hole fill		
5.4	834	Stake-hole		
4.3?	835	Clay & chalk deposit	57	Roof. A920, A921; An. (2)
5.4	836	Clay surface	59	Med. 1:21; Tile (2); BS; Coal 3g
5.4	837	Clay surface	59	PM 2:69; Brick (1); Copper A670; Iron A278; Tile (1); An. (2); BS; Cin. 7g; Coal 24g; Fish
5.4	838	Clay surface	59	Med. 2:5; PM 1:11; Tile (1); An. (2); Cin. ≤1g; Coal 3g
1	839	Post-hole fill	65	
1	840	Post-hole	51	
1	841	Depression fill		
1	842	Depression		
1	843	Post-hole fill		
1	844	Post-hole	50	
1	845	Stake-hole (cut and fill)		
2.1	846	Post-hole fill		Char. ≤1g
2.1	847	Post-hole		
1	848	Pit fill	50	An. (23); Char. 3g
1	849	Pit	48, 50	
2.1	850	Post-hole fill		
2.1	851	Post-hole fill		
2.1	852	Post-hole	49	
1	853	Stake-hole (cut and fill)		
1	854	Post-hole fill		Char. ≤1g
1	855	Post-hole	48	
2.1	856	Post-hole fill		
2.1	857	Post-hole		
1	858	Post-hole fill		An. (1)
1	859	Post-hole		
5.4	860	Pit fill		Med. 1:2; Iron A1023; Tile (1); An. (1); BS; Coal 1g
5.4	861	Pit		
5.1	862	Terrace	51, 58	
2.1	863	Post-hole fill		
2.1	864	Post-hole		
2.2	865	Stake-hole		Cin. ≤1g
2.1	866	Stake-hole		
2.1	867	Post-hole fill		Char. 6g
2.1	868	Post-hole		
1	869	Post-hole fill		Char. ≤1g
2.1	870	? Weathered natural	49	
4.3?	871	Post-hole fill		An. (2)
4.3?	872	Post-hole	57	
2.1	873	Post-hole		
2.1	874	Post-pipe	49	An. (6)
2.1	875	Post-hole fill		
2.1	876	Post-pipe	49	
2.1	877	Post-hole fill		Char. 2g
2.1	878	Post-hole		
1	879	Post-hole		
4.3?	880	Post-hole fill		
4.3?	881	Post-hole		
5.4	882	Demolition debris		Med. 3:4; Sst. A356; An. (1); BS; Cin. 2g
2.4	883	Post-hole fill		
2.4	884	Post-hole		
3.3	885	Surface		Rom. 1:5; Med. 1:6; An. (2)
2.1	886	Clay & chalk deposit		
2.1	887	Post-pipe		
2.1	888	Post-hole fill		
2.1	889	Post-hole	49	

Phase	Context	Description	Fig. Nos	Artefacts and environmental remains
1	890	Post-hole fill		
1	891	Post-hole		
1	892	Stake-hole (cut and fill)		
1	893	Stake-hole (cut and fill)		
1	894	Stake-hole		
1	895	Post-hole fill		An. (2)
1	896	Post-hole	50	
2.4	897	Stake-hole		
2.3	898	Levelling dump	53	An. (10)
4.1	899	Surface	56	
5.4	900	Clay & chalk pebble deposit		
1?	901	Stake-hole fill		
1?	902	Stake-hole		
2.4	903	Post-hole fill		
2.4	904	Post-hole		
2.4	905	Post-hole fill		Wood A98; An. (1); Char. ≤1g
2.4	906	Post-hole		
1	907	Post-hole fill		
1	908	Post-hole	48, 49, 50	
2.1	909	Post-hole fill		
2.1	910	Post-hole		
5.4	911	Clay deposit		
2.4	912	Post-hole fill		
2.4	913	Post-hole		
2.4	914	Post-hole fill	51	An. (2); Char. 1g
2.4	915	Post-hole	51	
2.1	916	Post-pipe		Iron A211; An. (33); Char. 7g; Slag 68g
2.1	917	Post-hole fill		
2.1	918	Post-hole	49	
4.1	919	Stake-hole	56	
1	920	Scoop fill		Med. 3:4; An. (35); Char. 16g; Cin. 41g
5.4	921	Surface		Vess. 61
5.4	922	Demolition debris		Med. 2:4; Wood A99
5.4	923	Silty clay & chalk deposit		
2.4	924	Post-pipe		
2.1	925	Scoop fill		
2.1	926	Scoop		
2.1	927	Post-pipe	49	An. (3)
2.1	928	Post-hole fill		An. (10); Char. ≤1g; Fish
2.1	929	Post-hole		
2.1	930	Stake-hole (cut and fill)		An. (3)
1	931	Post-hole fill		
1.1	932	Stake-hole		
2.2	933	Stake-hole		Brick (1)
2.1	934	Redeposited chalk/?nat. surface	49	Char. ≤1g
2.1	935	Post-hole fill		An. (10)
2.1	936	Post-hole		Wood A100
4.3?	937	Surface	57	Med. 7:24; PM 6:15; Copper A1017; Iron A1383; Roof. A922, A923; An. (7); Char. 5g; Cin. 12g; Coal 1g; Plas.
5.4	938	Post pad	59, 60	Sst. A357
1	939	Post-hole fill		An. (5); Char. 2g
1	940	Post-hole	48	
2.1	941	Stake-hole		Char. ≤1g
2.1	942	Stake-hole		
2.1	943	Stake-hole		
2.1	944	Stake-hole		
2.1	945	Post-hole fill		Iron A1125; An. (22); Char. 2g
1	946	Stake-hole (cut and fill)		Med. 3:15; Char. 2g
2.1	947	Post-hole fill		
2.1	948	Post-hole	49	
1	949	Stake-hole		
1	950	Scoop	48	
2.4	951	Stake-hole		
2.4	952	Stake-hole		
2.1	953	Post-hole fill		An. (13)
2.1	954	Post-pit	49	
2.1	955	Post-hole fill		
2.1	956	Post-hole		
2.1	957	Post-hole fill		An. (1)
2.1	958	Post-hole	49	
2.1	959	Post-hole fill		An. (1); Slag 17g

416

Phase	Context	Description	Fig. Nos	Artefacts and environmental remains
4.3?	960	Hearth	57	
1?	961	Post-hole fill		Med. 1:1
1?	962	Post-hole		
4.3?	963	Surface		Med. 1:5; Char. ≤1g; Coal 4g
4.3?	964	Silty clay & sandy mortar deposit		Med. 1:8; Cin. 2g; Fish; Mortar
2.1	965	Surface	49, 50	
2.2	966	Post-hole fill		An. (2)
2.1	967	Post-pipe		An. (1)
2.1	968	Post-pipe		
2.1	969	Post-pipe		An. (12)
2.1	970	Post-hole	49	
2.1	971	Post-pipe		An. (2); Slag 127g
2.1	972	Post-pipe		
2.1	973	Post-hole fill		Rom. 1:3; An. (11)
2.1	974	Post-hole fill		
2.1	975	Post-hole		
2.1	976	Post-hole fill		
2.1	977	Post-hole	49	
1	978	Stake-hole		
2.1	979	Scoop fill		
2.1	980	Scoop		
2.1	981	Post-hole fill		
2.1	982	Post-hole		
1	983	Stake-hole (cut and fill)		
4.3?	984	Stake-hole fill		
4.3?	985	Stake-hole	57	
4.3?	986	Stake-hole fill		
4.3?	987	Stake-hole	57	
4.3?	988	Silt & chalk deposit		Med. 1:9; Tile (3); BS; Char. 1g; Cin. 2g; Slag 23g
4.3?	989	Surface		PM 1:2; Copper A671; An. (3); Char. ≤1g; Coal 3g
5.4	990	Post pad		Coin med. 35; An. (1); Char. 3g
5.4	991	Cut for post pad	59, 60	
5.4	992	Sandstone dump		
5.4	993	Pit		
1	994	Post-hole fill		
1	995	Post-hole		An. (2)
1	996	Post-hole fill		
1	997	Post-hole	48	
1	998	Post-hole fill		
1	999	Post-hole		Char. ≤1g
1	1000	Stake-hole (cut and fill)	48	
1	1001	Post-hole fill		An. (10); Char. ≤1g
1	1002	Post-hole	48	
1	1003	Post-hole fill		An. (5)
1	1004	Post-hole	48	
1	1005	Post-pipe	48	
1	1006	Post-pipe		
1	1007	Gully fill/post-hole		An. (1)
1	1008	Gully/post-hole	48	
1	1009	Stake-hole (cut and fill)		An. (1)
1	1010	? Natural	48	
1	1011	Post-hole fill		Rom. 1:5; An. (3)
1	1012	Post-hole	48	
1	1013	Post-pipe		
3.4?	1014	Topsoil & demolition debris		
3.4?	1015	Surface	51	Med. 31:166; Tile (9); An. (3)
3.4?	1016	Stake-hole		
3.4?	1017	Stake-hole fill		
3.4?	1018	Stake-hole		
6.3	1019	Terrace	51	
1	1020	Stake-hole		
1?	1021	Stake-hole fill		
1?	1022	Stake-hole		
3.4?	1023	Stake-hole fill		
1?	1024	Stake-hole fill		
1	1025	Stake-hole		
1?	1026	Stake-hole fill		
1?	1027	Stake-hole		
1?	1028	Post-hole fill		Tile (1)
1?	1029	Stake-hole		
1?	1030	Stake-hole fill		

Phase	Context	Description	Fig. Nos	Artefacts and environmental remains
1?	1031	Stake-hole		
1	1032	Post-hole fill		
1	1033	Post-hole		
1	1034	Post-pit fill		
1	1035	Post-pit		
1	1036	Post-pipe		Wood A137; An. (3)
1	1037	Post-pipe		
1	1038	Post-pipe		
-	1039	Post-hole fill		
-	1040	Post-hole		
1	1041	Stake-hole (cut and fill)		
4.3?	1042	Gully fill		PM 1:1; Coal ≤1g
4.3?	1043	Gully		
3.4?	1044	Stake-hole		
5.4	1045	Post pad		
5.4	1046	Post pad		
4.3?	1047	Silty clay deposit		An. (1); Coal ≤1g
4.3?	1048	Surface		BS; Cin. 2g; Coal ≤1g
4.3?	1049=533	Clay & chalk deposit		PM 1:8
4.3?	1050	Post-hole fill		Med. 1:1; Cin. 1g; Coal ≤1g
4.3?	1051	Post-hole	57	
4.3?	1052	Post-hole fill		An. (3); Cin. ≤1g; Coal 1g
4.3?	1053	Post-hole	57	
4.3?	1054	Post-hole fill		
4.3?	1055	Post-hole	57	
	1056	Unused context		
4.3?	1057	Silt & pebble deposit		An. (1)
1	1058	Natural Chalk		
4.3?	1059	Scoop fill		
4.3?	1060	Scoop	57	
1?	1061	Post-hole fill		
1?	1062	Post-hole		
1?	1063	Pit fill		
1?	1064	Post-hole fill		
1?	1065	Post-hole		
1?	1066	Pit fill		Rom. 2:10; An. (2); Char. 2g
1?	1067	Pit		
-	1068	Post-hole fill		
-	1069	Post-hole		
1?	1070	Stake-hole fill		
1?	1071	Stake-hole		
1?	1072	Stake-hole fill		
1?	1073	Stake-hole		
1?	1074	Stake-hole fill		
1?	1075	Stake-hole		
1?	1076	Pit fill		Char. ≤1g
1?	1077	Pit		
1?	1078	Post-hole		
1?	1079	Pit fill		
1?	1080	Pit		
1?	1081	Post-hole fill		An. (1); Char. 1g; Coal 2g
1?	1082	Post-hole		
1?	1083	Dump		
1?	1084	Post-hole fill		
1?	1085	Post-hole fill		
1?	1086	Stake-hole		
1?	1087	Post-hole fill		Coal 3g
1?	1088	Post-hole		
1?	1089	Stake-hole fill		
1?	1090	Stake-hole		
1?	1091	Stake-hole fill		
1?	1092	Stake-hole		
1?	1093	Stake-hole fill		
1?	1094	Stake-hole		
1?	1095	Stake-hole fill		
1?	1096	Stake-hole		
1?	1097	Pit fill		
1?	1098	Pit		
1?	1099	Pit		
1?	1100	Stake-hole fill		
1?	1101	Stake-hole		

Phase	Context	Description	Fig. Nos	Artefacts and environmental remains
1?	1102	Pit fill		
1?	1103	Pit		
	1104	Unused context		
2.1	1105	Stake-hole		
1	1106	Stake-hole (cut and fill)		
1	1107	Stake-hole (cut and fill)		
1	1108	Stake-hole (cut and fill)		
1	1109	Stake-hole (cut and fill)		
1	1110	Stake-hole (cut and fill)		
1	1111	Stake-hole (cut and fill)		
1	1112	Stake-hole (cut and fill)		
1	1113	Stake-hole (cut and fill)		
	1114-19	Unused contexts		
2.1	1120	Post-hole	49	
4.3?	1121	Post-hole	57	
	1122-29	Unused contexts		
5.2	1130	Unexcavated deposit	58, 59	
7.1	1131	Ash pit	63	
7.8	1132	Drain/gully		
8.3	1133	Post-hole		
8.3	1134	Post-hole		
8.3	1135	Post-hole		
7.1	1136	Pad stone	63	
5.2	1137	Unexcavated deposit	58, 59	
8.2	1138	Demolition debris		
5.2	1139	Terrace cut		
5.2	1140	Silty clay & chalk deposit	50	
6.2	1141	Post-hole	60	
7.1	1142	Stake-hole (cut and fill)	63	
	1143-1200	Unused contexts		
u/s	9000	Unstratified		Med. 2:21; PM 6:45; Lst. A654-658; Mem. 36, A175, A176; Roof. A924, A925; Tile (3); Burnt (4)

Site 55

Phase	Context	Description	Fig. Nos	Artefacts and environmental remains
-	26	From dump between cottages and Vicarage		Stone 25
-	27	No context information		Sst. A583
-	39	Rabbit hole on hillside down to stream		Coal 6g
-	41	No context information		Iron A988

Site 75

Phase	Context	Description	Fig. Nos	Artefacts and environmental remains
-	1	No context information		PM 3:17; Iron A516; Vess. (1)
-	2	No context information		PM 2:25; Vess. (1)
-	3	No context information		Bone 54
u/s	u/s	No context information		PM 2:13

Site 77

Phase	Context	Description	Fig. Nos	Artefacts and environmental remains
6	1	Turf and topsoil	45, 46	Rom. 1:2; Med. 1:92 (38); PM 35:266; Brick (4); Copper 9, 84, 90, A854, A915, A943; Iron A147, A308, A559, A878, A940, A1052, A1238-1240, A1463; Nail 27:3; Roof. A939-942, A1548; Sst. A384-386; Tile (29); Vess. (10); BS; Char. ≤1g; Cin. ≤1g; Coal 60g; Slag 114g
5.2	2=28=29 =30=32 =66=67	Hillwash		Med. 9:128; Quern A139
1-5	3	Occupation surface		Med. 3:41; Brick (2)
1-5	4	Rubble & humic deposit		
1-5	5	Chalk & humic deposit		
1-5	6	Natural		
1-5	7	Weathered surface		
1-5	8	Chalk & humic deposit		Cp (1)
1-5	9	Rubble deposit		
1-5	10	White deposit		
	11	? Unused context		
1-5	12	Marl layer		
1-5	13	Displaced bedrock layer		
1-5	14	Marl layer		Med. 2:4; PM 4:169 (74); Cp (1); Tile (2)
1-5	15	Layer		
1-5	16	Marl layer		

Phase	Context	Description	Fig. Nos	Artefacts and environmental remains
1-5	17	Layer		
1-5	18	Layer		
1-5	19	Marl layer		
1-5	20	Layer		
1-5	21	Layer		
1-5	22	Layer		
1-5	23	Humus & chalk rubble		
1-5	24	Humus & chalk rubble		
5.1/5.2	25	Loam & chalk rubble		PM 1:3
6	26	C20 tree root disturbance		
1-5	27	Humus deposit		
5.2	28=2=29 =30=32 =66=67	?Hillwash deposit		
5.2	29=2=28 30=32=66 =67	?Hillwash deposit		
5.2	30=2=28 =29=32 =66=67	?Hillwash deposit		
5.2	31	Loam and rubble deposit		
5.2	32=2=28 =29=30 =66=67	?Hillwash deposit		
-	33	Wall		
1-5	34	Hearth stones		
5.2	35	Wall		
5-6	36	Humic layer		
5-6	37	Loam & chalk pebble deposit		
5-6	38	Loam deposit		
5-6	39	Revetment wall		
5-6	40	Loam & chalk deposit		
5-6	41	Chalk pebble deposit		
5-6	42	Chalk pebble deposit		
5-6	43	Loam & chalk rubble deposit		
5-6	44	Loam deposit		Lst. A687
5.1	45	Loam deposit		Slag 5g
5-6	46	Loam & chalk rubble deposit		
5.1	47	Foundation trench fill		
5.1	48	Pad-stone	44	
5.2	49	Humic layer	45	
5.1/5.2	50=51=52 =53=54= 84=92=93 =94=95= 99	Hillwash	45	Med. 20:449 (23, 28); PM 1:15; Cp (1)
5.1/5.2	51=50=52 =53=54= 84=92=93 =94=95= 99	Hillwash		
5.1/5.2	52=50=51 =53=54= 84=92=93 =94=95 =99	Hillwash		
5.1/5.2	53=50=51 =52=54= 84=92=93 =94=95 =99	Hillwash		
5.1/5.2	54=50=51 =52=53=84 =92=93=94 =95=99	Hillwash		Med. 1:4
5.2	55=?203	Chalk deposit		Rom. 1:16
1	56=641	Wall	38, 39, 43, 45	
1-5	57	Wall tumble		
5.1?	58	Chalk block deposit		
5.1?	59	Burnt sandstone & charcoal		
5.1?	60	Loam & chalk deposit		

Phase	Context	Description	Fig. Nos	Artefacts and environmental remains
5.1	61	Chalk rubble deposit		
-	62	Quarry fill		
1-5	63	Chalk & humic deposit		
-	64	Layer		
1-5	65	Rubble		
5.2	66=2=28 =29=30 =32=67	?Hillwash deposit		
5.2	67=2=28 =29=30 =32=66	?Hillwash deposit		
1-5	68	Loam & chalk rubble deposit		Med. 3:7; PM 1:7; Brick (1); Nail 1:-
1-5	69	Loam & chalk pebble deposit		
-	70	Chalk quarry pit		
-	71=8999	Natural		
5.2	72	Robber trench		
5.2	73	Robber trench fill		Med. 8:34; PM 1:1; Brick (6); Sst. A387; Coal 5g
5.2	74	Robber trench fill		Med. 3:6; PM 1:6; Nail 1:-
5.1	75	Wall demolition rubble		Med. 11:51; Nail 2:-
5.2	76	Topsoil		Med. 9:16; PM 3:36; Copper A916, A986; Iron A1384, A1464; Nail 2:-; Sst. A388; Vess. (5); Coal 4g
5.1	77=117	Wall	44	
5.2	78	Demolition rubble		Med. 9:28 (22 pt); Iron A1151, A1385; Nail 1:-; Roof. A1549
4	79=175 =177	Sandstone steps		Sst. A389, A570
5.2	80	Demolition debris		Med. 8:120; Nail 7:-; Roof. A943, A1550; Sst. A390; Tile (7); An. (12); Char. 50g; Cin. 3g; Coal 19g
4-5	81	Hillwash		Med. 7:85; An. (4)
1-5	82	Pit		Sst. A391
1-5	83	Pit fill		
5.1/5.2	84=50=51 =51=52 =53=54 =92=93 =95=94 =99	Hillwash		Med. 84:1351 (9); PM 26:323; Brick (11); Copper 118, A944; Cp (1); Iron 108, A528, A1111, A1152, A1465-1467; Roof. A944-948; Sst. A392; Tile (13); Vess. (1)
5.2	85	Compacted road surface		Med. 151:1654 (5, 16, 26, 34); PM 26:249 (68); Brick (3); Coin pm 5, 30; Copper A855, A1018; Cp (1); Iron 65, A504, A1024; Nail 11:-; Roof. A949; Tile (28); Vess. (3); An. (37); Burnt (1); Coal 59g
5.2	86	Chalk pebble surface	46	PM 25:426; Brick (2); Clay A32; Copper 85; Cp (4); Iron 59, 63, 66, 90, 102, A560, A879, A1112, A1165; Nail 5:-; Roof. A1513; Tile (7); Vess. (6); An. (15); Cin. 3g; Coal 14g
5.1	87	Cut of hollow		
5.1	88	Hollow fill		Med. 17:81; PM 3:74
5.1	89	Beaten earth surface		Med. 2:8; PM 1:4; Nail 2:-; Tile (1); An. (8)
5.1	90	Trackway cleaning deposit		Roof. A1514; An. (3)
5.1	91	Humic loam, chalk & slate deposit		Med. 7:152; PM 5:142 (69); Iron 68, A148, A880, A1241, A1242, A1386; Lst. A742; Nail 1:-; Roof. A950; Vess. (1)
5.1/5.2	92=50=51 =52=53 =54=84 =93=94 =95=99	Hillwash		
5.1/5.2	93=50 =51=52 =53=54 =84=92=94 =95=99	Hillwash		Med. 16:187; PM 2:78; Brick (2); Iron A881; Stone 8
5.1/5.2	94=50 =52=53= 54=84 =92=93 =95=99	Hillwash		
5.1/5.2	95=50=51 =52=53 =54=84 =92=93 =94=95 =99	Hillwash		
5.2	96	Hillwash		Med. 7:32; Copper A987; Nail 1:-
-	97=?112	Horse burial		

Phase	Context	Description	Fig. Nos	Artefacts and environmental remains
-	98	Loam & rubble deposit		Med. 1:2
5.1/5.2	99=50=51 =52=53 =54=84 =92=93 =94=95	Hillwash		Med. 2:12; PM 1:45; Copper A856; Tile (1)
-	100	Loam & chalk pebble deposit		Med. 19:98; Tile (1); Char. 1g; Cin. 2g; Coal 13g
5.1	101	Terrace extension of imported soil		Med. 64:662; Bone 12; Coin pm 47; Iron A224, A1057; Nail 1:-; Quern 31, A140; Roof. A951; Tile (1); Coal 36g
5.1	102	Trampled surface layer		Med. 2:10; An. (1)
5.1	103	Loam & chalk pebble deposit		Med. 6:13; Nail 3:-; Tile (1)
6	104	Demolition rubble		Med. 8:140; PM 3:7; Nail 2:-; Roof. A1551; Stone 21; An. (4); Coal 4g
5.2	105	Upper fill of conduit	46	Med. 37:755; PM 8:151; Nail 3:-; Roof. A952, A953; Sst. A393; Tile (3); Vess. (5); BS; Coal 16g
5.2	106=457	Conduit	42, 44, 46	
-	107	Post-hole		
-	108	Post-hole fill		Nail 1:-; Char. 4g
-	109	Post-hole fill		Iron A517
-	110	Post-hole		
-	111	Post-hole fill		
-	112=?97	Animal burial		
-	113	Horse burial fill		Med. 18:184; Copper A694; Iron A1387; Nail 31:-; Roof. A954
6	114	? Old archaeological dump		Med. 18:316 (55); PM 38:820 (73); Brick (1); Copper 82, A917; Cp (5); Iron A309, A655, A882, A941; Nail 1:-; Quern A141; Roof. A1515, A1552; Tile (11); Vess. (6); Char. 2g; Coal 31g
5.1	115	Loam & chalk rubble deposit		Med. 9:142; PM 2:33; Iron A960; Nail 1:-
5.1	116	Loam & chalk rubble deposit		Med. 6:85; Copper A976, A988, A1019
5.1	117=77	Wall	44	Med. 4:33
5-6	118	Wall		
	119	? Unused context		
5-6	120	Wall tip		
5-6	121	Revetment bank		
5.1	122	Demolition rubble		Med. 1:11; PM 2:47; Nail 1:-
5.1	123	Rubbish pit		
5.1	124	Pit fill		Med. 3:36; PM 8:45; Copper A857; Nail 1:1; Tile (1); Vess. (1)
5.1	125	Pit fill		
5.1	126	Pit		
-	127	Wall fill		Med. 1:18 (62 pt)
5.1	128=227 =228	Wall matrix	46	Med. 1:27
1-5	129	Rubble deposit		Copper A1036
5.1	130	Pit fill		PM 1:2; Coal 1g
3-5	131	Loam & chalk deposit		Med. 1:12
5.2	132=?154 =?155	Conduit backfill	46	Rom. 1:5; Med. 48:595 (62 pt); PM 5:127 (66); Cp (2); Iron 21, A273, A883; Nail 4:-; Quern A142, A143; Roof. A955-957; Sst. A394; Tile (24); Vess. (3); Coal 45g
1-5	133	Demolition rubble		
-	134	Residue from attempted cremation		Nail 1:-
1-5	135	Post-hole		
5.1	136	Robber trench fill		Cp (1); Roof. A958, A959; Tile (1)
1-5	137	Pit/robber trench		PM 3:12; Nail 1:-; Vess. (2); Coal 7g
1-5	138	Fill of 137		
5.1	139	Wall tumble		
5.1	140	Silt deposit		
1-4	141	Demolition debris		Med. 2:13; Nail 1:-
1-4	142	? Old turf line		
1-3	143	Weathered rubble deposit		Med. 1:87; PM 1:9; Tile (1)
5.1	144=168 =185	Surface	44, 45	Med. 122:1319; PM 8:142 (67); Copper A858, A1020; Iron A149, A150, A942, A1388, A1468; Nail 75:3; Quern A144; Roof. A960-962; Tile (44); An. (52); Char. 9g; Cin. 26g; Coal 8g
5.1	145	Wall		
3.1	146	Wall	40	Nail 1:-; Tile (1)
5.1	147	Pad-stone		
5.1	148	Pad-stone		
5.1	149	Pad-stone	44	
-	150	Pad-stone		
5.1	151	Wall		
1-5	152	Chalk rubble deposit		
5.1	153	Wall chalk core	44	

Phase	Context	Description	Fig. Nos	Artefacts and environmental remains
5.2	154=?132 =?155	Conduit fill		Med. 16:227; PM 3:23; Iron 104, A1153; Nail 5:-; Sst. A395; Tile (6); Coal 9g
5.2	155=?132 =?154	Conduit fill		
-	156	Post pad		
-	157	Post-hole/stake-hole		
-	158	Post-hole/stake-hole fill		
-	159	Wind blown hillwash		Med. 9:278; Coal 6g
5.2	160	Loam & rubble deposit		
-	161	Silt & pebble deposit		
5.1	162	Silt & pebble deposit	44, 46	
5.1	163	Loam & chalk rubble deposit	44	
5.2	164	Silt deposit		Med. 18:184; PM 1:15; Iron A1126, A1127; Nail 6:-; Roof. A963; Tile (10); Cin. 2g; Coal 7g
5.1	165=181	Surface deposit	44, 46	
-	166	Loam deposit		Med. 2:2; Coal 2g
-	167	Animal skeleton		
5.1	168=144 =185	Surface	44	Med. 62:522 (41 pt); PM 1:1; Brick (2); Copper A1021; Iron A738; Nail 15:-; Roof. A964-971; Tile (53); An. (21); Char. 2g; Coal 16g
6	169	Excavation trench		
6	170	Excavation trench backfill		
5.1	171	Wind blown soil		
5.1	172	Foundation trench		
-	173	Post-hole		
-	174	Post-hole fill		
4	175=79 =177	Chalk rubble steps		
5.2	176	? Building rubble		Nail 1:-
4	177=79 =175	Sandstone landing for steps		
1-5	178=193	Hillwash		Med. 6:38; PM 5:61
u/s	179=250 =9000	Unstratified deposit		Med. 3:37; PM 1:2; Iron A1469; Nail 3:-; Roof. A972
5.1	180	Hillwash		Med. 171:2355 (35 pt, 59, 63); PM 8:185; Brick (2); Iron A726; Lst. A688, A743; Roof. A973, A974; Tile (4); Wood. A101; Slag 295g
5.1	181=165	Levelling layer	44, 46	Med. 56:720 (22 pt, 35 pt); PM 1:9; Nail 14:-; Roof. A975; Tile (4); An. (17)
3.1	182	Wall	40, 43	Med. 10:62; Lst. A689, A690; Nail 4:-; Quern A145; Roof. 40, A976-979; Sst. A396-406
5.2	183=216 =255	? Yard surface	41	
5.2	184	Floor surface/burnt deposit		
5.1	185=144 =168	Surface	44	Med.53:713 (41 pt, 72); PM 3:15; Brick (10); Iron A215, A424; Nail 6:-; Tile (58); An. (31); Char. 2g; Cin. 3g; Coal 2g
5.1	186	Pea-grit deposit		Cin. 44g
4	187=?213	Wall		
5.1	188	Rubble deposit		Med. 7:121; Iron A961; Nail 2:-; Roof. A980-982; Sst. A407
1-5	189	Wall		
5.2	190	Chalk deposit/? Natural		Med. 3:21; Nail 1:-; An. (1)
1-5	191	Hillwash		Rom. 2:12; Med. 143:1665 (29, 48); PM 4:45; Iron A1113; Nail 1:-; Stone 22; Slag 57g
1-5	192	Pea-grit deposit/? bonding material		Med. 5:24; Clay 3
1-5	193=178	Hillwash		Med. 37:519 (59); PM 2:38; Char. 6g
1-5	194	? Natural	45	
1-5	195	Hillwash		
5.1	196	Demolition deposit		Med. 22:162; PM 2:3; Nail 1:-; Tile (1); An. (2); Cin. 3g; Coal 7g
5.1	197	Wall		
5.1	198	Wall		
5.1	199	Hillwash		Med. 6:29; PM 3:27
5.1	200	Hillwash	45	Med. 86:727 (33 pt, 66); Nail 7:-; Roof. A983-986; Stone A186; An. (19); Cin. 1g
1-5	201	Hillwash		
1-5	202	Silt & chalk deposit	45	
5.1/5.2	203=55	Hillwash/levelling deposit	45	Med. 54:1263; Brick (1); Nail 1:-; Roof. A987, A988; Stone A66; Tile (9); Coal 15g
2	204	Levelling deposit		Med. 5:59; Lst. A691-696; Nail 9:-; Roof. A989-1003; Sst. A408, A409; Tile (4); An. (7)
5.1	205	Rubble deposit		
5.1	206	? Weathered surface		An. (21)
5.1	207	Packed chalk surface		
5.1	208	Chalk rubble deposit		Med. 19:139; Nail 2:-; Tile (1)

Phase	Context	Description	Fig. Nos	Artefacts and environmental remains
5.1	209	Destruction debris		Med. 140:2408 (30, 42 pt, 70); PM 3:114 (70); Brick (2); Clay 4; Iron 39, 62, A274, A727; Lst. A697, A744; Nail 103:-; Quern A146; Roof. A1004-1020, A1553; Sst. A410-413; Tile (80); Wood A102; An. (94); Char. 54g; Cin. 4g; Coal 18g; Fish; Slag 313g
5.1	210	Burnt deposit		
5.1	211	Chalk surface		
5.1	212	Silt & chalk deposit		BS
4	213=?187	Base for steps		
5.1	214	Pack material/? levelling deposit		
5.1	215	Chalk rubble deposit		
5.2	216=219 =255	Compacted surface/demolition debris	46	Rom. 1:12; Med. 31474; :PM 4:49; Brick (1); Lst. A698, A699; Nail 17:-; Roof. A1021-1028; Tile (15); An. (18); Char. 1g
5.1	217	Pea-grit deposit		
5.1	218	Chalk pebble deposit		Med. 14:102; Roof. A1029-1031; An. (6)
5.2	219=216 =255	Demolition debris		Med. 5:202 (10); Iron A1114; Nail 3:-; Tile (1); An. (6); Char. ≤1g
3.1	220	Wall	40	Med. 2:168; Sst. A141-417
3-5	221	Pea-grit deposit		Med. 1:59; Nail 1:-; Roof. A1032
1-5	222	Chalk & pea-grit deposit		
5.1	223	Clay & chalk deposit		Med. 21:349; PM 1:33; Brick (4); Copper A1022; Iron A1154; Lst. A700; Nail 3:-; Quern A148; Roof. A1033-1047; Sst. A418, A419; Tile (61); Wood A103; Char. 2g; Cin. 10g; Coal 5g
5.1	224	Robber trench		
5.1	225	Robber trench fill		Med. 5:40 (47 pt)
5.1	226	Pea-grit deposit		Med. 49:1163 (32 pt, 40, 54 pt, 65, 69); PM 1:4; Iron 56; Nail 26:-; Roof. A1048-1050; Tile (1); Cin. 9g
5.1	227=128 =228	Clay & chalk deposit		Med. 1:12
5.1	228=128 =227	Clay & chalk deposit		
5.1	229	Robber trench		
5.1	230	Rubble deposit		BS
5.1	231	Wall	44, 46	
5.1	232	Robbed wall		
5.1	233	Depression		Iron 109, A1025, A1026, A1389
5.1	234	Depression fill		Med. 12:252 (11, 54 pt); Copper A223; Nail 1:-; BS; Cin. 7g; Coal 6g
1-5	235	Silt lens	45	Med. 1:6 (17)
5.1	236	Hillwash	45	
1-5	237	Hillwash		Char. ≤1g
1-5	238	Periglacial natural chalk		
	239	? Unused context		
-	240	No context information		Rom. 1:5; Sst. A420
	241	? Unused context		
	242	? Unused context		
	243	? Unused context		
	244	? Unused context		
	245	? Unused context		
	246	? Unused context		
-	247	No context information		Roof. A1051
	248	? Unused context		
	249	? Unused context		
u/s	250=179 =9000	Unstratified		Med. 44:908 (33 pt, 42 pt, 49); PM 5:306 (72); Brick (7); Copper A250; Cp (2); Iron A739; Lst. A701; Nail 38:-; Roof. A1052-1082; Sst. A421-423; Tile (43); Char. ≤1g; Cin. ≤1g; Coal 4g; Slag 3g
1-5	251	Trampled surface		
5.1	252=254 =?292 =?305	Levelling material		
5.1	253	Rubble deposit		Med. 36:420 (32 pt, 52); Lst. A702; Nail 7:-; Roof. A1083; Sst. A424; Tile (4); Coal 1g; Slag 136g
5.1	254=252 =?292=?305	Levelling material		Med. 7:217; Iron A529, A1128; Nail 4:-; Tile (1); An. (18)
5.2	255=216 =219	Hillwash/demolition debris		Med. 15:115 (42 pt); Nail 1:-; Roof. A1084, A1085; An. (13)
1-5	256	Wall		Med. 10:148; Nail 1:-; Roof. A1086-1092; An. (10); Coal 3g
5.1	257	Robber trench		
5.1	258	Demolition debris		Med. 3:54; Brick (6); Lst. A703-705; Nail 1:-; Tile (6); An. (6); Coal 6g
5.1	259	Burnt surface deposit		Copper 12
1	260	Wall	38	
1	261	Wall	38, 39	Sst. A425
5.1	262	Levelling deposit		Med. 8:229; Nail 4:-; Wood A104; An. (2)

Phase	Context	Description	Fig. Nos	Artefacts and environmental remains
5.1	263	Levelling deposit		Med. 16:297; Iron A225; Nail 12:-; Tile (2); Wood A105; Char. 3g; Cin. 5g; Coal 5g
5.1	264	Levelling deposit		Med. 2:306; Nail 1:-
1-3	265	?Wall		
1-5	266	Hillwash lens		Wood A106
1-5	267	Hillwash lens		
1-5	268	Hillwash lens		
1-5	269	Hillwash lens		Nail 7:1
1-5	270	Hillwash/natural layer		
5.1	271	Trampled clay surface		
4	272	Packed surface	43	
5.1	273	Terracing dump/levelling		Med. 5:42; Wood A107; Coal 9g
51/5.2	274	Demolition debris		
5.1	275	Levelling deposit		Med. 10:228; Iron A226, A884, A1129; Nail 8:-
5.1	276	Irregular area dump		Med. 3:34; Tile (2)
5.1	277	Rubble/levelling dump		Med. 4:51; Nail 5:-; Roof. A1093; An. (5)
5.1	278	Clay & chalk deposit		Med. 1:1; Brick (1)
5.1	279	Clay & chalk deposit		
4	280	Wall	43	
4	281	Wall	43	
4	282	Wall	43	
5.1	283	Rubble deposit		
5.1	284	Clay & chalk deposit		Tile (1)
5.2	285	Pit fill	46	
5.2	286	Pit	46	Brick (2)
5.2	287	Rubble deposit		
5.1	288	Silt & chalk deposit	46	
5.1	289	Silt & chalk deposit	46	
5.1	290	Silt & chalk deposit	46	
5.1	291	Silt & chalk deposit	46	
5.1	292=?252 =254=305	Silt & chalk deposit	46	
5.1	293	Silt & chalk deposit	46	
-	294	Silt & chalk deposit	46	Med. 5:52; PM 2:2; Iron A1058; Nail 3:-
5.1	295	? Feature fill	46	
5.1	296	Silt & chalk deposit	46	
5.2	297	Silt & chalk deposit		Med. 5:29; PM 19:392; Cp (2); Iron A583, A885, A962, A1115; Nail 9:-; Roof. A1554; Tile (5); Vess. (2)
5.2	298=?328	Conduit fill		
5.2	299	Silt & chalk deposit		
5.1	300=?323	Silt & chalk deposit		PM 1:11
5.1	301	Silt & chalk deposit		
-	302	Silt & chalk deposit		
5.2	303=333	Silt & chalk deposit	42	
5.1	304	Robbed feature fill	42	PM 13:316 (71); Cp 16 (3); Nail 1:-
5.1	305=?252= 254=292	Silt & chalk deposit	42	
5.1	306	? Feature fill	42	
5.1	307	Silt & chalk deposit	42	
5.1	308	Robber trench fill	42	
5-6	309	Silt & chalk deposit		
5-6	310	Silt & chalk deposit		
5-6	311	Silt & chalk deposit		
5-6	312	Silt & chalk deposit		
5-6	313	Silt & chalk deposit		PM 4:51
5-6	314	Silt & chalk deposit		
5.1	315	? Levelling layer		
3-5	316	Occupation layer		
5.1	317	Levelling deposit		
2	318	Demolition debris		
5.1	319	Levelling dump		
2	320	Demolition debris		Med. 1:184; Nail 62:-; Sst. A426; Char. 109g
2	321	Clay & chalk deposit		Nail 7:-; Cin. ≤1g
6	322	Barrow run deposit		
5.1	323=?300	Barrow run deposit		Med. 104:895 (36 pt); PM 1:1; Iron A1130; Nail 5:-; Roof. A1094; Tile (5); BS; Cin. 4g; Coal 1g
3-5	324	Silt & chalk deposit		Med. 70:610 (15, 53 pt); PM 1:3; Brick (5); Copper 20, 119; Iron A530, A886, A1243; Nail 13:-; Quern A149; Roof. A1095-1101; Tile (53); BS; Char. 4g; Cin. ≤1g; Coal 8g
3-5	325	Clay & chalk deposit		Med. 3:21; PM 2:12
3-5	326	Wall		

Phase	Context	Description	Fig. Nos	Artefacts and environmental remains
5.1	327	Foundation rubble		
5.2	328=?298	Conduit fill		
5.1	329	Wall fill		Nail 1:-; Tile (1); An. (1); Char. 90g
	330	? Unused context		
5.1	331	Levelling deposit		Med. 3:97; Nail 16:-; Roof. A1102-1104; Sst. A427; Tile (6); Char. 3g
5.1	332	Buried soil layer		Med. 1:4; PM 5:80; Nail 2:-; Tile (1); Cin. 9g; Coal 45g
5.2	333=?303	Conduit fill		Med. 19:360; PM 1:10 (65); Nail 6:-; Tile (7); Vess. (4); Coal 6g
5.1	334	Construction debris		Med. 5:14; PM 1:4; Iron A963; Lst. A732; Nail 2:-; Roof. A1105, A1106; Tile (4); Wood A108; An. (1); Cin. 12g; Coal 29g; Slag 24g
5.1	335	Humic loam deposit		Med. 19:157 (42 pt); PM 24:500; Cp (3); Nail 8:-; Sst. A428; Tile (1); Coal 8g
1-5	336	No description		
1	337	Pad stone impression		
5.1	338	Wall		Nail 1:-
5.1	339	Robber trench fill	44	Med. 1:12; Brick (2); Nail 5:-; Sst. A429
5.1	340	Loam & chalk deposit		
5.2	341	Conduit fill		Med. 3:15 (50 pt); PM 1:13; Iron 111; Tile (1)
5.2	342	Conduit fill		Iron A1131
5.2	343	Conduit fill		
5.1	344=345	Loam & chalk deposit		Med. 5:52; Brick (1); Cp (1); Nail 2:-; Roof. A1107, A1108; Sst. A430; Tile (3); Cin. 11g; Coal 15g
5.1	345=344	Loam & chalk deposit		Roof. A1109-1112
3-5	346	No description		
3.2	347	Demolition debris		
3.1	348	Wall	40	
3.2	349	Fill of robber trench/demolition debris		
5.1	350	Hillwash		Med. 8:53; Tile (1); An. (6); Slag 293g
5.1	351	Natural silting and erosion		Med. 3:17; Nail 7:-
5.1	352	Dumped material		
5.1	353	Dumped material		Rom. 1:3; Med. 1:2
5.1	354	Wall collapse/?dumping		Med. 2:125 (43 pt); Roof. A1113-1134; Tile (1); Char. 5g
5.1	355	Wall collapse/?dumping		Med. 8:58
5.1	356	Wall demolition		Brick (1); Nail 3:-; Roof. A1135-1146; Sst. A431; Tile (10); Wood A109; An. (1); Coal 21g
5.1	357	Demolition rubble/robbing backfill		Med. 1:16 (50 pt); Brick (1); Nail 1:-; Sst. A432; Tile (2); Coal 33g
4	358	Wall	43	Med. 1:23; Nail 3:-; Roof. A1147-1150; Sst. A433; Tile (10); An. (7); Char. ≤1g; Coal 18g
5.1	359	Rubble dump		Roof. A1151; Tile (1); An. (1)
5.1	360	Wall collapse/?dumping		Med. 11:345; Brick (1); Lst. A706, A707; Nail 1:-; Roof. A1152-1171; Sst. A434-436; Tile (17); An. (15)
1-5	361	Silt & cobble deposit		Med. 3:48
1-5	362	Silt & cobble deposit		
5.1	363	Trampled deposit		Med. 6:70; Brick (2); Lst. A708; Nail 3:-; Roof. A1172-1181; Tile (10); An. (1)
5.1	364	? Yard surface	364	Med. 3:39; Roof. A1182, A1183; Sst. A437; An. (3)
4	365	Terracing cut		An. (2)
4	366	Loam & chalk deposit		
4	367	Silt & cobble deposit		
5.1	368	Silt & gravel deposit		
4	369	Terracing cut backfill		
5.1	370	Clay & chalk rubble deposit		Med. 6:85; Nail 2:-; Quern A150; Roof. A1184; Tile (2); BS; Char. 1g; Coal 8g
5.1	371=414	Terracing cut backfill		Med. 3:30 (42 pt); PM 8:107; Roof. A1185-1188; Sst. A438; Tile (1); Cin. 2g; Coal 76g
5.1	372	Feature fill		Med. 2:9; Nail -:1
5.1	373	Feature		
5.1	374	Compacted cobble layer		Med. 2:13; Cp (2); Nail 1:1; Roof A1189; Tile (2); BS; Char. 3g; Coal 4g
3.2	375=377	Wall collapse/?dumping		Med. 4:50 (43 pt); Roof. A1190-1195; Tile (19); Char. 3g
1-5	376	Wall rubble/?over-excavation		
3.2	377=375	Wall tumble/dumping		Med. 2:119; Brick (5); Nail 2:-; Roof. A1196-1203; Sst. A439; Tile (43); Char. 4g; Coal 5g
1-5	378=379	Clay silt with pebbles		Med. 23:188; Nail 2:1; Quern A151, A152; Coal ≤1g
1-5	379=378	Clay silt with pebbles		
5.1	380	Wall tumble/dump		Med. 9:67 (43 pt); Bone 3; Copper A695; Nail 6:-; Roof. A1204-1261; Tile (42); An. (5)
5.1	381	Floor levelling/?dump		Med. 6:173 (46 pt); Nail 8:-; Roof. A1262-1264; Tile (9)
5.1	382	Feature		
-	383	Sand deposit		
1-5	384	Clay & pebble deposit		
5.1	385	Silt & chalk deposit		

Phase	Context	Description	Fig. Nos	Artefacts and environmental remains
4	386	Terracing backfill		
4	387	Terracing cut		
3.2	388	Sandy deposit		Med. 9:77; Brick (4); Iron A227; Nail 3:-; Roof. A1265-1269; Tile (30); An. (3); Coal 1g; Char. 5g
5.1	389	Wall	44	Tile (1); Char. 23g
5.1	390	Rubble dump		
5.1	391=408	Rubble backfill of 382		Med. 1:24; Sst. A440; Coal 3g
5.1	392	Rubble dump		
3-5	393	Silt & cobble deposit		Med. 1:2; Nail 1:-; Roof. A1270; Tile (7); Slag 17g
5.1	394	Wall collapse/?dumping		Roof. A1271-1273
5.1	395	Wall collapse/?dumping		Med. 2:18; Mem. A179; Nail 1:-
3-5	396	Silt & pebble deposit		Med. 1:3; Brick (1); Iron A964; Nail 2:-; Roof. A1274
5.1	397	Clay & pebble deposit		Nail 2:-
5.1	398	Demolition deposit		Nail 3:-; Char. 3g
5.1	399	? Old barrow run		Med. 1:2
3-5	400	Clay & pebble deposit		Med. 33:688 (42 pt, 47 pt); PM 2:13; Nail 2:-; Quern A153; Roof. A1275-1278
5.1	401	Wall debris	44	
	402	Deleted context		
u/s	403	Unstratified		Rom. 1:6; Med. 19:195 (42 pt, 47 pt); Quern A154, A155; Roof. A1279-1289; Tile (4); Char. 1g
4	404	Wall tumble	43	
5.1	405	Clay & pebble deposit		Med. 6:62; Brick (9); Nail 1:1; Roof. A1290; Tile (7)
3-5	406	Rubble deposit	44	
5.1	407	Rubble deposit		Rom. 1:6; Med. 21:252; Nail 67:-; Quern A156; Roof. A1291-1294; Sst. A441; Stone A67; Char. 16g; Slag 16g
5.1	408=391	Sand & cobble deposit		Nail 2:-
3-5	409	Rubble deposit		Tile (1)
5.1	410	Rubble deposit		Med. 9:47; Nail 5:1; Tile (3); Coal 38g
1-5	411	Silt & cobble deposit		Med. 2:12
5.1	412	Rubble deposit		Nail 1:-
3-5	413	Rubble deposit		Med. 6:31
5.1	414=371	Rubble deposit		Med. 1:2; Coal 6g
3-5	415	Clay & pebble deposit		
1-5	416	Silt & pebble deposit		
3.1	417	Rubble dump		Nail -:1
3-5	418	Chalk & pebble deposit		
	419	Unused context		
5.1	420	Rubble deposit		Med. 1:6; PM 1:3; Nail 1:-; Sst. A442; Burnt (1); Coal 4g
3-5	421	Pebble deposit		Med. 12:289 (47 pt); Nail 6:-; Roof. A1295; Char. 5g
5.1	422	Clay & pebble deposit		Med. 14:480; Nail 2:-; Tile (27); Coal 16g
3.1	423	Clay & cobble deposit		
5.1	424	Impacted pebble deposit		Med. 5:62; Brick (2); Lst. A726; Nail 2:1; Sst. A443; Tile (3); Cin. 2g
3-5	425	Silt & pebble deposit		Med. 12:148; Nail 3:1; Roof. A1296, A1297; Tile (10); Char. 8g; Cin. 6g
5.1	426	Build-up deposit		Med. 23:401 (19, 22 pt, 46 pt); Copper A251, A679, A1023; Iron A1132; Lst. A709; Nail 12:-; Roof. A1298, A1299; Sst. A444; Tile (2)
3-5	427	Rubble deposit		Med. 10:86; Roof. A1300; Stone A68; Cin.; Slag 219g
5.1	428	Demolition debris		Iron A216
3-5	429	Rubble deposit		Med. 6:108 (42 pt); Lst. A710; Nail 3:-; Char. ≤1g
	430	No context information		Med. 1:3; Nail 4:-; Tile (6); Char. 3g; Coal 2g
3-5	431	Compacted deposit		
-	432	Silt & pebble deposit		Nail 2:-
5.1	433	Wall tumble		Med. 4:111 (45 pt)
	434	No context information		Med. 1:3; Nail 1:-; Roof. A1301-1304; Tile (4); Char. 3g
3.1	435	Robber trench fill/?bedding material	40	Med. 1:13; Nail 12:-; Quern A157; Sst. A445; Tile (2); Char. 2g; Cin. 2g
3-5	436	Rubble deposit		Med. 2:17; Brick (1); Iron A1390; Nail 14:-; Roof. A1305-1322; Tile (10); Char. 22g
1-5	437	Rubble deposit		Med. 1:1
3-5	438	Rubble deposit		
5.1	439	Silt lens		Med. 1:25
3-5	440	Rubble deposit		Med. 1:26; Char. 2g; Coal 27g
4	441	Terracing cut fill		Med. 5:62; Brick (1); Copper A977; Tile (2); Burnt (1); Cin. 1g; Coal 9g
1-5	442	Chalk block structure		
3-5	443	Rubble deposit		Med. 1:3
1-5	444=?448	Compacted clay chalk deposit		Med. 1:4
1-5	445	? Hillwash		
4	446	Chalk block structure	43	Med. 6:39; Brick (1); Copper A252; Lst. A711; Roof. A1323-1325; Sst. A446-472; Tile (4); An. (9); Char. 20g; Coal 3g
5.1	447	Rubble deposit		Nail 4:-; Roof. A1326; An. (2); Cin. 1g
1-5	448=?444	Compacted clay chalk deposit		Quern A158; Sst. A473

Phase	Context	Description	Fig. Nos	Artefacts and environmental remains
2	449	Demolition debris		Nail 8:-; Sst. A474; Char. 49g
-	450	Structure		
3.2	451	Pebble deposit		Med. 5:44; Iron A305; Nail 6:-; Roof. A1327-1331; Stone 18; Tile (3); An. (12); Char. 27g
1-5	452	Silt & cobble deposit		Med. 1:2; Roof. A1332, A1333
1-4	453=535= 577=578	Rubble deposit		
3-5	454	Wall tumble		
3.1	455	Wall repair		Nail 1:-
3-5	456	Rubble dump		Med. 35:581 (42 pt); Nail 3:-; Sst. A475-478; Tile (11)
5.2	457=106	Conduit		
4	458	Rubble dump		Nail 5:-; Tile (4); Coal ≤1g
-	459	No context information		Nail 3:-; Char. 9g
3-5	460	Rubble dump		Med. 4:43; Nail 1:-; Roof. A1334; Tile (1); Coal 6g
3.1	461	Structure	40, 41	Med. 1:2; Iron A965, A966; Nail 2:-; Sst. A479, A480; Tile (1); An. (7)
1-5	462	Deposit		
5.1	463	Rubble dump		Med. 2:4; Roof. A1335; Tile (1); Coal 6g
1-5	464	Clay & pebble deposit		
4	465	Robber trench fill		
4	466	Excavation backfill		Med. 8:69; Nail 1:-; Roof. A1336-1338; Sst. A481; Tile (1); Coal 22g
3-5	467	Impacted pebble deposit		
1-5	468	Clay & pebble deposit		
-	469	Rubble dump		
1-5	470	Clay & pebble deposit		
4	471	Construction trench		
3-5	472	Rubble deposit		Med. 1:2; Iron A943; Lst. A712; Roof. A1339
5.1	473	Stone dump		Iron A1391
4	474	Deposit		
4	475	Rubble dump		
1-5	476	Post-hole fill		
4	477	Compacted rubble deposit		Roof. A1340
5.1	478	? Structure	44	Med. 3:80; Nail 2:-; Sst. A482; Tile (3); An. (1); Char. ≤1g
4	479	Rubble fill		Med. 9:156 (45 pt, 60); Roof. A1341; Sst. A483, A484; Tile (3)
3-5	480	Construction trench		
1-5	481	Post-hole		
5.1	482	? Robber trench fill		Med. 1:6; Iron A944; Nail 2:-; Roof. A1342-1351; Tile (2)
3-5	483	Sand & chalk deposit		Med. 30:239 (42 pt); Nail 2:-; Roof. A1352; Tile (1); An. (15)
1-5	484	Shallow feature		
1	485	Rubble dump		Nail 5:-
3-5	486	Rubble dump		
5.1	487	Hillwash & rubble dump		Med. 39:215; Copper 10; Iron A967; Lst. A733; Nail 1:1; Sst. A485; An. (16); Burnt (1); Cin. 4g; Coal 1g; Fish; Slag 12g
4	488	Rubble dump		Med. 12:101; Lst. A713, A714; Nail 2:-; Roof. A1353-1355; Tile (2); An. (1); BS
3-5	489	Clay & cobble deposit		Tile (1)
3-5	490	Rubble deposit		Med. 5:89; Nail 1:-; Roof. A1356-1358
4	491	Clay & cobble deposit		
3-5	492	Wall tumble		
3.1	493	Rubble deposit		Med. 2:26; PM 1:5; Brick (4); Nail 7:-; Roof. A1359; Sst. A486-489; Tile (13); An. (6); Char. 11g; Coal 119g
3.2	494	Robber trench backfill		Med. 26:382 (13, 39 pt); Nail 10:-; Roof. A1360; An. (16); Char. 10g; Fish; Slag 8g
1-5	495	Rubble dump		Med. 40:422; Nail 4:-; Roof. A1361-1372; Slag 8g
4	496	Clay & pebble deposit		
1-5	497	Clay & pebble deposit		Nail 1:-; Char. 3g
1-3	498	? Wall/rubble dump		Med. 4:23; Brick (1); Nail 1:-; Quern 29; Roof. A1373; Sst. A490-492; Tile (4); An. (4)
4	499	Collapsed wall		Lst. A715; Nail 1:-; Roof. A1374, A1375, A1555; Sst. A493-497; Tile (2); An. (6); Coal 18g
5.1	500	? Remnant of 354		Tile (1)
4	501	? Robber trench fill		Nail 1:-; Roof. A1376; Tile (1); Char. 2g
1-3	502	Clay & cobble deposit		Rom. 3:5; Med. 23:150; Quern A159; An. (20); Slag 1g
4	503	Robber trench	43	
3-5	504	Rubble deposit		Sst. A498
1-5	505	Rubble deposit		Nail 1:-
4	506	Wall	43	
1-5	507	Burnt deposit		Med. 2:1
2	508	Rubble deposit		Nail 4:-; An. (42); Char. 45g
4	509	Large rubble dump/wall tumble		Med. 1:18; Nail 1:-; Sst. A499-501; Cin. 2g; Coal 12g
3-5	510	Silt & cobble deposit		
5.1	511	Clay & chalk deposit		

Phase	Context	Description	Fig. Nos	Artefacts and environmental remains
5.1	512	Clay & chalk deposit		
5.1	513	Clay & chalk deposit		
6	514 (Site 99/514)	Topsoil		Iron A1100
5.1	515	Feature		
5.1	516	Feature fill		
5.1	517	Shallow gully		
5.1	518	Gully fill		
5.1	519	Clay & chalk deposit		
1-5	520	Compacted pebble deposit		
4	521	Clay deposit		Nail 2:-
4	522	Soil & pebble deposit		Med. 9:44 (41 pt); PM 1:36; Iron 91; Nail 3:-; Roof. A1377, A1378; Sst. A502-509; Stone A106; Tile (1); An. (7); Burnt (5); Char. 2g; Coal 98g; Fish; Plas.
5.1	523	Rubble deposit		Brick (1); Nail 36:-; Quern A160; Roof. A1379, A1380; Sst. A510-512; Tile (1)
5.1	524	Wall tumble		Med. 5:40; Copper A678, A859; Iron A428, A728, A1392; Lst. A716; Nail 7:-; Sst. A589; Slag 10g
1-5	525	Silt & pebble deposit		
1-5	526	Feature		
1-5	527	Feature fill		
1-5	528	Clay & cobble deposit		
1-5	529	Clay & pebble deposit		
-	530 (Site 99/530)	Silt & pebble deposit		
1-5	531	Clay & cobble deposit		
-	532	Deposit		
3.1	533	Wall		Nail 5:-; Sst. A513-516; An. (1); Char. 1g; Coal 18g; Slag 208g
1-5	534	Compacted cobble deposit		
1-4	535=453 =577=578	Wall tumble & levelling dump		Med. 1:8; Roof. A1381
4	536	Clay & pebble deposit		
6	537	Topsoil		Med. 5:9
6	538	Hillwash		Med. 3:22; Coal 12g
	539	Unused context		
-	540	No context information		Roof. A1382; Sst. A517
-	541	Rubble deposit		
1-3	542	Clay & pebble deposit		
1-5	543	Clay & pebble deposit		
-	544	Rubble deposit		
2	545	Rubble & hillwash/? Levelling		Med. 5:20; Brick (3); Nail 1:-; Roof. A1383, A1384; Tile (14); BS; Char. 20g
3.1	546	Ash/charcoal deposit		
3.2	547	Rubble deposit		Med. 4:25; Nail 1:-; Roof. A1385
4	548	Rubble overspill		Roof. A1386; Sst. A518; Tile (1)
4	549	Silt & chalk deposit		Med. 5:31 (21); Roof. A1387, A1388; Sst. A519-521; Coal 23g
5.1	550	Rubble deposit		
4	551	Charcoal deposit		
4	552	Rubble dump		Med. 4:17; Brick (12); Copper A675, A1024; Lst. A717; Nail 6-; Sst. A522-525; BS
2	553	Demolition debris & hillwash/? Levelling		Med. 10:228; Bone 5; Nail 6:-; Roof. A1389-1397; Sst. A526, A527; Tile (4); Char. 206g
-	554	Clay & cobble deposit		
-	555	Clay & pebble deposit		Rom. 1:10
1-4	556	? Natural		Sst. A528
3.2	557	Silt & cobble deposit		
5.1	558	Silt & pebble deposit		
2	559=643	Burnt deposit	39	Med. 4:39 (39 pt); Iron A616, A1133, A1134; Lst. A718; Mem. A173; Nail 474:2; An. (2); Char. 274g; Fish
5.1	560	Rubble dump		Med. 53:864 (45 pt); Lst. A745; Nail 14:-; Roof. A1398-1401; Tile (3); Char. 1g
2	561	Demolition deposit		Med. 8:89; Roof. A1402-1406; Tile (15); Char. 79g; Coal ≤1g
1-5	562	Sand & pebble deposit		Sst. A529, A530
1-5	563	Rubble deposit		Nail 1:-
-	564	Deposit		Med. 1:1; Roof. A1407-1410; Char. 2g
3.2	565	Rubble fill	40	Nail 4:-
-	566	No context information		Med. 5:88; Nail 9:-; Quern A161; Roof. A1411-1423; Sst. A531; Tile (7); Char. 23g; Coal 1g
-	567	Cobble deposit		Med. 14:321; Copper A676, A677, A1025; Nail 9:-; Roof. A1424; Sst. A532-534; Mortar
5.1	568	Clay & pebble deposit		Sst. A535

Phase	Context	Description	Fig. Nos	Artefacts and environmental remains
4	569	? Structure	43	
	570	Unused context		
	571	Unused context		
-	572	Deposit		
4	573	Chalk & pebble deposit		Nail 1:-; Roof. A1425; Tile (1); An. (2); Coal ≤1g
4	574	Demolition debris		
4	575	Foundation layer		Med. 6:78
5.1	576	Rubble dump		Nail 1:-
1-4	577=453 =535=578	Rubble dump		
1-4	578=453 =535=577	Rubble dump		Med. 3:97; Copper 52, A696; Iron 52, A212; Nail 4:-; Sst. A536, A537; Char. 1g
4/3	579	Wall	43	
1-5	580	Rubble dump		
5.1	581	Robber trench		
3.1/2	582	Loam & cobble deposit		
5.1	583	Robber trench fill		
-	584	Structure		
-	585	Pea-grit & pebble deposit		Sst. A538
1	586	Wall	38, 39, 43	Nail 1:-; Char. 4g
1-5	587	Clay & pebble deposit		Med. 1:5
-	588	Wall		
1	589	Wall	38	Med. 1:7; Sst. A539-542; Coal 8g
3.2	590	Rubble dump		An. (1)
4	591	Rubble fill of robbed out wall	43	
5.1	592	Rubble deposit		Med. 1:4
3.1	593	Construction debris		Nail 4:-
3.1	594	Wall foundation		
3.1	595	Hearth structure	40	
3/1	596	? Compacted chalk floor		
-	597	Deposit		
3.1	598	Hearth stones	40	Sst. 38
1-3	599	Deposit		
1-3	600	Deposit		Stone 26
1-3	601	Deposit		
1-3	602	Deposit		
1-5	603	Rubble dump		Copper A674; Char. ≤1g
3.1	604	Levelling dump		Nail 2:-; An. (7)
4	605i	Structure		
4	605ii	Rubble foundation		Med. 2:17 (37); Roof. A1426-1428; Sst. A543, A544; Tile (1); An. (2)
2	606	Rubble deposit		Nail 1:-
3.1	607	Levelling dump		Med. 4:55; Nail 3:-; An. (1)
1	608	Construction debris		
1-5	609	Rubble deposit		
2	610	Rubble deposit		Nail 1:-
3.1	611	? Hearth setting		
2	612	Rubble deposit		
4	613	Wall tumble		Quern A162; An. (1)
3/1	614	? Hearth remains		
1-3	615	Rubble deposit		Iron A1135
3/1	616	Hearth pit	38	
2	617	Wall tumble		Med. 1:3; Sst. A545; Tile (2); Char. 34g
3.2	618	? Hillwash & rubble terrace		Med. 6:18; PM 1:3; Nail 1:-
4	619	? Robber trench fill	43	
	620	Now Context 1, Site 100		
1-5	621	Rubble dumps		Med. 1:2; PM 1:1; Nail 2:-
2	622	? Make-up deposit	39	Nail 40:-; Sst. A546-549; Tile (3); Char. 281g
1-4	623	Sand & cobble deposit		Med. 2:57; Nail 2:-; Roof. A1429
3.1	624	Base setting for hearth stones		
6	625	Old spoil heap of topsoil		Med. 3:22; PM 2:14; Nail 1:-; Roof. A1556; Vess. (1); Coal 7g; Slag 49g
-	626	Deposit		Med. 1:2
1-3	627	Silt & pebble dump		
4	628	? Demolition debris		Roof. A1430; An. (1)
2	629	Wall tumble & burnt debris		Nail 18:-
-	630 (Site 99/630)	Rubble dump		Med. 2:3; Roof. A1557
1	631	Rubble deposit		Nail 1:-
-	632	Clay & pebble deposit		
-	633 (Site 99/633)	Silt & cobble deposit		
1-3	634	Rubble dump		Rom. 1:2; Med. 1:2; Roof. A1431

Phase	Context	Description	Fig. Nos	Artefacts and environmental remains
-	635 (Site 99/635)	Silt & cobble deposit		
1-5	636	Rubble dump		Nail 1:-
1-5	637	Rubble dump		Med. 7:19
4	638	Wall		Sst. A550
-	639	Deposit		PM 1:32
1-3	640	Sand & pebble deposit		Med. 2:4
1	641=56	Wall	38	Med. 2:9
1	642=649	Wall/division	38, 39	Med. 8:34; Nail 2:-; Tile (1); An. (5); Fish
2	643=559	Charcoal deposit	39	Nail 9:-; Char. 8g
2	644	Chalk rubble, wall tumble & ? hillwash	39	
3.2	645	Rubble deposit		
1-5	646	Rubble dump		Nail 2:-; Stone 3
2	647	Burnt deposit		
3.2	648	Rubble dump		Med. 1:11
1	649=642	Continuation of 642		Nail 3:-
-	650	Structure		
4	651	Rubble dump		Iron A531; Nail 4:-
5.1	652	Rubble dump		Med. 6:225; Nail 2:-; Tile (2)
2	653	Cobble deposit		Iron 103; Nail 8:-
-	654	Deposit		
-	655	Deposit		
-	656	Deposit		
-	657	Deposit		
-	658	Deposit		
2	659	Charcoal deposit		Char. 7g
1	660=716 =719	Floor level	38	Med. 5:40; Roof. A1432, A1433; Sst. A551
3-5	661	Rubble dump		
1-3	662	Rubble dump		Med. 2:45; Roof. A1434
3-5	663	Pea-grit deposit		
2	664	Silt & pebble deposit		Nail 2:-; Char. 64g
2	665	? Robber trench fill	39	
1	666=?681	? Tumble/blocking of doorway		
2	667	Rubble dump/wall collapse		Char. 14g
1-5	668	Rubble dump		Med. 5:90; Copper 58, A672, A673, A697, A860-864, A1026; Iron A429; Lst. A719; Nail 22:-; Roof. A1435; Char. ≤1g; Slag 4g
-	669	Rubble dump		Med. 1:2
4	670	Rubble dump		Nail 2:-
-	671	Structure		
3-5	672	Robber trench		
1	673	? Floor surface		Nail 2:-
1	674	Wall	38	
-	675	Rubble and hillwash		
-	676	Clay & pebble deposit		
-	677	Wall tumble		
-	678	Pea-grit lens		
-	679	Sand & pebble deposit		
1	680	Floor surface		
1	681=?666	Wall	38, 39	Copper A989; Nail 2:-; Roof. A1436; Sst. A552; An. (2)
4	682	Unexcavated rubble spread		Med. 5:112 (20); Brick (1); Nail 2:-
3-5	683	Pea-grit lens		
3-5	684	Trampled surface		
3-5	685	? Wall tumble		
2	686	Rubble dump	39	
-	687=694	Rubble deposit		
4	688	Rubble deposit		
1	689	Deposit		
4	690	Cobble & pebble deposit		Rom. 1:19; Med. 5:23; Nail 1:-; Roof. A1437-1439
5.1	691	Rubble dump		Nail 1:-
3.2	692	Rubble dump		Med. 1:6
1	693	Structure		
-	694=687	Rubble deposit		
3.2	695	Rubble dump		
2	696	Wall tumble	39	
1	697	Burnt area		Nail 10:-; Char. 69g
1	698	Rubble dump		Nail 5:-
3-5	699	Rubble deposit		
2	700	? Wall tumble		Nail 1:-
-	701	Rubble dump		Nail 1:-

Phase	Context	Description	Fig. Nos	Artefacts and environmental remains
1	702	Floor surface		
-	703	Rubble dump		
1	704	Rubble dump		Med. 16:131; An. (3)
5.1	705	Rubble dump		Med. 2:38; Nail 2:-
2	706	Rubble dump		
1	707	Rubble dump		
3-5	708	Rubble dump		
5.1	709	Rubble dump		
1	710	Rubble dump		
1	711	Wall	38	
3/1	712	Pit/post-hole	40	
1	713	Wall bonding material	38, 39	
3.1	714	Wall	40	
2	715	Rubble dump		
1	716=660=			
	719	Barn floor	38	Med. 11:64; Nail 3:-; Roof. A1440-1442; An. (2)
1	717	Linear feature	38	
4	718	Feature		
1	719=660=			
	716	Surface	38	
3.2	720	Rubble dump		
1	721	Wall		
Nat.	8999=71	Bedrock/natural		
u/s	9000=179=			
u/s	-	-		Rom. 1:5; PM 46:1315; Brick (15); Copper 112, A865, A866, A918, A945, A990, A991, A1027-1030; Cp (7); Iron 97, 112, A181, A275, A279, A372, A380, A425, A656, A672, A729, A887-890, A945, A968, A969, A1027, A1059, A1060, A1136, A1137, A1393-1396, A1470, A1471; Lst. A720; Nail 250:3; Quern A163-165; Roof. A1443-1484, A1558; Sst. A553-568; Stone 5, 27; Tile (300); Vess. (12); Wood A110; Burnt (6); Char. 76>g; Cin. 3g; Coal 178g; Plas.; Slag 9g

Site 79

Phase	Context	Description	Fig. Nos	Artefacts and environmental remains
-	1	No context information		PM 38:334
-	10	No context information		PM 7:525
-	16	No context information		PM 1:10
-	21	No context information		Rom. 1:5

Site 99

Phase	Context	Description	Fig. Nos	Artefacts and environmental remains
-	514 (Site 77/514)	Topsoil		Brick (2); Tile (1); Coal 5g
-	530 (Site 77/530)	Silt & pebble deposit		Nail 1:-
-	630 (Site 77/630)	Rubble dump		Tile (1)
-	633 (Site 77/633)	Silt & cobble deposit		Sst. A569
-	635 (Site 77/635)	Silt & cobble deposit		Lst. A721; Quern A166; Tile (1); Cin. 2g

Site 100

Phase	Context	Description	Fig. Nos	Artefacts and environmental remains
-	1	Hillwash		Nail 3:-; Roof. A1516; Tile (28); Coal 6g
-	2	Clay & chalk pebble deposit		Iron 67, A357; Quern A167; Coal 1g
-	3	Clay & chalk pebble deposit		Nail 1:-
-	4	Rubble surface deposit		
	79	Steps	40	
u/s	9000	Unstratified		Nail 2:-

Bibliography

Abbreviations

Borthwick, Borthwick Institute for Archives, University of York

Cal IPM, Calendar of Inquisitions post mortem

Cal PR, Calendar of Patent Rolls

Interim Report, Interim Reports for the the years 1958 and 1985-9

LP Henry VIII, Letters and Papers (State Papers), foriegn and domestic, Henry VIII, 1509-1560

MPRG 1998, Medieval Pottery Research Group, *A Guide to the Classification of Medieval Ceramic Forms*, Occ. Pap. 1

NYCRO, North Yorkshire County Record Office, ZAZ = Hutton of Marske, ZQG = Cholmeley of Brandsby, ZPD = Fitzwilliam of Malton

Opgravingen in Amsterdam 1977, Baart, J., (Fibula-van Dishoek, Haarlem)

Reading UL, Reading University Library, EN = Englefield of Wootton Bassett

Reg Corbridge, Brown, W. (ed.), 1925, *The Register of Thomas Corbridge, Lord Archbishop of York (1286-1296) Part II*, Publ. Surtees Soc. 151

Reg Greenfield, Brown, W. and Thompson, A.H. (ed.), 1936, *The Register of William Greenfield, Lord Archbishop of York 1306-1315*, Part III, Publ. Surtees Soc. 151

TNA PRO, The National Archives, Public Record Office

YVBSG, Yorkshire Vernacular Buildings Study Group

References

Adams, H., 1913, *Practical Surveying and Elementary Geology*

Albarella, U. and Davis, S.J.M., 1996, 'Mammals and birds from Launceston Castle, Cornwall: decline in status and the rise of agriculture', *Circaea* 12 (1), 1-156

Alcock, N.W. and Blair, J., 1986, 'Crucks: New Documentary Evidence', *Vernacular Archit.* 17, 36-8

Allan, J.P., 1984, *Medieval and Post-Medieval Finds from Exeter, 1971-1980*, Exeter Archaeol. Rep. 3

Allison, K.J, 1976, *East Riding of Yorkshire Landscape*

Almeida Ferreira, M.M.L., 2005, 'Eighteenth-century wheel-engraved glassware from Lisbon', *Post-Medieval Archaeol.* 39/2, 233-42

Amis, P., 1968, 'Some domestic vessels of southern Britain: a social and technical analysis', *J. Ceram. Hist.* 2

Andrews, D., 'Bone Objects', in *Wharram I*, 128-130

Archer, M., 1997, *Delftware. The Tin-Glazed Earthenware of the British Isles*

Armstrong, J., 1991, 'The Clay Roof Tile' in Armstrong, P., Tomlinson, D. and Evans, D.H., *Excavations at Lurk Lane, Beverley*, Sheffield Excavation Rep. 1, 199

Armstrong, P., 1977, *Excavations in Sewer Lane, Hull, 1974*, Hull Old Town Rep. Ser. 1

Armstrong, P. and Ayers, B., 1987, *Excavations in High Street and Blackfriargate*, East Riding Archaeol. 8, Hull Old Town Rep. Ser. 5

Armstrong, S. and Armstrong, J., 1992, 'Clay Roof Tile and Roof Furniture' in Evans, D.H. and Tomlinson, D.G. (eds), *Excavations at 33-35 Eastgate, Beverley, 1983-86*, Sheffield Excavation Rep. 3

Atkins, C., 1986, 'The Archaeology of a Medieval Roof Tile Factory Site in Grovehill, Beverley'. Humber Archaeology Unit Developer's Report

Austin, D., 1989, *The Deserted Medieval Village of Thrislington County Durham Excavations 1973-74*, Soc. Medieval Archaeol. Monogr. 12

Baildon, W.P., 1895, *Notes on the Religious and Secular Houses of Yorkshire* I, Yorkshire Archaeol. Soc. Rec Ser 17 (for 1894)

Baildon, W.P., 1920, 'Compositions for not taking knighthood at the coronation of Charles I', *Miscellanea I*, Yorkshire Archaeol. Soc. Rec. Ser. 61 (for 1920), 84-107

Bailey, G., 2004, *Buttons and Fasteners 500 BC - AD 1840*

Bailey, M., 1988, 'The rabbit and the medieval East Anglian economy', *Agric. Hist. Rev.* 36, 1-20

Baines, E., 1823, *History, Directory & Gazetteer of the County of York etc. Vol. II: East and North Ridings*

Baker, D., Baker, E., Hassall, J. and Simco, A., 1979, 'Excavations in Bedford 1967-1977', *Bedfordshire Archaeol. J.* 13

Baker, E. and Hassall, J., 1979, 'The Pottery', in Baker *et al.*, 147-240

Baker, J. and Brothwell, D., 1980, *Animal Diseases in Archaeology*

Baker, J.C., 1984, *Sunderland Pottery*, Tyne Wear Cty Counc. Mus.

Barclay, C., 'A Review of the Medieval Coins and Jetons from Wharram Percy', in *Wharram XI*, 301-304

Bartels, M., 1999, *Steden in Scherven*, Stichting Promotie Archeologie en de Rijksdienst voor het Oudheidkundig Bodemonderzoek (Zwolle)

Barnwell, P.S. and Giles, C., 1997, *English Farmsteads 1750-1914*, R. Comm. Hist. Monuments Engl.

Barrett, J.H., 1997, 'Fish trade in Norse Orkney and Caithness: A zooarchaeological approach' *Antiquity* 71, 616-38

Barrett, J.H., 2005, 'The fish bone,' in *Wharram X*, 169-75

Belcher, J. and Jarrett, M.G., 1971, 'Stem-bore diameters of English clay pipes: some northern evidence' *Post-medieval Archaeol.* 5, 191-93

Bennett, A., 2005, *Shops, Shambles and the Street Market. Retailing in Georgian Hull 1770-1810*

Beresford, M. and Hurst, J.G., 1990, *Wharram Percy Deserted Medieval Village*

Berthoud, M., 1982, *An Anthology of British Cups*

Biddle, M., 1961/2, 'The deserted medieval village of Seacourt, Berkshire', *Oxoniensia* 26/27, 70-201

Biddle, M., 1990, *Object and Economy in Medieval Winchester*, Winchester Stud. 7ii

Biddle, M. and Brown, D., 1990, 'Writing Equipment and Books', in Biddle, M. (ed.), *Artefacts from Medieval Winchester: Object and Economy in Medieval Winchester, Part II*

Biddle, M., Hiller, J., Scott, I. and Streeten, A., 2001, *Henry VIII's Coastal Artillery Fort at Camber Castle, Rye, East Sussex*

Bilson, J., 1896, *The North Bar, Beverley*, Trans. East Riding Antiq. Soc. 4

Blair, J. and Ramsey, N., 1991, *English Medieval Industries*, 229

Boardman, S. and Jones, G., 1990, 'Experiments on the Effects of Charring on Cereal Plant Components'. *J. Archaeol. Sci.* 17, 1-11

Bowie, G.G.S., 1990, 'Northern Wolds and Wessex Downlands: contrasts in sheep husbandry and farming practice, 1770-1850', *Agric. Hist. Rev.* 38, 117-26

Brears, P.D., 1967, Appendix 3: 'Clay pipe making' in Brears, P.D., 'Excavations at Potovens, near Wakefield', *Post-medieval Archaeol.* 1, 40-43, (3-43)

Brears, P.C.D., 1971, *The English Country Pottery: its History and Techniques*

Brewster, T.C.M. and Hayfield, C., 1988, 'Cowlam deserted village: a case study of post-medieval desertion' *Post-medieval Archaeol.* 22, 21-109

Brooks, F.W., 1951, 'East Riding muster roll, 1584' *Miscellanea, V* (Yorkshire Archaeol. Soc. Rec Ser 116 (for 1949), 69-116

Brooks, C.M., 1987, *Medieval and Later Pottery from Aldwark and Other Sites*, Archaeol. York 16/3, Counc. Br. Archaeol.

Brown, D., 1990, 'Dice, a Games-Board, and Playing Pieces', in Biddle, 692-706

Brown, D.H., 2002, *Pottery in Medieval Southampton c.1066-1510*, Southampton Archaeol. Monogr. 8, Counc. Br. Archaeol. Res. Rep. 133

Brown, P., 2001, *British Cutlery*

Bryant, A., 1829, *Map of the East Riding of Yorkshire from an Actual Survey by A. Bryant, In the years 1827 and 1828*, scale one inch to a statute mile [1:63360]

Buczacki, S., 2002, *Fauna Britannica*

Carruthers, W.J., 2005, 'Environment and Economy: Evidence from the Pond and Dam samples' in *Wharram X*, 214-19

Castle, H.J., 1847, *Engineering Field Notes on Parish and Railway Surveying and Levelling*

Celoria, F.S.C. and Kelly, J.H., 1973, *A post-medieval pottery site with a kiln base found off Albion Square, Hanley, Stoke-on-Trent, Staffordshire, England SJ 885 474*, City Stoke-on-Trent Mus. Archaeol. Soc. Rep. 4

Celoria, F. and West, H.W., 1967, *A Standard Specification for Tiles in 1477*, Trans. J. Br. Ceramic Soc. 4, 218

Cerón-Carrasco, R., 2005, 'Marine shells' in Pollard, T., *The Excavation of Four Caves in the Geodha Smoo near Durness, Sutherland*, Scott. Archaeol. Internet Rep. 18, 32-5 (http://www.sair.org.uk/sair18)

Challis, A.J. and Harding, D.W., 1975, *Later Prehistory from the Trent to the Tyne*, Br. Archaeol. Rep. 20

Charles, B.H., 1974, *Pottery and Porcelain. A Dictionary of Terms*

Charleston, R.J., 1975, 'The glass', in Platt, C. and Coleman-Smith, R., *Excavations in Medieval Southampton 1953-69, Volume 2: The finds*, 204-26

Charleston, R.J., 1986 'Glass from Plymouth', in Gaskill-Brown, C., *Plymouth Excavations. The medieval waterfront Woolster Street, Castle Street. Finds Catalogues*, 36-52

Chesney, K., 1970, *The Victorian Underworld*, History Book Club

Clarke, H. and Carter, A., 1977, *Excavations in Kings Lynn 1963-1970*, Soc. Medieval Archaeol. Monogr. Ser. 7

Clay, J.W. (ed.), 1889, 'Paver's Marriage Licences', *Yorkshire Archaeol. J.* 10

Clay, J.W. (ed.), 1903, 'Paver's Marriage Licences', *Yorkshire Archaeol. J.* 17, 155-91

Clutton-Brock, J., 1999, *Domesticated Mammals*

Collins, F. (ed.), 1888, 'Feet of Fines for the county of York', *Yorkshire Archaeol. Soc. Rec. Ser.* 5

Cook, G.H., 1947, *Medieval Chantries and Chapels*

Corder, P. and Kirk, J.L.,1932, *A Roman Villa at Langton, near Malton, East Yorkshire*. Roman Malton Dist. Rep. 4

Cowgill, J., de Neergaard, M. and Griffiths, N., 1987, *Knives and Scabbards*. Medieval Finds from Excavations in London 1

Coysh, A.W., 1972, *Blue-Printed Earthenware 1800-1850*

Coysh, A.W. and Henrywood, R.K., 1982 (repr. 1983), *The Dictionary of Blue and White Printed Pottery 1780-1880 Vol. 1*, Antique Collectors' Club

Crummy, N., 1983, *The Roman Small Finds from Excavations in Colchester 1971-9*, Colchester Archaeol. Rep. 2

Crummy, N., 1988, *The post-Roman Small Finds from Excavations in Colchester 1971-85*, Colchester Archaeol. Rep. 5

Cunningham, C.M., 1985, 'Bone Objects', in Cunningham, C.M. and Drury, P.J., *Post-Medieval Sites and their Pottery: Moulsham Street, Chelmsford*, Counc. Br. Archaeol. Res. Rep. 54, 57-9

Cushion, J.P., 1976 (1988 reprint), *Pocket Book of Ceramic Marks* (3rd ed.)

Davey, P.J. (ed.), 1979, *The Archaeology of the Clay Tobacco Pipe I*, Br. Archaeol. Rep., Br. Ser. 63

Davey, P.J. (ed.), 1987, *The Archaeology of the Clay Tobacco Pipe X*, Br. Archaeol. Rep. Br. Ser. 178, 110-138

Davey, P.J., 1999a, 'A 19th-century export ceramic assemblage from Poyll Vaaish', in Davey (ed.), 281-302

Davey, P.J. (ed.), 1999b, *Recent Archaeological Research on the Isle of Man*, Br. Archaeol. Rec. Br. Ser. 278

Davey, P.J., forthcoming, Clay pipes from recent excavations in Ripon

Davey, P. and Hodges, R. (eds), 1983, *Ceramics and Trade*

Davey P.J. and Pierce T.J., 1977, 'The clay pipes', in Leigh, A., 'Excavations at St Elphin's Rectory, Warrington', *J. Chester Archaeol. Soc.* 60, 94-128

Davey, P.J., Freke, D.J. and Higgins, D.A., 1996, *Excavations in Castletown, Isle of Man, 1989-1992*

Davies, I., 1973, 'Window Glass in Eighteenth-Century Williamsburg' in Hume, I.N. (ed.), *Five Artifact Studies*, Colonial Williamsburg Occas. Pap. Archaeol. I, 82

Davis, W.J., 1904, *The Nineteenth Century Token Coinage of Great Britain, the Channel Islands and the Isle of Man*

de Rougemont, G.M., 1989, *A Field Guide to the Crops of Britain and Europe*

de Saye Hutton, A., 1990, *A Guide to New Hall Porcelain Patterns*

Dickinson, M., 1992, *Seventeenth Century Tokens of the British Isles and Their Values*

Diderot, D. and d'Alembert, J. le R. (eds), 1772, *Encycopédie ou Dictionnaire Raisonné des Sciences, des Arts et des Métiers. Recueil de Planches* (Paris), in Davies 1973

Didsbury, P., 2000, Unpublished assessment reports for Northern Archaeological Associates on Don Pottery waster deposits from Thurnscoe

Didsbury, P., 2004, 'The Iron Age and Roman pottery', in *Wharram IX*, 139-183

Didsbury, P., forthcoming, 'Report on the medieval and post-medieval pottery from excavations by Northern Archaeological Associates at Blanket Row, Hull', *East Riding Archaeol.*

Dobney, K.M., Jaques, S.D. and Irving, B.G., 1996, *Of Butchers and Breeds: Report on Vertebrate Remains from Various Sites in the City of Lincoln*, Lincoln Archaeol. Stud. 5

Dobson, E., 1850, *A Rudimentary Treatise on the Manufacture of Bricks and Tiles,* Part II, 114

Doncaster Library Service, 1983, *Don Pottery Pattern Book*

Douglas, G. and Oglethorpe, M., 1993, *Brick, Tile and Fireclay Industries in Scotland*, R. Comm. Anc. Hist. Monuments Scotland

Draper, J., 1977a, *Mugs in Northampton Museum. A Jubilee Celebration*, Northampton Mus. Art Gallery

Draper, J., 1977b, *Eighteenth Century Earthenware Tea and Coffee Pots in Northampton Museum*, Northampton Mus. Art Gallery

Driver, J.C., Rady, J. and Sparks, M., 1990, *Excavations in the Cathedral Precincts 2: Linacre Garden, 'Meister Omers' and St Gabriel's Chapel*, Archaeol. Canterbury 4

Duco, D.H., 2003, *Merken en merkenrecht van de pijpenmakers in Gouda*, (Pijpenkabinet, Amsterdam)

Duncan, H., 2002, 'Domestic Metalwork', in Roberts, I., *Pontefract Castle. Archaeological Excavations 1982-86*, Yorkshire Archaeol. 8, 249-80

Dunning, G.C., 1961, 'Stone mortars', in Hurst, J.G., 'The Kitchen Area of Northolt Manor', *Medieval Archaeol.* 5, 279-84

Dunning, G.C., 1976, 'Aardenburg ware from Manningtree, Essex and finds of Aardenburg ware and other pottery imported from the Low Countries', *Essex Archaeol. Hist.* 8, 184-99

Dyer, C., 1997, 'Bredon Barn in History', *in* Charles, F.W.B., *The Great Barn of Bredon, its fire and reconstruction.* Oxbow Monogr 76, 21-28

Dyer, C., 2000, *Everyday Life in Medieval England* (London and New York)

Dykes, W., 1836a, 'Plan of an Estate comprising Wharram Percy, Bella and Wharram Grange in the East Riding of the County of York, the Property of Henry Willoughby Esqre', Birdsall Estate Office, Bi M 21

Dykes, W., 1836b, 'Plan of an Estate comprising Wharram le Street (*sic*), Bella and Wharram Grange in the East Riding of the County of York, the Property of Henry Willoughby Esqre', surveyed 1836, Borthwick PR WP9/5

Earnshaw, J.R. and Watkins, J.G., 1984, *An Excavation at Kirkgate, Bridlington, 1980-81*, Humberside Heritage Publ. 6

Edelen, G. (ed.), 1994, *The Description of England*, (New York)

Edwards, D. and Hampson, R., 2005, *White Salt-Glazed Stoneware of the British Isles*, Antique Collectors' Club

Egan, G., 1998, *The Medieval Household. Daily Living c. 1150 – c. 1450*, Medieval Finds from Excavations in London 6

Egan, G., 2005, *Material Culture in London in an Age of Transition. Tudor and Stuart period Finds c. 1450 - c. 1700 from Excavations at Riverside Sites in Southwark*, Mus. London Archaeol. Serv. Monogr. 19

Egan, G., 2008, 'Metal fixtures and fittings', in Mann, J. (ed.), *Finds from the Well at St Paul-in the-Bail, Lincolnshire*, Lincolnshire Archaeol. Stud. 9

Ellenberg, H., 1988, *Vegetation Ecology of Central Europe*

Elliott, G., 1998, *John and David Elers and their Contemporaries*

Evans, J. with Creighton, J., 1999, 'The Hawling Road ceramic series', in Halkon and Millett 1999, 200-229

Faull, M. and Moorhouse, S., 1981, *West Yorkshire: an Archaeological Survey to AD 1500*

Fairclough, G., 1979, *Plymouth Excavations. St Andrew's Street 1976*

Flood, R.J., 1976, *Clay Tobacco Pipes in Cambridgeshire*

Fox, R. and Barton, K.J., 1986, 'Excavations at Oyster Street, Portsmouth, Hampshire, 1968-71', *Post-Medieval Archaeol.* 20, 31-255

Gaimster, D., 1997, *German Stoneware 1200-1900*, Br. Mus.

Gallagher, D.B., 1987, 'The 1900 list of the Pipe Makers' Society', in Davey (ed.)

Gallagher, D.B., and Price, R., 1987, 'Thomas Davidson & Co., Glasgow' in Davey (ed.)

Garner, F.H. and Archer, M., 1972, *English Delftware*

Garrard, P. and Elder, J., 1988, 'The Small Finds', in Blockley, P., 'Excavations at No. 41 St. George's Street, Canterbury, 1985', *Archaeologia Cantiana* 105, 107-50

Gauch, H.G., 1984, *Multivariate Analysis in Community Ecology*

Gerrard, C.M. with Aston, M., 2007, *The Shapwick Project, Somerset. A rural landscape explored,* Soc. Medieval Archaeol. Monogr. 25

Gibson, M., 1999, *Lustreware*

Godden, G.A., 1968, *The Handbook of British Pottery and Porcelain Marks*

Goodall, A.R., 1979, 'Copper alloy objects' , in *Wharram I*, 108-114

Goodall, A.R., 1987, 'Copper alloy objects', in *Wharram III,* 171-73

Goodall, A.R., 1989, 'Copper alloy objects', in *Wharram VI,* 46-48

Goodall, A.R., 2007, 'Non-ferrous metal objects', in *Wharram XI,* 304-308

Goodall, A.R. and Paterson, C., 2000, 'Non-ferrous metal objects', in *Wharram VIII,* 126-32

Goodall, I.H., 2005, 'Iron objects excluding nails' in *Wharram X,* 132-39

Gooder, E., 1984, 'Finds from the cellar of the Old Hall, Temple Balsall', *Post-Medieval Archaeol.* 18, 149-250

Grant, A., 1988, 'Animal resources', in Astill, G. and Grant, A., *The Countryside of Medieval England*, 149-87

Green, C., 1999, *John Dwight's Fulham Pottery. Excavations 1971-79*, Engl. Heritage Archaeol. Rep. 6

Greenwood, C., 1818, *Map of the County of York,* surveyed in 1815, 1816 and 1817 [1:87120]

Greep, S., 2004, 'Catalogue of Objects of Bone and Antler', in Dalwood, H. and Edwards, R., *Excavations at Deansway, Worcester, 1988-89. Romano-British Small Town to late medieval City,* Counc. Br. Archaeol. Res. Rep. 139, 490-506

Griffin, J.D., 2001, *The Don Pottery 1801-1893*, Doncaster Mus. Service

Griffin, J.D., 2005, *The Leeds Pottery 1770-1881,* Leeds Art Collections Fund

Guerin, P., 1899, 'The probable causes of the poisonous effects of the Darnel (*Lolium temulentum L.*), *Bot. Gazette* 28, 136-8 (Chicago)

Gurney, J.H., 1921, *Early Annals of Ornithology*

Halkon, P. and Millett, M., 1999, *Rural Settlement and Industry: Studies in the Iron Age and Roman Archaeology of Lowland East Yorkshire.* Yorkshire Archaeol. Rep. 4

Hall, L., 2005, *Period House Fixtures and Fittings 1300-1900*

Halstead, P., 1985, 'A study of mandibular teeth from Romano-British contexts at Maxey' in Pryor, F., French, C., Crowther, D., Gurney, D., Simpson, G. and Taylor, M., *Archaeology and Environment in the Lower Welland Valley Volume 1*, 219-24

Härke, H., 1995, 'Weapon Burials and Knives', in Boyle, A., Dodd, A., Miles, D. and Mudd, A., *Two Oxfordshire Anglo-Saxon Cemeteries: Berinsfield and Didcot*, Thames Valley Landscapes Monogr. 8, 67-75

Harland, J.F., Barrett, J.H., Carrott, J., Dobney, K. and Jaques, D., 2003, 'The York System: An integrated zooarchaeological database for research and teaching', *Internet Archaeol.* 13: http://intarch.ac.uk/journal/issue13/harland_index.html

Harris, A., 1961, *The Rural landscape of the East Riding of Yorkshire, 1700-1850*

Harrison, B. and Hutton, B., 1984, *Vernacular Houses in North Yorkshire and Cleveland* (Edinburgh)

Hassall, T.G., Halpin, C.E. and Mellor, M., 1984, 'Excavations in St. Ebbe's Oxford, 1967-1976: Part II: Post-Medieval Domestic Tenements and the Post-Dissolution Site of the Greyfriars', *Oxoniensia* 49, 153-277

Hayes, R.H., 1978, 'Post-medieval pottery at Grimstone Manor Farm, near Gilling', *Trans. Scarborough Archaeol. Hist. Soc.* 21, 1-10

Hayfield, C., 1988, 'Cowlam deserted village: a case study of post-medieval desertion', *Post-Medieval Archaeol.* 22 , 21-109

Hayfield, C., 1991, 'Manure factories? The post-enclosure High Barns of the Yorkshire Wolds', *Landscape Hist.* 13, 33-45

Hayfield, C., 1994, 'Farm Servants' Accommodation on the Yorkshire Wolds', *Folk Life* 33, 7-28

Hayfield, C., 1998 'Vessey Pasture: the development of a Yorkshire Wold farmstead', *Yorkshire Archaeol. J.* 70, 109-23

Hayfield, C. and Brough, M., 1986-7 'Dewponds and pondmakers of the Yorkshire Wolds', *Folk Life*, 25, 74-91

Hayfield, C. and Buckland, P., 1989, 'Late Medieval Pottery Wasters from Firsby, South Yorkshire', *Trans. Hunter Archaeol. Soc.* 15, 8-24

Hayfield, C. and Wagner, P., 1998, 'The use of chalk as a building material on the Yorkshire Wolds', *Vernacular Archit.* 29, 1-12

Henig, M., 1977, 'Objects of Bone, Antler and Shell', in Durham, B., 'Archaeological Investigations in St Aldates, Oxford', *Oxoniensia* 42, 162-4

Henkes, H.E., 1994, *Glas Zonder Glans. Vijf eeuwen gebruiksglas uit bodem van de Lage Landen 1300-1800*, Rotterdam Pap. 9

Higgins, D.A., 1992, 'Clay Pipes', in 'Speke Hall: Excavations in the West Range, 1981-82', *J. Merseyside Archaeol. Soc.* 8, 68 (47-84)

Hildyard, R., 1985, *Browne Muggs. English Brown Stoneware*, Victoria and Albert Museum

Hinks, S., 1995, *A Structural and Functional Analysis of Eighteenth Century Buttons*, South Carolina Inst. Archaeol. Anthropol., Volumes in Historical Archaeol. 32, (Columbia)

Hinton, P. (ed.), 1988, *Excavations in Southwark 1973-76 Lambeth 1973-79*, London Middlesex Archaeol. Soc. Surrey Archaeol. Soc., Joint Publ. 3

*Holland Catalogue, c.*1915, Appendix 11, in Jung 2003, 313-63

Horsey, I.P., 1992, *Excavations in Poole 1973 – 1983*, Dorset Natural Hist. Archaeol. Soc. Monogr. 10

Hudleston, N.A., 1962, *History of Malton and Norton*

Hughes, B. and Hughes, T., 1968, *The Collector's Encyclopaedia of English Ceramics*

Hume, I.N., 1970, *A Guide to Artifacts of Colonial America*

Hume, I.N., 1991, *A Guide to Artifacts of Colonial America* (New York)

Hume, I.N., 2001, *If These Pots Could Talk*. The Chipstone Foundation (Hanover NH and London)

Hurley, M.F., 1997a, 'Artefacts of Skeletal Material', in Cleary, R.M., Hurley, M.F. and Shee Twohig, E., *Skiddy's Castle and Christ Church Cork. Excavations 1974-77 by D.C. Twohig*, 239-73 (Cork)

Hurley, M.F., 1997b, 'Bone and Antler Artefacts', in Hurley, M.F., *Excavations at the North Gate, Cork, 1994*, 144-8 (Cork)

Hurley, M.F., 2004, 'Bone Artefacts', in FitzPatrick, E, O'Brien, M. and Walsh, P., *Archaeological Investigations in Galway City, 1987 – 1998*, 463-76 (Bray)

Hurst, J.G., 1984, 'The Wharram Research Project: results to 1983', *Medieval Archaeol.* 28, 77-111

Hurst, J.G., Neal, D.S. and Van Beuningen, H.J.E., 1986, *Pottery Produced and Traded in North-West Europe 1350-1650*, Rotterdam Pap. 6 (Rotterdam)

Jacomet, S., 1987, *Prähistorische Getreidefunde*. Botanisches Institut der Universität Abteilung Pflanzensystematik und Geobotanik (Basel)

Janssen, H.L., 1977, 'Bewerkt been', in Janssen, H.L., *Van Bos tot Stad. Opgravingen in s'-Hertogenbosch*, 293-301 (S'-Hertogenbosch)

Janssen, H., 1983, 'Later medieval pottery production in the Netherlands', in Davey and Hodges, 121-85

Jarrett, M.G., 1970, 'The deserted village of West Whelpington, Northumberland: second report' *Archaeologia Aeliana* 48, 183-302

Jefferys, T., 1775, *The County of York*, survey'd in MDCCLXVII, VIII, [X and MDCCLXX]. Engraved by Thomas Jefferys, Geographer to His Majesty. MDCCLXXI, Corrected and Published according to Act of Parliament 25 March 1775. [1:63360] Sheet IX covers Wharram Percy

Jennings, S., 1981, *Eighteen centuries of pottery from Norwich*, East Anglian Archaeol. Rep. 13

Jennings, S., 1992, *Medieval Pottery in the Yorkshire Museum*

Jennings, S. and Boyles, G., 1995, 'Evidence for the manufacture of Ryedale ware recovered from the village of Coxwold', in Vyner (ed.), 228-34

Jones, J., 2005, 'Plant macrofossil Remains from Site 71'. in *Wharram X*, 214-19

Jones, R.T., Sly, J., Simpson, D., Rackham, J. and Locker, A., 1985, *The Terrestrial Vertebrate Remains from The Castle, Barnard Castle*, Ancient Monuments Lab. Rep. 7/85

Jung, S.P., 2003, 'Pollocks of Manchester: Three Generations of Clay Tobacco Pipemakers', in Higgins, D.A. (ed.), *The Archaeology of the Clay Tobacco Pipe XVII*, Br. Archaeol. Rep. Br. Ser. 352

Kaner, J., 1980, *Medieval Brickmaking*, Sciant Presentes, 8, 4

Kelly, J.H., 1973, *A rescue excavation on the site of Swan Bank Methodist Church, Burslem, Stoke-on-Trent, Staffordshire, England SJ870 499*, City of Stoke-on-Trent Mus. Archaeol. Soc. Rep. 5

Kelly, J.H. and Greaves, S.J., 1974, *The Excavation of a Kiln Base in Old Hall Street, Hanley, Stoke-on-Trent, Staffs. SJ 885745*. City of Stoke-on-Trent Mus. Archaeol. Soc. Rep. 6

King, H. and Harris, A., 1962, *A Survey of the Manor of Settrington*, Yorkshire Archaeol. Soc. Rec. Ser. 126

Klippel, W.E. and Schroedl, G.F., 1999, 'African Slave Craftsmen and single-hole Bone Discs from Brimstone Hill, St. Kitts, West Indies', *Post-Medieval Archaeol.* 33, 222-32

Korf, D., 1968, *Haarlemse majolica- en tegelbakkers* (Haarlem)

Korf, D., 1973, *Nederlandse Majolica* (Bussum)

Kybalová, J., 1989, *European Creamware*

Larkham, P.J., 1992, 'Facadism and a Vernacular Farmhouse: An Example in East Yorkshire', *Trans. Anc. Monuments Soc.* 36, 119-28

Lawrance, N.A.H. 1985 *Fasti Parochiales, V, Deanery of Buckrose*, Yorkshire Archaeol. Soc. Rec. Ser. 143 (for 1983)

Lawrence, H., 1974, *Yorkshire Pots and Potteries*

Lawrence, S., 1973, 'Clay Tobacco Pipe Makers in West Yorkshire' Yorkshire Archaeol. J., 45, 189-93

Lawrence, S., 1979, 'York pipes and their makers', in Davey, 67-84

Leadam, I.S. (ed.), 1892, 'The Inquisition of 1517. Inclosures and Evictions I', *Trans. R. Hist. Soc.* 6, 167-314

Leadam, I.S. (ed.), 1893, 'Yorkshire' in 'The Inquisition of 1517. Inclosures and Evictions II', *Trans. R. Hist. Soc.* 7, 127-292

Leaf, H, 2006, 'English Medieval Bone Flutes – a Brief Introduction'. *Galpin Soc. J.* 59, 13-19

Leatham, I., 1794, *General View of the Agriculture of the East Riding of Yorkshire, and the Ainsty of the City of York, with Observations on the Means of its Improvement*

Le Cheminant, R., 1982, 'The development of the pipeclay hair curler - a preliminary study' in Davey, P.J. (ed.), *The Archaeology of the Clay Pipe VII*, Br. Archaeol. Rep. 100, 345-54

Le Patourel, H.E.J., 1968, 'Documentary Evidence and the Medieval Pottery Industry' *Medieval Archaeol.* 12, 101-26

Le Patourel, H.E.J., 1979, 'Medieval Pottery' in *Wharram I*, 74-107

Letts, J.B., 1999, *Smoke Blackened Thatch*

Luthi, A.L., 2007, *Sentimental Jewellery: Antique jewels of love and sorrow*, Shire Book 366

MacGregor, A., 1985, *Bone, Antler, Ivory and Horn. The Technology of Skeletal Materials since the Roman Period*

MacGregor, A., 1987, 'Bone and Ivory Objects', in *Wharram III*, 176

MacGregor, A., 1992, 'Bone and Antler Objects', in *Wharram VII*, 54-58

MacGregor, A., 1995, 'Roman and Early Medieval Bone and Antler Objects', in Phillips, D. and Heywood, B., *Excavations at York Minster. Volume I. From Roman Fortress to Norman Cathedral*, 414-27

MacGregor, A., 2000a, 'Bone and Antler Objects', in *Wharram VIII*, 148-54

MacGregor, A., 2000b, 'Objects of Bone, Antler and Ivory', in Ellis, P., *Ludgershall Castle. Excavations by Peter Addyman 1964-1972*, Wiltshire Archaeol. Nat. Hist. Soc. Monogr. 2, 160-68

MacGregor, A. and Riddler, I.D., 2005, 'Bone and Ivory Objects', in *Wharram X*, 143-45

MacGregor, A., Mainman, A.J. and Rogers, N.S.H., 1999, *Craft, Industry and Everyday Life: Bone, Antler, Ivory and Horn from Anglo-Scandinavian and Medieval York*, Archaeol. York 17/12

Margary, H., 1991, *The Old Series Ordnance Survey Maps of England and Wales*, 8 (Lympne Castle)

Margeson, S., 1993, *Norwich Households: Medieval and Post-medieval Finds from Norwich Survey Excavations 1971-78*, East Anglian Archaeol. 58

Marshal, C.T., 1924, 'A medieval pottery kiln discovered at Cheam', *Surrey Archaeol. Collect.* 35, 79-94

Martin, P., 1987, 'Alphabetical list of pipemakers in Scotland', in Davey, P. (ed.), *The Archaeology of the Clay Tobacco Pipe X*, Br. Archaeol. Rep. Br. Ser. 178, 337-350

Matheau-Raven, E.R., 1997, *The Identification and Dating of Sheffield Electroplated Wares, 1843-1943*

McCarthy, M.R. and Brookes, C.M., 1988, *Medieval Pottery in Britain AD 900-1600*

McConnel, B., 1995, *The Collector's Guide to Thimbles*

McCormick, F., 2002, 'The distribution of meat in a hierarchical society: the Irish evidence' in Miracle, P. and Milner N. (eds), *Consuming Passions and Patterns of Consumption*, 25-31

McLaren, G., 1997, *Ceramics of the 1950s*

Meaney, A.L. and Hawkes, S.C., 1970, *The Anglo-Saxon Cemeteries at Winnall, Winchester, Hampshire*, Soc. Medieval Archaeol. Monogr. 4

Megginson, I., 1987, *Mud on My Doorstep, Reminiscences of a Yorkshire Farmwife*

Moffett, L., 1991, 'The archaeobotanical evidence for free-threshing tetraploid wheat in Britain' in Hajnalová, E. (ed.), *Palaeoethnobotany and Archaeology*, Acta Interdisciplinaria Archaeologica VII, 233-43 (Nitra)

Monaghan, J., 1997, *Roman Pottery from York*, Archaeol. York 16/8

Moore, S., 1999, *Cutlery from the Table*

Moorhouse, S. and Roberts, I., 1992, *Wrenthorpe Potteries*, Yorkshire Archaeol. 2

Moorhouse, S. and Slowiskowski, A.M., 1987, 'The pottery' in Moorhouse, S. and Wrathmell, S., *Kirkstall Abbey Volume 1 The 1950-64: excavations: a reassessment*, 59-116

Moorhouse, S. and Slowikowski, A.M., 1992, 'The Pottery', in Moorhouse and Roberts, 89-149

Myerscough, R., 2001, Field Meeting Report, Ryedale Vernacular Building Materials Research Group, 20 October 2001

Myerscough, R., 2005, 'The Geology and Building Stones of Southern Ryedale', *Yorkshire Build.* 33, 33-41

Neave, D., 1991, 'Pantiles: their use and manufacture in the Humber Region', in Tyszka, D., Miller, K. and Bryant, G. (eds), *Land, People and Landscapes*, Lincolnshire County Counc., 93-8

Neave, D., 2002 '"The Melancholy Contagion": cattle plague in the East Riding, 1747-56', *East Yorkshire Hist.* 3, 22-8

Neave, S., 1990, 'Rural Settlement Contraction in the East Riding of Yorkshire c. 1660-1760', Ph.D Thesis, Univ. Hull

Neave, S., 1993a, 'Rural settlement contraction in the East Riding of Yorkshire between the mid-seventeenth and mid-eighteenth centuries', *Agric. Hist. Rev.* 41, 124-36

Neave, S., 1993b, 'Thatched cottages of the East Riding' *Yorkshire J.* 3, 43-9

Neave, S. and Ellis, S., 1996, *An Historical Atlas of East Yorkshire*

Neave, S. and Neave, D., 2006, 'The East Riding of Yorkshire' in Barnwell, P.S. and Airs, M. (eds), *Houses and the Hearth Tax*, Counc.Br. Archaeol. Res. Rep. 150

Newman, C., 1996, 'Clay tobacco pipes' in Newman, R. and Wilkinson, P., 'Excavations at Llanmaes, near Llantwit Major, South Glamorgan, *Post-medieval Archaeol.* 30, 224-6 (187-233)

Northern Ceramic Society, 1997, *A Celebration of Yorkshire Pots*

O'Connor, S. and Duncan, H., 2002, 'The Bone, Antler and Ivory Artefacts', in Roberts, I., *Pontefract Castle. Archaeological Excavations 1982-86*, Yorkshire Archaeol. 8, 300-308

O'Connor, T.P., 1982, *Animal Bones from Flaxengate, Lincoln c. 870-1500*, Archaeol. Lincoln 18/1

O'Connor, T.P., 2000, *The Archaeology of Animal Bones*

Oliver, R., 1996, 'Six-inch sheet: "Surveyed" or "Fair drawn" ?', *Sheetlines* 47, 65-66

Ordnance Survey 1854, *Yorkshire, sheet 143*, surveyed in 1850-51, scale six inches to one statute mile [1:10560]

Ordnance Survey 1890, *Yorkshire (East Riding), Sheet CXLIII.9*, surveyed in 1888, Scale 1:2500

Ordnance Survey 1910, *Yorkshire (East Riding), Sheet CXLIII.9*, re-surveyed in 1888, revised in 1909, edition of 1910, Scale 1:2500

Orton, C., 1988, 'Post-Roman Pottery', in Hinton (ed.), 295-363

Oswald, A., 1975, *Clay Pipes for the Archaeologist*, Br. Archaeol. Rep. 14

Oswald, A., Hildyard, R.J.C. and Hughes, R.G., 1982, *English Brown Stoneware*

Ottaway, P. and Rogers, N.S.H., 2002, *Craft, Industry and Everyday Life: Finds from Medieval York*, Archaeol. York. The Small Finds 17/15

Payne, S., 1973, 'Kill-off patterns in sheep and goats: the mandibles from Asvan Kale', *Anatolian Studies* 23, 281-3

Pearce, J., 1992, *Border Wares*

Percival, J., 1948, *Wheat in Great Britain*

Pevsner, N. and Neave, D., 1995, *The Buildings of England: Yorkshire, York and the East Riding*

Pigot & Co., 1829, 1834, *National Commercial Directory*

Pinter-Bellows, S., 2000, 'The animal remains', in *Wharram VIII*, 167-84

Plan of the Church Yard & Glebe Land adjoining situate at Wharram Percy referred to in the preceding Terrier, 1855, [1:3168], Borthwick PR WP1

Platt, C. and Coleman-Smith, R., 1975, *Excavations in Medieval Southampton 1953-1969. Volume 2. The Finds*

Pretty, J.N., 1990, 'Sustainable Agriculture in the Middle Ages: The English Manor', *Agric. Hist. Rev.* 38, 1-19

Price, R.M., 1963, 'English Redware', *Apollo*, April 1963, 310-313

Purdy, J.D., 1991, *Yorkshire Hearth Tax Returns*

Purvis, J.S., 1949, *Select 16th-century Causes in Tithe*, Yorkshire Archaeol Soc Rec. Ser., 104 (for 1947)

Purvis, J.S., 1953, *An Introduction to Ecclesiastical Records*

Raphaël, M., 1991, *La pipe en terre*, (Rognac)

Rath, J.A., 1979, *Antique and Unusual Thimbles* (Cranbury, New Jersey)

Redfern, M. and Shirley, P., 2002, 'British Plant Galls. Identification of galls on plants and fungi' *Field Studies* 10, 267

Reineking-von Bock, G., 1976, *Steinzeug* (Köln)

Richardson, J., 2001, 'The animal bones from West Heslerton - The Anglian Settlement', unpubl. rep. for D.J. Powlesland, Landscape Research Centre

Richardson, J., 2004a, 'The animal remains', in *Wharram IX*, 257-72

Richardson, J., 2005a, 'The animal remains', in *Wharram X*, 153-69

Richardson, J., 2005b, 'Appendix 1: The animal remains from Sites 9 and 12 (Areas 10 and 6)' in *Wharram X*, 229-42

Riddler, I.D., 2001, 'The Small Finds', in Hicks, M. and Hicks, A., *St Gregory's Priory, Northgate, Canterbury. Excavations 1988 – 1991*, Archaeol. Canterbury New Ser. II, 267-87

Riddler, I.D., 2004, 'Bone, Antler and Ivory Objects', in *Wharram IX*, 251-54

Riddler, I.D., 2006, 'Objects and Waste of Bone and Antler', in Cramp, R.J., *Wearmouth and Jarrow Monastic Sites. Volume 2*, 267-81

Riddler, I.D., 2007a, 'Stone, Bone, Antler and Ivory Finds', in Saunders, D., *Excavations at Launceston Castle, Cornwall*, Soc. Medieval Archaeol. Monogr. 24, 357-80

Riddler, I.D., 2007b, 'Objects of Antler and Bone', in *Wharram XI*, 313-17

Riddler, I.D. and Trevarthen, M., forthcoming, *The Prehistoric, Roman and Anglo-Saxon Funerary Landscape at Saltwood, Kent*, Channel Tunnel Rail Link Monogr.

Riddler, I.D., Trzaska-Nartowski, N.T.N. and Hatton, S., forthcoming, *An Early Medieval Craft. Antler and Boneworking from Ipswich Excavations 1974-1994*, East Anglian Archaeol.

Rivington's Series of Notes on Building Construction, 1910, Part III Materials, 7th ed., (new impress. 1919)

Rixson, D., 1989, 'Butchery evidence on animal bones', *Circaea* 6 (1), 49-62

Roberts, G.B., 1998, *True Blue. Transfer Printed Earthenware*

Roes, A., 1963, *Bone and Antler Objects from the Frisian Terp Mounds* (Haarlem)

Roper, H. and Kitching, C., (ed.), 2006, 'Feet of Fines for the county of York', *Yorkshire Archaeol. Soc. Rec. Ser.* 158

Roussel, D.E., 1982, *The Castleford Pottery 1790-1821*

Rushton, J., 2003, *The History of Ryedale From the Earliest Times to the Year 2000*

Sahlberg, I., 1960-61, 'Om Kammakare I Åbo och deras Arbete', *Åbo Stads Historiska Museum Årsskrift 1960-1*, 36-58

Salzman, L.F., 1952, *Building in England down to 1540*

Scott, S., 1991, 'The animal bones' in Armstrong, P., Tomlinson, D. and Evans D.H., *Excavations at Lurk Lane, Beverley, 1979-82*, Sheffield Excavation Rep. 1, 216-227

Seaby P. and Purvey P.F., 1984, *Standard Catalogue of British Coins 2: Coins of Scotland, Ireland and the Islands*

Seewaldt, P., 1990, *Rheinisches Steinzeug. Bestandskatalog des Rheinischen Landesmuseums Trier* (Trier)

Sellwood, L., 1984, 'Objects of Bone and Antler', in Cunliffe, B. (ed.), *Danebury Excavation Report Volume 2*, Counc. Res. Rep. 52, 371-8

Shaw, J.T., 1973, *Sunderland Ware. The Potteries of Wearside,* Sunderland Public Libraries, Mus. Art Gallery

Sherlock, D. and Woods, H., 1988, *St Augustine's Abbey: Report on Excavations, 960-78*, Kent Archaeol. Soc. Monogr. 4

Silver, I.A., 1969, 'The ageing of domestic animals' in Brothwell, D. and Higgs, E. eds., *Science in Archaeology*, 283-302

Sitch, B., 'Coins: a Review of the Iron Age and Roman Coins from Wharram Percy', in *Wharram IX*, 234-40

Slowikowski, A.M., 1989, 'The Pottery' in *Wharram VI*, 35-38

Slowikowski, A.M., 1991, 'The Archaeological Evidence for the Character and Uses of Medieval Pottery in the Lowlands of West Yorkshire' unpubl. MPhil Thesis, Univ. Leeds

Slowikowski, A.M., 2000 , 'The Anglo-Saxon and medieval pottery' in *Wharram VIII*, 60-100

Slowikowski, A.M., 2005, 'The Anglo-Saxon and medieval pottery', in *Wharram X*, 73-121

Slowikowski, A.M., 2007, 'The Anglo-Saxon and medieval pottery', in *Wharram XI,* 251-68

Slowikowski, A.M., forthcoming, *Late Medieval Reduced Ware: A Regional Synthesis*, Medieval Pottery Res. Group Occas. Pap.

Smith T.P., 1985, *The Medieval Brickmaking Industry in England 1400-1450*, Br. Archaeol. Rep. 138, 48

Snodin, M., 1974, *English Silver Spoons*

Southey, J.F., 1972, *Anguina tritici.* Commonwealth Institute of Helminthology Descriptions of Plant-parasitic Nematodes Set 1, No.13

Spall, C. A. and Troop, N.J. (eds), 2005, *Blue Bridge Lane and Fishergate House, York*, Report on Excavations: July 2000 to July 2002, 295

Steane, J.M., 1975, *Excavations at the Deserted Medieval Settlement at Lyveden*, 95

Taylor, S. and Gault, W.R., 1979, 'Late Nineteenth Century Clay Tobacco Pipes from Warwick', in Davey, 279-93

Ter Braak, C.J.F. and Smilauer, P., 2002, *CANOCO Reference Manual and CanoDraw for Windows User's Guide* (Wageningen)

Theuerkauff-Liederwald, A-E., 1994, *Venezianisches Glas der Kunstsammlungen der Veste Coburg. Die Sammlung Herzog Alfred von Sachsen-Coburg und Gotha 1844-1900*

Thomas, R. and Locock, M., 2000, 'Food for the dogs? The consumption of horseflesh at Dudley Castle in the eighteenth century', *Environ. Archaeol.* 5, 83-91

Thompson, A., Grew, F. and Schofield, J., 1984, 'Exavations at Aldgate, 1974', *Post-Medieval Archaeol.* 18, 1-148

Thomson, R.G. and Brown, D.H., 1992, 'Archaic Pisan Maiolica and related Italian wares in Southampton', in Gaimster, D.R. and Redknap, M. (ed.), *Everyday and Exotic Pottery from Europe* c. *650-1900: Studies in honour of John G. Hurst*, Oxbow Monogr. 3, 177-85

Tibbles, J., 2001a, 'The Ceramic Building Material', in George, R., *Trial Excavations at County Hall Beverley, East Riding of Yorkshire*, Humberside Archaeol. Partnership Rep. 84

Tibbles, J., 2001b, *The Ceramic Building Materials from Bridgegate Howden, East Yorkshire*, JTCeramics Rep. 2019

Tibbles, J. 2003, *The Ceramic Building Materials from Bishop Lane, Hull East Yorkshire*, JTCeramics Rep. 2042, 32

Tibbles, J., in prep, *Regional Brick and Roof Tile Typology*

Towner, D.C., 1957, *English Cream-Coloured Earthenware*

Trimpe Burger, J.A., 1962-3, 'Ceramiek uit de blaeitijd van Aardenburg (13de en 14de eeuw)', *Berichten van de Rijksdienst voor het Oudheidkundig Bodemonderzoek*, (12-13) 495-548

Tyrell, R. and Zeepvat, R. J., 1991, 'The Finds', in Mynard, D.C. and Zeepvat, R.J., *Excavations at Great Linford, 1974-80. The Village*, Buckinghamshire Archaeol. Soc. Monogr. Ser. 3, 137-240

Ulbricht, I., 1984, *Die Verarbeitung von Knochen, Geweih und Horn im mittelalterlichen Schleswig,* Die Ausgrabungen in Schleswig. Berichte und Studien 3, (Neumünster)

Van Trigt, J., 2003, *Cutlery - From Gothic to Art Deco: the Hollander Collection*

van Vilsteren, V.T., 1987, *Het Benen Tijdperk. Gebruiksvoorwerpen van been, gewei, hoorn en ivoor 10,000 jaar gelden tot heden*, Drents Museum

van Vilsteren, V.T., 1988, 'De botte benen botermesjes', *Westerheem* 37, 213-21

von den Driesch, A., 1976, *A Guide to the Measurement of Animal Bones from Archaeological Sites* (Cambridge, Massachusetts)

Vyner, B. (ed.), 1995, *Moorland Monuments: studies in the archaeology of north-east Yorkshire in honour of Raymond Hayes and Don Spratt*, Counc. Br. Archaeol. Res. Rep. 101

Walton Rogers, P., 1997, *Textile Production at 16-22 Coppergate*, Archaeol. York 17/11

Waterman, D.M., 1959 , 'Late Saxon, Viking and Early Medieval Finds from York', *Archaeologia* 97, 59-105

Watkins, J.G., 1987, 'The Pottery', in Armstrong and Ayers, 53-181

Watts, S., 2007, 'Milling stones', *in Wharram XI,* 295-6

Weatherill, L., 1971, *The Pottery Trade and North Staffordshire 1660-1760*

Wharram I (Andrews, D.D. and Milne, G., 1979) *Wharram. A Study of Settlement on the Yorkshire Wolds, I. Domestic Settlement 1: Areas 10 and 6*, Soc. Medieval Archaeol. Monogr. 8

Wharram III (Bell, R.D., Beresford, M.W. and others, 1987) *Wharram. A Study of Settlement on the Yorkshire Wolds, III. Wharram Percy: The Church of St Martin*, Soc. Medieval Archaeaol. Monogr. 11

Wharram VI (Wrathmell, S., 1989) *Wharram. A Study of Settlement on the Yorkshire Wolds, VI. Domestic Settlement 2: Medieval Peasant Farmsteads*, York Univ. Archaeol. Publ. 8

Wharram VII (Milne, G. and Richards, J.D., 1992) *Wharram. A Study of Settlement on the Yorkshire Wolds, VII. Two Anglo-Saxon Buildings and Associated Finds*, York Univ. Archaeol. Publ. 9

Wharram VIII (Stamper, P.A. and Croft, R.A., 2000) *Wharram. A Study of Settlement on the Yorkshire Wolds, VIII. The South Manor Area*, York Univ. Archaeol. Publ. 10

Wharram IX (Rahtz, P.A. and Watts, L., 2004) *Wharram. A Study of Settlement on the Yorkshire Wolds, IX. The North Manor Area and North-West Enclosure*, York Univ. Archaeol. Publ. 11

Wharram X (Treen, C. and Atkin, M., 2005) *Wharram. A Study of Settlement on the Yorkshire Wolds, X. Water Resources and their Management*, York Univ. Archaeol. Publ. 12

Wharram XI (Mays, S., Harding, C. and Heighway, C., 2007) *Wharram. A Study of Settlement on the Yorkshire Wolds, XI. The Churchyard*, York Univ. Archaeol. Publ. 13

Wharram XIII forthcoming, (synthesis)

White, S.D., 2003, 'Clay Tobacco Pipes from Excavations in Nursery Street, Sheffield', archive report prepared for Archaeol. Res. Consultancy Univ. Sheffield

White, S.D., 2004, *The Dynamics of Regionalisation and Trade: Yorkshire Clay Tobacco Pipes 1600-1800*, The Archaeology of the Clay Tobacco Pipe XVIII, Br. Archaeol. Rep. Br. Ser. 374

White, S.D., 2005a, 'Doncaster North Bridge Project: The Clay Tobacco Pipes', archive report prepared for Archaeol. Res. Consult. Univ. Sheffield

White, S.D., 2005b, 'Clay Tobacco Pipes from Excavations in London Road, Sheffield', archive report prepared for Archaeol. Res. Consult. Univ. Sheffield

White, W., 1840, *History, Gazetteer, and Directory of the East and North Ridings of Yorkshire*

Whitehead, R., 2003, *Buckles 1250-1800*

Whyman, M., 1997, 'Excavations in Deanery Gardens and Low St. Agnesgate, Ripon, North Yorkshire', *Yorkshire Archaeol. J.* 69, 119-64

Willmott, H., 2002, *Early Post-Medieval Vessel Glass in England, c. 1500-1670*, Counc. Br. Archaeol. Res. Rep. 132

Willmott, H., 2004, 'The post-Roman glass', in *Wharram IX*, 233-4

Willmott, H., 2005, *A History of English Glassmaking AD 43-1800*

Willmott, H., 2007a, '17 Glass', in Gerrard with Aston, 765-78

Willmott, H., 2007b, 'Glass Objects', in *Wharram XI*, 299-301

Wise, R., 1845, Malton and Driffield Junction Railway, Sheet M&D, No 5, [1:3960], House of Lords Record Office Floor 5 1846 M5

Wondrausch, M., 1986, *Mary Wondrausch on Slipware*

Woodeford, J., 1976, *Bricks to Build a House*, 136

Woodfield, P.,1963-64, 'Yellow-glazed wares of the seventeenth century', *Trans. Birmingham Warwickshire Archaeol. Soc.* 81, 78-87

Woodward, D. (ed.), 1984 (2006 reprint), *The Farming and Memorandum Books of Henry Best of Elmswell 1642*, Rec. Soc. Econ. Hist. New Ser. 8

Wright, T., 1880, *Dictionary of Obsolete and Provincial English*

Young, C.J., 2000, *Excavations at Carisbrooke Castle, Isle of Wight, 1921-1996*, Wessex Archaeol. Rep. No. 18

Index
by S. Atkin

Page numbers of illustrations and plates are in italics.
In the pottery and small finds reports, the periods cited in the catalogue entries have not been indexed.

maiolica 102

Martincamp flasks (MCAMP) 158, 176, 177

Midland Yellow ware (MYEL) 158, 177

Pearlware (PEARL) 158, 161-4, 172, 176, 178
    PEARL1 158, 165, 174, 178, 182, 196
    PEARL2 158, 163, 171, 175, 176, 178, 180, 190, 193
    PEARL2a 159, 178, 196
    PEARL3 159, 162-4, 168, 169, 171, 172, 174, 175, 178
    PEARL4 159, 178, 193
    PEARL5 159, 161, 171, 173, 178, 182, 198

Porcelains and bone china (PORC) 159, 161-6, 170, 172, 174-6, 178, 180, 182, 196, 364

Post-medieval local coarsewares (PMLOC) 159, 167, 169, 180

Purple-glazed earthenwares (PURP) 159, 176

Raeren stoneware (RAER) 159, 169, 170, 172, 176-7, 185, 198

Ryedale ware (RYED) 98, 102, 112, 156, 159, 161-77, 182, 184, 185, 188, 190, 193, 351, 354, 355

South Yorkshire gritty ware (SYG) 159, 185

Staffordshire slipwares (STAFS) 36, 159, 161, 163, 165, 166, 169-71, 173-5, 177
    STAFS1 159, 167, 169, 171, 173-5, 180, 190, 196
    STAFS2 159, 164, 173, 190, 193
    STAFS3 159, 169, 171, 173-5

Tin-glazed earthenwares (TIN) 159, 161-3, 165, 169, 171-3, 175, 177, 180, 185, 188, 190, 193, 196

Trailed slipwares (TRSL) 159, 180

Unattributed chafing dish (UCD) 159, 185

Unattributed post-medieval slipware (UNATSLIP) 159, 175

Unattributed (UNAT) 159

Unglazed red earthenwares (UGRE) 159, 166, 172, 185, 193

Weser slipware (WESER) 160, 162, 177, 180

Westerwald stoneware (WEST) 160, 167, 170-7, 188, 190, 193

Whieldon-type wares (WHIEL) 160

White-dipped wares (WHDIP) 160, 161-3, 169, 173, 174, 182, 184

le Prestehous 16

privy, farmer's 28, 29, 32

probate inventories *see* inventories

Purbeck Marble 204

purse-ring 256

querns 363

rabbit warrens 15, 335

railway 204, 209; *see also* Wise's railway plan

Read, Mary 5

Read, William 5, 7

rectory 2, 16, 17, 19, 22, 343

rectory barn 17

residues
    salt 41
    in wine bottle 249, 251

Reves, John 17

Richardson family 341, 368

Richardson, John 3

Richardson, Petronel 3

rings
    iron 266, 273, 362, 363
    non-ferrous 265
    see also finger-rings

rivet, copper alloy 259

Rivis, Thomas 13

rods, iron 270

Roman/Romano-British period
    animal bone 117, *319*
    coins 252, 253, *257*, 258
    finds 362
    molten glass 252
    nail 275
    Site 26: 88, 117
    Site 54 Romano-British levels 88, 117, 345
    stone 204
    see also pottery

roof tiles 14
    ceramic 206-8

roofing stone 78, 204, 349

Rose's brewery, Malton 167

rove, iron 270

Rowland, William 12, 13

ruler 259

Ryvar, Robert 21, 22, 349, 351

St Katherine's chapel, Towthorpe 17

St Martin's Church 15-16, 19
    cartographic evidence 26, *26-7*
    chantry 2, 3, 349
    clay pipes 217, 227, 234, 236
    combs 279
    harmonium 261
    lead window cames 264
    revenues 22
    sandstone from 80
    Scrope chantry 349
    stonework reused 54, 80, 118, 204, 349, 363, 368
    tile 206
    see also Churchyard

salting of meat 41, 336

salt residues 41

Salvayn, Gerald and George 16

sarcophagus fragment 204

Saxon *see* Anglo-Saxon/Saxon period

Sayers, Tom, boxer 231-2, *231*, 236

school 365

scissors, iron 269, *272*, 365

Scorah, Richard, pipemaker 228, 236

Scrope, Sir Geoffrey and Yvette 16, 349

Scrope, William and Constance 16

spur buckles, iron 266, *267*, 365
spurs, iron 266, 274
stables
    Bella Farm (Monkman's) 12-13, 14
    farmer's stable (and Site 73) 27, 28, 29, 32, 66, 68, 345
    Monkman's 343
    Site 26: 112
    Site 51, Period 2.3: *44, 50*, 52, 343
    Site 54: 112
    vicar's stable 19, 20, 22, 25, 26-7, 345, 347
    Wharram Grange 10
Stanesby, William, vicar 2, 20, 312
staples, iron 270
stick handle *see* walking-stick handle
stirrups 274
stone bearing 202
stone objects 200-5, 363
stonework, reused 54, 62, 80, 94, 96, 110, 118, 347, 349, 363-4, 368
strap ends, copper alloy 256, *257*
strap fastener, iron 266
strap fragments, iron 271
Structure P *see* conduit
studs
    copper alloy 259
    iron 271, 362
styli
    bone 275, *277, 278*, 362
    lead 259
sundial *see* pocket sundial
syringe, bone 285, 365

Tailor (Taylor), Michael 3, 18, 20-1
taps and tap fitting *262, 263*, 273, 364
terriers *see* glebe terriers
thatch 10, 14, 25, 117, 287, 297, 301-2, 304-5, 343, 357, 358
    'thack' 349
thimbles, copper alloy *262, 263*, 365
Thirk, William 13
Thixendale
    barley 306, 309
    farmhouse 358, *361*
Thorpe, John 2, 3, 22, 341
Tibthorpe, farmhouse 358, *361*
tile
    ceramic 206-8, 343 (*see also by type*)
    stone 364
timber, for building 357-8
timber-framing 357-8
tin openers 269
tithe causes 2-3, 7, 22, 24
tongs 269, 362, 363
tools 362
    agricultural *272*, 273-4, 362
    building, crafts and unknown function 269-70
Tournai 'Marble' 204
Towthorpe, chantry and chapel 17, 349

trade tokens 253, 254, 255, 366
traps *see* animal traps
tubes, copper alloy 265
turkey 335
tweezers, copper-alloy 258

undercroft *see* Site 51, West Range, Period 1
upholstery tacks 264, 363

valuation book of the estate (1806) 13, 37, 308, 343, 367
vessels 364-5
    copper-alloy 365
    iron and cast-iron *267, 269*, 365
Vessey Pasture 343
vicarage 345-55, 367
    building materials and construction 357-8
    cartographic evidence 26-32
    census 14
    demolition (*c.*1834/35) 24, 29, 118, 355
    destroyed by fire (1553) 22
    dimensions 22, *23*, 351, 355-6
    documents 25, 356 (*see also* glebe terriers)
    final abandonment 117
    medieval activity 362
    medieval and 1440 ordination 16-17, 118, 341, 345
    mid-16th-century documents 17-22, 367
    outshots built (pre-fire) 21, 22, *23*
    parlours with chimneys built (pre-fire) 22, *23*
    post-fire construction 22, *23*, 351
    pottery 138-51, *153*, 154-5, 156, 167-78, 185-98
    pre-fire 19-22, *23*, 78, 117, *346*, 347, *348*, 349, 355
    pre-vicarage features (Site 54, Structures A-C) 88-93, 345
    roofing materials 349
    rooms and use of 25, 356
    ruin 15, 19, 24-5, 355
    tenants 3
    thatched 25, 349, 358
    see also Site 54, Structure K; Site 77
vicarage barn *see* Site 77, Period 1 (pre-1553) *and* Period 2 (1553)
vicars 15-17, 24-5
    diet 335-6, 339-40
    income reduced 341
    pottery 368
    security 363

wagon shed 12, 343, 358
Waite, Richard 12, 13
Wake, Thomas 16
walking-stick handle, antler 285, 365
wall hooks, iron 270, 363
washer, iron 270
water supply 10, 341
Weddell, Ellen 3
Weddell, Leonard 3, 24
Weddell, Margery 3, 24

Weddell, Robert 3, 24
weedhook 273, 362
weights
    iron 269, 362
    lead 263
    stone 201, 202
Welburn, Matthew, curate 25
well 10, 28, 29, 351
West Pasture 7, *8*
Westerdale family 234
Westow 355
Wharham, Thomas 7
Wharram Grange farm 5, *8*, *11*, 27
    'ablemen' 3
    estate valuation (1806) 13, 308, 343
    improvements to buildings 10, 14
    new barn 12
    thatched 358
Wharram le Street
    barley 306
    Buck family 5
    Buck rental 10
    building materials 357, 358

    farmers 5
    hearths 356
Wharram Percy Farm 5, 10, 27-8, *27*
    estate valuation (1806) 14, 308
wheat-seed gall nematode *311*, 312
wheel depressions (Site 49) 65
wheel-ruts (Site 77) 82
wig curler *see* hair curler
window, stone reused 62, 204, 363-4
window cames and ties, lead 264, 362, 363
window fastening, iron 270, 363
window stay, iron 270, 363
wire, non-ferrous 258
Wise's Railway Plan (1845) 15, 28, 29
witness statements *see* cause of dilapidations
Wood, the 24
Wood & Sons 166
wool 5, 356
Worthy Close 7, *8*, *9*, *11*
writing leads or pencil 259, 365
writing slates and 'slate' pencils 200, 365

Yedingham 355, 356